GOVERNMENT AND LABOR

IN EARLY AMERICA

GOVERNMENT AND LABOR IN EARLY AMERICA

By Richard B. Morris

With a New Foreword by the Author

OCTAGON BOOKS

A DIVISION OF FARRAR, STRAUS AND GIROUX

New York   1975

Reprinted 1965
by special arrangement with Richard B. Morris

Second Octagon printing 1975

OCTAGON BOOKS
A DIVISION OF FARRAR, STRAUS & GIROUX, INC.
19 Union Square West
New York, N.Y. 10003

Library of Congress Cataloging in Publication Data

Morris, Richard Brandon, 1904-
   Government and labor in early America.

   Reprint of the ed. published by Columbia University Press, New
York.

   Includes bibliographical references.
   1. Labor and laboring classes—United States—History.
   I. Title.
HD8068.M65   1975   331′.0973   74-28200
ISBN 0-374-95890-4

Printed in USA by
Thomson-Shore, Inc.
Dexter, Michigan

To JEFFREY and DONALD

FOREWORD TO THE SECOND OCTAGON REISSUE

THE TWO HUNDREDTH anniversary of American independence prompts a reappraisal of this nation's past and a reexamination of the role of labor in its transforming society. For the latter task it might well be profitable to examine afresh the findings and conclusions of *Government and Labor in Early America,* a pioneer monograph first published in 1946.

Government and Labor in Early America informed us that the government's role in the economy has deep roots, anticipating by some three centuries the innovations of the New Deal era. It documented the not infrequent interventions on the part of government—whether the administrative branch, the provincial legislatures, or the courts—to set guidelines, legal or hortatory, governing the relations of employer and workman. Finally, it demonstrated the ways in which the unpublished records of inferior courts can be mined by the social as well as the legal historian to secure data about the ordinary workingman and woman. Ofttimes court records are the only available source for his or her side of the story, absent diaries, correspondence, and account books, in which employers, plantation owners, small farmers, mine operators, master craftsmen, and merchants set down in considerable detail their business transactions and their dealings with free workers, indentured servants, apprentices, and slaves.

Research over the past quarter century has not measurably changed the findings or altered the conclusions of this book. Thus, Mary Roys Baker's investigation of early trade union roots in Massachusetts documents in detail some of the antecedent examples of concerted action treated in this volume. Much attention has been focused upon slavery, slave resistance, slave profitability, mobility, and competition of black artisans with white free labor. In essence, these in-depth studies have not altered the account in this volume of the impact of slavery upon white labor in the colonial period, a subject to be treated in a sequel, *Freedom and Bondage in the Slave States.*

Some recent penetrating studies, notably by Aubrey C. Land and James C. Henretta, suggest that the laboring class, while continuing to enjoy upward economic mobility in the eighteenth century, was steadily losing ground relative to the more affluent planters and merchants, but these conclusions were anticipated in *Government and Labor in Early America,* which pointed to the rise in the number of indigent persons, particularly in seaport towns on the eve of the American Revolution and the growing insecurity of labor dependent to so considerable a degree on the vagaries of the import trade.

Lastly, the broad outline of the workingman's role in the coming of the Revolution, notably of the town "mechanics" and the seamen, is underscored in *Government and Labor*. Subsequent investigations by Jesse Lemisch, Staughton Lynd, Alfred Young, Roger J. Champagne, Pauline Maier, and Richard Walsh, among others, have spelled out in fine detail that remarkable phenomenon, the combined activism of laboring and mechanic-employer groups, providing the initial momentum for resistance to British imperial measures. Temporary in character, to be sure, such combinations in the leading cities served to blur class lines in the revolutionary struggle for American independence.

RICHARD B. MORRIS

October 1, 1974

PREFACE

JAMES MADISON, writing in 1787, made explicit the fundamental role of government as a regulator of economic and class interests.[1] The relations, prior to the rise of trade unionism, between labor, one of these economic classes, and government are analyzed in the present study. Although unorganized in the main and largely inarticulate in America of the seventeenth and eighteenth centuries, labor has been nevertheless considered here as a social unit, for, as Arthur F. Bentley stated many years ago, groups not fully enjoying political and civil rights are a factor in government if only because of their potentialities for affecting other groups.[2] While labor had certain separate and distinct interests in the colonial and Revolutionary periods, its members were not precluded from making common cause with others, as, notably, in joining with the commercial interests to protest the British policy on the eve of the Revolution. A fuller understanding of the part the worker played in the fashioning of our early American institutions should serve to introduce a note of greater realism into the study of American history.

Government in this volume is not considered in monistic terms. The British imperial machinery, the Continental Congress, the colonial and early state governments all concerned themselves with labor relations, as did the county, the town, and the parish. In the seventeenth and eighteenth centuries there was no simple tripartite form of government to deal with labor problems, although the principal supervisory responsibility devolved upon the courts. To a very considerable degree the courts acted as administrative as well as judicial bodies, and there was no sharp line of demarcation separating the areas of judicial action from those of administration. Governors served as chancellors, mayors and aldermen as judges of inferior courts, legislatures acted as appellate courts, town and county conventions adopted economic regulations which had some sanctions behind them, and local emergency committees at times assumed judicial powers. The problem of appeals from administrative tribunals to the courts is not novel to the twentieth century. Sessions courts had the right to review the actions taken by the

[1] *The Federalist*, No. 10.
[2] See Arthur F. Bentley, *The Process of Government: a Study of Social Pressures* (Chicago, 1908), pp. 211, 269, 271.

local justices, although in certain areas the right of appeal was circumscribed by statute.

From the modern era when the employment relationship is terminable at will it may seem a long road back to the days when the master had the right to sell or assign a servant for the remaining term of service and to secure the specific performance of a personal service contact. Conversely, it may seem a long journey forward from the time when the master could discipline a disobedient servant to the National Labor Relations Act which defines as an unfair labor practice the employer's refusal to bargain collectively with representatives of his employees. Actually, as this study discloses, the hand of the past is still writ large in the labor law and labor relations of this country, and the early concepts and procedures often forecast the shape of things to come. The experience of government with labor in the first two centuries of American history holds numerous clues to later developments and provides significant parallels to current patterns. Wage- and price-fixing and economic stabilization, the right of workers to take concerted action for their own advancement, child labor, absenteeism in industry, pirating of workers, restrictions on admission to a trade, restraints upon dismissals, conscription of labor—all contemporary labor problems accentuated by the crisis of the second World War—constitute the core of the master-servant relations that were supervised by colonial and Revolutionary governments.

In considering early American labor relations this study is confined to an analysis of the legal and social position of free and bound labor. Except in so far as its impact was felt directly upon the free and bound labor systems, slavery is not accorded special treatment; ample documentary sources and secondary accounts of slavery are available. The early free and bound labor systems, have far greater significance to the student of contemporary social and governmental problems. Phases of the free labor and indentured servant systems which have been competently surveyed in the pioneer studies of Sartorius von Waltershausen, Geiser, Herrick, Jernegan, Seybolt, Saposs, McKee, and other investigators are alluded to briefly. Fuller exposition is reserved for areas not previously explored to any extent. Throughout the volume an attempt has been made to give adequate recognition to the economic and regional diversities prevailing along the Atlantic seaboard and to consider the problems of government and labor in relation to these diverse conditions as well as to the English social, economic, and legal heritage of the American colonists.

Some twenty thousand cases, largely unpublished, have been reviewed in the course of the investigation of which this volume is the end product. The principal source has been a field largely unexplored —the unpublished inferior court records of the American colonies. To examine these, the writer traversed the Eastern seaboard from Wiscasset, Maine, and Woodsville, New Hampshire, to St. Augustine, Florida. Statutes, town ordinances, and vestry books complemented the judicial records.[3] Wherever possible these sources were supplemented by contemporary newspapers, accounts of travelers, diaries, letter books, military order books, and business papers.

Paper restrictions imposed by our wartime emergency dictated a drastic reduction of the size of this book. Subjects cognate to labor relations, such as price regulation, the responsibility of the employer for injuries to his employee, and the impact of the white labor system upon slave labor, have therefore received brief allusion only. It was necessary to omit numerous tables illustrating the business of the colonial courts in the labor field and the specific action taken in such fields as absenteeism, servitude in satisfaction of criminal sentence, apprenticeship, grounds for granting relief to servants, and wage suits brought by mariners.[4] Nevertheless, the general trends and conclusions to which these tables point have been included, and the actual cases have been cited in compact footnotes.

This study was in considerable measure made possible by grants received from the Social Science Research Council and the American Philosophical Society. I have benefited materially from the generous cooperation of a number of scholars. I am particularly indebted to three former students—my colleague, Dr. Jonathan Grossman, for assistance in gathering data relating to wage- and price-fixing, and to Mr. Lester Jayson, Special Assistant to the Attorney General, and Technical Sergeant Martin Kleinbard, U.S. Army Air Force, both of the New York bar, for helpful suggestions at other points in the investigation.

[3] The documentation to this volume should serve as a guide to the unpublished judicial sources available for the prosecution of social, economic, and legal studies in the area of American history in the seventeenth and eighteenth centuries. For general suggestions, see R. B. Morris, "Early American Court Records: a Publication Program," *Anglo-American Legal History Series,* No. 4 (New York, 1941). The main regions traversed for this study are surveyed therein. The published official sources—imperial, colonial, county, town, and parish—which were examined in the preparation of the present work are listed in E. B. Greene and R. B. Morris, *A Guide to the Principal Sources for Early American History (1600–1800) in the City of New York* (New York, 1929).

[4] These tables and other unpublished illustrative documents have been placed on file with the American Labor Archive and Research Institute, New York City, in the belief that they may be effectively utilized by research workers in the field of early American labor history.

Professor Abbot Emerson Smith of Bard College very graciously allowed me to consult data he had gathered in the preparation of his forthcoming study of colonial immigration, and Professor Lawrence A. Harper of the University of California and my colleague, Lieutenant John M. Cox, U.S. Army Air Force, turned over for my use microfilm of the British Naval Office lists which they had jointly prepared. I have enlisted the aid of a number of experts in contemporary labor law, among them Professor Arthur Lenhoff of the University of Buffalo School of Law, who read and criticized the chapter dealing with the enticement and pirating of workers. At a number of points in the course of this investigation I had occasion to consult Professor Eli Heckscher of the University of Stockholm, the late Dr. Charles M. Andrews, New Haven, Conn., Dr. Evarts B. Greene, Croton-on-Hudson, N.Y., and my colleague, Professor Michael Kraus.

Archivists, librarians, and staffs of county seats facilitated research in the field at every point. Virtually all the state directors of the Historical Records Survey in the thirteen original states allowed me to consult the useful inventories of the public records (many of which remain unpublished) that have been prepared under their direction. Thanks are especially due to the National Directors of that project, Dr. Luther Evans, now Librarian of Congress, and Mr. Sargent Child. I am also indebted for aid in the field to Miss Mary T. Quinn, Archivist of Rhode Island, to Mr. Norbert Lacy, New Haven, Conn., and Mrs. Louise G. Newton, Connecticut State Library, to Professor John T. Farrell, College of New Rochelle, to Mr. Maxwell Vollins, Hall of Records, New York City, and to Mr. George J. H. Follmer, clerk of the United States District Court for the Southern District of New York, to Mr. George J. Miller of the New Jersey bar and Professor H. Clay Reed of the University of Delaware, to Mr. Leon de Valinger, Jr., Archivist of Delaware, and to the late Dr. James Robertson, Archivist of Maryland, and his successor, Dr. Morris L. Radoff, to the late Hon. Carroll T. Bond, Chief Judge of the Maryland Court of Appeals, and to Hon. Emory H. Niles, Judge of the Supreme Bench of Baltimore City, to the late Mr. Morgan Robinson, Virginia State Library, to Dr. C. C. Crittendon, North Carolina Historical Commission, to Mr. A. S. Salley, Jr., South Carolina Historical Commission, and to Mrs. Katherine F. Lawson, St. Augustine Historical Society.

Special thanks are due the record custodians or librarians of a number of repositories visited in Great Britain, including the Guildhall, London, the British Museum, the Public Record Office, and the Bodleian Library. In this country acknowledgment is gratefully made to the librarians of the New Hampshire Historical Society, Concord, the Baker Library, Dartmouth College, the Athenaeum, Boston, the Boston Public Library, the Harvard Law School Library, the Newport Historical Society, the New York State Library at Albany, the New York Historical Society, the New York Public Library, the Association of the Bar of the City of New York, the College of the City of New York, Columbia University, the Historical Society of Pennsylvania, the Library of Congress, the Virginia Historical Society, the Charleston Library Society, the Georgia Historical Society, and the Henry E. Huntington Library, San Marino, California, among many private repositories visited, for courtesies extended. Acknowledgment should also be made to the editors of the *Political Science Quarterly* and the *New England Quarterly* for their permission to use the substance of articles which appeared in those periodicals.

Dean Harry J. Carman and Professor J. Bartlett Brebner of Columbia University and Professor Lawrence A. Harper of the University of California generously undertook the laborious task of reading the original manuscript, and I am indebted to them for their keen and incisive suggestions for revising this study. Dean Carman's faith in this enterprise, and the encouragement of other friends, including Frank G. Sommer, former Dean of New York University School of Law, Mr. Jacob Billikopf of Philadelphia, and Mr. John Dickinson, General Counsel of the Pennsylvania Railroad, will remain treasured pages in the memory of one scholar. Throughout the long years of investigation the writer received very substantial help and encouragement from his mother and his wife, who too often sacrificed other interests to share the labors of uncovering, copying, and collating documentary sources. To them he will always be deeply grateful. The valued editorial assistance of Miss Matilda L. Berg of the Columbia University Press is also gratefully acknowledged.

RICHARD B. MORRIS

December 15, 1945
New York City

CONTENTS

Introduction

free workers, and other landsmen in the navy, 294; Nonmilitary
services of artificers, laborers, and servants in the army, 295;
Artificers and laborers in the Continental and British armies during
the American Revolution, 297

Part II: Bound Labor

Conclusion

ABBREVIATIONS

A.P.C.,Col.	*Acts of the Privy Council of England, Colonial Series* (*Rolls Series*), edited by W. L. Grant and James Munro (6 vols., 1613–1783; Hereford, England, 1908–12)
Assistants	*Records of the Court of Assistants of Massachusetts Bay* (3 vols., Boston, 1901–28), I, 1673–92; II, 1630–44; III, 1642–73
C.C.	Common Council
C.O.	Colonial Office Papers, Public Record Office, London
Co.	County; Company (in Virginia only)
Col.	Colonial
Coll.	Collections
C.P.	Common Pleas
CSPA	*Calendar of State Papers, Colonial Series; America and West Indies* (Rolls Series, London, 1860–)
Essex	*Records and Files of Quarterly Courts of Essex County, Massachusetts, 1638–83* (8 vols., Salem, 1911–21)
G.S.	General Sessions
Hening	W. W. Hening, comp., *The Statutes-at-Large, Being a Collection of All the Laws of Virginia* (1619–1792; 13 vols., Philadelphia and New York, 1823)
HMC,*Rep.*	Royal Commission on Historical Manuscripts, *Reports,* and other publications (London, 1874–)
M.C.C.	*Minutes of the Common Council of the City of New York, 1675–1776* (8 vols., New York, 1905)
N.Y.M.C.M.	Minutes of the Mayor's Court of New York City
O.B.	Order Book
Q.S.	Quarter Sessions
R.N.A.	*Records of the Court of Burgomasters and Schepens of New Amsterdam, 1653–74,* edited by H. B. Dawson (Morrisania, N.Y., 1867)
Suffolk	"Suffolk County, Massachusetts, Court Records, 1671–80," edited by Z. Chafee and S. E. Morison, Colonial Society of Massachusetts, *Publications,* XXIX, XXX

VMH *Virginia Magazine of History and Biography* (1893–)

WMCQ *William and Mary College Quarterly Historical Magazine* (1st
Ser., I–XXVII, 1892–1919; 2d Ser.. I–X, 1921–1943; 3d Ser., I–,
1944–)

INTRODUCTION

THE MERCANTILIST BACKGROUND OF
AMERICAN LABOR RELATIONS

THE REVOLUTION in the government's relations with business and labor, inaugurated in 1933 and gaining increased momentum in the course of the Second World War, does not mark the first appearance in this country of a system of elaborate governmental controls over the economic order. Prior to laissez faire capitalism, both business and labor considered government regulation the normal order. This was particularly true in the age of colonial settlement, an era when business enterprise was regulated in the interest of a political program. Then the entrepreneur was not free to carry on his business as he saw fit, nor was the worker free to withhold his labor or to demand any working conditions he wished. The controls for the regulation of commerce, industry, and labor which were introduced in the English colonies in the New World were to a large degree rooted in English and continental experience. However, in studying these controls it must be borne in mind that the labor problem was only one phase of the general problem of economic regulation under mercantilism.[1] A study of the labor codes apart from these general controls would serve to give to labor matters a false emphasis for that time and place.

Mercantilism had as its objective the creation of a prosperous and powerful national state or self-sufficing empire. According to the prevailing thought of the day, such prosperity and power were to be obtained by maintaining an adequate system of national defense and an adequate stock of precious metals, by affording protection to home industries against foreign competition, and by making it possible for home industries to compete successfully in foreign markets through assurance of necessary raw materials and low production costs. Hence, mercantilism in England may be said to have rested upon two main pillars

---

[1] The term "mercantilism" has been criticized by some recent students of the period because of its vagueness. See E. A. J. Johnson, *Predecessors of Adam Smith* (New York, 1937), pp. 3–5. However, despite this difficulty the term is used in the present study to identify a group of writers and a body of doctrine. In support of this position, see P. W. Buck, *The Politics of Mercantilism* (New York, 1942), p. 4n. The procedural side of mercantilism has more significance for us today than its body of substantive regulations. See L. A. Harper, "Geopolitics and Mercantilism," Amer. Hist. Assn., *Ann. Rep., 1942*, III, 121n.

—the Acts of Trade and the Tudor industrial code. The former provided for the external regulation and control of foreign trade and the subordination of colonial interests to those of the mother country.[2] The latter sought to assure profit to the English entrepreneur by guaranteeing him an adequate labor supply at a subsistence wage[3] and at the same time to safeguard the worker against unrestrained exploitation in order that agricultural and industrial labor needs might continue to be met over the long term.

The Tudor industrial code patterned colonial legislation and administrative practice, although both the colonial entrepreneur and the free

[2] The paramount principle of settlement was that it must prove advantageous to the mother country. See Hillsborough to Gage, *Correspondence of General Thomas Gage*, ed. C. E. Carter (2 vols., New Haven, 1931, 1933), II, 108, 109 (1770). Wrote Gage to Barrington in 1772: "I [think it would] be for our interest to Keep the Settlers within reach of the Sea-coast as we can; and *to cramp their Trade as far as it can be done prudentially. Cities flourish and increase by extensive Trade, Artisans and Mechanicks of all sorts are drawn thither, who teach all sorts of Handicraft work before unknown in the Country, and they soon come to make for themselves what they used to import. I have seen this Increase, and I assure your Lordship that Foundations are laid in Philadelphia, that must create Jealousy in all Englishmen."* Ibid., pp. 615, 616 (1772). (Italics mine.) See also HMC, *Rep.*, XLV, Pt. I, 735.
In 1774 the Marquis of Carmarthen, aghast at the rioting in America on the eve of the Revolution "by a people sent out from this country, as it were from our own bowels," undubitably expressed public sentiment in a rhetorical question which he phrased in Parliament in debating the bill for the administration of justice in Massachusetts: *"For what purpose were they suffered to go to that country, unless the profit of their labour should return to their masters here?* I think the policy of colonization is highly culpable, if the advantages of it should not redound to the interests of Great Britain." *The Parliamentary History of England*, XVII (London, 1813), 1208, 1209.
See also G. L. Beer, *Origins of the British Colonial System* (New York, 1908) and *The Old Colonial System* (2 vols., New York, 1912); Jacob Viner, "Early English Theories of Trade before Adam Smith," *J. Pol. Econ.*, XXXVIII (1930), 249–301, 404–457; C. M. Andrews, *The Colonial Period of American History* (New Haven, 1938), IV, ch. x; L. A. Harper, *The English Navigation Laws* (New York, 1939); "The Effect of the Navigation Acts on the Thirteen Colonies," in *The Era of the American Revolution: Studies Inscribed to Evarts Boutell Greene*, ed. R. B. Morris (New York, 1939), pp. 3–39; Curtis Nettels, "The Menace of Colonial Manufacturing," *N.E.Q.*, IV (1931), 230–269. For the contemporary writers on the Navigation Acts and the colonial system, see Buck, *op. cit.*, pp. 202–204.
[3] In general, the mercantilists favored an economy of low wages as a preventive of poverty and vice, an assurance of a favorable trade balance, and as serving to keep the labor classes in their place. Increasing wages was considered a "notorious prejudice to the Commonwealth" and "the support of all the Insolence of Servants." Thomas Manley, *Usury at Six Per Cent. Examined* (London, 1669), pp. 17–20, *passim;* [Daniel Defoe], *The Great Law of Subordination Consider'd* (London, 1724), pp. 79–80. However, there was no agreement on this point among mercantilists, just as on many other subjects. Some of the best known, such as Child and Cary, opposed the subsistence wage program. Eli F. Heckscher, *Mercantilism*, trans. M. Shapiro (London, 1935), II, 152, 163–172, 297–301; E. S. Furniss, *The Position of the Laborer in a System of Nationalism* (Boston, 1920), chs. vi, vii; Witt Bowden, *Industrial Society in England towards the End of the Eighteenth Century* (New York, 1925), pp. 231–233; W. Hasbach, *History of the English Agricultural Laborer* (London, 1908), p. 100n. See also E. Lipson, *The Economic History of England* (3 vols., London, 1927, 1931); L. Brentano, *Geschichte der Wirtschaftlichen Entwicklung Englands* (Jena, 1927), Vol. II; M. T. Wermel, *The Evolution of the Classical Wage Theory* (New York, 1939), pp. 21–27.

worker, owing to widely divergent conditions obtaining in this country, enjoyed a larger measure of freedom from restriction than they would have if they had remained at home. Even in the colonies there were many vestigial remains of medieval town regulations alongside a vigorous program of centralizing mercantilism. Because of the failure to effectuate any true measure of colonial unification, mercantilism as a system of internal regulation for the strengthening of the national economy never attained in colonial life a fullness of vigor comparable with its counterpart in the mother country, where town regulatory activity was in the course of time subordinated to a broad national policy.[4] Typical urban regulations, such as those sustaining the craft monopolies, were introduced into some of the colonies for a brief period at best, although by regulating admission to freemanship the colonial towns were long able to check competition in the crafts and retail trades. However, while the craft guild system was not successfully re-created at the time of settlement, vigorous enforcement was given to colonial and local regulations against forestalling, engrossing, and regrating, and establishing the assizes of bread.[5] In England the enforcement of the industrial code was relegated to such local agencies as the borough, the guild, newly incorporated companies, the justice of the peace, and other local authorities. In the colonies the codes were largely in the hands of town and parish officials and county justices.

The keystone of the Tudor industrial code was found in the Statute of Artificers,[6] which restated and modified the medieval Statutes of Labourers, and in the Poor Laws.[7] Let us consider the basic principles laid down by this legislation and the extent of their adoption in this country.[8]

COMPULSORY LABOR

IN THE FIRST PLACE, the Elizabethan statutes maintained the principle of compulsory labor for able-bodied persons falling into certain designated categories.[1] The Statute of Artificers provided that persons be-

---

[4] Thus, it had been the aim of European mercantilists such as Colbert to abolish local tolls and tariffs impeding national trade. For the colonial problem, see *infra*, pp. 21, 118.

[5] See *infra*, pp. 60, 126.   [6] 5 Eliz. c. 4.   [7] 39, 40 Eliz. c. 3; 43 Eliz. c. 2.

[8] In the preface to Greenleaf's edition of *An Abridgment of Burn's Justice of the Peace and Parish Officer* (Boston, 1773), the editor declares: "What we have rejected related to acts made for the regulating their woolen manufactory . . . weights and measures, vagrants, . . . shoemakers, servants, seamen, . . . linen cloth, leather, . . . and a number of articles under other heads of no possible use or importance to us in America." Nevertheless, in a number of the named fields parallel legislation was enacted in the colonies.

[1] Vagrants under the act of 1547 were subject to branding and a two-year sentence as a "slave." *Stat. at Large* (Pickering), V, 246. This statute was repealed within two years because

tween twelve and sixty not employed otherwise were to be servants in husbandry. Youths refusing to serve as apprentices were subject to impressment. Any one below the rank of yeoman was forbidden to withdraw from an agricultural pursuit in order to be apprenticed to a trade.[2] In the Elizabethan act for the punishment of rogues, vagabonds, and sturdy beggars [3] wandering persons and common laborers who refused to work at the ordinary rate of wages were included, along with beggars, peddlers, palmists, gypsies, fences, petty chapmen, and others, in a comprehensive list of persons who fell into these categories and were subject to whipping and to sentence to labor in the house of correction. Children of persons who could not maintain themselves were to be taught a trade and set to work, for the mercantilists strongly advocated the labor of women and children of the working classes. In short, those living "without a calling" were compelled to work or were punished by the criminal machinery.[4]

It is readily understandable why the colonies, constantly short of manpower and pervaded by that intense resentment of idleness often associated with pioneer lands, should have largely taken over this program. Not alone in Puritan New England was idleness stigmatized as "the parent of all Vices," [5] but throughout the length and breadth of the North Atlantic seaboard idleness was discountenanced. As in the Elizabethan code, Rhode Island classified together "any Rougs, vagabonds, Sturdy beggars, masterless men, or other Notorious offenders whatsoeuer." [6] Penn's Frame of Government provided that "all children within this province of the age of twelve years, shall be Taught some useful trade or skill, to the end none may be idle, but the poor may work to live, and the rich, if they become poor, may not want." [7]

---

of its severity, but in 1572 a statute made vagabonds found at large liable to one year's service to responsible property owners willing to give bond to maintain them. If no property owner would accept a culprit, he was to be whipped and burnt through the gristle of the right ear. Death was the penalty for a third offense. *Ibid.*, VI, 299, 311, 392.

[2] See also 12 Ric. II, c. 5 (1388). For the rationale of this restriction, see R. H. Tawney and Eileen Power, eds., *Tudor Economic Documents* (London, 1924), I, 354, 355.

[3] 39, 40 Eliz. c. 4.

[4] For example, the overseers of Turvile declared that one spinster's refusal to enter the service they had found for her on the ground that she was unwilling to labor was "of ill example to lazy and thriftless people." She was committed to the workhouse. G. R. Crouch, ed., *Calendar to the Buckingham Session Records* (Aylesbury, 1935), II, 222. See also HMC, *Rep.*, XIV, Pt. VIII, 193; "Manchester Sessions, 1616–1622/3," Record Society, *Publications*, XLII (1901), 58 (1618).

[5] See report adopted by the town of Boston in 1769. Record Commissioners of the City of Boston, *Reports* (Boston, 1876–), XVI, 273, 274.

[6] *Early Records of the Town of. Providence* (20 vols., Providence, 1892–1909), XVII, 5, 6 (1682).

[7] *Pa. Arch.*, I, 42. To discourage idleness Philadelphia suppressed theatrical performances. *M.C.C. Phila., 1704–76* (Philadelphia, 1847), p. 523 (1750). Cf. also *Pa. Col. Rec.*, IX, 166 (1764). In Southern towns the sale of liquor to servants as well as slaves was sharply cur-

Colonial almanacs were studded with aphorisms on the sinfulness of being unemployed. "Leisure is the Time for doing something useful," Poor Richard put it. The Ameses, father and son, remind their readers that "The Law of Nature so ordains, *Toil, and be Strong.*" "By the sweat of thy brow thou shalt eat thy bread," the colonial child entered in his copybook.[8]

Early statutes generally punished idleness by whipping or fine,[9] but later enactments provided for forced labor[10] or commitment to the workhouse.[11] Where the unemployed were recent arrivals, statutes authorized their transportation to the colony whence they came.[12] Some

---

tailed. Norfolk C. C. Mins., f. 11 (1738); *S.C. Gazette*, Oct. 31, 1774; *Ordinances of the City Council of Charleston, S.C.* (Charleston, 1802), pp. 15, 149. Cf. also *Gazette of the State of S.C.*, Dec. 12, 1785, and *Mass. Centinel*, Dec. 23, 1786.

[8] Sam Briggs, *The Essays, Humor, and Poems of Nathaniel Ames, Father and Son, of Dedham, Massachusetts, from their Almanacks, 1726–1775* (Cleveland, 1891), pp. 258, 260, 261 (1755), 274 (1757), 377 (1766), 412 (1770). It must be borne in mind, as Carl Van Doren points out, that the earlier Poor Richard was not always on the side of calculating prudence. On the eve of his execution a burglar exhorted the good citizens of Boston to:

> Shun vain and idle Company;
> They'll lead you soon astray;
> From ill-fam'd Houses ever flee,
> And keep yourselves away.

> With honest Labor earn your Bread,
> While in your youthful Prime;
> Nor come you near the Harlot's Bed,
> Nor idly waste your Time.

.   .   .   .

> The dreadful Deed for which I die,
> Arose from small Beginning;
> My Idleness brought poverty,
> And so I took to Stealing.

Broadside, Pa. Hist. Soc., also in Ola E. Winslow, ed., *American Broadside Verses from Imprints of the 17th and 18th Centuries* (New Haven, 1930). See also Sister Monica Kiefer, "Early American Childhood in the Middle Atlantic Area," *Pa. Mag. of Hist. and Biog.*, LXVIII (1944), 5. Conservative ministers attacked the evangelical fervor of the Great Awakening on the ground that religious meetings kept the multitude from their work. See L. W. Labaree, "The Conservative Attitude toward the Great Awakening," *WMCQ*, 3d ser., I, 341–343.

[9] For typical examples see *Plymouth Col. Rec.*, XI, 32, 90 (1639), 143, 144 (1658), 206 (1661–63); *R.I. Col. Rec.*, III, 452 (1702); *Conn. Pub. Rec.*, I, 528 (1650), VI, 82 (1718).

[10] See N.C. Laws of 1755, c. 4; Laws of 1760, sess. 4, c. 13; Laws of 1766, c. 17; Laws of 1770, c. 79—on failure to betake himself to some "lawful calling," the vagrant was to be hired out for one year. Virginia, by executive order in 1692, impressed idle seamen. Henrico O.B., lib. I, f. 491 (1692). For conscription of vagrants into the armed services, see *S.C. Stat.*, IV, 51, 52 (1758); Hening, IX, 216, 217 (1776); *N.C. State Rec.*, XXIV, 157 (1778). See also Critchton's case, Guilford, lib. 1781–88, f. 10 (1781). Cf. also *S.C. Gazette*, Dec. 2, 1773, Dec. 12, 1785; *Charleston Ordinances*, pp. 141, 143 (1796).

[11] For workhouse statutes, see *infra*, pp. 12, 13.

[12] The New England Confederation had set an example by a mutual agreement to this end. *Conn. Pub. Rec., 1678–89*, p. 489 (1673). See also *N.Y. Col. Laws*, II, 56 (1721); Allinson, *N.J. Acts*, pp. 418, 419 (1774); but cf. *Newcastle, Del., Court Rec.* (Lancaster, 1904), I, 421 (1680). For the transportation to the West Indies of an "idle person that refuseth to work," see *Boston Town Rec.*, VII, 162 (1683).

of these statutes were frankly based upon the Tudor and Stuart legislation; others borrowed the identical phraseology of some of these
English enactments. A Virginia act of 1672 directed the justices of the
peace to "put the lawes of England against vagrant, idle and disolute
persons in strict execution." [13] An act of the same province of 1728
incorporated the principle laid down in 39, 40 Eliz. c. 4 by including in
its definition of vagabonds "all persons, able in body, and fit to labour,
and not having wherewithal otherwise to maintain themselves, who
shall be found loitering, and neglecting to labour for the usual and
common wages." [14] In 1750 the legislature of Rhode Island resolved to
introduce into the colony all the British statutes "related to the poor and
relating to masters and their apprentices, so far as they are applicable
in this colony, and where we have no law of the colony." [15] The effectiveness of such statutes in curbing demands on the part of workmen for
higher wages was dependent upon the degree of vigilance exercised by
the justices. A New Haven quarter sessions court in 1688 cited the
statutes of Elizabeth and James I regarding vagabonds as being in
operation in the colony; to bring about proper observance of the statutes
the town constables were instructed to publish the court order that
"none may plead Ignorance in not doeing their duty." [16] In the main
these statutes and local regulations were strictly enforced by the courts
and town authorities, who were diligent in seeing that laborers were
employed and "attended to their callings." [17]

The compulsory labor program was by no means confined to the unemployed. Generally in the colonies all male inhabitants between sixteen

[13] Hening, II, 298 (1672); *VMH*, IX, 374. Cf. also act of 1619, implying the right of the
governor to conscript servants. L. G. Tyler, ed., *Narratives of Early Virginia, 1606–1625* (New
York, 1907), p. 273. Barbados made provision in 1652 for putting vagrants to work in defense
of the island. Richard Hall, *Acts Passed in the Island of Barbados, 1643–1762* (London, 1764).
By an act of 1688, authority was given to any two justices to bind out any loose, idle, or unsettled persons under the age of twenty-one to apprenticeship "in the manner prescribed by the
Stat. 5 Eliz. c. 4." *Ibid.*, No. 83, cl. IV.

[14] Hening, IV, 208–214 (1728).   [15] *R.I. Col. Rec.*, V, 288 (1750).

[16] New Haven Q.S., New Haven Co. Court, lib. I, f. 4 (1688).

[17] For typical prosecutions for vagrancy and idleness, see York, Me., Sess., *York Deeds*, V, Pt. II,
f. 51 (1695); *Assistants*, II, 14 (1631), 70 (1637), 84 (1639), 123, 126 (1642); *Plymouth Col.
Rec.*, I, 163 (1640), II, 36 (1642), III, 127 (1658), delinquent debtor; *Boston Town Rec.*, II,
132, 133; *Boston Selectmen Rec., 1701–15*, p. 17 (1701); New Haven Co. Court, lib. I, 1666–98,
f. 54 (1672); Hartford Co. Court, "Conn. Prob. Rec.," lib. III, f. 166 (1677); Hartford Co. Court,
lib. 1706/7–18, f. 91 (1709); New London Co. Court, lib. III, f. 47 (1672); Conn. Superior
Court Rec., lib. 1710–49, f. 68 (1712); Newport Court of Trials, lib. I, f. 141 (1701); Gravesend, L.I., Town Rec., lib. IV, 1662–99, f. 25 (1669); N.Y.G.S., lib. 1694–1731/2, f. 524 (1730),
1722–42/3, f. 272 (1739); Burlington, West Jersey, Court Bk., f. 79 (1688); Monmouth, N.J.,
C.P. and Q.S., lib. 1688–1721, f. 443 (1718); Talbot, Md., Co. Court, lib. NN, No. 6 (March 5,
1687); York, Va., O.B., 1706–10, f. 83 (1707).

and sixty were required to work on certain occasions during the year on public works projects.[18] In the Northern colonies this compulsory labor program embraced master as well as servant, freemen as well as inhabitants.[19] In addition to public works projects, Massachusetts, in order to assure a food supply for the colony during the Pequot and King Philip's Wars, impressed men to carry on "the husbandry of such persons" as were in the armed services.[20] At the same time men in the militia might be subject to assignment to labor projects. An act of 1646 authorized the constables of every town to require artificers and handicraftsmen "to work by the day for their neighbours in mowing, reaping of corn and inning thereof." This law was justified by the fact that the harvest of hay, corn, flax, and hemp usually came so close together "that much losse can hardly be avoyded." Compensation was to be paid by the farmers to their conscripted workers. A fine of double the usual daily wage was fixed for noncompliance, "provided no artificer or handycrafts-man shall be compelled to work . . . whiles he is necessarily attending on the like business of his own." [21] New Haven colony provided that the governor or magistrates could require the captain on training day to send as many fit men as the public work required. For this work they were to be reimbursed "vpon just pay." All private contracts were "suspended" until the public service was performed, after which they were to "return to their full force as if the presse had not bin." [22] The burgomasters and schepens of New Amsterdam actually avoided a private contract committing men to go into service in Virginia on the ground that the governor had impressed the defendants for public work.[23] The Duke's Laws authorized the sending of warrants to any justice, and by the justices in turn to the town constable, to procure "so many Labourers and Artificers as the warrant shall direct," at wages judged proper by the constable and overseers. Provision was made

[18] See, e.g., *Records of the Town of Southampton, 1639–1870* (6 vols., Sag Harbor, N.Y., 1874–1915), I, 41 (1644); *Records of the Town of Jamaica, L.I., 1656–1751* (3 vols., New York, 1914), I, 61 (1674); "Newark Town Rec., 1666–1836," N.J. Hist. Soc., *Coll.*, VI, 60 (1675).

[19] See *Assistants*, II, 38 (1633); *Conn. Pub. Rec.*, II, 229; *New Haven Col. Rec.*, I, 55, 227, 231; *Providence Town Rec.*, II, 94 (1656); *R.N.A.*, V, 105 (1664).

[20] "Early Records of the Town of Dorchester, 1632–87," Boston Rec. Commissioners, *4th Rep.* (Boston, 1880), p. 32 (1637), where the order applied also to masters whose servants had gone into military service. See also *Mass. Bay Rec.*, V, 78 (1676), where the conscripts were to be compensated at a rate of 18*d.* a day for their work "to be payd by the respective persons for whom they worke." For the impressment of artificers and laborers for military duties, see *infra*, pp. 279 *et seq.*

[21] *The Laws and Liberties of Massachusetts, 1648* (Cambridge, 1929), p. 55; *Mass. Bay Rec.*, II, 180–181. 12 Ric. II, c. 5 (1388) was a good precedent for such conscription.

[22] *New Haven Col. Rec., 1638–49*, p. 213 (1645).   [23] *R.N.A.*, V, 131 (1664).

"that no Ordinary Labourer" should be compelled "to work from home above one week." [24] It should be noted that the Massachusetts act of 1646 and this provision of the New York code were discriminatory as they applied only to the working class.

In the early days of settlement Virginia authorized the general impressment of inhabitants for public service, but provided that such impressment was to be conducted "least burthensome to the people, and most free from partialitie." [25] The Grand Council of South Carolina in 1672 required all persons, with a few exceptions noted, to work at planting until the next crop had been gathered. Loiterers were liable to be disposed of by the council to the care of some industrious planter.[26] Occasionally Southern county courts required tithables to do the farm work for those who went off to fight.[27] However, the general practice was to require the master to send his "laboring servant or slave" for public works projects.[28] Masters of two or more tithable male laboring servants were excepted from such public works.[29]

A Maryland impressment act for the building of a town house provided that the housekeepers be required to contribute "stuff, workmanship, labor or tobacco in such manner and after such rates proportional to each man's personal estate" as the authorities assessed, and that no man, "artificers excepted," be pressed to labor on the building before November and after February, the artificers and laborers "to have such for their work as are reasonably used within the colony." [30] Under this project the artificers and laborers really carried the load of personal service. In 1699 that colony set a fine for laborers refusing to obey the overseer and for masters who refused to send all their taxable male servants to him.[31] An act of 1750 required the overseers of iron works to send one out of every ten laboring persons to the overseer of the highways.[32] In colonial, Revolutionary, and post-Revolutionary South Carolina laborers could be conscripted for public works,[33] and in Georgia slaves were included among the "hands" impressed for road work.[34]

---

[24] *N.Y. Col. Laws*, I, 38 (1665).   [25] Hening, I, 196 (1632).
[26] *Journal of the Grand Council of South Carolina, 1671–1680*, ed. A. S. Salley, Jr. (Columbia, S.C., 1907), p. 27.
[27] Accomac, Va., O.B., I, f. 105 (1638).   [28] See Hening, X, 368 (1780).
[29] *Ibid.*, VI, 66 (1748); X, 164, 165 (1779).   [30] *Md. Arch.*, I, 75 (1639).
[31] *Ibid.*, XXII, 546–554 (1699).
[32] *Ibid.*, XLVI, 294 (1749). In the West Indies Negroes could be impressed. *CSPA, 1681–85*, No. 1259, p. 499; No. 1291, p. 511 (1683). A master might be required to send one Negro out of every twenty or thirty.
[33] *S.C. Stat.* (Cooper and McCord), IV, 441 (1728); *Gazette of the State of S.C.*, Feb. 9, 1780; March 16, 1786.
[34] Chatham Co. Court Mins., lib. 1774–79 (1774); lib. 1781–85 (1783, 1786); lib. 1782–90,

Hence, the conclusion may be drawn that, except for the early settlement years, impressment for service on public works in the Southern colonies was a class obligation involving principally laborers, servants, and slaves.

The kind of public works projects for which labor could be impressed included, first and foremost, road and highway construction and repair.[35] The courts were vigilant in seeing that the impressment was equitably administered and that inhabitants were not compelled to labor on the highways "but in their Respective Turns Justly and Equally as the said Law Directs." [36] When a person had not completed his share of the work, some of the towns authorized the constable to hire other labor and held the absentee liable for the wages of such hired hands as well as for the constable's time; elsewhere he could pay a definite rate —two or three shillings a day—in lieu of personal services. In the Northern colonies the size of one's estate often determined the extent of one's obligations for road work. This in effect amounted to an assessment, which in some colonies could be worked off at a specified daily rate of pay.[37] The obligation to work on roads has carried down to the twentieth

---

f. 252 (1786). For the impressment of Negroes for public works elsewhere, see *M.C.C.*, I, 225, 226 (1691); Tonyn to Knox, Sept. 26, 1778, Turnbull MSS, Shelburne Transcripts, St. Augustine Hist. Soc.

[35] Compulsory labor on highways was enforced throughout contemporary England. See 14 Car. II, c. 6; Mary S. Gretton, "Oxfordshire Justices of the Peace in the Seventeenth Century," Oxford Rec. Soc., *Publications*, XI (Oxford, 1934), lxvii, lxviii.

[36] N.Y.G.S., lib. 1694–1731/2, f. 546 (1732); lib. 1732–62, f. 82 (1738).

[37] For the general practice, see James Parker, *Conductor Generalis or the Office, Duty and Authority of Justices of the Peace* (Andrew Bradford: Philadelphia, 1722), p. 123. For orders, prosecutions, and assessments, see *Maine Prov. and Court Rec.*, I, 304 (1667); York Sess., lib. VI, f. 402 (1715); Gloucester Co. Court Rec., Vermont Hist. Soc., *Proceedings, 1923–25*, pp. 171, 172 (1773); Worcester, Mass., G.S., lib. 1778, f. 425; *Records of the Court of Nathaniel Harris, Justice of the Peace for Middlesex County . . . 1734–61* (Watertown, Mass., 1938), pp. 59, 60, 62, 64, 65 (1741); *Boston Town Rec.*, II, 62, 63 (1641); *Muddy River and Brookline Rec., 1634–1889* (4 vols., Brookline, 1875–89), pp. 90, 171; *Watertown Rec. from 1634* (3 vols., Watertown, 1894–1904), III, 219; IV, 35, *passim; Records of the Town of Lee, 1777–1801* (Lee, Mass., 1900), pp. 20, 107. See also *New Haven Town Rec.*, I, 354–356, 391 (1658–59), rates payable in labor or money levied "in every man's proportion"; *Providence Town Rec.*, III, 55 (1664); N.Y.G.S., lib. 1683–94 (1694); lib. 1694–1731/2, f. 322 (1716); Westchester G.S., Westchester Co. Hist. Soc., *Coll.*, II, 40–42 (1687); 74, 75 (1693); Dutchess G.S., Bk. C, 1758–66, f. 67 (1764); Bk. E, 1771–75 (1771); *Records of the Town of East Hampton, L.I., 1648–1900* (5 vols., Sag Harbor, N.Y., 1887), I, 27 (1652), 71 (1654); *Jamaica Town Rec.*, I, 26 (1663), 31 (1673), 34 (1683), 137 (1685); *Records of the Town of Brookhaven* (3 vols., New York, 1930–32), Bk. C, pp. 15 (1693), 43 (1704) 51 (1707), 207 (1738); *Brookhaven Town Rec., 1662–79*, I (New York, 1925), 95 (1704); *Southampton Town Rec.*, III, 332 (1790); Newark, N.J., Rec., N.J. Hist. Soc., *Coll.*, VI, 20, 21 (1669), 52 (1674); Burlington, West Jersey, Court Bk., f. 19 (1684); *N.J. Gazette*, Oct. 28, 1778.

In Philadelphia prior to 1712 the inhabitants were obliged to "Send Able Labourers" to work on road construction projects, but the common council, for reasons of economy, authorized overseers to take 1s. 6d. from those who were willing to pay to be excused from a day's labor. *M.C.C., Phila.*, p. 80. For instances of forced labor on the roads in Pennsylvania, see Bucks Q.S., lib.

century, and in recent years the compulsory requirement that certain persons labor annually on public highways has been held not to violate prohibitions against involuntary servitude, but is considered in the same category as training in the militia.[38] The inhabitants might also be impressed to work on bridges [39] or fortifications,[40] required to construct or repair dams, weirs, and dikes,[41] clear a commons, make a pound, or set up a sufficient fence,[42] deepen or broaden a river's channel,[43] cut brush,[44] build a meeting house,[45] cart materials for the parsonage,[46] and repair prisons, stocks, whipping posts "or other Instruments of Justice." [47] The wages to be paid for such work were set by the local authorities.[48]

1715–53, f. 373 (1745); *Records of the Courts of Chester Co., 1681–97* (Philadelphia, 1910), p. 244 (1691); Lancaster Road and Sess. Docket, No. 3, 1760–68 (1761); West Chester Q.S., lib. 1714–23 (1715). For Delaware, see *Some Records of Sussex, Del.* (Philadelphia, 1909), pp. 65 (1682), 116 (1684).

For examples of impressment for road and highway projects in the South, see, e.g.: *Virginia:* Caroline O.B., 1732–40, Pt. II, f. 439 (1737), 1777–80, f. 6 (1777); Charles City O.B., 1655–65, f. 357 (1663); Fairfax O.B., 1768–70 (Lib. of Cong.), f. 74 (1768); Fincastle O.B., 1773–77 (1773, 1776). *North Carolina:* Bertie, lib. 1724–69 (1732, 1736, 1758); Bute, lib. 1767–76, fols. 79 (1769), 361 (1775); Cartaret, lib. 1764–77 (1764, 1768); Caswell, lib. 1770–80 (1777), 1777–81 (1777); Craven, lib. 1767–75 (1768); Guilford, lib. 1781–88 (1782, 1783); Rutherford, lib. 1780–82 (1782); Tyrrell, lib. 1770–82 (1777). Occasionally motions of inhabitants for exemption from forced labor on the roads were considered (Onslow, lib. 1741–49, f. 37 [1741]), and frequently overseers of the roads were indicted for not doing their duty; see, e.g., Rex v. Daniel, Halifax Reference or Prosecution Docket, lib. 1759–70 (1770). During the Revolution, South Carolina imposed a fine of $200 for failure to respond to a call for work on roads, bridges, etc. *S.C. Gazette*, Feb. 24, 1779.

[38] *In re* Dassler, 35 Kan. 678 (1886), at p. 684; Dennis v. Simon, 41 Ohio St. 233 (1894); Butler v. Perry, 240 U.S. 328 (1916). But cf. Rex v. Gay, Quincy Rep. (Mass.) 91–93 (1763), which decided that a capias would not issue in Massachusetts for neglect in mending a highway. This decision was indicative of a trend away from impressment for public works by the end of the colonial period.

[39] *Plymouth Col. Rec.*, III, 13 (1652); *Essex*, VI, 317 (1677).

[40] *Boston Town Rec.*, II, 8 (1635); *Mass. Bay Rec.*, IV, Pt. II, 42, 43 (1662); *R.N.A.*, VII, 30, 31 (1673); Albany Mayor's Court Mins., J. Munsell, *Annals of Albany* (10 vols., Albany, 1850–59), II, 98 (1687); *M.C.C.*, I, 329–330; Hening, II, 257, 258 (1667); Jamaica Council Mins., *CSPA, 1693–96*, p. 133 (1693).

[41] *Derby, Conn., Rec., 1655–1710* (Derby, 1901), p. 121 (1681); *Southampton Town Rec.*, I, 40 (1644); *Brookhaven Rec., 1662–79*, I, 117 (1674); *Newcastle, Del., Court Rec.*, I, 57 (1677); *Pa. Stat. at Large*, IV, 265 (1734).

[42] *Conn. Pub. Rec., 1678–89*, p. 91 (1681); *Derby, Conn., Rec., 1655–1710*, p. 120 (1681); York Court of Associates, *York Deeds*, Pt. I, f. 19 (1676); *Brookhaven Rec., 1662–79*, I, 53 (1678).

[43] *Gazette of the State of S.C.*, Oct. 21, 1778.

[44] *Jamaica Town Rec.*, I, 145 (1691).

[45] *Derby, Conn., Rec., 1655–1710*, p. 127 (1682); *Jamaica Town Rec.*, II, 344 (1693).

[46] "Kingston Dutch Rec.," N.Y. State Hist. Assn., *Proceedings*, XI, 40, 41 (1662).

[47] *Plymouth Col. Rec.*, XI, 164 (1658), 258 (1682).

[48] For example, in New Castle, Del., wages and hours were fixed; in 1767 they were 3s. for a day's work from 7 A.M. to 6 P.M. The wages were raised to 4s. in 1770, and both wages and hours scales appear to have been retained until the Revolution. In 1778 the wages were raised to 18s., reflecting inflationary developments. Newcastle Town Rec., lib. I, fols. 26, 28, 30, 34, 42, 43, 45.

Forced labor for private profit was legal during the colonial period.[49] In order to induce an entrepreneur to engage in an undertaking desired by the locality, the authorities might promise him that he could count upon impressed labor. To dig a channel three entrepreneurs asked the New Haven colony in 1644 to "grant them 4 dayes worke for every man in the towne from 16 to 60 yeares olde." The government agreed, and permitted "those that cannott worke, to hyre others to worke in their stead," but required "those that can, to worke in their owne person." [50] In Newark, as an inducement to the entrepreneurs to set up a corn mill the town offered them "3 days Work of every Man and Woman that Holds an Allotment in the Town." [51] This is one instance where women as well as men were required to perform public work.

In the course of time it was shown to be thoroughly unrealistic to insist upon compulsory labor unless permanent employment was available. The enclosures, the rising cost of living consequent upon the Financial Revolution, and the marked fluctuations in the business cycle were creating a serious unemployment problem in England. It was less than objective, in view of changing social and economic conditions, to maintain, as did certain leading mercantilists, that poverty was due to a defect in character. If the "duty to labor" was to be fulfilled and local communities, so far as possible, freed of the burden of caring for the unemployed, a more constructive program was essential. The statute of 1535–36 first recognized the principle that work should be provided for the able-bodied. In the absence of any mechanism this law remained largely a dead letter until the establishment of such workhouses as the Bridewell in London.[52] By an act of 1575–76 this institution was made a part of the national program of poor relief. We are indebted to the parochial reports, diligently gleaned by Sir Frederic Eden, for a description of these insanitary, vermin-infested workhouses, which gen-

---

[49] While in the Spanish colonies a distinction was made between the "public service" industries, comprising chiefly agriculture, mining, and public works, in which forced Indian labor could be required, and other occupations in which compulsory service was prohibited, nevertheless the *mita* system of native forced labor employed under Spanish rule was far more extensively adopted than the English system of impressment of European colonists. See J. J. Carney, "The Legal Theory of Forced Labor in the Spanish Colonies," University of Miami, *Hispanic-American Studies*, No. 3 (1942), pp. 26, 27, 29, 30. One argument raised by labor leaders in opposing national service legislation during World War II was that forced labor for private profit was involuntary servitude, and therefore unconstitutional.

[50] *New Haven Col. Rec., 1638–49*, p. 143. [51] N.J. Hist. Soc., *Coll.*, VI. 30, 31 (1670).

[52] E. M. Leonard, *The Early History of English Poor Relief* (Cambridge, 1900), pp. 30–36, 65; Buck, *Politics of Mercantilism*, p. 91. For Coke's endorsement of the workhouse program, see Lipson, *Econ. Hist. of Eng.*, III, 426.

erally concentrated on the manufacture of textiles and often imparted a small amount of trade instruction.[53] The London Bridewell offered training in a considerable number of trades.[54]

The workhouse program was also introduced in the colonies. As early as 1658 Plymouth colony passed an act providing for a house of correction where vagrants, idle persons, rebellious children, and stubborn servants who refused "to work to earne theire own bread" were to be employed.[55] During the latter part of the seventeenth and the early part of the eighteenth century royal instructions were issued to colonial governors to have laws enacted for the erection of workhouses; this fact, coupled with the increase of unemployment and poverty in many colonial communities, explains the conspicuous trend toward the workhouse system in eighteenth-century American towns.[56] The general Parliamentary law of 1722 giving permission to parishes to establish workhouses [57] may well have served as a model for some of the colonial legislation. By the middle of the eighteenth century workhouses had been erected in Boston, New York, Philadelphia, and Charleston.[58] The Montgomerie charter of 1731 authorized the New York City authorities

[53] Sir Frederic M. Eden, *The State of the Poor,* ed. A. G. L. Rogers (New York, 1929); Oliver J. Dunlop, *English Apprenticeship and Child Labour* (New York, 1912), p. 248.

[54] Leonard, *op. cit.,* p. 354. For Coke's endorsement of the workhouse program, see Lipson, *op. cit.,* III, 426.

[55] We have no information about the operations of this institution. *Plymouth Col. Rec.,* XI, 120 (1658). Cf. also *Boston Town Rec.,* VII, 157, 158 (1682), 204 (1690).

[56] See L. W. Labaree, *Royal Instructions to British Colonial Governors* (New York, 1935), I, 342, 343; *Md. Arch.,* VIII, 279, XXII, 287; VMH, XXVIII, 44.

[57] Stat. 9 Geo. I, c. 7 § iv; Eden, *op. cit.,* pp. 47–51, *passim;* Sir George Nicholls, *A History of the English Poor Law* (London, 1904), II, 16–17.

[58] For colonial legislation establishing workhouses, see *Mass. Acts and Resolves,* I, 67 (1692–93), 654 (1710–11), II, 756; III, 108, 926, V, 46; *Acts and Laws of New Hampshire,* I, 73 (1718); *Conn. Pub. Rec.,* V, 383, VII, 127, 530, VIII, 137–139, 505, X, 159, 206, XIII, 237; *R.I. Col. Rec.,* IV, 365, V, 157, 378, VI, 598; Allinson, *N.J. Acts,* pp. 179 *et seq.* (1748); *Pa. Stat. at Large* (Mitchell and Flanders), V, 84, 85 (1749), VII, 15 (1766), 85–88 (1767); *Pa. Col. Rec.,* XIV, 354 (1785); Hening, VI, 475 (1755); *S.C. Stat,* VII, 90.

For local regulations of workhouses, spinning schools, etc., including commitments, see *Boston Selectmen Rec., 1701–15,* p. 20 (1702), *1716–36,* pp. 66, 108, 137, 275, 293, 296, 297; *Boston Town Rec.,* VIII, 93, 96, 97, 101 (1712–14), 147–148 (1720); *M.C.C., N.Y.,* III, 362, IV, 308 (1736); D. M. Schneider, *The History of Public Welfare in New York State, 1609–1866* (Chicago, 1938), pp. 119–120. Philadelphia as early as 1712 provided for the establishment of a workhouse to employ the idle poor. *M.C.C., Phila.,* pp. 80, 229, 230, 279. See also comment in *Phila. Directory, 1794.* According to the vestry records, six Virginia parishes had workhouses or poorhouses before the American Revolution. See G. F. Wells, *Parish Education in Colonial Virginia* (New York, 1923), p. 66. See also *Bristol Parish Vestry Book and Register, 1720–89* (Richmond, 1898), p. 160. As early as 1735 the Charleston, S.C., grand jury returned that, for want of a workhouse to punish the idle, the poor were flocking to the town. *S.C. Gazette,* March 23–30, 1734. See also presentments of 1768, *ibid.,* Jan. 25–Feb. 1, 1768; *S.C. Council J., 1764–68,* fols. 252, 255 (1768). See *S.C. Gazette, passim,* for regular lists of those committed to the workhouse. See also M. W. Jernegan, *Laboring and Dependent Classes in Colonial America* (Chicago, 1931), pp. 201 *et seq.*

to erect an almshouse, which, when completed in 1735, was used as both a house of correction and a workhouse for "Beggars, Servants running away or otherwise misbehaving themselves, Trespassers, Rogues, Vagabonds, and poor people refusing to work." [59] With the establishment of workhouses, short-term labor sentences were frequently imposed for minor offenses.[60]

The nonimportation agreements were a fillip not alone to domestic manufactures but also to the promotion of plans for the employment of the poor on such favored or subsidized projects as the manufacture of woolens, linen, and cotton goods. By the eve of the Revolution leading colonial towns had set up establishments for such manufacturing. These projects, privately operated, undoubtedly drew upon the town workhouses and helped lighten the local community's poor relief burden, while at the same time assuring a cheap labor supply.[61]

[59] *N.Y. Col. Laws,* III, 645.

[60] Mary Atkinson's case is doubtless typical of many friendless laboring people and vagrants. She was committed to gaol by the following *mittimus* made up by a justice of the peace:

City of   To the Keeper of the House of Correction or Brideswell
New York   You are hereby Required and Commanded to take into the Bridewell the Body [of] Mary Atkins [*sic*] and her keep to Hard Labour During the Space of Forty Days given Under my Hand and Seal this 19 Day of December in the thirteenth year of His Majesty Reign A:D 1772

John Dykeman

Mary's mother petitioned the attorney-general that her daughter had been sent to the Bridewell "without any Crime," and that Alderman Brewerton had accordingly obtained her release. Whereupon the justice had her recommitted. As a result, her mother charged, "she's hindred from her Service besides hurting her Caracter which is tender to those that Live by their Labour." Kempe MSS, A–B, N.Y. Hist. Soc.; see also *ibid.,* W–Y, order regarding vagrants John Willson *et al.* (1774).

[61] The undertakers of such a project in Boston in 1768 disclaimed any profit motive, stating that their design was solely to employ "the many Poor we have in the Town and giving them a Livelihood." *Boston Town Rec.,* XVI, 226, 227, 230–232, 249. As unemployment increased, the responsibilities of the entrepreneurs were enhanced. In April, 1769 it was reported that over 200 unemployed in Boston were desirous of securing work at spinning and carding and that "their Numbers are dayly increasing." Funds were provided for setting up spinning schools to train children and for securing machinery, etc., to take care of the unemployed. This, it was reported by the committee, would not only reduce the numbers in the almshouses but would "habituate the People to Industry, and preserve their Morals who instead of their continuing a burden to society will become some of its most useful Members." *Ibid.,* pp. 272–276. For other similar Boston projects, see *ibid.,* XVIII, 70, 71 (spinning wool, 1772; building ships and wharves and paving streets to care for unemployed sufferers from the Port Bill, 1774). Peter Curtenius of New York City made a series of remarkable proposals to the Boston committee responsible for this program. His idea was that these work projects should be self-sustaining, that the ships built by the ship carpenters be sold and the proceeds used again; similarly with house carpenters, who should be employed "to keep them in a good humour." Set the unemployed blacksmiths to work making nails which were assured a profitable market, he recommended. Sell the yarn and thread made by the poor and unemployed women spinners, or have the material woven and sell the cloth. Peter Curtenius to William Cooper, August 26, 1774, N.Y. Pub. Lib.

The sum of £1,000 voted by the New York Provincial Congress in 1775 for the relief of the poor was placed in the hands of John Ramsey, a woolen merchant, to employ them in making linen and tow cloth. His own fee was five per cent of all moneys turned over to him. A further

POOR RELIEF

A PROGRAM which favored compulsory labor for the unemployed was by iron logic compelled to advocate the regulation of poor relief, and to keep it within strict limits. The medieval Statute of Labourers prohibited all almsgiving except to the impotent poor, who were to remain at their place of residence or be sent to the place of their birth.[1] The poor law code inaugurated at the end of Elizabeth's reign placed responsibility upon the parish to maintain and set to work children whose parents were unable to support them, to purchase stocks of material to carry on work for the poor, and to relieve the impotent and unemployable through general taxation.[2] A logical consequence of this principle of local responsibility was the Law of Settlement of 1662, which authorized the overseer to expel from the parish any person occupying property renting for less than £10 a year who was deemed likely at some future time to be in need, and to convey such person to the parish where he had last legally settled.[3]

The scrutiny to which strangers entering New England were subjected was in large measure due to a reluctance on the part of the local authorities to be burdened with the maintenance of immigrants incapable of supporting themselves and their families.[4] Where the immigrant became chargeable before gaining a residence, the burden of support fell upon the person responsible for his entry.[5] The old English custom of "warning out" was practiced in New England to avoid responsibility

---

sum of £1,000 was granted him in March, 1776. *J. N.Y. Prov. Cong.*, I, 231; *Cal. Hist. MSS Rel. to the War of the Revol.* (Albany, 1868), I, 311; Schneider, *op. cit.*, pp. 97, 98.

The Continental Congress officially encouraged the formation of societies throughout the colonies for the promotion of manufactures. See John Adams, *Works*, ed. C. F. Adams (Boston, 1850–56), II, 487; VI, 235, 252.

A venture for the production of coarse linen was established in Philadelphia in 1764 with the ostensible object of relieving unemployment. Buildings were erected and more than 100 persons employed. The House of Employment eventually ran into financial difficulties. J. T. Scharf and T. Westcott, *History of Philadelphia, 1609–1884* (Philadelphia, 1884), III, 2309, 2310; *Pa. Col. Rec.*, IX, 567; *M.C.C., Phila.*, p. 799.

[1] 12 Ric. II, cc. 3 and 7.

[2] 43 Eliz. c. 2. See also Tawney and Power, *Tudor Econ. Docs.*, II, 296–369.

[3] 13 and 14 Car. II, c. 12. See also Karl de Schweinitz, *England's Road to Social Security* (Philadelphia, 1943), pp. 39–47.

[4] For example, in 1713, the selectmen of Boston proposed that a committee be appointed "to consider Some Expedient for the more Effectual preventing of the Poor belonging to other places, from Obtruding them Selves on the Town." *Boston Selectmen Rec.*, 1701–15, p. 178 (1713). See also *infra*, pp. 148, 219 n., 416.

[5] See Jernegan, *Laboring and Dependent Classes*, p. 192 and note. Residence requirements ranged from three months to a year. The law required close relatives to support their dependents. See *Mass. Acts and Resolves*, IV, 705 (1764); Providence, R.I., Superior Court Rec., 1769–90, fols. 186–189 (1773).

for the support of prospective paupers.[6] Generally the New England colonies required the towns to maintain their own poor.[7] Ultimately the workhouse was set up for the tramp and vagrant whereas the pauper remained under the care of town officials.[8] In some New England towns the practice of binding out indigent widows to service was so successful that poorhouses were not built.[9]

While in New England the supervision of the poor remained a responsibility of town government, the English parish system, which was responsible for administering poor relief in the mother country, was duplicated in the Southern colonies.[10] The vestries could apprentice poor children,[11] make levies for the poor, and allot aid according to the needs of individual cases. In turn, the vestries could be called to account by the county courts, which on occasion administered poor relief.[12]

[6] See *Mass. Acts and Resolves*, I, 67, 378–381, 538–539, II, 42, IV, 735 (1765), 911 (1767); J. H. Benton, *Warning Out in New England* (Boston, 1911); *Essex*, VIII, 45 (1680); York, Me., Court Rec., lib. II (transcribed), f. 379 (1680); Hampshire, Mass., C. P., lib. 1728/9–35, f. 7 (1729); *Boston Town Rec.*, II, 10 (1636), 90 (1647), VII, 134, 135 (1679); VIII, 102 (1714), 177 (1723). For the English background, see J. H. Thomas, *Town Government in the Sixteenth Century* (London, 1933), pp. 117, 118, 132, 133.

[7] *Plymouth Col. Rec.*, XI, 41 (1642); *Conn. Code of 1673*, p. 57; *Conn. Code of 1702*, p. 94; *Mass. Acts and Resolves, 1692–93*, c. 28. The *Boston Town Records* have innumerable references to poor relief. See, e.g., VII, 214, 215 (1693), 231 (1698); VIII, 3 (1700), 23 (1702), 43, 44 (1707), 93 (1713); *Boston Selectmen Rec., 1701–15*, p. 23 (1702); *1716–36*, pp. 122 (1723), 146 (1725), 237 (1733). Beginning with 1736 and running down to the Revolution, the selectmen found it necessary to take more frequent action with reference to poor relief as the problem became steadily more acute. There are forty instances of action being taken by the selectmen between 1736 and 1742; thirty instances between 1742 and 1753; twenty-six between 1754 and 1763, some involving ten or a dozen persons; and fifty instances between 1764 and 1768, some involving two or three persons. See *ibid., 1736–42, 1742–53, 1754–63, 1764–68, passim*. For poor relief in other Massachusetts towns, see Chatham Town Rec., lib. I, fols. 51 (1731), 123 (1745), *passim;* II, fols. 17, 19 (1752); Falmouth Town Book, lib. II (May 1, 1775; Dec. 15, 1777). For Rochester, see W. R. Bliss, *Colonial Times on Buzzard's Bay* (Boston, 1900), p. 40 (1729). See also Hampden Co., Mass., Court Mins., lib. 1710, 1714–84, f. 16 (1721).

[8] E. W. Capen, *The Historical Development of the Poor Law of Connecticut* (New York, 1905), pp. 17, 18.

[9] The poor widows of Wareham, Mass., were sold at auction annually to reimburse the town for sums advanced them. Bliss, *op. cit.*, pp. 97–100. See also Wareham Town Rec., lib. I (1782). For an instance of the binding out of a married couple, see *Plymouth Col. Rec.*, III, 37, 38 (1653).

[10] See, e.g., Hening, I, 433, II, 25, 356, III, 264, VI, 29, 32; *S.C. Stat.*, II, 116 (1695), 593 (1712), 606 (1713).

[11] See *infra*, p. 386n.

[12] A frequent form of relief was exemption from levies. See, e.g., Ann Arundel, 1720–21, fols., 48, 49 (1720), 260 (1721); Charles, 1674–76 (1675); Frederick, 1750–51, f. 295 (1751); Prince George, lib. A, 1696–1702, f. 51 (1696), 1746–47 (Nov., 1746); *Minutes of the Council and General Court of Colonial Virginia*, ed. H. R. McIlwaine (Richmond, 1924), p. 248 (1671). "Augusta Parish Vestry Book," *Chronicles of the Scotch-Irish Settlement in Virginia, extracted from the Original Court Records of Augusta County, 1745–1800* (hereafter *Augusta County Rec.*), ed. Chalkley (3 vols., Rosslyn, 1912), II, 451 (1756), 455 (1767); *Bristol Parish Vestry Book and Register, 1720–89* (Richmond, 1898), pp. 1 (1720), 16 (1724), 28 (1726), 38 (1728); J. S. Moore, *Annals of Henrico Parish* (Richmond, 1904), pp. 1, 11, 12, 42, 98, 145, 162; *VMH*,

In the Middle colonies poor relief administration combined features of the New England town system and the parish system of the Southern colonies.[13] Persons obtaining relief were required to wear a badge. In New Jersey the pauper had to wear on the shoulder of the right sleeve a large blue or red "P" together with the first letter of the name of the city or county in which he resided.[14] Owing to the heavy immigration to these areas, the legislation of the Middle colonies was especially distinguished for its restrictions on entertaining persons not legally settled in the colony, on allowing servants procured from gaols, hospitals, or workhouses of neighboring colonies to gain a settlement, and its requirements that importers give security to indemnify the province if the person imported became a public charge.[15]

Throughout the colonies the binding out of poor children and orphans as authorized by the English Poor Laws was the regular practice of town officials, parish vestries, or county courts.[16] The preamble of a Virginia statute of 1646 providing for the binding out of poor children to be employed in public flaxhouses pays tribute to the parliamentary acts "with great wisdome ordained," which served as a pattern for this statute, according to which the county commissioners were given the same powers of binding out as had been conferred by the English legislation upon the justices of the peace.[17]

XII, 183 (1739); XIII, 26 (1718); *S.C. Gazette,* April 2, 1744. For municipal regulations in the South, see Norfolk C.C. Mins., fols. 367–369, 375, 376 (1798).

[13] A New York act of 1683 provided for local supervision of the poor; that of 1691 made support of the poor a town charge only; and the act of 1693 provided for poor relief to be administered by a board of vestrymen and church wardens elected annually by the freeholders of every city or county. In New York City the common council named the church wardens overseers of the poor in 1736 and they continued to serve in this capacity until the act of 1784 which abolished that office and substituted a public administrative system for the previous combination of church officers and overseers. By that act the overseers of the poor were to be elected at the annual meetings of inhabitants and freeholders. The principle of local responsibility was clearly embodied in the act and strict provisions were laid down for the legal settlement and removal of the unsettled poor. A good deal of charitable relief was administered by the mayor's court. See R. B. Morris, ed., *Select Cases of the Mayor's Court of New York City, 1674–1784 (American Legal Records,* II, Washington, D.C., 1935), pp. 29, 67–71; *N.Y. Col. Laws,* I, 328–333; *M.C.C.* IV, 309, 310; *Laws of New York* (Holt, 1784), p. 146; R. F. Seybolt, *Apprenticeship and Apprenticeship Education in Colonial New England and New York* (New York, 1917), pp. 67, 68; A. E. Peterson and G. W. Edwards, *New York as an Eighteenth Century Municipality* (New York, 1917), pp. 182–199, 296–308; Martha Branscombe, *The Courts and the Poor Laws in New York State, 1784–1929* (Chicago, 1943), pp. 13, 14.

[14] *M.C.C.,* II, 330; *Pa. Stat. at Large,* III, 224, 225 (1718); Allinson, *N.J. Acts,* pp. 410, 411 (1774).

[15] Allinson, *op. cit.,* p. 404 (1774); *Pa. Stat. at Large,* IV, 139, 167 (1729), 266–277 (1735). See also Gloucester, N.J., Q.S., lib. 1771–83 (Sept., 1771); Kent, Del., Co. Court, lib. 1703–17, f. 48 (1706); Newcastle, Del., G.S., lib. 1778–93, f. 175 (1782). Servants and apprentices were denied legal settlement by virtue of their service. Van Schaack, *Laws of N.Y.* (1774), I, 753 (1773); Nevill, *Acts of N.J. General Assembly* (1761), II, 218 (1758).

[16] See *infra,* pp. 384, 385.   [17] Hening, I, 336 (1646).

RESTRAINTS ON DISMISSALS

To PROTECT the workman and curb unemployment the Tudor acts restrained the wrongful dismissal of employees.[1] Early American legal authorities closely followed the English law. By Rhode Island law a master could not put a covenant servant away before the end of his term without reasonable and sufficient cause and the written approval of the chief officer of the town and "three or foure able and discreet men of the Common Council or Towne." [2] The Boston town authorities in 1657 made a sweeping order requiring employers who set servants at liberty "to see after their imployment, and to secure the Town from any charge that might otherwise be occasioned by such." [3] Governor Oglethorpe of Georgia expressed a responsibility to the trustee servants to give those dismissed a month's pay.[4] Even in the case of free workmen the colonial authorities placed curbs on irresponsible dismissals as leading to unemployment and imposing great burdens on the poor relief agencies. In addition to allowing Thomas Marvin wages for the period he had served, the Massachusetts Court of Assistants in 1642 awarded him twenty shillings "for being turned away in winter, unprovided." [5] Workmen under contract were not to be dismissed without reason.[6] Modern factory executives who have found it expedient to dismiss workmen over forty with little or no regard to the social responsibilities of business enterprise might be surprised to read in the quarterly court records of Essex County, Massachusetts, among depositions of

[1] Cunningham cites instances of action by the Council in 1528, 1586, 1591, 1622, and 1623 requiring manufacturers to go on manufacturing even though there was no market for their goods. W. Cunningham, *Growth of English Industry and Commerce in Modern Times* (3d ed., 2 vols., Cambridge, 1903), II, 50; Leonard, *Eng. Poor Relief*, pp. 47–49, 147–149, 152, 153; W. S. Holdsworth, *A History of English Law* (Boston, 1923), IV, 380, 381 (hereafter cited as *H.E.L.*), See also Joan Wake, ed., *Northampton Record Society* (Hereford, 1924), I, 60 (1630); J. C. Atkinson, ed., *North Riding Quarter Sessions*, VI, 136 (1669), 148 (1670); C. E. Longmore, ed., *Session Books of Hertford County* (Hertford, 1935), VI, 405–407; "Manchester Sessions, 1616–1622," *loc. cit.*, p. 106 (1620). Once the coercive authority of the Council had disappeared employers generally were no longer obliged to employ. Holdsworth, *H.E.L.*, VI, 348, 349.

[2] The penalty was 40s. *R.I. Col. Rec.*, I, 182, 183 (1647).

[3] *Boston Town Rec.*, II, 141, 142 (1657). But cf. Abigail Littlefield's case, Suffolk G.S., lib. 1680–92, f. 302 (1686).

[4] *Ga. Col. Rec.*, XXII, Pt. I, 280 (1738).   [5] *Assistants*, II, 120 (1642).

[6] This applied also to workers who had temporarily incapacitated themselves in service. Willemsen v. Cloete, *Albany, Rensselaerswyck, and Schenectady Court Minutes*, trans. and ed. A. J. F. Van Laer (2 vols., Albany, 1926, 1928), II, 320, 321 (1678). The Kent County, Del., court ordered one mistress to take back her employee, "who appears not to be in his right Sences" until she could appear in person in court to give reasons for dismissing him. Cullins's case, Kent, Del., Court Rec., lib. 1699–1703, f. 18 (1700). The authorities of Georgia specifically enjoined the principal trader from discharging any of "his Men" in the Indian country from his service. *Ga. Col. Rec.*, I, 40.

workmen employed at the ironworks, one by Henry Stick, "aged about one hundred and two years," who deposed that he was employed by John Giffard "in the mystery of coaling."[7]

The master as a general rule could not discharge a servant for an incurable illness, and he was obligated to provide him with medical, surgical, and nursing treatment when injured in his employ.[8] In some jurisdictions masters were penalized for turning away servants who had not completely recovered from illness.[9] On rare occasions, but without sufficient consistency to affect the general policy, the court might require the public authorities to maintain and cure the sick or injured servant.[10] It is by no means clear that the government accepted responsibility for injuries to workers engaged in public works projects,[11] although there is some evidence after 1776 of a willingness of town authorities to assume such responsibility.[12]

MAXIMUM WAGE-FIXING AND RESTRAINTS ON COMBINATIONS

THE MERCANTILISTS concretely implemented the medieval policy which sought to prevent the engrossing of indispensable necessaries, of which labor, like food and raw materials, was a basic element. Central control

[7] *Essex*, II, 96 (1653).

[8] 1. Str. 99; William Simpson, *The Practical Justice of the Peace and Parish Officer* (Charleston, S.C., 1761), p. 236; J. Davis, *The Office and Authority of a Justice of the Peace* (New Bern, N.C., 1774), p. 311; William Graydon, *The Justices and Constables Assistant* (Harrisburg, Pa., 1803), p. 15; J. F. Grimké, *The South-Carolina Justice of the Peace*, 3d ed. (New York, 1810), p. 9, and *New Conductor Generalis* (Albany, 1819), p. 29. By court order in 1656 New Haven differentiated between strangers, whose mishaps might have been borne by the public, and servants whose illnesses placed a responsibility on their "Governor" rather than on the colony. *Assistants*, II, 53 (1635); *Essex*, I, 109 (1646), III, 322 (1666); *New Haven Town Rec.*, I, 58 (1650); Bucks County, Pa., C.P. (1684), (1698); *Newcastle, Del., Court Rec.*, I, 173 (1678); *Md. Arch.*, IV, 268 (1644), X, 452 (1656), LVII, 322 (1668). *In re* Laurence Evans, cf. Pennypacker, *Pa. Col. Cases*, p. 86 (1685) and Corbett's case, *Md. Arch.*, LVII, 182, 368–369 (1667–68).

[9] *Laws of Barbados, 1648–1718* (Baskett ed., London, 1732), Law No. 21, cl. x (1661); *Acts of Assembly Passed in the Island of Jamaica, 1681–1737* (Baskett ed., London, 1738), pp. 2–5 (1681); *Acts of Assembly Passed in the Charibbee Leeward Islands, 1690–1732* (Baskett ed., London, 1734), p. 160 (1716); *Laws of Antigua* (London, 1805), I, 185 (1716), 320 (1755). The penalty was 2,200 lbs. of sugar to be paid by the master to the overseer of the poor in Barbados; £20 current in Jamaica, Antigua, and South Carolina, and £5 in North Carolina. James Iredell, *Laws of the State of North Carolina* (Edenton, 1791), c. xxiv. For Florida, see Cecil Johnson, *British West Florida* (New Haven, 1942), p. 179.

[10] *Assistants*, II, 125 (1642).

[11] See petition of the selectmen of the district of Palmer, Mass. Arch., lib. 303 (Petitions, 1659–1786), f. 128 (1761).

[12] See *S.C. Gazette*, Dec. 30, 1778; Pear's petition, N.Y. Common Council Rec., Jan. 29, 1785, Record Room 250, Municipal Building. No reference to this petition is in the *Minutes*. See also Common Council Rec., File Box 14, Bundle 4, *M.C.C., 1784–1831*, I, 658 (1791), where an award was made to a laborer injured in a public works project.

over the regulation of wages and prices was first seriously attempted in England in the medieval Ordinance of Labourers and the Statute of Labourers, enacted in 1349 and 1351, respectively. Statutes of 1351 and 1388 established specific maximum wage scales, but this policy was dropped in 1390, when the justices of the peace were authorized to impose wages "according to the dearth of victuals." Between 1455 and 1515 maximum wage scales were once more set by statute, but the great Statute of Artificers of 1563, which laid down principles determining the legal relations of master and servant for more than a century and a half, threw specific maximum scales overboard and authorized the justices of the peace to fix wages according "to the plenty or scarcity ·of the time." [1]

Whether or not the government was genuinely concerned about improving the condition of the workers, as some writers maintain, there is no question that the Tudor program did restrain unconscionable landowners. The Privy Council insisted that workers were not to be "uncharitably dealt with." [2] On a few rare occasions minimum wages were prescribed by law.[3] But in general the program was restricted to the levying of maximum wages. The Statute of Artificers (§ 16) provided that none should "geve any more or greater wages, then by proclamacion shall be limited, upon payne that the maister shall forfaite five pounds. And the servant shall suffer one and twentye days imprisonment without baile or mayneprice." In every wage assessment is found the provision that workmen in a particular category were *"not to be paid more than"* specific wages stated. The explanation for the fact that the wage assessments had the effect of assuring a constant cheap labor supply lay in the relaxation of control over the program by the Privy Council and the conferring of authority upon the justices of the peace to fix the rates of wages. By law the justices of the peace were required to be men of property and prominence in their respective localities.[4] The

[1] Stat. of Labourers, 23 Edw. III, cc. i-viii; 25 Edw. III, stat. 1; 12 Ric. II, cc. 3–5; 13 Ric. II, stat. 1, c. viii; 3 Hen. V, c. 4; 6 Hen. VI, c. 3; 4 Eliz. c. 4, § 11. See also Richard Burn, *The Justice of the Peace* (London, 1800), IV, 206 *et seq.* The regulatory background in England and on the continent has been treated in the studies of Tawney, Hauser, Heckscher, Lipson, Bertha H. Putnam, Estelle Waterman, and Knoop and Jones, among others. For a bibliography of mercantilist writings on the subject, see Buck, *Politics of Mercantilism,* p. 201.

[2] See Lipson, *Econ. Hist. of Eng.,* III, 257. For the Stuarts, see *ibid.,* pp. 258, 259. See also Holdsworth, *H.E.L.,* II, 463, 464.

[3] 1 Jac. I, c. 6; Lipson, *op. cit.,* III, 251–254. See also draft bill fixing minimum rates for spinners and weavers and restraining speculation in yarn (April, 1593). Tawney and Power, *Tudor Econ. Docs.,* I, 371–376.

[4] C. A. Beard, *Origin and Duties of the Justice of the Peace* (New York, 1904), pp. 51, 54.

country gentry could hardly be expected to make decisions consistently against their own interests.[5] Where, as in the industrial communities, the justices were apt to be impartial, they were likely to be indifferent, negligent, or corrupt.[6] As Holdsworth has observed, "the capitalist had in substance freed himself from the obligations which the Tudor scheme imposed upon him; but the workmen still remained liable to them." [7] The English colonies experimented quite extensively with wage fixing. Such experiments were by no means confined to Great Britain and her colonies, but were familiar to continental countries and at various times were introduced by the French and Spanish into their New World possessions.

Throughout the colonial period, and long after general legislative wage fixing had been discontinued, colonial towns and villages or other licensing bodies customarily set the wages or fees of certain quasi-public functionaries, such as porters, carmen, draymen, millers, smiths, chimney sweeps, gravediggers, pilots, and others. Fees for many public services, such as slaughtering, sawing wood, and grinding corn, were customarily fixed by public authority. The legal fare was set for ferries, and seaport towns fixed wharfage and storage rates. In addition, the prices of certain necessaries were determined by public authority. While bread was the most consistent subject of regulation, assizes of meat, leather, bricks, and other products were frequently set.[8] In addition, the prices of liquors, food, and lodging to be charged in taverns and or-

[5] For evidence of partiality on the part of the justices in deliberately curbing wage rises, the records of Hertford, Buckinghamshire, Middlesex, North Riding, Nottingham, West Riding, and Wiltshire provide us with abundant illustrations. See, e.g., J. D. Chambers, *Nottinghamshire in the Eighteenth Century* (London, 1932), pp. 279, 280; Lincoln Record So ety, *Quarter Sessions of Lincoln*, XXV, 4. The justices were primarily worried about *"excessive* wages" rather than *inadequate* wages. See "Quarter Session Records, County Palatine of Chester, 1559-1769," ed. J. H. E. Bennett and J. C. Dewhurst, Record Society, *Publications*, XCIV (1940), p. 68 (1609). In an emergency the justices of the peace were supported by the militia, officered by men of the same general background as themselves. M. Beloff, *Public Order and Popular Disturbances, 1660-1714* (Oxford, 1938), pp. 152, 153.

[6] Heckscher, *Mercantilism*, I, 247; E. Dowdell, *One Hundred Years of Quarter Sessions* (Cambridge, 1932), p. 49. The statute, 1 Jac. I, c. 6 (1604), provided, however, that no justice of the peace who was by trade a clothier could be a "rater" of wages of workers in the clothmaking industry.

[7] H.E.L., VI, 348, 349.

[8] In England the assizes were not limited to bread, but included meat, wine, cheese and butter, wool, lead, ale and beer. See John Powell, *Assize of Bread* (1626, ed.); also "Surrey Quarter Sessions Records, 1569-1661," Surrey Rec. Soc., *Publications*, XXXV, 25 (1660); "Quarter Session Records, County Palatine of Chester, 1559-1769," Record Society, *Publications*, XCIV (1940), 43 (1604). For criticism of the operation of the assize in 18th-century Britain, see D. G. Barnes, *A History of the English Corn Laws from 1660-1846* (New York, 1930), p. 34. Pennsylvania furnishes an interesting example of maximum price legislation for both leather and shoes. See *Pa. Stat. at Large*, II, 257 (1721); VIII, 223 (1772). See also *Md. Arch.*, XIX, 183 (1695); Hening, III, 75 (1691); VI, 133 (1748).

dinaries were universally regulated. In the Southern colonies the setting of tavern rates was the most consistent example of price regulation undertaken by the county or sessions courts right through the Revolutionary period. Aside from regulating the prices of basic products and services, the colonial authorities, notably in Maryland, Virginia, and North Carolina, laid down standards of quality and measure for commodities and certain manufactured articles, passed laws impeding the free traffic of commodities and manufactured goods, and enacted legislation curbing production. These economic controls of goods and labor services were buttressed by a popular demand for a regulated market which found expression in the continuation of prohibitions on forestalling, engrossing, regrating, and monopolizing necessaries,—restraints which were to enjoy enormous vitality in Revolutionary days.[9] While such regulations directly affected the independent producers in certain fields and only indirectly their hired workmen, many of the articles regulated were processed materials or involved a considerable amount of labor services, and therefore such regulation had a tendency to limit the wages which the producer in such regulated trades or monopoly fields could pay.

Tudor legislation buttressed the wage assessment procedure by making the refusal to work at the statutory rate a criminal offense, just as an earlier act had declared it illegal for workmen to combine in order to secure higher wages.[10] No workman was to depart before the end of his agreed term, and then he was required to produce letters testimonial to show that he was free to hire himself out. Employers were prohibited from engaging workmen who could not produce such a testimonial.[11] The courts interpreted these statutes to give a right of action against a master who enticed a servant away from another. The present study considers in detail the extent to which the colonies introduced the English restraints against concerted action on the part of workers to better their working conditions.[12] The vigilance of colonial courts in giving masters a remedy against those who enticed servants or workmen away from them or who otherwise induced a breach of a labor contract bespeaks eloquently the influence of the Tudor industrial code upon the colonial labor system.[13]

---

[9] A multiplicity of examples of price regulation, inspection laws, and trade regulations are found in R. B. Morris, ed., *Era of Amer. Revol.*, pp. 76, 77, 83–89, 123, 124.
[10] 2, 3 Edw. VI, c. 15.   [11] 5 Eliz. c. 4 §§ 7, 8.   [12] See pp. 136–207.   [13] See pp. 414–434.

THE SUPPLY OF SKILLED LABOR

FINALLY, the Tudor industrial code was the culmination of a program initiated in the Middle Ages to assure an adequate supply of skilled workmen and good quality in the manufactured product. Such a program served to protect consumers, but it was calculated at the same time to assure a continued demand for English exports in foreign markets. The statute of 1562–63 set the term of apprenticeship at seven years and avoided contracts not in accordance with this act.[1] In general, this traditional term of service, borrowed from the "custom and order of the city of London," was widely adopted in the American colonies. However, the colonies differed from the mother country in their refusal to impose property qualifications for parents as prerequisite to admitting children to apprenticeship,[2] although in practice colonial parents frequently were required to pay masters to accept their children as apprentices in the more highly skilled crafts or in such professions as the law.[3] In order to assure good workmanship a long series of statutes were passed under the Tudors and James I supervising specific industries. This was also true in America, where inspection laws were widely adopted, particularly for processed products exported from the colonies.

In the early years of settlement the home authorities sought to encourage colonization. It was widely believed, although as we know now erroneously, that England was overpopulated [4] and that the unemployed poor and vagrant class should be shipped to the colonies to produce the raw materials needed at home and to consume England's surplus manufactured products.[5] Gradually, with England's rise to commercial and industrial leadership, the official attitude changed.[6] The government now sought to restrain the colonies when they tried to follow the shrewd advice of James I to

---

[1] 5 Eliz. c. 4 §§ 19, 24, and 34.

[2] The English statute set a property qualification for the trade of a merchant, mercer, draper, goldsmith, ironmonger, embroiderer, clothier, and cloth weaver. See also 7 Hen. IV, c. 17 (1405), setting such qualifications as a prerequisite to putting a son to any craft or labor in any city or borough.

[3] See *infra*, pp. 369–370.

[4] See, e.g., *Nova Britannia* (1609) in Peter Force, *Tracts and Other Papers Relating Principally to the Colonies in North America* (4 vols., Washington, 1836–46), I, 19; *Winthrop Papers*, II (Mass. Hist. Soc., 1931), 111, 114, 118, 139 (1629).

[5] For mercantilist statements of the advantage of colonies as a means of taking care of population, see Buck, *Politics of Mercantilism*, pp. 60, 204; K. E. Knorr, *British Colonial Theories* (Toronto, 1944), pp. 41–48.

[6] Roger Coke, an economic heretic, anticipated this governmental somersault. *A Treatise Wherein Is Demonstrated That the Church and State of England Are in Equal Danger with the Trade of It* (London, 1671), pp. 1–36. See also Knorr, *op. cit.*, pp. 68–81.

take example of England, how it hath flourished both in wealth and policie, since the strangers craftsmen came in among them; therefore not only permit, but allure strangers to come here also; taking as strait order for the repressing the mutining of ours at them, as was done in England, at their first bringing there.[7]

In 1699 the Board of Trade urged Parliament that workers engaged in the manufacture of woolens be prohibited from leaving England.[8] As early as 1718 Great Britain began to impose restrictions on the free emigration of skilled artisans; in 1750 its restrictions were specifically applied to workers in certain textile industries. In 1765 Parliament forbade the emigration of trained operatives, both to prevent the spread of closely guarded industrial secrets and to maintain an adequate supply of highly trained labor at home.[9] This was followed by statutes of 1774 and 1781, forbidding the exportation of textile machinery, plans, or models. An act of 1782 prohibited the emigration of artificers in the textile fields or in the manufacture of machinery for these industries; three years later this prohibition was extended to workmen in the iron and steel industry; and four years later it was extended to coal miners.[10]

This changing attitude was clearly apparent by the middle of the eighteenth century. Postlethwayt, writing in 1745, opposed furnishing the colonies with white labor either from the mother country or the Continent on the ground that such emigration would serve to make the colonies manufacturing rivals of England. Instead, he favored slave importations as tending to keep the colonies agricultural.[11] For a forthright expression of the official attitude we are indebted to the commander

---

[7] *The Workes of the Most High and Mightie Prince James* (London, 1616), p. 164.

[8] See *CSPA, 1699*, No. 32, pp. 17, 18.

[9] Under 22 Geo. II, c. 60, it was a crime to entice artificers out of England. For the first offense the penalty was £500 and 12 months' imprisonment per workman enticed, and for each successive offense a fine of £1,200 and a similar term of imprisonment. European ship captains appear to have been adept at evading this act. See A. H. Cole, *Industrial and Commercial Correspondence of Alexander Hamilton Anticipating His Report on Manufactures* (Chicago, 1928), pp. 109–112 (1791). See also *ibid.*, p. 185.

[10] Actually as far back as 1666 and again in 1686 the king, at the urgent request of the Society of Frame Work Knitters, issued proclamations prohibiting the transportation to the colonies of frames for knitting and making silk stockings and wearing necessaries. See 5 Geo. I, c. 27; 14 Geo. III, c. 71; 15 Geo. III, c. 5; 22 Geo. III, c. 60; 25 Geo. III, c. 67. See also *J. Commrs. Trade and Plantations, 1722/3–28*, p. 132 (1724). Despite these prohibitions Arkwright's machinery was available in this country in the post-Revolutionary period. *Md. Gazette* (Baltimore), August 21, 1789, reported: "Carding machines are made as cheap and as well at Philadelphia, as in Europe."

[11] *The African Trade the Great Pillar and Support of the British Plantation Trade in America* (London, 1745). This view was widely held in the English newspaper and periodical literature of the day. See F. J. Hinkhouse, *The Preliminaries of the American Revolution as seen in the English Press, 1763–1775* (New York, 1926), pp. 107, 108.

in chief of the British armies in North America, Major General Thomas Gage, who wrote Barrington in 1768:

I have never heard of a people . . . who could manufacture without hands, or materials; We read also that many Manufacturers embark for America, but can't discover where they land. . . . It would be well, if the Emigrations from Great Britain, Ireland and Holland, where the Germans embark for America, were prevented; and our new settlements should be peopled from the old ones, which would be a means to thin them, and put it less in their power to do Mischief.[12]

Despite the growing hostility to the emigration of skilled workmen the home government down until the eve of the Revolution placed no obstacles on the emigration of vagabonds and the unemployed poor, and, beginning with the latter half of the seventeenth century, stepped up the pace of shipments of convicted felons to the colonies.[13] But by the eve of the conflict with the colonies the government felt it necessary to curb all emigration. Governors were forbidden to assent to bills of naturalization or issue patents for lands, and, finally in 1774, a prohibitive per capita tax was imposed on all emigrants to the colonies from Great Britain and Ireland. These measures were attacked in the Declaration of Independence.[14]

However, despite official obstructions, the importation of skilled craftsmen went on virtually unabated throughout the colonial period. The Virginia Company brought over Dutchmen to erect sawmills, Polish workers for the naval stores industry, "vigneroones from Languedoch," and Italians to establish a glassworks.[15] More widely publicized examples include Peter Hasenclever, the Prussian ironmaster who transported from Germany to America over five hundred miners, forgemen, colliers, carpenters, masons, and laborers, together with their wives and children;[16] "Baron" Stiegel, the fabulous glassmaker and ironmaster from Cologne; the North of Ireland flaxworkers who developed the linen industry in New England as well as on Maryland's Eastern Shore

---

[12] *Gage Corr.*, II, 450 (1768). [13] See *infra*, pp. 323–326.

[14] E. E. Proper, *Colonial Immigration Laws* (New York, 1900), p. 75, considers these as political rather than economic measures, but in the light of the extensive restrictions on the movement of craftsmen this must be considered as too circumscribed a view of British policy.

[15] *The Records of the Virginia Company of London*, ed. Susan M. Kingsbury (4 vols., Washington, 1906–35), I, 251, 252 (1619); III, 278, 315 (1620), 474, 475, 477 (1621), 640 (1622); IV, 522 (1625).

[16] *The Remarkable Case of Peter Hasenclever, Merchant; Formerly One of the Proprietors of the Iron Works, Pot-Ash Manufactory, etc. Established and Successfully Carried On under His Directors, in the Province of New York, and New Jersey, in North America, 'till November 1766* (London, 1773), p. 5.

and in South Carolina; [17] the Moravian craftsmen of Bethlehem; [18] the artisans of Germantown; the Huguenots of South Carolina who pioneered in salt manufacturing and indigo production; [19] and the Italians trained in silk culture and brought over to establish that industry in Georgia.[20]

To begin with, every single workman had to be imported. The apprenticeship system never proved completely adequate to meet colonial needs for trained workers. Special efforts were constantly made to attract craftsmen from England and the Continent. Many craftsmen were transported to Virginia in the early years of settlement.[21] Those coming over on the *Ann* and the *Bonny Bess* to James City in 1623, for example, were almost all craftsmen. Only ten were listed as "gentlemen" as against twenty-four tradesmen, one student, four husbandmen, one servant, and a lad from "Christ's Hospital." [22] As late as 1662 William Hatton was presented in the York County court for calling several justices of that county "Coopers, Hoggtrough makers, Pedlars, Coblers, Tailors, weavers and saying they are not fitting to sit where they doe sit." [23] A great majority of the passengers of the Winthrop Fleet of 1630 belonged to the families of artisans or tillers of the soil.[24] To seventeenth-century Massachusetts came English shipwrights, ironmasters, posters, and Yorkshire woolen workers.[25] As a result of this immigra-

[17] See W. R. Bagnall, *The Textile Industries of the United States* (Cambridge, 1893), pp. 16–18; *N.J. Arch.*, V, 204; *CSPA, 1720–21*, No. 153, p. 68 (1720). For the German glassmakers at Braintree, see *Boston Gazette*, Sept. 26, 1752.

[18] J. J. Sessler, *Communal Pietism among Early American Moravians* (New York, 1933), and *infra*, pp. 145, 146.

[19] See A. H. Hirsch, *Huguenots of South Carolina* (Durham, N.C., 1928), pp. 214, 215, 245, 246; Cooper, *S.C. Stat.*, II, 132.

[20] See *Ga. Col. Rec.*, I, 100 (1733); XXII, Pt. I, p. 169 (1738). For an earlier proposal to import Italian silk workers, see *CSPA, 1669–74*, No. 737 (1672). For the importation to Georgia of German Protestants skilled in the making of wines and silk, see Hester W. Newton, "The Industrial and Social Influence of the Salzburghers in Colonial Georgia," *Ga. Hist. Q.*, XVIII, 348–349.

[21] See Force, *Hist. Tracts*, No. 5, pp. 5, 15, 17. Thirty-five different trades were listed among tradesmen "to be entertained" in 1620. *Va. Co. Rec.*, III, 317 (1620).

[22] *Va. Gen. Court Mins.*, p. 6 (1623).

[23] York O.B., 1657–62, f. 175 (1662).

[24] See C. E. Banks, *The Winthrop Fleet of 1630* (Cambridge, 1930), p. 52. A list of those who were in New England in 1634, while incomplete, reveals a heavy majority of cloth workers and husbandmen. J. Savage, "Gleanings for New England History," Mass. Hist. Soc., *Coll.*, 3d ser., VIII, 270–275. For poor economic conditions in the English cloth industry at the time of the early migrations, see *Victoria History of Suffolk* (London, 1907, 1911), I, 676, 677; II, 265; *Victoria History of Kent* (London, 1908), III, 407–408. 63 per cent of the 1,600 male emigrants sailing from Bristol, 1654–61, whose status can be determined, were from the farming classes. See Mildred Campbell, *The English Yeoman* (New Haven, 1942), p. 215.

[25] See *infra*, p. 57. See also *CSPA, 1574–1660*, No. 72, p. 158 (1633); *N.E. Hist. and Geneal. Register*, XXXIX, 33–48; Capt. Edward Johnson, *Wonder-Working Providence of Sion's Savior in New England* (London, 1664; reprinted Andover, 1867), p. 183; *Essex*, VI, 82 (1675).

tion trained artisans were found even in such New England frontier communities as York County, Maine, whose court records for the mid-seventeenth century list twenty trades, including a physician, surgeon, and schoolmaster, while for the same period the court records of more populous Essex County mention at least fifty-three trades.[26] Governor Rising of New Sweden wrote home in 1654 for potterymakers, brickmakers, limeburners, cabinetmakers, shoemakers, and tanners, as well as for a French hatmaker, among others.[27] A proposal in 1657 for the setting up of ironworks in Virginia was based on the importation of virtually all skilled artisans and laborers from England, as "Artists are not to bee had at any rate." [28] In a suit instituted against a potter brought over from London, who, one person attested, was "as good a work man as James Budd the Plaintiffe can finde in England," a Burlington (West Jersey) court jury in 1686 was unable to render a final verdict "untill materialls requisite shall come from England to prove the skill of the Defendant." [29] To activate a virtually nonexistent shipbuilding industry Virginia imported ship carpenters at the end of the seventeenth century.[30]

The importation of skilled workmen, attracted by the lure of higher wages and the opportunity to set up in independent business or to acquire a homestead, continued throughout the colonial period. In 1702 the Board of Trade reported that "of late years great numbers of people are enticed over to your M. Northern Colonies in America, and particularly those under Propriety and Charter governments. . . . Divers manufacturers and workmen also are carried over upon specious pretence of more easie livelihood in those parts." [31] Despite official reluctance, the authorities were obliged to issue a call for trained artisans to emigrate to areas newly settled in the eighteenth century.[32] Lack of trained hands was assigned by Governor Hunter as one of the reasons for the collapse of the government-sponsored naval stores project in New York, as the Palatines, brought over for this industry, had had no previous experience in it. Governor Spotswood of Virginia told the Board of Trade that tar could not be made with the kind of labor

[26] See *Me. Prov. and Court Rec.*, I, *passim*; *Essex*, V, *passim*. One hundred different trades and professions are mentioned in the Surrey (England) Q.S.O.B., 1659–1661. Surrey Record Society, *Publications*, No. 35.

[27] A. C. Myers, ed., *Narratives of Early Pennsylvania, West New Jersey and Delaware, 1630–1707* (New York, 1912), p. 142.

[28] *WMCQ*, 2d ser., I, 100 *et seq.* (1657).

[29] Budd v. Randall, Burlington, West Jersey, Court Book, fols. 41, 42 (1686).

[30] *CSPA, 1696–97*, No. 1131, p. 530 (1697).   [31] *CSPA, 1702*, No. 1103, p. 695.

[32] See *J. Commrs. Trade and Plantations, 1749/50–53* (March 30, 1750).

available in the plantations and urged that tar burners be brought from Finland for that purpose.[33] When machinery was imported it was not infrequent to send along a skilled mechanic who could assemble it in this country.[34]

When colonial industrialists wanted English artisans they did not stop to haggle over the price, as this news story in the *New-York Journal* for October 8, 1767, would indicate:

Thirteen of the best Hammer-men and Forge-men in the Iron Manufactory have been engaged to come from Sheffield to America, for which a handsome premium is given them; and great wages for two years certain, and six shillings a week to each of their wives and families as stay behind for that time. They have also given one hundred guineas for each of the best Saw-makers, and the same money for their wives that stay. (If provisions are kept up at the rate they are, the Americans will soon have enough to carry on the manufacture, without giving premiums.) [35]

A few months later a New York newspaper reported a news item from London to the effect "that in the course of this week, upwards of 100 Journeymen weavers have engaged to go to New-York and Boston, where they are promised constant employment." [36] "Numbers of our manufacturers are daily shipping themselves off for the regions of America," London reported in 1768,[37] notwithstanding official opposition of mercantilist nationalism.[38]

Colonial advertisements bear testimony to the variety of crafts plied by foreign workmen in this country. A tailor in Charleston announced that he had been "foreman to the most eminent master-taylors in London and Paris, and by them acknowledged to be as compleat a workman

---

[33] See H. L. Osgood, *American Colonies in the Eighteenth Century* (New York, 1924), II, 333; W. A. Knittle, *Early Eighteenth Century Palatine Emigration* (Philadelphia, 1937), pp. 177, 178.

[34] See *HMC, Rep.*, LIX, Pt. I, p. 29.

[35] French refugees brought over to cultivate silkworms in New York and South Carolina were also reported to have secured very advantageous terms. *N.Y.J.*, Sept. 23, 1774. A mason who was brought over from England to build a furnace in Virginia was paid a daily wage from the time he left Gloucestershire until his return home, unless he chose to remain in Virginia after he had completed his contract. J. S. Bassett, ed., *The Writings of "Colonel William Byrd of Westover in Virginia Esqr."* (New York, 1901), p. 375 (1732).

[36] *N.Y. Gazette or the Weekly Post-Boy*, Feb. 1, 1768.

[37] *S.C. Gazette*, Feb. 29–March 7, 1768.

[38] British emigration lists, 1773–76 (Treasury Papers, 47, Bundles 9–11) confirm this charge. The bulk of the emigrants in this period were tradesmen—coopers, hatters, stocking weavers, woolcombers, blacksmiths, laborers,—or husbandmen. Only a very small number were accounted "gentlemen," merchants, or professional men. For the wide variety of crafts plied by the redemptioners and, in some instances, transported convicts, see *Boston News-Letter*, June 18–25, 1716; Oct. 31, 1763; *Md. Gazette* (Annapolis), June 26, 1760; March 11, 1762; Feb. 24, 1774.

as ever they employed, particularly in the art of cutting."[39] A Dublin linen printer and dyer told the Bostonians that he was ready to produce colors "as good and as lasting as any that comes from Europe."[40] Workmen frequently advertised that they had served a regular apprenticeship in a London shop.[41] A cabinet- and chairmaker who came to New York from London advertised that he had brought along six journeymen, and was prepared to manufacture furniture according to the prevailing mode set by Chippendale.[42] English and French silversmiths opened shops in the leading colonial towns and made "Queen Anne" tankards and Meissonier candlesticks. The proprietors of a china factory established in Philadelphia in 1770 advertised for workmen, with the stipulation that "none will be employed who have not served their apprenticeship in England, France, or Germany."[43]

The process of importing trained operatives was accelerated after the close of the American Revolution when American agents in English manufacturing towns sought to persuade large numbers of trained mechanics to emigrate.[44] A highly competent observer reported in 1790 that "a large proportion of the most skillful manufacturers in the United States are persons who were journeymen and in a few instances were foremen in the workshops and manufactories of Europe."[45]

Not only were workmen imported from Europe, but efforts were made to attract skilled workmen from other colonies. New Englanders migrated to the Carolinas, Philadelphia manufacturers sought to attract craftsmen from Charleston, Virginia cabinetmakers sought to lure journeymen from Maryland, and an effort was made to get journeymen shoemakers from Charleston to go to East Florida. When wages declined in Savannah, the artisans left for Charleston or New York.[46]

[39] *S.C. Gazette*, March 21, 1768.   [40] *Boston Gazette*, Supp., May 7, 1759.
[41] E.g., *Pa. Packet*, Jan. 30, 1775; *Pa. J.*, Oct. 31, 1771; *Md. J. and Baltimore Advertiser*, Dec. 5, 1783. Cf. Pa. Mus. of Art, *Picture Book of Philadelphia Chippendale Furniture* (1931).
[42] *N.Y. Mercury*, May 31, 1762; see also *N.Y. Gazette or Weekly Post-Boy*, August 5, 1762; June 13, 1765; Sept. 11, 1766. For other instances of European artisans establishing themselves in the colonies, see *Boston News-Letter*, Oct. 6–13, 1707, Nov. 3–10, 1712; March 4–11, 1717; April 21–28, June 23–30, 1735; Feb. 9, 1769; Nov. 26, 1772; *Boston Gazette*, Nov. 5, 1764; *Pa. J.*, Oct. 24, 1771; *S.C. Gazette*, Jan. 18, 1768. See also *infra*, pp. 217, 421–423.
[43] *S.C. Gazette*, March 15, 1770. When English workmen did come over, they were impelled to complain of this firm's mistreatment of them. *Pa. Gazette*, Nov. 4, 1732.
[44] See V. H. Clark, *History of Manufactures in the United States, 1607–1860* (Washington, 1916), pp. 399, 400.
[45] Tench Coxe, *A View of the United States of America* (Philadelphia, 1794), p. 443. "Our Mechanics are ruined by British Importations!" was a frequent cry. See *Mass. Centinel*, April 6, 1785. See also *Mass. Spy* (Worcester), Feb. 18, 1790; *N.J. Gazette*, Sept. 12, 1785; *Pa. J.*, Oct. 24, 1771; *Md. J. and Baltimore Advertiser*, Dec. 5, 1783; *Charleston City Gazette and Advertiser*, Feb. 4, 1797.
[46] See *Boston News-Letter*, Aug. 23–30, 1714; *S.C. Gazette*, Nov. 16–23, 1734, Nov. 22– Dec. 6, 1735, March 15, 1770, May 30, 1774; *Md. Gazette*, June 22, 1762; *Ga. Col. Rec.*, XXII,

Silversmiths like Samuel Soumain were as much at home at Annapolis as at Philadelphia, and Cornelius Kiersteade plied his craft at both New Haven and New York.

The bound-labor system was devised to attract workmen from Europe and to assure a cheap labor supply in the colonies. Although skilled workmen were more reluctant than plowmen and laborers to go to the colonies as redemptioners, a status which soon gained an unsavory reputation,[47] German artificers were a notable exception. Indentured servants, whose status is the subject of detailed consideration in Part II of this study, were employed throughout the colonies, but their use was more circumscribed in New England than in the Middle colonies and the South. By and large they were employed in semiskilled and unskilled occupations. In the seventeenth century such servants were used on the plantations for both husbandry and the crafts, but with the advent of Negro slavery they were gradually supplanted as field workers and were principally retained as overseers, foremen, or herdsmen. Bound white artificers were still employed to train Negroes in the crafts, but were gradually displaced as this task was performed. By the latter part of the colonial period many indentured servants moved to the upland regions, and the bulk of them survived as the "poor whites" of the South.[48]

In the Southern plantations geographical factors and the trend toward husbandry discouraged the development of a skilled white artisan class. These difficulties were described by contemporaries, writing at the close of the seventeenth century, who reported:

For want of Towns, Markets, and Money, there is but little Encouragement for Tradesmen and Artificers, and therefore little Choice of them, and their Labour very dear in the Country. Then a great deal of Tradesman's Time being necessarily spent in going and coming to and from his Work, in dispers'd County Plantations, and his Pay being generally in straggling Parcels of Tobacco, the Collection Whereof costs about 10 per cent, and the best of this Pay coming but once a year, so that he cannot turn his Hand frequently with a small stock, as Tradesmen do in England and Elsewhere, All this occasions the Dearth of all Tradesmen's Labour, and likewise the Discouragement, Scarcity, and Insufficiency of Tradesmen.[49]

Pt. I, pp. 69 (1738), 366 (1740). The manager of the Hibernia Furnace in New Jersey wrote Lord Stirling, the proprietor, of the need of acquiring the services of a New York blacksmith named Lawrence, reputed to be "the best judge of Blister'd Steel of any there." Stirling MSS, lib. IV, f. 13 (1774), N.Y. Hist. Soc.

[47] For the experience in New Netherland, see *Doc. Rel. to the Col. Hist. of N.Y.*, XIV, 401 (1656).

[48] See *WMCQ*, 1st ser., II, 146.

[49] H. Hartwell, Rev. J. Blair, and E. Chilton, *The Present State of Virginia* (London, 1727), p. 8.

Various methods were employed to counteract the scarcity of skilled workmen. In the first place, artificers in the early days of settlement were required to stick to their lasts. In Virginia craftsmen were required by law to work at their trades and were not permitted to turn to husbandry.[50] Acts of 1726 and 1748 penalized by extra service persons imported into the colony as "tradesmen or workmen in wages" who refused to work,[51] and a South Carolina statute of 1741 forbade artisans in certain enumerated trades from keeping taverns.[52] Not only were handicraftsmen expected to stick to their trades, but, because of the shortage of men and materials, the Plymouth court went so far in 1626 as to forbid them to work for "any strangers or foreigners till such time as the necessity of the Colony be served." [53] Sometimes the legislation applied to one specific trade: a Virginia statute of 1632 and a Rhode Island act of 1647 set a penalty of £5 to go to the employer of artificers or laborers in the building trades who left their work,[54] while Maryland legislation required coopers to complete work on hogsheads and barrels by specified dates during the year of the order.[55] These acts unquestionably outlawed strikes and effectually forestalled labor combinations in the trades enumerated.

Secondly, many of the colonies experimented for a time in the seventeenth century with maximum wage programs, which were again brought forth during the years of the Revolution.[56]

Thirdly, attempts were made in the Southern colonies to encourage manufacturers and craftsmen by setting up towns, programs which were largely confined to the paper on which they were written.[57] Annap-

[50] Hening, I, 115–118 (1621); *Va. Co. Rec., III*, 586 (1622): instructions to Gov. Wyatt regarding apprentices; Hening, I, 208 (1633): instructions to Gov. Berkeley, *VMH*, II, 287; MacDonald MSS, Va. State Library.

[51] Hening, IV, 168–175 (1726); V, 556, 557 (1748). See also the injunction of James Blair, *CSPA, 1696–97*, No. 1411, p. 670 (1697).

[52] *S.C. Stat.*, III, 583.   [53] *Plymouth Col. Rec.*, XI, 3, 4 (1626).

[54] Hening, I, 193 (1632); *R. I. Col. Rec.*, I, 183 (1647); code of 1663, Rider, *Laws of R.I., 1636–1705* (reprinted, Providence, 1896), p. 11.

[55] The penalty was 100 lbs. of tobacco for every ton unfinished, payable to the person placing the order, unless the cooper could show that the delay was due to illness or some other "Lawful Impediment." *Md. Arch.*, II, 288, 289 (1671), 511 (1676); XIII, 552, 553 (1692). In the licensed trades workmen could be kept at their tasks under strict penalties. Carters, porters, sawyers, and chimney sweeps were required to work at specified rates under penalty of a fine for noncompliance. *Philadelphia Directory, 1791*.

[56] See *infra*, pp. 55–135.

[57] For Virginia's ambitious plans, see Captain John Smith, "The Generall Historie of Virginia," in *Narr. of Early Va.*, ed. L. G. Tyler, p. 391; also *VMH*, III, 29 (1639). For the attitude of the Somerset County court toward the acts of 1699 for encouraging the manufacture of linen and woolen cloth and "for Erecting some new necessary Towns," see R. B. Morris, "Judicial Supremacy and the Inferior Courts in the American Colonies," *Pol. Sci. Q.*, LV (1940), 429–434. See also *Md. Arch.*, XIII, 111–120, 132–139, 218, 220–222; *CSPA, 1661–68*, No. 32, p. 11 (1661),

olis, Williamsburg, Norfolk, and Charleston attracted numerous craftsmen, but in general the program was a failure.

Failing to maintain an adequate number of white artisans, the Southern colonies then trained Negro slaves for the skilled trades. The files of the *South Carolina Gazette* reveal that Negroes were trained and practicing virtually all the crafts needed for maintaining the plantation economy. In addition to those engaged in husbandry, the well-organized plantation employed carpenters, coopers, stonemasons, a miller, a blacksmith, shoemakers, spinners, and weavers. The wealthier planters often carried on industrial enterprises on a considerable scale, necessitating the employment of a sizable number of skilled workmen. One must, therefore, revise the traditional picture of the planter solely dependent upon the vagaries of the tobacco market for the livelihood of his family and workmen.[58] Some white artificers were generally needed to start such enterprises, but they were in the main carried on almost exclusively by Negro slaves who were often hired out by their masters to others in need of skilled help.[59] Futile efforts were made by the white artificers of the Southern towns to check the encroachments of slavery upon the skilled trades.[60] Among planters the belief was prevalent that slave labor was more economical than free labor.[61] Not only did free

Nos. 301, 333, pp. 90, 98, 99 (1662), Nos. 975, 1030, pp. 290, 291, 316 (1665), No. 1241, p. 396 (1666), No. 1410, p. 446 (1667); *VMH*, II, 387; *WMCQ*, 2d ser., X, 332; *Calendar of Virginia State Papers*, ed. by W. P. Palmer *et al.* (11 vols., Richmond, 1875–93), I, 137 (1709); S.C. Council J., lib. 1737–41, f. 529 (1741).

[58] Indeed, a study of exports based upon the British Naval Office lists has disclosed that by the mid-eighteenth century Virginia led all the original states in the export of Indian corn, with Maryland second and Pennsylvania only third. See W. E. Bean, "War and the British Colonial Farmer: A Reëvaluation in the Light of New Statistical Records," *Pacific Hist. Rev.*, XI (Dec., 1942), 439–447.

[59] For typical newspaper references to skilled Negro artisans, see *Cape Fear Mercury*, Nov. 24, 1769; *S.C. Gazette*, Jan. 27–Feb. 3, Dec. 2–9, 1732, May 25, Oct. 5, 1734, Aug. 2–9, 1735, Dec. 15–22, 1739, Jan. 12–19, 1740, Nov. 1, 1742, Feb. 27, May 14, 1744, Oct. 23, 1762, June 21, 1773, April 24, 1774; *Gazette of the State of S.C.*, April 9, 29, 1777, Nov. 3, 1779, Dec. 25, 1783, July 1, 1784; *Ga. Gazette*, June 15, Nov. 9, 1774. See also *The Negro in Virginia*, comp. by the Writers' Program of the Work Projects Administration in the State of Virginia (New York, 1940), pp. 47–49; F. J. Klingberg, *An Appraisal of the Negro in Colonial South Carolina: a Study in Americanization* (Washington, 1941), p. 45. W. H. Brown, "The Education and Economic Development of the Negro in Virginia," University of Virginia, *Publications* (Phelps-Stokes Fellowship Papers), No. 6, pp. 12, 13, 18, 19, R. B. Pinchbeck, "The Virginia Negro Artisan and Tradesman," *ibid.*, No. 7, pp. 11–15, 21. Jernegan, *op. cit.*, ch. i. For the employment of slaves in the colonial iron industry, see Byrd, *Writings*, p. 345; in the 19th century, see Kathleen Bruce, "Slave Labor in the Virginian Iron Industry," *WMCQ*, 2d ser., VI, 21–31, 289–307. But cf. T. J. Wertenbaker, *Labor Costs and American Democracy* (Princeton, 1938), p. 5.

[60] See *infra*, pp. 184–188, 388, 524.

[61] See H. J. Carman, ed., *American Husbandry* (New York, 1939), p. 302. The service of a young, healthy slave was estimated at from 30 to 40 years. Klingberg, *op. cit.*, p. 113. For comparative wage statistics of Negro and white artisans in one region in the Revolutionary period, see W. H. Siebert, "Slavery and White Servitude in East Florida, 1726–1776," *Florida Hist,*

white labor demand higher wages than Negro workmen, but their up-keep was higher, for the latter, "even when well treated," as Washington observed, were fed the simple diet of Indian corn bread, buttermilk, pickled herrings, and meat "now and then," "with a blanket for bedding." [62] White workmen demanded more discriminating and varied fare, as numerous servant "strikes" on Southern plantations attest.[63]

Part of the labor shortage in the unskilled and semiskilled trades and in the household crafts was made up by the use of women and children. This was normal European practice, even more typical of the Continent than of England. Andrew Yarranton, a seventeenth-century observer, reported that in Germany a child that was sent to a spinning school at six could earn 8*d.* a day when he or she was nine years of age. He applauded a system wherein "a man that has most children lives best." [64] Defoe was gratified over the fact that in the vicinity of Taunton there was not a child of five years of age but could, if properly reared, "earn its own bread." In the colonies women and children were employed in many occupations.[65] A colonial wife was expected to live up to the ambitious standards set in the Book of Proverbs.[66] Generally speaking, she was not allowed to eat "the bread of idleness," and, aside from her extensive household and family duties, might be called upon to help in the fields.[67] The demand for child labor on the expanding frontier provided an incentive, if any was needed, for the high birth rate and large families of colonial times.[68]

In order to induce skilled workmen to settle in this country or to engage in a particular trade, colonies as well as local communities offered them exemption from taxation for a specified period of years,[69]

Soc. Q., X (1931), 156. Benjamin Franklin asserted that slave labor was expensive, when one took into account, in addition to the element of risk upon the slave's life, the expense of clothes and diet, the loss of time due to illness, as well as other losses due to negligence, indifference, and theft, and the cost of "a driver to keep him at his work." *Writings*, ed. A. H. Smyth (New York, 1905), III, 63–73.

[62] U.S. George Washington Bicentennial Commission, *Pamphlets* (Washington, 1932), Nos. 1–16, p. 40.

[63] See *infra*, pp. 167–182.

[64] Andrew Yarranton, *England's Improvement by Sea and Land . . .* (London, 1677), pp. 46, 47.

[65] See *infra*, pp. 321, 322, 384–387, 517, 518.   [66] Prov. 31:10–31.

[67] John Hammond painted a rosy picture of colonial labor conditions when he asserted that in Virginia women were not "put into the ground to worke" but merely assigned to domestic duties. "Leah and Rachel, or the Two Fruitful Sisters, Virginia and Mary-land" (1656), in Force, *Hist. Tracts*, III, 12, 14. As a matter of fact the Virginia authorities resented the presence of women who did "nothing but to deuoure the food of the land without dooing any dayes deed." *Va. Co. Rec.*, IV, 231, 232 (1623).

[68] See A. W. Calhoun, *A Social History of the American Family* (Cleveland, 1917), I, 124, 125.

[69] Hening, II, 85 (1662).

exemption from labor on roads and highways [70] and from military training,[71] land grants or leases,[72] and other attractive subsidies and bounties.[73] This mercantilist program in the colonies paralleled the grants of subsidies in the mother country to domestic manufacturers and the bounties granted by Great Britain to colonial producers of naval stores. However, the practice of issuing patents of monopoly to founders of new industries which proved so objectionable in England [74] never took deep root in the colonies.

While there never was an adequate supply of trained workmen to meet the needs of the expanding colonial economy, the quality of the work was often excellent and many native artisans attained eminence in their crafts.[75] In silverwork there were some distinguished craftsmen,

[70] *Md. Arch.*, XLVI, 212–470, *passim*. Under the Maryland act of 1750, c. 14, one tenth the number of workmen at each iron works were liable for service on public roads and bridges.

[71] See *infra*, pp. 279–281.

[72] *Boston Town Rec.*, II, 34 (1638); Falmouth Proprietors' Book (1677); *Brookhaven Rec.*, Bk. A, p. 28 (1667); *Easthampton, L.I. Rec.*, I, 338 (1671); *Jamaica Town Rec.*, I, 17 (1667); *Md. Arch.*, XIII, 534–536 (1692); *VMH*, II, 160 (1618); *S.C. Gazette*, May 13–20, 1732. For opposition to such grants as favoritism, see Munsell, *Annals of Albany*, IV, 88 (1653). In 1719 the common council of New York City permitted William Dugdale and John Searle to use certain lands as tenants at will for setting up a building for the making of rope. The petitioners had urged that the project should be considered as being in the public interest as it would give "encouragement to the raising of Hemp, Tar, etc., as also by employing of Journey Men and Labourers, and Bringing up of Boys." Original Records of the Common Council of New York City, File Box No. 1, Bundle 10, Board of Aldermen and City Clerk's Records; *M.C.C.*, III, 195 (1719). For the West Indies, see C.O. 154: 1, p. 18 (1668).

[73] E.g., *Plymouth Col. Rec.*, I, 159 (1640); IV, 45 (1663); *Mass. Acts and Resolves*, II, 28 (1716); XI, 241 (1727–28); *Boston News-Letter*, Dec. 13, 1750; *Boston Gazette*, Aug. 7, 1753; *Derby, Conn., Rec., 1655–1710*, p. 120 (1681); *R.I. Col. Rec.*, VII, 430 (1776); *Jamaica Town Rec.*, I, 67 (1676); Baltimore County Court Rec., lib. H.S., No. 7, 1730–32 (March, 1731); Ann Arundel, lib. 1745–47 (August, 1746); *Md. Arch.*, XI, 30 (1775), 77 (1776); *S.C. Gazette*, Feb. 23, 1734; Aug. 23, 1760; Cooper, *S.C. Stat.*, II, 370 (1712), 385 (1716); IV, 10 (1754); *Ga. Col. Rec.*, I, 507 (1748); XXIV, 227 (1744); *Laws of the Island of Antigua* (London, 1805), I, 276 (1740–41); Stock, *Proc. Brit. Parl.*, V, 539 (Jamaica, 1749). For typical bounties to war industries during the Revolution, see "Proceedings of the Committees of Safety of Cumberland and Isle of Wight Counties, Virginia, 1775–1776," Va. State Library, *Ann. Rep., 1918* (Richmond, 1919), pp. 7, 43 (1775); *J. Prov. Cong.*, N.Y., I, 105, 106 (1775), 366, 697 (1776). For an offer of a loan by the state of a sum of money without interest for the erection of powder mills, see *ibid.*, I, 349, 365 (1776); of rolling and slitting mills, *Amer. Arch.*, 4th ser., VI, 1467; 5th ser., I, 1349. See also A. C. Bining, *British Regulation of the Colonial Iron Industry* (Philadelphia, 1933), pp. 94–95. Hamilton in his Report on the Subject of Manufactures urged that bounties or subsidies be paid to induce skilled artisans to migrate from Europe. The early Federal exemption of tools and implements from duty was an indirect subsidy. Cole, *Hamilton Corr.*, pp. 294, 295; also *ibid.*, p. 183.

[74] W. R. Scott, *English, Scottish and Irish Joint Stock Companies to 1720* (Cambridge, 1910–12), I, ch. vi. For a short-lived salt monopoly to a private entrepreneur on Virginia's Eastern Shore, see Hening, II, 122, 186, 236. For other instances of exclusive privileges to manufacture in the colonies, see Clark, *Hist. of Mfgrs.*, pp. 47–53.

[75] William Williams was an unusual example of a colonial house carpenter who went to London to study architecture. *Pa. Packet*, Jan. 4, 1773. Other native carpenters who stayed at home had access to leading European architectural works, although they were by no means slavish copyists. T. J. Wertenbaker, *Golden Age of Colonial Culture* (New York, 1942), p. 99.

particularly in Boston and New York. In the colonial period Boston boasted such superb exemplars of the craft as Edward Winslow, Jeremiah Dummer, Jacob and Nathaniel Hurd, and Samuel Burt; while New York took pride in the achievements of Myer Myers, Adrian Bancker, Simeon Soumain, Charles Le Roux, Bartholomew Schaats, Benjamin Wynkoop, Cornelius Vanderburgh, Jacobus Van Der Spiegel, and Peter Van Dyck.[76] Were the list to be extended to other crafts we would have to include cabinetmakers like Joshua Delaplaine of New York and William Savery, Charles Gillingham, and David Rittenhouse of Philadelphia, and a number of celebrated New England families of clockmakers, including the Claggetts and the Willards.[77]

On the other hand, too often was versatility encouraged at the expense of quality. As a result of the failure to establish a permanent craft guild system, the constant shortage of skilled labor, and the rise of laissez faire tendencies workers frequently performed more than one industrial process. The blacksmith was a toolmaker, the soap boiler a tallow chandler, and, despite restrictive legislation,[78] the tanner often acted as a currier and shoemaker. At times the trades were not in the least related. A cabinetmaker might run a grocery shop, a house carpenter act as an undertaker, and a silversmith sell toothache remedy.[79] Joshua Hempstead, of New London, Conn., was a farmer, surveyor, house and ship carpenter, stonecutter, sailor, trader, and an attorney. He generally held three or four town offices, was a justice of the peace, a judge of probate, and frequently acted as executor or guardian. In addition, he served as business agent of the Winthrop family.[80] When John Julius Sorge advertised in the New York newspapers in 1755 that he could

[76] One should not omit mentioning the names of Francis and Joseph Richardson of Philadelphia, Samuel Vernon of Newport, and Samuel Soumain of Annapolis.

[77] As a result of the widespread adoption of Oliver Evans' grain elevator American flour mills in the early Federal period were considered definitely superior to those of Great Britain. Oliver Evans, *The Young Mill-Wright and Miller's Guide* (9th ed., Philadelphia, 1836), Preface. Shortly after the close of the Revolution a correspondent in a New England paper declared it to be a matter of "some surprise" that American artificers should be regarded as inferior to those of Europe, "for had they proper encouragement they could produce work that would defy all the workmen of Europe to outdo. The article of carriages will prove the assertion, as there are several now running in this town, that for neatness, convenience and shew, need not yield the palm to any foreign production whatever." *Mass. Centinel*, Aug. 10, 1785. See also *Mass. Spy* (Worcester), Sept. 24, 1789. George Cabot wrote Hamilton in 1791 that thirty-nine out of the forty persons employed in his cotton mill at Beverly, Mass., were natives of the vicinity, as the Irish artisans who were imported "proved deficient in some quality essential to usefulness." Cole, *Hamilton Corr.*, p. 62.

[78] See *infra*, pp. 153–154. See also Clark, *Hist. of Mfgrs.*, pp. 161, 162.

[79] See, e.g., *N.Y. City Directory, 1786; Pa. J.*, May 24, 1775; *S.C. Gazette*, March 12, 1737.

[80] See *Diary of Joshua Hempstead of New London, Conn., 1711–1758*, New London Hist. Soc., *Coll.*, I (1901).

make artificial fruit, do japan work, manufacture cleaning fluid, toilet water, soap, candles, insecticides, and wine and remove hair from ladies' foreheads and arms,[81] there is no reason to believe that New Yorkers were taken aback by this display of diverse talents. Household servants might be called upon "to wait at table, curry horses, clean knives, boots and shoes, lay a table, shave and dress wigs, carry a lanthorn, and talk French." [82] Paul Revere, the distinguished silversmith, who gained greater renown for carrying the messages of the Committees of Correspondence and the Sons of Liberty, was also a well-known copperplate engraver, although not a very good one, a dentist who set false "foreteeth," a manufacturer of clock faces for clockmakers, of branding irons for hatters, and of spatulas and probes for surgeons. After the Revolution, while continuing his workshop craft as a silversmith, he branched out into large-scale industry, setting up a foundry and later a mill for rolling copper into sheets; this has now become one of the greatest establishments of its kind in the country.

THE LABOR POPULATION AND THE SIZE OF THE INDUSTRIAL UNIT

IT IS VIRTUALLY IMPOSSIBLE to obtain any reliable statistics on the relative extent of free labor or indentured servitude in the colonies. The first general census, the Federal Census of 1790, ascertained the number of free whites, of other free persons, and of slaves, but, undoubtedly the journeyman as well as the indentured white servant was included in the first category.[1] A further difficulty is that the status of servitude, as distinguished from slavery, was only a temporary one, nor was the journeyman's status as relatively permanent and fixed as that of the wage earner of the present day. Relatively few indentured servants were employed on the New England farms. The average small farm probably got along with the labor of the proprietor and his large family and one or two hired hands. Of the 12,000 men available for military service in New England in 1665, it was estimated by a contemporary that two thirds were masters and one third were servants.[2] This was undoubtedly a high estimate. A report to the Board of Trade in 1721 stated that, out

[81] *N.Y. Gazette or Weekly Post-Boy*, June 16, 1755.
[82] See advertisement in the *Md. Gazette*, cited by E. S. Riley, *The Ancient City: a History of Annapolis in Maryland, 1649–1887* (Annapolis, 1887), p. 13.
[1] The French census of the Illinois country in 1723 included both settlers and white workmen. See E. B. Greene and Virginia D. Harrington, *American Population before the Federal Census of 1790* (New York, 1932), p. 186.
[2] Greene and Harrington, *op. cit.*, p. 9.

of a total population of some 9,000 people for New Hampshire there were very few white servants.[3] However, in Pennsylvania, where by 1755 it was estimated that almost one half of the 220,000 white inhabitants were Germans,[4] it is apparent that a very considerable proportion of the population must at one time or another have been bound out to service to pay the cost of transportation to the colonies.[5]

According to a report of 1697, the bulk of the workmen of Maryland were employed in planting tobacco. The artificers were estimated at not "more than the 60th part of such laborers." [6] In early years the ratio of servants to freemen was about six to one, but despite the sizable importations of bound labor this ratio was not maintained. Governor Seymour reported in 1707 that Maryland had 3,003 white servants and 4,657 slaves out of a total population of 33,833.[7] Since during this period it is estimated that a minimum of 500 servants were coming into Maryland each year,[8] it would appear from his compilation that after the expiration of their service they were listed as freemen in population returns. A Maryland census for 1755 gives the following figures:

	Free	*Servants*	*Convicts*	*Total*
Men	24,058	3,576	1,507	29,141
Women	23,521	1,824	386	25,731
Boys	26,637	1,049	67	27,753
Girls	24,141	422	21	24,584
Total Whites	98,357	6,871	1,981	107,209
Total Negroes				46,356 [a]

[a] Greene and Harrington, *op. cit.*, p. 126. This census fails to distinguish between "hired" and "indented" servants. The former category may well have included some free laborers.

While it is apparent that by the mid-eighteenth century the Negro population had outstripped many times the white laboring class, it should be borne in mind that the ratio of servants to slaves was not a

[3] *Ibid.*, p. 71.

[4] *Ibid.*, p. 115. Franklin in an overcautious estimate in 1766 gave a somewhat lower proportion to the Germans. *Writings* (Smyth ed.), IV, 415–416.

[5] At that time it was estimated that some 60,000 white servants had been imported into the province during the previous twenty-year period. *Pa. Col. Rec.*, IV, 468. In the early period of settlement Penn stated that there were on an average two servants to a family of five. Until the arrival of the German Palatines in large numbers beginning in 1708 Geiser estimated that at least a third of the early immigrants were servants. The German immigration, especially after 1728, was very largely a redemptioner immigration. K. F. Geiser, "Redemptioners and Indentured Servants in the Colony and Commonwealth of Pennsylvania," *Yale Rev.*, Supp., X, No. 2 (Aug., 1901), 26, 27, 36. On the proportion of redemptioners to general immigration, see *infra*, p. 315n.

[6] *Md. Arch.*, XIX, 540 (1697).　　　　　　　[7] *Md. Arch.*, XXV, 258.

[8] See *CSPA, 1697–98*, No. 670, p. 390 (1698), in which Governor Nicholson estimated annual servant immigration, chiefly Irish, at 600 to 700.

proper criterion of the relative importance of the two labor systems, for the term of the slave was for life.[9]

Figures on the laboring population of Virginia offer wide discrepancies. A census of 1625 disclosed that out of 1,202 English inhabitants there were 487 servants, but actually more adult male servants than freemen. At that early date there were only 23 Negroes.[10] One estimate submitted to the authorities in 1665 gave 15,000 men available for muster, of whom two thirds were servants and one third masters, whereas Governor Berkeley placed the total population of Virginia in 1671 at 40,000, including 2,000 Negro slaves and 6,000 short-term white servants.[11] Lord Culpeper in 1681 gave 15,000 servants and 3,000 Negroes out of a total population of some seventy or eighty thousand.[12] For years the annual average importation of indentured servants ranged between 1,500 and 2,000,[13] which would make the Culpeper estimate approximately correct. However, by the end of the century, slave importations increased with great rapidity and white servant importations correspondingly declined. In 1712 Governor Spotswood stated that there were 12,501 freemen fit to bear arms and an equal number of Negroes and other servants,[14] but the Negro population, which was less than one third of the white in 1715, rose to about 47 per cent of the total by the eve of the Revolution.[15] A report of the Governor and Council of South Carolina to the Lord Proprietors in 1708 gave 2,400 adult freemen and women and 200 white servants as against 2,400 adult Negroes.[16] However, by the eve of the Revolution the Negro population outnumbered the whites by almost two to one.[17]

Similar difficulties confront the investigator seeking information on the number of workers employed in typical colonial industrial enterprises.[18] In the first place, we do know that the unit of industrial enterprise as compared with modern times was not large. The colonial pe-

[9] L. C. Gray, *History of Agriculture in the Southern United States* (2 vols., reprinted, New York, 1941), I, 348.

[10] Greene and Harrington, *op. cit.*, p. 144.   [11] *Ibid.*, p. 136; Hening, II, 515.

[12] *CSPA, 1681–85*, No. 320, p. 157.

[13] J. C. Ballagh, *White Servitude in the Colony of Virginia* (Baltimore, 1895), p. 41.

[14] Greene and Harrington, *op. cit.*, p. 139.

[15] Thomas Jefferson, "Notes on Virginia," *Writings* (P. L. Ford, ed., 10 vols., New York, 1892–99), III, 187–192.

[16] T. D. Jervey infers that "a very substantial portion" of the white settlers had served their terms as indentured servants. "White Indentured Servants of South Carolina," *S.C. Hist. and Gen. Mag.*, XII (1911), p. 165.

[17] Greene and Harrington, *op. cit.*, pp. 173, 175, 176. See also estimates of slave population in the colonies in Gray, *op. cit.*, II, 1025. In North Carolina servants were never very numerous. See J. S. Bassett, *Slavery in the State of North Carolina* (Baltimore, 1899), p. 76.

[18] See also R. B. Morris, "The Organization of Production during the Colonial Period," in H. F. Williamson, *The Growth of the American Economy* (New York, 1944), pp. 58–62.

riod was the age of the individual entrepreneur, who, in such industries as the workshop crafts, performed the labor as well as put up the capital for the venture himself. The joint-stock company or corporation was not widely employed for financing industrial ventures. Trading corporations, fire insurance, and water-supply companies, a few of the early mining companies, and the land companies were exceptions rather than the rule. Joint-stock companies for manufacturing were given a fillip in the Revolutionary era, but by and large productive enterprises were sufficiently small that they could be adequately financed by individuals or partnerships.[19]

The greatest concentration of labor was found on the larger plantations where industrial enterprises were carried on in addition to the production of an agricultural staple. Colonel Scarburgh, a seventeenth-century planter-industrialist, employed nine shoemakers on his plantation alone.[20] Robert Carter, the Virginia planter, had an interest in the Baltimore Iron Works organized in 1731; he used part of his shares of the iron to manufacture implements at his own smithy on his plantation. In addition, he set up a fulling mill and employed ten Negro women at spinning wool in a tobacco house assigned for that enterprise. During the Revolution he engaged six white workers who were expert spinners and weavers and proceeded to manufacture cloth. He also built a grain mill, had two bake ovens, and set up complete equipment for the manufacture of salt. Aside from a considerable number of white artisans and laborers employed for these varied enterprises, it is estimated that by the eve of the Revolution Carter employed some 350 slaves on his plantations.[21] Washington also had an establishment on his plantations for the manufacture of woolen, cotton, and linen cloth, employing at least one white woman and five Negro girls.

The efficient operation and management of a plantation might very well bring about a certain amount of labor displacement. The speed-up or "Bedaux system" is rooted in the American tradition of efficiency, which antedates Frederick W. Taylor by many generations. Washington carefully calculated that, allowing for a full day's work "from Sun to Sun" and two hours for breakfast, each of his carpenters ought to

[19] The number of American business corporations rose from seven in 1780 to at least 335 by 1800. J. S. Davis, *Essays in the Earlier History of American Corporations* (Cambridge, 1917), p. 22.

[20] See Northampton, Va., Co. Court O.B., 1682–97, f. 213. He also operated a malthouse.

[21] Louis Morton, *Robert Carter of Nomini Hall* (Williamsburg, 1941), p. 99. For an account of the manufacture of homespun clothing on the plantations, see Governor Spotswood's letter to the Board of Trade in Va. Hist. Soc., *Coll.,* I, 72–74 (1710). See also Broadus Mitchell, *The Rise of Cotton Mills in the South* (Baltimore, 1921), pp. 12, 13.

saw 180 feet of plank, taking into consideration the difference between poplar and other wood.[22] In harvesting his wheat he observed that nine or ten cradlers were sufficient to keep the rest of his hands employed, and that two "brisk" stackers would stack as fast as the wheat was cut. He further observed:

> From experience it has been found advantageous to put the Cradlers and their attendants into at least 3 Gangs. The Stops and delays by this means are not so frequent, and the Work much better attended to, as every Mans work is distinguishable, and the whole Cradlers not always stopping for every little disorder that happens to each respective one, as is the case when they cut altogether.

If these methods were followed he could get along at harvest time without having to employ extra hands at "exorbitantly high wages." [23] The adages of the day held out to masters the advantages of careful supervision. "Not to oversee your workmen is to leave them your purse open." "The diligent eye of the master will do more work than both his hands." [24]

Next to the great plantations, the furnace and forge industries called for the greatest concentration of labor of a semiskilled character working along rather specialized lines under one employer. In a proposal drawn up in 1657 by Anthony Langston for establishing an ironworks in Virginia, it was estimated that in order to produce 500 tons of iron annually—a figure only slightly in excess of the rate of production of the Lynn ironworks [25]—he would need forty men to cord, a similar number of laborers to carry the coal, eight stone-diggers, eight loaders and drivers, three men to dig limestone and nine to transport it, a founder and his mate for the furnace, who "must be good Artists," for upon them "the whole design depends much," a clerk at the forge, another at the furnace, four furnacemen and eight forgemen, and twenty men for emergencies and substitutions,—in all 144 workmen (not counting a chirurgeon and a minister), involving an expenditure of

[22] J. C. Fitzpatrick, ed., *The Diaries of George Washington, 1748–1799* (New York, 1925), I, 122 (1760).

[23] *Ibid.*, pp. 338, 339 (1769). Jefferson was constantly on the lookout for labor-saving machinery adaptable to farm operations, and prepared schedules to determine "the proportioning the labor to the size of the farm" to assure "a more judicious employment" of such labor. E. E. Edwards, "Jefferson and Agriculture," U.S. Dept. of Agriculture, *Agric. Hist. Series*, No. 7 (1943), pp. 39, 75, 76.

[24] Briggs, *Ames Almanacks*, p. 412 (1770). Cf. *Winthrop Papers*, III (Mass. Hist. Soc., 1943), 248 (1636).

[25] Even before the middle of the 18th century the larger Pennsylvania furnaces at Warwick and Reading were producing 800 tons annually. Maryland furnaces averaged better than 300 tons annually. Bining, *Col. Iron Industry*, p. 27.

£2,700! [26] Hasenclever's iron ventures involved the operation of six blast furnaces, seven forges, a stamping mill, three sawmills, and a gristmill. His undoubtedly was the largest payroll of any industrial enterprise in America prior to the Revolution.[27] Actually, the iron industry of the Middle colonies and the South was centered on the "iron plantations," tracts of several thousand acres of land which comprised largely self-sufficing, quasi-feudal communities.[28]

The average colonial shipyard was small, employing from five to ten workers and rarely exceeding twenty-five. At least as many men were employed on an average in the ropewalks, sizable establishments for the manufacture of standing and running rigging.[29] Such colonial industries as distilleries and breweries, paper and gunpowder manufacture, and the production of candles required considerable capital for equipment and some concentration of workers for successful operation.

The mill industries in general did not require a large number of employees per unit. A fulling mill to pound cloth required very few operatives. One entrepreneur announced that his fulling mill in Pitt County, North Carolina, had "a workman that is equal if not superior to any in the state." [30] The simpler sawmills attended by a man and a boy could in a working day saw one thousand feet of pine lumber. The use of gangs of saws was very common in the colonial period, and actually such mills were looked upon as displacing the labor of sawyers.[31] Grain mills were relatively smaller employers of labor than sawmills and iron

[26] *WMCQ*, 2d ser., I, 100 *et seq.*

[27] The Sterling Iron Works advertised in 1763 for "founders, miners, mine burners, pounders, and furnace fillers, banks-men, and stock-takers, finers of pigg, and drawers of bar; smiths and anchor smiths, carpenters, colliers, woodcutters, and common labourers." *N.Y. Gazette and Weekly Post-Boy*, Supp., Nov. 4, 1763. In 1766 Samuel Ogden of Boonetown, Morris County, N.J., advertised for fifteen or twenty persons who could work flat iron into kettles. *N.Y. Gazette and Weekly Mercury*, Aug. 12, 1776. Cf. also *N.J. Arch.*, XXVI, 361, 368 (1769). The Loyalist Samuel Smith, who, on the eve of the Revolution was the overseer of an ironworks in New Jersey, testified before the Royal Commission on Loyalist Claims that fifty of his workmen signed a paper opposing independence. H. E. Egerton, ed., *The Royal Commission on the Losses and Services of American Loyalists, 1783–1785* (Oxford, 1915), p. 320. Hundreds of workers were employed at the royal smelter and forges of St. Maurice, in French Canada, on the eve of the French and Indian War. L. H. Gipson, *The British Empire before the American Revolution*, V (New York, 1942), 18.

[28] See A. C. Bining, "The Iron Plantations of Early Pennsylvania," *Pa. Mag. of Hist. and Biog.*, LVII (1933), 117–137; C. S. Boyer, *Early Forges and Furnaces in New Jersey* (Philadelphia, 1931), pp. 26–33, 225, 226; Joseph Tuttle, "Hibernia Furnace," *N.J. Hist. Soc., Proceedings*, 2d ser., VI, 150. In the South slaves were extensively employed on the "iron plantations." See Kathleen Bruce, *The Virginia Iron Manufacture in the Slave Era* (New York, 1931), pp. 12–16.

[29] J. G. B. Hutchins, *American Maritime Industries and Public Policy, 1789–1914* (Cambridge, 1941), pp. 105, 125. Cf. also *Mass. Centinel*, April 30, 1785.

[30] *N.C. Gazette*, Nov. 14, 30, 1778.

[31] Clark, *Hist. of Mfgrs.*, pp. 176, 177; J. L. Bishop, *A History of American Manufactures from 1608 to 1860* (3 vols., Philadelphia, London, 1866), I, 105.

furnaces. The seventeenth-century gristmills were generally operated by the owner, his family, and one or two assistants. In the course of the eighteenth century the size of these enterprises increased, particularly in the Middle colonies, where the gristmill owner frequently operated a bolting mill to produce high-grade flour, a cooper shop, and at times a bakery.[32]

The application of power to milling machinery in the colonial period resulted in some displacement of labor. Oliver Evans, a pioneer in the use of high-pressure steam, invented a device for cleaning, grinding, cooling, bolting, and barreling grain without the intervention of any manual operation. It cut labor requirements of a flour mill by one half. Where the work of one man was formerly required for every ten barrels of flour, with Evans's invention, one man was sufficient for twenty barrels. It was estimated that six men, mostly employed in closing barrels, could convert annually 100,000 bushels of grain into flour.[33] Other pioneers in the use of steam power were William Henry, a Pennsylvania gunsmith who had known Watt in England and was reputed to have devised labor-saving machinery, and John Fitch, the steamboat pioneer, who managed a gun factory during the Revolution.[34] Washington observed that Winlaw's threshing machine not only saved labor in the mills, but made it possible to substitute women and boys for men in its operation.[35]

It is very likely that the introduction of labor-saving machinery was on so modest a scale that workmen had little ground to protest.[36] A let-

[32] *N.Y. Weekly Post-Boy*, May 20, 1745; C. B. Kuhlmann, *The Development of the Flour Milling Industry in the United States* (Boston, 1929), ch. i. In the environs of Wilmington and Baltimore the most extensive developments in this industry took place in the later period. See also M. Tyson, *A Brief Account of the Settlement of Ellicott's Mills* (Baltimore, 1870).

[33] The mill elevator was not in operation until a few years after the close of the Revolution. The Ellicott brothers on the Patapsco River were among the first to introduce Evans' improvement in their mills. See Oliver Evans, *The Young Mill-Wright and Miller's Guide* (9th ed., Philadelphia, 1836), pp. 203, 239; G. and D. Bathe, *Oliver Evans: a Chronicle of Early American Engineering* (Philadelphia, 1935), pp. 11, 23, 24, 26, 29. Duc de la Rochefoucault, *Travels through the United States of North America* (2 vols., London, 1799), II, 250–253; Clark, *Hist. of Mfgrs.*, pp. 179, 180. Another labor-saving device was Evans's invention in 1777 or 1778 of a machine which could complete 150 pairs of cotton or wool cards from wire per day. Bathe, *op. cit.*, p. 8.

[34] E. B. Greene, *The Revolutionary Generation, 1763–1790* (New York, 1943), p. 65; Bining, *Col. Iron Industry;* Lord Sheffield, *Observations on the Commerce of the American States* (6th ed., London, 1784), p. 14. For Silas Deane's proposal in 1785 to introduce the steam engine into the United States as a labor-saving device, see N.Y. Hist. Soc., *Coll.*, XXIII, 460.

[35] *Diaries*, IV, 72, 73 (1790).

[36] In England fear of technological unemployment caused widespread discontent and brought on riots and property destruction in the 17th and 18th centuries. See G. N. Clark, *Science and Social Welfare in the Age of Newton* (New York, 1937), p. 97; Beloff, *Public Order and Popular Disturbances*, pp. 88, 155.

ter from Baltimore published in the *Boston News-Letter* in 1772 describes the importation into the colonies by an English manufacturer of machinery which would "spin ten, and others from twenty to one hundred threads at one time, with the assistance of one hand to each machine." The writer shrewdly observed:

These machines are not allowed at home, and so inveterate are the common people against them, that they burn and destroy not only them, but the houses wherein they are found. The Americans being able to purchase cotton to more advantage than the Europeans, a manufactory of this kind will doubtless be properly encouraged by the well-wishers of America.[37]

The prevailing mode of production in the colonial towns was the workshop craft, employing generally one or two journeymen and a like number of apprentices.[38] In such trades as carpentry and cabinetwork there was some concentration of employees, however. The Loyalist house carpenter and joiner of New York City who claimed to have employed as many as twenty journeymen and three apprentices was by no means exceptional.[39] In Salem the Sandersons, prominent cabinetmakers, acted as wholesale distributors to foreign markets for the productions of other cabinetmakers, gilders, turners, and upholsterers. In Roxbury a considerable number of craftsmen obtained work from the Willard clockmakers.[40] Hewson, a calico printer who emigrated to America around 1772, opened a shop at Philadelphia with six English journeymen.[41]

The textile industries did not require a large concentration of labor, for, as stated in a Virginia act "for Weavers and Loomes" passed in 1666, "five women or children of 12 or 13 yeares of age may with much ease provide suffitient cloathing for thirty persons, if they would betake themselves to spinning." [42] As long as an operative was required for every spindle, there was no economy in applying water power to spinning or incentive to the setting up of factories. Hence, spinning was largely carried on in colonial households. Governor Moore of New York, a shrewd observer of economic trends, reported on the

[37] *Boston News-Letter*, Feb. 20, 1774. The manufacturer also planned to bring six journeymen along with him, doubtless to operate this machinery.

[38] See Lechford, *Note-Book*, p. 91 (1639).

[39] Loyalist Transcripts, XIX, 281. See also *infra*, p. 422; *Boston News-Letter*, March 10, 1768; *Pa. Packet*, March 1, 1794; *Daily Advertiser* (New York), July 9, 1798. Silversmiths and jewelers increased their staffs and expanded their facilities considerably after the Revolution. See *Pa. Packet*, July 8, 1795. This was also true of hatters once the Hat Act was technically inoperative. See Cole, *op. cit.*, p. 21.

[40] *Essex Inst. Hist. Coll.*, LXII (1934), 323-364.

[41] Clark, *Hist. of Mfgrs.*, p. 547. [42] Hening, II, 238 (1666).

eve of the Revolution that "every house swarms with children, who are set to work as soon as they are able to Spin and card; and as every family is furnished with a Loom, the Itinerant Weavers who travel about the Country, put the finishing hand to the work." [43] Indeed, home manufactures made big strides in the Revolutionary era, and were regarded by some as "the Most Direct Road to National Prosperity." [44]

Weaving required more mechanical equipment and greater skill than spinning. In England clothmaking tended to become specialized and to be produced in workshops or factories. In the colonies the putting-out or domestic system developed rapidly by the end of the colonial period for weaving and in the shoe industry. [45] The weaver or shoemaker would work at home but would be dependent for stock upon an entrepreneur who in some cases furnished implements as well. In the shoe industry there was a considerable concentration of labor in Lynn, which, by the eve of the Revolution, had become the most highly developed center for the domestic system in that field of manufacturing; but other towns in the Bay colony were also by this time manufacturing quantities of shoes for the wholesale trade. [46]

In such industries, as Herbert Heaton has observed, "while much material went to the worker many workers came to the material." The nonimportation agreements proved an incentive not alone to domestic

[43] *Docs. Rel. to the Col. Hist. of N.Y.,* VII, 888, 889 (1767). See also letter of Comptroller Weare to the President of the Board of Trade, Mass. Hist. Soc., *Coll.* 1st ser., I, 74, 79. An idea of the magnitude of such household manufactures can be gained from estimates of the production of cloth for the town of Lancaster alone between May, 1769 and May, 1770. During that period it was reported that 27,790 yards of cloth were woven, with an additional six or seven thousand yards still on the looms and sufficient yarn in the homes of the inhabitants to weave another thousand yards. *N.Y.J. or Gen. Advertiser,* June 28, 1770; J. O. Knauss, "Social Conditions among the Pennsylvania Germans in the Eighteenth Century, as Revealed in German Newspapers Published in America," Pa.-German Soc., *Publications,* XXIX (1918, Lancaster, 1922), p. 132. For impressive production figures in such communities as Woodbridge, N.J., and Newport, R.I., see *N.Y. Gazette or Weekly Post-Boy,* Jan. 18, 1768; *N.Y. Gazette and Weekly Mercury,* Feb. 1, 1768.

For silk manufacture as a household industry, see *Mass. Spy* (Worcester), Dec. 24, 1789, where it is asserted that one woman, assisted by two or three children could tend sufficient silkworms to make ten or twelve pounds of silk.

The difference between the old and new spinning processes was described by Washington in 1789 when he contrasted a duck manufactory at Haverhill conducted by Samuel Blodgett, an inventor, where "one small person turns a wheel which employs eight spinners, each acting independently of each other, so as to occasion no interruption to the rest if any one of them is stopped," with a duck factory at Boston where "each spinner has a small girl to turn the wheel." *Diaries,* IV, 47 (1789).

[44] Winslow, *Amer. Broadside Verses,* pp. 198, 199.

[45] For the domestic system of production of cotton thread and cloth, see *Mass. Spy* (Worcester), April 16, 1788; Jan. 29, Aug. 27, 1789.

[46] See Blanche E. Hazard, *Organization of the Boot and Shoe Industry in Massachusetts before 1875* (Cambridge, 1921), p. 29.

manufacturing but also to the establishment of larger units of production employing more labor. Informal spinning groups made up of ladies who felt the patriotic urge to spin in the company of others or to engage in spinning matches sprang up throughout the colonies.[47] Largely as a result of the activities of the New York Society for the Promotion of Arts, Agriculture and Oeconomy in granting premiums for local manufacture and in establishing spinning schools, it was estimated that some three hundred persons were employed in the making of linen alone from the middle of 1765 to the close of the following year.[48] In the "Manufactory House" built by the Boston Society for Encouraging Industry and Employing the Poor, a spinning school was opened by William Molineaux in 1769. There were four hundred spinning wheels, many looms for weaving, and furnaces, hot and cold presses for finishing the goods, and a complete dye house. While this machinery was not power-driven, it was concentrated in one establishment and operated under centralized direction by a sizable labor force. As one economic historian remarks, "if this was not a factory, it was a near approach to it." [49] The same description would apply to the factory set up by the United Company of Philadelphia for Promoting American Manufacture, the first joint-stock company for the manufacture of cotton goods and reputedly the first in the country to use a spinning jenny; in its initial year, 1775, it employed 400 women.[50] A like number of women spinners were said to have been employed by another Philadelphia company formed the same year to encourage woolen manufactures.[51] Finally, it should be borne in mind that war industries necessitated by the American Revolution generally involved a considerable concentration of employees in single units.[52]

COMPARATIVE LABOR CONDITIONS

THE SCARCITY AND HIGH COST of labor served as a brake upon the rapid expansion of colonial production, but by the same token assured the workman of a higher standard of living than was obtainable by a per-

[47] *N.Y.J.*, Supp., May 11, 1769.

[48] *N.Y.J.*, Dec. 17, 31, 1767; A. M. Schlesinger, *The Colonial Merchants and the American Revolution, 1763–1776* (New York, 1917), p. 77.

[49] E. C. Kirkland, *A History of American Economic Life* (rev. ed., New York, 1939), p. 91.

[50] J. L. Bishop, *History of American Manufactures, 1608–1860* (rev. ed., Philadelphia, 1866–1868), I, 384. See also Scharf and Westcott, *Hist. of Phila.*, III, 2314.

[51] *Ibid.*, p. 2301.

[52] A gun factory in Virginia employed at one time 19 workmen and 5 apprentices. *Cal. Va. State Papers*, III, 305 (1782). See also *Md. Arch.*, XII, 519 (1776). Unemployed Negro workmen to the extent of one hundred were required for the Aera Furnace erected in South Carolina during the Revolution. *Charleston Gazette*, Jan. 11, 1780. See also *infra*, pp. 301–303.

son of similar employment in England or on the Continent. Describing conditions in Virginia, Peter Arundle reported early in 1622: "Yea I say that any laborious honest man may in a shorte time become ritche in this Country." [1] Poverty was the exception rather than the rule, especially in the seventeenth century. Governor Leete of Connecticut reported to the Committee for Trade and Plantations in 1680: "There is seldom any want relief; because labor is deare, vis., 2s., and sometimes 2s. 6d. a day for a day labourer, and provision cheap." [2] Maryland reported in 1699 that the "Province wants workmen, workmen want not work; here are no beggars, and they that are superannuated are reasonably well provided for by the country." [3] That enthusiastic promoter of immigration, Gabriel Thomas, exhorted the "Poor Labouring Men, Women, and Children in England" that in Pennsylvania there were "no Beggars to be seen (it is a Shame and Disgrace to the State that there are so many in England) nor indeed have any here the least Occasion or Temptation to take up that Scandalous Lazy Life." [4] John Bolzius, writing in 1743 of pioneer days in Georgia, gave much the same picture. "All industrious people," he stated, "live more comfortably here than in their native country, and beg in their letters frequently that their relatives might follow them to this colony." [5]

The scarcity of labor, particularly of skilled workers, created a labor market which favored the laborer rather than the employer. The colonial workman commanded real wages which exceeded by from 30 to 100 per cent the wages of a contemporary English workman. All authorities agreed on the relatively high wages prevailing in the colonies. John Winthrop records the answer made by a servant to a master who had been obliged to sell a pair of oxen to meet his wages. The master told the servant that he saw no prospect of being able to continue to pay him. "Sell more cattle," said the workman. "What shall I do when they are gone?" "You can serve me and get them back," was the reply. [6] John Winter wrote from Maine in 1639 that if the current high rate of wages continued, "the servants wil be masters and the masters servants." [7]

---

[1] *Va. Co. Rec.*, III, 589.　　　　　[2] *Conn. Pub. Rec.*, III, 300.

[3] *CSPA, 1699*, No. 581, p. 320. See also *ibid.*, No. 317, p. 176. Answer to the queries of the Board of Trade, 1697: "The scarcity of Artificers and labourers and their high wages is the chiefe and onely difficulty in procuring those things of which there is an inexhaustible quantity." *Md. Arch.*, XIX, 540 (1697). Cf. also Hugh Jones, *Present State of Virginia* (Sabin's reprint, New York, 1865), pp. 53, 54.

[4] Myers, *Narr. of Pa.*, pp. 332, 333.　　　[5] *Ga. Col. Rec.*, XXIV, 41 (1743).

[6] John Winthrop, *History of New England from 1630 to 1649* (cited as *Journal*), ed. J. Savage (2 vols., Boston, 1853), II, 220. Servants were preferred to cash. See *Essex*, III, 371 (1666).

[7] "Trelawny Papers," Me. Hist. Soc., *Coll.*, III, 164, 200.

One discouraged New Englander wrote in 1660 that "help is scarce and hard to gett, difficult to please, uncertaine, etc." Samuel Sewall sought to solve his household servant problem by paying court to a likely prospect, and noted in his diary that it was "hard to find a good one" even in the year 1687.[8] "Poor People," Gabriel Thomas wrote of Pennsylvania workmen, "can here get three times the wages for their Labour they can in England." High labor costs to some extent impaired the ability of colonial producers to compete with English manufacturers and rendered competition with continental producers in some fields virtually hopeless without subsidies. It was reported in 1694 that "Labour costs but one sixth of the price (in Sweden and Denmark) as it does in New England," and William Byrd 2d abandoned plans for the introduction of hemp. "Labour being much dearer than in Muscovy, as well as Freight, we can make no Earnings of it," he wrote in 1737.[9]

Those were the days when help-wanted advertisements vastly outnumbered notices inserted by artisans seeking employment. The cry, "help is not to be had at any rate," [10] was not unusual. Journeymen had to be offered "good," "generous," or "great" wages and "constant employ." [11]

After the Revolution American workmen continued to enjoy considerably higher wages than the workers of Great Britain.[12] While Hamilton in his Report on the Subject of Manufactures indicated that in certain heavily populated areas of the country the labor shortage appeared to be disappearing, he nevertheless reassured business that "un-

[8] Cotton Mather, reporting in his diary on the scarcity of household servants, declared, with characteristic piety: "I resolve, if God bless me with Good *Servants*, I will serve Him with more Fidelity and activity." "Diary of Cotton Mather, 1681–1708," Mass. Hist. Soc., *Coll.*, 7th ser., I, 554 (1706). Cf. also *Winthrop Papers*, IV (Mass. Hist. Soc., 1944), 139 (1639), 273 (1640).

[9] See, e.g., *Va. Co. Rec.*, III, 457; *Essex*, V, 50, 51 (1672); *Conn. Pub. Rec.*, 1678–89, p. 293 (1680); *CSPA, 1693–96*, No. 967, p. 263 (1694), *1696–97*, No. 108, p. 54 (1696), No. 783, p. 392 (1697), *1697–98*, No. 25, pp. 9, 10 (1697), *1699*, No. 769, p. 428, *1711–12*, No. 454, pp. 305–306 (1712), *1716–17*, No. 402, p. 205 (1716), *1719–20*, No. 564, p. 357 (1719), *1720–21*, No. 206, p. 173 (1720), No. 656, pp. 413–414 (1721); *N.J. Col. Docs.*, V, 126, 127 (1773); *WMCQ*, 2d ser., I, 196 (1737); *Ga. Col. Rec.*, XXIII, 170 (1741), 352, 444 (1742); *Amer. Husbandry*, pp. 8, 30, 127, 128, 253; *N.J. Arch.*, 1st ser., XX, 256–261 (1758). In 1732 Byrd observed that labor costs in Virginia were five times as great as in Riga. Byrd, *Writings*, p. 367.

However, as Hasenclever observed, American ironmasters made up in part for the "exorbitant wages" by selling goods and provisions to their workers, averaging profits on such sales estimated at £1 10s. sterling per ton of bar iron. *Remarkable Case of Peter Hasenclever*, p. 80.

For a typical mercantilist denunciation by a colonist of the effect of high wages, see *Pa. Chronicle*, March 12, 1769.

[10] F. L. Hawks, *History of North Carolina* (Fayetteville, N.C., 1859), II, 215.

[11] See, e.g., *Boston News-Letter*, Aug. 23–30, 1714; *Pa. Evening Post*, Oct. 14, 1777; *N.C. Gazette*, Dec. 26, 1777; Nov. 30, 1778; *Md. J. and Baltimore Advertiser*, April 20, 1784; Dec. 6, 1785.

[12] See Cole, *Hamilton Corr.*, pp. 42, 64, 90, 192, 220–221.

dertakers of manufactures in this country can, at this time, afford to pay higher wages to the workmen they may employ, than are paid to similar workmen in Europe." [13]

However, all was not beer and skittles in the life of a colonial workman. "In this Country is no living without hard labour," a pioneer labor overseer complained.[14] Too often were indentured servants treated in a degrading manner and denied even a subsistence livelihood.[15] In the eighteenth century the number of indigent persons increased considerably, particularly in the seaport towns, where poor immigrants collected and employment was dependent to a considerable degree upon the vagaries of the import trade. Currency depreciation and cyclical factors, becoming more marked as the Revolution drew near, created some degree of working-class insecurity.[16]

Much spade work will have to be done before we can ascertain the prevailing scale of wages in the various trades in colonial America. Available compilations are unsystematic and lacking in comprehensiveness, nor do they take into account varying living costs in diverse areas and the highly complex colonial currency. Adequate consideration has not as yet been given to the role of subsistence farming in the colonies in supplementing the income of wage earners. The decline of this supplementary income in eighteenth-century England owing to the effects of the enclosures and agricultural capitalism contributed materially to weakening the economic position of the English working class.[17]

[13] *Ibid.*, pp. 268, 270.

[14] "Trelawny Papers," *Doc. Hist. of Maine*, III, 313 (1642).

[15] See *infra*, pp. 470–500.

[16] See Jernegan, *Laboring and Dependent Classes*, pp. 197, 198; *Boston Selectmen Rec., 1742–53*, p. 161 (1747). See also *Boston Town Rec.*, VII, 190 (1686); *S.C. Gazette*, Aug. 3, 1738. For the petition of the ministers, wardens, and vestry of the parish of Bruton in which there is reference to the increase in the number of vagabonds in the parish, see *Journals of the House of Burgesses, 1752–55*, p. 260 (1753).

[17] U.S. Bureau of Labor Statistics, *Bulletin*, No. 449 (1929) contains some tables, but the study is very partial. Even less satisfactory and of doubtful utility are the tables compiled by W. B. Weeden, *Economic and Social History of New England, 1620–1789* (2 vols., Boston and New York, 1890). To satisfy the formidable criteria for wage scales laid down by Mantoux in *The Industrial Revolution in the Eighteenth Century* (rev. ed., London, 1928), pp. 430–431, it will be necessary to pursue intensive regional studies by crafts, as Mrs. Gilboy did for eighteenth-century England. Such an investigation should parallel the price studies conducted by Arthur H. Cole of wholesale commodity prices for the period down to 1861, and the special regional studies conducted by Anne Bezanson, Robert D. Gray, and Miriam Hussey for Pennsylvania, and by Herman M. Stoker, G. F. Warren, and F. A. Pearson for New York. While newspapers provide a mine of information of wholesale commodity prices, they will not be of much utility for a wage study. Instead, account books and business papers, court records, and administrative records should prove very useful to such compilers. Of great utility for a limited area is T. M. Adams, "Prices Paid by Vermont Farmers for Goods and Services; Wages of Vermont Farm Labor, 1780–1940," *Vt. Agricultural Experiment Station, Bull.*, No. 507 and Suppl. (1944). For some suggestive comparisons of English and colonial wage rates, see also Myers, *Narr. of Pa.*, pp.

The assumption that high wages, by attracting many immigrants, would in the long run glut the labor market and thus bring down the wage rate is contrary to the facts. In the main, the ultimate economic objective of colonial workmen was security through agriculture rather than industry. As this was the age of the enclosures when the yeoman was being displaced from his land in Britain, the attitude of the immigrant was quite understandable.[18] As soon as a workman had accumulated a small amount of money he could, and in many cases did, take up a tract of land and settle on it as a farmer. This was the paradox of the high wage scale, for, as the author of *American Husbandry* pointed out, "nothing but a high price will induce men to labour at all, and at the same time it presently puts a conclusion to it by so soon enabling them to take a piece of waste land."[19] A high colonial official reported to the Board of Trade in 1767:

the genius of the People in a Country where every one can have Land to work upon leads them so naturally into Agriculture, that it prevails over every other occupation. There can be no stronger Instances of this, than in the servants Imported from Europe of different Trades; as soon as the Time stipulated in their Indentures is expired, they immediately quit their Masters, and get a small tract of Land, in settling which for the first three or four years they lead miserable lives, and in the most abject Poverty; but all this is patiently borne and submitted to with the greatest chearfulness, the Satisfaction of being Land holders smooths every difficulty, and makes them prefer this manner of living to that comfortable subsistence which they could procure for themselves and their families by working at the Trades in which they were brought up.

The Master of a Glass-house; which was set up here a few years ago, now a Bankrupt, assured me that his ruin was owing to no other cause than being deserted in this manner by his servants, which he had Imported at a great expence; and that many others had suffered and been reduced as he was, by the same kind of Misfortune.[20]

---

326 *et seq.*; *CSPA, 1675–76,* No. 628, pp. 259, 260 (1675); *1696–97,* No. 1285, p. 591 (1697); *1702,* No. 1135, p. 710 (1702); *1711–12,* No. 192, pp. 166, 167 (1711). See also Stock, *Proc. Brit. Parl.,* III, 304n. (1713); I. N. P. Stokes, *Iconography of Manhattan Island* (New York, 1915–28), IV, 554 (1737).

[18] Rack-renting and the enclosures were among the principal reasons assigned in the Emigration Lists, 1773–76, for migrating to America. Treasury Papers 47: 9–11.

[19] *Amer. Husbandry,* pp. 52, 54. Cf. also *Lloyd's Evening Post,* Aug. 12, 1768; *London Chronicle,* April 21, 1774. Franklin, who in later years developed the theory of the economics of high wages, concurred. *Some Observations Concerning the Increase of Mankind, Peopling of Countries, etc.,* (Boston, 1755).

[20] *Docs. Rel. to the Col. Hist. of N.Y.,* VII, 888, 889. A frequent ground for cancelling indentures of apprenticeship was the abandonment by a master of his trade for the "Business of Farming." See, e.g., Lane's case, N.Y.G.S., lib. III (Aug. 6, 1755).

This favored position of agriculture was maintained long after the Revolution. Talleyrand, an acute observer of economic conditions in America in the last decade of the century, observed that as long as farming "calls to it the offspring of large families it will obtain preference over industrial labor. It requires less assiduity, it promises greater independence, it offers to the imagination at least a more advantageous prospect, it has in its favor priority of habits." [21] Thus, in a great many cases the opportunity of acquiring good land in freehold tenure rather than the prospects of higher wages attracted immigrants. This was all to the good in the opinion of men like Jefferson, by whom agriculture was not only considered a more profitable occupation than manufacturing, but one offering a sounder prospect upon which to build a social and political order. "Let our workshops remain in Europe," he once declared.[22]

On the other hand, as very little capital was required for the handicraft trades when they merely served their local communities, journeymen did not take long to accumulate adequate funds, and, in turn, in preference to husbandry, might in some cases choose to open up shops for themselves. There were constant opportunities for the artisan-entrepreneur in the expanding economy of the colonial and Revolutionary periods.

The fluid character of the colonial labor system offers a splendid field for research in which some of the techniques of the genealogist can be put to good use by the social historian. How many convict servants settled down and became substantial citizens? We know of only a few, notably Andrew Lamb, the transported convict, who settled in Philadelphia and acquired a reputation as an instrument-maker and teacher of mathematics, surveying, and navigation. His son, John, was a general in the Continental army. How many indentured servants actually took up land and settled down to husbandry at the expiration of their terms? Abbot Emerson Smith suggests that few did in seventeenth-century Maryland, perhaps 8 per cent was "a fair estimate of the proportion of indentured servants who achieved a reasonably stable position in the

[21] H. Huth and Wilma J. Pugh, "Talleyrand in America as a Financial Promoter, 1794–96: Unpublished Letters and Memoirs," II, Amer. Hist. Assn., *Ann. Report, 1941* (Washington, 1942), p. 127.

[22] In his earlier years Jefferson felt that urban industrialization, with its accompanying evils, was to be avoided at all costs. *Writings,* ed. P. L. Ford, III, 268–270, IV, 87–90, 449; *Writings,* ed. A. A. Lipscomb and A. E. Bergh (Washington, 1903), V, 93–96. For a similar view, see Briggs, *Ames Almanacks,* pp. 448–449. However, Jefferson in his more mature period came to defend manufactures and the laboring classes, whose interests he regarded as threatened by excessive commercialism. See *Writings,* III, 319, XIV, 387–393, XV, 28; also Adrienne Koch, *The Philosophy of Thomas Jefferson* (New York, 1943), pp. 170, 173.

colonies." [23] More studies remain to be made in this field if we are to be able to evaluate the economic and social role of the common man, the "village Hampden" and the "mute inglorious Milton."

A traditional theme of English and American ballads is that of the poor farmhand who marries the farmer's daughter and the apprentice boy who falls in love with his young mistress.[24] The story was given a reverse twist in the cases of Benjamin Franklin's maternal grandmother, Mary Morrils, whom Peter Folger had bought as an indentured servant for £20 and afterward married, and of Eleanor Stevenson, a runaway servant girl of Sir Edmund Plowden, who married William Branthwait, a relative of Lord Baltimore, and Deputy-Governor of Maryland.[25] How many journeymen actually set up in trades for themselves? Roger Sherman, apprenticed as a shoemaker, who worked at the trade until he was twenty-two, then turned to law and became both a Signer and a delegate to the Constitutional Convention, is an outstanding case. The meteoric career of Benjamin Franklin, the printer's apprentice, was certainly extraordinary and not typical of the times, nor was that of another Signer, the lawyer, George Walton, of Georgia, who had been apprenticed to a carpenter upon being left an orphan and was to a great extent a self-made man. Oliver Evans started his brilliant career as inventor and engineer by serving an apprenticeship to a wheelwright and John Fitch, steamboat inventor, was apprenticed to two different clockmakers before setting up his own brass foundry.[26]

However, we can safely conclude that the high wages commanded by colonial workmen, the relative independence enjoyed by them, and the

---

[23] "The Indentured Servant and Land Speculation in Seventeenth Century Maryland," *Amer. Hist. Rev.*, XL (1935), 467–472. In the early pioneering days a heavy proportion of bound laborers appear to have returned to England when their terms were up. See "Trelawny Papers," *Me. Hist. Soc. Coll.*, III, 204 (1639).

[24] See Louise Pound, *American Ballads and Songs* (New York, 1922), pp. 69, 71, 74–76; *J. of Amer. Folk-Lore*, XXVI (1913), 363.

[25] *WMCQ*, 1st ser., IV, 29.

[26] William Price, murdered in 1668, had risen from indentured servitude to become a landowner and practicing attorney before the Charles County court. *Md. Arch.*, LVII, xxvii–xxviii. Daniel Dulany the elder was reputed to have come over to Maryland from Ireland as an indentured servant—a story perpetuated by his son's political opponent, Charles Carroll of Carrollton. Ellen H. Smith, *Charles Carroll of Carrollton* (Cambridge, Mass., 1942), pp. 101, 106. However, because of his family background he was not typical of the run of the redemptioners. See *Md. Hist. Mag.*, XIII, 20 *et seq.* Thomas Ferguson began as a sawyer and plantation overseer and ultimately acquired nine plantations and married Christopher Gadsden's daughter. Connor Dowd came from Ireland as a laborer, and by the time of the American Revolution had established himself as a substantial plantation owner. Egerton, *Royal Commission*, pp. 216, 218. John Hennessey was an Irish redemptioner, bound for a four-year term. After twenty years he accumulated enough money as a carter and auction dealer in Charleston to buy a house in 1775 for £3,000 current. *Ibid.*, p. 285. For further instances of "gentlemen" as bound servants, see *WMCQ*, 1st ser., XXVI, 31.

wide recognition of the importance of labor accounted in large part for the greater esteem accorded workmen, particularly skilled craftsmen, in the colonies than in the mother country.[27] Hence, class attitudes were not as sharply accentuated as in contemporary England, where men of property thought of the laborers as a composite class—"the lower orders" and "the meaner sort," who, according to eighteenth-century mercantilists, were more in need of discipline than employment. In certain occupations, such as coal mining, they were widely regarded as not only uncouth, but also degraded.[28] A number of observers asserted that these sharpened class differences were leading to mounting industrial clashes in Britain. George Blewitt complained of "idle and rioting Vermin," [29] and Daniel Defoe castigated the "Lab'ring Poor" for being "saucy, mutinous, and beggarly," in spite of "double pay." [30] Describing labor conditions in the west of England in 1757, Josiah Tucker observed that the increase in the number of workmen in shops and factories was leading to a rise in union activity and rioting "upon every little Occasion."

The master—however well-disposed in himself, is naturally tempted by his Situation to be proud and over-bearing, to consider his People as the Scum of the Earth, whom he has a Right to squeeze whenever he can; because they ought to be kept low, and not to rise up in Competition with their Superiors. The Journeymen on the contrary, are equally tempted by their Situation, to envy the high Station, and superior Fortunes of their Masters; and to envy them the more, in Proportion as they find themselves deprived of the Hopes of advancing themselves to the same Degree by any Stretch of Industry, or superior Skill.[31]

Mob activity and rioting in Great Britain became more marked on the eve of the American Revolution in no small part as a result of the unusual number of bad crops between 1756 and 1773.[32]

[27] See "Report of the Journey of Francis Louis Michel from Berne, Switzerland, to Virginia, Oct. 2, 1701–Dec. 1, 1702," *VMH*, XXIV, 287, 288. For the attractive position of the artisan during and after the Revolution in a booming town, see T. J. Wertenbaker, *Norfolk: History of a Southern Port* (Durham, N.C., 1931), pp. 94 *passim*.

[28] Henry Fielding, *Enquiry into the Late Increase in Robbers* (London, 1751); Elizabeth W. Gilboy, *Wages in Eighteenth Century England* (Cambridge, Mass., 1934), pp. xviii, xixn.; D. Marshall, *The English Poor in the Eighteenth Century* (London, 1926); M. D. George, *London Life in the XVIIIth Century* (London, 1926), *passim;* Furniss, *The Position of the Laborer in a System of Nationalism*, p. 104; J. U. Nef, *The Rise of the British Coal Industry* (London, 1932), II, 151 *et seq.*, 175.

[29] *An Enquiry whether a General Practise of Virtue Tends to the Wealth or Poverty, Benefit, or Disadvantage of a People?* (London, 1725), p. 208.

[30] *The Great Law of Subordination Consider'd* (London, 1724), pp. 79–80.

[31] Josiah Tucker, "Instructions for Travellers" (Dublin, 1758), in R. L. Schuyler, ed., *Josiah Tucker: a Selection from His Economic and Political Writings* (New York, 1931), pp. 244, 245.

[32] Barnes, *English Corn Laws*, p. 31.

Despite the social stratifications that pervaded almost all areas of colonial settlement, the bulk of the settlers in this country had a greater respect for the dignity of hard labor,[33] and the working class in turn was possessed of a greater spirit of independence. From early settlement they had participated in town government in New England and on Long Island. This led Governor Nicolls in 1666 to observe that "Democracy hath taken so deepe a Roote in these parts, that the very name of Justice of the Peace is an abomination!" The American Board of Customs Commissioners saw reason for alarm in reporting in 1768 that these town meetings were being diverted to "political purposes." "At these meetings, the lowest Mechanicks discuss upon the most important points of government, with the utmost freedom." [34] English officialdom had little sympathy with the strivings of the working class in the colonies for political influence. It was fitting, one official observed, that "the lives and fortunes" of the settlers should be entrusted to persons "who have the best abilitys and the best estates." [35] By the eve of the Revolution "democracy" and mob rule were considered one and the same thing by British officials.[36] Men of wealth in America shared these views; [37] but in the era of the American Revolution it became increasingly fashionable to acclaim the "virtuous" mechanics and to cloak them with respectability, even though social distinctions between "gentle" and "simple" were by no means obliterated. In the very same year in which one English writer stated that it was essential to "a flourishing state" that there be at the base of the social pyra-

[33] This was natural in a society where idleness was regarded as sinful. Jefferson declared at a later period: "My new trade of nail-making is to me in this country what an additional title of nobility is, or the ensigns of a new order are in Europe." *Writings* (Ford ed.), VII, 14 (1795). In fact, merchants and professional men were regarded by some as "supernumeraries" and "idlers" who should be put to work as farmers or mechanics. See *Mass. Spy* (Worcester), Sept. 11, 1788.

[34] Report to the Treasury, Feb. 12, 1768, cited by L. H. Gipson, *Jared Ingersoll* (New Haven, 1920), p. 270.

[35] Opinion of Sir William Thompson, Dec. 19, 1717. Va. Hist. Soc.

[36] See *Gage Corr.*, I, 205, 358, 359; II, 29 ("that insolent and infatuated Mob"). For references by royal governors to "the dastardly Spirit of our common People" and the "rabble," see *Md. Arch.*, IX, 59; William Smith, *History of New York* (New York, 1830), p. 333; *Amer. Arch.*, 4th ser., I, 775, 1062; Ga. Hist. Soc., *Coll.*, III, 228; J. K. Hosmer, *The Life of Thomas Hutchinson* (Boston, 1896), pp. 103, 104; C. L. Becker, *The History of Political Parties in the Province of New York, 1760–1774* (Univ. of Wisconsin, *Bulletin*, No. 286, Madison, 1909), p. 115; N.Y. Hist. Soc., *Coll.* (1875), pp. 127, 128. Somewhat earlier Governor Lewis Morris of New Jersey had referred to the majority as "the meanest of the people," and was easily persuaded by Eccles. 38:25, 26, 33 that the "plowmen" who made up the legislature should be deprived of a voice in public affairs. N.J. Hist. Soc., *Coll.*, IV, 40, 277, 278.

[37] Gouverneur Morris, for example, considered the people as a "mob" and "poor reptiles," and denounced "this cursed spirit of levelling." Jared Sparks, *Life of Gouverneur Morris* (Boston, 1932), I, 23–25; *Pa. Packet*, April 29, 1776. Some observers noted a growing hostility between labor and employer on the eve of the Revolution. J. Boucher, *A View of the Causes and Consequences of the American Revolution* (London, 1797), p. 306.

mid "a large and solid basis of the lower classes of mankind," [38] a Yankee almanac editor urged his countrymen "to prevent the execution of that detestable maxim of *European* policy amongst us, *viz:* That the common people, who are three quarters of the world, must be kept in ignorance, that they may be slaves to the other quarter who live in magnificence." A high standard of living would be the reward of the masses if trade and commerce, merchants and artificers were encouraged, and "foreign luxury, effeminacy, immorality, and idleness" banished. "He that will not work neither shall he eat." [39] The notable role of the town mechanics in developing a revolutionary spirit in the colonies is now fully recognized, but it also must be born in mind that this labor group, though generally unenfranchised, supported the ratification of the Federal Constitution while at the same time insisting upon a bill of rights. [40]

Democracy, as we understand the term today, was not by any means achieved with the Revolution, [41] but the process of freeing the individual from restraints that were external in origin was accelerated, and mercantilism was one of the principal casualties. [42] At the same time the relation between the government and popular associations organized

[38] Sir James Stewart, *Principles of Political Economy* (London, 1767), I, 73–75.

[39] Briggs, *Ames Almanacks*, pp. 382, 383 (1767). See also *Brutus to the Free . . . Inhabitants.* Lenox Broadsides, N.Y. Pub. Lib.; Thomas Young to John Lamb, Newport, Oct. 4, 1774. Lamb MSS, N.Y. Hist. Soc. With these views compare the charges of William Goddard, Loyalist printer, who in 1777 published a list of the names and vocations of the members of the Baltimore Whig Club, comprising sailors, haberdashers, tailors, and watchmakers, and asked how a man who was only fit to "patch a shoe" could have the temerity to attempt to patch the state. "Papers relating to the Whig Club," April 8–17, 1777, in Maryland Misc. MSS (1771–1838), Lib. of Cong.; also cited by E. P. Link, *Democratic-Republic Societies, 1790–1800* (New York, 1942), p. 26. See also Greene, *Revol. Generation*, p. 97.

[40] New York is the most clear-cut illustration, for in that state alone the principle of manhood suffrage was adopted in the election of delegates to the ratifying convention. In New York County, chief seat of the artisan class, the highest Federalist vote for delegates totalled 2,735; the highest anti-Federalist vote, 134. Following a large working-class demonstration in Baltimore, the Federalist delegate received 962 votes as against 385 votes for his leading opponent. See C. A. Beard, *An Economic Interpretation of the Constitution of the United States* (New York, 1929), pp. 241, 244, 247. The contrary view of F. T. Carlton—*Organized Labor in American History* (New York, 1920), p. 52—is not supported by the evidence available. For the participation of masters, journeymen, and apprentices in the processions celebrating the ratification of the Federal Constitution, see *Md. J.*, May 6, 1788; *Mass. Spy* (Worcester), May 29, 1788; *Pa. Gazette*, July 9, 1788. It must be borne in mind, however, that the workers generally supported the Republican Societies in their opposition to the Hamiltonian program of the new Federal government. See Link, *op. cit.*, pp. 31, 93, 94, 96.

[41] The Pennsylvania Constitution of 1776 was the greatest triumph of the democratic movement. See F. N. Thorpe, ed., *The Federal and State Constitutions, Colonial Charters, and Other Organic Laws* (7 vols., Washington, 1909), V, 3084; J. C. Miller. *Origins of the American Revolution* (Boston, 1943), ch. xxi; also *infra*, pp. 503–506.

[42] See C. M. Andrews, *Col. Period of Amer. Hist.*, IV, 423n. To Lorenzo Sabine "the great object of the Revolution was to release labor from these restrictions," *The American Loyalists* (Boston, 1847), pp. 1, 2.

both for economic and political ends was becoming increasingly significant. The history of labor in Great Britain and the United States was to pursue a number of parallel courses. Clues to the points of departure are found in the greater economic and social democracy which prevailed in America in the Revolutionary and early Federal periods [43] and in the continually expanding economy on this side of the Atlantic. With the rise of trade unionism these differences became even more accentuated.[44]

[43] For egalitarian trends among the working class and the decline of the term "servant," see Elkanah Watson, *Men and Times of the Revolution* (New York, 1857), pp. 169–170; J. F. Watson, *Annals of Philadelphia* (Philadelphia, 1830), p. 165; Albert Matthews, "Hired Man and Help," Col. Soc. of Mass., *Transactions* (1897–98), pp. 225–254 at p. 250. There were no "masters" in America, Martin Chuzzlewit found out—only "owners"!

[44] In the 19th century the availability of land was an indirect, rather than an immediate, cause of the maintenance of higher labor standards in this country than prevailed abroad. The free-land alternative helped to maintain wages and served to direct native workers away from the laborious, unskilled jobs. See C. R. Daugherty, *Labor Problems in American Industry* (5th ed., New York, 1941), p. 246; Malcolm Keir, *Labor's Search for More* (New York, 1937), p. 4. There is a good deal of contemporary evidence from the West which casts grave doubt on the "Safety-Valve Doctrine" that the American workman solved his difficulties by moving Westward, unless he settled in other industrial centers. For an analysis of this doctrine, see Carter Goodrich and S. Davidson, "The Wage Earner in the Westward Movement," *Pol. Sci. Q.*, L (1935), 161, LI (1936), 61, F. A. Shannon, "The Homestead Act and the Labor Surplus," *Amer. Hist. Rev.*, XLI (1936), 637–651. See also E. E. Edwards, "References on the Significance of the Frontier in American History," U.S. Dept. of Agriculture, *Bibliographical Contributions*, No. 25 (Washington, 1939). Labor historians such as Carlton (*op. cit.*, pp. 7, 82–107) and Mary Beard—*A Short History of the American Labor Movement* (New York, 1920), p. 3—place considerable stress upon this doctrine. A more realistic attitude is taken by Marjorie R. Clark and S. Fanny Simon, *The Labor Movement in America* (New York, 1938), p. 19.

For the role of labor as a democratic leaven in the society of the post-Revolutionary period, see *infra*, pp. 200, 201; Link, *op. cit.*, ch. iv.

I. THE REGULATION OF WAGES PRIOR TO
THE REVOLUTION

H ISTORIANS have devoted considerable attention to the impact of external mercantilist regulation upon the life of the American colonists, but the subject of internal economic controls has been treated far more casually. Wage and price controls have been cavalierly dismissed as abortive economic experiments. In point of fact, wages and prices were regulated in many of the colonies at various times in the seventeenth century. It must be borne in mind that in England wage assessments in one branch or another of industry continued down to the third decade of the nineteenth century, although as early as the latter part of the seventeenth century the system had become largely ineffective and the scale set by the justices is believed to have lagged behind the amounts actually paid.[1] As time went on assessments became increasingly haphazard. In Middlesex, for instance, after 1725 there was not "the faintest sign of the most perfunctory action." The desuetude of the "sleeping law," as one writer called it late in the century, brought cheer to Adam Smith, who felt that the law never could regulate wages properly, though it often pretended to do so.[2]

NEW ENGLAND

THE MOST SIGNIFICANT experiment in colonial wage and price control took place in Massachusetts Bay, the happy hunting ground for paternalistic controls over religion, morals, and business. It is generally known that, in the first decade of the colony's history, ambitious legislation was launched to establish maximum wages, but it is commonly thought that these laws were not enforced and were quickly discarded. A recent careful student of the field maintains that "by 1640 . . . the trend of thought was away from the fixation of prices" and "men of affairs" had

---

[1] The total known assessments for the 18th century run to about fifty. Estelle Waterman, "Some New Evidence on Wage Assessments in the 18th Century," *Eng. Hist. Rev.*, XLIII (1929), 399, 403.

[2] Adam Smith is corroborated in this view by such recent investigators as Lipson, Heckscher, and Dowdell, among others.

discredited price and wage controls.[1] For this impression the early writers are largely responsible. Hubbard looked back with nostalgia upon that first decade as the "golden age of New England, when vice was crushed . . . especially oppression and extortion in prices and wages." [2] Winthrop admitted as early as 1640 that the General Court,

> having found by experience, that it would not avail by any law to redress the excessive rates of labourers' and workmen's wages, etc. (for being restrained, they would either remove to other places where they might have more, or else being able to live by planting and other employments of their own, they would not be hired at all), it was therefore referred to the several towns to set down rates among themselves. This took better effect, so that in a voluntary way, by the counsel and persuasion of the elders, and example of some who led the way, they were brought to more moderation than they could be by compulsion. But it held not long.[3]

In reality, the rulers of the Bay colony and the early settlers in her towns, possessed of unusual powers of supervision over strangers, vagrants, and the idle, the authority to establish compulsory labor, and the right to impress men to pursue fugitive servants on land and over water, appear to have experimented in the matter of maximum wages with some measure of persistence for several generations. Their efforts did not fully cease until the last quarter of the century. As late as 1670 the Assistants proposed a sweeping regulatory measure. Although defeated in that year and again two years later when they presented the bill in revised form, they retrieved some measure of victory in the passage of extensive legislation during King Philip's War. The consequences of introducing maximum wage legislation in a country where land was reasonably plentiful and labor scarce would seem to us, gifted with opportunities of hindsight, fairly obvious. These comparative bounties of nature offset in large part the absence from the Massachusetts labor system of certain safeguards found, at least on paper, in the Tudor labor code, such as general or local regulations preventing dismissals [4] and the setting on rare occasions of wage minima.[5]

That the colonists borrowed heavily from medieval economic thought

---

[1] E. A. J. Johnson, *American Economic Thought in the Seventeenth Century* (London, 1932), pp. 129–130 and 210–212. It is true that in the forties the authorities were confronted with more serious problems created by the exodus of settlers from Massachusetts, the fall in the values of land and cattle, and the scarcity of money and foreign commodities. Winthrop, *Journal* (ed. Savage), II, 103.

[2] William Hubbard, *A General History of New England from the Discoverie to 1680* (reprinted Boston, 1848), p. 248.

[3] Winthrop, *Journal*, II, 29.

[4] See *supra*, p. 17.   [5] *Supra*, p. 19.

and current mercantilist ideology is now well established.[6] They were unquestionably influenced by contemporary local English practices. The settlers of the Bay colony had come in considerable part from East Anglia and its neighborhood, including Norfolk, Suffolk, Essex, and southern Lincolnshire,[7] and considerable evidence is at hand of wage assessments in these centers of the manufacture of woolen cloth on the eve of the great Puritan migration.[8] Some of the leaders doubtless had had firsthand experience with the legal technicalities of the prevailing labor code. Such were John Winthrop, who had served as a justice of the peace in the mother country; Richard Bellingham, who had been recorder of the borough of Boston in Lincolnshire; and Nathaniel Ward, who had enjoyed the advantages of legal education in England. Aside from their probable acquaintance with the English statutes and practices of the country justices, the American Puritan leaders, in legislation and public utterance, mirrored the prevailing views of the mercantilists as to "the lower orders," who were enjoined to obedience and honest carriage.[9] Maximum wage regulation was thoroughly consistent with that social attitude.

When the program was initiated in Massachusetts, the regulation of wages and prices was placed in the hands of the central authorities. In medieval England this program had originated in the towns, but was later adopted as a general policy by the central government. Ultimately the central authorities in England found it expedient to authorize the local justices to set the assessments. After a short experience with maximum wage scales set by legislative fiat the authorities in Massachusetts found it more practicable to confer upon administrative officials discretionary authority to levy assessments. Let us pursue the course of this legislative program, first in the General Court, and then in the towns, after which sporadic instances of enforcement in the law courts will be examined.

Owing to the scarcity of skilled craftsmen in the early days, the first series of enactments, launched in 1630, was directed toward regulating

[6] See Johnson, *op. cit., passim.*

[7] Suffolk and Essex headed the English counties represented in the early migrations. C. E. Banks, *The Winthrop Fleet of 1630; Planters of the Commonwealth, 1620–1640* (Cambridge, Mass., 1930), p. 14.

[8] See Lipson, *Econ. Hist. of Eng.,* III, 259. However, it is interesting to note that in the West Riding of Yorkshire the textile groups disappeared as early as 1671 from the list of industries in which wages were assessed, although statutes regulating wages in the woolen industry were enacted in the century following. H. Heaton, "The Assessment of Wages," *Econ. J.,* XXIV, 228; and *The Yorkshire Woollen and Worsted Industries* (Oxford, 1920), pp. 313 *et seq.*

[9] *Mass. Bay Rec.,* I, 397. See also E. S. Furniss, *The Position of the Laborer in a System of Nationalism* (Boston, 1920), and Johnson, *op. cit.,* p. 31.

wages in the building trades. Carpenters, joiners, bricklayers, sawyers, and thatchers were limited to two shillings a day. Both giver and taker of higher rates were subject to a fine of ten shillings. For piece work, the wages for sawyers were established at 4*s*. 6*d*. per hundred for boards (at six score to the hundred) if they had their wood felled and squared for them, and not above 5*s*. 6*d*. if they did these extra tasks themselves. The governor and deputy governor for the time being and four others were named justices of the peace with power "in all things . . . that Justices of peace hath in England." Hardly a fortnight elapsed before the rates of master carpenters, masons, joiners, and bricklayers were leveled down to 16*d*. a day with meat and drink, while assistants or journeymen as well as laborers were restricted to 12*d*. a day. Similar fines for violations were set. Shortly thereafter it was enacted that sawyers should not take more than 12*d*. a score for sawing oak boards, and 10*d*. for pine boards, if they had their wood felled and squared for them.[10]

After slightly more than six months' experience with these regulations, the General Court abolished them in 1631, without even providing posterity with a good rationalizing preamble, and ordered that "the wages of carpenters, joyners, and other artificers and workmen . . . shall nowe be lefte free and att libertie as men shall reasonably agree."[11] Similarly in regard to prices, the rate of 6*s*. per pound for beavers was dropped and every man was "hereafter lefte free . . . to make the best proffit and improuement of it that hee can";[12] the price of corn formerly set at 6*s*. the bushel was "sett at liberty to be solde as men can agree."[13] This did not involve any repudiation of the general program of wage-fixing, for very shortly thereafter the rates of sawyers were re-established at twelve pence a score for boards, and if they did their own felling and squaring, at not above seven shillings the hundred, five score to the hundred.[14] Massachusetts Bay was now embarked upon a building program of some magnitude, and the scarcity of labor and the relatively high wage scale obtaining spurred the magistrates to new legislative restrictions. Writing in the fall of 1633, Governor Winthrop reported that carpenters were demanding three shillings a day and laborers two shillings, six pence. As they could make enough in four days to keep them a week, he reported that they spent the reminder of their time in idleness and their surplus money in tobacco and strong waters.[15]

[10] For these successive enactments, see *Mass. Bay Rec.*, I, 74, 76, 79, respectively; II, 3, 5, 29.
[11] *Mass. Bay Rec.*, I, 84; *Assistants*, II, 12.   [12] *Assistants*, II, 8 (1630).
[13] *Ibid.*, II, 31 (1633), 43, 44 (1634).   [14] *Mass. Bay Rec.*, I, 91.
[15] Winthrop, *Journal*, I, 138.

The governor's observations reflected the hostility shared by Puritan and mercantilist alike toward leisure and toward expenditures above mere subsistence on the part of the laboring class, The General Court adopted the same tone. Alleging "great extortion used by divers persons of little conscience" and great disorder resulting from "vain and idle waste of much precious time" for which "immoderate gains" were responsible, it enacted the most comprehensive of its first series of wage statutes. Carpenters, sawyers, masons, clapboard rivers, bricklayers, thatchers, joiners, wheelwrights, and mowers were limited to two shillings a day without board and to fourteen pence a day with refreshment. "The best sorte of labourers" were forbidden to accept more than eighteen pence a day without board and eight pence with it. The wages of tailors were limited to twelve pence and board for the master, and eight pence and board for the journeyman. A constable and two others were given authority under the act to regulate the wages of inferior laborers, and the constable was further empowered to summon idlers before two assistants to deal with as they thought meet. It was also ordered "that all workmen shall worke the whole day, alloweing convenient tyme for foode and rest." [16] The Statute of Artificers defined a normal working day for artificers and laborers hired by the day or week as from 5 A.M. to 7 or 8 P.M. from the middle of March to the middle of September, allowing two and one half hours off for breakfast, dinner, and drinking. From the middle of September to the middle of March the hours were "from the spring of the day until night." [17]

Having set maximum bounds for wages, the General Court deemed it only fair to make certain that "honest and conscionable workemen should (not) be wronged or discouraged by excessive prizes of those comodityes, wch are necessary for their Life and comfort." Accordingly the 1633 wage regulations were accompanied by a prohibition of the sale of commodities at prices higher than one third above those prevailing in England, with the exception of cheese, liquors, oil, and vinegar, for which the hazard of transportation and dangers of leakage justified maintaining a free market. In the absence of such hazards, as with linen goods, the General Court ordered the settlers "not to exceede the bounds of moderation" under threat of severe punishment.[18] In connection with

[16] *Mass. Bay Rec.*, I, 109; *Assistants*, II, 36 (1633). This rate was double that of skilled workmen in England at that time and almost treble that of laborers. See *HMC, Rep.*, XXIX, Pt. III, 31 (April 10, 1632).

[17] 5 Eliz. c. 4, f. 12. During the summer months the time off included a half hour's nap. See also assessment of Hertfordshire, 1687, W. Hardy and C. E. Longmore, eds., *Session Books of Hertford County* (Hertford, 1935), VI, 405-407.

[18] *Mass. Bay Rec.*, I, 111; *Assistants*, II, 39.

public works projects, the court in the following year empowered the overseer of the works, in conjunction with an assistant, to award "such extraordinary wages as they shall judge the worke to disserve," and armed them with the authority to issue warrants to constables of adjacent locations for laborers and artificers as need arose.[19]

As far back as 1633 it was recognized that a fixed wage basis and a runaway price scale would throw the labor system out of equilibrium. Hence, the early statutes included elaborate regulations of the prices of basic commodities, for in a general way such leaders of early American Puritan thought as Winthrop and Cotton accepted the medieval doctrine of the "just price."[20] In 1641 the General Court conferred on the towns power over the regulation of the prices of commodities as well as wages. The assize of bread was the most persistent regulatory measure, but other price, quantity, and quality regulations included the assizes of casks, leather, wood, and bricks. Oppression in price was punished by the court on numerous occasions. Michael Wigglesworth, in *The Day of Doom,* placed those who acquired wealth by "oppression" in the same category with adulterers and whoremongers.

As time went on, the founding fathers wrestled continually with the problem of scarcity and high wages. It is quite clear that the wage law of 1633 was generally ineffective and that current wages exceeded the levels laid down by 50 per cent.[21] The entering wedge to broad class discrimination was contained in the act of September, 1634, which abolished the penalty against employers for giving wages in excess of the law, but left untouched the penalties against workers. As a matter of fact, no employer was ever penalized under this act. English statutes provided ample precedent for such class discrimination.[22] In order to counteract labor scarcity, the Massachusetts statute of 1634 attempted to restrict the trend of workers toward agriculture by the provision that no servant could be allotted land until he had "approved his faithfulness to his master during his time of service."[23]

[19] *Mass. Bay Rec.,* I, 124.

[20] See *Mass. Bay Rec.,* I, 115; *Essex,* I, 34, 49; II, 69, 100, 117–119; VI, 72; *Suffolk,* p. 632.

[21] U.S. Bureau of Labor Statistics, *Bull.,* No. 449 (1929), pp. 9–10.

[22] While the act of 1349 provided penalties for both master and workman violating the wage-freezing law and the act of 1388 provided that both parties would have to pay the wages paid in excess of the rate set therein (for the second offense double, and for the third offense treble the value of the excess), a statute passed in 1416 exempted employers from the penalty set in the 1388 act and provided "that the pain contained in the said statute shall run only upon the taker." An act of 1427 imposed the penalty solely upon laborers, asserting, in justification, that previous ordinances had been too harsh on the master and too lenient on the servants. But cf. *North Riding Sessions Rec.,* I, 105, 127.

[23] *Mass. Bay Rec.,* I, 127. According to the same act, workmen boarding themselves were to be allowed 2d. extra a day in wages.

The trend of legislation was now definitely turning toward discretionary rates and to the decentralization of the administrative system. This was foreshadowed in the provision in the September, 1634, enactment that, if a wage contract proved inequitable to either party, three men appointed by the town should be empowered to set a new rate. In September, 1635, the General Court repealed the law which "prohibited taking above iiij*d* in the shilling proffitt for commodities, and that wch restrained workemens wages to a certainety." [24] In the same month, however, the court, despite the recent repeal of the wage and commodity laws, provided that "such ill disposed persons as may take liberty to oppresse and wronge their neighbrs, by takeing excessiue wages for worke, or vnreasonable prizes for such necessary merchandizes or othr commodyties as shall passe from man to man" should be "punished by Fine or imprisonmt, according to the quallity of the offence." [25] Thus, discretionary penalties were substituted for fixed penalties. In 1636 John Cotton, member of a committee appointed "to make a draught of laws agreeable to the word of God, which may be the Fundamentals of this Commonwealth," [26] presented to the General Court a copy of his proposed code, "Moses his Judicialls," largely based upon Biblical precedents.[27] Cotton proposed specifically a plan which was in substance embodied in the act of 1636. Dealing with the subject of commerce, his code provides:

To the intent that all oppression in buying and selling may be avoided, it shall be lawful for the judges in every town, with the consent of the free burgesses, to appoint certain selectmen, to set reasonable rates upon all commodities, and proportionably to limit the wages of workmen and labourers; and the rates agreed upon by them, and ratified by the judges, to bind all the inhabitants of the town. The like course to be taken by the governor and assistants, for the rating of prizes throughout the country, and all to be confirmed, if need be, by the general court.[28]

Along the lines of Cotton's proposal, the magistrates, in October, 1636, turned the regulation of wages over to the freemen of the towns, with

[24] *Ibid.,* I, 159.   [25] *Ibid.,* I, 160.   [26] *Ibid.,* I, 147; Winthrop, *Journal,* I, 191.

[27] Insufficient weight has been given by historians to the non-common-law elements in Cotton's code; for example by Charles M. Andrews, *The Colonial Period of American History* (New Haven, 1936), II, 156–157.

[28] Mass. Hist. Soc., *Coll.,* 1st ser., V, 180; Peter Force, *Tracts,* III (Washington, 1844), ch. ix, pp. 10–11; "Hutchinson Papers," I, Prince Society, *Publications* (Albany, N.Y., 1865), p. 194. W. B. Weeden (*Econ. . . . Hist. of N.E.,* I, 167n.) quite carelessly attributes this reference to the Body of Liberties, the official code of 1641, which, as a matter of fact, is silent on this point. Probably his mistake arose from the fact that in 1641 Cotton's proposed, but unadopted, code was published in London under the misleading title *An Abstract of the Laws of New-England, as They Are Now Established.*

discretionary punishment to be vested in the court "according to the quality and measure of the offence." Anticipating possible competition of town against town for the services of badly needed workers, the General Court made provision that the court or the governor and assistants might hear complaints against towns "For alowing greater rates or wages then themselves." [29] This attempt at local regulation, according to the admission of the court in 1638, resulted in "divers complaints made concerning oppression in wages" and in prices, particularly in the wages of smiths and the rates of cartage and teams, "to the great dishonour of God, the scandoll of the gosple, and the greife of divers of Gods people, both heare in this land and in the land of our nativity." A distinguished committee headed by Endecott, Bellingham, Saltonstall, and John Winthrop, Jr., was appointed to propose remedies,[30] but no report of their findings is in the records.

For all practical purposes the General Court had turned wage regulation over to the towns; yet there was no official renunciation of authority. Because of crop conditions in 1640 and 1641, the General Court in the latter year, pointing to the lower commodity prices then prevailing, enacted that laborers should be "content to abate their wages according to the fall of the commodities wherein their labors are bestowed." The court announced its firm intention of proceeding against those laborers who acted contrary to this order, although no specific penalties were provided. Workers were to be paid in commodities (according to a subsequent act of the same year, in corn), the price, where agreement could not be reached, to be set by two "indifferent freemen," one chosen by the master, the other by the workman.[31] The codes of 1648 and 1660, and the supplement of 1672, continued substantially the basic law of 1636 against oppression in wages and prices, leaving to the freemen of each town the authority to settle the rates of pay. This policy of local regulation found further expression in a clause empowering the selectmen of Boston and Charlestown to regulate the wages of porters, "who many times do require and exact more than is just and righteous for their labours." The specific provisions of the act of 1636 permitting discretionary fines or imprisonment to be imposed and turning regulation over to the towns were retained, and county courts were authorized to punish violations at their discretion.[32] These codes also

[29] *Mass. Bay Rec.*, I, 182.   [30] *Mass. Bay Rec.*, I, 223.   [31] *Ibid.*, I, 326, 340.

[32] *The Laws and Liberties of Massachusetts, 1648* (Cambridge, Mass., 1929) (*Mass. Laws, 1648*), pp. 38, 39, 43; *The Colonial Laws of Massachusetts, Reprinted from the Edition of 1660, with the Supplements to 1672*, ed. W. H. Whitmore (*Mass. Col. Laws, 1660–72*) (Boston, 1889), pp. 174, 185, 187.

contained the provision that "workmen shall work the whole day, allowing convenient tyme for food and rest." The emphasis upon discretionary rather than fixed penalties accorded both with experience and with
the legal philosophy of the leading magistrates, who opposed definite
penalties except in capital cases in order to strengthen their own authority at a time when it was being challenged on all sides, and also out of
deference to theories of individualizing punishment. Thus, John Winthrop pointed to the case in which a penalty "hits a rich man" and "pains
him not; but if it lights upon a poor man, it breaks his back." [33]

In the years before King Philip's War the authorities continued to be
greatly exercised over the need for wage fixing. In 1655 a committee on
trade was directed to consider "some way to regulate workmen's wages,
if any way be found." [34] In general, however, the problem was left to
the localities. In the seventies there was a revival of activity on the part
of the central government. On May 15, 1672, the General Court passed
an act which, while specifically prohibiting the giving of wine or strong
liquors to workmen, was only in part a sumptuary measure; from its
phraseology it appears to have been motivated by a desire to curtail the
demands of the workers:

Whereas there have binn sundry and frequent complaints prefferred to this
Court of oppression by excessive wages of worke men and labourers, which,
notwthstanding the endeavours of this Court to redress such oppressions, continue, and further increase, by a dangerous imposition of such persons on those
they worke and labour for, by demanding an allowance of licquors or wine
every day, over and above their wages, wthout which it is found, by too sad
experience, many refuse to worke. Now, forasmuch as such a practize of
drincking licquors and wine tends much to the rooting young persons in an
evill practise, and by degrees to trayne them vp to an habittt of excesse, it is
therefore ordered by this Court and by the authority thereof, and be it hereby
enacted, that if any person or persons, after the publication hereof, shall give
wine or strong liquers to any workmen or boyes that worke wth them, except
in cases of necessity, shall pay twenty shillings for every such offence. [35]

The town of Ipswich drew up a regulation in similar tenor. [36] Elsewhere, however, the act of 1672 was not enforced. In Watertown, only
one year after its passage, the town granted Isaac Micktur the sum of

---

[33] "Arbitrary Government Described," 1644, in R. C. Winthrop, *Life and Letters of John
Winthrop* (2 vols., Boston, 1869), II, 445 *et seq.*

[34] *Mass. Bay Rec.*, IV, Pt. I, 247.

[35] *Ibid.*, IV, Pt. II, 510. Back in 1640 the Assistants fined one employer £3 for giving a gallon
of "strong water" to workmen at his house. Barnard's Case, *Assistants*, II, 94 (1640).

[36] J. B. Felt, *History of Ipswich, Essex, and Hamilton* (Boston, 1834), p. 105.

five shillings in lieu of a gallon of liquor owing for work on a bridge.[37] Again, in 1679, the town allowed 9s. 2d. for liquors for labor at the mill bridge; and in 1681, to push forward work on the bridge, the selectmen gave Caleb Church, the miller, fourteen shillings to procure good liquor as cheaply as possible to be disbursed in such manner as would best aid the work. It is clearly apparent that the exception in the statute for cases of necessity was generously interpreted.[38]

Two years earlier, on May 17, 1670, there had been introduced in the General Court a bill which went to the heart of wage and hour regulation. This proposed legislation is included in the Massachusetts Archives, but was omitted from the published record of the colony's proceedings. Because of the sweeping character of these proposals, the complete text [39] is herewith given:

This Court considering the great difficultie and discouragemnt, that at prsent lyes pressing vpon many inhabitants of this jurisdiction especially vpon Such, as whose callings are in husbandry, not onely by reason of the afflicting hand of God vpon them severall yeares in blasting thier principall grayne and abating their increase in other Corne, and Slowenes of market and exceeding low price for that the husbandman can raise; vnto whose afflicting hand all ought to Submitt and humble themselves and yet with the prophet confesse, Thou, Lord, hast afflicted vs lesse then we deserve, but also Difficultie and discouragemt is yet heaped and increasing vpon them and others by reason of the excessive deerenes of labour by artifficers, Labourers, and Servants, contrary to reason and equitie, to the great prejudice of many householders and their Familyes, and tending to their vtter ruein and vndoeing, and the produce thereof is by many Spent to mayntayne Such bravery in Apparell which is altogether vnbecomeing thier place and ranck, and in Idleness of life, and a great part spent viciously in Tavernes and alehouses and other Sinful practices much to the dishonour of God, Scandall of Religion, and great offence and griefe to Sober and Godly people amongst vs. All which timely to prevent,

---

[37] *Watertown Rec.,* I, 116, 132; II, 10.

[38] For a discussion of the temperance movement in Massachusetts in this period, see J. A. Krout, *The Origins of Prohibition* (New York, 1925), pp. 51–53. In 1674 Increase Mather delivered two sermons, published as *Wo to Drunkards* (Cambridge, 1673), in which he enjoined his listeners to "Kill this Serpent, before it be grown too big for you" (p. 29). See also K. B. Murdock, *Increase Mather* (Cambridge, 1925), pp. 103–104.

[39] Vol. CXIX, fols. 28–29. Joseph B. Felt published this bill with certain editorial emendations in his *Historical Account of Massachusetts Currency* (Boston, 1839), pp. 243–245. Felt listed nine sections, but the original has ten, of which the fifth, providing restrictions on the tanning of hides, was deleted. The editors of the Bureau of Labor Statistics *Bull.* No. 499, reprinted in the appendix Felt's version of this bill, and then added quite unwarrantably the curious statement that the bill was "introduced into the Court of Essex County, Massachusetts, in 1670 and again in 1672." As a matter of fact, both bills were proposed in the General Court. This error is repeated in the revised bulletin, No. 604 (1934).

this Court account it their duty carefully by all good meanes to provide, and therefore doe order as followeth,

It is therefore ordered by this Court and the Authoritie thereof that no person within this Jurisdiction, directly or indirectly, shall hereafter either paye or receave for worke, labour or comoditie, more or aboue, then is in this present order appointed, and that vpon the penalties therein heere after expressed.

	s.	d.

Imprimis. Labourers by the daye from the end of September
to the end of March dyeting themselves . . . . . . 1 — 3 per day
From the end of March to the end of June . . . . . 1 — 8 .
From the end of June to the end of September they workeing 10 houres in the daye besides repast . . . . . . 2 — 0

2. Taske worke. One Acre of salt marsh, and one Acre of English grasse well mowen . . . . 2 — 0 per acre
one Acre of wheat well reapeing . . . . 4 — 0
one Acre of Rye well reapeing . . . . 3 — 0
one Acre of Barly, and one Acre of oats, each well moweing 1 — 0
one Acre of peas, cutting . . . . 3 — 0
one Coarde of woode, cutting, and well Coarding . . . 1 — 3
This wages is allowed as above to workemen Dyeting themselues.

3. Carpenters and Masons and Stonelayers, from 1 March to 10 of October . . . . 2 — 0 per day
and all worke taken by the great or peice by Carpenters, masons, joyners, or shinglers, is to be apportioned according to the equitie of the value of Daye's worke as above they dyeting themselves.

4. Master Taylors, and Such as are fully workmen of that Trade for one daye's worke of 12 hours . . . . . . 1 — 8
Apprentices to that trade the first 4 yeares, the like daye . 1 — 0
And all weavers for thier worke at 12 hours per day, are to have the like wages as Taylors.

6. All men and women Servants shall in their respective wages be moderated according to the proportion of labour above limitted.

7. No person shall pay, neither shall any Shoemaker receave, more than 5s. for men's Shoes of elevens or twelves,[40] nor for women's Shoes of Seavens or Eights more than 3s.–8d.

---

[40] This would indicate an increase in the price of shoes as compared with the value of 4s. 4d. and 4s. 8d. respectively fixed by the Suffolk Co. probate court in 1651 for men's shoes of sizes 11 and 12. See inventory of Robert Turner of Boston, shoemaker, in *Suffolk Co. Prob. Rec.,* Vol. II (1651); also G. E. Dow, *Every Day Life in Massachusetts Bay Colony* (Boston, 1935), p. 243.

And all bootes and shoes of other Sizes proportionable to the rates abovesaide.

8. Cowpers shall not receave nor any person paye for a thight barrel of 32 gallons above 2–8, and other Cowper's worke proportionable in price to barrels.

9. Smythes Shall not take nor any person paye for great worke, as for Ships, Mills, plough Irones, all Irones for Cart wheeles well layd vyon the wheeles, and other the like great worke, aboue 5d. per lb. For smaller worke as Chaynes and other the like Solde by weight, not aboue 6d. per lb. For the largest horse shoe well set with 7 nayles, not above 6d. per shoe. For removeing a horse shoe, 2d. For an ordinary felling axe, 3s. 6d. For one broade axe, 5s. 6d., one broade hough 3s., all being good and well steeled, and all other Smithe's worke not named to be proportioned according to the prices aboue-Said.

10. And whereas it apears that Glovers, Sadlers, Hatters, and Seuerall other artifficers doe at present greatly exceed the rules of equitie in their prizes, they are all required to moderate the Same according to the rules prescribed to others, or know that in neglect thereof they are lyeable to presentment and proceeded against according to the Lawe,—Title, opression.

Inkeepers and ordinary keepers are required to attend the dutie of them expected according to Lawe—Title Inkeepers, Sect. 11,[41] which order ought more carefully and strictly to be executed for the prevention of oppression in Selling of wine, and as for Selling beere they are to attend the Lawe that orders what quantitie of malte is to be putt into each hogshead of beere, and that when malt is vnder 4s. per bushell then to Sell no lesse then one quarte for 1s.–½d., and for the entertaynmt of horses in Summer not to take more then 4d. for one daye and night, and in winter not to exceed 6d. for the like time.

All these paymts are to be made in merchantible Corne at the price from yeare to yeare, set by the Generall Courte, prouided that when the materials are brought from the market by the artifficer, as shoemakers, Smythes, and the like, allowance may be made for that Charge by the buyer according to what the transportation may be.

If any person shall paye or receave more then according to the rates aboue

41 The law referred to provides that "no Taverner, seller of wine by retaile, Licensed as aforesayd, shall take above *nine pound profit,* by the Butt or Pipe of wine (and proportionably for all other Vessels) towards his wast and drawing, and otherwise, out of which allowance, every such Taverner or Vintner, shall pay *fifty shillings* by the Butt or Pipe, and proportionably for all other Vessels to the Country, for which they shall account with the Treasurer or his Deputy every six months, and discharge the same, all which they may do by selling *six-pence a quart* in retaile (which they shall no time exceed) more then it cost by the Butt." *Mass. Col. Laws, 1660–72,* p. 165.

expressed, he or they, both buyer and Seller, shall forfeit the full treble value of what Shall be payed or receaved, one-halfe to the enformer and the other halfe to the Treasurer of the Seuerall Countie Courts.

The President of euery Countie Courte shall at euery such Court giue in charge to the Grand Jury to enquire into the breach of this order in euery particular thereof.

And all Grand Jurymen are required vpon their oath to present all offences against this Lawe, and if it shall apeere to the Court of the Countie at any time within one yeare after the offence is comitted, that any Juryman have knoweingly neglected his dutie heerein, he shall vpon conuiction before the Courte be fined Tenn times So much as the offenders should have payed whome he ought to have prsented.

The division of opinion between the upper and lower houses in the court is represented in the ensuing record:

The Deputyes having Considered of this Bill regulating workmen's wages, doe think it meete to Referre the same to consideration vntill the next Court of election, o[u]r honored magistrates Consenting.   Wm. Torrey, Cleric

May 17, 70. The Magistrates haue passed this Bill for an order of this Court, desiring the consent of our brethren the deputyes.

John Pynchon, per order.

The Deputyes Consent not hereto.

William Torrey, Cleric.

When the proposals in this bill are compared with corresponding assessments set only the year before in East Yorkshire, both husbandman and skilled worker in Massachusetts appear at a decided advantage.[42] Carpenters by the day, for example, were allowed 1s. in the English county as against the rate of 2s. proposed in Massachusetts, and agricultural laborers in the Bay colony were to be permitted wages from three to four times greater than those prevailing under the English assessment. Nevertheless it is highly probable that the Massachusetts proposals were considerably below prevailing wage scales in that colony.[43]

The wage proposals of 1670 were reintroduced, but with several

---

[42] See R. K. Kelsall, "Two East Yorkshire Wage Assessments, 1669, 1679," *Eng. Hist. Rev.*, LII, 283–289. The assessments were somewhat higher in Hertford around this time. W. J. Hardy, ed., *Notes and Extracts from the Hertfordshire Session Rolls* (Hertford, 1905), I, 292; C. E. Longmore, ed., *Session Books of Hertford County*, VI, 400–405. Such detailed wage assessments for a variety of categories of labor were customary in contemporary England. Cf. Gretton, *op. cit.*, pp. lxiii, lxiv (1687— Oxfordshire).

[43] For example, one Braintree account book reveals that common male labor received 2s. per day or £10 per year, considerably higher than the schedule proposed. W. S. Pattee, *A History of Old Braintree and Quincy* (Quincy, Mass., 1878), p. 541.

important changes, in 1672.[44] The preambles of the two bills are similar, but there are a number of differences in detail, and with one exception when rates were changed, they were revised downward.[45] Again the bill failed of passage in the lower house. According to the entry, dated August 11, 1672:

> The magists haue past this wt the payne affixt as an order of the Court. Their brethren the deputyes hereto Consenting.
>
> Edward Rawson Secret.
>
> The Deputyes Consent not hereto
>
> William Torrey Cleric.

In the absence of a record of debates, some obvious questions cannot be answered definitively. Was the 1670 proposal altered in minor details to meet the objections of the deputies? Did the veto of the lower house rest on any fundamental opposition to wage regulation? This much is clear in the light of the legislative record of the General Court in this period: neither deputies nor assistants opposed wage regulation in principle.

As a matter of fact, in the very same year, 1672, the whole question of wage, price, and sumptuary controls was brought to a head when the General Court investigated labor and commodity costs of tanners, glov-

---

[44] Mass. Arch., CXIX, fols. 32–33. Felt completely ignored the differences between the two proposals and treated the 1672 bill as a mere duplicate of the 1670 measure, an error into which the editors of the Bureau of Labor Statistics, *Bull.*, Nos. 499 and 604, likewise fall.

	1670	1672
	s. d.	*s. d.*
[45] One acre of wheat "well reapt"	4–0	5–0
One acre of peas, cutting	3–0	2–6
Shoemakers, for shoes of elevens or twelves	5–0	4–0
for women's shoes of sevens and eights	3–8	3–0
Smiths, for iron work	5–0 per lb.	4–½ per lb.
for smaller work such as chains	6–0	5–½
for the largest horseshoe	6–0	5–½
for removing a horseshoe	2–0	1–½
for an ordinary felling axe	3–6	3–0
for a broad axe	5–6	4–6
for a broad hoe	3–0	2–6

In Sections 1 and 3 changes are also made in the dates of the working season. In Section 4 the following additional provision regulating tailors is inserted: "and to regulate work on making garments or weaving by the sq. yard to the same rate proportably." Among the artificers specified in Section 10 who were not to exceed the rules of equity in setting prices are included, in addition, brickmakers and limeburners. The innkeepers' law referred to in Section 11 of the 1670 bill includes also a citation of Section 8, referring to drunkenness. There is the further provision that, when malt is under 4s. a bushel, beer is to be sold for no more than 1d. a quart instead of 1½d. as in the earlier proposal. Oats were not to be sold "aboue 8d. per peck." The 1672 bill provides for payments in merchantable corn at the price set by the General Court from year to year "according to our valluation in mony." The later bill omits the earlier provision allowing the seller transportation charges.

ers, shoemakers, and hatters. A petition of the hatters was dismissed with the declaration "that when the hatters shall make as good hats and sell them as cheape as are affoorded from other parts, they shall be willing and ready to answer their petition." [46] The shoemakers pointed out that the current French styles involved the use of more leather than previous fashions; that long credits were customarily extended in the trade; that curriers were paid 4*s.* a hide, whereas in England the cost was only 2*s.* 8*d.*; and that thread was also much dearer than in England. The glovers pointed out that alum and lime were much higher, and likewise silk, but that to a large degree excessive costs were due to "the bad flayeing the skinnes by gashes and holes whereby they must Sell the tanned skinnes that are good and well flayed at Such a price as may make good for the loss by them that are full of holes." They complained further that "labour is very deere and help hard to attayne." The tanners suggested that none but skilled men be permitted to tan and that no raw hides be dried before tanning. They also charged that labor costs comprised a heavy item, some workers receiving £30 per annum, "some more."

In regard to the quality and condition of hides and skins used in these three occupations, the General Court acted at once, specifically ordering that searchers be appointed by the selectmen of the towns to inspect hides and skins before they left the butchers' hands. The Committee of Nine which investigated these industries, in summing up its findings, reported that tanners, glovers, and shoemakers were all oppressed by the high wages demanded by journeymen, and took occasion further to criticize "the excesse of pride of meane people that will weare no other shoes generally but of the newest fashion and highest price." Hence such people would not work "but for Such wages wt will mayntaine them in this profuse expensive manner." They concluded these mercantilist lamentations with a specific recommendation that a law be enacted providing a maximum sales price for shoes of elevens or twelve at 5*s.* a pair and other sizes in proportion, "upon penaltie of forfeiting the value of the whole price of those Solde aboue those values." This was similar to the recommendations embodied in the proposed bill of 1670 and somewhat higher than the scale fixed in the 1672 proposal, neither of which was adopted. The committee further proposed

that Some effectuall meanes be used to Suppresse the groweing excesse in Aparrell in this Countrey, pride and Idleness beginning to be the prevayling evils and shames of the people especially of the younger and meaner Sorte,

[46] *Mass. Bay Rec.,* IV, Pt. II, 527 (1672).

and it is feared they are Some of the provoking Sinnes that procure the Frownes of our God upon us." [47]

This recommendation was incorporated by both houses in a compromise plan adopted to meet the labor scarcity during the Indian War of 1675, when the court passed a series of laws for the reformation of "Provoking Evils," with the express purpose of enforcing virtue and avoiding God's wrath. The "Provoking Evils" denounced "the evil pride in Apparel, both for Costliness in the poorer sort, and vain, new strange Fashions both in poor and rich." Its numerous provisions embraced wage fixing, price regulation, and sumptuary legislation. Of all sections of the statute, these sumptuary provisions were the most widely enforced.[48] Article XI of the "Provoking Evils" authorized selectmen to hear complaints against takers of excessive wages, and empowered such officials not only to require the offending laborers to make double restitution to their employers, but also to pay double the excess value of their work as a fine.[49] This compares with the treble damages assessed in the 1670 bill, which were to be shared by informer and county court. No penalties were exacted of masters who competed for the labor of artisans by offering excessive wages. Under this act a new machinery for price regulation was set up; complaints were to be directed to the grand jurors. It is a fair inference from the broad mercantilist controls set up under the act of 1675 that the objections in 1670 and again in 1672 by the deputies, representing the more democratic elements in the colony, were not to the principle of wage regulation, but rather to the specific wage provisions of the proposed code. As late as 1675 there was clearly no expressed objection to a flexible system of control to be administered in the localities.[50]

[47] Mass. Arch., CXIX, fols. 40, 41. The General Court had been concerned with the regulation of quality, price, and wages in the leather industry at least as far back as 1648, when the shoemakers' guild had been chartered. See *Mass. Bay Rec.*, III, 132; Mass. Arch., LIX, fols. 29–32, 125, 126, 227–233, and 413. Johnson testified early to the high prices prevailing in this trade. *Wonder-Working Providence* (London, 1664; reprinted Andover, 1867), pp. 207–209.

[48] The English authorities had already found it impossible to enforce an extensive system of sumptuary legislation. See F. E. Baldwin, *Sumptuary Legislation and Personal Regulation in England* (Baltimore, 1926).

For sumptuary legislation in Massachusetts against extravagance in dress, see *Mass. Bay Rec.*, I, 126, 183, 274; II, 84; III, 243; IV, 41, 42, 60. See also *Plymouth Col. Rec.*, IX, 81. Numerous instances of enforcement are found in the records of the quarterly court of Essex Co. shortly after enactment (See *Essex*, I, 257, 271–275, *passim*), but no convictions are found between 1663 and 1675. For the enforcement of the provision of the "Provoking Evils" against excess in dress, see *Suffolk*, pp. 698, 751, 752; *Essex*, VI, 26, 73, 135; VII, 291. For enforcement in Hampshire Co., see Sylvester Judd, *History of Hadley* (Northampton, 1863), pp. 90–92. By 1690 enforcement seems to have become ineffective and was no longer seriously attempted.

[49] *Mass. Bay Rec.*, V, 62–63; *Mass. Col. Laws, 1660–72*, p. 236.

[50] Other events in the year 1675 indicate that the "Provoking Evils" was merely one phase

While the central government on numerous occasions between 1630 and 1675 regulated the wages of workers and the prices of commodities, the same function was also being performed by the towns of the Bay colony. Almost a year before the General Court authorized the towns to regulate wages, Boston, probably exceeding its authority at the time, appointed in November, 1635, a committee which, among other things, was to set "prices upon . . . laborer's and workingmen's wages" as well as certain commodities, and ordered "that noe other prices or rates shal be given or taken." [51] Dorchester was one of the first towns to take advantage of the authority granted by the act of 1636, and in May of the following year, used the Pequot War as a pretext, ordering

that any of the members or house keeprs wch shal be Chosen to goe for a Souldier and have a Charge of busenesse to leaue behind him, he may commend the Care of his busenesse to some friend which he shall nominate, who, if he cannot of himself or p'cure others to doe it at the same wages that is giuen to the souldiers it shall be lawful for Henery Withington, Mr Brankard, Mr Bates and Nathan duncan or any of them to enjoyne any one they shall thinke fitt to worke in this k[ind] for the helpe of such as [shall] need, and if any being so joyned shall refuse to worke he shall pay five shill. for Such refusall, to be levied by distresse.

It is ordered, also, that any that haue servants or any other which goe in the Services shall haue the Benfitt of this order.[52]

This order illustrates the practice of labor impressment combined with that of wage regulation, but it is surpassed in scope by the regulation of 1642, in which the town set a specific wage scale for common laborers, including hoers, reapers, and tailors. The prevailing wages of 2*s.* per day for the period from March 25 to October 25 were reduced to 28*d.*, and other seasonal variations were taken into account as follows:

	Rate per diem
Oct. 25–Dec. 1	15*d.*
Dec. 1–Feb. 1	12*d.*
Feb. 1–March 15	25*d.*

of a broad program to keep down wages and maintain a large labor market by discouraging idleness and labor monopoly. In that year the selectmen were ordered to check on idlers (*Mass. Bay Rec.*, IV, 62); and a group of ship carpenters who had ridden an interloper out of Boston on a rail because he had worked in the yard without having served his full seven years' apprenticeship were fined five shillings apiece payable to the government and a like amount to the victim. *Suffolk*, p. 603.

[51] *Boston Rec.*, II, 5.

[52] *Early Records of the Town of Dorchester*, ed. W. B. Trask (Boston, 1867), p. 32; *Boston Rec.*, IV, 23, 24.

By the same order these proportionate wage reductions were extended to "those that doe other mens worke at thire owne houses." Finally, the order provided that "al men Com in due tyme to thire labor uppon such penalty as the Court vppon iust Complaint made shal be pleased to inflyct." [53] There was good precedent in the Elizabethan statute for combining maximum wage regulations with an hours schedule.

Hingham in 1641 ordered "by a joint consent" that "the prices of labourer's wages and commodities . . . should be abated 3 pence upon the shilling of what has been formerly taken." Wages of common labor were fixed at 1s. 6d. per diem, of mowers and wheelwrights, 2s., and of carpenters 1s. 10d. Specific rates were also established for work of field teams of men and oxen. The flat percentage reduction was also held to apply to tailors and shoemakers. The interesting provision is also found that "they are to work eight hours a day," but this probably referred to the field teams rather than to the craftsmen generally, who were customarily required to work much longer hours.[54] The phraseology of the ordinance is indicative of previous wage-fixing activity by the town. Salem acted in specific cases when necessary. In 1643 that town set the wages of one Tom Tuck, ironworker, and in the following year ruled that the wages of two carriage makers conform to the prevailing Boston scale.[55] Rowley, a leading town in the manufacture of cloth, settled by Yorkshire families quite familiar with wage regulation at home, established the wages of various categories of workers in 1651. The town mowers were limited to 20d. a day; laborers to 18d. in summer, 14d. in the months of October and November, and 12d. in the three winter months; and "Reapers and other tradesmen, excepting Taylors, to have the same wages." [56] As late as 1668 the town of Ipswich was moved to set the maximum wage for laying a thousand shingles at 7s. 6d.[57]

For several generations the Puritans were in dead earnest about their wage codes. Both the Court of Assistants and the inferior county courts enforced on occasion the specific penalties of the law or drew upon their discretionary authority to discipline refractory workers. The first case on the records of the central courts occurred four years after the earliest wage statute. At a session of the court held at Boston on March 4, 1634, John Chapman was fined 20s. for charging the rate of 8s. per hundred

[53] *Boston Rec.*, IV, 51.
[54] Solomon Lincoln, Jr., *History of the Town of Hingham* (Hingham, 1827), p. 52n.
[55] *Salem Town Rec.* (2 vols., Salem, 1913), I, 134.
[56] *The Early Records of the Town of Rowley, 1639–1672*, I (Rowley, 1894), 72.
[57] Felt, *Ipswich*, p. 104.

for boards. Upon his promise to contribute three hundred feet of four-inch plank toward the building of the "sea fort,"—one of several charter violations charged up to Massachusetts by her overseas enemies—the fine was remitted.[58] As this case indicates, where the rates in question were those charged by masters, the borderline between price and wage regulation was extremely shadowy. On August 5 of the same year, Francis Godson was haled before the Court of Assistants and compelled to give bond for his appearance at the October session "to answer for breach of an order of Court in takeing to greate wages." [59] No further entry dealing with this case is found. On the same day James Rawlens was fined 5*s.* for charging 18*d.* a day and meat and drink for ten days' work of one of his servants whom he hired out "for weeding corne." Here the master was acting as a labor contractor and was fined as a receiver rather than as a taker of excessive wages.[60]

After the General Court abolished the penalty against employers who gave excessive wages but retained the fine against workers, a master named Hutchinson brought charges in the Court of Assistants on August 4, 1635, against four workmen for taking wages of 2*s.* 6*d.* per diem for their services. James Hawkins was accused of receiving this exorbitant wage for thirty-six days, and Arthur Holbridge, Thomas Munt, and Richard Bulgar, for thirty, nine, and six days, respectively. Another employer named Cogan also appeared on the scene and denounced Hawkins for having extorted similarly oppressive wages from him for fourteen days' labor. The court fined each violator, in accord with the law, 5*s.* per diem. These were grossly excessive penalties, as Hawkins was required to pay more than £12 and Holbridge close to £8, as much as they could be expected to earn under the legal wage scale during an entire season. Not being able to pay the fines, Holbridge and Hawkins were imprisoned, but on September 1 the court ruled that all four could pay the marshal 3*s.* weekly until the fines were discharged.[61] Whether or not these tremendous fines shocked the Puritan conscience will probably never be known, but shortly thereafter the law restraining "workingmen's wages to a certainty" was repealed, and discretionary penalties substituted.[62]

In these early years prosecutions for infractions of the price code vied with complaints for taking excessive wages for the attention of the

---

[58] *Assistants*, II, 40, 42.   [59] *Ibid.*, p. 48.   [60] *Ibid.*, p. 47.
[61] *Mass. Bay Rec.*, I, 153–154; *Assistants*, II, 53, 56–57. Shortly thereafter Bulgar appears to have been denounced as a follower of Anne Hutchinson. Winthrop, *Journal*, I, 297n.
[62] *Mass. Bay Rec.*, I, 159–160.

higher courts.[63] Most celebrated of these prosecutions was the complaint against Robert Keayne, who was charged at the General Court in 1639 with "oppression in the country in sale of foreign commodities." [64]

There were a few prosecutions by the General Court under the law substituting discretionary penalties for fixed penalties. In 1639 the General Court fined Edward Palmer £5 for charging an excessive price for the plank and woodwork on the Boston stocks, and with grim Puritan humor sentenced him, in addition, to sit in the stocks he himself had made. Through his lawyer, the outspoken Thomas Lechford, Palmer petitioned the Court for remission of the fine, setting forth that he was "poor and no wayes able to pay the said fine having a wife and six children all or some of which he expects to come forth of England to him shortly." Having forced the culprit to eat humble pie, the Puritan magistrates, who preferred exemplary or humiliating punishments to any other sort, reduced the fine to a mere 10s.[65] Hubbard, the Puritan historian, appears to have derived much satisfaction from this case. He thoroughly approved the severity of the punishment on the ground that "oppression and extortion in prices and wages" were an "injustice to the public." [66] In 1642 William Shepheard was fined £2 "for covenanting for £15 wages per annum," and Laurence Copeland similarly for an identical contract of wages, in both cases their employer having agreed to release them half of their working time.[67] In 1643 Anker Ainsworth was presented for taking excessive wages, and at the same session one Stodder for selling cloth at an excessive price; but the oppression was proved in neither case, and both were discharged.[68] Later in the year six persons, including a man and wife, were presented for "taking too

[63] Those exceeding the legal scale for wine and beer were prosecuted. See *Assistants*, II, 59 (1635), 67, 84 (1637, 1639); *Note-Book Kept by Thomas Lechford, Esq., Lawyer* (Cambridge, 1885), p. 85; *Mass. Bay Rec.*, I, 266. Cf. also *Assistants*, II, 80 (1638), 84 (1639), where the prosecutions failed for want of adequate proof. Millers likewise were fined for taking excessive tolls.

[64] This case is too well known for extended comment here. It is perhaps significant that one of the grounds advanced by the magistrates for leniency in this case was that there was no law in force limiting profits in trade. Cotton held a stricter view of this offense than did the magistrates. Winthrop, *Journal*, I, 58 *et seq.* Keayne charged in his will that he had been unfairly slandered. Boston Record Commissioners, *Report* (1886), pp. 27–35. Cf. also *Assistants*, II, 91. A law of 1641 determined the basis for the "markett or true price" of cattle. *Mass. Bay Rec.*, I, 331. Another *cause célèbre* was the prosecution before the Maine court of John Winter, overseer of Robert Trelawny, for charging excessive prices for commodities, for refusing to accept beaver at the current rate, and for forestalling and regrating. The court dismissed the case on the ground that it was not proper to regulate a man's profit in trade. Cleve v. Winter, "Trelawny Papers," Me. Hist. Soc., *Coll.*, III, 212, 215, 240 (1640).

[65] *Mass. Bay Rec.*, I, 260, 291; Lechford, *Note-Book*, p. 242.

[66] Hubbard, *General History*, p. 248.   [67] *Assistants*, II, 128.   [68] *Ibid.*, p. 131.

much wages," [69] but the final action of the court is not found in the record. These were the last cases to come before the central authorities.

There is no reason to believe that the absence of prosecutions in the central courts indicated a willingness on the part of the workers to moderate their demands. John Winthrop cites one instance from the year 1643, the last one in which the court busied itself with wage violations:

One Richard ——, servant to one —— Williams of Dorchester, being come out of service, fell to work at his own hand and took great wages above others, and would not work but for ready money. By this means in a year, or little more, he had scraped together about 25 pounds, and then returned with his prey into England, speaking evil of the country by the way. He was not gone far, after his arrival, but the cavaliers met him and eased him out of his money; so he knew no better way but to return to New England again, to repair his loss in that place which he had so much disparaged.[70]

For thirty-five years longer the inferior courts and local authorities prosecuted violators of the wage code, the principal prosecutions occurring in the quarterly court of Essex County between 1635 and 1676. Under the act of 1635 setting discretionary penalties,[71] the quarterly court at Salem at a single session in 1636 fined William Dixie, John Stone, and Jonathan Sibley 3s. apiece for taking the oppressive wages of 3s. a day, while James Smith, for taking "too great wages," did not get off so lightly, but was fined 20s.[72] In a case in 1651 in which Mark Symonds was fined £1 5s. for lying and 5s. for "railing" against the magistrates, depositions were made that the culprit had lied about the wages he was paid for the use of his boy and cattle by one Kimball, in order to secure a similar rate from Goodman Beals, who felt that "it was too much and that none in the town would give it." This is not a prosecution under the wage code, but it is doubtful whether the authorities would have concerned themselves with the deceit if they did not feel that Symonds had set a bad example by his oppressive demands.[73]

Under the authority of the act of 1636, John Alderman in 1652 charged Thomas Trusler before the magistrates at Salem with taking excessive wages from him.[74] No further action is recorded. In 1653 Humphrey Wilson prosecuted James Wall for taking excessive wages

---

[69] *Ibid.*, p. 135, cases of Loranson, Callwell, Danford, Gill *et ux.*, and Pope.
[70] *Journal*, II, 119.   [71] *Mass. Bay Rec.*, I, 160; *Mass. Col. Laws, 1660–72*, p. 120.
[72] *Essex*, I, 3.   [73] *Ibid.*, pp. 226–227.   [74] *Ibid.*, p. 247.

in building a sawmill. It is not clear from the record whether this is an action of contract, as the work was alleged to be "insufficient," or a criminal prosecution, and the action was withdrawn.[75] In 1658 the Ipswich court discharged William Godhue of the complaint that he took excessive wages for his son [76] and the next year the court admonished John Applefourd for taking excessive wages.[77] Somewhat analogous was the case of the attorney and deputy marshal who, in 1669, was given the choice of a whipping or a fine of £10 with costs.[78] In 1672 the Ipswich court dismissed the several charges against Lawrence Clenton, among which was the accusation that he took the high wage of 16s. and his dinners for three and a half days' work in painting a room. The charge was not proved.[79] In 1675 a man named Dennis was presented "for oppression in his trade," [80] and the following year, shortly after the passage of the sweeping general wage code enacted during King Philip's War, one Richard Scammon was presented for charging too much for repairing a pistol lock, among other work. According to the evidence, he took 500 feet of boards for his labor—for work, which by his own statement was "not worth more than 6s. 6d.,"—and as a punishment was ordered to return 250 feet to his employer and fined the remaining 250.[81] In 1679 John Wilkinson was prosecuted in the Salem court for "entertaining other men's servants" without their master's knowledge. According to one deponent, Wilkinson, a barber, started to shave him and then refused to finish unless he gave him one shilling, which he was thus forced to do or "he would have had to go away in that condition to another barber." [82] While the case does not appear to have turned on this point in the testimony, it bears evidence that at this late date such acts of oppression were still looked upon as contrary to the public welfare. Curiously enough, no case under the wage acts was reported in the early records of the Suffolk County court, although as late as 1675 there is a prosecution for oppression in the price of cloth,[83] and the accused was fined 10s. to the county, a like amount to the buyer of the cloth, together with costs and fees. Occasionally the selectmen of the towns were moved to act, as in Woburn in 1676, when they fined Hopestill Forester for oppression in exacting "inordinate wages" in

---

[75] *Ibid.*, p. 281.
[76] *Essex*, II, 119. At the same session William Bartholomew was fined 10 shillings "for selling dear." In a suit brought by Jonathan Wade against John Fuller for false testimony, evidence was presented that the plaintiff had been charged in court with "dear selling of grindstones," linen, and cotton cloth. *Ibid.*, 117 (1658).
[77] *Ibid.*, p. 152.   [78] *Ibid.*, IV, 178, 198: Godfrey v. Ela (1669).   [79] *Ibid.*, V, 37.
[80] *Ibid.*, VI, 72 (1675).   [81] *Ibid.*, VI, 142.
[82] *Ibid.*, VII, 326, 327n.   [83] Batt's case, *Suffolk*, II, 632.

making boards, nails, and other carpentry work, a portion of the fine being assigned by the court to the two injured complainants.[84]

The act of 1675 for the reformation of "Provoking Evils" marked the culmination of wage regulation in the pre-Revolutionary period. Only four years later a synod held in Boston considered the need for a reformation of social and moral conditions in the community and wrestled with two great questions: "1. What are the evils that have provoked the Lord to bring his Judgements on New England? 2. What is to be done so that these Evils may be Reformed?" In answer to the first, the elders found that sabbath-breaking, intemperance, gaming, and "mixed dancing" were provocative of God's wrath, manifest in plagues, fire, and war. In addition, they pointed to "Inordinate affection of the World," as evidenced in the "oppression which the land groaneth under," owing, among other things, to the fact that "Day Labourers and Mechanics are unreasonable in their demands." [85] As a program of action, the synod recommended adherence to the laws which had been passed a few years earlier "for Reformation of Provoking Evils," not mentioning the regulation of wages specifically, but singling out for emphasis the act of 1672 which aimed to curb immoderate drinking in order to check the demands of workers. Thereafter the church, according to Cotton Mather,[86] took it upon itself to see that such "evils" were eliminated. As late as 1690 Mather justifiably complained that the good old laws for the reformation of "provoking evils" had been indifferently enforced.[87]

Despite the continued regulation of certain public services and quasi-public utilities, and the regular setting of the assize of bread throughout the colonial period, all signs point to the disintegration in the eighteenth century of the general scheme of wage and price fixing in Massachusetts. Notwithstanding, the basic system embodied in the codes of 1648 and 1660 remained on the law books unrepealed. Although the candidates for master's degrees at Harvard in 1725 agreed that prices could be regulated by law, and that it was not always lawful to give and take the market price,[88] the absence in eighteenth-century Massachusetts of extensive regulatory codes, except for the Revolutionary period, considered in conjunction with other factors, is evidence of the breakdown of mercantilism as a system of internal regulation and of the rise of

---

[84] Samuel Sewall, *History of Woburn* (Woburn, 1868), p. 58; *Woburn Rec.*, II, 58.
[85] *The Necessity of Reformation . . . Synod at Boston* (Boston, 1679).
[86] *Magnalia Christi Americana*, II, 287–289.
[87] Mather, *The Present State of New-England* (Boston, 1690).
[88] Weeden, *Econ. . . . Hist. of N.E.*, II, 524.

laissez-faire practices in industry and commerce considerably before the Revolution.[89]

To a somewhat lesser degree this same pattern of wage and price regulation is found among the Bay colony's neighbors. The commissioners of the New England Confederation recommended to their respective governments in 1646 that "some serious provision be speedily made against oppression" in wages;[90] but as a matter of fact Plymouth, New Haven, and Connecticut had already anticipated this recommendation. In Plymouth as an independent colony the court on a number of occasions sentenced culprits who profiteered.[91] But the only reference to a wage prosecution is found in 1643 when the court declared: "Mowers that haue taken excessive wages, vizt, 3*s.* per diem, are to be presented, if they make not restitution."[92]

By an order of the New Haven General Court in 1640 retail profits were limited to 3*d.* in the shilling on commodities imported from England; for wholesale business a lesser profit was considered adequate. Exception was made for perishable commodities, but neither buyer nor seller was to "suffer in the rates." Commodities brought from Massachusetts, Connecticut, or Virginia were "to be in proportion moderated in the prises, according to the adventures of the commodityes." Sweeping regulations were included in this order as regards the wages of laborers and artificers:

> In callings wch require skill and strength, as carpenters, joyners, plasterers, bricklayers, Shipcarpenters, coopers and the like, ma'r [master] workemen

[89] Professor E. A. J. Johnson, emphasizing colonial industrial self-sufficiency, regards the second decade of the eighteenth century as marking "the highest point of development of the Massachusetts mercantilist ideas," and sees a gradual breakdown thereafter to the sixties. "Some Evidence of Mercantilism in the Massachusetts-Bay," *N.E.Q.*, I, 395.

[90] *Plymouth Col. Rec.*, IX, 81.

[91] For Plymouth legislation, see *ibid.*, XI, 30 (1638), setting a rate of 12*d.* a day with board for laborers, 18*d.* without board; repealed in 1639. John Barnes was presented for selling rye for 5*s.* per bu. which he had bought for 4*s.*, "without adventure or long forbearance in one and the same place," but was acquitted. *Ibid.*, II, 5 (1640); VII, 19. Again acquitted on a profiteering charge. *Ibid.*, II, 12 (1641). See also presentment of Stephen Hopkins for selling a looking glass for 16*d.* sold elsewhere in the colony for 9*d. Ibid.*, I, 137 (1639). Goodwife Knowles was fined 10*s.* for selling strong waters for 5*s.* or 6*s.* a bottle which had cost her only 35*s.* a case. *Ibid.*, II, 174 (1651).

[92] *Ibid.*, p. 60 (1643), based on the 1638 act setting wages of day laborers. In a suit arising in 1672 Francis Baker of Yarmouth sued William Nicarson in an action "of the case" for £10 for six meat barrels and for the labor on some tar barrels. The jury gave him a verdict for 5*s.* and costs. Nicarson thereupon turned around and sued Baker for £30, alleging that the tar barrels were defective and above the ordinary gauge and that he had been overcharged "six pence vpon a barrell more than men ordinarily payed for tarr barrells."

The relative paucity of prosecutions in Plymouth affords little substantiation for Mr. Kittredge's statement that "the records are full of cases where men were fined for charging too much either for their work or for their wares." H. C. Kittredge, *Cape Cod: Its People and Their History* (Boston and New York, 1930), p. 86.

not to take above 2*s*. 6*d*. a day in sumr, in wch men may worke 12 howers, butt less than 10 howers dilligently improved in worke cannot nor may be admitted for a full dayes worke, nor in winter above 2*s*. a day, in wch att least 8 howers to be dilligently improved in work. And by advice of approved M'r workemen the names of others who in there severall trades are to be allowed for m'r workemen are to be sett downe. But all workemen in the former and like trades, who are not as yet allowed to passe under the names of ma'r worke-men, not to take above 2*s*. a day in sumr and 20*d*. a day in winter, they im-proving their time in worke both sumr and winter as above expressed.

Planters and laborers, experienced and dilligent in their way, not to take above 2*s*. a day in sumr, and not above 18*d*. in winter, improveing their time as above, and others in proportion, as they may deserve, and boyes to have wages in sumr and winter in seurall imploymts according to the service they doe, wch shall be judged (when any doubt ariseth) by honest and indifferent men.

Wages for special tasks such as mowing, fencing, sawing timber, and the like were also set, and it is of some interest to compare the scales set at this time with the new schedule adopted in 1641, which marked a scaling down of the maximum wages fixed in the initial regulation:

		Maximum Wages	
		1640	*1641*
Skilled workmen	summer:	2*s*. 6*d*.	2*s*.
	winter:	2*s*.	20*d*.
Journeymen in skilled trades	summer:	2*s*.	20*d*.
	winter:	20*d*.	16*d*.
Farmers and laborers	summer:	2*s*.	18*d* [a]
	winter:	18*d*.	14*d*. [a]
Sawing			
by the hundred, for boards		4*s*. 6*d*.	3*s*. 8*d*.
for planks		5*s*.	4*s*.
for slitwork		5*s*. 6*d*.	4*s*. 6*d*.
by the day, top man or foreman (summer) [b]		2*s*. 6*d*.	2*s*.
pit man, less skill (summer) [b]		2*s*.	18*d*. [c]
Felling of timber, 2 feet or more		3*d*. a foot	2½*d*.
between 18 inches and 2 feet		2*d*. a foot	1½*d*.
Hewing and squaring of timber, at least 15 in. sq.		18*d*. tun girt measure	15*d*.

[a] The 1641 act puts in this category plasterers, haymakers, fellers of timber, and laborers. "Unskillful negligent laborers and boyes, both in somr and winter in several imploymts, accord-ing to the service they doe, wch when any doubt ariseth shalbe judged by able and indifferent men."

[b] "Proportionable in winter as before."

[c] Where of equal skill, each to get 22*d*. in summer and 18*d*. in winter by the act of 1641 as against 2*s*. 3*d*. in the previous scale.

	Maximum Wages	
	1640	*1641*
Sills, beams, plates, etc.	1*d.* a foot	3*f.*
Mowing, by the acre, salt marsh	3*s.*	3*s.* 6*d.*
fresh marsh	2*s.* 6*d.*ᵈ	3*s.*
Thatchers	2*s.* 6*d.*	
Fencing, with pales (pales and carting not included)	2*s.* a rod	18*d.*
with five rails	2*s.* a rod	18*d.*
with three rails	18*d.* a rod	14*d.*
Lime, by the bushel	9*d.*	7*d.*
by the hogshead	5*s.*	4*s.*

ᵈ By the day 2*s.* 6*d.*

The second schedule also included wages for sawn timber, hewing and nailing clapboards, lathing and shingling, and other work connected principally with the building trades and carpentry. It also provided that the food, lodging, and washing for a laboring man should be no more than 4*s.* 6*d.* by the week. It was further provided that all commodities and wages—"henceforward, till some other course be settled by order" —should be paid for either in corn at the prevailing price, in labor according to rates settled by the court, in cattle "as they shall be in differently prized, or in good march'table bever according to its goodnes." [93]

Nine months after the passage of the second schedule the court ordered that the regulatory laws passed "concerning wares and workes" be henceforth considered "voyd and of no force till the court see cause to the contrary." [94] After 1641 no further comprehensive regulations were enacted in New Haven, although in 1648 the authorities took action "to moderate the price of leather and shooes," [95] and as late as 1657 the court took action to prevent oppression among shoemakers.[96] The law against oppression included in the New Haven Code of 1656 declared it to be "much sin against God, and much damage to men" to take "excessive wages for work, or unreasonable prises for commodities." Offenders were liable to fine or imprisonment "according to the quality and measure of the offence as the Court shal judg meet." [97]

A number of prosecutions of the wage and price codes are found in the brief judicial history of New Haven colony. Under the act of 1640 the colony court early the following year fined John Reader 40*s.* "for breaking the order of the court in exacting greater wages (then

[93] *New Haven Col. Rec., 1638–49*, pp. 35 (1640), 52–56 (1641).
[94] *Ibid.*, p. 61 (1641).   [95] *Ibid.*, p. 161.   [96] *Ibid., 1653–65*, p. 215 (1657).
[97] *Ibid., 1653–65*, p. 604 (1656).

the court had determined) for 20 dayes worke wch he confessed he had received mony for." [98] The bulk of the prosecutions involved violations of the price code.[99]

The Connecticut experiment in price and wage regulation also runs closely parallel to that of the Bay colony. Apparently a wage regulatory order was promulgated sometime prior to June 15, 1640, for on that date the colony records indicate that the "Order concerneing artificers and laborers for wages, is renewed dureing the pleasure of the court." No text of the earlier order is found in the records. A half year later this order was "dissolued." [100] However, again in June of 1641 the court found it necessary to announce its "apprehensions to the country conserning the excesse in wages amongst all sorts of artifficers and workemen," indicating that "men would haue bine a law unto themselves." It confessed to "finding little reformation therein," and therefore enacted a maximum scale as follows:

Skilled artificers (carpenters, ploughwrights, wheelwrights, masons, joiners, smiths, coopers)	Summer (Mar. 10– Oct. 11):	20*d*. per diem 11 hours daily
	Winter:	18*d*. per diem 9 hours
Mowers		20*d*. per diem

All other artificers, handicraftsmen, or "chief laborers" were forbidden to take above 18*d*. a day for the first half of the year and not above 14*d*. for the latter portion. Piecework was to be valued in proportion, but in some instances was particularized as follows: sawyers, 4*s*. 2*d*. for slit-work or 3 in. planks; 3*s*. 6*d*. for boards by the hundred.[101] The maximum rate for a day's use of oxen and horses was also specified for a stated number of hours. As in the case of the earliest regulatory order in Massachusetts, this act provided that any person who "either directly or indirectly, shall giue or take any greater wages for the worke either of men or cattle than the pryses before mentioned, shall abyde the censure of the Court." The substitution of censure for fine undoubtedly weakened the regulation.

Owing to the scarcity of currency in the colony, the effective en-

[98] *Ibid., 1638–49*, p. 51.

[99] Cases of Turner, *et al., ibid.*, p. 161 (1645); Turner v. Mistress Stolion, *ibid.*, pp. 174–176; Gregory's case, *ibid.*, p. 358 (1648). See also H. W. Farnam, *Chapters in the History of Social Legislation in the United States to 1860* (Washington, 1938), p. 75; Tomlinson's case, *New Haven Col. Rec., 1653–65*, pp. 182, 185 (1656).

[100] *Conn. Pub. Rec.*, I, 52 (1640), 61 (1641).

[101] Boards were not to be sold above 5*s*. the hundred. *Ibid.*, I, 65 (June 7, 1641).

forcement of maximum wage legislation turned on the price established for commodities used as currency, notably Indian corn, wheat, and rye. No man was permitted to refuse merchantable Indian corn at the rate of 2*s.* per bushel "for any contracte made for the labour of men or cattell or commodityes sold after the publishing this order." [102] Within six months this rate was repealed and "all sorts of Corne"—summer wheat at 4*s.* 4*d.* per bushel, rye at 3*s.*, peas at 3*s.*, Indian corn at 2*s.* 8*d.*,—were made legal tender for labor contracts as well as for payment of town rates.[103] Thereupon workmen complained that the chapman paid them less for their corn than it represented as wages. As a result the Connecticut authorities found it necessary to order that all sales of commodities or other contracts payable in corn should be governed by the legally established country rate.[104] A slight reduction of the former rate was made in 1644 with regard to wheat and Indian corn.[105]

The experiment in comprehensive wage fixing by the legislation of a central governmental body was abandoned in Connecticut in March, 1650, when, according to the records of the colony:

> The order about the wages of men and cattle is repealed. Allso, the order about the prises of all corne is repealed; whereby all persons are left at libberty to make theire bargaines for corne, provided where no price is agreed betwixt persons, corne shall bee payable according to the former order, that is to say, wheat at 4*s.*, pease at 3*s.*, rye at 3*s.*, and Indian at 2*s.* 6*d.* pr bush.[106]

But this did not necessarily mean that the central authorities had abdicated their authority over wages in specific crafts. In 1677 maximum scales were set for the products of shoemakers and tanners as follows:

Shoemakers
   Plain and wooden-heeled shoes (all sizes above men's sevens) . . 5½*d.*
   French falls, well wrought . . . . 7½*d.*
Tanners
   Tanning hides
      green hides . . . . 2*d.* per lb.
      dry hides . . . . 4*d.* per lb.
   Sale of hides [a]
      green hides . . . . 3*d.* per lb.
      dry hides . . . . 6*d.* per lb.

[a] It was further provided that the tanner "set downe the price payd to the butcher or owner, or to be payd, vissibly upon the hide, that the price of the hide being tanned may be truly knowne."

[102] *Ibid.*, I, 72 (May 11, 1642).   [103] *Ibid.*, p. 79 (1642).   [104] *Ibid.*, p. 100 (1643).
[105] *Ibid.*, p. 118 (1644).   [106] *Ibid.*, p. 205 (1650).

This act further provided that, where a tanner or owner sold leather for more than the price fixed, such leather or its value should be forfeited, one third to go to the complainant, the rest to the county treasurer.[107]

Of wider significance was the action taken the same day, when the court appointed five persons "to be a committee to treat wth the most prudent and conscienscious of each calling, and to prepare such orders and instructions for the regulateing and stateing of trades and workmen, so as that all oppression may be removed from us and that righteousnes may be advanced, and to present the same to the next Court." [108] However, there is no report of this committee's activity.

As in Massachusetts Bay and New Haven, the Connecticut authorities finally substituted for specific wage regulations a general act against oppression, which came down unchanged to the Revolutionary period. Oppression was declared a "Mischievous Evil the Nature of Man is prone unto." Those taking "excessive" wages or "unreasonable" prices were to be punished by fines or imprisonment "according to the quality of the Offences" and at the discretion of the trial court. In deciding such complaints, the court was required to consult "two or three of the same Occupation or Trade" as the person complained of for oppression. These experts were to give their opinion under oath as to the price of the goods sold or the labor done, "which opinion and judgment shall be the ground of legal conviction." One assistant or justice of the peace was empowered to hear cases not exceeding 40s.; above that amount cases were to be tried by the county court. The penalty was not to exceed threefold "the wrong done" and was to be divided equally between the complainant and the poor of the town where the offender dwelt, the offender to pay all other charges.[109]

Occasional prosecutions under Connecticut's wage and price codes are found. In 1642 one Thomas Hurlburt was fined 40s. for taking higher wages than those fixed by statute.[110] At least one prosecution for violation of the price code has been uncovered in the unpublished court records of the colony. At a court held at Hartford, April 1, 1673, John Wilkins was accused of "oppression and extorsion among our people by the extream sales of his wares." Wilkins confessed in court that he had sold pins at the rate of 2s. the half thousand, and indigo at 12d. per ounce, and had also profiteered on tin pans. The judgment of the court

---

[107] *Ibid.*, II, 325. [108] *Ibid.*, pp. 324, 325.
[109] *The Laws of Connecticut of 1673* (Brinley reprint of 1865), p. 55; *Acts and Laws of His Majesties Colony of Connecticut in New England* (revision of 1702), p. 91.
[110] *Conn. Pub. Rec.*, I, 81.

was that this practice was "evill," but that, as he was a stranger who had claimed that he had "sold some Goods at good rates by which he was looser the Court saw cause to reproue him sharply for his extorting prices and remitt all Further punishment." [111]

THE MIDDLE COLONIES

THE MIDDLE COLONIES did not, prior to the Revolution, enact colony-wide regulations fixing the wages of workmen. The bulk of such regulations were established by the localities, and in most cases applied to specific callings. A number of examples of general wage and hour regulations were found during the Dutch period. For example, in 1639 it was provided that mechanics and laborers in the employ of the West India Company at New Amsterdam were to begin and end their labors at the ringing of a bell. Gilles de Voocht was appointed their superintendent "to go around and note those who are in default and report their names" to the director-general and the council.[1] In 1648 the court of Rensselaerswyck conferred upon Jan Verbeek and Jan Michielsz the exclusive privilege of engaging in the tailor's trade. Each was permitted a helper. Provision was made that neither tailor should receive more than 36 stivers for a day's work, and the helper 30 stivers.[2] This in effect set up a tailor's guild at Rensselaerswyck, but a more sweeping resolution was adopted by the burgomasters of New Amsterdam on July 11, 1658, when that body resolved "that the Board of Burgomasters and Schepens should fix Certain hours of the day when working people should go to their work and come from their work, as well as their recess for meals. Wherein the Board resolved to draft a petition to the Director General and Council to establish Guilds." [3]

An illustration of detailed regulation of hours is furnished by the personal instructions of the burgomasters of New Amsterdam to the porters of the weighhouse and the beer carriers "to report every morning at six o'clock before the Company's Warehouse or Scales and remain there until 12 noon, coming back at 1 o'clock to remain until sunset." The porters were required to keep at work continually from job to job, reporting each time upon their return to their foreman. Fines were provided for inattention, insolence, and tardiness. The porters were

---

[111] "Conn. Prob. Rec.," lib. III, f. 130.

[1] *Laws and Ordinances of New Netherlands, 1636–74,* comp. and trans. by E. B. O'Callaghan (Albany, 1868), p. 20; Stokes, *Iconography,* IV, 90.

[2] *Minutes of the Court of Rensselaerswyck, 1648–52,* trans. and ed. A. J. F. Van Laer (Albany, 1922), p. 28 (1648). The court denied their request to prohibit anyone from employing some other tailor in Fort Orange.

[3] *R.N.A.,* II, 410; VIII, 189 (1658).

not to take more than the wages prescribed by the burgomaster, and if they did, they would be dismissed.[4] These wages or rates to be charged by the porters or laborers at the weighhouse were set down a few days later.[5] The fixing of the hours of the weighhouse and beer porters was frequently done in New Amsterdam. These were monopolistic callings. The porters themselves were charged with the responsibility of seeing that no one but themselves should work at their trade. Dismissal was the usual penalty for taking more than the fixed rate of wages.[6]

As in New England and Virginia, the setting of maximum wages was accompanied by experimental efforts to control profits derived from trade. In 1653 the Council of New Netherland prohibited the sale of goods, except in the Indian trade, at more than 100 (temporarily 120) per cent advance above the invoice value.[7]

The period of English control which followed was characterized by less frequent instances of the fixing of wages and hours. But there is on record one unusual instance when the governor in 1672 confirmed an order of the town of Southampton fixing maximum wages for Indians engaged in whaling. Because it appears to be unique it is reproduced in full.

A confirmation of an ord'r made at the East End of Long Island, about whaling.

Whereas there was an ord'r made at the Towne Meeting in South Hampton, upon the Second Day of May last relating to the Regulation of the Whale Fishing, and Employment of the Indyans therein, wherein particularly it is mentioned That whosoever shall Hire an Indian to go a whaleing, shall not give him for his Hire, above one Trucking Cloath Coat for each whale hee and his Company shall Kill, or halfe the Blubber, without the Whale Bone, under a Penalty therein Exprest; upon Consideration had thereupon, I have thought good allow of the said order and do hereby Confirme the same, untill some inconvenience therein shall bee made appeare; And do also order that the like Rule bee followed at East Hampton and other places, If they shall find it practicable amongst them. Given under my hand in New Yorke, the 28th day of November 1672.

Fran: Lovelace [8]

However, examples of such intervention on the part of the governor to regulate wages or prices in colonial New York were exceptional.[9]

[4] *Minutes of the Orphanmasters of New Amsterdam, 1655–1663*, trans. and ed. B. Fernow (2 vols., New York, 1902), II, 98–101; Stokes, *Iconography*, IV, 213.
[5] *Mins. Orph. Court*, II, 102–103.   [6] *R.N.A.*, V, 256–258 (1665).
[7] *Laws and Ord. of New Neth.*, pp. 149–151.
[8] N.Y. State Hist., *Ann. Rep., 1896, Col. Ser.*, I, 363 (1672).
[9] In 1745 the Esopus Indians complained to the Kingston Sessions that their produce was

Prosecutions for "extortion" or "oppression" generally involved violations of wage or price codes or local assizes. They are less frequent in the court records of the Middle colonies than in New England, but occasionally are found in New Jersey quarter sessions.[10]

Prior to 1682 laborers and servants in Pennsylvania settlements were required to work at their callings the "whole day, the Master or Dame allowing time for food and rest."[11] The Pennsylvania Assembly in 1682 debated the setting of a maximum wage for all artificers. A committee of two was chosen to decide "Whether every Man may agree with his Artificer to his best Advantage, or that a general salary be put upon all Artificers."[12] Apparently no colony-wide legislation was enacted, but two years later an act was passed empowering the justices of each county court to set the wages of workmen and servants and affix a penalty for violation.[13] But there is no evidence that the county courts actually enforced this measure. In 1685 Penn wrote that "the hours for work and meals of Labourers are fixt, and known by Ring of the Bell."[14]

THE TOBACCO PROVINCES

WHILE THE TOBACCO PROVINCES regulated fees and wages in special callings throughout the colonial period, experimentation with colony-wide comprehensive wage and price fixing was somewhat more short-lived than in New England. The issue of the hours of work of servants was raised in the Maryland Assembly in 1638. According to the proceedings, "upon a question moved touching the resting of servants on Saturdays in the afternoon, it was declared by the house that no such custom was to be allowed."[1] In October, 1640, the Maryland legislature passed an "act for rateing artificers' wages." This act empowered the county courts to "moderate the bills, wages and rates of artificers, labourers and chirurgeons according to the most current rate of tobacco

---

priced too cheaply and the Christian goods too dear, "and Therefore they desire that their produce may be Dearer and the Christians Commodity Cheaper." But the court refrained from fixing prices and merely ordered that the price of goods on both sides "be regulated according as Parties on both Sides Can Agree," Ulster Sessions, 1737–50 (May 7, 1745).

[10] See Rex v̇. King, Burlington Q.S., 1764–87, fols. 116, 117 (1771); fined £5 and 2 weeks imprisonment. See also Rex v. Eldridge, f. 119 (1771).

[11] *Duke of York's Book of Laws and Charter to William Penn and Laws of the Province of Pennsylvania Passed between 1682 and 1700* (Harrisburg, 1879), p. 37.

[12] *Pa. Arch.*, 8th ser., I, 9, 10 (1682). At the same session it was voted not to put a price upon grain, although prices for malt beer and molasses beer were fixed.

[13] *Pa. Col. Rec.*, I, 98, 102 (1684). At the same time the Council passed a bill providing that the prices of linen and woolen cloth were to be fixed by the county courts; the price for hemp was set at 5d. per lb. and flax, 8d. per lb.

[14] *Narratives of Pennsylvania*, p. 262.　　　　　[1] *Md. Arch.*, I, 21 (1638).

proportioned to the rate of the price of the same or the like art, labour, or workmanship in England."[2] This was a temporary law to endure for two years. A careful examination of the county court records fails to reveal instances of the execution of such powers in Maryland.

Virginia was more enterprising in her early efforts to restrain wages and prices. Here the experiment antedated by a good many years that of the Bay Colony. In the early period of settlement the Company set a limit of 25 per cent on its profits in trade and established rates on commodities.[3] In order to enforce discipline and put an end to idleness Governor Gates ordered the colonists to go to work and set their hours from six to ten in the morning and from two to four in the afternoon—hardly an overly strenuous day![4] In 1621 the Governor and Council "with the advise of such discreet persons, as they then thought fitt to call unto them" laid down for that year and the next ensuing a schedule of wages as follows:

A mr Carpenter with meat and drinke by the day	3s.
And without meate and drinke by the day	4s.
A mr Bricklayer by the day with meate and drinke	3s.
And without meate etc.	4s.
A mr Shipwright by the day with meate etc.	3s.
And without meate and drinke	4s.
A mr Tailour by the day with meate etc.	2s.
And without meate etc.	3s.
A labourer in husbandry by the day with meate etc.	2s.
And without meate etc.	3s.
A mr Joyner by the day with meate etc.	4s.
And without meate etc.	5s.
A mr Mason by the day with meate etc.	3s.
And without meate etc.	4s.
A mr Couper by the day with meate etc.	3s.
And without meate etc.	4s.
A Sawyer to be allowed for sawing 100 foote with meate etc.	6s.
And without meate and drinke	8s.

The servants of all tradesmen abovesaid to be allowed by the day one 4th part lesse then theire mrs.

[2] *Ibid.*, p. 97 (1640). In 1692 the legislature was memorialized to regulate the fees of physicians and surgeons, allowing the medical practitioner "the first Costs of his Medicines administred to his patients and thereto add soe much more as his Costs, and for every Visitt to Charge Tenn pounds of Tobacco for every Mile that he shall Ride to Visitt his Patients." *Md. Arch.*, XIII, 357 (1692).

[3] P. A. Bruce, *Economic History of Virginia in the 17th Century* (New York, 1895; reprinted in 1935), II, 260 *et seq.*, 286.

[4] Force, *Hist. Tracts*, III, 19, 20.

This rate was to be proclaimed in the four "cities" of the colony.[5] It was followed up in 1623 by a proclamation by Governor Wyatt setting maximum prices for numerous commodities. Prices had risen, deplored the governor, to "excessive and unconscionable height." The "common sort of people" would pay any price rather than be wanting in strong drinks. Accordingly, maximum prices were fixed both in ready money and in tobacco for wines and beers, including sherry, canary, malaga, muscatel, whisky, wine vinegar, beer, and cider. In addition, ceiling prices were set for loaf and powdered sugar, butter and cheese, and Newfoundland and Canada fish. Finally, it was conceded that it was impossible to set specific prices "upon all sorts of goods, wares and commodities by reason of the difference of kinds, and degrees in goodness." Accordingly profits on the sale of all goods and commodities were from this time forward restricted to 10s. in the pound in money, and 20s. in tobacco.[6] Two years later Wyatt and his Council were forced to admit that the strict enforcement of the proclamation of 1623 might, in view of the drop in the price of tobacco, "hinder trafficke, and shorten supplies in our great necessities." A modified scale of prices was accordingly established.[7] Actually the price fixing of tobacco preceded by a few years the regulation of corn as well as of the wages of workmen. A tobacco price scale was legislated in 1619, followed by further acts over a twenty-year period. However, in 1641 a royal ordinance inspired by the merchants at home put an end temporarily to these attempts at statutory price fixing.[8] Nevertheless the baneful effects of the Navigation Acts on the Virginia tobacco industry served to keep alive efforts at price fixing, coupled with a broad program of crop curtailment that involved agreements with other tobacco colonies.[9]

Wyatt's initial comprehensive wage-fixing program was never re-

---

[5] Wyatt MSS in possession of the Earl of Romney, *WMCQ*, 2d ser., VII, 246; *Va. Co. Rec.*, III, 590. The names of the following officials were attached to the schedule: George Thorpe, Thomas Nuce, Francis Wyatt, John Berkley, Christopher Davison, George Yeardley, John Pott, and J. Pountis. For the wage scale in 1623, see *Va. Co. Rec.*, IV, 65.

[6] Forfeiture of all money and tobacco received for commodities sold contrary to this order was the penalty, with one half going to the informer, the other half to the government. *WMCQ*, 2d ser., VII, 250, 251; Randolph MSS, *Va. Hist. Soc.*; *VMH*, XVI, 3, 4.

[7] *WMCQ*, 2d ser., VIII, 50 (1625); *VMH*, XV, 369. In 1655 the act limiting profits in merchandise to 50 per cent was repealed. Bruce, *Econ. Hist. of Va.*, II, 289, 336n.; Hening, I, 413.

[8] Hening, I 162 (1632), 188, 206 (1633), 206 (1639), 225, 226 (1640); *J. of the House of Burgesses, 1619–1658/9*, p. 124; *VMH*, II, 287. In 1632 the legislature removed price limitations on corn on the ground that such practices were "contrary to the president of other countryes and kingdoms." Hening, I, 197.

[9] See L. C. Gray, "The Market Surplus Problem of Colonial Tobacco," *WMCQ*, 2d ser., VIII, 10; *A.P.C., Col.*, I, No. 478; Bruce, *op. cit.*, I, 389–395, 401–407; *Cal. Va. State Papers*, I, 20, 68; *Md. Arch.*, XXXVIII, 441.

newed. However, in 1662 the legislature passed an act for the building of a town at James City. This act provided that each of the seventeen counties in the province build one house, and that in each county there be impressed "bricklayers, carpenters, sawyers, and other tradesmen." In order to obviate "exaction of workemen, the price of bricks, the wages of workemen and labourers and their diett at the ordinaryes" were not to exceed an enumerated schedule.[10] Three years later an act for the building of a fort empowered the governor "to press carpenters labourers and other workemen, and that the carpenters finding themselves dyett and lodging be allowed Forty five pounds of tobacco per day." [11]

Wage and price regulations in certain fields appear to have been enforced during this period on Virginia's Eastern Shore. In 1663 the Northampton County court directed a tanner to curry leather in accord with the law and at maximum prices specified by the court. The record is included in full because of the reference by the court to Parliamentary statute and the scale of prices prevailing in the mother country as well as because it involved that pioneer industrialist among the great planters, Colonel Edmund Scarburgh.

Upon the Petition of Coll. Edm: Scarburgh declareing and Complaineing that hee hath bin at a Vast charge for tanning and makeing shooes, and that hee hath at this present nine shoomakers that doe noe worke, for want of Leather curried wch is and hath bin through the neglect of Nathaniell Bradford Currier who by Act of Parliamt is ingaged wthin sixteene daies in Winter and eight daies in Summer to curry all hides brought to him upon the Pennalty of paying Ten shillings per hide for his default The Court takeing the premisses into their serious Consideration Order that the sherriffe cause the Statute to be produced to the said Nathaniell Bradford that hee may not pretend Ignorance, and also that John Turnor and Robert Richardson be appointed veiwers and approvers both of the Leather sufficient Tanning and well and Sufficient currying, and in case of the absence of either of them John Tizard to bee assistant therein. And that the said Nathaniell Bradford bee paid for every hide, well and sufficiently curried thirty pounds of tobacco or a paire of shooes for each large hide, as the Imployer shall thinke fitt, and this by the Court allowed as the greatest of payments, and to Continue untill the Court shall be better informed of the prizes in England.[12]

A year before Maryland authorized the county courts to regulate the fees of surgeons, Virginia instituted the regulation of fees in the medical profession. An enactment of 1639 provided that the fees of physicians

---

[10] Hening, II, 172, 173 (1662).   [11] *Ibid.*, p. 220 (1665).
[12] Northampton O.B., 1657–64, f. 153.

could be evaluated by the courts—specifically, under act of 1646, the county courts. The Assembly was moved to declare that as a result of "the said intollerable exactions that the hearts of divers masters were hardened rather to suffer their servants to perish for want of fitt meanes and application than by seeking reliefe to fall into the hands of griping and avaricious men." [13] The law of 1639 was constantly reenacted, and an act of 1736 set the fees for the services of physicians, surgeons, and apothecaries, taking into account distance travelled.[14] It should also be noted that in some of the colonies, signally in Maryland, the fees of lawyers were regulated for a time.[15]

THE RICE AND SUGAR COLONIES

IN THE VERY EARLY YEARS of settlement South Carolina operated under emergency conditions. In December, 1671, the Grand Council appointed a committee to draft a bill setting "at what rates Artificers and Labourers shall worke." [1] The following July the Council ordered two of its members to recommend a scale of reasonable payments to be charged by the smiths, who, not having been previously regulated, were charging "unreasonable rates." [2] As time went on, interest in wage regulation disappeared.

In early Georgia, the Company operated the colony's economy. Servants and laborers were directly employed by the overseer of the Trust and their wages were set by the authorities.[3] Provision was made in 1739 for paying male servants at the rate of 8d. a day, without maintenance, females at the rate of 6d. a day, and children 4d. a day with maintenance, except in the case of children under six whose parents were trust servants and were to maintain them out of their wages.[4] Annual wages of £4

[13] Hening, I, 316–317; *WMCQ*, 1st ser., XIX, 148, 149.

[14] Hening, IV, 509–510; also F. R. Packard, *History of Medicine in the United States* (New York, 1931), I, 164–166.

[15] For enforcement of the Maryland act of 1674 fixing 200 lbs. of tobacco as the maximum attorney's fee, see *Md. Arch.* XL, xx. The Maryland act of 1725 to that end was disallowed by the Proprietary. In the 17th century attempts were made unsuccessfully to prevent attorneys from charging any fees whatsoever. The "Fundamental Constitutions" of Carolina, for example, forbade lawyers to plead for fees. See R. B. Morris, *Studies in the History of American Law*, (New York, 1930), pp. 43, 44; Charles Warren, *History of the American Bar* (Boston, 1911), p. 39. For efforts along these lines in New England, see *Plymouth Col. Rec.*, XI, 251 (1679); *Acts and Laws of Conn., 1796*, p. 36.

[1] *J. of the Grand Council of South Carolina, 1671–1680*, ed. A. S. Salley, Jr. (Columbia, S.C., 1907), p. 17.

[2] *Ibid.*, pp. 39, 40.

[3] The overseer was required to keep a "Weekly Book of Labour by Task'd Work." *Ga. Col. Rec.*, II, 274 (1739).

[4] Similar arrangements were made for 21 male servants and 17 females employed at Frederica. *Ibid.*, pp. 277, 280.

were set by resolution in 1741 for a group of servants, not to exceed sixty, who were to be sent over to serve five years.[5] These Georgia regulations seem to have been founded upon some contractual relationship between the trustees and the workers.

Dependent almost entirely upon imported supplies and labor, the British West Indian colonies found it expedient to establish minimum scales of wages and maintenance for servants in order to assure an adequate supply of white labor for the colonies and to restrain masters from exploiting their servants. This program affords notable contrast with the mercantilist regulations in force in the French Caribbean colonies during the corresponding period, where the objective was the restraining of excesses in the wage and price scale.[6] In the British West Indies the legislatures set minimum wages, either in money, goods, or land, for servants imported without indentures or contract, and also stipulated minimum weekly or monthly wages or allowances for servants generally.[7] While food and clothing allowances were invariably considered minimum requirements, a Barbadian act of 1696 set wages of £1 5s. per annum "and no more . . . provided no other Wages be contracted for." [8]

---

[5] An additional £1 per annum was to be paid to defray passage. *Ibid.*, p. 368.

[6] In the French West Indies, as in New England, maximum scales were in force. The Council of Martinique in 1666 declared that it was necessary to fix the wages and food of artisans, especially masons and carpenters, "because of their dearness, their insolence, and their laziness." Hours of labor were set from one-quarter hour before sunrise to one-quarter hour after sunset, with two hours off for lunch, and artisans were forbidden to stop work during working hours. The regulation was renewed in 1678. See M. L. E. Moreau de Saint-Méry, *Loix et constitutions des colonies françoises* (6 vols., Paris, 1784–90), I, 150–151; C. W. Cole, *Colbert and a Century of French Mercantilism* (New York, 1939), II, 37, 38. In the Spanish colonies the viceroy determined wages, prices, and hours. These regulations appear to have had at least some effect, although most students stress the fact that the royal commands on economic matters were not generally obeyed. See Carney, Univ. of Miami, *Hispanic-Amer. Studies*, No. 3 (1942), pp. 32, 33. For an account of an interesting attempt at price fixing in Spanish California in the 18th century, see G. Mosk, "Price Fixing in Spanish California," *Calif. Hist. Soc. Q.*, XVII (1938), 118–122.

[7] C.O. 139:1, fols. 60b–63, 126b, 161; C.O. 139:5, fols. 6–9; Baskett, ed., *Acts of Assembly Passed in the Island of Barbadoes, 1648–1718* (London, 1721), p. 22 (1661); C.O. 154:1, f. 98 (1672); *CSPA, 1669–74*, No. 1013 (1672); C.O. 28:3 (1696). By an act of 1703 Barbados provided a fine of 10s. to the poor for violations of the clothing and provision allowances; 2d offense 20s.; subsequent violations 40s. Richard Hall, *Acts Passed in the Island of Barbados from 1643 to 1762* (London, 1764), p. 157; Baskett, *Acts*, p. 204 (1703). For St. Christopher, see *J. Commrs. Trade and Plantations, 1722/3–1728*, p. 76 (1723). See also *Laws of the Island of Antigua, 1690–1804* (London, 1805), I, 320 (1755), 388 (1767). The Montserrat act of 1673 empowering justices of the peace "to order Labourers' Wages" appears to have conferred upon them jurisdiction in wage disputes not exceeding 1,000 lbs. of sugar rather than to have given them authority to fix wages. Baskett, ed., *Acts of Assembly Passed in the Island of Montserrat, 1668–1740* (London, 1740), p. 31.

[8] C.O. 28:3 (1696).

II. THE REGULATION OF WAGES DURING THE REVOLUTION

REGULATION BY THE STATES AND CONGRESS

By the eve of the Revolution wage regulation was confined to the licensed trades and in effect amounted to a regulation of prices, fees, or services in special callings. The situation was abruptly reversed with the crisis of the American Revolution, when, owing to the rapid depreciation of the currency, a program of regulation, virtually nation-wide in scope, was launched the very first year of the war. The program was initiated by the Northern states, acting together in regional conventions, but the Continental Congress lent encouragement. Here, as in the earlier controls, labor regulation was one phase of the larger program which had as its aim compulsory circulation of paper money by legal tender laws, buttressed by price and wage regulations and restraints against monopolistic practices. Therefore, while due emphasis will be given the labor codes set up in regional conventions, enacted in state statutes, or adopted by county conventions and town meetings and carried through by local committees, the close relationship of such regulation to the larger program will·be constantly borne in mind. In the light of these comprehensive programs, it is proposed to evaluate and determine the role of mercantilist theory at this time of grave constitutional difficulties and military crisis when such theories were definitely on the wane among the nations of western Europe.

Although the states were to serve as the springboard for such regulation, the Continental Congress had, as a matter of fact, pointed the way in price control as early as 1774 by incorporating in the articles of association stipulations not to sell merchandise at rates in excess of those prevailing during the previous twelve months and to sell domestic manufactures "at reasonable prices, so that no undue advantage be taken at a future scarcity of goods." [1] Prices for tea, coffee, salt, pepper, sugar, and other imports were set both by Congress and by local committees in 1775 and 1776, violators of such orders being con-

---

[1] W. C. Ford and G. Hunt, eds., *Journals of the Continental Congress* (34 vols., Washington, 1904–37), I, 78, 79. The nonconsumption agreements enforced by the towns frequently, as in Connecticut in September, 1774, embodied prohibitions against forestalling and engrossing. W. G. Sumner, *The Financier and Finances of the American Revolution* (New York, 1891), I, 53.

sidered "enemies of the American cause" to be "treated accordingly." [2] In the course of 1776 Congress had occasion to rule that the military pay no higher prices for goods furnished the soldier "than the first cost of them, and five percent for charges," [3] and on October 31, 1776, that body recommended that "the assemblies, conventions, councils or committees of safety of the several states" take suitable measures for obtaining engrossed goods for the use of the army, allowing to the owners a reasonable price for them, and enact laws preventing monopolies. [4] Local committees enforced the congressional resolves and also set prices in some instances. In March, 1776, the Albany committee of correspondence asked Congress for an interpretation of its regulations as to whether they related "to the profits on such Goods or to the accustomed prices Goods were sold at in 1774." [5] On a number of occasions during the year that body and its Schenectady counterpart set the price of tea, salt, pepper, sugar, and numerous other imported items. [6] In the spring of 1776 the committees of inspection of fifteen towns in Hartford County met at Hartford and fixed the prices for certain commodities. [7] In April the Philadelphia committee of inspection inquired whether they should continue to exercise the power of setting the price of goods in instances other than green tea. Congress replied that the association by its very nature was temporary, and, as supplies were now largely consumed and the risks of enterprise were to be encouraged, the power of such local committees to regulate prices in general ought, therefore, to terminate. [8] Nevertheless, within a month, on hearing that profiteers were monopolizing shoes, stockings, and other necessaries for the army, Congress recommended that the assembly of Pennsylvania adopt immediate measures adequate to remedy the evil. [9]

Of all areas, early New England had experimented most broadly with price and wage controls, so that it was in a way natural that the leadership in this movement should now be assumed by that section. At the outbreak of the Revolution, Connecticut passed a number of such laws. At the May session of the General Assembly in 1776, an

---

[2] Newport *Mercury*, March 25, 1775; May 13, June 13, 20, 1776; *N.Y. Gazette*, April 22, 1776.
[3] *J. Continental Cong.*, V, 591.   [4] *Ibid.*, VI, 915, 916.
[5] *Minutes of the Albany Committee of Correspondence*, ed. J. Sullivan (Albany, 1923), I, 358.
[6] *Ibid.*, I, 385, 511, 512, 556, 601; II, 1067. For price regulation in Newark, N.J., at this time, see *N.Y. Gazette and Weekly Mercury*, April 22, 1776. See also *Pa. Packet*, April 22, 1776.
[7] R. R. Hinman, *Historical Collection* (Hartford, 1842), p. 83.
[8] *J. Continental Cong.*, IV, 320; *Pa. Gazette*, May 6, 1776. For local regulation of the price of salt in Virginia at a somewhat later date, see Chesterfield O.B. (January Court, 1777), *VMH*, XIV, 328.
[9] *J. Continental Cong.*, VI, 980, 981.

old statute concerning oppression in exacting high prices or wages was amended so as no longer to require the appraisers appointed by the authorities to be men of the same occupation or trade as the person complained of.[10] In October, penalties were prescribed against those who discriminated against continental bills in setting prices,[11] and in the following month a statute was enacted fixing the maximum price of farm labor in the summer season at 3s. per diem,

and so in the usual proportion at other seasons of the year; and other labor to be computed, and of mechanics and tradesmen according to the usages and customs that have heretofore been adopted and practised in the different parts of this state compared with farming labour and the prices hereafter set and established.

Prices for numerous commodities were also fixed and violations of either the wage or price scales were to be punished by the state law against oppression.[12]

The Providence Convention. Interstate action was initiated by Massachusetts. The first two conventions were called on her initiative,[13] in direct response to petitions for relief from high prices from some score of Massachusetts towns and four towns in New Hampshire.[14] The meeting at Providence at the close of 1776, comprising committees from New Hampshire, Massachusetts, Rhode Island, and Connecticut, was the first of these regional sessions. In addition to recommending military measures and taking steps to stabilize the credit of the paper bills in circulation, the Providence convention, under the presidency of William Bradford, adopted at its session of December 31, 1776, wage and price regulation as follows:

This Committee taking into Consideration the unbounded Avarice of many Persons, by daily adding to the now most intollerable exhorbitant Price of every necessary and convenient article of Life, and also *the most extravagant Price of Labour, in general,* which at this Time of Distress unless a speedy and effectual Stop be put thereto will be attended with the most Fatal and Pernicious consequences As it not only Disheartens and Disaffects the Soldiers who have Nobly enter'd into Service, for the best of Causes, by obliging them to give such unreasonable Prices for those things that are absolutely needful for their

[10] *Conn. Sess. Laws*, 1776, p. 422.　　　　[11] *Ibid.*, p. 434.

[12] *Conn. State Rec.*, I, 62, 63 (Nov. 19, 1776).

[13] *Mass. Acts and Resolves*, V, 669. Connecticut first declined on the ground that Congress was considering the currency question and that state activity might foster jealousy and endanger the union. *Amer. Archives*, 5th ser., III, 1077. Rhode Island proposed broadening the scope of the convention to include (in addition to price measures) embargoes, regulation of public auctions, etc.—a view which prevailed.

[14] *Mass. Acts and Resolves*, V, 669–673.

very existence that their Pay is not sufficient to Submit them, but is also very Detrimental to the Country in General.

Wherefore it is recommended by this Committee, that the Rates and Prices hereafter enumerated be affixed and settled within the respective States in New England, to wit:

Farming Labour in the Summer Season shall not exceed Three Shillings and Four Pence per Diem, and so in the usual Proportion at other Seasons of the Year, and the Labour of Mechanics and Tradesmen and other Labour to be computed according to the Usages and Customs that have heretofore been adopted and practised in different Parts of the several States compared with Farming Labour.[15]

The committee also set the prices for some twenty-seven domestic commodities, including wheat, corn, and wool, and for a few manufactured items such as shoes, stockings, and cloth. It recommended that, "notwithstanding the great risque of a voyage to and from Europe, the high rate of insurance, the difficulty of procuring articles suitable for that market, the loss upon those exported, the increased expence and length of the voyage, and the real necessity of importing many commodities" from Europe, the wholesale price of imported goods should not exceed by from 250 to 275 per cent the original cost, and the retail price should be no more than 20 per cent greater than the wholesale. In addition to this comprehensive schedule, the committee further recommended that the respective state legislatures fix the price of wood, hay, pine boards, plank, joist, hoops, shingle, charcoal, tanned leather, cotton and linen cloths, mutton, veal, and flour, "and also the Rates of carting, which can be much better done in the several States than by this Committee." Severe penalties for violations were also proposed.

The states represented at the meeting acted with commendable speed. Connecticut immediately set up a wage and price scale, raising the maximum for farm labor to accord with the new schedule to 3*s*. 4*d*. from the 3*s*. set the previous month, in fact repealing the previous act.[16] New Hampshire, Massachusetts, and Rhode Island likewise fell into line at once.[17] Under the Massachusetts statute, rates of labor were only

[15] MS Journals of the Convention of the New England States with Accompanying Resolutions, 1776–80, Rhode Island State Archives; Force Transcripts, Vol. XIII, Lib. of Cong.; also in modernized form in *Conn. State Rec.*, I, 592–96; *Mass. Acts and Resolves*, V, 670.

[16] *Conn. State Rec.*, I, 98–100; R.V. Harlow, "Aspects of Revolutionary Finance, 1775–83," *Amer. Hist. Rev.*, XXXV, 57. The wages of farm labor appear to have been accepted as a standard of value, commodity prices being ascertained with reference thereto.

[17] *Laws of N.H.*, IV, 78–82; *Prov. Papers of N.H.*, VIII, 455–456, 471; *Mass. Acts and Resolves*, V, 583–589. The Massachusetts act as originally passed had no time limit, but later a time limit of three years was set. *Ibid.*, V, 647; MS, R.I. Col. Rec., 1772–77, fols. 548 *et seq.*; *R.I. Col. Rec.*, VIII, 85.

3s. per diem [18] as compared with the 3s. 4d. in the Providence recommendation, but in other respects the act conformed to the price schedule for manufactured goods. In addition, the price of refined and bloomery iron was fixed. The prices set in this law applied to Boston; in other towns the selectmen were authorized to regulate prices in accordance with this scale, making the necessary allowance for differences in the cost of transportation. Rhode Island, in addition to setting the established scale for farm labor, specified wages as follows:

per diem

Teaming work, the teamster finding himself and cattle, for one Hand with Cart or Waggon, one Yoke of Oxen, and a good draught-Horse, or two Yoke of Oxen 13/

Teaming to and from Sea Port Markets and for the army per Ton per Mile, if not more than one mile 4/. For every Mile after the first mile out 1/6.

Horse-keeping, at Sea Port Towns per Night or 24 Hours, 2/6.

Horse-shoeing all round, with steel Corks, Heel and Toe, 6/.

Ox-Shoeing and other Blacksmith's Work in the same Proportion.

Ships Iron-work—weight-work at 3d. per lb. and all light work in the same Proportion, excepting cast Iron.

House-Carpenters, finding themselves 5/

Ship-Carpenters,   "   " 6/

Caulkers,   "   " 7/

Masons,   "   " 6/6

Taylors making a plain suit of best Broadcloth Cloths, 24/ and their daily wage, the employer finding them at 3/

Trucking, 1/6 per Hogshead, and other things in Proportion

Best Beaver Hats, at 42/. Best Felt Hats at 8/.

Coopers, finding themselves 5/
setting and finding Hogshead Hoops, 3d. each
setting and finding Barrel hoops, 2d. each

Barbers for shaving. 3d.[a]

a Prosecutions for violation could be brought in any court of record.

By March of the following year Rhode Island found it necessary to raise maximum wages in some categories and at the same time to ascertain more precisely the seasonal wages of farm labor, as follows:

The Price of Farming Labour, viz. for Mowing and Reaping in their Season, shall not exceed three Shillings and six Pence per Day, and in the three Winter Months one shilling and six pence per Day, and at all other Times of the Year

18 This had been the prevailing rate the previous year. *Essex Inst. Hist. Coll.*, II (1860), 259.

two Shillings per Day: That for the Three Summer Months the Price of Labour by the Month shall not exceed forty-eight shillings when found, and at all other Seasons in the same Proportion compared with Day Labour: That Common Labour in the Town of Providence shall not exceed four shillings and six Pence per Day, they finding themselves, and three shillings when found. . . .[19]

The proceedings of the convention were laid before Congress on January 28, 1777, and evoked a spirited debate. William Ellery wrote Governor Cooke of Rhode Island that he had no doubt that they would be approved.[20] As to their reception, the partisan Samuel Adams reported that they were "much applauded as being wise and salutary." [21] Nonetheless, over the course of the next few weeks the issue was warmly debated on at least three occasions. As the arguments formulated were fairly representative of the division of opinion on the wisdom of regulation, it seems desirable to consider them in some detail. On February 4, a resolution of the Committee of the Whole was debated setting forth the opinion of the committee

that the peculiar Situation of the New England States, whose Communication with Congress was in a great Measure cut off, and who were invaded or threatened with an immediate Invasion by the Enemy, rendered the Appointment and Meeting of the Committee proper and necessary, and consequently worthy of the Approbation of Congress.[22]

For the affirmative, Sam Adams defended as the privilege of freemen the right of assembly "upon all occasions to consult measures for promoting liberty and happiness," and Richard Henry Lee maintained that, as the states were not yet confederated, no law of the union was infringed. As the New England program of price regulation was very popular with Congress, according to the admission made on February 7 by John Adams, who himself felt that no permanent good could come of it,[23] it was necessary for the opposition to muster an impressive array of talent. Those arguing in the negative were in general to prove op-

---

[19] MS, R.I. Col. Rec., 1772–77, f. 641 *et seq.*; *R.I. Col. Rec.*, VIII, 183. Within less than three months after the passage of her price-regulatory law, New Hampshire also found it necessary to legislate a new and higher set of maximum rates. *Acts and Laws of New Hampshire*, IV, 88 1777).

[20] E. C. Burnett, comp., *Letters of Members of the Continental Congress* (8 vols., Washington, 1921–36), II, 227.

[21] *Ibid.*, II, 233.

[22] *J. Continental Cong.*, VII, 80, 81. Benjamin Rush reported the motion as: "Whether it did not stand in need of the Approbation of Congress to make it *valid*," thus raising a nice constitutional question. Burnett, *Letters*, II, 234.

[23] *Familiar Letters of John Adams and His Wife Abigail Adams during the Revolution* (New York, 1876), p. 239.

ponents of mercantilist controls, although favoring a stronger political union—a point of view which ultimately prevailed in 1787. Thus, Wilson maintained that, as the business transacted was "continental" in scope, it required the approval of Congress. John Adams, while defending the convention as "founded in necessity," conceded "that the four New England States bore the same relation to the Congress that four counties bore to a single state. These four counties have a right to meet to regulate roads, and affairs that relate to the poor, but they have no right to tax or execute any other branch of legislation." Since the convention had dealt with continental as distinguished from local matters it stood in need of approbation. Dr. Benjamin Rush regarded the Providence meeting as "full of great and interesting consequences, which should be regarded with a serious and jealous eye." He charged that body with usurping the power of Congress, just as four counties would usurp the power of the state legislature if they attempted to tax themselves. He also accused the convention of contravening an express resolution of Congress by regulating the price of goods.

The motion was decided in the affirmative on February 4, but, when reconsidered, was defeated a few days later by one vote, only to be reopened on February 14.[24] At that time the opponents of the motion were reinforced by additional men of eminence in Congress. James Smith maintained that a recommendation to the other states would be an interference with their "domestic police," a subject of "too delicate a nature to be touched by Congress."[25] Benjamin Rush left off constitutional grounds and turned to economic history and theory. He cited the experiment in the reign of Edward II, the failure of Congress to keep down the price of tea, or of the Philadelphia committee to restrain a price rise in West Indian imports. In his opinion, the "extortion" was the direct result of "the excessive quantity of our money," and therefore the proposed remedy was merely an opiate. Richard Henry Lee promptly replied that the continent labored under a spasm, "and Spasms

[24] *J. Continental Cong.*, VII, 87; Burnett, *Letters*, II, 234, 235; Benjamin Rush, Diary (Library Co. of Philadelphia, Ridgway Branch). According to Thomas Burke, some of the states, including North Carolina, voted against approbation for fear that further disputes might arise. Burnett, *Letters*, II, 249; *N.C. State Rec.*, XI, 389. After a favorable vote by the committee of the whole on February 5, the proceedings of the Providence convention were referred to a committee of five: Richard Henry Lee, James Wilson, Samuel Chase, John Adams, and Roger Sherman. Its report of the following day was tabled for the time being. *J. Continental Cong.*, VII, 93, 97. The report of James Wilson is in Papers of the Continental Congress, No. 24, f. 375, Lib. of Cong.

[25] These constitutional arguments were doubtless very influential with certain opponents of the resolution, who felt that its purpose was to secure for the Congress the power to disapprove other state acts as occasions arose. See M. Jensen, "The Idea of a National Government during the American Revolution," *Pol. Sci. Q.*, LVIII (1943), 364.

. . . require *palliative* medicines." Samuel Chase took up the defense at this point, arguing from utter necessity, and urging that the "mines of Peru would not support a war at the present high price of the necessaries of life," and that unless the prices of clothing and other articles were limited the pay of soldiers would have to be raised. Sergeant, Wilson, and Witherspoon denied the practicability of the measure. Sergeant insisted that "the price of goods cannot be regulated while the quantity of our money and the articles of life are allowed to fluctuate." James Wilson stated dramatically:

There are certain things Sir which Absolute power cannot do. The whole power of the Roman Emperors could not add a single letter to the Alphabet. Augustus could not compel old batchelors to marry. He found out his error, and wisely repealed his edict least they should bring his authority into contempt.

Witherspoon's argument was perhaps the most forceful. He pointed out that regulated articles had risen in price more than unregulated items and that the failure of this proposed program would weaken the authority of Congress. John Adams expressed doubt as to "the justice, policy and necessity of the resolution," and pointed out that the experiment "was tried in vain even in the absolute government of France. The high price of many Articles arises from their scarcity. If we regulate the price of imports we shall immediately put a stop to them for ever." [26] Rush, in closing for the negative, supported Adams in the view that the rise in prices in Philadelphia was not due to Tory monopolizers and speculators, but rather to the constant emissions of currency which led to speculation. The Philadelphia committee supported by the "country people" had attempted unsuccessfully to sustain prices. Then, retorting to Lee, he diagnosed the malady of the continent as "not a spasm, but a dropsy," for which he wrote the following prescription:

(1) Raising the interest of the money we borrow to 6 per cent. This like a cold Bath will give an immediate Spring to our affairs; and (2) *taxation.* This like *tapping,* will diminish the Quantity of our Money, and give a proper value to what remains. [27]

As a result of this debate, the resolution was amended. In so far as it related to wages and prices, the Providence plan was not specifically

[26] Shortly thereafter Adams referred to the wage and price codes as "mere temporary Expedients" and palliatives, and advised a radical cure—ceasing to emit paper currency and redemption in gold and silver through importation of the precious metals. John Adams to Joseph Palmer, Feb. 20, 1777. Myers Coll., N.Y. Pub. Lib.

[27] Burnett, *Letters,* II, 250 *et seq.;* Rush, Diary, Feb. 14, 1777.

endorsed, as historians have insisted,[28] but "the propriety of adopting similar Measures" was "referred" to the "serious Consideration" of the other states.[29] Congress then proceeded to call a meeting to be held in March, 1777, at York, Pa., for commissioners from New York, New Jersey, Pennsylvania, Delaware, Maryland, and Virginia; and at Charleston, S.C., for commissioners from North and South Carolina and Georgia, in both cases to adopt "such a System of Regulation as may be most suitable to those States."

The York Convention. At the York meeting a report was brought in establishing a maximum price tariff for goods needed for the military services. It was further recommended that the respective legislatures fix the prices of other articles to bear the same relation to the prices that obtained before the war as did the enumerated items. Likewise, in order to make certain that "the price of labor and of manufacture" would be "proportionate to each other," it was proposed that prices of goods bear the same relation to wages as they did before the conflict. The delegates from Pennsylvania, Delaware, and Maryland voted to reject the report, while New York, New Jersey, and Virginia voted for adoption. Its opponents argued that regulation would be "productive of the most fatal consequences." The convention, hopelessly divided, contented itself, therefore, with sending copies of the proceedings to Congress and the states represented.[30] The failure of the Middle states to agree on a price and wage schedule deterred action by local committees in that area at this time. For example, in May, 1777, the Albany committee of correspondence resolved that "as the necessaries of Life and other Merchandize are not ascertained this Committee do decline to undertake the Task of Regulating and ascertaining the Prices or Wages to be allowed for Sloops in the public service." [31]

Revision of the Convention Schedules. Despite criticism in high places, these early conventions were clearly representative of a substantial body of public opinion which favored curbs on all sorts of profiteering; and the immediate reaction to the New England legislation incorporating the Providence proposals was distinctly cordial. The acts were praised for "rightly considering the several classes of men, allotting to the farmer, to the manufacturer, to the day laborer, and to the trader, the

[28] Sumner, *Financier and Finances of the Amer. Rev.,* I, 56; A. S. Bolles, *The Financial History of the United States* (New York, 1879), p. 159; Burnett, *Letters,* II, xii, xiii.

[29] *J. Continental Cong.,* VII, 124, 125; Papers of the Continental Cong., No. 24, f. 393. See also Burnett, *Letters,* II, 266; *N.C. State Rec.,* XI, 39.

[30] *Selections from the Correspondence of the Executive of New Jersey, 1776–86* (Newark, 1848), pp. 34–35; Burnett, *Letters,* II, 340; *J. Continental Cong.,* VII, 267.

[31] *Mins. Albany Comm. Corr.,* I, 772.

allowance respectively proper for them." [32] They weie endorsed at public meetings held in various towns, notably New Haven and Boston, which set up special committees to enforce the law—in the latter town, a committee of thirty-six persons not in trade to aid the selectmen and the committee of correspondence by furnishing information and legal assistance.[33] In Boston the act was not deemed sufficiently comprehensive, and on April 14 prices were laid down for at least fifty additional commodities and such services (as carting and trucking) not enumerated in the state law.[34]

Nevertheless the precipitate decline in the value of money soon created deep dissatisfaction with these measures in New England.[35] The Massachusetts farmers refused to bring produce to the markets and the townsmen charged them with bad faith; whereas the country people regarded the Bostonians as speculators and profiteers.[36] As early as January the Massachusetts House of Representatives found it necessary to revise some prices, and further modifications were proposed by a committee of the Council on March 17, including an increase for horsekeeping per night from 2s. to 2s. 8d., and for teaming per ton per mile from 1s. 6d. to 2s. The proposal was rejected, but a new committee on April 4 favored repeal of as much of the law as related to flour, a general revision of the price code, and the calling of a new intercolonial convention to meet that month.[37] On May 10 the act was revised. The new statute established maximum prices on some thirty enumerated articles and services (including teaming), and conferred broad powers upon the selectmen and committees of correspondence of the towns to fix bimonthly the "price of farming and other labor and of poultry, flour, and iron," and to seize the goods of engrossers and place them on the market. Under authority of the act the towns were to choose committees annually to aid in its enforcement. Certain labor services and prices generally were revised upwards. Thus, teaming per ton per mile was

[32] *Continental J.*, Feb. 6, 1777. See also appeal to farmers and laborers for support of the acts in *ibid.*, Feb. 13, 1777. See also *New Hampshire State Papers*, XIII, 284, 285.

[33] New Haven Town Rec., Jan. 30, 1777; *Independent Ledger*, April 24, 1777; *Boston Rec.*, XVIII, 260, 261; *Mass. Acts and Resolves*, V, 262–264. See also F. W. Caulkins, *History of Norwich* (Hartford, 1866), p. 243.

[34] *Continental J.*, April 17; *Boston Gazette*, April 28, 1777.

[35] Governor Trumbull, writing in February, 1777, attributed the rise in wages and prices to the scarcity of labor caused by the drawing off of so many workmen into the army. Paradoxically, the rapid rise of the cost of living "operated strongly to discourage soldiers from enlisting." Jared Sparks, *Correspondence of the American Revolution* (4 vols., Boston, 1853), I, 342.

[36] See R. V. Harlow, "Economic Conditions in Massachusetts during the American Revolution," Colonial Society of Massachusetts, *Publications*, XX, 167–271, and authorities cited.

[37] *Mass. Acts and Resolves*, V, 674, 723, 724; *Boston Gazette*, March 17, 1777; *Continental J.*, March 20, 1777.

raised from 1*s*. 6*d*. in the act of January 28 to 2*s*. in the act of May 10.[38] This gave rise to dissatisfaction in neighboring states which had been parties to the Providence convention. The governor of Rhode Island protested that he could not enforce his own wage and price codes if the larger states did not live up to their part of the bargain.[39] In some Massachusetts towns the response to the revised code was sympathetic. A convention of committees of correspondence in Plymouth, meeting on May 21, urged support and strict enforcement,[40] and the following week Watertown chose a committee of five to put the act into effect.[41] To criticisms made at the Plymouth sessions that the wages of labor were too high, a writer in the *Independent Chronicle* replied that the increased cost of provisions and depreciation of the currency justified the prevailing wages.[42] Another writer admitted that the workers were endeavoring to secure wages which would bear the same proportion to the price of imported articles and necessaries as they formerly did.[43] No sooner was the act passed, therefore, than revisions were considered by the General Court.[44]

Elsewhere the effects of the regulating acts set up under the Providence convention were denounced. The other New England states found it necessary in the spring of 1777 to authorize higher price levels.[45] Thus, the town of Providence specifically instructed her representatives in the legislature that the act was

so intricate, variable, and complicated, that it cannot remain any time equitable. . . . It was made to cheapen the articles of life, but it has in fact raised their prices, by producing an artificial and in some articles a real scarcity. It was made to unite us in good agreement respecting prices; but hath produced animosity, and ill will between town and country, and between buyers and sellers in general. It was made to bring us up to some equitable standard of honesty . . . but hath produced a sharping set of mushroom peddlars, who adulterate their commodities, and take every advantage to evade the . . . act, by . . . quibbles and lies. It was done to give credit to our currency; . . . but it tends to introduce bartering and make a currency of almost everything but money.[46]

The Springfield Convention. Those were days when official bodies did not hesitate to call a spade by its name. As the Massachusetts towns

---

[38] *Mass. Acts and Resolves*, V, 642–647; *Boston Gazette*, June 23, 1777.

[39] *Mass. Acts and Resolves*, V, 724; *Mass. Arch.*, Vol. 137, f. 50.

[40] *Boston Gazette*, June 16, 1777.   [41] *Watertown Rec.*, IV, Pt. VI, 161.

[42] *Boston Ind. Chron.*, Aug. 29, 1777.   [43] *Ibid.*, Sept. 11, 1777.

[44] *Mass. Acts and Resolves*, V, 810–813; *Mass. Arch.*, Vol. 137, f. 133.

[45] April 10, 1777, *Laws of N.H.*, IV, 88–92; March, 1777, *R.I. Col. Rec.*, VIII, 183–185; May, 1777, *Conn. State Rec.*, I, 230–231.

[46] *Providence Gazette*, June 21, 1777.

were in complete sympathy with these sentiments, on June 27 a joint committee of the Massachusetts Council and House of Representatives reported a motion for the calling of an interstate convention, including delegates from New Hampshire, Massachusetts, Rhode Island, Connecticut, and New York, to meet at Springfield on July 30 to consider such interstate problems as currency depreciation and monopoly.[47] The Springfield convention resolved on August 4 that the acts against monopoly and oppression, being "attended with inconveniences," be repealed "so far as they relate to affixing the prices at which the articles therein enumerated shall be sold, and creating penalties for not observing the same." Severe penalties were urged for engrossers and profiteers.[48] As a matter of fact the states outdid the Springfield proposals and repealed the entire act, including, generally, restrictions upon engrossers and public auctions as well as price and wage controls.[49] This ended direct regulation of prices and wages by the central government in Massachusetts, although further legislation regulating engrossing and monopolizing, establishing embargoes, and restricting public auctions was passed from time to time during the Revolution. One of the methods of dealing with engrossers and profiteers adopted in Connecticut was to empower the town selectmen acting as assessors to increase their assessment by an additional £50 minimum—a crude form of war profits tax.[50]

The New Haven Convention. In the face of widespread popular support of such measures at the beginning of the war the Continental Congress had refused by a close vote to endorse the original Providence plan; but in November, 1777, after the New Englanders had found it expedient to scuttle the price and wage codes, it came out with a recommendation for a broad scheme of price and wage regulation. A call was issued for three interstate conventions: (1) for South Carolina and Georgia to meet at Charleston on February 15; (2) for North Carolina, Virginia, and Maryland to meet at Fredericksburg, Va., on January 15; and (3) for the remaining eight northern states to meet on the latter date at New Haven "to regulate and ascertain the price of labour, manufacturing, internal produce" and imported commodities, and also to

---

[47] *Mass. Acts and Resolves*, V, 812, 813.　　　[48] *Conn. State Rec.*, I, 599–606.

[49] *Mass. Acts and Resolves*, V, 733–734; *Laws of N.H.*, IV, 126; *Conn. State Rec.*, I, 366. In accord with the Springfield resolutions Massachusetts, by a resolve of Sept. 29, 1777, empowered the selectmen to call meetings of the town voters to provide for supplying the families of non-commissioned officers and privates in the Continental army with provisions at the rates set in the repealed act to prevent monopoly and oppression. *Mass. Acts and Resolves*, V, 812.

[50] "And others in like proportion according to their gains." *Conn. State Rec.*, I, 365, 366. See also *Mass. Acts and Resolves*, V, 924.

determine innkeepers' tariffs.[51] Despite the demonstrated futility of such legislation in the face of unsound fiscal policies, some prominent members of Congress, notably Richard Henry Lee, were optimistic about regulation and were not easily swayed by economic theories or theorists. Thus, Lee wrote Sam Adams, another warm advocate of regulation, on November 23:

I know my friend Mr. John Adams will say the regulation prices wont do. I agree it will not singly answer, and I know that Taxation with Oeconomy are the radical cures. But I also know that the best Physicians sometimes attend to Symptoms, apply palliatives and under favor of the Truce thus obtained, introduce cause removing medicines. Let us for a moment check the enormity of the evil by this method, whilst the other more sure, but more slow methods secure us against a return of the mischief. The middle and southern States (particularly the insatiable avarice of Pennsylvania) having refused to join in the plan formerly, rendered the experiment on your part inconclusive and partial; therefore I do not think Mr. Adams's argument drawn from that trial quite decisive against the Measure. I incline to think that the necessity of the case will now procure its adoption universally, and then we shall see what great things may be effected by common consent. The American conduct has already shattered and overset the conclusions of the best Theorists, and I hope this will be another instance.[52]

The New Haven meeting, the only one of the three actually held, resulted in the addition of a group of the Middle states to the numbers enacting wage and price codes. The New Haven convention went on record excoriating engrossers as enemies of the cause and not unlike "the man who, zealously professing Christianity, lives in continued practice of the breach of its precepts." Conceding that in the long run the reduction of the circulating medium and the meeting of expenditures through adequate taxation and loans were the essential remedies, it vigorously defended price regulations as founded in necessity, rhetorically asking:

Why do we complain of a partial infringement of liberty manifestly tending to the preservation of the whole? Must the lunatick run uncontrouled to the destruction of himself and neighbours merely because he is under the operation of medicines which may in time work his cure? and indeed without the use of those medicines will the confinement cure him? Must we be suffered to continue the exaction of such high prices to the destruction of the common

[51] *J. Continental Cong.*, IX, 956; *Mass. Acts and Resolves*, V, 1012; Papers of the Continental Cong., No. 19, III, fols. 155–163.
[52] Samuel Adams Papers, N.Y. Pub. Lib.; *Letters of Richard Henry Lee*, ed. J. C. Ballagh (New York, 1911–14), I, 353.

cause, and of ourselves with it, merely because the reduction of the quantity of our currency may in time redress the evil; and because any other method may be complained of as an infringement of liberty?

The commissioners observed that their wage and price schedules were "much higher than anyone will suppose they ought to be." As to labor, the New Haven meeting set up the following schedule: (1) labor of farmers, mechanics, "and others" at rates not exceeding 75 per cent advance over those obtaining in the several states in 1774; (2) teaming and all land transportation not to exceed the rate of five twelfths of a continental dollar for the carriage of 2,000 "neat weight per mile, including all expences attending the same." Manufactures and domestic produce were likewise allowed a 75 per cent advance over 1774; trades were allowed 25 per cent increases, with additions for cost of transportation; and innholders were allowed not more than 50 per cent advance on liquors, and for other articles of entertainment, refreshment, or forage not more than 75 per cent over the 1774 prices. In setting prices for the enumerated commodities, variations were made on the basis of three zones: (1) New Hampshire; (2) Massachusetts and Rhode Island; (3) Connecticut, New York, New Jersey, and Pennsylvania, although throughout the constituent states one price was to obtain for such manufactured products as tanned leather, shoes, iron, steel, and a few other articles. The idea of price and wage differentials thus clearly antedates the New Deal program. As Delaware did not send a delegate, the convention at its closing session on January 31, 1778, transmitted a copy of the proceedings and noted in a covering communication that, while they had "omitted to regulate the prices of labour, etc. for your State," they did not doubt but that from her "zealous attachment to the common cause similar measures would be immediately adopted by her." [53]

The resolves of the New Haven convention met a mingled reception. New Hampshire, Massachusetts, and Rhode Island took no action. In Massachusetts it was claimed that the public was sharply divided on the program,[54] and her two neighbors deferred to her leadership.[55] Governor Trumbull of Connecticut cautioned the legislature that "if we

[53] Lib. of Cong. transcript of the journal of the New Haven convention; *Conn. State Rec.*, I, 607–620; S. E. Baldwin, "The New Haven Convention of 1778," New Haven Hist. Soc., *Papers*, III, 33–62; *Mass. Acts and Resolves*, V, 1013–1015.

[54] *Mass. Acts and Resolves*, V, 1016, 1017. The inhabitants of Boston had come out strongly for a continuation of regulation and had urged that farm labor be reimbursed at the previously prevailing rate of a bushel of corn for a day's work.

[55] Henry Phillips, Jr., *Historical Sketches of the Paper Currency of the American Colonies* (Roxbury, Mass., 1865–66), II, 243; Sumner, *Financier and Finances of the Amer. Revol.*, I, 66.

affix a low price to provisions and articles of importation, we shall find that the Farmer will cease to till the ground for more than is necessary for his own subsistence, and the merchant to risque his fortune on a small and precarious prospect of gain." [56] Nonetheless the Connecticut General Assembly incorporated the New Haven recommendations in its enactments, specifically authorizing the selectmen to determine such wages of labor, prices of commodities, and charges of innholders as were not specifically enumerated. The act further provided that no resident of the state could sue in law or equity before taking oath that he had not willingly "received or contracted to receive for any labour done or article sold" more than the rate fixed by this law. Statutes were also passed in New York, New Jersey, and Pennsylvania establishing rates of wages and prices in close conformity to the New Haven proposals. [57]

Opponents of regulation in Congress had seen nothing in the recent course of events to shake them in their opposition. John Witherspoon, writing at the end of January, expressed the view that the New Haven scheme was "impracticable and absurd," as "fixing prices by Law never had nor ever will have any Effect but stopping Commerce and making Things scarce and dear." [58] The regulating act was the Achan, troubler of Israel, Oliver Wolcott wrote his wife, and stated that "no Regard is paid to any Act of this Kind in this State [Pennsylvania]. No such Act to the Southward of it Exists nor ever will." [59] On the other hand, Eliphalet Dyer, in justifying the calling of the New Haven convention, attributed the price rise not to the large emissions of bills or the scarcity of goods but to "that corrupt, avaricious, unnatural, infectious Disease, which was spread'g thro every State, and which Nothing but extraordinary Remedies could check and Controul." [60]

When Thomas Cushing, president of the New Haven convention,

[56] Conn. State Arch., Revolutionary War, X.

[57] *Conn. State Rec.*, I, 524–528; *Conn. J.*, March 4, 1778. Copies of this act were ordered to be sent to the legislature of the constituent states. *Ibid.*, p. 536. 1 *Laws of N.Y.*, 1st sess., c. 34; *N.J. Laws* (Wilson ed.), p. 34; *N.J. Arch.*, 2d ser., I, 519; *Pa. Stat. at Large*, IX, 236–238, 283–284. Reports of proceedings of the Poughkeepsie convention of Jan. 11, 1778, and of the General Assembly of Pennsylvania of Jan. 30, 1778, enacting this program, are in the Rhode Island State Archives. See also *Mins. of the Del. Council*, pp. 194 ff., *passim*. On May 19, 1778, Governor Trumbull wrote a letter rebuking Massachusetts for her failure to carry out "the United voice of these States," and to cooperate with New York, New Jersey, and Pennsylvania. In reply, the Massachusetts authorities asserted that, while the question was still undecided, they had been informed by the Purchasing Commissary of the Continental Army that, if the regulatory measures were renewed, it would become impossible to purchase provisions for the troops. *Mass. Acts and Resolves*, V, 1016–1018.

[58] Burnett, *Letters*, III, 57.

[59] *Ibid.*, III, 167, 168; Oliver Wolcott MSS, II, 51, Conn. Hist. Soc.   [60] *Ibid.*, III, 125, 126.

under date of January 30 sent a report of the proceedings to Congress, that body referred the matter to a committee. Witherspoon, leading opponent of regulation, was a member for a time but was later replaced. On April 8, the committee recommended that the proceedings be transmitted to the states from Maryland to Georgia inclusive, "with the Propriety of adopting similar Measures to be referred to their serious Consideration, and that it be recommended to Delaware, Pennsylvania and the States eastward thereof to suspend the Execution of the Plan of the Convention, for regulating Prices, until Congress shall inform them of the Proceedings of the Southern States on the same subject." [61] Action was delayed until June, when Congress decided to follow the second recommendation of the committee and to ignore the first on the ground that "it hath been found by Experience that Limitation upon the Prices of Commodities are not only ineffectual for the Purposes proposed, but likewise productive of very evil Consequences to the great Detriment of the public Service and grievous Oppression of Individuals." It thus reversed its action of the previous January and recommended that the states repeal such laws "limiting, regulating, or restraining the Price of any Article, Manufacture or Commodity." [62] Wages of labor were not specifically singled out, but were understood by the states to be included in the repeal recommendation. Those states that had enacted the New Haven schedule promptly repealed their statutes.[63]

Regulation by Town Convention. For the better part of a year no broad wage or price regulations were enacted by any state legislature. From this it might be inferred that the disapproval expressed by Congress of the sad experience with earlier measures had brought regulation into disrepute. However, as a matter of fact, through the instrumentality of town meetings and county and regional conventions, wage and price regulation was revived within the year with considerable éclat.[64] The catastrophic decline of paper currency was mainly responsible for the renewed activity. Notable in adopting such measures were the

[61] *J. Continental Cong.*, X, 172, 260, 322–324. The report, in the writing of Elbridge Gerry, is in the Papers of the Continental Cong., No. 24, f. 393.

[62] *Ibid.*, XI, 472, 569. The report, in the writing of Gouverneur Morris, is in the Papers of the Continental Cong., No. 19, VI, f. 123.

[63] Conn. State Arch., Revolutionary War, XIII, f. 126; *Session Laws, 1778*, p. 499; Pa. Mins. House of Rep., I, 211, which suspended the act in May. The Northern states were convinced that those to the south would never adopt these regulations. See letter of Connecticut delegates to Governor Trumbull, York, April 29, 1778, in Burnett, *Letters*, III, 202.

[64] One writer in the *Conn. J.*, under date of Oct. 14, 1778, maintained that prices ought to be fixed at what they were before the war and kept so until the conflict was over. See also Phillips, *Continental Paper Money*, p. 84.

towns of Massachusetts, which state actually passed for the remainder of the war no more legislation fixing wage or price levels.[65] On May 25, 1779, the town of Boston adopted the report of a committee enumerating the prices of some fifteen articles on a month-to-month basis.[66] A few weeks later a group of Boston merchants agreed at a public meeting to a scale of prices to be in force among themselves and to a further limitation of prices, after July 1 next ensuing, to levels which had prevailed on the first of May, provided other Massachusetts towns cooperated.[67] These resolves were promptly endorsed at a Watertown meeting, where a pledge was given that if the Boston prices remained constant both the farmers and the mechanics of Watertown would lower their prices in accord with the decline in foreign commodity rates. A committee was appointed to fix prices, and the meeting declared that persons selling their goods at excessive rates would be deemed "enemies of their country and cried as such by the town clerk for six months after every public meeting of the town." [68] Pursuant to a general endorsement, on the part of the town of Boston, of the merchants' price agreement, with specific instructions to seek the advice of other local committees as to the best measures to be adopted in the emergency, the Boston committee of correspondence called a convention to be held at Concord on July 14 to consider the regulation of the wages of labor and the prices of produce and manufactured articles. This call was widely endorsed.[69] At the July Convention at Concord some 140 Massachusetts towns from eight counties were present. By general agreement the convention set maximum prices for certain enumerated commodities (violators to have their names published in the newspapers as enemies of the country) and directed the towns to fix the wages of labor, the prices of innholders, teaming, manufactures, and goods "in Proportion to the rates of the Necessaries of Life, as stated in the above Regulations," cautioning them "to keep a watchful Eye over each other, that no Evasion or infringement of these Resolutions may escape Nature." [70] The convention's resolves were endorsed enthusiastically by town after town, which proceeded to set prices on nonenumerated arti-

---

[65] A number of towns, including Rehoboth, petitioned the legislature at this time for a new price regulation law, but, although the committee considering the matter reported favorably, the legislature remained adamant. *Mass. Acts and Resolves*, V, 1019, 1243.

[66] *Ind. Chron.*, June 10, 1779. A few weeks later Mendon set prices. *Continental J.*, July 1, 1779.

[67] *Ind. Chron.*, June 24; *Boston Gazette*, June 21; *Massachusetts Spy*, July 1, 1779.

[68] *Watertown Rec.*, IV, Pt. VI, 203–204.

[69] *Continental J.*, July 15, 1779 (Roxbury); *Records of the Town of Plymouth, 1636–1783* (3 vols., Plymouth, 1889–1903), III, 375; *Watertown Rec.*, IV, Pt. VI, 206.

[70] *Boston Gazette*, Aug. 2, 1779.

cles and appointed committees to enforce price regulations.[71] At least seventy-five towns ratified the convention.[72] To avoid great disparities in labor and price scales, counties also held regulating conventions. As regards wages, there were some differences in the prevailing scales, especially in the skilled crafts. Common labor generally received £3 per day, and skilled workers £4 in Falmouth, £3/18 in Boston, and £3/18 in Plymouth. Variations were noted also in wages for such enumerated trades as barbers, hatters, tanners, curriers, butchers, and tailors, and in certain labor services, such as carting [73] and horseshoeing.[74] These conventions sought to stabilize wages and prices within the counties and to iron out discrepancies wherever possible. Thus, the Worcester County convention of August 11, in which thirty-eight towns participated, set maximum wages for common labor at £2 4s. per diem during the best season; female labor was to receive a mere £2 a week, and mechanics and skilled workers were to be paid proportionately. A convention on August 31 of Middlesex and Suffolk County towns sought wage and price uniformity and recommended fixed prices even for such articles as drugs and medicines.[75]

In the face of the express disapproval of the Continental Congress and repeal by the state legislatures, wage- and price-fixing conventions were held not alone in Masschusetts but also in New Hampshire, Rhode Island, New York, New Jersey, Pennsylvania, and Delaware in order to check the rapid descent of the currency. The Providence action, taken on August 31, was in response to a resolve adopted at a convention of Rhode Island towns held at East Greenwich on August 10, parallel to the Concord convention in Massachusetts.[76] The wage code adopted is typical of New England at this time, but its sweeping enumerations and careful gradations are worthy of separate examination:

	per diem
Common laborers, "finding themselves"	48s.
Ship-carpenters, caulkers, masons	73s.
House-carpenters, ship-joiners, riggers	72s.
Blacksmiths, :os. per lb. "For shoeing a horse all round, 4l./10. For steeling and corking all round, 6l. For new setting all round 1l. 7s.	

---

[71] *Boston Gazette*, Aug. 9, 1779; for Hingham, see Col. Soc. of Mass., *Publications*, X, 116–119.

[72] See *Boston Gazette*, Aug. 16, 30, Sept. 6, 1779; *Watertown Rec.*, IV, Pt. 6, 206–210; *Mass. Spy*, Aug. 16, 1779; *Ind. Chron.*, Aug. 19, Sept. 16, 1779; *Boston Rec.*, XXVI, 80, 81; *Plymouth Town Rec.*, III, 379–381.

[73] Watertown, 18s.; Plymouth, 13s.　　　[74] Watertown, 5s.; Plymouth, 4s.; Boston, 6s.

[75] *Mass. Spy*, Aug. 19, 26, 1779; *Ind. Chron.*, Sept. 6, 9, 23, Oct. 14, 1779; *Boston Gazette*, Sept. 6, 1779; A. A. Lovell, *Worcester in the War of the Revolution* (Worcester, 1876), pp. 96–98.

[76] *Pa. Packet*, Sept. 2, 1779.

For a good ax well steeled, 6*l*. and other work in proportion.

Tanners, 18*s*. per pound for good sole leather and other leather in proportion.

Shoemakers. For best customers shoes 6*l*. 6*s*. per pair, and other work in proportion. Best boots 25*l*. per pair.

Printers, Physicians, Apothecaries, Blockmakers, Cabinetmakers, Pewterers, Rope-makers, Boat-builders, Tinmen, and Painters, shall reduce their prices Twenty per cent.

Leather-Dressers. For the best Deer's Leather breeches, 33*l*. and other work in proportion.

Hatters. For the best Beaver hats, 35*l*.; best castor ditto, 21*l*. Best Felt ditto, 4*l*.

Taylors. For making a plain suit of broadcloth cloaths, 17*l*. and other cloaths in proportion.

Card makers. For best wool-cards, made in this State, 39*l*. 12*l*. per doz. pair, and 72*s*. per single pair.

Glaziers. For setting glass and finding puttey not more than 4*s*. per square.

Innholders and Victuallers, shall reduce their prices for victualling and horse-keeping Twenty per cent.

Goldsmiths shall not take more than the weight of the plate they work, and sixteen times what they had for their labour in the year 1774.

Saddlers. For a good man's saddle, with a housing or saddle cloth, £43.

For a good man's bridle, 4*l*. 10*s*. and all other work in proportion.

Sail-makers. For working new duck 5*l*. 8*s*. per bolt. . . .

All other tradesmen and mechanics not before mentioned shall reduce their work and manufactures in average proportion with the above.[77]

While the scale for common labor was considerably lower than that adopted in Massachusetts as a result of the Concord convention, both common and skilled labor were allowed a wage level some fifteen times higher than that which had obtained in the beginning of 1777—eloquent testimony to the extent of currency depreciation.

Philadelphia had acted in the meantime. Mass meetings, parades, and handbills during May of 1779 announced the determination of the inhabitants to regulate prices. The action of a meeting held in the State House yard, at which a committee was appointed to fix a scale of prices, was referred to by Daniel of St. Thomas Jenifer as that of a "Mob . . . assembled to regulate prices." Members of Congress were alarmed. "What will be the issue God knows," said one at this time.[78] The com-

[77] *Amer. J. and Gen. Advertiser*, Sept. 2, 1779.
[78] *Ibid.*, IV, 232; *Md. Arch.*, XXI, 417. See also *Pa. Packet*, June 22, 26, 1779.

mittee published its scale on June 29, along with a refutation of the view that "trade will regulate itself." To do so, ran the argument, trade must not be "clogged with a disease." It favored action by similar committees in every state and county to the end that the prices obtained in 1774 might be multiplied by some certain number to be agreed upon by all in order to ascertain the regulated price.[79] The artillery company of Philadelphia promptly passed resolutions offering, if necessary, to support the committee with their arms.[80] In June, 1779, a price schedule was adopted at a town meeting in Lancaster and the same month a committee in Newcastle County, Delaware, took similar measures and adopted a resolution regarding wages couched in the following language:

Resolved also, That it be recommended to the good people of this county, not to give a higher price to labourers the ensuing harvest, than one bushel of wheat, or the value thereof as above stipulated, for two days reaping or mowing, or one day's cradling; nor to give the mechanicks higher prices than were current the first day of May last.[81]

One Albany correspondent, writing in June, 1779, reported that "all our districts have chosen Committees, and are regulating the prices of country produce." [82] During the summer, meetings were held in upstate New York, notably in Albany, Orange, and Dutchess counties, to consider the problem of depreciation, profiteering, and hoarding; and specific measures were adopted by the Schenectady committee of correspondence.[83] The Dutchess County committees, meeting at Poughkeepsie on August 14, restricted the increase of prices of imported articles as follows: "dry goods at 12½% retale, to be added to the first cost on the original invoice, and the cost of transportation." It was further resolved "that it be recommended to the mechanicks, labourers and others, to regulate their prices according to the above price." [84] During the summer also the Essex County, New Jersey, committee fixed rates for transportation and wholesale and retail prices for numerous commodities and, in accordance with instructions from the county, ruled

---

[79] *Pa. Packet*, June 29, 1779. For the pro-regulation arguments of "Philodemus" at this time see *ibid.*, June 19, 1779.

[80] *Ibid.*, May 27, June 29, July 1, 1779; A. McF. Davis, "Limitation of Prices in Massachusetts, 1776–79," Col. Soc. of Mass., *Publications*, X, 12, 13; Sumner, *Financier and Finances of the Am. Rev.*, I, 72, 73; Bolles, *Financial Hist. of the U.S.*, pp. 162, 163.

[81] *Pa. Packet*, July 3, 1779.   [82] *Ibid.*, June 29, 1779.

[83] *N.Y.J.*, July 19, 26, Aug. 2, 16, 1779; *Mins. Schenectady Comm. Corr.*, II, 1146–48, 1157, 1158; *Pa. Packet*, June 20, 1779. For arguments at this time urging limitation and trade regulation, see *N.Y.J.*, April 26, Oct. 11, 1779.

[84] *N.Y.J.*, Aug. 16, 1779.

that "not more than fifteen for one from the price of 1774, ought to be demanded or given" for labor, produce, and manufactures, "which it is expected will very soon be reduced." [85] On the other hand, a meeting of the General Committee of Burlington County on July 21, 1779, set the wages of common labor for the month of August at £2 10s., and provided that weavers, tailors, carpenters, and "such other mechanicks as do not work their own stuff" were to have sixteen times the prevailing rates of wages of the year 1774.[86]

This spontaneous convention activity was viewed with apprehension by opponents of regulation in Congress, among them William Ellery, who condemned such "unnatural restraints" which "eventually do no good," at the same time conceding that only through universal adoption of regulation could its efficacy be fairly tested.[87] Meriwether Smith, writing to Thomas Jefferson in the summer of 1779, expressed alarm at the growth of the activities of local committees: "The most pernicious Effect will flow from the establishment of those Bodies." He quoted Gerard as charging that they were in fact "instruments in the Hands of designing Men." [88]

The Concord convention, resuming sessions in October, adopted a new schedule of wages and prices reflecting further the steady rise in the premium of gold and silver and also the trend toward increasing by many times the number of enumerated commodities.[89] The towns were authorized to fix the wages of common labor and mechanics and the rates of innkeepers. Immediate response to the second convention program was cordial,[90] but considered reflection led to the abandonment of serious attempts to enforce the code. A Boston committee reported to its town meeting that they had found it impracticable to fix the prices of goods which they had been requested to do.[91] Shortly thereafter the publishers of the five Boston newspapers announced that they were forced to raise the price of their papers, as regulation had been "of no effect for them to stem the tide of avarice alone." [92] A published observation commented on "the various evasions by which the resolves of the late Convention . . . which with apparent cheerfulness and unanimity

[85] *N.J.J.*, July 20, 1779.

[86] Piece-work rates were also set for various items and prices laid down for various commodities. Violators of the schedules would be "held up to the publick in a manner adequate to their offence." *N.J. Arch.*, 2d ser., III, 538–540. Morris County also set up a regulatory committee. *N.Y. Gazette and Weekly Mercury*, August 2, 1779.

[87] To John Langdon, York, March 2, 1778. Burnett, *Letters*, III, 105.

[88] *Ibid.*, IV, 348 (July 26, 1779).   [89] *Mass. Spy*, Nov. 5, 1779.

[90] *Boston Gazette*, Oct. 25; *Ind. Chron.*, Oct. 21, 1779; *Boston Town Rec.*, XXVI, 98, 99.

[91] *Boston Town Rec.*, XXVI, 100, 101.   [92] *Ind. Chron.*, Nov. 25, 1779.

were adopted by their constituents, have in many instances failed of their desired effect." [93] In New Jersey, voluntary associations were proposed as a substitute for penal laws which, one proponent conceded, had failed to restrain "exorbitant prices." [94] In July the master tanners, curriers, and cordwainers met and denounced the action of the price-regulation committee as contrary to free trade principles. They threatened that, if price regulation were to be continued, they would shut their shops and discharge their journeymen.[95]

But the cause of regulation was not permitted to die. "Crito," writing in the *New Jersey Gazette,* June 16, 1779, urged joint action on the part of New York, New Jersey, and Pennsylvania to regulate wages and prices. In October, 1779, New Jersey and New York strongly urged upon Congress a renewed program of regulation. New Jersey had never repealed her regulatory act, but merely suspended it until other states adopted similar programs, for, in the words of Woodbury Langdon, it was deemed "very impolitic for any particular state to regulate Prices unless it becomes general throughout the United States." [96] On the twentieth of October commissioners from the New England states and New York met at Hartford and defended the necessity of regulation,

especially when it is considered that the engrosser, monopolizer, opulent farmer and trader, will be induced, and it will be in their power (unless restricted) to encrease the price of the articles they have on hand in proportion to the encrease of their taxes, which will not only defeat the end and the purpose of taxation, oblige Congress to make further emissions, or the army be left destitute, but too great a burden of the taxes will be cast on the poor and middling farmer, and will produce a further depreciation of our currency, which if not prevented may soon end in very unhappy effects.

It was the sense of the meeting that price limitation would have a tendency to prevent further depreciation of the currency, and that "to render such limitation permanent and salutary" all the states, or at least "as far westward as Virginia," should accede to the program. To this end it urged that a convention of the Northern and Middle states and Maryland and Virginia be held in Philadelphia in January, 1780. In the light of price-fixing action taken by conventions in New Hampshire, Massa-

[93] *Boston Gazette,* Oct. 25, 1779.

[94] *N.J.J.,* June 20, 1779. However, "A Tradesman of New Jersey" had only a short time before urged Congressional action. *N.J. Arch.,* 2d ser., III, 389–391.

[95] *Pa. Packet,* July 15, 1779.

[96] *N.J. Exec. Corr.,* pp. 195–197; Burnett, *Letters,* IV, 485, 495; MS, R.I. Archives, Letters to the Governors, 1779–80, f. 19; W. R. Staples, *Rhode Island in the Continental Congress* (Providence, 1870), pp. 253, 254.

chusetts, and Rhode Island, the remaining constituent states—Connecticut and New York—were urged to adopt similar measures.[97] If additional prompting were needed, it was provided by Congress, which considered the report of the Hartford meeting, transmitted by its president, Stephen Hopkins, and promptly resolved that a general limitation be enacted throughout the states, whereby wages and prices for farming and common labor, tradesmen and mechanics, water and land carriage, and domestic produce were "not to exceed twenty-fold of the prices current through the various seasons of the year 1774." [98] The Hartford proceedings were specifically endorsed and recommended to the nonparticipant states.[99] In justification of this recommendation, Congress maintained that the advance of prices was due to "unprincipled and disaffected people"—a view not unlike that of President Hoover, who attributed the stock market débacle after 1929 to bear raids rather than to fundamental economic causes. The argument *ad hominem* is always good politics, if unsound economic thinking. This view was held by Congress as late as January, 1780.[100] As to the value of this latest resolve, some members of Congress reserved judgment. Samuel Huntington felt that only time and experience would "bring all men to agree in Judgment" as to the wisdom of this plan.[101] Allen Jones, who entered Congress a few weeks later, was unenthusiastic and convinced that the plan would not be generally adopted.[102]

In response to the joint urgings of the Hartford convention and Congress, Connecticut and New York took prompt action. At the January session, 1780, Connecticut passed "An act for a general limitation of prices, to prevent the withholding from sale the necessaries of life." [103] This was endorsed: "To lie unpublished till further order from the Governor," who was to so order on receiving word that the other New England states and New York had passed similar acts of limitation agreeable to the Congressional resolves. But this statute was neither printed nor recorded. New York, on February 26, 1780, passed "An act for a general limitation of prices, and to prevent engrossing and with-

[97] *Conn. State Rec.*, II, 566–569. "There is not a doubt but the proposition will be cheerfully acceded to by this state." *N.Y.J.*, Nov. 30, 1779.

[98] *Mass. Acts and Resolves*, V, 1261, 1262; *Conn. State Rec.*, II, 562, 563; *N.C. State Rec.*, XIV, 214; Burnett, *Letters*, IV, 514, 519, 522; *J. Continental Cong.*, XV, 1289.

[99] Burnett, *Letters*, IV, 542.

[100] *J. Continental Cong.*, XVI, 57–59. See also *Boston Gazette*, April 6, 1778, for a similar view, charging depreciation of the currency to avarice.

[101] Burnett, *Letters*, IV, 527; V, 1.   [102] *Ibid.*, IV, 548.

[103] Conn. State Arch., Revolutionary War, XVIII, f. 71; *N.Y.J.*, April 10, 1780.

holding within this State." [104] Under this act a penalty of treble the value or price of the services or commodities could be exacted, but actually the "wages of tradesmen and mechanics," though mentioned, were not ascertained in the statute, which dealt primarily with commodities. This act was not to be effective until twenty days after proclamation by the governor stating that information had come to him that Massachusetts, Connecticut, and Pennsylvania had passed laws for the like purpose. New Jersey likewise fell into line, and in Maryland a bill limiting prices was proposed, but never enacted.[105]

The drama of futility was drawing to a close. In its instructions to delegates to the final price-fixing convention the Massachusetts General Court advised them to consider the advantages of such a plan and to give "equal attention" to the question of "the practicability of its being carried into execution," being careful to point out that previous efforts had "Shut up our Granaries, discouraged Husbandry and Commerce and starved our Sea Ports," creating "such stagnation of Business and such a withholding of articles as has obliged the People to give up its measure or submit to starving." [106] James Lovell, in a letter to Sam Adams, dated January 28, 1780, prophesied just what would take place. "I do not know," he wrote, "but the regulating Convention may again get effectively together, but if they do, I suspect the Consequences will not only be to let *us* and *themselves* down easily." [107]

At the final Philadelphia session in February, 1780, New York and Virginia did not attend, although the former gave pledges that she would carry into effect a general plan for regulating prices. Both states were requested to appoint commissioners, a committee was set up to propose a general plan for price limitation and to report back, and the convention adjourned to the fourth day of April, but never appears to have reassembled.[108] On February 15 the Connecticut delegates wrote Governor Trumbull: "We hope that some Measures will be soon adopted for introducing a stable Medium of Trade that will render a limitation of prices unnecessary." [109] Such measures were soon taken by Congress, which apparently did not subscribe to the optimistic view of the North Carolina delegates that, even among the affluent, prices would "find limits beyond which they cannot go, and Commerce will so regulate itself that even paper money will find a certain fixed value as a general

[104] *Laws of N.Y.*, 3d sess., c. 43.
[105] Burnett, *Letters*, IV, 550; V, 4, 6.
[106] *Mass. Acts and Resolves*, V, 1263.
[107] Samuel Adams Papers, N.Y. Pub. Lib.
[108] Mass. Hist. Soc., *Coll.*, 7th ser., III, 15; *Conn. State Rec.*, II, 577-579; Staples, *Rhode Island in the Continental Congress*, p. 272; Burnett, *Letters*, V, 16, 23, 27.
[109] Burnett, *Letters*, V, 36.

representative of Industry." [110] The action of Congress on March 18 fixing the value of continental bills in circulation at not more than one-fortieth of their denominational value and requesting the states to call in and destroy their bills in circulation did not end the price crisis at once. For some time thereafter continental bills still in circulation continued to depreciate, and the view of Davis that "prices would now take care of themselves and be governed by natural laws" [111] is by no means borne out by the facts.

Throughout the price crisis in the winter of 1780 one member of Congress, John Armstrong, stubbornly maintained his advocacy of regulation in the face of increasing opposition. Regulation, he urged, was founded in critical necessity. "The Hacknied Maxim, that Trade must always Regulate itself, Is in our situation as impolitick as it is arrogant and absurd, and patience but scarcely restrains from bestowing upon it the severer epithets due to a possession So very ill-timed." The blockade, speculation, and hoarding forced this exception to the "Mercantile rule." Opposition was due in good part, according to Armstrong, to "an idle refinement of civil rights and lethargic timidity." [112]

Regional meetings held subsequent to the Philadelphia fiasco demonstrate that Armstrong's views were still popular. In February, 1780, Nathanael Greene wrote Washington that the people did not object to a limitation of prices, but were insistent that it should not be binding upon them until in effect throughout the states. "People will withhold their services in this State," he asserted, "as long as they receive a less compensation than their neighbours." [113] On the other hand, some students of finance were distinctly hostile. Pelatiah Webster, whose first *Essay on Free Trade and Finance,* published in July, 1779, had wide influence, clearly understood the relation between paper money and the price structure and likened the "utmost effect" of these laws to "that of water sprinkled on a blacksmith's forge, which indeed deadens the flame for a moment, but never fails to increase the heat and force of the internal fire." [114]

[110] Burnett, *Letters,* V, 57 (Feb. 29, 1780).

[111] Col. Soc. of Mass., *Publications,* X, 20; Harlow, "Revol. Finance," *Amer. Hist. Rev.,* XXXV, 60.

[112] Burnett, *Letters,* IV, 490; V, 8, 13, 14, 38, 76–78; Reed MSS, lib. VI, and Gates MSS, lib. XVI, N.Y. Hist. Soc.

[113] Sparks, *Corr. of Amer. Revol.,* II, 393, 394.

[114] *Political Essays on the Nature and Operation of Money, Public Finances, and Other Subjects* (Philadelphia, 1791), pp. 11–18, 128n., 129, 132. Alden Bradford, *History of Massachusetts, 1775–89* (3 vols., Boston, 1822–29), II, 172, 173, puts the blame for the failure of this "salutary" law upon the "many citizens of Massachusetts" who disregarded it and upon the officers who were remiss in enforcement. See also W. B. Reed, *Life and Correspondence of Joseph Reed*

Such arguments were rooted in laissez faire reasoning. Occasionally, however, resort was had to constitutional principles. For example, one writer as early as May, 1777, maintained that the regulating of price by penal statute "always has and ever will be impracticable in a free country, because no law can be framed to limit a man in the purchase or disposal of property, but what must infringe those principles of liberty for which we are gloriously fighting." [115] Again in August, 1779, a group of Philadelphians memorialized the city for repeal of regulation, emphasizing the argument that limitation violated property rights by compelling a person to accept less in exchange for his goods than he could obtain in an uncontrolled market and therefore operated as a class tax. In reply, a committee of thirteen defended limitation upon historical grounds, citing instances in the past, such as usury laws and limitations of porters' and carriers' charges and of ferry rates, among other examples, and urging the parallel to general trade prices on the ground that restraints must be imposed to prevent a favored group from taking unjust advantage of the necessity of the public. In conclusion, the committee asserted: "We have had the experience of four years without limitation or regulations; the consequence of which had very nearly been the total ruin of the currency and resting it here, we prefer this single case to all the arguments that can be produced against it." In 1783 the Pennsylvania Council of Censors declared that such regulations constituted "invasions of the right of property." [116]

The very same men who viewed wage and price controls as an invasion of property rights also expressed concern over the tendency of states to act in combination. Later New England conventions in 1780 and 1781, while not attempting to enforce further price codes, did make important recommendations of an economic nature and favored stronger Federal government.[117] The Articles of Confederation con-

(Philadelphia, 1847), II, 140; Franklin, *Writings* (Smyth ed.), IV, 468–471. Cf. also the interesting debate between "Honestus" and "True Patriot." *N.J. Gazette,* Dec. 8, 1779; March 29, 1780. See also *ibid.,* March 1, 17, 1780. "Eumenes" made a contribution to the confusion, pointing out that periodic revisions of the regulatory schedules with the idea of gradual price reductions would actually curb trade and manufactures and deter the farmer from producing more than his immediate needs. *N.Y.J.,* Dec. 21, 1779.

[115] *Conn. Courant,* May 12, 1777.

[116] *Pa. Packet,* Aug. 10, 1779; *Proceedings of the Constitutional Conventions of 1776 and 1790* (Harrisburg, 1825), pp. 86, 87; R. C. Bull, "The Constitutional Significance of Early Pennsylvania Price-fixing Legislation," *Temple Law Quarterly,* XI, 327–329. Historical arguments supporting regulation were also advanced in the 19th century in Munn v. Illinois, 94 U.S. 113 (1876), where opponents of regulation supported their case on common law grounds.

[117] "Doings of the Committee of the States of New Hampshire, Massachusetts, and Connecticut, assembled at Boston, August, 1780, to consider the Affairs relating to the War," Force transcripts. Vol. XIV, Library of Congress; *R.I. Col. Rec.,* IX, 153, 161. For the Hartford meeting of Nov., 1780, see Conn. State Arch., Revolutionary War, Vol. XIX, fols. 13, 250, 282, 285.

tained a prohibition of such combinations between states, and Hamilton and Madison were clearly opposed.[118] Nevertheless, the convention idea survived within the states, even though the original objectives were no longer determining. Local conventions within the counties continued to deal with economic and social grievances in such states as Massachusetts, and Shays's rebellion can trace its lineage to a long line of county meetings starting in Revolutionary times. At the same time, the road for the Constitutional Convention of 1787 was actually paved by the interstate conventions on economic affairs, most notable being the last at Annapolis. From the failure of these experiments with economic controls, two consequences followed: (1) the creation of a strong Federal government; and (2) the crystallization of sentiment among members of the Convention in favor of laissez faire policies in the internal economic life of the nation.

Before considering the extent to which the wages and price schedules were actually enforced by the courts or other agencies, it should be borne in mind that, along with the regulatory code, there was enacted during the Revolution in virtually every state extensive legislation against forestalling, engrossing, and regrating, against selling for a lower price in specie than in paper money, against refusing to accept paper currency, imposing restrictions upon public auctions, and establishing embargoes on exports.[119] Such measures, though instigated at the time of the nonimportation agreements,[120] were in harmony with the general course of colonial legislation. In some communities these "violators" were still subject to prosecution considerably after the close of the war.[121] Some of these war measures actually specified the rate of profit considered legitimate for a licensed trader.[122] Monopolizers

[118] *Madison Papers*, I, 429; Sumner, *op. cit.*, I, 93.

[119] See, for example, act of Nov. 27, 1777, *Laws of N.H.*, IV, 115 (repealed May 23, 1778); act of Jan. 2, 1778, *ibid.*, IV, 139; act of April 3, 1779, *ibid.*, IV, 209; act of June 23, 1779, *ibid.*, IV, 211. *Mass. Acts and Resolves*, V, 483 (1775–76, c. 18, sec. 5), 924, 1073, 1114 (1779, repealed 1780, p. 1395). *R.I. Col. Rec.*, IX, 92 (June, 1780). Act of Dec. 11, 1777, Wilson, *Acts of N.J. Ass.*, p. 34; act of June 22, 1778, *ibid.*, p. 54; act of Oct. 7, 1778, *ibid.*, p. 58; act of Dec. 3, 1778, *ibid.*, p. 62; act of Dec. 21, 1779, *ibid.*, p. 104. Act of Jan. 2, 1778, *Pa. Stat. at Large*, XII, 177; act of April 1, 1778, *ibid.*, IX, 245–247; act of April 5, 1779, *ibid.*, IX, 387; act of Oct. 8, 1779 (repealed March 22, 1780), *ibid.*, IX, 421; act of March 22, 1780, *ibid.*, X, 175. Act of Oct., 1777, carefully defining forestallers, regrators, and engrossers, Hening, IX, 382–384; act of Oct., 1778, *ibid.*, pp. 581, 584; act of Oct., 1779, *ibid.*, X, 157; act of May, 1781, *ibid.*, X, 425. Proclamation of Sept. 5, 1777, *N.C. Gazette*, Sept. 5, 1777; of Feb. 1, 1778, *ibid.*, Feb. 6, 1778. Acts of 1777, *Gazette of the State of S.C.*, April 28, Sept. 15, Nov. 12, Dec. 15, 1777. Act of 1780, S.C. Journal of the House of Representatives, Vol. CV, f. 160; *Gazette of the State of S.C.*, Feb. 9, 1780. See also the proposal of Richard Adams in *VMH*, V, 293 (1778). Engrossing and kindred activities were branded as "distressing and ruinous to the industrious poor, and most heinously criminal." *Pa. Col. Rec.*, XI, 671.

[120] *S.C. Gazette*, Oct. 3, 1774. [121] *Columbian Herald* (S.C.), Sept. 21, 1786.

[122] See, e.g., act of 1780, *N.C. State Rec.*, XXIV, 318; repealed, p. 354.

and forestallers were universally reprobated as creating "artificial scarcities and taking advantage of people's necessities." In the north in the early years of the war this legislation was largely inspired by resentment on the part of urban groups against profiteering by farmers and middlemen.[123] In the south hostility was manifest early in the struggle against merchant profiteers, many of whom were felt to be loyalist in sympathy.[124]

ENFORCEMENT OF ECONOMIC CONTROLS

THE PRICE REGULATION and antimonopolizing statutes were closely related. Both often specifically empowered courts of record and local justices to punish violators. But instances of enforcement by the courts are rare. Pennsylvania's experience appears exceptional. In March, 1780, the legislature of that state empowered the courts of quarter sessions to fix the "price of common labor then current" in their respective counties. This rate was to determine the amount of fines payable under that act for neglect of or absence from militia duty.[1] In accordance with this statute the June session of the Philadelphia quarter sessions [2] fixed wages as follows:

Pursuant to the Directions of an Act of the General Assembly of the Commonwealth of Pennsylvania, passed at Philadelphia the twentieth Day of March last past, entitled "An Act for the Regulation of the Militia of the Commonwealth of Pennsylvania," We the Subscribers, being a Majority of the Justices attending at the Court of General Quarter Sessions of the Peace now held at Philadelphia for the County aforesaid, have this Day ascertained and do hereby fix and determine the Average Price of Common Labour at this Time by the Day to be Twenty Dollars within the said County. Witness our Hand and Seal at Philadelphia this sixth Day of June Anno Domini 1780.

Isaac Howell [LS]	John Ord [LS]
William Rush [LS]	And^w Knox [LS]
Seth Quec [LS]	Willm McMullan [LS]
Benjamin Paschall [LS]	David Kennedy [LS]

[123] See V. L. Johnson, *The Administration of the American Commissariat during the Revolutionary War* (Philadelphia, 1941), pp. 127, 143, 151.
[124] See the debate between "A Carolina Planter" and a "Merchant," *N.C. Gazette*, Dec. 12, 26, 1777. It was only natural that "monopolizers" should bitterly oppose regulation. See G. H. Ryden, ed., *Letters to and from Caesar Rodney, 1756-1784* (Philadelphia, 1933), p. 303 (May 22, 1779).
The British military authorities enforced similar regulations against forestalling in the occupied cities. HMC, *Rep.*, LIX, Pt. I, 186 (1778). A proclamation prohibiting the export of wheat was necessary in Quebec in 1781 owing to the activities of engrossers of wheat and flour. *A.P.C. Col., Unbound Papers*, VI, No. 1001, p. 582.
[1] *Pa. Stat. at Large*, X, 144-173 (March 20, 1780).   [2] Lib. 1773-80.

During the same month the Northampton quarter sessions set the average daily wage of common labor at $17,[3] and the Bucks County justices set wages at $24.[4] In August the Lancaster quarter sessions, under authority of the same act, fixed the "price of common labor" at "ten pounds per day to the end of next Sessions."[5] In September the Philadelphia quarter sessions levied the wages of labor at the June rate.[6] Instances of the imposition of penalties by the courts for violations of wage assessments in these four Pennsylvania counties have not been found in the court records, and these assessments appear to have been in effect merely to determine military penalties rather than to provide a maximum scale for laborers. No such wage assessments appear to have been levied in the other Pennsylvania quarter sessions courts.[7] By the end of September, 1780, the legislature found that the experience with assessing wages had proved "inconvenient and unequal," and provided henceforth that the average daily price of common labor should be ascertained by the general assembly for purposes of assessing fines for absence from the militia.[8]

Despite the paucity of court convictions for violations of price and wage schedules, in a number of jurisdictions prosecutions were brought in this period under statutes imposing penalties for "selling for hard money,"[9] for forestalling,[10] and for regrating.[11] When in the April term, 1778, George Mitchell and three others entered an appeal in the Essex County, N.J., quarter sessions court "from Judgments given against them on the regulating Law," the court, doubtful of the pro-

---

[3] Northampton Q.S. (June session, 1780).   [4] Bucks Q.S., lib. 1754–82, f. 627.

[5] Lancaster Road and Sessions Docket, No. 5, 1776–82 (Aug. session, 1780).

[6] Philadelphia Q.S., lib. 1773–80 (Sept. session, 1780).

[7] Dockets at West Chester, York, Reading, and Carlisle for this period give no hint of such activity.

[8] *Pa. Stat. at Large*, X, 225–227 (Sept. 22, 1780).

[9] Comm. v. Stapler, April, 1780, verdict: not guilty. Same v. Elizabeth Felfard, Philadelphia Q.S., 1773–80. For prosecutions for attempting to depreciate state or Federal bills of credit, see Hanks's case, Windham, Conn., Co. Court Rec., 1777–82, f. 15 (1777); Fitch's case, Conn. Superior Court Rec., lib. XIX (1778).

[10] The New Jersey courts took seriously the injunction to enforce this legislation strictly. *N.J. Arch.*, 2d ser., V, 25 (1778). State v. Nitingale, Gloucester Co., N.J., Q.S. and C.P., lib. 1771–82 (Dec., 1780), verdict: guilty, fined £3 hard money. Comm. v. Williams, Philadelphia Q.S., lib. 1779–82 (July, 1780), verdict: not guilty. The peak of such prosecutions occurred in the Morris Co., N.J., quarter sessions. For the year 1780 the docket reveals 18 indictments for forestalling. In two cases the juries returned not guilty verdicts; in one the prisoner was convicted and fined £50. In the remainder the accused were apparently never brought to trial. There were two indictments returned in 1781, both of which were quashed. Morris Q.S. and C.P., lib. 1778–82, fols. 78, 79, 81, 91, 93, 101, 130 (1780), 144, 145 (1781).

[11] State v. McCable, Same v. Barnes, Queen Ann, Md., lib. 1771–80 (June, 1779), both fined 7s. 6d. current money of Maryland. Same v. McCallister, *ibid.* (March, 1780). Philadelphia Q.S., lib. 1779–82, Comm. v. Williams and McKitterick (April, 1780); Comm. v. Burt (Oct., 1780); Comm. v. Burt (Jan., 1781), verdict: not guilty.

priety of such appeals, referred the matter to the consideration of a later sitting, but no further action in the matter appears in the record.[12]

In New York in April, 1779, the first judges of the courts of common pleas of Albany, Dutchess, and Orange levied an assize, ascertaining the pay and wages for teams, carriages, horses, and drivers impressed for the public service pursuant to an act of the state legislature. Rations to the amount of 8s. per day were to be deducted from the drivers' pay and "in Case of extraordinary services, or in very bad Weather, such Quantity of Liquor to be allowed to the respective Drivers, as has been heretofore customary in such Cases." [13] In April of the following year, at a time when the state regulatory legislation had been suspended, the first and second judges of common pleas in Dutchess and the Orange County third judge of pleas similarly fixed the pay for such services at a rate some five or six times higher than the schedule of '79. In addition, they ascertained the price of hay at $248 per ton, of rye at $32 per bushel, of Indian corn at $27 per bushel, and of oats and buckwheat at $16 per bushel.[14]

In May, 1780, Thomas Younghusband, a country justice, was indicted in the Edenton, N.C., district court for saying publicly: "Damn the Congress!" and "Damn the Currency!" and for refusing to take paper money for liquor purchased at his inn.[15] In Connecticut and Delaware, hoarding was criminally prosecuted,[16] and in the latter state a ferryman was presented for demanding a fare in excess of the legal rate for transporting passengers.[17] Considering the comprehensive set of economic controls in operation during this period, the relative infrequency of prosecutions, however, is conclusive that the common law courts functioned only in a minor way in enforcing these regulations.

State legislatures and local officials, such as committees of correspondence and of safety, selectmen, or town committees devoted more attention than did the courts to enforcing the system. Typical of countless instances was the action of the Providence town meeting which set up its price and wage code in August, 1779, and authorized its committee of inspection to receive complaints against offenders and report

---

[12] Essex Q.S. and C.P., lib. 1772–81 (April, 1778).   [13] N.Y.J., April 12, 1779.
[14] Ibid., April 10, 1780.   [15] Edenton, N.C., District Court Papers, 1751–87.
[16] Hayward's case, Windham Co., Conn., Court Rec., 1777–82, f. 47 (1778); Chandle's case, ibid., f. 202 (1780). Mervin's case, New Haven Co. Court Rec., 1774–83, f. 400 (1779). Delaware v. Moses Cochran, Newcastle G.S., lib., 1778–93, f. 125 (Nov. 1780).
[17] Delaware v. Haines, Newcastle G.S., lib., 1780–81 (May, Aug., 1781). For other prosecutions for profiteering or "oppression," see Prescott's case, New Haven Co. Court Rec., lib. 1778–83 (1777), fined £125 9s. and costs; Flint's case, Windham Co., Conn., Court Rec., 1777–82, f. 41 (1778); Smith's petition for relief from a sentence for profiteering, Conn. State Arch., Revolutionary War, lib. X, f. 319a (1778).

the same to the committee of correspondence, who were "empowered either to proceed to inflict a proper punishment, by advertising them as enemies to their country, or in cases of any peculiar difficulty to lay the whole before the town to be finally determined." [18] Expulsion, corporal punishment, or fines were not customarily meted out. Instead, publication of breaches of the schedules was normally the sole punishment. At a time when speculators and hoarders were linked in the public mind with Loyalists, when the opprobrium "Monopolizer" was one to be dreaded as suitable only for canker worms, "vermin," "rats," and "worse enemies to the country than Burgoyne," [19] this form of social ostracism might well have been effective. Actually, publication of profiteers went back to the regulations that were in force following the First Continental Congress.[20]

Numerous cases are on record where such bodies punished either by fine or public denunciation for charging higher than the regulated price for goods or for refusing to sell at such a price; [21] for refusing to accept specie in payment of debts or in exchange for commodities; [22] for valu-

[18] *Amer. J. and Gen. Advertiser* (Providence, R.I.), Sept. 2, 1779.

[19] *Boston Gazette*, Jan. 8, 1777. See also letter of John Penn to Governor Richard Caswell of North Carolina, Philadelphia, June 25, 1777, Emmett MSS, No. 3933—N.Y. Pub. Lib.

[20] See *Newport Mercury*, Nov. 28, 1774; Dec. 18, 1775.

[21] Massachusetts cases. Moses Fessenden: *Boston Gazette*, April 21, 1777, *Continental J.*, April 24, May 2, 1777. Stephen Hall: *Boston Gazette*, Aug. 30, Sept. 6, 1779, *Independent Chronicle*, Sept. 2, 1779, *Continental J.*, Sept. 9, 1779. Thomas Fessenden: *Ind. Chron.*, Sept. 23, Nov. 5, 1779; Gideon Putnam of Danvers (defense—price in accord with the Ipswich Convention): *ibid.*, Oct. 14, 1779. Josiah Draper (in this case the Attleborough committee of correspondence was divided, some members maintaining that Draper's salt was of high quality): *Continental J.*, Oct. 28, 1779.

New York cases. Robinson and Price, Nov. 3, 1775: *J. Prov. Cong., Provincial Convention, Committee of Safety and Council of Safety of the State of New York, 1775–77* (2 vols., Albany, 1842), I, 193, 349; Mrs. Jonathan Lawrence (complained of by the committee of New Windsor, June 14, 1776): *ibid.*, pp. 494, 495. Volkert P. Douw and six other merchants, March, 1776: *Mins. Albany Comm. Corr.*, I, 351; Robert McClallen, April 24, 1776: *ibid.*, p. 387; John Boyd, Sr., John Boyd, Jr., and Absalom Woodworth, May 8, 1776: *ibid.*, p. 540. Lewis Vincent, David Heusted, and Joseph Emory, Jan. 13, 1777: *Mins. N.Y. Comm. for Detecting Conspiracies in New York*, I, 96, 97. David Frank, July 2, 1779: *Mins. Schenectady Comm. Corr.*, II, 1147; Hugh Mitchell, July 8, 1779 (acquitted): *ibid.*, p. 1148; Mrs. Morton, Mrs. Robbison, and Caleb Beck, July 3, 1779: *ibid.*, p. 1155; John Van Antwerp, Aug. 3, 1779: *ibid.*, p. 1156. When in 1777 the committee of safety of Rhinebeck, Dutchess Co., instituted a complaint against Robert Livingston of Livingston Manor, accusing him of selling bar iron at excessive prices, he pleaded in extenuation that the higher wages he was compelled to pay his workmen increased considerably the cost of manufacturing bar iron over 1775 costs. *J. Prov. Cong.*, I, 1100.

New Jersey cases. David Layton, Jan. 24, 1778: *Mins. N.J. Council of Safety, 1777–78* (Jersey City, 1872), p. 196; John Smyth, Jan. 26, 1778: *ibid.*; Samuel Titus, Woolingston Redman, March 10, 1778: *ibid.*, pp. 212, 213; Samuel Smith, innkeeper (fines particularized, May 4, 1778): *ibid.*, p. 232. Curtis and Norris (Morris Co. Comm. cases): *N.J.J.*, Sept. 7, 1779.

[22] Capt. Thomas Harnot, May 28, 1775, *J.N.Y. Prov. Cong.*, I, 465; William Newton, May 25, 1776, Andrew Gautier's case, appealed from the general committee of N.Y. to the Provincial Congress, June 4, 1776, *ibid.*, pp. 461, 473; Cornelius Glen, June 4, 1776, *Mins. Albany Comm. Corr.*, I, 430; Abraham Jacob Lansingh, Feb. 18, 1777, *ibid.*, p. 680; cases of Samuel Car and Charles Barclay, June 16, 1778, *Mins. N.J. Council of Safety*, p. 255.

ing specie higher than paper currency;[23] and for attempting to corner or monopolize commodities.[24] In addition to publication, the offenders might be cried through the city, have the money in excess of the regulated prices returned, or suffer a fine, and in Albany further humiliating punishment might be exacted, such as being forced to stand on a scaffold erected in the market place and publicly swear obedience to the committee.[25] In New York and New Jersey the violator might also be imprisoned until he could post bond for his good behavior or "till farther orders."[26] On rare occasions the vendee in the illegal transaction might be fined along with the seller,[27] and the purchaser for hard money prosecuted as well as the taker.[28] Occasionally the jurisdiction of such committees was challenged, as by Nathaniel Pearce of Stoughton, who, when denounced for profiteering, retorted that "he would be damned if he went across the town to hear or be heard by the Committee," and that nobody could stop him from selling at any price he could obtain.[29]

Few cases of violations of the labor and service codes have been recorded, and these generally involve prices exacted by master workers for finished products or wages for piece work rather than per diem. As early as January 7, 1776, the Philadelphia committee censured a hatter, among others, for refusal on grounds of conscience to accept continental money.[30] For a similar offense, a cordwainer was declared an enemy of his country and committed to jail by the Pennsylvania Council of Safety.[31] In July, 1779, John Van Epps was cited to appear before the committee of correspondence of Schenectady for charging three dollars an ell for weaving striped coarse linen and twelve shillings an ell for very coarse plain linen. Two outside weavers were given the cloth to examine and estimate "how much they used to weave such cloth for." According to the record:

Hall said that He wove for grain and did not weave much for money. Wesselse said the one sort he wove for six shillings an Ell and the other for nine shillings

[23] Boston Committee of Public Safety: Abraham Salomon, *Ind. Chron.*, March 12, 1777; Bowle's case, *Continental J.*, Jan. 8, 1778; William Pemberton, June 5, 1776, *Mins. Albany Comm. Corr.*, I, 432; Marmaduke Abbot, Oct. 16, 1777, *Mins. N.J. Council of Safety*, p. 147.

[24] John Nazro, Martin Becker, and Enoch Brown felt impelled to deny publicly such accusations. *Continental J.*, Jan. 23, Oct. 2, 9, 1777; *Boston Gazette*, April 21, 28, 1777; *Ind. Chron.*, May 2, Oct. 9, 1777; *Boston Town Rec.* XXVI, *passim*.

[25] *Pa. Packet*, June 29, 1777.

[26] Van Vranken's case, *Mins. Albany Comm. Corr.*, I, 944 (March 18, 1778).

[27] William Sloan, fined £6 "for paying more for the sugar than the law allows." A similar fine and a huge forfeiture were exacted of the sugar merchant (June 19, 1778), *Mins. N.J. Council of Safety*, p. 257.

[28] See Glifford's case (July 20, 1779), *Mins. Schenectady Comm. Corr.*, II, 1152.

[29] *Ind. Chron.*, Oct. 14, 1779.

[30] See also *Amer. Arch.*, 4th ser., III, 1388; IV, 564 (Dover, Del., committee).

[31] *Pa. Col. Rec.*, X, 774, XI, 70; *J. Cong.*, II, 475.

an Ell. Thereupon Resolved that said John Bt Van Epps Junr do return the sum of twenty three pounds twelve shillings which in the opinion of this board was *extorted* from said De Graaf by said V. Eps Junr which we hope will prevent all extortioners from pursuing the same evil practices by which said V. Eps is become an object of public resentment.

Epps was published for this "extortion." [32] Offering "hard specie for work" was as serious an offense as offering specie for commodities, as the result would be the cornering of the labor market. During the same month just such a charge was brought against Elias Rosa before the Schenectady committee. [33]

Perhaps the most notable case in this category was that of Sarson Belcher of Boston, denounced in 1779 as an "enemy of his country" for selling a beaver hat for £48, £13 above the regulated price. Belcher, in a published refutation, claimed that the price of £35 set by the committee was ridiculously low as he had formerly received as much as £60 for beaver hats. The price he had charged, he claimed, amounted to a 20 per cent reduction from the former price and corresponded exactly to the amount by which other trades were forced to reduce their prices. Such a scale was needed to support his family and purchase necessaries, and in this contention, he had the solid support of the hatters' industry. Twenty hatters signed a statement justifying Belcher's action. Nevertheless the Boston town meeting voted to let the publication stand, denounced him for his attack upon the committee, and warned the other hatters that unless they retracted they would earn a similar public denunciation. Only four hatters retracted under pressure: the other sixteen, when denounced, defended Belcher's prices and countered that, as most hatters were withholding their products instead of placing them on sale at the stipulated price, Belcher was really doing a service by relieving the hat shortage. County hatters, they insisted, were selling no better hats for £50, and no hand was turned against them. Belcher himself appealed publicly to the town, claiming that actually only fifteen persons at an unusually small town meeting had voted against him. [34]

More drastic extralegal measures, such as expulsion and tarring and feathering, were occasionally taken. Such penalties were generally the result of vigilantist activity fostered by mounting popular indignation against profiteers. In Boston the activities of Joyce Junior and his cohorts in enforcing the state acts against monopoly enjoyed considerable

---

[32] *Mins. Schenectady Comm. Corr.*, II, 1150.   [33] *Ibid.*, p. 1152.
[34] *Boston Gazette*, Sept. 27, 1779; *Continental J.*, Sept. 23, Oct. 2, 7, 1779.

publicity. In April, 1777, under his leadership five "Tory Villains"—four Bostonians and one resident of Cape Ann—were carted over the Boston line for profiteering; warnings were issued to shopkeepers who had refused to sell dry goods and West Indian produce, had adulterated products, or had turned down paper money. Orders went out to all who had "left Butchering, Droving, Horse jockeying, Shoemaking, sand-driving, and assum'd selling by Wholesale or Retail West India Goods, and all others in the same Business, and of Huxtering, that they forthwith open their Stores and Shops," and sell commodities openly at the prices set by law.[35] Describing these carting incidents, Abigail Adams wrote that about 500 people followed "Joice Junior, who was mounted on horseback, with a red coat, a white wig, and a drawn sword, with drum and fife following." [36] Urging that "Connecticut take the Alarm!" and proudly claiming that opposition to the Stamp Act also had originated in Boston, "Vox Populi" warned that "an unabating vengeance" would descend "on the heads of monopolizers, as it did on the odious stamp masters." [37] Elsewhere riots against profiteers broke out. Peter Messier of New York charged, in May, 1777, that a party consisting of two continental soldiers and twenty-two women had descended upon his house, refused his wife the price that she had asked for tea, and seized as much tea as they wanted, leaving an amount that they judged fair, and that several other parties had visited him subsequently, searching the premises in the name of the committee for detecting conspiracies, beating the complainant and his servants, and committing acts of vandalism. These incidents were apparently not unusual.[38]

MILITARY REGULATION

CIVILIAN REGULATION was actually but one phase of the Revolutionary program of price and wage controls; for in addition to the courts, local officials and committees, and extralegal bodies, the armies, both Continental and British, were forced to set prices for articles required in the conduct of the war, to fix wage schedules and determine working hours for their artisans, and to seize hoarded goods needed in the military service. The British military authorities set prices for the purchase by the army of liquor, medicines, and provisions.[1] In New York City

---

[35] *Boston Gazette,* March 17, April 21, 24, 1777.
[36] *Familiar Letters during the Revolution* (New York, 1876), pp. 262, 263; Mathews, Col. Soc. of Mass., *Publications,* VIII, 94.
[37] *Pa. Packet,* June 22, 1779.   [38] *Mins. N.Y. Comm. for Detecting Conspiracies,* I, 301–303.
[1] See HMC, *Rep.,* LIX, Pt. I, 106, 154, 161 (1777).

the venerable practice of setting the assize of bread was observed by the commandant during the British occupation.[2] In the occupied cities the army also set the rate of wages of artificers working on military projects.[3] In the Continental army artisans needed to erect fortifications and for other military purposes were formed into companies with wages fixed, in the case of New York, by the Provincial Congress. In the company at Fort Constitution in 1776 ten dollars per month and one ration was established for artisan-privates.[4] The quartermaster general was empowered to regulate the prices of commodities purchased by the army.[5] This maximum wage legislation was enforced by military penalties.[6] Hours were also fixed for artificers and for fatigue parties.[7] At times the military authorities also found it necessary to fix maximum prices or wages of civilian tailors and washwomen accompanying the army or living at camp.[8] A Virginia statute of May, 1779, authorized the county courts to set the rate of compensation for workmen employed by the commissaries.[9] As reward for working on the road over the Cumberland Mountains to Kentucky, Virginia agreed to give the laborers and militia guard 300 acres of any waste or unappropriated land within the state or £120 at the option of the claimant.[10] In 1780 the legislature of the state listed the prices for provisions impressed for the use of the army,[11] and the following year empowered the governor and council to fix a reasonable price in specie for all impressed articles enumerated in the previous statute.[12] In addition to setting prices for a great many impressed provisions, an act of 1782 also fixed the rate of compensation for certain public services, notably

[2] *N.Y. Gazette,* August 9, 16, 1779.

[3] "Letters of General Pattison," N.Y. Hist. Soc., *Coll.* (1875), pp. 67, 68. For rates of wages for carting on Staten Island in 1779, see HMC, *Rep.,* LIX, Pt. II, p. 73 (1779). For the futile attempts made by the British army to regulate prices north of the Ohio, see N. V. Russell, *The British Régime in Michigan and the Old Nothwest, 1760–1796* (Northfield, Minn., 1939), p. 120.

[4] *J.N.Y. Prov. Cong.,* I, 299.

[5] *Amer. Arch.,* 5th ser., II, 616 (1776).

[6] At times the military authorities stepped in to enforce the laws against extortion and oppression. In April, 1776, a Military Court of Enquiry was held in Princess Anne County, Virginia, which acquitted Thomas Talbot of the charge of "extortion from the people." Va. State Arch.; *VMH,* XV, 409. Where local committees of correspondence engaged artificers for military tasks, they customarily determined the wages to be paid. *Mins. Albany Comm. Corr.,* I, 160 (1775).

[7] For the building of Fort Golgotha on Long Island in 1782 8 carpenters were ordered to report to Captain Conkling "by 8 o'clock ever morning with their tools to work said Fort in Town . . . and not go away till Dismissed or they will not be Credited for a full Days work." *Huntington Town Rec.,* III, 81 (Nov. 26, 1782). See also Orderly Book of the 1st Pennsylvania Regiment, *Pa. Arch.,* 2d ser., XI, 475 (1779).

[8] Orderly Book of the 7th Pennsylvania Regiment, *Pa. Arch.,* 2d ser., XI, 423.

[9] Hening, X, 81 (1779).   [10] Hening, X, 144 (1779).

[11] *Ibid.,* p. 345 (1780). Cf. also *Mins. Albany Comm. Corr.,* I, 714, 715 (1777).

[12] Hening, X, 437 (1781). See also *Cal. Va. State Pap.,* I, 431 (1781).

waggon-hire, with a full team and driver and finding provisions and forage, fifteen shillings per day; waggon-hire, with a full team and driver and found by the public, eleven shillings per day . . . horseshoes, one shilling and six pence each . . . common labourer, two shillings per day; tradesmen or watermen, five shillings per day.[13]

CONSEQUENCES OF REGULATION

WHEN ALL KNOWN prosecutions, both civil and military, are taken into consideration, there is no justification for Pelatiah Webster's charge that these regulations were "executed with a relentless severity." [1] In Massachusetts as early as 1777 it was necessary to defend labor against the charge of demanding excessive wages. Such defense rested on the cost of provisions and the depreciation of the circulating medium. A large part of the working population, one writer admitted, was only striving to boost wages to the former level in relation to imported articles and necessaries.[2] In March, 1778, the town of Boston memorialized the general court against the rise in farm prices, pointing out that labor had not shared in that price rise; customarily farm labor had received the equivalent of one bushel of corn for a day's work, but at that time the daily wage was equivalent to only three pecks of corn.[3] Conditions were similar as to wages of town mechanics. According to one informer, the price scale prevailing in Boston in 1779 was reducing many to beggary.[4] "Mobility," in the *Boston Gazette,* warned hoarders that "Hunger will break through stone walls, and the resentment excited by it may end in your destruction." [5] John Eliot wrote: "Did the country farmers *feel* like the Bostonian mechanics, I don't know what would be the consequence." [6]

The gap between wages and prices was patent at the time of the New Haven convention. There were so many exceptions to the rule limiting

[13] Hening, XI, 79 (1782). Cf. the 1781 schedule, setting daily wages for laborers at 2*s.* or 10 lbs. of tobacco; of the best artificers at 5*s.* or 25 lbs. of tobacco, and of ordinary artificers at 3*s.* 9*d.* or 18¾ lbs. of tobacco. *Cal. Va. State Papers,* I, 495. For the ineffectiveness of such regulations, see *infra,* pp. 127–132.

[1] *Political Essays,* p. 129n.

[2] *Ind. Chron.,* Aug. 27, Sept. 11, 1777. In Pennsylvania during the same period, farm laborers and teamsters were similarly charged with demanding exorbitant rates. *Pa. Arch.,* 1st ser., VI, 116, 128.

[3] *Mass. Acts and Resolves,* V, 1016n.

[4] Harlow, Col. Soc. of Mass., *Publications,* XX, 178, quoting from Pickering MSS, XVII, fols. 242–243 (Feb. 28, 1779).

[5] *Boston Gazette,* April 26, 1779; see also *ibid.,* June 24, 1779.

[6] Mass. Hist. Soc., *Coll.,* 6th ser., IV, 176–183 (March 29, 1780). "Tradesmen and salary men grumble at the Countrymen's extortion, and threaten to join the Regulars against them." *The Diary of William Pynchon of Salem* (Boston, 1890), p. 52 (March 8, 1778). See also Winslow, *Amer. Broadside Verses,* pp. 188, 189.

advances in produce to 75 per cent over 1774 that the wage restriction to that level operated to the disadvantage of labor. As a matter of fact, wages of skilled artisans were about three times as high in 1778 as in 1774. Boston newspapers were in the later year advertising carpenter's wages at nine shillings a day, with board, as against between three and four shillings in 1774.[7] Under the Concord scale of 1779, common labor received from three to four pounds a day, but in Watertown the authorities fixed a rate of pay for road work of only forty shillings. On the other hand, the recommendation of Congress that common labor for 1780 should not exceed by twentyfold the scale of 1774 was disregarded in that town, where road wages rose from three shillings before the war to nine pounds in 1780.[8] However, before any definitive conclusion could be drawn as to the effect of regulation on real wages, it would be necessary to compare wages and prices in all communities where regulation was in effect. From the very limited evidence at hand, admittedly conflicting, it may be tentatively inferred, though, that the regulatory program in Massachusetts actually checked real wages, which suffered a decline during this period.[9]

In New York, as early as 1776, one prosecution witness in an action for profiteering in tea brought on appeal to the Provincial Congress testified that he replied to a demand for hard money for tea in this manner: "Mr. Sickles, I thought you was joking; where should cartmen get hard money; we work for the Continent and get Continental money," and further that it was hard "not to be able to purchase" with that currency "the necessaries for his family."[10] The Albany committee of correspondence attempted to meet "exorbitant Prices" in setting service and labor schedules.[11] That delicate balance between prices and wages was carefully analyzed by "Rationalis" in a contribution to the *New Jersey Gazette*. Although maintaining that "trade can best regulate it's own prices," that writer conceded that on extraordinary occasions legislative intervention was justifiable. Such schedules, he urged, should bear equitably on all groups in the community and

[7] *Boston Gazette*, March 9, 1778. For wages in Salem in 1775, see Essex Institute, *Hist. Coll.*, II, 259. Governor Trumbull stated in Feb., 1777, that at the commencement of hostilities a common laborer received 40s. per month while at the time of writing he was getting $10. Seamen were offered $20 per month, "and tradesmen and artificers in proportion." Sparks, *Corr. of Amer. Revol.*, I, 342.

[8] *Watertown Rec.*, IV, 72, 194, 221.

[9] However, for the view that "things in general were raised fifty per cent" by the Connecticut regulating act of 1777, see *Conn. Courant*, May 12, 1777.

[10] *J. Prov. Cong. of N.Y.*, I, 473.   [11] *Mins. Albany Comm. of Corr.*, I, 915 (Jan. 31, 1778).

should favor the production of necessaries. His calculations, however, are so pertinent to this general question of the disparity between wage and price levels that they are worthy of inclusion *in extenso:*

. . . in order to find out how to proportion the limitations duly, it may be necessary to have recourse to calculation.

By the law lately passed for regulating prices, the legislature seem to have aimed at fixing most of the articles of internal produce at double the former prices. This may perhaps be a proper standard for some articles; but when the matter is fairly considered, it will be found that the same reasons which require the prices of some things to be doubled, will call for a similar advance on some others, and on others again a much greater. Of the latter kind are such articles as derive their value chiefly from labour, and require the use of some commodity, either imported from abroad, or which, from it's scarcity, cannot be obtained but at a very high price. To explain my meaning I shall subjoin a few calculations.

I. As to farmers. Let us suppose a farm, the annual produce of which is for sale, exclusive of what was necessary for the consumption of such parts of the family as do not labour, would sell in former time for £300.0.0

It is said to be a large allowance, to admit that one half of this value is paid for labour, supposing the whole to be done on hire . •. . 150.0.0

Annual profit remaining 150.0.0

Supposing the price of labour to be doubled, the labour on the same farm will be worth 300.0.0

The consumption of the family will be the same, and allow the same annual profit as formerly 150.0.0

The extraordinary price of salt may be 15.0.0

Allow, moreover, the use of as much rum, tea, sugar, and other luxuries that will cost extra 35.0.0

500.0.0

The farmer ought therefore to have for his produce on an average now 5*s.* for what he would formerly have sold for 3*s.* or 1*s.*8 now for 1*s.* formerly.

II. As to labourers. Let us suppose a labourer, finding his own provisions and cloathing, formerly earned per annum 45.0.0

That his provisions cost him 20.0.0

And his cloathing 10.0.0

Profit toward maintenance of his family 15.0.0

45.0.0

Provisions at double price will be 40.0.0

Cloathing will cost at least three times the old price . . . 30.0.0
His profit for the use of his family ought to be at least double
   as they must purchase all they consume 30.0.0

                                     £100.0.0

His wages therefore ought to be increased to 10s. for every 4s.6 he would formerly have received; or 1s.8 now for 9d. formerly.

The same proportion will be requisite for mechanicks, handicraftsmen, lawyers, clerks, etc. so far as their several productions derive their value from labour; making the proper additions or deductions for what the prices of their respective materials may exceed or fall short of that proportion.

It will be observed that I have stated the price of labour at double the former price to the farmer, though I have shewn it must cost more to others; and that I have stated provisions at double to labourers, etc. though I have said the farmer ought to sell them at a lower rate. A little reflection will justify these diversities. As to the first, the farmer having the advantage of feeding; and, in a great measure, clothing and paying his labourers from his own produce without purchase, (to say nothing of the advantage he may derive from the labour of his children and servants) can always procure at a much cheaper rate than a person of any other class. And as to the second,—Suppose the price of the common articles of provisions should be fixed at the rate of 5s. now, for 3s. formerly, as above stated, if we move but a small allowance for the extraordinary prices of salt, sugar, tea, rum, etc.—and some of these must and will use as their neighbours,—we shall find the average price of provisions to labourers, mechanicks, &c. will not be less than doubled. I have heard it remarked that a great majority of the members of the legislature being farmers, their limitations are calculated greatly in favour of that class of men. If there is any truth in the remark, I am persuaded it must arise from their want of proper information, as I cannot suppose they would designedly oppress others for their own emolument. As faithful representatives of the people, I should suppose they would be particularly watchful that no just ground should be given for a suspicion of this kind. . . .[12]

Workers themselves were moved to express dissatisfaction with the price schedules ascertained for various manufactured products. These protestants were usually master artificers or pieceworkers, but they regarded their interests as identical with the journeymen's. For example, in July, 1779, ten Philadelphia cordwainers publicly declared that they had subscribed to the town regulations of May 25 as regards the prices of shoes in the expectation that others would deal likewise with them for articles needed in their trade or for their families. They were joined a few days later by the tanners and curriers in their open opposition

---

[12] *N.J. Gazette,* March 11, 1778.

to the price schedules on the ground that they were detrimental to the labor interests:

Our business requires a considerable number of journeymen, who after labouring the whole week, with unabated diligence, have usually found themselves where they began, not being able to lay up any thing out of their scanty wages; this useful body of men will be immediately thrown out of employ, if the regulations take place; they must seek bread elsewhere, and will leave their employers in a state of poverty, and want, and the citizens barefooted; this is by no means exaggeration or ill grounded surmise, but may be fairly deduced as a necessary consequence from the following prices.

They then proceeded to point out that, in general, commodities, according to the schedule, were increased in price by twenty times, whereas the prices for their products were held down to fourteenfold. While it is not usual for labor groups in this period to advance laissez faire arguments, these remonstrants urged:

It is absurd and contrary to every principle of trade, where no man will purchase if he knows the market is falling. It will destroy every spring of industry, and will make it the interest of every one to decline all business. . . . Trade should be free as air, uninterrupted as the tide, and though it will necessarily like this be sometimes high at one place and low at another, yet it will ever return of itself, sufficiently near to a proper level, if the banks and dams, or, in other words, injudicious attempts to regulate it, are not interposed; this maxim, we apprehend, admits of no exception but in the case of a besieged city.

To the "Whig Shoemaker" who charged them with Toryism, they retorted that they were acting in defense of their families. In championing their chairman, who had been accused by "Justice" of selling his shoes in excess of the regulated price, they pointed out that others had not obeyed the schedules, and that therefore in raising his prices he was acting out of necessity.[13]

As for commodities, the rare instances when merchants made a point of stipulating in their advertisements that produce was for sale at the regulated price is indicative that these were unusual bargains to be parceled out in small quantities—as, in the case of tea, one pound to a family.[14] On one occasion the governor of Rhode Island protested to Massachusetts that he could not enforce his own wage and price law if the larger states did not keep to their schedules.[15] In addition to with-

[13] *Pa. Packet,* July 15, 20, 1779.
[14] *Pa. Packet,* April 22, 1776; *Continental J.,* Feb. 27, March 6, 1777, Aug. 12, 19, 1779, *Boston Gazette,* April 28, 1777; *Ind. Chron.,* May 2, 1777.
[15] *Mass. Acts and Resolves,* V, 724; Mass. Arch., Vol. 194, f. 50.

holding produce from the market, many persons endeavored to evade the price and wage schedules by resorting to barter.[16] Enumerated articles could usually be purchased with hard money at far below the stipulated rate.[17] Whether or not these price schedules were effective in braking the price rise, it is clear that within a very short time after their promulgation they were obsolete. Thus, prices obtaining in Boston within three months after the passage of the Massachusetts regulating act of 1777 were from 20 to 140 per cent higher than the legal schedule.[18] A resolve of the town meeting of Portsmouth, New Hampshire, in 1780, declared that where goods had been sold at the stipulated prices they could not be replaced for five times the sum within a month or two afterwards.[19] In short, just as twentieth-century minimum-wage scales have in effect set a maximum in certain industries, so, too, it appears likely that the maximum-wage scale set during the Revolution proved to be the minimum actually paid.[20]

Economic historians have been harsh in their judgment of these wage and price controls. "All such methods," declares Bullock, "were as idle as attempts to violate the natural laws of money have always proved to be." [21] Even if one were to concede the theoretical soundness of their position, it is nonetheless clear that it is unrelated to reality. In the stress of war, nations cannot be guided exclusively by theoretical considerations; for, apart from budgetary abnormalities, such crises bring about an unhealthy stimulation of industry which in turn is reflected in greater purchasing power and a sharp upward surge in prices and wages. At other times and in other places, in like military emergencies, similar regulatory measures were tried. The maximum price legislation adopted by the Committee of Public Safety in France in 1793 ran parallel to the earlier American program, and the spontaneous rise of antihoarding sentiment in French municipalities at that time is indicative of the popular support behind the program.[22]

In the twentieth century such controls have been widely adopted under

[16] See, e.g., *Continental J.*, Aug. 12, 1779; *Mass. Spy*, July 29, Aug. 5, 12, 1779.

[17] *N.Y. Gazette and Weekly Mercury*, August 4, 1777.

[18] For other instances, see table of prices in Harlow, Col. Soc. of Mass., *Publications*, XX, 168.

[19] *N.H. State Papers*, XIII, 287, 288.

[20] The following advertisement under date of April 20, 1778, seems to bear this out: "*Wanted:* Tanners. Greatest wages allowed by law will be paid." *N.J. Arch.*, II, 180. For frequent allusions to the rapid rise in prices, see *Despatches and Instructions of Conrad Alexandre Gerard, 1778–1780* (Baltimore, 1939), pp. 304, 580–581, 584–585 *passim*.

[21] C. J. Bullock, *Essays on the Monetary History of the United States* (New York, 1900), p. 66. See also J. Backman, *Government Price Fixing* (New York, 1939).

[22] See Bourne, "Maximum Prices in France," *Amer. Hist. Rev.* (Oct., 1917), pp. 110, 112, 133, and "Food Control and Price Fixing in Revolutionary France," *J. Pol. Econ.* (Feb., March, 1919).

stress of emergency. During the first World War it was necessary to regulate profiteering and hoarding and to fix prices for many commodities and manufactured products.[23] Through labor boards, Great Britain established maximum wages.[24] "Perhaps the greatest economic lesson the war has taught," wrote one authority, "is how inadequate and inequitable the fixing of prices by the law of supply and demand becomes when one party is under pressure of absolute necessity, and either supply or demand is limited." [25] Another writer finds in the regulatory practices of the first World War a curious commentary on the "eternal" truths of economics that the heretical doctrine of regulation enjoyed "a greater vogue and more important practical consequences than many of the abstract generalizations which are supposed to be true for all time but are never strictly applicable except in a hypothetical world." [26] Then, as in Revolutionary times, it was clearly recognized that the principal factor in price appreciation was currency inflation.[27] As a matter of fact, the failure to check inflationary trends in industry and finance during and after the first World War brought on a major depression.[28]

As a result, the movement for minimum-wage legislation for the protection of workers was accelerated. The first truly comprehensive program of minimum wages was established in 1933 under the codes of the NRA. Although this program was declared unconstitutional, the Supreme Court in 1937 upheld a Washington minimum wage act, thereby reversing a decision of fourteen years previously and providing a fillip to state wage regulation. Meanwhile, in 1936 the Walsh-Healey Public Contracts Act established as a minimum the prevailing wage, the eight-hour day, and the forty-hour week in government contracts. Finally, in 1938 the Fair Labor Standards Act was passed, establishing minimum standards for wages and hours and proscribing the use of child labor in interstate commerce or in producing goods entering into such commerce.[29]

[23] F. W. Taussig, "Price Fixing as Seen by a Price Fixer," *Q.J. Econ.* (Feb., 1919), p. 238; S. Litman, *Prices and Price Control in Great Britain and the United States during the World War* (New York, 1920), p. 318; E. M. H. Lloyd, *Experiments in State Control at the War Office and the Ministry of Food* (Oxford, 1924), pp. 50–64; E. J. Howenstine, Jr., *The Economics of Demobilization* (Washington, 1944), pp. 217–236.

[24] M. B. Hammond, *British Labor Conditions and Legislation during the War* (New York, 1919), pp. 100, 188, *et seq.*

[25] C. W. Baker, *Government Control and Operation of Industry in Great Britain and the United States during the World War* (New York, 1921), p. 126.

[26] Lloyd, *op. cit.*, p. 283. See also G. P. Adams, Jr., *Wartime Price Control* (Washington, 1942).

[27] *Parl. Debates, House of Lords*, XXVI, 1077 (Nov. 20, 1917).

[28] The removal of price fixing upon the cessation of hostilities contributed to a sharp increase in prices. *Hearings before House Committee on Banking and Currency on H.R. 5479* (superseded by H.R. 5990), 77th Cong., 1st Sess. (1941), p. 345.

[29] 52 Stat. 1060 (1938), 29 U.S.C.A., §§ 201–219.

On the outbreak of the second World War, public opinion had been already prepared for the sweeping price- and wage-fixing regulations of the Director of Economic Stabilization. Price fixing had become implicit in a war regime.[30] The National War Labor Board was the agency designated to carry out the wage policies of the anti-inflation program. The Board strove to deny all demands for wage increases which did not correct maladjustments. In effect, labor's wartime bargaining power was seriously curtailed.[31]

Except for these wartime analogies, the objectives of the modern legislation and of the measures of the Tudor and colonial periods are diametrically opposed. Minimum-wage legislation aims at assuring workmen decent living conditions in an era of unemployment and increasing industrial insecurity, whereas, as Adam Smith observed, the early wage fixing was for the purpose of lowering rather than raising wages, for, as he aptly pointed out, "whenever the legislature attempts to regulate the difference between masters and their workmen, its counsellors are always the masters." [32] On the other hand, the objective of the program of the first and second World Wars was in many respects the same as that of the Revolutionary War. The second World War brought about a huge demand for goods and services and a decreasing supply of labor. This labor shortage could not be met by merely turning to new sources of labor. General manpower conscription was proposed and maximum wage and price controls soon proved necessary.

[30] See Emergency Price Control Act of 1942, Pub. L. No. 421, 77th Cong., 2d Sess.; amended on October 2, 1942, by Pub. L. 729, which authorized the President "to issue a general order stabilizing prices, wages, and salaries, affecting the cost of living . . . so far as practicable . . . on the basis of levels which existed on September 15, 1942." See also C. W. Wright, ed., *Economic Problems of War and Its Aftermath* (Chicago, 1942).

[31] See Executive Order 9250, Title II (2), 7 Fed. Reg. 7871 (1942); NWLB, B284. The "Little Steel" formula was an attempt to give labor a parity as well as agriculture, and allowed it to retain the same purchasing power it had in Jan., 1941. It was clearly recognized that a condition precedent to wage stabilization was the stabilization of the cost of living. See Julius Hirsch, *Price Control in the War Economy* (New York, 1943), pp. 243–254; William Green, "Should Wages be Frozen?" Amer. Acad. Pol. Science, *Annals* (Nov., 1942), p. 60; W. H. Davis, "Aims and Policies of the War Labor Board," *ibid.*, pp. 141–146. The difficulties attendant upon stabilizing prices impelled labor to demand a modification of the "Little Steel" formula. In practice the War Labor Board found it difficult to stabilize wages at the Sept., 1942, level as authorized by the amended Price Control Act. Many upward adjustments were permitted, particularly through the extension of paid vacations, granting of overtime and night shift premiums, equal pay for equal work without regard for race or sex, and the elimination of substandards of living and of intra-plant wage-rate inequities. See Jane C. Record, "The War Labor Board: an Experiment in Wage Stabilization," *Amer. Econ. Rev.*, XXXIV (1944), 98–110. Executive Order 9328 of April 8, 1943, was much more restrictive. This authorized the War Labor Board to grant no further wage increases except such as were clearly necessary to correct substandards of living or to give effect to the Little Steel formula. The WLB showed considerable ingenuity in bending this formula without breaking it.

[32] *Wealth of Nations*, Bk. I, ch. x, Pt. II.

The regulatory program embraced, in addition, heavy taxation of industry and labor as a further means of controlling the price and wage structure during the military emergency.[33]

Few will argue today that the laissez faire doctrine presents a satisfactory program for capitalism in crises. One should be generous, therefore, in evaluating a comprehensive experiment in regulation during the greatest military crisis in American history when any program along truly national lines was virtually impossible to effectuate.

Those who have opposed controls have at times been forced to concede that at certain periods in American history regulation was very much in evidence. Chief Justice Chapman of Massachusetts, commenting on a much later occasion on the practice of fixing wages by the towns during the Revolution, said: "Experience and increasing intelligence led to the abolition of all such restrictions, and to the establishment of freedom for all branches of labor and business. . . . Freedom is the policy of this country." [34] Those who demand a free market have also postulated a "natural rate of wages." Needless to say, some reflection on the sources of wages and the degree to which determining factors are subject to control should lead to the conclusion that any dichotomy into "natural" and "artificial" wage categories is clearly unreal, and, in the words of two close students of the problem, " 'the natural rate of wages,' like the 'normal' world to which it belongs, exists only in books and in the minds of men." [35]

[33] See Anderson, *TNEC Report: Taxation, Recovery, and Defense,* Monograph No. 20 (1940), pp. 242 *et seq.;* also H. J. Tobin and P. W. Bidwell, *Mobilizing Civilian America* (New York, 1940). Even in the Revolution the idea of taxing excess profits to underwrite the war was considered. William Whipple wrote James Barrett, May 21, 1779: "If the whole sum could be drawn from those speculating miscreants, who have been sucking the Blood of their country, it would be a most happy circumstance." Burnett, *Letters,* IV, 223. In Connecticut special taxes on profiteers were levied. *Conn. State Rec.,* I, 365, 366.

[34] Carew v. Rutherford *et al.,* 106 Mass. 1, 14, 15 (1870). See also Taft, *C.J.,* in Wolff Packing Co. v. Court of Industrial Relations, 262 U.S. 522 (1923).

[35] Walton Hamilton and Stacy May, *The Control of Wages* (New York, 1928), p. 112. Cf. also H. A. Millis and R. E. Montgomery, *Labor's Progress and Some Basic Labor Problems* (New York, 1938), pp. 278, 279.

III. CONCERTED ACTION AMONG WORKERS

To ACT IN CONCERT or collectively to redress grievances both economic and political has been a deeply rooted tradition of American life. As a "nation of joiners" we have always utilized voluntary organizations, open or secret, formal or impromptu, permanent or temporary. While the resort to collective action has characterized every range of social and cultural activity,[1] this study is confined to an analysis of instances of concerted action taken by the artisan and working classes, generally, in early American history prior to the rise of trade unions in relatively permanent form.

These economic combinations or associations of workers fall into distinct categories:

1. Combinations by master workers in certain trades to secure and maintain a monopoly of business operations and to restrain freedom of vocational choice.[2] Against such monopoly combinations, whether of labor or of capital, those who favored freedom of trade and of occupational choice made increasing headway in the course of the eighteenth century.

2. Concerted action by workers (normally masters) in licensed trades to secure better fees or prices, customarily regulated by local authority. Such trades were regarded as invested with a public interest.

3. Concerted action by bound servants to secure a redress of grievances. Such action generally took the form of strikes, insurrectionary uprisings, or conspiracies to desert or break the contract of employment.

4. Combinations of free white workmen to resist encroachments on their trades by Negro artisans. Such action paralleled the efforts of artisan monopolists to exclude others from admission to their trades, but it was chiefly manifest in regions where Negro labor competition was especially keen.

5. Joint political action by workmen and employers in the Revolutionary years.

6. Combinations by journeymen workers to secure better working conditions—excessively rare prior to the American Revolution, but increasingly significant after that conflict had ended.

---

[1] See A. M. Schlesinger, "Biography of a Nation of Joiners," *Amer. Hist. Rev.*, L (1944), 1–25.

[2] Major E. A. J. Johnson suggests the term *laissez-travailler* for this freedom. See F. K. Henrich, The Development of American Laissez Faire," *J. Econ. Hist.*, Supp., Dec., 1943, p. 52.

THE COMMON LAW AND COLLECTIVE ACTION

BEFORE CONSIDERING these various manifestations of collective action in the colonies and early states, it would be well to ascertain the attitude of contemporary English law courts toward combinations, whether on the part of masters or of workers. It was the view of the early nineteenth-century British and American courts that the crime of conspiracy at common law embraced virtually all forms of economic combinations to raise prices or wages.[1] It has since been established that the inclusion of labor combinations as conspiracies at common law stems from an ambiguous statement of Hawkins, in his *Pleas of the Crown* published in 1716, to this effect: "There can be no doubt, but that all confederacies whatsoever, wrongfully to prejudice a third person are highly criminal at common law." [2] This bare statement, founded on precedents of dubious value, was widely reiterated.[3] Within a few years it was reinforced by the decision in *Rex v. Journeyman Tailors of Cambridge*,[4] which blazed the trail for a long line of decisions. The majority of scholars who have studied this subject do not support this view, but hold that the extension of criminal conspiracy to include acts in restraint of trade actually began in the Court of Star Chamber early in the seventeenth century; and that such jurisdiction was claimed and ultimately absorbed by King's Bench. Up to that time, apart from the Statute of Labourers

[1] For a detailed discussion of these cases, see R. B. Morris, "Criminal Conspiracy and Early Labor Combinations," *Pol. Sci. Q.,* LII (1937), 52–57.

[2] W. Hawkins, *A Treatise of the Pleas of the Crown* (1st ed., London, 1716), Bk. I. ch. 72. For the authorities in support of this statement, see F. B. Sayre, "Criminal Conspiracy," *Harvard Law Rev.,* XXXV, 402, 403.

[3] Richard Burn, *The Justice of the Peace* (4th ed., London, 1755), p. 276; Matthew Bacon, *Abridgement* (London, 1832), IV, 409; J. Chitty, *A Practical Treatise on the Criminal Law* (1st ed., London, 1816), III, 1139. Early law books published in America did not follow Hawkins, but incorporated instead the early common-law definition of conspiracy. See James Parker, *Conductor Generalis* (Philadelphia, 1722), p. 52; George Webb, *The Office and Authority of a Justice of the Peace* (Williamsburg, Va., 1736), p. 88; Burn, *Justice of the Peace Abridgment* (Boston, 1773), p. 100. Hawkins's definition was adopted by Parker, *op. cit.,* (ed. Woodbridge, N.J., 1764); Richard Starke, *The Office and Authority of a Justice of the Peace* (Williamsburg, Va., 1774), pp. 100–102; J. F. Grimké, *The South-Carolina Justice of the Peace* (Charleston, 1788), p. 114, and by James Wilson (*Works* [Philadelphia, 1804], III, 118), but it is interesting to note that Z. Swift, in his *A System of the Laws of the State of Connecticut,* published in 1796, considered conspiracy merely "as a combination to indict or procure to be prosecuted an innocent man falsely and maliciously, and who is accordingly indicted, and acquitted" (II, 356).

[4] 8 Mod. 10 (1721). Certain workers were indicted and found guilty of conspiracy to raise their wages. In the preceding year a statute had been passed in England expressly making it criminal for the journeymen tailors of *London* and *Westminster* to enter into any agreement "for advancing their Wages or for lessening their usual Hours of Work." 7 Geo. I, c. 13 (1720). However, the indictment could not have been based upon this statute, which was inapplicable, nor was it based upon any other statute, but lay at common law. The court, however erroneously, decided, according to the available report, that the indictment need not conclude *contra formam statuti,* because conspiracy was a common law offense.

and the subsequent line of labor statutes, the only conspiracies known to the law or commonly treated as crimes, according to this view, were conspiracies to prevent, obstruct, or defeat the course of justice, or conspiracies by officials to defeat or delay justice or to extort under color of office. Even such conspiracies were statutory in origin, they contend, and unknown to the early common law.[5]

While there is much merit in this position, it does not give sufficient weight to the fuller significance of trial court judgments and policies as expressed in statutes.[6] For whether or not the common law did consider a combination of workers to raise wages a criminal act, there is no question that under such basic labor laws as the Statute of Labourers of 1349 and the Tudor Statute of Artificers such concerted action was regarded as criminal and seditious.[7] It would hardly be logical to expect that the mercantilists, who advocated forced labor and a low wage scale as a preventive of poverty and vice and an assurance of favorable competition for industry in foreign markets, would tolerate combinations by workers to better their conditions of employment. To crush the rapidly expanding labor movement, a series of acts was passed in the eighteenth century outlawing combinations in particular crafts.[8] Where workers

[5] Maitland points out that Coke's view that even before the Edwardian statutes the writ of conspiracy was already in existence is based upon the fables of the *Mirror of Justice*. Sir Frederick Pollock and F. W. Maitland, *The History of English Law* (Cambridge, 1923), II, 539n. See also P. H. Winfield, *The History of Conspiracy and Abuse of Legal Procedure* (Cambridge, 1921), p. 37; R. S. Wright, *The Law of Criminal Conspiracies and Agreements* (Philadelphia, 1887), p. 5; Sir James Stephen, *History of the Criminal Law of England* (London, 1883), III, 209–210; Sayre, "Criminal Conspiracy," *loc. cit.*, pp. 395, 400 *et seq.*; David Harrison, *Conspiracy as a Crime and as a Tort in English Law* (London, 1924), p. 10.

The process of analogical extension began with the Poulterers' Case, 9 Co. Rep. 55b; Moore, 814 (1611), where a mere agreement or act of combination, not followed by acts in furtherance of its object—in this case to indict falsely—was punished criminally. In Rex v. Starling, 1 Sid. 174; 1 Keb. 650, 655 (1665), the defendants were convicted for conspiring to interfere with the farming of the public revenue. Here was an offense, as Holt pointed out, which was directly leveled at the government. Reg. v. Daniell, 6 Mod. 99, 100 (1703). From this, by analogy, combinations directed against the public welfare were later prosecuted.

[6] See J. M. Landis, *Cases on Labor Law* (Chicago, 1934), p. 12; also M. Sharp and C. O. Gregory, *Social Change and Labor Law* (Chicago, 1939), p. 90.

[7] Going back to the Middle Ages, both journeymen guilds that sought to use the power of combination to improve laboring conditions and masters who combined to drive wages or prices to the level they thought appropriate (notwithstanding town ordinances fixing their wages or prices) were regarded by the courts as illegal combinations. See George, "The Combination Laws Reconsidered," *Econ. Hist.*, I (1927), 223. Among the early statutes the principal ones were: 23 Edw. III, c. 9 (1349); 3 Hen. VI, c. 1. 2, 3 Edw. VI, c. 15 (1549), though aimed primarily at combinations of journeymen craftsmen to keep up wages or reduce hours, outlawed combinations of "artificers, workmen, or labourers." As a matter of fact, as early as 1383 the Corporation of the City of London prohibited all "congregations, covins, and conspiracies of workmen." Sidney and Beatrice Webb. *The History of Trade Unionism* (rev. ed., London, 1920), pp. 2–6.

[8] See, e.g., 7 Geo. I, c. 13 (1720), amended by 8 Geo. III, c. 17, journeymen tailors; 12 Geo. I, c. 34 (1725), amended in 1756 and 1757 by 29 Geo. II, c. 33 and 30 Geo. II, c. 12, woolen industry. See also 22 Geo. II, c. 27, amended by 17 Geo. III, c. 55 and c. 56 (1777); 13 Geo. III,

opposed the scale of wages fixed by the justices of the peace, they were prosecuted for mutiny, riot, or criminal conspiracy. Many such prosecutions could be culled from the local court records of Hogarthian England, indicative of an impressive amount of labor unrest, and demonstrating that in effect combinations were illegal.[9]

COMBINATIONS TO MAINTAIN CRAFT MONOPOLIES

ONCE THE GREAT EMIGRATION to Massachusetts got under way measures were adopted to preserve trade monopolies and to restrain nonresidents from entering the trades. These monopoly groups in the early colonial towns were patterned after the European craft guilds. Massachusetts for a time experimented also with the chartered company, following the English pattern. In 1644 shipbuilding was placed under the supervision of such a chartered company.[1] Next followed the Boston shoemakers' guild, chartered in 1648.[2] The Boston shoemakers had petitioned the court that, on account of the poor quality of shoes being sold in that town, they be formed into a company with power to regulate their calling within the town. This petition was opposed by the country shoemakers, who advanced, in a petition signed by six of their number, several reasons for their stand. Very few of the Boston shoemakers, they contended, were members "of Such a body in o'r [our] Native Country," and therefore inexperienced in guild management. According to the country shoemakers, the real trouble was not poor workmen, whom the Boston shoemakers wanted to suppress, but the poor quality of leather, which should be the subject of closer official inspection. Instead of conferring upon the Boston shoemakers exclusive jurisdiction over the industry, their opponents urged that the country shoemakers and those of Boston be given the privilege of examining the shoes made by the other group. If the shoes of either group were pronounced poor, the

---

c. 68; 33 Geo. III, c. 67; 36 Geo. III, c. 111. For a list of these statutes, see R. Burn, *The Justice of the Peace* (26th ed., 1831).

[9] For 17th-century prosecutions, see *Session Books of Hertford County*, VI, 405–407; *Records of the Borough of Nottingham* (London, 1882–1914), IV, 362; J. C. Jeaffreson, *Middlesex County Records* (London, 1886–92), IV, 61–65; and *Cal. State Pap., Dom.*, Aug. 11–13, 1675. For 18th-century instances, see, e.g., E. G. Dowdell, *A Hundred Years of Quarter Sessions: the Government of Middlesex from 1660 to 1760* (Cambridge, 1932), pp. 154, 155; H. Heaton, *The Yorkshire Woollen and Worsted Industries from the Earliest Times up to the Revolution* (Oxford, 1920), pp. 316, 317; A. P. Wadsworth and J. de L. Mann, *The Cotton Trade and Industrial Lancashire* (Manchester, 1931), p. 342; *London Chron.*, Dec. 12, 1761, cited by M. Dorothy George, *London Life in the XVIIIth Century* (London, 1930), p. 368.

[1] *Mass. Col. Laws, 1660–72*, Introd., p. 72; J. J. Babson, *History of the Town of Gloucester, Cape Ann* (Gloucester, Mass., 1860), p. 187; Clark, *Hist. of Manufactures*, p. 66.

[2] See *Mass. Bay Rec.*, III, 132; Mass. Arch., lib. LIX, fols. 29–32; Blanche E. Hazard, *The Organization of the Boot and Shoe Industry in Massachusetts before 1875* (Cambridge, 1921), p. 9.

decision as to whether they were to be confiscated was to be put up to an impartial shoemaker. It was further urged that the Bostonians be denied the power "to hindre a free trade,"—that is, to keep country shoemakers from coming into the town. Unless that were done, either the country shoemakers would be ruined or forced to migrate to Boston to the detriment of other towns.

Notwithstanding these forceful arguments, a committee of the General Court recommended that a charter be granted to the Boston shoemakers; the General Court adopted the recommendation.[3] The charter conferred self-government upon the guild, including the right to elect their own officers, to pass regulations for their trade subject to the approval of the Assistants or the county court, to affix penalties for breach thereof and to levy fines by distress after a trial before the masters and wardens of the guild. In addition, it gave the craftsmen a monopoly and provided that the county court, on complaint of the masters and wardens, should have the power to "suppresse" shoemakers not approved by the guild. It is most significant that the authorities included a clause prohibiting unlawful combinations to raise the price of shoes, boots, or wages and expressly denying shoemakers the right to refuse to make shoes for a customer of the leather he provided and at a reasonable rate.[4] Finally, the charter was to be in force for three years only. At the same session the General Court granted an identical charter to the coopers of Boston and Charlestown.[5] In neither case does it appear that the charters were renewed at the end of the three-year period. These charters set up guild constitutions based on the contemporary English pattern,[6] in which the administrative functions were in the hands of the masters and wardens. The oligarchical type of control established in the two Massachusetts charters was actually under heavy attack in England at that time, when the cleavage between wage earners and employers was

[3] Mass. Arch., lib. LIX, fols. 29–32.

[4] John R. Commons suggests that this provision was the result of a compromise, as the shoemakers wanted to give up working as itinerant cobblers and to work instead in their own shops using their own leather. This provision is reminiscent of earlier European statutes imposing penalties upon guild members who refused to work in the homes of their customers. J. R. Commons, "American Shoemakers, 1648–1895; a Sketch of Industrial Evolution," *Q.J. Econ.*, XXIV, 41. However, the arguments advanced by both sides in this controversy make it appear that the authorities, having granted a monopoly to the Bostonians, were anxious to protect the consumer interest against strikes or combinations. The issue here was regulation of monopoly rather than shopmen versus itinerant cobblers.

[5] *Mass. Bay Rec.*, III, 132.

[6] Coyne's reference to this coopers' guild as "the first labor union" seems wide of the mark. F. B. Coyne, *The Development of the Cooperage Industry in the United States, 1620–1940* (Chicago, 1940), p. 11.

more clearly marked than in the American colonies during the period of the Puritan Revolution.[7] These guilds did not last long enough in Massachusetts for the rank and file of the membership to resent the power of the governing body. In addition to the coopers and shoemakers, Edward Johnson in his *Wonder-Working Providence* implied that the tanners also enjoyed virtual guild powers to determine standards and prices—their products being double the prices obtaining in England at that time—and suggests that other crafts were also organized, although, in the absence of records, it is not possible to pursue his leads.[8] A quarter century after the grant of charters to the shoemakers and coopers the hatters of Massachusetts Bay petitioned for similar privileges, but were refused until they could show that they could produce as good hats priced as cheaply as those imported.[9]

The guild organization of master craftsmen was exceedingly rare in other colonies save for licensed trades clothed with a public interest. In the colony of New York evidence has been uncovered pointing to an organization of weavers in the Borough Town of Westchester. The mayor's court minutes of that town have the following entry for July, 1702:

Wm Bennet Weaver makes his Application to this Court to be Admitted a freeman of the Guild of the Weavers in this Corporation. The Mayr and Alderman hauing heard a good Character of the said Wm Benet and that he is a man of Honest Life and Conversation and followes his trade of a plain Weaver do Admitt the s'd Wm Bennett to be a freeman in said Corporation and to have the Rights and Libertyes as any free man in any the like Corporations within her Majesties Realm of England.[10]

Apart from this cryptic entry, no further record has been found of this, the only known weavers' guild in colonial America.

Somewhat more craft guild activity was found in the province of Pennsylvania. The Philadelphia Common Council granted the petitions of the cordwainers and tailors for corporate privileges to regulate their

---

[7] See *The Case of the Commonalty of the Corporation of Weavers* (c. 1650), p. 1 (Guildhall Library, London). Cf. also Margaret James, *Social Problems and Policy during the Puritan Revolution, 1640–1660* (London, 1930), pp. 196 *et seq.;* I. B. Choate, "The Town Guild," *N.E. Hist. and Gen. Reg.,* LVII (1903), 168–177 at pp. 172, 173.

[8] *Wonder-Working Providence of Sion's Savior in New England* (ed., 1654), Bk. III, ch. vi, pp. 207–209.

[9] *Mass. Bay Rec.,* IV, Pt. II, 527 (1672); J. B. Felt, *Annals of Salem* (2d ed., Boston, 1845–49), II, 170; cf. Weeden, *Econ. . . . Hist. of N.E.,* I, 274.

[10] Minutes of the Mayor's Court of the Borough Town of Westchester, 1696–1706 (1702), N.Y. Hist. Soc. For New Netherland guilds, see *supra,* pp. 84, 85.

crafts, and formulated a policy of chartering other craft guilds if the artisans concerned desired "the better to serve the Publick in their Respective Capacities." [11]

The most important of these guilds or combinations of artisans in Philadelphia was the Carpenters' Company, formed in 1724 "for the purpose of obtaining instruction in the science of architecture, and assisting such of their members as should by accident be in need of support," or the widows and minor children of the members. In order to qualify for membership one must have been a master for six years.[12] The early members appear to have been master architects and builders like James Portius and Edmund Wooley. The admission fee was 30s., and restrictions imposed upon membership led to the formation of a rival association known as "The Second Carpenters' Company," which, after a few years of separate existence, merged with the older society. When, in 1769, the admission fee was raised to £4, "The Friendship Carpenters' Company" was established which admitted members for an inconsequential fee of 5s. But in 1785 members of the rival association were admitted into the parent society.[13]

The most significant activity of the company was the establishing of a "Book of Prices" for both employers and workmen with the avowed object of assuring the latter "a fair recompense for their labour and the owner . . . the worth of his money." [14] The minutes of the company from 1724 to 1763 have unfortunately been lost, but the extant minutes beginning with the latter year indicate that the appointment of a standing committee to set prices for carpenters' work to be laid

[11] *M.C.C., Phila.*, pp. 34, 145–147 (1718). Of the 17 fire companies in the city by the eve of the Revolution, all of which had social and political interests as well as fire prevention among their objectives, one, the Cordwainers' Fire Company, organized in 1760 by 39 master shoemakers, was set up along guild lines and concerned with controlling apprentices and servants in addition to fire fighting. See Cordwainers' Fire Company Mins., 1760–73, Pa. Hist. Soc. Even though the principal activity of this society appears to have been fire fighting and the protection of members' property, one could not be elected to the company if he had not served a regular apprenticeship. *Ibid.*, f. 22 (1762). For labor activities, see *infra*, pp. 445, 446.

[12] There is no evidence to support the position of Norman J. Ware, *Labor in Modern Industrial Society* (New York, 1935), p. 127, and Herbert Harris, *American Labor* (New Haven, 1938), p. 5n., that the society originally included journeymen as well as masters.

[13] The company was incorporated in 1792. In the course of time the entrance fee was raised to $100, although the bylaws provided that the eldest son of a deceased member might be admitted without a fee. See *An Act to Incorporate the Carpenters' Company of the City and County of Philadelphia* (Philadelphia, 1866), pp. vi, vii, 3, 14, 21; *Reminiscences of Carpenters' Hall* (Philadelphia, 1858), pp. 4, 5. In 1783 the Company appointed a committee to act with other committees of manufacturers and mechanics to memorialize the Assembly to lay such duties on imported manufactures as might be deemed necessary. *Act to Incorporate*, p. 47.

[14] In other trades without such price lists as, for example, the upholsterers, there might be severe price-cutting competition. See *Pa. Chron.*, July 13, 1767.

before the whole company for their approval was regularly carried out. The bylaws of the company stated the function of the committee on the book of prices to be "to fix a price on all new-fashioned Carpenter work, that may be introduced from time to time; and further to equalize such of the prices as may be requested, and to enter the same in the manuscript book to be kept by them in the Hall for that purpose for the use of the members of the Company," who were permitted to make copies. Furthermore, the committee was charged with the settlement of any differences arising in the valuation of carpenter's work, both between carpenters and their employers or between members of the company. Their decision as respects the price of such work was to be binding on the parties. Any member of the company desirous of evaluating carpenter's work who had been a member for at least five years was eligible to receive a certificate from the committee under the seal of the company provided that the applicant made oath or affirmation before an alderman or justice of the peace that he would "well and truly measure and value Carpenter work, agreeably to the standard Book of Prices of this Company, to the best of his judgment and ability, always having special regard to the quality of the work." Any member measuring work without such certificate was liable to be fined ten dollars for the first offense and to be expelled for the second. Fines were also imposed upon members for showing the book of prices to non-members.[15] It is therefore apparent that the publication of these price lists was not a policy of the company in the early period.[16]

In emulation of the Philadelphia Carpenters' Company, associations of master carpenters in other towns in the colonies began in the course of the eighteenth century to establish price scales, many of which were published. In the post-Revolutionary period it was quite customary for carpenters to issue detailed schedules of prices. In the *Rules for House-Carpenters' Work in the Town of Providence,* issued in that city in 1796, there is an introductory note to this effect:

The Committee appointed in February, 1796, to revise the rules of carpenters' work have found upon examination that the former rules begun in the year

[15] *Act to Incorporate,* pp. 20, 35, 41, 43, 48, 60; Richard K. Betts, *Carpenters' Hall and Its Historic Memories* (Philadelphia, 1891), p. 4.

[16] The late Alexander J. Wall reported the existence of a volume in preparation, dated about 1775, bearing a bookplate of the Carpenters' Company of Philadelphia and the name of Thomas Savery, a prominent carpenter; it has 36 plates and a leaf of text containing a price list. "Books on Architecture Printed in America, 1775–1830," *Bibliographical Essays: a Tribute to Wilberforce Eames* (Cambridge, Mass., 1924), p. 299. This was probably the text in preparation for publication for the company's members.

1750 and continued down to the present date, were calculated upon a scale of five shillings per day; and have made the following calculations upon the same principles.

In 1800 the Boston carpenters issued a book of prices which was a revision of rules adopted in that town in 1774. In an introductory statement the committee which drew up the rules discussed the principles which guided them and added:

Upon these principles *"the Carpenters rules of work in the Town of Boston"* were formed and published in the year 1774; and several have held them up as a direction at this day, not considering that they were calculated upon a scale which bears no proportion to the price of other labor *now,* and which is by no means an equivalent compensation for the service, in reference to the raised price of the necessaries of life; and that, not only the low rate at which they were cast render them a very incompetent guide at present, but that they are besides greatly defective in not specifying one quarter part of the work now in demand. Wherefore, the Carpenters of the Town have met at sundry times to consider the propriety of forming new arrangements, and Rules, more accurate and more complete, and calculated on a scale better adjusted to the means of an honest livelihood in an equitable reward to faithful industry. They chose, accordingly, a large and respectable committee, out of their number, to form such Rules; which, being reported and unanimously approved by the whole body, they now publish for the service of the Craft,—expecting that all work will be measured by them, and executed in the best possible manner.[17]

At a meeting of the Boston Carpenters at Mareau's Hall, August 21, 1800, it was voted that the names of the committee of twenty-one who drew up the rules be published in the book.[18] These rules are very detailed, and lay down a schedule of prices per item rather than per diem. For example, the price schedule covers such work as framing floors of all kinds, side and ends, and roofs, laying rough boarding, putting up window frames, sashes, clapboarding, and laying shingles (per square), building stairs, wainscoting, dadoing rooms and stairs. This volume is representative of a considerable number of publications reproducing price scales agreed upon by master carpenter organizations going back as far as 1790 and continuing well down into the middle of the nineteenth century.[19] It is apparent from the extensive schedules that were

[17] *The Rules of Work of the Carpenters in the Town of Boston* (Boston, 1800), pp. iii, iv, Harvard Coll. Lib.

[18] *Ibid.*, p. 2.

[19] Price books have in general been omitted from the compilation of H. R. Hitchcock. See *Constitution, Rules, Regulations of the Carpenter Society of Baltimore* (Baltimore, 1790); *The Constitution of the Associated Body of House Carpenters of the City of New-York* (New York, 1792); *A Price-Book, in Alphabetical Order, of Sundry Carpenters' Work, Collected, Calculated, and Now, by the Authority of an Angry Block-Cornice Architect, Dictated for the Carpenters of*

published that master house carpenters, along with cabinet- and chair-makers, had begun to organize by the eve of the Revolution, and that in some cases these organizations included journeymen or were supplemented by journeymen's organizations.[20]

Unique among colonial combinations were the Moravian collective ventures set up at Savannah in 1735, at Bethlehem, Pennsylvania, in 1744, and in North Carolina in 1753. Spangenberg's "General Plan," the most celebrated of these projects, brought all trades and industries at Bethlehem and Nazareth under church control and operated through a *Hausgemeine,* really a central guild council comprising representatives from each of the crafts meeting in regular sessions. The proposals of the *Hausgemeine* had to be approved by the central board, an executive body. The Moravians were obligated to work in the General Economy merely by a verbal contract under which they donated their time and labor in exchange for no material compensation other than food, clothing, and shelter for themselves and their families and protection in old age. In the Brotherly Agreement of 1754 the members stated that they had joined not "for the sake of wages" nor to "demand hire or pay for their labor," but rather for spiritual satisfaction. While looking upon themselves as "free people" rather than as "men-servants and maid-servants," they specifically agreed not to oppose "those persons who have been appointed our leaders." Having agreed to "a willing and

---

Baltimore-Town . . . (Baltimore, 1792); *The Carpenters' Rules of Work, for the Town of Boston* (Boston, 1794); *The Journeymen Cabinet and Chair-Makers' Philadelphia Book of Prices* (2d ed., corrected and enlarged, Philadelphia, 1795, Hist. Soc. of Pa. [the first edition, printed in 1795, was called *The Philadelphia Chair-Makers Book of Prices*]); *The Constitution of the Carpenters Society of Carlisle* [cut of house] (Carlisle, Pa., 1785); *The Carpenters' Rules of Work, in the Town of Boston, with Great Addition to the Work* (Boston, 1795), Lib. of Cong.; *The Journeymen Cabinet and Chair-Makers' New-York Book of Prices* (New York, 1796); *Rules for House-Carpenters' Work in the Town of Providence* (Providence, 1796), Brown University, R.I. Hist. Soc.; *The Philadelphia Cabinet and Chair-Makers' Book of Prices, Instituted March 4, 1796* (Philadelphia, 1796), Hist. Soc. of Pa.; *Regulations, Ascertaining the Work and Wages of House-Joiners and Cabinet Makers; Agreed upon at Hatfield in the County of Hampshire, March 2, 1796* (Northampton, Mass., 1796); *Regulations Ascertaining the Work and Wages of House-Joiner and Cabinet Makers; Agreed upon at Hatfield, in the County of Hampshire, March 2nd, 1796. A Paper Very Useful Both for Workmen and their Employers* (Rutland, 1797); *A Bill of Rates for Carpenter and House Joiner Work Settled and Agreed on, by the Subscribers, Chambersburg, April 13, 1790* (Chambersburg, 1799). See also William Norman, *The Builders' Easy Guide, or Young Carpenter's Assistant; . . . To Which Is Added a List of the Price of Carpenter's Work, in the Town of Boston* (Boston, 1803), N.Y. Hist. Soc. (lacks the list of carpenters' prices); James Gallier, *American Builders' General Price Book and Estimator* (New York, 1833); *The Book of Prices of the House Carpenters and Joiners of the City of Cincinnati, Adopted Monday, January 4, 1819*, revised in 1844 by Louis H. Shally (Cincinnati, 1844), N.Y. Pub. Lib.; J. Wilson, *The Mechanics' and Builders' Price Book, Showing in Detail the Price of Wood, Brick and Stone Work* (New York, 1859).

[20] See the *Journeymen Cabinet and Chair-Makers' New-York Book of Prices* (New York, 1796).

childlike subordination," they could have no moral right to combine for wages. Under this agreement strikes would have been regarded as impious as well as immoral.[21]

In these Moravian communities a virtual guild system was maintained, with rank in the crafts divided between masters and apprentices. Conferences of masters regulated prices, agreed upon standards of quality, and set up facilities to provide proper training for apprentices. Considerable dissatisfaction arose in the General Economy because the farmers and craftsmen were burdened with the support not only of the church in Europe but also of the Pilgrims' Congregation, an unproductive group in their own community, which devoted itself to religious affairs. When the General Economy was dissolved in 1762, the crafts and trades returned to private management, with the church retaining a goodly measure of control. Until the end of the eighteenth century, religious exclusiveness dominated the economic life of these Moravian settlements and interlopers were not tolerated. When the policy of exclusion was abandoned many outsiders moved into Bethlehem.[22]

The craft guilds did not take root in the South. While it is true that the incorporated trades of London were the chief subscribers to the Virginia Company venture, the guilds of mercers, grocers, fishmongers, merchant tailors, ironmongers, and clothworkers all supporting the colonization program,[23] there is no evidence of guilds of master workmen in seventeenth-century Virginia. The merchant guilds provided for in the act of 1705 "for establishing ports and towns" appear to have been designed more as an instrument of government than as monopoly combinations.[24]

---

[21] When the Single Brothers struck at Salem, N.C., in 1778, Moravian leaders called the "audacious combination" sinful, but increased the annual bonus. See A. L. Fries, ed., *Records of the Moravians of North Carolina*, III (Raleigh, 1926), 1211, 1212, 1226, 1259.

[22] Besides the farms, 32 trades provided the General Economy with a source of income in 1749, 40 in 1752. A similar distribution of crafts was found among the brethren at Nazareth, Gnadthal, Christiansbrunn, and Friedensthal.

Between Jan., 1787, and Feb., 1788—within a year after the policy of exclusion had been abandoned—150 strangers entered the town. The chief authority for the Moravian economic program is J. J. Sessler, *Communal Pietism among Early American Moravians* (New York, 1933), pp. 19, 79–81, 85–87, 89, 90, 192–202, 207, 229–231. The rules of the General Economy found in the Archives at Bethlehem are in substance translated by J. M. Levering, *A History of Bethlehem, Pa., 1741–1892* (Bethlehem, 1903), pp. 178, 179. Typical management contracts after the breakdown of the General Economy are found in the Archives at Bethlehem for 1763 and 1764.

[23] See Brown, *Genesis of the U.S.*, I, 250 *et seq.*, 277, 278, 291, 302, 306, 309; II, 857 *et seq.*

[24] This act provided that each town was to have a merchant guild and community "with all customs and libertys belonging to a free burgh." In communities of thirty families or more, eight of the principal inhabitants were to be chosen by the freeholders and inhabitants who had reached twenty-one years of age, "not being servants or apprentices." The eight were designated "benchers of the guild hall" and entrusted with the government of the town. Hening, III, 408 (1705).

In medieval England local craftsmen were protected from nonresidents entering the crafts in their towns. In fact, restrictions became more
onerous in the course of time.[25] As Salzman points out, the traditional
attitude of the Englishman toward a stranger had always been to "heave
half a brick at him." [26] In the early colonial period the town authorities
protected local workmen from interlopers. When they failed to do so,
local workers took concerted action for their own protection. This
medieval principle of monopolistic exclusiveness found expression in
regulations of colonial towns limiting admission to the crafts to those
who enjoyed the freedom of the town. Boston, for instance, made the
completion of a term of apprenticeship a prerequisite to opening up a
shop and limited the trades and crafts to those who had been admitted
as inhabitants.[27] During the early years the apprenticeship requirement
appears to have been strictly enforced.[28]

In 1675 a group of ship carpenters who had ridden an interloper out
of Boston on a rail because he had worked in the yard without having
served his full seven years' apprenticeship were fined five shillings apiece
payable to the government and a like amount to the victim.[29] John
Roberts and the eight other defendants admitted the charge of having
forcibly carried John Langworthy "upon a pole and by violence" from
the north end of Boston to the town dock. This "occasioned a great
tumult of people, meeting there with the Constable who did rescue
him." The defendants justified their conduct on the ground that "hee
was an interloper and had never served his time to the trade of a Ship
carpenter and now came to work in theire yard and they understood
such things were usuall in England."

[25] O. J. Dunlop, *English Apprenticeship and Child Labour* (New York, 1912), p. 37n. See
petition of the coopers and tailors in J. S. Davies, *A History of Southampton* (London, 1883),
pp. 273, 276; complaint of the citizens of London against alien handicraftsmen (1571), Tawney
and Power, *Tudor Econ. Docs.*, I, 309, 310. For 17th-century protests against French artisans, see
Beloff, *Public Order and Popular Disturbances*, p. 82.

[26] L. F. Salzman, *English Industries of the Middle Ages* (Oxford, 1923), p. 333.

[27] *Boston Town Rec.*, II, 135 (1657), 156, 157 (1660)—setting an age minimum of 22 years
and an apprenticeship of 7 years. For early Plymouth legislation, see *Plymouth Col. Rec.*, XI, 33,
108, 191 (1636), requiring a servant to serve his master "for some time" before being admitted
"to bee for himselfe," with the broad exception: "except hee haue bin an houskeeper or master
of a family or meet or fitt to bee soe."

[28] See *Boston Town Rec.*, II, 137 (1657); VII, 142 (1680). In 1664 the town enjoined Josiah
Clarke from opening a cooper's shop before attaining the minimum age and serving out his
time. *Ibid.*, VII, 21 (1664). The authorities were especially alert to see that these requirements
were not waived by master craftsmen in favor of their own sons or other close relatives. *Ibid.*,
pp. 19, 39, 88 (1663, 1668, 1674). The master was warned that he would be subjected to a
penalty of 10s. per month for each month his son illegally plied the trade of a cooper. See also
ibid., p. 35 (1667).

[29] Cases of Roberts *et al.*, *Suffolk*, pp. 602, 603 (1675).

Down through the colonial period artisans and laborers were expected to get permission from the Boston town authorities before plying their trades.[30] Such permission was at times withheld, and violators of the town ordinance fined.[31] In line with this policy of maintaining intact the craft and trade monopolies was the general restriction on the movements of strangers. Among those warned to depart the town were numerous laborers and artisans.[32] In addition to the competitive motive, the authorities also wished to make reasonably certain that strangers would not be a charge upon the town.[33] By the mid-eighteenth century the population trend which favored the growth of other colonial towns at the expense of Boston and the increase of a laissez faire spirit in that town were signalized by a noticeable decline in the number of prohibitions to exercise trades and in "warnings out."

It seems likely that in Boston as well as in other colonial towns the artisan, having served an apprenticeship and having been admitted as a freeman, could and did at times practice more than one craft or transfer to other crafts or trades if he wished.[34] A Boston pamphlet of 1714 protested against the proposed incorporation of the town, objecting to "paying for our Freedom, that was Freeborn and in bondage to no man," and also to the possibility that shopkeepers and artisans who were undertaking several trades would have to give up the practice.[35]

In New York the local monopoly of trades and handicrafts stemmed directly from the "burgher-right," a privilege of the inhabitants of New Amsterdam,[36] which, after the English conquest, was carried over into

---

[30] The crafts and retail trades were restricted to the inhabitants—persons formally admitted to the town by the selectmen or in town meeting or freeholders, including persons born in the town and those having served an apprenticeship in the town. *Mass. Province Laws*, I, 452 (1710); *Mass. Acts and Resolves*, V, 38, 39, 259, 460, 903, 1123. See also *Boston Town Rec.*, VIII, 104 (1714). For admissions of tradesmen, artisans, and laborers, see *Boston Selectmen Mins.*, *1716–36*, *1736–42*, *1742–53*, *1754–63*, *1764–68*, *passim*. New Haven admissions show a big increase beginning around 1742. New Haven Town Rec., lib. 1684–1765, e.g., fols. 461, 463, 469, 490, 497, *passim*.

[31] *Boston Town Rec.*, VII, 121, 122 (1678), where the authorities investigated George Jay, "said to be in the rebellion of Nathl Bacon there," *ibid.*, p. 22 (1664), layman appointed to determine whether a craftsman possessed the proper degree of skill in his craft. See also *ibid.*, VII, 49 (1669), 125 (1678), 171 (1684); XIII, 31, 33.

[32] See *Boston Selectmen Mins.*, 1716–36, pp. 2, 11, 14, 26, 30–33. See also *Suffolk*, p. 108 (1672), a weaver.

[33] See *supra*, p. 14.

[34] In England an early statute barred such changes of employment. 37 Edw. III, c. 6 (1363).

[35] N. Mathews, Jr., "Attempts to Incorporate Boston," Col. Soc. of Mass., *Publications*, X, 345. See also *Boston Town Rec.*, *passim*; "Burghers and Freemen of New York," N.Y. Hist. Soc., *Coll.* (1885), pp. 103, 179–180; Samuel McKee, Jr., *Labor in Colonial New York, 1664–1776* (New York, 1935), p. 54. Cf. also *N.Y. Gazette and Weekly Post-Boy*, Aug. 26, 1751, where John Tremain, an actor, announced that he was setting himself up in business as a cabinetmaker.

[36] *R.N.A.*, I, 10, 44–46; III, 250, 270; V, 166, 169; VII, 232–236.

the freemanship.[37] However the cost of purchasing the freedom was nominal,[38] and the city followed a liberal policy in admitting outsiders,[39] both skilled and unskilled workmen.[40] As a matter of fact, for many years prior to the Revolution the authorities admitted without cost those unable to pay the freedom dues.[41] As the price of freemanship was low in relation to the relatively high wage scale of New York's craftsmen, it is clear that the freemanship opened the polls to all classes of citizens, including a good proportion of artisans and laborers.[42]

Nevertheless, despite the declining legal significance of the freemanship on the eve of the Revolution, at times it was still essential for a workman who wished to secure work in New York to establish the fact that he had been an inhabitant of the city for some time prior to his application. This is the clear implication of the following advertisement in the *New-York Gazette or Weekly Post-Boy* for May 8, 1766 (Supplement):

A Large quantity of good well drest spinning Flax is wanted for the Factory in New-York: All Persons who have such to dispose of, at reasonable rate, by applying to Obadiah Wells, in Mulbery-Street, near the Fresh Water, may have ready Money for it. N.B. None but the best sort will have the preference. Also

[37] N.Y.M.C.M., lib. 1674–75 (June 5, 1675); Rec. Wills, lib. XIXB, f. 617 (1675), Surrogate's Court, N.Y. Co. The New York City charter granted this monopoly, and set a fine of £5 for engaging in any craft or trade without being free of the city. *N.Y. Col. Laws*, I, 181–195; *M.C.C.*, I, 290–306 (1686); also pp. 222, 228 (1691).

[38] *M.C.C.*, II, 198–199. The fee for handicraftsmen was raised from 6s. to 20s. in 1730. *Ibid.*, IV, 96–97; VI, 308–310.

[39] McKee has found 582 persons admitted to the freedom of the city between March 27, 1694, and Sept. 3, 1706, representing 80 different trades (*op. cit.*, p. 30). "Burghers and Freemen," *loc. cit.*, pp. 77–82.

[40] In 1756 thirty-one common laborers, almost half of the admitted freemen, secured the freedom of the city. *Ibid.*, pp. 183 *et seq.*; N.Y.G.S., 1732–62, fols. 276, 295, *passim*.

[41] *M.C.C.*, V, 326 (1762). The practice prevailed in the mayor's court long before that date. See, e.g., R. B. Morris, ed., *Sel. Cases, Mayor's Court*, p. 178, where a former servant was made a freeman "Gratis, being a Poor Man." The relative decline of the number of laborers securing admission after 1765 is attributed by McKee to the likelihood that it was gradually becoming unnecessary for a common laborer to become a freeman in order to earn a living, and he naturally wanted to avoid the expense of freemanship, by that time principally of political significance. The increase in the number of admissions at the time of the agitation over the Stamp Act (*N.Y. Mercury*, Oct. 7, 1765) was very likely due to a desire to secure the franchise during those critical days. McKee, *op. cit.*, pp. 40, 41.

[42] Beverly McAnear, in a suggestive article, contends that during the 18th century there was a constantly growing percentage of men engaged in retailing or handicrafts who had not gained the freedom of the city. "The Place of the Freeman in Old New York," *N.Y. Hist.* (October, 1940). The price of the freedom was halved in 1801. "Burghers and Freemen," *loc. cit.*, pp. 240, 249, 275, 399.

The course of the freemanship in Albany pretty closely paralleled the trend in New York City. On occasion handicraftsmen were barred from plying their trades until licensed. Munsell, *Annals*, VI, 257, 258 (1711), 268 (1712); VII, 11 (1713); VIII, 297 (1724). The price of the freedom was reduced for handicraftsmen from 16s. to 12s., but later raised to £1 16s. *Ibid.*, X, 134 (1748), 150 (1752), 153 (1781). See also *Brookhaven Rec.*, I, 36 (1662).

the spinners in New-York, are hereby notified, that due Attendance will be given, every Tuesday, Thursday, and Saturday, in the Afternoon, to give out Flax and receive in Yarn; by said Wells, and to prevent Trouble, no Person who has not been an Inhabitant in this City ever since May last, will be admitted as a Spinner in the Factory. Also the said Wells, still continues receiving and selling in the Market, all sorts of Country Manufactories, such as Linens and Woollen Cloth, Stockings, etc. etc. at five per cent for Sales and Remittances.

While the principal complaints against interlopers came from the licensed trades, other groups sought protection well along into the eighteenth century, by which time laissez faire trends resulted in a greater degree of freedom of occupational choice. The General Court of Assize, sitting in New York in 1675, found Cornelius Steenwyck and six others guilty of having engaged in "divers Trades and occupations," "being aliens . . . contrary to the several Statute Lawes in such cases enacted." Their goods and chattels were accordingly forfeited to the crown.[43]

In 1747 a large number of building-trades workers petitioned Governor George Clinton against the encroachments of interlopers from the Jerseys who came into the city "in Several numerous Companys," exercising the trades of carpenter, bricklayer, etc. "after the laying of our Taxes yearly." By offering their services at drastically lower wages (for example, at a rate per job or per specific article of workmanship of £20 or £30 less "than has been agreed for by us") and by bringing their own nails and building materials from other provinces, the outsiders constituted a serious threat to local labor.[44] Implied in this petition is the existence of a combination of carpenters, bricklayers, and kindred workers to set a scale of wages or prices. The existence of such a combination would, aside from the concerted actions of licensed guilds such as the carmen, porters, butchers, and bakers, represent what was probably the first temporary labor union in the history of the city. Certainly the public authorities gave not the slightest encouragement to such activities, but viewed this evidence of industrial solidarity with marked suspicion. The petition was submitted to rigid scrutiny. The authorities noted that, of the ninety-nine signatures on the petition, two of the

[43] N.Y. State Hist., *3d Ann. Report* (1897), p. 431 (1675). See also presentment of James Grayham, Rec. Wills, lib. XIXB, f. 289 (1680), Surrogate's Court, N.Y. Co.

[44] "Burghers and Freemen of New York," *loc. cit.,* pp. 507–511; "Calendar of Council Minutes," p. 363. A copy of the petition is in the Horsmanden Papers, fols. 175–177, N.Y. Hist. Soc. The document is endorsed in Horsmanden's handwriting: "Report upon it verbally 10 April 1747. Advised the Gov. to give for answer to the petitioners that they should pursue the ordinary and regular method prescribed by the Law of the City."

workers had "signed twice," that three names were "feigned," that one signature represented a non-existent person, another a "highlander" and accordingly suspect, that two were mere "labourers," and that one was actually a "cordwainer," and clearly out of place in the building trades. Less attention, however, was devoted to the economic issues raised by the carpenters and allied workers. The governor referred the petition to a committee, which advised the petitioners to seek their remedy under the city charter, which provided that strangers who exercised a trade in the city and failed to take up their freedom could be fined five pounds. The committee's further observation betrayed a somewhat patronizing class bias:

Secondly, The Council observe there are about Ninety nine Names to this Petition. That the Bulk of the persons who may be supposed to have subscribed their Names are obscure people altogether unknown to us in person and name, excepting very few of them. If they are Freemen and there be at this time any real cause for such complaint, they must be ignorant and forgetful of the Obligations of the Oath of a Freeman of this City which is "The Franchise and Customs thereof to maintain and the City to keep harmless in that which in there is" and therefore the Council are of Opinion it becomes the Duty of every Freeman when the priviledges of the Citizens are invaded (to use the words of the petition) and who is apprized thereof to warn the Mayor that the Remedy given by Charter may be applyed.

In 1769 Thomas Hardenbrook and other house carpenters, by petition to the common council, similarly complained against unfair competition of country carpenters coming to the city in the summer season. The council courteously referred the matter to a committee, and then let it die.[45] But at least the applicants were spared a lecture on their civic duty.

The ship carpenters also endeavored to confine their occupation to inhabitants. Jeffrey Amherst wrote to Mayor John Cruger on August 10, 1763, that he was fitting out some transports for immediate service and that the carpenters employed on them would not venture to work without a license from the mayor. He went on to say: "I should be glad you would give them Permission, as it is of real consequence to the King's Service that those Vessels are got ready by the utmost expedition." [46]

In 1784 a group of ship carpenters complained to the public authorities

[45] *M.C.C.*, VII, 177; McKee, *op. cit.*, p. 43. Stokes (*Iconography*, IV, 797, 798) observes that "the situation appears to have been settled by private agreement, as the committee made no report of record." This is hardly convincing evidence of agreement or of any action whatsoever.
[46] MSS Coll., N.Y. Pub. Lib.

that George Gar shipwright lately (about sixteen or eighteen Months) from Scotland carries on his business in a manner hurtful to the Petitioners and their Brother Shipwrights: And that as the said George is not a Freeman but an Alien they conceive he is not entitled to carry on the said Busines therefore they pray that he may [be] fined and prevented for the future from carrying on the said Business, as the Charter directs.[47]

The master workmen of Philadelphia made similar strenuous efforts to maintain the exclusive privileges to ply their trades. Shortly after the incorporation of Philadelphia the mayor and Common Council issued an ordinance forbidding nonfreemen from keeping "Open Shops, or to be master workmen." Many of the immigrants after 1716 were regarded by the town craftsmen as "not quallify'd to Exercise thear Trades." Nevertheless, the bars to the freemanship were let down early.[48]

In general, the effect of these local regulations was to curb freedom of occupational choice until well along into the eighteenth century, by which time the authorities appeared reluctant to protect local craftsmen against transient workers and were lax in enforcing apprenticeship requirements. These laissez faire trends parallel a similar trend in contemporary England, where, despite the rise of combinations formed primarily to maintain the earlier restrictions against interlopers, the authorities encouraged the rise of a free labor market and large-scale industry.[49]

The general restrictions against admission to the crafts were implemented by certain European guild notions about the strict separation

[47] N.Y.C.C. Rec., File Box 10, Bundle 3, Record Room 250, Municipal Building.

[48] Between April 16 and May 27, 1717, 426 persons were admitted to the freedom, including laborers and a variety of artificers. *M.C.C., Phila.*, pp. 117–135.

[49] As early as 1615 the London mayor's court in Tolley's Case, a proceeding on the apprenticeship clauses of the Statute of Artificers, sustained a plea in bar that there was a custom of London according to which any freeman of that city who had been apprenticed to one trade for seven years might lawfully relinquish that trade and take up another. Tawney and Power, *Tudor Econ. Docs.*, I, 378–383. Instances multiplied in 17th-century England of workers setting up trades for themselves without having served their apprenticeship. In the period 1659–61 there were twelve cases in the Surrey quarter sessions of infringement of apprenticeship laws. *Surrey Quarter Session Records, Order Book, 1659–61* (Surrey Record Society, No. 35), *passim*. For instances of late 17th- and early 18th-century organizations of workers in England to exclude outsiders, see G. Unwin, *The Gilds and Companies of London* (London, 1909), p. 343, and *Industrial Organization in the Sixteenth and Seventeenth Centuries*, pp. 212, 213; Wadsworth and Mann, *op. cit.*, pp. 341, 343; Lipson, *Woollen and Worsted Industry*, p. 211; Dunlop, *Eng. Apprenticeship*, pp. 225 *et seq.* For the treatment of such petitions by the courts, see Heaton, *Yorkshire Woollen and Worsted Industries*, pp. 309, 310; Wadsworth and Mann, *Cotton Trade and Indust. Lancashire*, p. 351; Dowdell, *Hundred Years of Quarter Sessions*, pp. 174, 175; Lipson, *op. cit.*, pp. 85, 116, 117. For the decline of the guild monopolies in the 17th and 18th centuries, see Stella Kramer, *The English Craft Guilds: Studies in their Progress and Decline* (New York, 1927), pp. 176, 177, 205, 208, 210. See also Adam Smith, *Wealth of Nations*, Bk. I, ch. x, pt. ii. For the problem in France in the late 17th century, see C. W. Cole, *French Mercantilism, 1683–1700* (New York, 1943), pp. 187, 193.

of related trades. Edward Johnson in his *Wonder Working Providence* states that in Massachusetts Bay carpenters, joiners, glaziers, and painters "follow their trades only," implying such strict specialization had been achieved by the time he was writing. The leather industry furnished the most notable example of rigid separation of crafts. Throughout the colonies legislation was enacted time after time strictly separating the various branches of that industry. Precedent for such legislation was a series of English statutes forbidding tanners from working as shoemakers or shoemakers as tanners, keeping the crafts of tanner and currier strictly separate, and denying to both curriers and cordwainers the right to poach on the territory of the other.[50] By the early seventeenth century these irksome restrictions were being circumvented in England,[51] but the colonists persisted for a long time thereafter in the attempt to maintain tanning, currying, and shoemaking as separate trades.[52] Certain towns, notable among them New Haven, restricted tanners to those who were licensed by the authorities, generally after having served a term of apprenticeship in that craft.[53] But with the spread of laissez faire trends in eighteenth-century New England rigid craft differences were slowly eliminated. Attempts were made in Massachusetts in the years 1731 and 1732 to renew the regulations of the previous century preventing butchers, curriers, and shoemakers from pursuing the tanners' "mystery," but without success.[54] However, as late as 1784 a Great Barrington shoemaker was prosecuted in the Berkshire court for serving as a tanner as well as a shoemaker and for tanning one hundred hides in the course of a year.[55]

Likewise in the Middle colonies the attempt to maintain this separation of crafts proved futile in the long run. As early as 1680, for having "countenanced and suffered" the shoemakers to tan hides contrary to law, the governor and council in New York punished the tanners by forfeiting their "Pretended Dues" (which were to have been paid them

[50] For the English statutory background, see 13 Rich. II, st. I; 2 Hen. VI, c. 7 (1423); 1 Hen. VII, c. 5 (1485); 19 Hen. VII, c. 19 (1503); 22 Hen. VIII, c. 6 (1530); 5 Eliz., c. 8 (1562); 1 Jac. I, c. 22 (1604). See also Salzman, *Eng. Industries,* pp. 328–333.

[51] The cordwainers and curriers of London came to a tacit agreement in 1616 to ignore them after much litigation, and amalgamations of curriers, shoemakers, and skinners and glovers were established to safeguard their mutual business interests. See Unwin, *Industrial Organization,* pp. 21–22; Kramer, *op. cit.,* p. 94.

[52] *Mass. Laws and Liberties* (1672), pp. 88–90; *Acts and Laws of N.H.,* I, 12, 13 (1701); *Conn. Pub. Rec.,* IV, 78, 83 (1692).

[53] See New Haven Co. Court Rec., lib. II, fols. 349 (1708), 432 (1710), III, 1713–39, fols. 32 (1714), 128 (1721), 363, 364 (1732), 411, 412 (1734), IV, fols. 346 (1749), 676 (1754); Hartford Co. Court Rec., 1706/7–18, f. 183 (1711).

[54] *Mass. Acts and Resolves,* I, 312–314; *House of Rep. J.,* X, 43; XI, 159.

[55] Comm. v. Nast, Berkshire G.S., lib. B, f. 260 (1784).

by the shoemakers at an agreed rate of 6*d*. per hide) and ordered the shoemakers to pay them to the "Church or Charitable uses." [56] Freedom of occupational choice in the crafts meant freedom for the domestic system of manufactures to develop despite the opposition of some workers and craftsmen. Both in New York and New Jersey the artificers resented farmers who acquired some proficiency in several trades. One writer in a New York newspaper of the period declared that

It should not be permitted for one man to carry on the Business of Tanning, Currying and Shoemaking; much less ought a Farmer to do one, or all those Occupations within himself. . . . A Farmer also ought to employ himself in his proper occupation without meddling with Smiths, Masons, Carpenters, Coopers, or any other mechanical Arts, except making and mending his Plow, Harrow, or any other Utensil for Farming.[57]

In 1772 "a Number of Weavers and Inhabitants" of Somerset County, New Jersey, petitioned the legislature for a law "to prohibit Farmers and others keeping Looms in their Houses, and following the Weaving Business." In defense of this practice, a large number of freeholders and others from Somerset, Morris, Hunterdon, and Cape May counties petitioned against the enactment of such a law or against a similar proposal to prevent private persons from tanning their own leather. Apparently in deference to the views of the farmers, the legislature took no action.[58] The patriotic upsurge of the Revolutionary era brooked no check from the craft monopolies, and brought about a great expansion of home manufactures.[59]

The British Parliament, in accord with its evolving colonial economic policy, imposed legislative restrictions upon the freedom of the inhabitants of the colonies to follow the hatmakers' trade. These restrictions, embodied in the Hat Act of 1732, ran counter to the general trend in the colonies. That statute not only prohibited the exportation of American-made hats from the colony in which they were produced, but also restricted each hatmaker to two apprentices and required a seven-year apprenticeship.[60] The objective was the restriction of large-scale production in the colonies by discouraging labor from entering this industry. There were precedents in English mercantilism for this enact-

[56] For the governor's order (1681) and execution granted against the shoemakers (1682) to the extent of £1,699, see Rec. Wills, lib. XIXB, fols. 43, 44, Surrogate's Court, N.Y. Co.

[57] *New-York Post-Boy*, March 19, 1753. For Pennsylvania legislation rigidly separating the crafts in the leather industry, see *Pa. Stat. at Large*, II, 257 (1721). See also *ibid.*, VIII, 223 (1772); *Md. Arch.*, XIX, 183 (1695); Hening, III, 75 (1691), VI, 133 (1748).

[58] Notes of N.J. Assembly, Sept. 3, Nov. 1, 12, 17, 18, 23, 1772, N.J. State Lib. Home manufacture of textiles was frequently advocated in the magazines of the period. See, e.g., *The New Amer. Mag.*, July, 1758.

[59] See *supra*, pp. 43, 44.   [60] 5 Geo. II, c. 22.

ment,[61] but actually before the passage of the Hat Act the British courts had begun to disregard such limitations.[62]

Under this act there were at least three prosecutions in the province of New York in the late 1760s. One of them was brought against a New Yorker, a second was brought against a resident of Dutchess County, and a third against a hatter working across the river in Ulster County. Each was charged with making hats without having served a legal apprenticeship. All were *qui tam* actions brought on the statute by John Ogden, represented by John Tabor Kempe, attorney-general of the province. Among Kempe's rich collection of legal papers and briefs are notes on these three cases enabling us to follow the pleadings in at least one of the actions. William Smith, Jr., pleaded that the defendant had been bound by an indenture, dated July 10, 1764, to serve one William Wells, a feltmaker, for a term of seven years, in which capacity he had continued to serve. According to his notes, Kempe's argument on demurrer was along these lines:

1. It amounts to the General Issue.
2. It has not traversed the making Hats ag't [against] the Form of the Statute as charged.
3. Justifies as an Apprentice, without a profert of the Indenture.
4. Tis an affirmative Plea to an Affirmative Charge and on which no Issue can be joined.

Coke Lit. 303a
5. That the plea is argumentative.

Yelv. 223.
6. Tis an affirmative Pregnant.

See Statute 4 and 5 Anne, cap. 16, by Virtue of which Pleading double is permitted. Sect. 7. Except suits on penal Laws out of this Act.

To the 1st Point that it amounts to the general Issue.

10 Co. 95a
Hob. 127
If all was true, which he intended to establish by the plea it amounts to Nil Debet, a not Guilty.

Cro. Car. 257
To the 2d Point, the Want of the Traverse.

1 Sid. 106
Salk. 394
The Charge is making Hats, ag't the Form of the Statute—not having served a 7 yrs apprenticeship.

The Plea is that he was an apprentice, and made Hats

[61] Stat. 2 and 3 Phil. & M., c. 11 provided that country weavers could keep only one loom and city weavers two, and limited the number of apprentices for each master to two at one time. English guild restrictions had frequently limited the number of apprentices which a master might have. Such regulations not only served to keep down the number of master craftsmen, but also protected adult workmen from the competition of cheap child labor. Dunlop, *op. cit.*, pp. 43–46; Salzman, *op. cit.*, pp. 338–340; Adam Smith, *Wealth of Nations*, Bk. I, ch. x, pt. ii. For like restrictions by modern trade unions, see *infra*, p. 524.

[62] See Highamshire v. Baskin, 12 Mod. 46 (1693). The large-scale employment of apprentices in the English textile industry provoked riots among unemployed journeymen frame-work knitters. Beloff, *Public Order and Popular Disturbances*, pp. 81–87.

as an Apprentice—without traversing the making
them ag't the Form of the Statute—The Fact charged
is not declared and all may be true as set forth in the
plea, and all may be true nevertheless which is
charged in the Declaration.
Vidi Croke James 365, pl. 5. Syvedale versus Sir Edw'd
Levthall. Information on a penal Stat. exhibited personally beyond a year,—adjudged good for the King
tho bad for the Informer.[63]

CONCERTED ACTION BY WORKERS IN LICENSED TRADES

CERTAIN TRADES or occupations were in the colonial period conceived as
being clothed with a public interest. They were licensed and regulated
as are public utilities at the present day. The fees which they might command for their services were regulated by the town authorities and their
monopolistic privileges were in some cases maintained for a considerable time after the colonial period had ended. The principal trades enjoying such monopolistic privileges were the porters, carters, butchers,
and bakers, although other groups sought recognition as guilds. The
monopoly trades were accustomed from earliest times to acting in concert by way of petition or even to striking to enforce their demands for
higher wages or fees for services, for higher prices for their products,
or to bar interlopers from working in their trades. Requirements of space
have limited illustrations of such concerted action to New York City,
although a few instances are also cited from other leading colonial
towns, where franchised groups adopted parallel techniques of collective action.

Porters and Carmen. Going back to the Dutch period and continuing
down through colonial times, the authorities of New Amsterdam and
New York specifically designated the weighhouse and beer porters and
laborers at the public scales, limited their number, and allowed vacancies to be filled only by express permission.[1] In November, 1662,

---

[63] Smith· apparently moved to strike out one of the pleas, which motion Kempe opposed,
citing the exception for suits on penal statutes in stat. 4 and 5 Anne, c. 16, §§ 4, 7. Ogden v.
Allison (1767), Ogden v. Woolley (1768), Ogden v. Suidam (1769), Kempe MSS, N.Y. Hist.
Soc. In the Allison case defendant was permitted to compound with the prosecution pursuant to
statute. N.Y. Sup. Court of Judic., 1766–69, fols. 256, 314 (1767). In addition to compounding
with the prosecutor for 20*s.*, he paid costs of suit and a fine of 10*s.* A petition to the New Jersey
Assembly in Dec., 1771, by five tanners proposed the enactment of a law requiring all persons
entering their trade in the future to serve an apprenticeship. A motion to introduce such a bill
was tabled. Notes of N.J. Assembly, Dec. 10, 1771, N.J. State Library.

[1] In 1657 Stuyvesant, with the approval of his council, increased the number of licensed
laborers employed at the company's warehouses and scales for carrying beer and wine from two
to nine. They were required to work together "in one common purse." *R.N.A.*, VII, 144–146

at the request of Joost Goderis, foreman of the porters at the weigh-house, the burgomasters decreed that the porters should each pay eight stivers weekly into a common fund established for the benefit of such of their group as were taken ill. Those "unwilling" were to be assessed double.[2] This is probably the earliest instance of a friendly society plan in any of the colonies along the Atlantic seaboard. The carters were likewise given a franchise in this period, and those engaged in public carting were limited to the "appointed carmen." [3]

Both groups employed concerted action to better their working conditions. In 1657 the porters refused to carry salt on the ground that they had never been required to do so in the past.[4] In 1674 the mayor's court acted upon a petition of the corn and wine porters, and ordered that brewers, bakers, and others refrain from employing any but the corn porters or their own servants in carrying their products.[5] In 1685 the porters petitioned that a committee be appointed as nominated by them to investigate regulations and rates prevailing in their guild.[6] When they appeared before the common council a few months later and refused to comply with the regulations concerning the cording of wood, they were dismissed from the service.[7] At the beginning of the following year, the council, acting upon recommendations of a committee of two, neither of whom was on the list of nominees sent up by the porters, approved a new schedule of rates, which apparently was an increase over the fees prevailing.[8]

More than once the carters resorted to a threat to stop work and on some occasions actually did go out on strike. At the time of the Dutch reoccupation of the town they complained to the court "that there were some who intruded in that employment," and upon their departure sold their carts, horses, and privileges to cart to nonlicensed carters; in addition, they charged that certain boys were also engaged in trucking. The court decreed that these boys were not to "ride Cart any more." [9] In 1674 they were complained of for unwillingness "to ride timber,

(1657); also *ibid.*, V, 246–258 (1665), 347 (1666). For filling vacancies by the authorities, see *ibid.*, VI, 177 (1669), 231 (1670); see also *ibid.*, p. 402 (1673).

[2] *Mins. Orphanmasters Court*, II, 163–164; Stokes, *Iconography*, IV, 222 (1662).

[3] *R.N.A.*, VI, 73, 74, 76 (1667). A maximum fee of ten stivers sewan (wampum) was set for each load within the city's gates. Their privileges were confirmed again in 1670 on condition that they assist in street construction. *Ibid.*, pp. 272–273. During the same year the eleven carters signed an agreement to work for the city one day each week gratis, and the four newly admitted carters agreed to work without compensation two days a week. *Ibid.*, p. 401 (1673). For the conferring of monopolistic privileges upon the carters of Albany, see Munsell, *Annals*, II, 98 (1687); IX, 44, 45, 63; X, 77.

[4] *R.N.A.*, VII, 239, 240.   [5] N.Y.M.C.M., lib. 1674–75 (Dec. 1, 1674).

[6] *M.C.C.*, I, 146.   [7] *Ibid.*, p. 149.   [8] *Ibid.*, pp. 174–176.   [9] *Ibid.*, VII, 122.

stone and other materials for the city and public service." The court decreed that upon "their first refusal or exhibition of unwillingness, their horses" should "be immediately untackled, and they be deprived of their places as carters." [10] What would seem to have been the first criminal prosecution for a "strike" occurred in New York City in 1677. The prosecution appears to have been founded on the idea of contempt rather than conspiracy. The common council dismissed twelve carmen, or truckmen, "for not obeying the Command and Doing their Dutyes as becomes them in their Places," and, to quote the record,

for Such their contempt fyne either and every of them, three shillings a peece or els to carry fifteen Loads apeece to the Wharf of the Said Citty. And the said Persons being called into Cort and hearing their Discharge read unto them, They either and every of them for himself prayed to be admitted and that they would Submitt to the Judgmt of the Cort and Submitt to such Condicons as the Cort should order and direct, Upon their Admittance and for the Fees of their doeing and performing their Dutyes for the Citties buisines.[11]

Upon submission, the court admitted them to their old places at the same rates and required them to carry the same loads on pain of losing their places and of further prosecutions for contempt.

Again in 1684 fifteen carmen went on strike and refused "to Obey, Observe and follow the Laws and Orders" of the city relating to their guild. They were "Suspended and Discharged from being any Longer Carmen" by the common council, which issued a proclamation giving "free Liberty and Lycence" to all except the discharged strikers and slaves "to Serve for Hyre or wages as Carrmen." [12] On acknowledging their fault and paying a fine of 6s., three out of the fifteen carters were readmitted. The justification for this punishment probably rested upon their contempt of authority rather than upon their conspiracy.[13]

In the post-Revolutionary period the carters still sought to maintain

---

10 *Ibid.*, VII, 51; Stokes, *Iconography*, IV, 297 (1674). See also Gibbs, Sheriff v. Sigismundus, Carman, N.Y.M.C.M., lib. 1674–75 (Dec. 22, 1674).

11 *M.C.C.*, I, 64, 65.

12 Common Council Rec., File Box 1, package 1C; *M.C.C.*, I, 147–148.

13 This view finds confirmation in an order of general sessions in 1692 requiring all carmen to repair certain highways. Upon refusal, they were liable "to such penalty and Fines as the Mayor shall Judge requisit for the said Contempt." N.Y.G.S. Mins., 1683–92 (1692). Again in 1695 the carmen petitioned for an increase in wages and for a limitation of their numbers to 24, but the request was flatly denied. *M.C.C.*, I, 393. At Kingston carters refusing to cart firewood for the watch were threatened by the authorities that others would be hired to perform this task at the expense of those not complying. Ulster Dutch Transcripts, lib. II, f. 487 (1668).

In the 18th century the carters continued to act in concert. One writer depicted the mayor and aldermen as men "who stand in more Awe of a Band of Carmen than of an Armed Host; because that proceeds not so much from natural Timidity, as a more political Reason." *Independent Reflector*, Sept. 13, 1752.

their monopoly intact. In 1785 they petitioned the council against the practice of farmers taking up temporary residence in the city during the summer season and following the carters' trade, returning to their farms later in the year. The council was stirred by the plea that the number of carters greatly exceeded the demand, "insomuch that none of them can support their Families thereby," and accordingly resolved that no addition to the number be authorized and that those who left the city with their families to reside in the country during the winter should be "deemed to have forfeited their licenses." [14] When it appeared in 1797 that the carmen were charging extortionate fees and in many cases operating without licenses, the city authorities revoked all licenses and reorganized the carters into companies of 49, each under the supervision of a foreman.[15]

Coopers. In 1675 the coopers of South and East Hampton requested that coopers who were not inhabitants of the Hamptons or had not served their time as apprentices be forbidden to work there. During the winter Boston coopers, who had paid neither town nor county taxes, came to the Hamptons and worked at their trade; but the Hampton coopers in turn were not accorded reciprocal privileges in Boston. The General Court of Assize ordered "that noe Cooper Shall bee admitted to make Cask without the Consent of the Magistrates and Officers of the Respective Townes." [16]

The prosecution in 1680 of the coopers' combination was the first in the history of New York City to rest clearly on grounds of criminal combination. The coopers, twenty-two in number, "subscribed a paper of combination" not to sell casks except in accordance with rates established by themselves under penalty of 50s. to the poor. The text of the agreement reads:

ARTICKLES OF AGREEMENT Made By and Beetwixt Wee, the Coopers in this Citty Underwritten, Doe Agree upon the Rate and Prizes of Caske that Is to Say, for euery Dry half Barll one shilling Six Pence, for euery titte Barll For Beefe or porke Three Shillings; And Wee, the Vnder Written, Doe Joyntly and Seaverally Bind ourselfes, that for Euery one that shall sell any cask Beefore

[14] N.Y.C.C. Rec., File Box 10, Bundle 5; *M.C.C., 1784–1831*, I, 117. For additions to the carters, see *ibid.*, File Box 7, Bundle 2; N.Y.C. Misc. MSS, Box 14, N.Y. Hist. Soc.

[15] By 1800 there were twenty companies, or one thousand carmen. *M.C.C., 1784–1831*, I, 629; II, 405–406; S. I. Pomerantz, *New York: an American City, 1783–1803* (New York, 1938), p. 213; *N.Y. Directory, 1799*, p. 126, *1800*, pp. 92–108. A parable, seemingly indicating a successful strike by the Boston carters, appeared in the *Mass. Centinel*, March 12, 1785. Annapolis licensed certain trades engaged in public services, including carmen, far beyond the colonial period. See Annapolis Court Mins. (1828).

[16] *Docs. Rel. to Col. Hist. of N.Y.*, XIV, 701, 702; *M.C.C.*, I, 3, 4.

mentioned under the Rate or prizes aboue Sd., that for euery Such Default Fiuety Shillinges he or they shall pay for the vse of the poore, as Wittnes our hands, this 17th Day of December, 1679.[17]

When summoned before the governor's council they acknowledged their subscription, but denied any "ill intent." One cooper testified that the paper was written at Peter Stevenson's home, and another that a seaman, the brother of the cooper Crooke, had drafted it. The court declared the agreement null and void and fined all the subscribers 50s. "to the Church or Pious uses." Those in public employment were dismissed. Two of their number, Richard Ellyot and Andries Brestee, were in addition barred from acting as packers or cullers in the future.[18] A combination such as this for the maintenance of prices was indubitably illegal by that time in English law.

Butchers. In 1665 the New York City authorities decreed that none but licensed butchers would be allowed to slaughter within the city except with the consent of the licensees.[19] Repeatedly the sworn butchers of New Amsterdam and New York appeared before the authorities requesting an increase in fees for slaughtering [20] and for other trade advantages.[21] In 1763 a group of prominent "freemen and Freeholders" petitioned the council for a downward revision of the assizes,[22] complaining particularly of the price of meat, which, they charged, "would have fallen by the greater plenty of Provisions necessarily consequent on the conclusion of a peace, yet they are surprized to find that the same continues as high as it was in time of much greater consumption and

---

[17] 21 signatures follow. Only four of the coopers had to use marks. Valentine, *Manual of the Corporation of the City of New York for 1850* (New York, 1850), pp. 450, 451.

[18] The governor's order and the order to the sheriff to levy on the delinquent coopers' goods are found in Rec. Wills, lib. XIXB, fols. 43, 44, Surrogate's Court, N.Y. Co. See also Valentine, *op. cit.*, pp. 450, 451; Mrs. Schuyler Van Rensselaer, *History of the City of New York* (New York, 1909), II, 219, 220.

[19] *R.N.A.*, V, 312 (1665). Restrictions on the licensing of butchers were not lifted until 1795. In England in early modern times the butchers were closely regulated. They were well organized and not infrequently resorted to the strike or boycott when town authorities sought to open the market to country butchers. See J. H. Thomas, *Town Government in the Sixteenth Century* (London, 1933), pp. 73–75.

[20] *Mins. Orphanmasters' Court*, II, 163, 165; Stokes, *Iconography*, IV, 222 (1662); *R.N.A.*, V, 312 (1665).

[21] As late as 1735 we find the butchers collectively petitioning the city to maintain the market houses and keep them in repair. C.C. Rec., File Box 2, Bundle 3, Record Room 250, Municipal Building.

[22] For high wholesale prices in this period, see H. M. Stoker, "Wholesale Prices at New York City, 1720–1800," Cornell University Agricultural Experiment Station, *Memoirs*, CXLII (Ithaca, 1932); Anne Bezanson, R. D. Gray, and M. Hussey, *Prices in Colonial Pennsylvania* (Philadelphia, 1935), pp. 422, 424; A. H. Cole, *Wholesale Commodity Prices in the United States, 1700–1861* (Cambridge, Mass., 1938), p. 120, and *Statistical Supplement*, pp. 49, 50.

scarcity." [23] As a result, a drastic ordinance was adopted regulating the prices of foodstuffs, more sweeping in character than any of the previous limited assizes. Two of the most important butchers of the day, John Carpenter and Jacob Arden, openly declared their intention of violating the assize. They were both punished by being turned out of the markets, and the former was disfranchised. But the very same day the council changed the prices of beef to satisfy the protestants. [24]

Bakers. Of all the licensed groups of master workers or producers the bakers were most consistently subjected to official regulation in colonial towns. Such regulation generally took the form of setting the assize of bread. Collective action by master bakers to adjust the assize in their own interest was a most common occurrence in the colonies. Relations between the public authorities and the bakers were frequently tense, and at times culminated in actual strikes of master workers. [25] The bakers of Boston on numerous occasions petitioned for relief from the assize. [26] When one of the Boston bakers attempted to undersell his competitors in 1722, the others retaliated by offering to meet his price with a better quality loaf—evidence of a price-quality combination on their part. [27]

In New Netherland after 1656 the bakers were in many respects a licensed guild [28]—a status which they continued to enjoy after the English occupied the town. A good deal of self-regulation was practiced in the bakers' guild, which supervised quality and recommended eligible new masters to the council. [29]

A favorite technique of the New York bakers was to stop baking bread when the prices were not satisfactory from their point of view. Twice in 1659 the bakers went on strike, winning from the burgomasters

[23] C.C. Rec., File Box 5, Bundle 2. The complaint was made six months after the close of the French and Indian War.

[24] *M.C.C.*, VI, 336, 337; Stokes, *Iconography*, IV, 737; T. F. DeVoe, *The Market Book* (New York, 1862), I, 148 *et seq*. For a later assize of meat, butter, and milk, see Common Council Rec., File Box 2, Bundle 1; *M.C.C.*, VI, 374–375.

[25] For a bakers' strike in Tudor England against the assize of bread, see Tawney and Power, *Tudor Econ. Docs.*, I, 124, 125. See also J. H. Thomas, *Town Government in the Sixteenth Century* (London, 1933), pp. 72, 73.

[26] *Suffolk Court*, p. 126 (1672); *Mass. Bay Rec.*, V, 272, 317 (1680); *Mass. Acts and Resolves*, VII, 162 (1697), VII, 567, IX, 145; Mass. Arch., lib. LIX, fols. 225, 248. As late as 1765 the Boston selectmen refused to accede to petitions to alter the assize of bread. Only the year before they had granted the bakers a 50 per cent rise in the assize of wheat. *Boston Selectmen Mins.*, 1764–68, pp. 96 (1764), 148, 149 (1765).

[27] *N.E. Courant*, Sept. 17, 24, 1722.

[28] *R.N.A.*, II, 207 (1656); also *ibid.*, VII, 224, 231. As a result of an order of March 25, 1661, the marks of seven bakers were registered. *Ibid.*, I, 46, III, 285.

[29] See N.Y.C.C. Rec., File Box 1, Bundle 8; *M.C.C.*, I, 172. Those eligible for admission were *"approved* by the rest of the bakers," according to the printed *Minutes*, whereas the files state: *"appointed* by the rest of the bakers." See also *M.C.C.*, I, 173.

on each occasion a favorable adjustment of the assize.[30] In 1661 the bakers appear to have been fined for refusal to bake and to have been specifically ordered to bake good bread on pain of not being allowed to bake for one year and six weeks after it had appeared to the court that there was economic justification at that time for such a work stoppage.[31] However, shortly thereafter the authorities were persuaded by representatives of the bakers to modify the price schedule in their favor, which they again did two years later.[32] The bakers were equally successful in prosecuting their petitions for higher prices before the English authorities.[33] Probably in order to forestall a strike of bakers the court of general sessions in 1696 ordered that "all Bakers within this City doe keep bread in their shops that the Inhabitants be supplied accordingly." [34]

Of these instances of concerted action, the combination of bakers in 1741 is the most notable. The *New-York Weekly Journal,* April 20, 1741, assigned the following item to an inconspicuous portion of the sheet: "Last Week there was a general Combination of the Bakers not to Bake, because Wheat is at a high price, which occasioned some Disturbance, and reduced some, notwithstanding their Riches, to a sudden want of Bread." The issue of law which resulted was uncovered by Colden, of counsel for the defense in *People v. Melvin* (the *New York Cordwainers' Case*),[35] who, in 1809, described the incident to the court of general sessions:

I have had an opportunity of examining the records of the criminal proceedings of our tribunals for a great number of years back. I have found an information which was preferred in the year 1741, against certain bakers, for combining not to bake bread but on certain terms. This indictment, however, concludes contrary to the form of the statutes. And it appears that no judgment was ever rendered upon it, so that it cannot be appealed to as an authority on either side; or if it is in favour of either, it must be the 'defendants, because it appears that the crime there charged was laid as an offence against some statutes, and not as an offence at common law.[36]

Emmet, special counsel for the prosecution, referred to this as

[30] *R.N.A.,* I, 43–44, VII, 206, 215, 219–220, 221.

[31] *Ibid.,* III, 354, 359, 360, 378 (1661).

[32] *Mins. Orphanmasters' Court,* II, 113–115; *R.N.A.,* I, 47–48; III, 378, 381–391; II, 119; IV, 218.

[33] *M.C.C.,* I, 254, 256; Albany Mayor's Court Mins., Nov. 3, 1691; Munsell, *Annals,* II, 115 (1691). See also *M.C.C.,* I, 329 (1693), 373–375 (1695).

[34] N.Y.G.S. Mins., 1694–1731/2 (Feb. 2, 1698).

[35] For a discussion of this case, see *infra,* pp. 206, 207.

[36] *Trial of the Journeymen Cordwainers,* p. 83.

an information against journeymen bakers for a conspiracy not to bake till their wages were raised. On this they were tried and convicted before the revolution; but, as the counsel says, it does not appear that any sentence was ever passed, from which he concludes that judgment was arrested. This undoubtedly is a *non sequitur.* The criminal may have become penitent, and the object of the prosecution having been obtained, judgment may never have been moved for; besides, it is well known that those records have been in such confusion that no one can tell what has happened in almost any case. But if judgment was arrested, let me point out the fault in the information on which it may have happened. It concludes against the form of the statute, whereas it should have concluded at common law, even if there had been a colonial statute regulating that subject, which does not appear. . . . On account of this defect, perhaps, judgment was never had; but the learned counsel, by relying on this record, admits that his clients' case is similar to that of the bakers; and contends that such a combination on their part is not indictable.[37]

The specious logic of the prosecution is of little help in determining why a conviction was not obtained. Colden's description of the information is in terms general enough to cover the strike of master bakers for higher prices recorded in the *New-York Weekly Journal.* On the other hand, there is no evidence to support Emmet's view that the case involved a strike of journeymen bakers for higher wages. The minutes of the court of general sessions contain no reference to this prosecution; those of the Supreme Court are missing for the year 1741; and the mayor's court minutes ignore the incident. No papers relating to the 1741 case are available today. The parchment information was doubtless removed from an old bundle of papers of that year by Colden in the course of his investigations and appended to the papers in the *New York Cordwainers' Case* by way of exhibit; but unfortunately the papers in the latter case are also missing. Nevertheless, the absence of the information and other papers does not preclude speculation, however, idle, as to the cause for prosecuting the bakers for criminal conspiracy.

The community which received news of the bakers' combination was already in the grip of a mass hysteria which, with the possible exception of the New England witchcraft episode and the Charleston slave riots of 1739, was unrivaled in colonial history. For many weeks fires, believed to have been of incendiary origin, laid waste a good part of the lower city. Rumors of a plot of Negro slaves to burn the city gained widespread acceptance. The reckless stories of informers added

---

[37] *Ibid.,* pp. 103, 104. Sampson, in refutation, properly pointed out that "the precedent produced by Mr. Colden, shows all it was cited for, that in the only record to be found of the kind, no conviction took place, or no judgment was given."

to the consternation. The very same issue of the *New-York Weekly Journal* that carried the story of the bakers' combination published a proclamation by Governor George Clarke offering a reward of £100 for information leading to the conviction of anyone who set the fires which had caused destruction of property in the lower part of the island. The militia was called out. Panic-stricken souls fled with their belongings to the refuge of the Bowery or Harlem. The rest awaited the impending insurrection. During the spring months many Negroes were convicted of seditious conspiracy on highly dubious evidence and burned at the stake; and the panic was not allayed until summer.[38]

To add to the general feeling of unrest, reports were filtering into the colony detailing the progress of the campaign against the Spaniards and vague uneasiness was felt as to the possibility of a naval attack upon the city. Wartime conditions were responsible for skyrocketing commodity prices. Wheat was at the highest level for over a generation,[39] and the price of bread in the provision colonies was up 50 per cent over the previous year.[40] The publication in the May 4th issue of the *Journal* of the drastic action taken a few months earlier by the court of sessions of Edinburgh to lower prices did not inspire the provincial authorities to similar action. It does show, however, that the colonists were aware of the crisis that arose in the mother country in the preceding year, when wheat prices soared to prohibitive figures and rioting broke out in the North of England and in Wales, especially in the coal fields.[41] These incidents were fresh in the minds of the members of the common council when on April 17 they petitioned the governor and council to prohibit

[38] See R. B. Morris, "Negro Conspiracy," in *Dictionary of American History;* D. Horsmanden, *Journal of the Proceedings in the Detection of the Conspiracy* (New York, 1744); Colden MSS, N.Y. Hist. Soc. *N.Y.J.*, March 23, 1740. Across the river in New Jersey during the decade prior to the "conspiracy" in New York the county justices had on a number of occasions to deal with refractory Negro slaves, and in 1741 the Bergen County justices sentenced two Negroes to be burnt for setting fire to seven barns. *Mins. of the Justices and Freeholders of Bergen Co., N.J., 1715–1795*, pp. 20–23 (1731), 30–33 (1735), 36–39 (1741).

[39] Bezanson, Gray, and Hussey, *Prices in Col. Pa.* Statistics gathered for New York City by Herman M. Stoker seem less satisfactory for this period. Stoker, *loc. cit.* See also G. F. Warren and F. A. Pearson, "Wholesale Prices in the United States," *ibid.*, Pt. I; Cole, *Wholesale Commodity Prices*, p. 120, *Supp.*, pp. 22, 23.

[40] Compare Morris, ed., *Sel. Cases, Mayor's Court*, p. 67, with *N.Y.J.*, May 18, 1741. The peak was recorded in June, and a gradual decline in the price of breadstuffs took place until December. Bezanson, Gray, Hussey, *op. cit.*, p. 381. In Albany the authorities found it expedient to resolve that "the chamberlain sell the remainder of the city's wheat in his custody to the poorer sort of people" at a specified rate below that at which he was permitted to sell to others after the poor had been supplied. Munsell, *Annals*, X, 96 (Nov. 28, 1741).

[41] T. Tooke, *History of Prices* (London, 1838), I, 35, 40, 43n., 46; T. S. Ashton and Joseph Sykes, *The Coal Industry of the Eighteenth Century* (Manchester, 1929), pp. 115–117. See also Barnes, *Corn Laws*, p. 15.

the exportation of wheat from the province;[42] but the council, impressed by the point of view of the back country wheat growers, refused to take the needed action.[43] Living in dread of arson and insurrection, strained by the stresses of war, and facing the prospect of an early famine, the population would not be expected to view with equanimity a combination in restraint of trade involving basic necessities of life, even though such combinations were not entirely unfamiliar. It is not difficult to understand, therefore, why the resolve of bakers not to bake until the city authorities raised the price of bread should, under the circumstances, have been prosecuted as a criminal conspiracy. The fact that no conviction was obtained is surprising in view of the hysterical tension which prevailed in the spring of 1741.

Precedents existed in English law for prosecuting criminally a combination of producers to raise the prices of necessities. The act of 27 Edw. III, st. 2, c. 3, against regrators, and of 37 Edw. III, c. 5, against engrossers, and more directly the act of 2 and 3 Edw. VI, c. 15, which was aimed primarily at combinations to keep up prices charged to consumers, were applicable in such a situation. There were a number of prosecutions under some one of these statutes.[44]

Other remonstrances on the part of the New York and Albany bakers against the prevailing price schedule are on record following the short-lived strike of 1741.[45] In the post-Revolutionary period, when collective action by handicraftsmen was of far more frequent occurrence, the bakers continued to act in concert as a group to advance their economic interests, requesting both price raises and the elimination of unlicensed competitors.[46] They actually proposed, without success, that price regulation be entrusted to the bakers' "Society."[47] As late as 1801 the master bakers ordered a stoppage of work in protest against the

---

[42] *M.C.C.*, V, 19; E. B. O'Callaghan, *Cal. of Hist. MSS*, Pt. II (Albany, 1866), p. 543. When in 1710 the price of wheat had soared in Boston, a ship laden with wheat for export was disabled. Samuel Sewall, "Diary," Mass. Hist. Soc., *Coll.*, 5th ser., VI, 280.

[43] "Calendar of Council Minutes, 1668–1773," N. Y. State Lib., *Bulletin*, LVIII (March, 1902), 111. For other sectional issues in provincial history, see C. W. Spencer, "Sectional Aspects of New York Provincial Politics," *Pol. Sci. Q.*, XXX, 397–424.

[44] Wright, *The Law of Criminal Conspiracies and Agreements*, p. 47. A leading case, decided subsequent to the New York bakers' combination, involved a successful prosecution of a combination of this character. See dictum of Lord Mansfield in Rex v. Eccles, 1 Leach 274 (1783).

[45] Munsell, *Annals*, X, 98, 99 (1742); Stokes, *Iconography*, IV, 598; *N.Y. Assembly J.*, II, 116 (1746); N.Y.C.C. Rec., File Box 4, Bundle 2 (1773); *M.C.C.*, VII, 434; Stokes, *Iconography*, IV, 835, 839; Virginia Harrington, *The New York Merchant on the Eve of the Revolution* (New York, 1935), p. 283.

[46] N.Y.C.C. Rec., File Box 7, Bundle 2 (Aug., 1786, June, 1787); *ibid.*, File Box 10, Bundle 6 (1789).

[47] *Ibid.*, File Box 18, Bundle 4 (*c.* 1796); also *ibid.*, File Box 20, Bundle I (1800).

assize, an action reminiscent of the hectic crisis of 1741.[48] In 1801 the assize was finally discontinued in New York City. The tactics adopted by the packers during the second World War in protesting against the proposals for subsidies on food products points the moral that even in our own generation food processors are prone to resort to the "strike" or to curtailment of production when they are not satisfied with the regulated price.

The Licensed Professions. Organization of the medical and legal professions appears well advanced by the end of the colonial period.[49] Efforts were made at various times by resident physicians and surgeons to keep newcomers from practicing before their qualifications were determined.[50] Eventually laws passed by the colonial and early state legislatures provided that no one would be admitted to the practice of medicine or surgery without governmental approval.[51] The legal profession set up the guild form of organization in various provinces. In New York, for example, a bar association was founded at the beginning of the eighteenth century, which strictly enforced apprenticeship or clerkship requirements.[52]

[48] Pomerantz, *op. cit.*, pp. 217, 225.

[49] As early as 1652 the surgeons of New Amsterdam petitioned Stuyvesant and the Council for the exclusive right to act as barbers. The authorities held that shaving was "not in the province of the surgeons, but is only an appendix to their calling, that nobody can be prevented to please himself" in the matter of shaving or from serving anybody else for friendship's sake, out of courtesy, and without payment. But they expressly forbade others from "keeping a shop to do it in," and in the interest of public health forbade ships' barbers from dressing any wounds, bleeding, or prescribing for any one without the consent of the surgeons or "at least Doctor La Montagne." *Docs. Rel. to Col. Hist. of N.Y.*, XIV, 155–156.

[50] Such a petition has been ascribed to the physicians and surgeons of Boston in 1653. They requested that the resident medical men determine the qualifications of prospective practitioners and that the magistrates then grant the approved candidates licenses to practice. They further urged that fines be imposed for practicing without a license. Mass. Arch., cited by F. R. Packard, *History of Medicine in the United States* (2 vols., New York, 1931), p. 167. Previously an act of 1649 had been passed to restrain excesses in the practice of the medical profession. *Mass. Col. Laws, 1660–72*, pp. 137, 138. This law was reproduced in the Duke's Laws, 1665.

[51] Such an act was passed in New York in 1760, but did not apply to those already in practice. A similar act was passed in New Jersey in 1772. Stricter qualifications were laid down by the New York acts of 1792 and 1797. See *N.Y. Col. Laws*, IV, 455–456; *Acts of N.J., 1702–1776* (Burlington, 1776), pp. 376–377. Even closer to the guild plan was the incorporation of the New Jersey Medical Society in 1766. Packard, *op. cit.*, p. 174; Stephen Wickes, *History of Medicine in New Jersey* (Newark, 1879), pp. 43–48. It was not until 1781 that a medical society was established in Massachusetts with the right to regulate medical practice. Mass. Medical Society, *Medical Papers* (Boston, 1790–1850), Preface, pp. viii–ix; H. B. Shafer, *The American Medical Profession, 1783–1850* (New York, 1936), p. 206.

[52] A bar association appears to have been formed in that city as early as 1710. See Morris, ed., *Sel. Cases, Mayor's Court*, Introd.; Paul Hamlin, *Legal Education in Colonial New York* (New York, 1940), pp. 35, 96, 158, 159.

CONCERTED ACTION BY BOUND SERVANTS

ONE TYPE of collective action which had no parallel in contemporary Britain was the participation by bound servants in conspiracies to run away and entice others to join in flight, occasionally encouraging Negro slaves to participate by violent means and for illegal ends. This type of concerted action was largely confined to the Southern colonies.[1]

Prosecutions for conspiracies to run away from service or to entice servants from their masters go back to the early history of Maryland.[2] One instance may be cited from the Provincial Court records of 1657. Robert Chessick, who had been captured and returned home after a runaway attempt, persuaded a group of servants of several different masters to "run away with him to the Sweades." About a dozen were implicated in the plot. Chessick, their leader, had been overheard to "Swear a Great Oath" that "If they had not better Store of Victualls, he would not Stay five days with his Master." They seized a boat from a master named Osbourne and took along a goodly supply of arms. Chessick's avowed intent was to use the arms in case anyone attempted to intercept them. One of the runaways was unaccountably lost. The rest were brought back, prosecuted, and sentenced by the court, which found "that there was a Conspiracie amongst the said Examins to run away and to steale and Carry with them Gunns powder Shott and Provision and Mr. Osburne's boat." Robert Chessick was found to have been not only "one of the Chief Acters in this late designe to endeavour his and the rest their running away, but hath formerly been the Chief Instigator and Actor in a former running away and stealing and carrying with him (and the rest that then run away) Guns powder shott, a boat and Provisions." He was sentenced to receive thirty lashes on the bare back with a whip, enjoined not to depart from his master's plantation without leave, and to civil and orderly behavior "upon pain of farther Censure." Corporal punishment was also meted out to the other culprits.[3]

[1] For an early New England plot to run away, involving 8 servants including one Negro, see Durall's case, *Suffolk*, pp. 249, 250 (1673). Whipping and multiple restitution (larceny was involved) were imposed by the court.

[2] In 1644 the Provincial Court issued a commission for apprehending Edward Robinson and two collaborators "to answer to their crime of open rebellion in armes to committ felony in carrying servants out of the Province and in Case of resistance to shoote them." *Md. Arch.*, IV, 280 (1644).

[3] For a previous runaway attempt and for "Concealing and Consenting to this last Combination" John Beale was required to execute the punishments decreed upon Chessick and a collaborator named Stephen Chaplin. *Md. Arch.*, X, 504, 505, 511–514.

Numerous instances are found in the *Md. Gazette* of two, three, or more servants, mainly

When the Maryland servant chose not to run away but instead went on strike in protest against working conditions he was subject to criminal prosecution. In 1663 Richard Preston petitioned the governor and council sitting as a Provincial Court that his servants did "peremptorily and positively refuse to goe and doe their ordinary labor," and declared "that if they had not flesh they would not worke." Preston reported that he told them that he had no meat to give them. He was called away from the plantation that day and, on his return, learned that the servants had not been at work in his absence. He charged that for the most part they had not been lacking in meat since the tobacco crop was in, and were given meat two or three times a week. They continued in their "obstinate rebellious condition," even though Preston provided them with sugar, fish, oil, and vinegar. Hence, he addressed himself to the court, but agreed that if they would be content with such provisions as he could provide, he was willing that all further proceedings be dropped. He reported an offer of a note under his hand "for three or Foure of them to take my Boate to spend a weekes time or more, to see, if they could buy any provision of flesh, or any thing else, and I would pay for it, though never soe deare bought." But as they remained on strike, he asked the court to censure them "according to equity and their demeritts . . . as shall be iudged equall for such peruerse servants; Least a worse euill by their example should ensue by encouraging other servants to doe the like."

John Smith, Richard Gibbs, Samuel Copley, Samuel Styles, Henry Gorslett, and Thomas Broxam, all servants of Preston, petitioned the court by way of answer that Preston did not allow them "sufficient Provisions for the inablem't to our worke, but streightens us soe far that wee are bought soe weake, wee are not able to performe the imploym'ts hee puts us uppon. Wee desire but soe much as is sufficient, but hee will allow us nothing but Beanes and Bread." They, in turn, requested the court to see that their wants were relieved by their master.

After considering the petitions and examining the servants in person, the court chose to take a serious view of the proceedings and sentenced all six to be whipped with thirty lashes each. The two "mildest (not soe refractory as the other)" were to be pardoned on condition that they

---

convicts, belonging to the same plantation, fleeing together. See issues of June 7, 1745; May 27, 1746; May 24, 31, June 16, Sept. 30, Oct. 7, 21, 1747; May 11, Aug. 24, 1748; Oct. 21, 1756; Aug. 18, Sept. 1, 1757; Oct. 5, 1758; Aug. 9, Sept. 6, Nov. 15, 1759. The authorities rarely resorted to conspiracy prosecutions in these cases, but seemed content with the capture of the runaways and the enforcement of the statutory extra service penalty for desertion (*q.v., infra,* pp. 434–461).

mete out the penalty to their companions. Thereupon all the servants fell on their knees and asked the forgiveness of their master as well as the court "for their misdemeanor and promising all complyance and obedience hereafter." Accordingly their penalty was suspended and they were placed on their good behavior "ever hereafter (uppon their promise of amendm't as afores'd) And Soe to bee Certifyed from Court to Court." [4]

After the restoration of Maryland to the proprietor a serious conspiracy was nipped in the bud. In 1721 a band of convict servants conspired to seize the magazine at Annapolis in a bold stroke for freedom. The mayor's court of the provincial capital acted swiftly. Only six weeks earlier that tribunal had required "all the Convicts and other Persons of ill fame Either freemen or Servants" that had not as yet given security to post bond in the amount of £10 current money for their keeping the peace. "Upon their refusing so to be convicted." The illuminating depositions reveal that at least one of the ringleaders, a servant named Emyson, threatened his master that, if he would not accept £20 for his freedom, he would run away. The masters of the convict servants implicated in the plot were required by the court to post £30 current for each of their servant's future peaceful behavior.[5]

The atmosphere of seventeenth-century Virginia was charged with plots and rumors of combinations of servants to run away. Discordant notes were sounded very early. All critics agreed that the early colonists were negligent and improvident. Sir Thomas Gates reported that he had seen some eat fish raw rather than fetch wood and cook it. Dissatisfied with conditions, numerous plots to desert were concocted by "mutinous loiterers," some stealing away by boat and entering upon careers of piracy, others returning to England where they proceeded to denounce conditions in Virginia.[6] The laws drawn up by Gates in 1610 and amplified by Dale the following year to end the disorders in the colony were based to a great extent upon the military codes of the low countries. They were extremely severe, but contemporaries justified

---

[4] *Md. Arch.*, XLIX, 8, 9 (1663).

[5] Annapolis Mayor's Court Mins., 1720–84, fols. 26, 27, 30–32 (1721). For an alleged plot in 1707 of a "gange of Runaway Rogues" to seize the magazine, burn Annapolis, steal a ship, and turn to piracy, see *Md. Arch.*, XXV, 263 (1707). In 1732 the government was forced to intervene when riots broke out in Prince George's County during which tobacco crops were destroyed. These riots were brought on by overproduction of tobacco accompanied by a severe decline in price (*ibid.*, XXVIII, 8).

[6] "A True Declaration of the Estate of the Colonie in Virginia . . . Published by the Advise and Direction of the Councell of Virginia" (London, 1610), in Force, *Hist. Tracts*, III, 15, 16. Dale reported the settlers to be "full of mutiny." *A.P.C., Col., 1574–1660*, p. 12 (1611).

them by prevailing conditions, although in the period of dissensions at the end of the company's history Sir Thomas Smith was criticized for having sanctioned such severe laws.[7] For mutiny against the authorities, resistance, disobedience, or neglect, the "Lawes Divine, Morall and Martiall" provided whipping for the first offense, three years in the galley for the second, and death for the third. A tradesman was required to attend to his occupation "upon perill," for the first lapse, "to have his entertainment checkt for one moneth"; for the second, for three months; the third, for one year; "and if he continue still unfaithfull and negligent therein, to be condemned to the Gally for three yeare." Overseers were to see that they executed the tasks assigned to them upon pain of such punishment as should be inflicted by a "Martiall Court." In obeying the call to work, no distinction was made by the code between soldiers and "tradesmen." Both were to be ready in the morning and the afternoon, "upon the beating of the Drum," to go to work and not return home until the drum beat again. For the first default, the culprit would be made to "lie vpon the Guard head and heeles together all night"; the second offense was to be punished by whipping, and the third by confinement to the galleys for a year. Likewise conspiracy against the public authorities was to be punished by death, and those withholding knowledge of such conspiracies were to be punished in the same manner as accessories.[8] This Draconic code did not end conspiracies and talk of conspiracies. Early in 1612, a number of "idell men" fled to the Indians. Those taken were executed under the Dale Code. This desertion is known as "Webbes and Prices designe."[9] The third Virginia charter of 1612 speaks of "divers lewd ill-disposed persons, both sailors and soldiers, artificers, husbandmen, labourers, and others," as having received their wages, apparel, and diet from the company in accordance with a contract to serve the company in the colony, and as having subsequently "either withdrawn, hid or concealed themselves," or "refused to go thither." Others who had gone at the expense of the company had, on arrival, "misbehaved themselves, by mutinies, sedition, or other notorious misdemeanors," or had "most treacherously" returned to England "by stealth" or without license of the authorities. Accordingly, the charter gave the Council, or any two of its members, the power to bind such recreants with good sureties for their good behavior, and, if they had already returned to England, to

[7] A. Brown, ed., *The Genesis of the United States* (Boston and New York, 1890), pp. 528–530.
[8] Force, *Hist. Tracts*, III, No. 2, §§ 26–28, 30.
[9] Brown, *The First Republic in America* (Boston and New York, 1898), p. 158.

have them sent back to Virginia, there to be proceeded against and punished as the governor and council should think fit or in accord with the laws in force in the colony.[10] In 1614, Coles, Kitchins, and others who had been guarding Don Diego de Molina, an important Spanish prisoner, were persuaded by that notable to flee to the Spanish settlement in Florida. They were captured after they had traveled about five days, were brought back to Jamestown, condemned, and executed.[11] There was considerable fear in 1619 that James I's plan to send over 150 "dissolute persons" would result in mutiny. It appears likely that, included in this company, were some of the dispossessed Irish who were sent to Virginia about this time.[12]

As far back as 1638 the servants of Captain Sibsey had "raised a mutiny" against his "agent." The Lower Norfolk court imposed a sentence of 100 lashes on each malefactor.[13] In 1640 complaint was made to the General Court by Captain William Pierce that six of his servants and a Negro belonging to a Mr. Reginald had plotted to flee to "the Dutch plantation." Examinations of the servants revealed that they had taken Pierce's skiff and some corn, powder, shot, and guns to carry out their design and were sailing down the Elizabeth River when they were taken. The court deemed that, if unpunished, such activity set "a dangerous precedent for the future time." Therefore it sentenced a Dutch servant named Christopher Miller, "a prime agent in the business," to 30 lashes, to be branded on the cheek with the letter "R," and to work with a shackle on his leg for a whole year, "and longer if the said master shall see cause." After the expiration of his service he was to serve the colony for an additional seven years. The others were sentenced to whipping and branding and service to the colony ranging from two and one-half years to seven years. The Negro "Emanuel" was also apparently a servant, and he likewise was sentenced to be whipped and branded and to work for a whole year for his master with a shackle on his leg "or more as his master shall see cause." [14]

However, far more serious insurrections of servants broke out in some of the Tidewater counties in the sixties. A forerunner was the trouble among Daniel Turner's servants which was litigated in the York County court in 1659. Robert Hersington, William Ives, and Edward Tomkins were boarded by their master, Jonathan Newell, at the house of Daniel Tucker and fared as Tucker's servants did, but when Newell

[10] Hening, I, 106, 107; Brown, *Genesis of the U.S.*, II, 550, 551.
[11] Brown, *First Republic in America*, p. 211.   [12] *Ibid.*, pp. 346, 348.
[13] Lower Norfolk Rec., April 2, 1638, lib. I, f. 12 (transcript).
[14] *Va. Gen. Court Mins.*, p. 467 (1640).

came over, probably to check up on their complaints, Hersington told him that he had given Tucker "notice in the presence of Mr Morecroft and William Hodges that if hee would not allowe them their dyet for theire worke this Depon't would provide for them elsewhere." According to other testimony, they were supposed to get their washing, lodging, and diet, and in turn were to do some of the chores. Instead, they refused to "helpe to beat their bread but twise and one of them spooken to to helpe to beat made answeare that hee would take a bagg and goe from house to house and begg my bread before I will beat." [15] The final outcome of this strike is not known. At the same session of court Richard Jones in the presence of others refused to "sett up his Caske" for John Roper on the ground that his pay was "not soe good as other mens." [16]

The affair of Turner's servants was a prelude to the first extensive servant plot which broke out in York County in 1661. As in the early Maryland strike, the issue here was a controversy over diet. It appears to have been customary to allow servants meat three times a week. William Barton stated on examination that he had heard William Clutton say "he would have Meat Three times a weeke or else hee used to Keep a clash and that hee had it soe and that if that when he was at worke in the woods if they sent him bread and cheese if he thought it too little he would send it back again." In fact, Barton asserted, he would not serve as Major Beale's overseer because he could not have meat for his servants three times a week and "as many Calves for Milk as hee himself thought good, and that wheresoever hee lived the servants should have meat three times a weeke." George White confessed that the reason why "hee broake of with Mair Beale was because he could not have meat for the Servants three times a week." Friend corroborated Barton's story, but in extenuation stated that William Clutton had told Goodwin's servant "that Servants ought to have pone and hominy and Meat twice a weeke." When Major Goodwin violated this custom by confining his servants to a diet of corn bread and water, much murmuring arose at his quarters. The ringleaders, Isaac Friend and William Clutton, proposed that they "should Joyne in a petition to send for England to the King" to have their conditions redressed. According to the examination of one Thomas Collins, Friend suggested "that they would get a matter of Forty of them together and get Gunnes and hee would be the first and lead them and cry as they went along *who would be for liberty and freed from bondage* and that there would enough come to them and they would goe through the Countrey and Kill those that

[15] York O.B., 1657–62, f. 149 (1659).   [16] *Ibid.*, f. 150 (1659).

made any opposition and that they would either be free or dye for it." Major Beale, when informed of the disorders, directed the servants to obey their overseer, but William Clutton arrived just at that time and demanded meat according to custom. As a result, he stirred up "a further discontent and murmuring amongst them."

In disposing of the cases, the York County court was unusually moderate. William Clutton was bound for "seditious words and speeches tending to Mutiny and tumultuous behavior of Divers Servants" who were thereby "encouraged to endeav'r and Plott to ioyne together in Companyes after a tumultuous manner by force of Armes to gaine their freedom from their Service." After several persons had declared in court that Clutton had "been accompted a very honest civill person," he was discharged by the court, on paying the sheriff's and clerk's fees. John Parker was ordered to "have a strict, dilligent eye upon Isaac friend his servant, who appears of a turbulent and unquiet spirit." Beyond that, the magistrates did not find it necessary or, perhaps, prudent to do more than to enter an order requesting "the several magistrates and masters of familyes . . . to prevent the like dangerous discourses in those parts and lawfully to look into the practice and behaviour of their severall servants." [17] Toward the end of 1662 a law was enacted restraining unlawful meetings of servants under heavy penalties.

The unrest of the servants in York appears to have communicated itself to the adjacent county of Gloucester to the north. It was at Poplar Spring, near Purton, that some servants who had been soldiers under Cromwell plotted an insurrection in 1663. The plotters seem to have been an Oliverian faction, and included Independents, Muggletonians, Fifth Monarchy men, and other dissident elements who had been sent to the colony on long terms of indentured servitude. They planned to capitalize on the very real economic and social discontent of the servant class, but it is believed that they aimed at something more than this—a plot to overthrow Berkeley and set up an independent commonwealth in Virginia. The night before the projected uprising the conspiracy was betrayed by an informer named Berkenhead, a servant of one John Smith. Militiamen were stationed at the rendezvous and a number of the conspirators were captured, though a majority were warned in time and escaped.

Actual accounts of the scheme vary. According to one of the plotters, Thomas Collins, the plan was for the band to march upon the governor

[17] York O.B., 1657–62, fols. 149 *et seq.* (1662); also *WMCQ*, XI, 34–37; Tyler's *Quarterly Historical and Genealogical Magazine* (hereafter Tyler, *Mag.*), I, 266, 267.

and demand release from serving one year of their terms. If the request was denied, they were to proceed to a designated island. Others, William Budell, William Poultney, and John Gunter, said nothing about seeking merely one year off, but declared that they had planned to demand their freedom, apparently unconditionally.

Indictments were returned against John Gunter, William Bell, Richard Darbishire, John Hayte, Thomas Jones, William Ball, William Poultney, William Bendell, and Thomas Collins—all styled laborers— for high treason in meeting together at Newman's Land in Gloucester County and plotting to break into the houses of Francis Willis, one of the members of the Governor's Council, and of Katherine Cooke, and to seize guns and ammunitions sufficient to arm some thirty persons who were prepared to march from house to house, seizing arms and killing any who offered resistance. Such action was deemed contrary to the statutes of 25 Edward III, c.2 and 13 Elizabeth. Of the nine indicted for high treason, four were condemned and executed. Berkenhead was given his freedom and 5,000 lbs. of tobacco, and his master was compensated for his time.

The whole episode made a profound impression on the colony. It was resolved that the thirteenth of September, the day fixed for the alleged rising, "be annually kept holy." Years later the General Court referred incidentally to the "horror yet remaining amongst us of the barbarous designs of those villaines in September 1663 who attempted at once the Subversion of our religion Lawes liberty and rights," when the colony was saved only by "God's mercy." [18]

The York conspiracy and the Gloucester plot were responsible for several statutes. Because of the special situation in Gloucester County, and in order to prevent "servants and other idlers running away in troops by a pursuit made at the charge of the county," the county court was empowered to make such laws as should be from time to time found necessary and convenient for the prevention, pursuit, or recovery of any such runaways.[19] A year or so later similar legislative powers were conferred on other counties in an act prohibiting servants from leaving their homes without license from their masters. Specifically, "the several respective counties (as they find cause) to take espetiall care to

[18] Hening, II, 191, 204, 510; *VMH*, VIII, 240, XV, 38–43, XXXII, 10; *WMCQ*, 1st ser., IV, 47, X, 3, XXII, 10. See also Robert Beverly, *The History and Present State of Virginia* (1705 ed.), p. 59; C. Campbell, *History of Virginia* (Philadelphia, 1860), p. 262; A. P. Scott, *Criminal Law in Colonial Virginia* (Chicago, 1930), pp. 155, 156. This attempted insurrection is the subject of an interesting historical novel by Mary Johnston, *Prisoners of Hope: a Tale of Colonial Virginia* (Boston and New York, 1902).

[19] Hening, II, 35.

make such by laws within themselves, as by the act dated the third of December 1662, they are impowered as may cause a further restraint of all unlawful meetings of servants and punish the offenders." [20]

Between the York and Gloucester episodes and Bacon's Rebellion there took place a number of combinations and conspiracies of white servants. In 1670 a group of servants led by one Thomas Miller were accused of conspiracy to steal some pipes of wine belonging to a master named Captain James Neale. Neale's servants were urged by the ringleader to do the same and conceal their acts.[21] In April of that year, as a result of complaints of servant trouble in the counties of York, Gloucester, and Middlesex, and with specific reference to the conspiracy of '63, the General Court issued its famous "order about Jayle birds," forbidding any person from bringing in any convict who deserved to die in England for his offense.[22] Again, in 1672, Katherine Newgent was sentenced to thirty lashes for complicity in a "confederacy" with other servants of Charles Scarburgh.[23] During this same period a number of Negro riots and insurrections were reported.[24]

Overshadowing all conspiracies and combinations of artificers and servants in Virginia was the insurrection known as Bacon's Rebellion. The details are too well known for extended comment here.[25] It is generally recognized that not only frontiersmen figured among supporters of Bacon, but the lower classes throughout the province rendered him some measure of support. William Sherwood and Philip Ludwell depict Bacon's men as ignorant rabble. The explanation for the support of Bacon by the lower classes in Virginia is found in the economic and social history of that colony in the decade and a half prior to the rebellion. In 1650 Virginia was a flourishing province. Tobacco commanded a high figure in the European market, hired men were scarce, and wages four times as great as in England.[26] However, the Navigation Acts depressed the tobacco plantations, and the lower classes seemed to have shouldered more than their proportionate share of the ensuing losses. Taxes were levied in each county for setting up tannery establishments, for converting wool, flax, and hemp into cloth, and for instructing poor children in the knowledge of spinning, weaving, and other useful trades. Unfortunately, as the inhabitants of Charles City County were moved

[20] *Ibid.*, p. 195.   [21] Charles City O.B., 1668–70, fols. 138 *et seq.* (1670).
[22] *Va. Gen. Court Mins.*, p. 209 (1670).   [23] Accomac O.B., 1671–73 (1672).
[24] Hening, II, 299, 481.
[25] See T. J. Wertenbaker, *Torchbearer of the Revolution: the Story of Bacon's Rebellion and Its Leader* (Princeton, 1940) and *Virginia under the Stuarts, 1607–1688* (Princeton, 1914).
[26] Wertenbaker, *Bacon's Rebellion*, p. 10.

to protest, none of the plants was completed or put in operation. The administrative ineptitude and graft associated with these projects aroused the underprivileged groups, including the servant class. Berkeley stated that he had "appeased" two mutinies, "raised by some secret villains who whispered among the people that there was nothing intended by the fifty pound [levy] but the enriching of some few people." [27] The forerunners of these outbreaks were the disturbances in the Tidewater counties in the sixties brought on by concerted action of servants and laboring men. When the rebellion broke out all servants did not have a free choice of action. Many of the leading planters fled to the Eastern Shore, taking their servants with them and lending Berkeley their support. Actually at one period Bacon was in command of all of Virginia except the Eastern Shore.

In February, 1677, the legislature enacted that pardon should not extend "to any servants who were ayders and assisters in the said rebellion; and by an act of this assembly were adjudged to make good the losse of tyme and damages done to their masters (or others) by leaving their masters service and imbezelling goods, or otherwise damageing their masters or others, but that they shalbe lyable to make good such damages as by the said act of assembly for that purpose shalbe provided." [28] Another statute provided for the return of servants and other property to loyal persons and those persons concealing such servants were to be punished as felons.[29] A statute passed in the same period "concerning servants who were out in rebellion" provided that servants who had served under Bacon, Ingram, or other rebels were punishable as runaways and were subject to prosecution at the expiration of their terms of service for whatever they plundered. The preamble to this act declares:

Whereas many evill disposed servants in these late tymes of horrid rebellion taking advantage of the loosnes and liberty of the tyme, did depart from their service, and followed the rebells in rebellion, wholy neglecting their masters imployment whereby the said masters have suffered great damage and injury.[30]

In order to bring about the return of the fugitive servants and share-croppers, the legislature enacted that persons who had others, not well

[27] *Ibid.*, p. 33.   [28] Hening, II, 372; repealed by proclamation, July 8, 1680.
[29] *Ibid.*, pp. 381–382; repealed by proclamation, July 6, 1680.
[30] *Ibid.*, p. 395; repealed by proclamation, July 8, 1680; L. W. Labaree, *Royal Instructions to Colonial Governors* (New York, 1935), I, 160. It should be borne in mind that in England many of the servants and apprentices had taken the Parliamentary side during the English Civil War. See M. G. Walten, *Thomas Fuller's The Holy State and the Profane State* (New York, 1938), I, 106.

known, residing in their houses for less than nine months, "whether as hired servant, sharer in the crop or otherwise," were required to give a description of such persons to the justice. For neglecting to do so, they would be liable to punishment for entertaining runaway servants. The declared object of this act was "to the end servants runaway and others Fled from debt in those late rebellious tymes be the better found out and discovered, and by that meanes reduced in their service and payment and their just debts, etc." [31] These statutes against the rebellious groups were repealed by proclamation in 1680, and in the "Act of free and general pardon, indemnity and oblivion" passed in that year there was a provision

that noe further punishment, satisfaction or damages shal be recovered or inflicted on any christian servants that have deserted their masters or bin active in the late rebellion, then that the time incurring betweene the said First day of May and the said sixteenth of January shal be accompted noe part of their tyme of service. [32]

Bacon's Rebellion and its ruthless suppression did not put an end to disorders among the poorer population. In October, 1681, in answer to a query as to whether it was necessary to continue the two companies of English soldiers in Virginia, it was reported to the Lords of Trade and Plantation that "Virginia is at present poor and more populous than ever. There is great apprehension of a rising among the servants, owing to their great necessities and want of clothes; they may plunder the storehouses and ships." [33] The plant-cutting riots of 1682, while by no means confined to servants and laboring men, were a further fresh manifestation of discontent on the part of the lower economic groups in the colony. [34]

---

[31] Hening, II, pp. 405, 406. [32] *Ibid.*, p. 462. [33] *CSPA, 1681–85*, No. 275, p. 134 (1681).

[34] By a proclamation of Aug. 12, 1682, all taking part in plant cutting were declared rebels. Orders were given to the justices to suppress the movement in accord with the provisions of stat. 13 Hen. IV, c. 7, against rioters. See *VMH*, III, 225, 226, XIII, 252 *et seq.*; *CSPA, 1681–85*, Nos. 493, 507; *Cal. Va. State Papers*, I, 181. To remove any doubts that such affairs were mere riots, the Assembly passed a law punishing as high treason the assembling together of eight or more persons and the cutting, pulling up, or destroying of tobacco plants, or the pulling down, burning, or destroying of tobacco houses. Hening, III, 10–12 (1684); *VMH*, X, 152. An instance of the burning of a tobacco warehouse occurred in Essex County in 1715. *Cal. Va. State Papers*, I, 181.

Numerous instances of mass desertions planned by white servants took place in the Southern colonies. For Virginia, see Lancaster O.B., lib. 1656–66, fols. 217, 264 (1663), lib. 1666–80, fols. 374 (1677), 487 (1679). See also, e.g., *Va. Gazette*, Nov. 11, 1737, June 2, 1738, June 15, 1739, Aug. 26, 1773, July 20, 1775; *VMH*, XXIV, 416, XXV, 12 (1755). For suggestion of a confederacy on the part of a number of North Carolina servants to jump their bonds, see *N.C. Gazette*, June 16, 1753, May 12, 1775; *Cape-Fear Mercury*, Dec. 29, 1773. For instances of servants banding together to effect their escape from South Carolina, see *S.C. Gazette*, June 29, 1734; Jan. 31–Feb. 7, 1735/6; April 2–9, 1737, March 12, 1743/4; April 30, 1744; April 1, 1745; Jan. 11–18, Feb. 1–8, 1768. For mass desertions in Georgia, see *Georgia Gazette*, May 25, 1774.

The most serious insurrection of white workers in the history of the British colonies on the North American mainland actually occurred in East Florida during the British regime. Under the administration of Governor Grant, group settlements were set up by Denys Rolle at Charlotia, on the St. Johns, and by that well-traveled Scotsman Dr. Andrew Turnbull at New Smyrna. The settlers of "Rollestown" were recruited from the English poor; discontent was rife, and ten years after its founding William Bartram reported that few inhabitants dwelt amid its ruins.[35] New Smyrna was founded with the support of a friendly governor, who appointed Turnbull to the Council, and with the financial sponsorship of Sir William Duncan and Sir Richard Temple, Turnbull's partners. Because of his acquaintance with Mediterranean lands, Turnbull recruited his servants from Greece and added to their number over one hundred Italians picked up at Leghorn and a larger group of starving Minorcans to whose pleas for aid Turnbull felt he could not turn a deaf ear. In all, some 1,400 settlers sailed from Minorca for Turnbull's colony. With the notable exception of the shipment of German Palatines to New York in 1710, this was perhaps the largest group of servants ever to emigrate to the British colonies in America in one expedition.[36] The heterogeneous group overtaxed the slender resources of the colony, and, within two months after landing, a revolt broke out, led by the Greeks and Italians. The timely aid of Grant prevented the colony from being completely destroyed.

We are indebted to the governor for a graphic report to Hillsborough and the Lords of Trade of the occurrence. Turnbull had brought some planters down from the Carolinas as his guests to see the progress the settlers had made, and had set out with his party for St. Augustine on the return journey, when at midnight on the nineteenth of August, 1768, he was aroused by a messenger who reported that Carlo Forni, one of the Italian overseers, had that very morning marched into the square at New Smyrna at the head of twenty malcontents and addressed the settlers, who left their work to hear him. He declared himself commander-in-chief of the Italians and Greeks, whom he intended to lead to Havana, confident of Spain's protection. He held out to them freedom from a life of hard work and stern masters. The crowd grew excited, the door of the storehouse was broken down, and casks of rum were rolled into the street. When Cutter, one of the English overseers,

[35] William Bartram, *Travels through North and South Carolina, Georgia, and East Florida, etc.* (Philadelphia, 1791), p. 97 Kathryn T. Abbey, *Florida: Land of Change* (Chapel Hill, 1941), p. 81.
[36] C.O. 5:541, pp. 423–424, 427; C.O. 5:549, p. 75.

intervened, he was seriously wounded and locked in one of the closets in the storeroom. About three hundred adherents of Forni—nearly all the Greeks and Italians in the colony—seized firearms and ammunition in the storehouse, plundered the dwellings of the Minorcans who re-fused to join the insurgents, and seized a ship loaded with provisions ly-ing in the river.

On hearing the news, Turnbull sent an express rider at top speed to Grant at St. Augustine. Meanwhile, instead of raising sail, the insur-gents caroused aboard the ship and were finally intercepted by govern-ment vessels. The rebels surrendered, and offered no further resistance, but some two score, including the leaders, escaped in an open boat. It took four months before they were overtaken on the Florida keys. When they were brought to trial at St. Augustine, the jurors were moved to compassion by their wretched condition. Three leaders were convicted of piracy. Two, including Forni, were executed, and the third pardoned on condition that he act as executioner of the other two. Three Greeks convicted of felonies were pardoned by Grant on the recom-mendation of Hillsborough, who insisted that amnesty be extended to all other participants.[37] Governor Grant summed up the affair in these words:

It was to be expected, My Lord, that so great a number of people collected to-gether in [*sic*] so many parts of the world, and imported into an infant Country at the same time might get into Riots and give Trouble at times, but I did not look for their carrying things to such a Height.

He recommended that a fort be built at New Smyrna to protect the settlers from the Indians and the other planters from these very same settlers.[38] A fort was started, but never completed, although a guard of eight men and a sergeant were stationed there permanently.

This was not the end of such disturbances at New Smyrna. The ar-rival of Patrick Tonyn as governor of East Florida in 1774 led to new dissension among the immigrant workers. Tonyn and Turnbull were personally antagonistic, whereas Turnbull had formerly enjoyed the complete cooperation of Governor Grant in dealing with the colony. With the outbreak of the American Revolution the Minorcans, hitherto

[37] C.O. 5:544, pp. 37–42, 95–96, 192–193; C.O. 5:549, p. 339; C.O. 5:550, pp. 72–73, 137–138; *S.C. Gazette*, Sept. 12, 19, 1768; *Georgia Gazette*, Oct. 19, 1768. See also Carita Doggett, *Dr. An-drew Turnbull and the New Smyrna Colony of Florida* (n.p., 1919), pp. 49 *et seq.* For a sympa-thetic account of the uprising, see Bernard Romans, *Concise Natural History of East and West Florida* (New York, 1776), pp. 268–273, whose account has been accepted as authentic by Bruno Roselli in an uncritical study, *The Italians in Colonial Florida* (n.p., 1940). A brighter side is presented in *S.C. Gazette*, Oct. 11, 1773.

[38] C.O. 5:544, pp. 37–42 (James Grant to Earl of Hillsborough, Aug. 29, 1768).

the most pacific element in the colony, were believed to have conspired with the Spaniards at Havana. Their loyalty to the British cause was suspect when they did not join the Loyalist militia organized for the defense of the border.

Of the many issues that arose between Turnbull and Tonyn, a number concern relations with the workers in East Florida. In 1776 Turnbull memorialized the Lords of Trade to remove Governor Tonyn from office. Among the various accusations of malfeasance leveled against that official was the charge that he had obtained through chicanery receipts for wages due to certain artificers for public work. As a result, it was asserted that "the Chief Master Builder in St. Augustine refused to repair the Platform for the Guns in the Fort on this Account." It was also charged that the "Governor brought up such Provisions as were much wanted by the Poor, that he put them into the Hands of a mean monopoliser, who sold them at double price, which was distressing to some Families." In addition, Turnbull accused the governor of treating his own servants and Negroes cruelly and of acting, himself, as executioner. Turnbull found it necessary for his own personal safety to flee to England to plead his cause in person, but during his absence conditions at New Smyrna grew serious. Charges of harsh treatment on the part of Turnbull's overseers of the servants in that colony were in some part politically inspired,[39] but such widespread unrest resulted that it was feared that the inhabitants might join the Revolutionary cause. Tonyn encouraged the settlers to repudiate their contracts and leave New Smyrna. He offered them freedom from indentures, land in St. Augustine, and assurances of protection if they ran away. Despite evidence of cruelty to the servants on the part of Turnbull's overseers (charges which are today believed to have been highly colored by Turnbull's political enemies), Tonyn's actions in encouraging mass desertions and enlistments of such servants in the militia were clearly illegal and without parallel in the history of the period. He was manifestly actuated by his enmity of Turnbull and his desire to bring about the Scotsman's ruin. Furthermore, since Chief Justice Drayton was a partisan of Turnbull and refused to consider these complaints of ill usage himself but directed them to be carried before some other magistrate,[40] Tonyn had to intervene in his capacity of Chancellor. Turnbull memorialized Shelburne that

the Settlement . . . was entirely abandoned by an insidious and underhand management of Governor Tonyn who had encouraged these Settlers by

[39] See *infra*, p. 499.   [40] C.O. 5:557, pp. 42 *et seq.*

specious promises to quit their labor and Plantations. He also encouraged them not to return to fulfill their contracts with your Memorialist, as was ordered by a Sentence of the Court of Sessions after a full investigation of that Business on a Hearing of their Complaints which were found to be frivolous and groundless, as appears by the Sentence of that Court.

Tonyn misrepresented the action of the court, reporting to the authorities at home that, between May and July, 1777, many of the settlers were freed by the courts and the rest set at liberty by Turnbull's attorneys.[41] But as a matter of fact, the only ones freed by the court were a few who had been contracted for by their parents when under age. The court of sessions declared the others legally bound to the proprietors of New Smyrna and ordered them back to the settlement. Tonyn deliberately defied the court. When the complainants were confined by the justices and ordered to live on bread and water until "they returned to their labour in order to fulfil their contracts," Tonyn sent them provisions from his own house.[42] Encouraged by the governor's defiance of the courts, the whole settlement moved to St. Augustine. There some sixty-five died because of inadequate food, shelter, and medical assistance.[43] Many were soon reduced to beggary, others enlisted in the corps of Rangers,[44] and still others built shacks on small lots assigned them north of St. Augustine. Hence, when Turnbull returned from England, he found his colony abandoned and his property and crops in serious condition. Tonyn, who had acted in a high-handed and illegal manner, wrapped himself in the mantle of patriotism and demanded Turnbull's dismissal from the Council on the ground of disloyalty. While admitting that Turnbull and his friends were "gentlemen," he charged that "in all the colonies, Georgia excepted, the principal people have been at the head of this rebellion." [45]

Insurrections of white servants were not confined to the mainland colonies. In the seventeenth century, white labor played an important role in the economy of the West Indies. There was a good deal of rest-

[41] C.O. 5:557, p. 42; HMC, *Rep.*, XLIX, Pt. II, 82.
[42] Lansdowne MSS, LXVI, fols. 729–732 (transcripts, St. Augustine Hist. Soc.).
[43] "Mrs. Stopford-Sackville MSS, America, 1775–77," HMC, *Rep.*, XLIX, Pt. II, 82.
[44] Lansdowne MSS, LXVI, fols. 725–727.
[45] C.O. 5:558, pp. 101–104; HMC, *Rep.*, LIX, Pt. II, 127, 128. Drayton was removed for his refusal to hear the Minorcans' cases in his court, and returned to Magnolia Gardens, then known as Drayton House, near Charleston. For Drayton's side of the controversy, see his "Inquiry into the present State and Administration of Affairs in the Province of East-Florida" (1778). Lib. of Cong. Turnbull was forced to give up the greater portion of his lands in order to secure his liberty. Lansdowne MSS, LXXXVIII, 189. Ultimately he recovered a Loyalist claim from the British government. C.O. 5:562, Reports of Commissioners for Florida Claims. See also Doggett, *Turnbull*, pp. 157 *et seq.*, 179 *et seq.*; C. L. Mowat, *East Florida as a British Province, 1763–1784* (Berkeley and Los Angeles, 1943), pp. 72, 106.

lessness among the white labor population, and insurrections were occasionally plotted. One such plot was uncovered in Barbados in 1649. According to the plan, on a given day all the masters were to be massacred by their servants, who were then to seize control of the island. The plot was frustrated at the last moment when one of the conspirators informed his master, Judge Hethersall, of his peril. Far more drastic measures were adopted by the court on that occasion than in the pre-Baconian insurrections in Virginia. Eighteen of the ringleaders were executed. According to one chronicler, "the reason why they made examples of so many was, they found these so haughty in their resolution and so incorrigible, as they were like to become Actors in a second plot."[46] After the Restoration there were occasional instances where white servants joined with Negroes in plotting rebellion,[47] but once the African slave trade had turned the balance of labor on the island from white servants to Negro slaves, threats of slave insurrections became alarmingly frequent and the white working class were used for garrisoning and overseeing the Negro population.

CONCERTED ACTION BY WHITE WORKMEN AGAINST NEGRO ARTISANS

LOCAL CRAFTSMEN in colonial towns sought not only to maintain their monopolistic privileges against nonresidents but also to control the labor market in general. One significant aspect of this struggle was the effort of white mechanics to keep free Negroes and Negro slaves from entering the skilled trades. While the issue of free mechanic versus slave was most sharply drawn in Charleston, center of a considerable slave population, and in the British West Indies, evidences of the conflict are found in virtually every sizable town on the Atlantic coast.

In New England servants from the British Isles were always preferred to Negro mechanics. Nevertheless, while the proportion of Negroes to whites in that area remained very small,[1] slave labor was highly diversified and employed in many of the New England trades, both skilled and unskilled.[2] Here as elsewhere white workers found Negro compe-

---

[46] Richard Ligon, *A True and Exact History of the Island of Barbados* (London, 1673), pp. 46–47. Cf. George Frere, *Short History of Barbados* (London, 1768), p. 12. See also V. T. Harlow, *A History of Barbados, 1625–1685* (Oxford, 1926), p. 305.

[47] *CSPA, 1685–88*, No. 572, p. 155 (1686), 1702, No. 210, p. 142.

[1] For estimates, see *CSPA, 1708–19*, Nos. 151, 155, pp. 110, 111 (1708), *1720–21*, No. 91, p. 46 (1720); *R.I. Col. Rec.*, IV, 131–135; W. A. Rossiter, *A Century of Population Growth, 1790–1900* (Washington, 1909), pp. 158–161. For the imposition by Massachusetts of a duty upon imported Negroes, see *Mass. Acts and Resolves*, I, 517, 981, 982.

[2] L. J. Greene, *The Negro in Colonial New England, 1620–1776* (New York, 1942), pp. 102, 103, 111 *et seq.*

tition objectionable.³ According to John Adams, the resentment of white labor toward Negro slaves was an important influence in the abolition of slavery in New England.⁴

In New York City the handicraftsmen bitterly opposed the employment of Negro slaves in the various trades. In 1686 representations were made to the common council that Negro and Indian slaves were regularly employed by their masters "to worke on the bridge Weighhouse and Markett House of this Citty about the goods of their Respective Masters." This resulted in "discourragement and Losse" to the "Sworne porters." Thereupon the council ordered that "noe Negro or Slave be suffered to work on the bridge as a Porter about any goods either imported or Exported from or into this Citty." ⁵ A similar complaint was made by the sworn porters in 1691, who declared that this practice "soe much impoverisht them, that they Cannot by their Labours gett a Competency for the Maintenance of themselves and Family's." ⁶ In 1737 Lieutenant Governor Clarke found it necessary to tell the legislature that "the artificers complain and with too much reason of the pernicious custom of breeding slaves to trades whereby the honest and industrious tradesmen are reduced to poverty for want of employ, and many of them forced to leave us to seek their living in other countries." ⁷ As in Boston, the post-Revolutionary trend toward emancipation of the Negro slave in New York was viewed by white workers as imperiling their economic status, and the mechanics led the opposition to laws gradually emancipating the Negro.⁸

Considerable hostility marked relations between white labor and Negroes engaged in the Philadelphia trades. It is believed that one of the motives for the Pennsylvania statute of 1712 placing a high duty on Negroes—an act passed soon after the insurrection in New York—was

³ *Ibid.*, p. 332. As far back as 1661 the Boston town authorities found that Thomas Deane had employed a Negro in the trade of a cooper contrary to the orders of the town. He was forbidden to employ him henceforth in any manufacturing capacity under penalty of 20*s.* for every day the Negro was retained in employment. *Boston Town Rec.*, VII, 5.

⁴ "If the gentlemen had been permitted to hold slaves, the common white people would have put the slaves to death, and their masters too, perhaps," Adams declared in 1795. "Belknap Papers," *Mass. Hist. Soc., Coll.*, 5th ser., III, 402.

⁵ N.Y.C.C. Rec., File Box No. 1, Bundle 8; *M.C.C.*, I, 179; Stokes, *Iconography*, IV, 339. Cf. also Munsell, *Annals*, VII, 172.

⁶ N.Y.C.C. Rec., File Box No. 2, Bundle 1, Library 357, Municipal Building; *M.C.C.*, I, 220.

⁷ C. Z. Lincoln, ed., *Messages from the Governors, 1683–1906* (Albany, N.Y., 1909), I, 260. See *ibid.*, p. 618, for Gov. De Lancey's proposal for a poll tax on slaves to encourage shipwrights and artificers.

⁸ N.Y. State Laws, 8 Sess., April 12, 1785, c. 68, prohibiting importation of slaves; *ibid.*, 22 Sess., March 29, 1799, c. 62, giving children born after July 4, 1799, the status of bond servants, the males until 28 years of age, the females until 25. By a law of 1817 slaves born before July 4, 1799, were to be free after July 3, 1827 (*ibid.*, 40 Sess., March 31, 1817), but slavery was not completely abolished until 1841 (*ibid.*, 64 Sess., May 25, 1841, c. 247).

the opposition of white workers to slave competition. This was crystal-lized in an Assembly resolve of 1722.[9]

In the Southern towns the authorities made vigorous efforts to pro-tect white craftsmen and traders from Negro competition.[10] The prob-lem was especially critical in Charleston. In 1744 a number of ship-wrights of that town petitioned the legislature for relief on the ground that they were reduced to poverty owing to competition from Negroes in the shipbuilding industry. The master shipwrights opposed the peti-tion and retorted that

Industry and a more frugal way of life [would cure the ills complained of and] that many times they have refused to work at all, or if obliged to it by necessity only on Extravagant wages, That his Majesty's Ships have been repaired and refitted only by the assistance of Our slaves, And that without these Slaves the worst Consequences might Ensue, his Majesty's Ships may remain by the Walls at their discretion: Merchants who are bound by Charter party to load Vessels within a limited time may be drawn into heavy demurrage, And no Mercht can have it in their power to take or refuse work upon their own terms. That there is business enough for three times the number of Carpenters, That the Complaints were with no other View than to Engross the whole Trade into their own hands and thereby to have it in their power to make their own price.

A committee of the Assembly reported it as their opinion "that the number of Negroes hired out, without a proportion of white men to do the business of ship-wrights or ship carpenters, is a discouragem't to white men of that business of ship-wrights." It further recommended that a bill be enacted for "the ascertaining [11] of wages for Ship-wrights, as well white men as Negroes." Both recommendations for limitation of Negroes in the industry and for wage regulation were unanimously agreed to.[12] It is thus clear that while the Assembly wished to control

[9] J. F. Watson, *Annals of Philadelphia* (Philadelphia, 1844) I, 98. In 1737 workers protested against the effect of Negro competition upon employment and wages. See also W. E. B. Du Bois, *The Philadelphia Negro* (Philadelphia, 1899), pp. 14–15.

[10] In Virginia restrictions were placed on the entry of Negroes into retail trades. Elizabeth City County O.B., 1684–99, fol. 11 (1693); Norfolk C.C. Mins., fols. 96 (1764), 128 (1773), 161 (1783). As late as 1786 Norfolk considered regulating the hiring out of slaves in the town. *Ibid.*, fols. 189, 190. For North Carolina, see New Bern Town Rec., lib. 1797–1825, fols. 7, 46, 47, 151.

[11] A reading of the text indicates that a bill was recommended to determine wages—not, as Jernegan suggests, to make "an inquiry." Jernegan, *Laboring and Dependent Classes in America* (Chicago, 1931), p. 21. "Ascertain" was at that time used synonymously with "fix," as in *Conn. State Rec.*, I, 595 (Providence Convention).

[12] S.C. Assembly J., 1743–44, fols. 159, 160 (Jan. 25, 1744); S.C. Council J., 1744, fols. 6–9 (Jan. 18, 1744).

the craft for the benefit of the white mechanics it had, at the same time, no desire to be faced with strikes and excessive wage demands, and in the latter point it yielded to the masters. Despite a similar proposal later in the year, the interests of the employer class prevented passage of such a bill.[13] The failure of the legislature to act left the matter up to the town, which in 1751 declared in sweeping language "that no Inhabitant of Charleston shall be permitted to keep more than two male Slaves, to work out for Hire, as Porters, Labourers, Fishermen or Handicraftsmen." [14] The *Gazette* of October 29–November 5, 1763, reported that Negro chimney sweepers were competing with the whites and actually "had the insolence, by a combination amongst themselves, to raise the usual prices, and to refuse doing their work, unless their exorbitant demands are complied with. . . . Surely, these are evils that require some attention to suppress." In 1764 the legislature prohibited Charleston masters from employing Negroes or other slaves as mechanics or in the handicraft trades, but placed no hindrance on the teaching by mechanics and artificers of their own Negroes or other slaves in their own respective trades, "so that they have and constantly employ, one white apprentice or journeyman for every two negroes." [15] In 1772 Charleston imposed a fine upon both master and employer, if a slave was hired out without license or badge.[16] In the post-Revolutionary period the amount of this fine was reduced, and by 1790 the city council abolished the license system entirely because the tax had been found to be "burdensome and unequal," and Negro slaves were entrenched in virtually all the crafts.

In North Carolina the same conflict between white and Negro labor arose by the eve of the Revolution. In 1773 the pilots of Oacock Bar petitioned the Assembly that Negroes, both free and slave, be denied licenses to pilot vessels up the rivers to Bath, Edenton, and New Bern,

[13] S.C. Assembly J., 1744, fols. 332–34.   [14] *S.C. Gazette*, May 6, 1751.

[15] *S.C. Gazette*, Aug. 25, 1764. The agreements of 1769 against the importation of Negro slaves were inspired apparently by a strong and unanimous stand of the mechanics, reinforced by some planters and merchants. *Ibid.*, July 6, 27, Dec. 21, 28, 1769; Jan. 25, 1770. The manufacture of candles and soap was opposed on the ground that the business was handled entirely by Negroes working at night as well as by day. *Ibid.*, Oct. 31, 1774. Time after time Charleston grand juries complained of Negroes being farmed out to do the work of artificers and of their irregularly selling produce and engaging in unfair trade practices. *Ibid.*, March 23–30, 1734; Oct. 29–Nov. 4, 1737; Jan. 25, 1770; March 24, 1773; Oct. 31, 1774; May 31, 1777.

[16] According to licenses issued to masters of slaves or free Negroes let out on hire in 1783, Negroes were employed in 23 occupations. See Leila Sellers, *Charleston Business on the Eve of the American Revolution* (Chapel Hill, 1934), pp. 101, 104, 105. For other drastic ordinances adopted in the post-Revolutionary period, including restrictions on the number of Negro servants that one might keep, see *Gazette of the State of S.C.*, Dec. 11, 1783, Aug. 3, 1786; *Columbian Herald*, July 31, 1786; *Charleston Ordinances*, pp. 164, 193, 194.

and charged that Negroes were unlawfully competing with them and manifesting an "Insolent and Turbulent disposition."[17] In Georgia, legislation forbidding the employment of Negroes and other slaves in the handicraft trades was enacted in 1758, and three years later a statute was passed against the hiring of Spaniards.[18] In West Florida, despite parallel legislation which proved difficult to carry out in practice, British army officers seem to have succeeded in 1767 in reducing the rate of wages of artificers engaged for the army by employing Negroes for certain tasks.[19]

One method adopted in most of the colonies to restrict Negro competition was to impose a duty on the importation of slaves, but such legislation was generally disallowed by the King in Council.[20] When in 1760 South Carolina prohibited the slave trade entirely, her action was promptly disallowed.[21]

The problem was intensified in the British West Indies, where white servants met ever-increasing competition from Negroes, and were required for garrison purposes as well as for labor. Despite the avowed preference of the planters for English and Scottish servants,[22] the scarcity of land deterred servants from emigrating to the British Caribbean possessions.[23] In addition to reducing the terms of service of servants engaged in garrison duty, to giving them land bounties, and to assuring them proper labor contracts and a suitable legal machinery for the recovery of wages, all the West Indian colonies adopted legislation providing that a minimum ratio of white workmen to Negroes be employed on the plantations or in the crafts. In the early years this ratio ranged from one white man for every Negro employed in the building and related trades in Barbados to the more typical ratio of one for every five or one for every ten slaves on the plantations. From time to time these ratios had to be modified owing to the impossibility of strict enforcement. Ratios of one to twenty, one to thirty, or even one to forty were ultimately substituted. In addition, legislation was enacted re-

[17] *N.C. Col. Rec.*, IX, 803–804.

[18] *Ga. Col. Rec.*, XIII, 276, 620. See also Jernegan, *Laboring . . . Classes*, p. 21.

[19] *Gage Corr.*, II, 405, 434.

[20] See *CSPA, 1717–18*, No. 660, p. 336 (1718); *1719*, No. 79, p. 44, No. 331, p. 177; *J. Commrs. Trade and Plantations, 1728/9–34*, pp. 64 (1729), 228, 231, 247 (1731), 298, 305, 307, 311, 316 (1732), 341, 366 (1733), 372, 401, 402, 417 (1734), *1734/5–41*, p. 3 (1735). Royal instructions to the governors forbade their consent to such acts. Labaree, *Royal Instructions*, II, 673, 674 (1731).

[21] A prohibitive duty of £100 was imposed in 1674. See W. E. B. Du Bois, *The Suppression of the African Slave Trade* (New York, 1896), pp. 9–11.

[22] See *CSPA, 1574–1660*, p. 443 (1656); *1675–76*, Nos. 682, 714, pp. 288, 304 (1675); *1681–85*, No. 1195, p. 474 (1683).

[23] C.O. 30:2, p. 78 (1670); *CSPA, 1675–76*, No. 1022, pp. 444, 445 (1676).

stricting the employment of Negroes in certain trades and crafts, particularly as porters, carmen, coopers, and boatmen.[24]

The wealthier planters set a poor example to the lower class whites by preferring in many cases to reside in England. In fact in 1761 the Board of Trade advised that a Jamaican act of 1760 providing for a minimum ratio of white settlers to Negroes and setting fines for deficiencies was contrary to the royal instructions as it "taxed absentees in greater proportion than residents."[25] The failure of all such efforts was not due to any lack of legislation but rather, as one royal governor put it, because there was no really "virtuous and strict execution of these laws" as well as of other statutes which assured servants in either planting or the trades a secure future when their terms expired.[26] Even had the laws been strictly enforced, they could never have stemmed the economic tidal wave which engulfed these islands. In the long run the serious lack of available freeholds as well as the ever-mounting competition of Negro slaves deterred the more industrious white servants from coming to the West Indies.[27]

Resentment against Negro slaves and free Negroes entering into the skilled trades lingered on in this country long after the colonial period. This resentment was founded not only upon economic rivalry,[28] but also upon a widespread belief in the South that the settling of Negroes in urban surroundings was bound to lead to the growth of a spirit of independence on the slave's part. Among the proposals inspired by the Vesey plot of 1822 which originated and centered in Charleston was the following:

The great fundamental principle should be that the slave should be kept as much as possible to agricultural labors. Those so employed are found to be

[24] *Barbados:* C.O. 30:2, pp. 89 *et seq.* (1671), C.O. 30:6, pp. 9, 43 *et seq.;* Baskett, ed., *Laws of Barbados* (Feb., 1699). *Jamaica:* C.O. 139:1, f. 138 (1672), C.O. 139:3, pp. 67 *et seq.* (1674); *CSPA, 1675–76,* No. 741, p. 315 (1675); C.O. 139:5, pp. 6–9 (1677), C.O. 139:6 (1678); Baskett, ed., *Acts of Jamaica, 1681–1737,* pp. 2–5 (1681), 99–101, also pp. 16, 17 (1681), 149–152 (1712); C.O. 139:9, p. 89 (1703); *J. Commrs. Trade and Plantations, 1722/3–28,* pp. 23 (1723), 116 (1724). *Antigua:* C.O. 154:2, p. 326 (1677), 340–342 (1679); *CSPA, 1675–76,* No. 929, p. 395; *Laws of the Island of Antigua, 1690–1798* (London, 1805), I, 272 (1740–41). *St. Christopher:* C.O. 154:2, pp. 23–24 (1679). South Carolina followed suit. An early ratio of 1 to 6 (*S.C. Stat.,* II, 153 [1698], 165 [1700]) was modified in 1716 to a 1 to 10 ratio (*ibid.,* p. 646).

[25] *A.P.C., Col., 1745–66,* p. 490 (1761).   [26] *Ibid., 1716–17,* No. 203, p. 113 (1716).

[27] Those who came despite these drawbacks were definitely of the less enterprising and industrious variety. See *ibid., 1719,* No. 209, p. 101.

[28] By 1819 the free Negroes of Charleston were engaged in 30 different trades. See E. H. Fitchett, "Traditions of the Free Negro in Charleston, S.C., in *J. Negro Hist.,* XXV (1940), 143. Before the Civil War the bulk of the mechanical trades in the South were manned largely by Negroes. See "The Negro American Artisan," ed. W. E. B. Du Bois and A. G. Dill, Atlanta University, *Publications,* No. 17 (Atlanta, Ga., 1912), p. 36.

the most orderly and obedient of slaves. . . . There should be no black mechanics or artisans, at least in the cities.[29]

Georgia in 1845 enacted legislation barring Negro mechanics from the building trades. In 1850 the white mechanics of the eastern part of North Carolina, resentful of the employment of Negroes in railroad building and public construction programs, petitioned the legislature that a tax be laid on free Negro mechanics for the purpose of colonizing them in Liberia. Shortly thereafter the mechanics of Rowan County declared their opposition to the competition of free Negro "mechanicks" on the ground that the Negroes were not only "a degraded class of men," but also that they were "never governed in fixing the prices for their labor by consideration of a fair compensation for the services rendered." Their proposal was that free Negro mechanics should be bound by law to an apprenticeship so long as they pursued their trade within the state and only be permitted to work under the direction of the master to whom they were bound.[30] This fear of competition in the skilled trades has doubtless influenced white Southerners in their opposition in more recent times to better educational facilities for Negroes [31] and has manifested itself concretely in the opposition of white labor to "upgrading" of Negro workers.[32]

POLITICAL ACTION BY WORKING CLASS GROUPS IN THE REVOLUTIONARY PERIOD

THE eve of the Revolution is marked by the appearance of numerous combinations of mechanics and laborers, masters and journeymen, primarily for political purposes. Together they protested against British imperial policy as it evolved after 1763. The course of this political op-

[29] Cited by Herbert Aptheker, *American Negro Slave Revolts* (New York, 1943), p. 115, from the *S.C. Gazette*.

[30] J. H. Franklin, *The Free Negro in North Carolina, 1790–1860* (Chapel Hill, 1943), pp. 137–139. For the protest in 1856 of the mechanics of Concord, N.C., see C. H. Wesley, *Negro Labor in the United States* (New York, 1926), p. 21. White mechanics also combined north of the Mason and Dixon line against Negro competitors. See Du Bois and Dill, *loc. cit.*, pp. 31–34. The fear of Negro competition in the labor market was an important factor in the New York draft riots of July, 1863. See *War of the Rebellion: Compilation of Official Records of Union and Confederate Armies* (128 serial vols., Washington, D.C., 1880–1901), 1st ser., XXVII, Pt. II, 938–939; D. M. Barnes, *The Draft Riots in New York, July 1863* (New York, 1863), pp. 113–116.

[31] See C. S. Mangum, Jr., *The Legal Status of the Negro* (Chapel Hill, 1940), p. 133. For the employment of Negro labor in the textile mills of the post-bellum South, see Broadus Mitchell, *The Rise of Cotton Mills in the South* (Baltimore, 1921), pp. 212–221. Industrial training has generally been restricted to training for cooking and menial service, and Negro education in the South has been principally "academic" and of a low order of effectiveness. Gunnar Myrdal, *et al.*, *An American Dilemma: the Negro Problem and Modern Democracy* (New York, 1944), II, 899.

[32] The Philadelphia transit strike of 1944 is a recent example.

position has been well charted by others and need not detain us. The pattern is now familiar. Leadership was gradually wrested from the conservative merchants by the more radical working class groups. Operating through committees of mechanics, these groups seized the initiative in the adoption and enforcement of the nonimportation agreements and in provoking incidents and organizing demonstrations. In this way the more conservative organs of protest were virtually supplanted.

The mariners were among the more radical and obstreperous element. In New York City they were organized as the Sons of Neptune, apparently antedating the Sons of Liberty, for whom they may well have suggested the pattern of organization.[1] Gage reported that the "insurrection" of November, 1765, in New York was supported by "great numbers of Sailors headed by Captains of Privateers, and other Ships." Shortly thereafter he referred to the sailors as "the only People who may be properly Stiled Mob," and charged that they were "entirely at the Command of the Merchants who employ them."[2] The rank and file of the Sons of Liberty throughout the colonies were workmen, although the organizing and directing was in large measure in the hands of master craftsmen, rather substantial merchants, and professional men.[3]

Certain outstanding examples may be considered to demonstrate the nature of working class cooperation for political ends and the solidarity

[1] See H. B. Dawson, *The Sons of Liberty in New York* (Poughkeepsie, 1859), pp. 51 *et seq.* For the part played by the mariners in New York City, see *N.Y. Gazette and Weekly Post-Boy,* July 12, 1764; Stokes, *Iconography,* IV, 843, citing *A Letter from Tom Bowline to His Worthy Messmates, the Renowned Sons of Neptune, Belonging to the Port of New York* (Dec. 12, 1773), original broadside, N.Y. Hist. Soc., *N.Y. Gazette,* Nov. 7, 1765.

[2] *Gage Corr.,* I, 71, 78, 79 (Nov. 4, Dec. 21, 1765). The master mariners shared the political sentiments of the seamen. When the Revolution broke out the members of the Marine Society were formed into a company of artillery. *J.N.Y. Prov. Cong.,* I, 41, 66 (1775).

[3] For Boston, see Force, *Amer. Arch.,* 4th ser., I, 506–508; Wells, *Adams,* I, 85, 86; J. C. Miller, *Sam Adams,* p. 39; J. K. Hosmer, *The Life of Thomas Hutchinson* (Boston, 1896), pp. 103–104; A. M. Schlesinger, *The Colonial Merchants and the American Revolution, 1763–1776* (New York, 1918), pp. 91 *et seq.* In Newport as well as Boston a group of shipwrights appears to have had an informal organization in the 18th century, meeting at the King's Head Tavern.

In New York the leadership of the Sons of Liberty was in the hands of merchants and lawyers. Out of 18 leaders of the society recently studied, 4 were lawyers, one a wealthy landowner and merchant, one a physician, and another, Abraham Brasher, a writer of popular ballads and possibly a mechanic by trade. The radicals who seized the helm during the later history of the organization comprised such leaders as Sears, Lamb, Allicocke, McDougall, and Willett, of whom four were prosperous merchants, although two had at one time worked as artificers. See H. B. Morais, "The Sons of Liberty in New York," *The Era of the American Revolution,* ed. R. B. Morris, pp. 272, 273; C. L. Becker, *History of Political Parties in the Province of New York, 1760–1776* (Madison, Wis., 1909).

For support by the Philadelphia mechanics of the nonimportation agreements, see *Pa. Gazette,* May 24, 1770; see also a broadside addressed "To the Tradesmen, Farmers, and Other Inhabitants

of the urban artisan group. The hostility of the Boston workman to the Red Coat on the eve of the Revolution stemmed in part at least from resentment of the interloper, for the men of the regular army were allowed to accept private employment when they did not have military assignments.[4] Quartered throughout Boston, the soldiers accepted work at very low rates of compensation. This sharp competition between soldiers and journeymen must be kept in mind in understanding the events leading to the Boston Massacre.

On the second of March, 1770, three British privates in the 29th Regiment went to the ropewalk belonging to John Gray looking for work. A journeyman by the name of William Green insulted one of them,[5] and the soldiers challenged him to a fight. After being worsted in fisticuffs, the soldiers ran back to the barracks in the immediate neighborhood and returned with several companions, who were driven off. The Red Coats then reappeared, reinforced to the number of some thirty or forty, armed with clubs and cutlasses, but the thirteen or fourteen hands of Gray's ropewalk were joined by fellow workers from neighboring ropewalks to the number of perhaps nine or ten, and the assault was again beaten off. Gray, the master, alarmed at the turn of events, made a personal complaint to Colonel Dalrymple, warning him that his soldiers were determined to even their score with the ropewalk work-

---

of the City and County of Philadelphia," Sept. 24, 1770, by "A Tradesman," in which it is asserted that the majority of the tradesmen of Philadelphia were enthusiastic in support of the nonimportation agreements (N.Y. Hist. Soc.), and C. H. Lincoln, *The Revolutionary Movement in Pennsylvania, 1760–1776*.

The direction of the radical town workmen of Charleston was assumed by Christopher Gadsden, a wealthy resident of that town, with Peter Timothy, printer of the *S.C. Gazette,* as his chief aide. They had first been organized by an influential mechanic named William Johnson. E. McCrady, *History of South Carolina under the Royal Government, 1719–1776* (New York, 1901), p. 589; R. W. Gibbes, ed., *Documentary History of the American Revolution* (New York, 1853–67), II, 10–11; D. D. Wallace, *The Life of Henry Laurens* (New York, 1915), p. 120; Sellers, *Charleston Business.*

[4] This practice was not new with the British army. As far back as 1717 the merchants and traders of Newfoundland urged the Board of Trade to restrain the soldiers from meddling with the fisheries or fishermen, from keeping any fishing boat, or from being employed in any other trade outside the limits of the fortifications. *CSPA, 1716–17,* No. 4, pp. 1, 2. See also Hillsborough to Gage *in re* a proposal "concerning the Mode of Discharging Soldiers having Trades." *Gage Corr.,* II, 60 (1768). See also "Kemble Diary," N.Y. Hist. Soc., *Coll., 1883,* p. 72. For an instance of a soldier of the 29th Regiment, which was involved in the Boston Massacre, working as a journeyman to a perukemaker of Boston, see F. Kidder, *History of the Boston Massacre, March 5, 1770* (Albany, N.Y., 1870). Permission was also given soldiers in the French garrisons in the Illinois country to work for the inhabitants. Gipson, *British Empire before the Amer. Revol.,* IV, 142. The custom also survived in the Continental army during the Revolution. See C. K. Bolton, *The Private Soldier under Washington* (New York, 1902), pp. 156, 157.

[5] According to the testimony of Samuel Bostwick at the Boston Massacre trial, Green, one of the hands, asked the soldier: "Soldier, will you work?" The soldier replied, "Yes." Whereupon Green retorted: "Then go and clean my s—t house." Kidder, *op. cit.,* p. 56.

ers. When Dalrymple placed the blame for instigating the riot upon Gray's journeyman, Gray discharged the accused on Monday morning, March 5th.[6]

Testimony is virtually unanimous that the soldiers nursed their humiliation at the hands of the ropewalks journeymen and were making rash threats of avenging the insult promptly.[7] On the evening of the fifth some British soldiers sallied out of Smith's barracks, beat up a number of persons, and were finally driven back to their barracks. Actually the incident followed the taunt of an apprentice boy hurled at a soldier, charging him with not paying a barber's bill to the lad's master. The soldier struck the apprentice, a general altercation ensued, and the exasperated soldiery fired, killing a number of persons, including Sam Gray, who had actively participated in the affray at the ropewalk on the preceding Friday. As to whether Gray was recognized and deliberately shot, or hit without special design, there was a conflict of testimony. Killroy, one of the soldiers positively identified as firing at the crowd, was known to have participated in the fight at the ropewalks, as was Warren, another soldier.[8]

The relationship of the ropewalk affair to the later massacre was admitted by the authorities, both British and colonial. Gage reported to Hillsborough:

A particular Quarrel happened at a Rope-Walk with a few Soldiers of the 29th Regiment; the Provocation was given by the Rope-Makers, tho' it may be imagined in the Course of it, that there were Faults on both Sides. This Quarrell it is Supposed, excited the People to concert a general Rising on the Night of the 5th of March.[9]

The Boston council also placed the blame for the affair of March 5, 1770, on the previous clash at the ropewalk, although on the details of the massacre civilians differed sharply from the military. According to the Boston authorities,

the affair which more immediately was introductory to the said Massacre was a quarrel between some Soldiers of the 29th Regiment and certaine Rope-

---

[6] For testimony and depositions relating to the affair at the ropewalks, see Kidder, *op. cit.*, pp. 13, 17, 48–51, 56; see also "A Short Narrative of the Horrid Massacre in Boston," reprinted in *ibid.*, p. 33.

[7] See *ibid.*, p. 34, where Matthew Adams stated that Corporal Pershall of the 29th Regiment had told him to stay at his master's house because the soldiers were determined to get satisfaction that very evening (the 5th); see also *ibid.*, pp. 49, 50, 53, 54. Samuel Quincy, in his charge to the jury, declared that the massacre could be directly traced to the earlier affray. *Ibid.*, p. 167.

[8] *Ibid.*, pp. 64, 80, 81, 151, 158, 159, 254. Matthew Killroy was one of the two soldiers—the other was Hugh Montgomery—who were found guilty of manslaughter, allowed their clergy, burnt in the hand, and discharged. The others were acquitted by the jury. *Ibid.*, p. 285.

[9] *Gage Corr.*, I, 249 (April 10, 1770).

makers at the Rope-walk of one Mr Gray. In the contest the Soldiers were worsted: and this reflecting, as they thought, on the honour of the Regiment there was a Combination among them to take vengeance on the Town indiscriminately. Of such a combination there is satisfactory proof.[10]

On a number of occasions mariners and town artificers struck in protest against British military preparations. Gage reported to Hillsborough in 1768 that transports would not proceed from New York to St. Augustine, because "the Troops are designed for Boston," and the mariners had been "threatened by Some of the Chiefs of the discontented," and dared not "incurr their Displeasure."[11] When, in 1774, Gage sought artificers to work on the fortifications of Boston, not only did the workers of that town refuse to work for him, but New Yorkers fully cooperated with the striking Bostonians.[12] Gage finally induced some Boston carpenters and masons to start work on the barracks, whereupon a joint committee of the Boston selectmen and members of the committee of correspondence persuaded them to quit.[13] Committees of correspondence of thirteen towns adjacent to Boston adopted joint resolutions deeming as "most inveterate enemies" any inhabitant of Massachusetts or the neighboring provinces who should supply the British troops at Boston with labor or materials.[14] Gage was forced to send to Nova Scotia for fifty carpenters and bricklayers, and through Governor Wentworth's aid, obtained a few additional ones from New Hampshire; but the troops did not get into barracks until November.[15] Early in the spring of 1775 mass meetings were held in New York City to protest the exportation of supplies for the use of the British garrison

[10] Kidder, *op. cit.*, p. 22; American Antiquarian Society, *Proceedings* (1937), pp. 290, 291. Randolph G. Adams refers to the Bostonians killed in the affray as "the dead mobsters." *Ibid.*, p. 264. A careful reading of the copious testimony available hardly justifies this epithet.

[11] *Gage Corr.*, I, 198.

[12] For the strike appeal, see *N.Y.J.*, Sept. 15, 1774. See also *Gage Corr.*, I, 376; Force, *Amer. Arch.*, 4th ser., I, 782. A broadside signed "Humanus" (Sept. 29, 1774) opposed the withholding of provisions and clothing from the troops in Boston on the ground that it would lead to rioting and hence fail in the end. Stokes, *Iconography*, IV, 867.

[13] Wrote Gage of this incident to Dartmouth, Oct. 3, 1774: "I was premature in telling your Lordship the Boston Artificers wou'd work for us. This Refusal of all Assistance has thrown us into Difficulties, but I hope to get through them, and to be able to put the Troops under Cover, tho' not so comfortably as I cou'd wish." *Gage Corr.*, I, 376, 377.

[14] Force, *Amer. Arch.*, 4th ser., I, 807–808; *N.Y.J.*, Oct. 20, 1774. The committee of the town of Rochester, N.H., found Nicholas Austin guilty of acting as a labor contractor for the army in Boston. He was made to pray forgiveness on his knees and to pledge that for the future he would never act "contrary to the Constitution of the country." *N.H. Gazette*, Nov. 11, 1774; Force, *Amer. Arch.*, 4th ser., I, 974; Schlesinger, *op. cit.*, p. 388n.

[15] Force, *Amer. Arch.*, 4th ser., I, 98, 991–992; *Mass. Gazette and News-Letter*, Nov. 10, 1774; *N.Y. Gazette*, Nov. 2, 1774. In October and November a considerable number of artificers shipped from New York to work upon the British barracks in Boston. *N.Y. Mercury*, Oct. 17, 1774; Stokes, *Iconography*, IV, p. 868.

at Boston. The supply ship was seized by the Committee and the crew forbidden to proceed on the voyage.[16]

At the very period when there was increasing concentration of workers in industrial establishments—a trend which was accelerated, first by the nonimportation agreements and subsequently by military needs —colonial journeymen put first things first, and combined *with* their employers in common political action rather than *against* their employers for economic advantages. In striking contrast was labor's role in Britain during those very same years. Franklin, writing in 1768, graphically described the lawless scenes in the British capital, where coalheavers and porters attacked the homes of coal merchants, while sawyers destroyed sawmills, watermen damaged private boats, and sailors would not permit ships to leave port unless their pay was raised.[17] When the Revolution began it was reported that Britain was drained of ships for transport purposes by combinations of workmen and sailors for raising their wages,[18] and strikers slowed down or disrupted production of English firms engaged in making clothing for the British army in America.[19] Gage reported that "the News of the Tumults and Insurrections which have happened in London and Dublin . . . is received by the Factions in America, as Events favorable to their Designs of Independency."[20]

CONCERTED ACTION BY JOURNEYMEN WORKERS FOR LABOR ENDS

Combinations by employers for purposes of trade monopoly, price fixing, and control of the labor market were more common in colonial times than combinations of journeymen and were unmolested by law. In certain fields such combinations were quite characteristic, particularly in the fisheries,[1] the spermaceti industry,[2] in the flour and baking

---

[16] Captain Isaac Sears, a ringleader, was arrested, but was rescued by the inhabitants and carried in triumph through the town. See *Gage Corr.*, I, 384, 408, 409; *N.Y.J.*, April 13, 1775; *N.Y. Gazette and Weekly Mercury*, April 17, 1775; H. B. Dawson, *The Park and Its Vicinity in the City of New York* (Morrisania, N.Y., 1867), pp. 70, 71.

[17] *Memoirs* (London, 1818), III, 315. Others reported widespread national distress and a "populace riotous." HMC, *Rep.*, XXXVIII, 30 (1766).

[18] HMC, *Rep.*, LIX, Pt. I, xviii, 59, 64 (1776). The authorities were also concerned at this time about preventing "combinations of merchants to raise the price" of provisions for the army in America. *Ibid.*, Pt. II, pp. 4–5 (1779).

[19] E. C. Curtis, *The Organization of the British Army in the American Revolution* (New Haven, 1926), p. 128, citing British Treasury and War Office papers.

[20] *Gage Corr.*, I, 197 (1768).

[1] For example, a Free New-York Fishery Company operated at Nova Scotia. *N.Y. Gazette and Weekly Post-Boy*, Sept. 9, 1751.

[2] The New England combine formed in 1761 included a group of Philadelphia manufacturers

trades,[3] and among tanners.[4] Employers combined to fix wages and control the labor market in the pre-Revolutionary period as well as during the war years that followed. For example, the *New-York Mercury* of August 7, 1758, carried the following item:

For the encouragement of Ship-Carpenters, able Seamen, and Labourers, in the Country, and the neighbouring Provinces, to repair to the City of New-York; The Merchants of this City have agreed to give to Ship-Carpenters 8*s.* per Day; able Seamen 8*s.* and Labourers 4*s.* with the usual Allowance of Provisions; and no other, or greater Wages whatsoever. And all Persons liking the above Proposals, may be certain of constant employment.

One of the significant rules laid down by the "Society for the Promotion of Arts, Agriculture and Economy," organized in New York in 1764, was "That no Member do receive unto his Service any Overseer, or Gardener, or white Servant, Male or Female, who shall not be able to produce a Recommendation in Writing, from the Master, or Mistress, whom they last served, in this Colony." [5] Agreements such as this, by no means unfamiliar to contemporary British industrialists,[6] constituted a standing threat to labor organizers and insubordinate workers.

In 1779 the New York Chamber of Commerce was instrumental in bringing about a reduction in the town rates for carmen.[7] In most

---

two years later. This combine agreed on a scale of maximum prices and commissions and was united to prevent "the setting up [of] any other Spermaceti works." "Commerce of Rhode Island, 1726–1800," I, Mass. Hist. Soc. *Coll.,* 7th ser., IX, 88–92, 97–100; Schlesinger, *Colonial Merchants,* p. 29; L. M. Friedman, *Jewish Pioneers and Patriots* (Philadelphia, 1942), pp. 309–315; G. C. Mason, "The United Company of Spermaceti Candlers, 1761," *Magazine of N.E. Hist.,* II, 165.

[3] For a price combination of Boston bakers, see *N.E. Courant,* Sept. 17, 24, 1722. The New York Chamber of Commerce, organized in the late sixties and chartered in 1770, effectively checked a combination among the bolters, millers, bakers, and flour merchants to raise the prices of flour and bread by making heavy purchases of flour in Philadelphia, forcing the New York flour combine to reduce prices. J. A. Stevens, Jr., *Colonial Records of the New York Chamber of Commerce* (New York, 1867), pp. 3–7, 21, 23, 32, 67, 89.

[4] For example, in 1747–48 tanners in the Boston area combined not to pay above an agreed price for leather. *Boston Gazette, or Weekly Journal,* Dec. 29, 1747; Jan. 5, 19, 1748; R. F. Seyboldt, "Trade Agreements in Colonial Boston," *N.E.Q.,* II, 307–309.

[5] *N.Y. Gazette,* Dec. 20, 1764. A somewhat similar joint action against workers was taken by a group of New Jersey ironmasters, who, at a meeting at Morristown in 1774, entered into an agreement to assist in collecting debts owing to the Hibernia Furnace by absconding workmen. Joseph Holt to Lord Stirling, March 2, 1774, Stirling MSS, lib. IV, f. 9, N.Y. Hist. Soc.

[6] J. U. Nef, *The Rise of the British Coal Industry* (London, 1932), II, 158.

[7] A penalty of imprisonment was set for nonobservance of these maximum rates. This was also imposed for refusal to haul the first load offered. For the inflated character of wages in this period, see H. Gaine, *Mercury,* Jan. 8, Dec. 14, 1778, Sept. 20, 1779; Rivington, *Royal Gazette,* Oct. 21, 1780; *Colonial Records of the Chamber of Commerce,* pp. 208–214; Loyalist Transcripts, XLI, 222.

colonial and post-colonial towns the master carpenters agreed upon a scale of prices or fees,[8] and on at least one occasion similar action was taken by the master barbers of Boston. Such an agreement was announced in the *New England Courant* for December 7, 1724:

On Tuesday the first of this Instant in the Evening, Thirty Two Principal Barbers of this Place, assembled at the Golden Ball, with a Trumpeter attending them, to debate some important Articles relating to their occupations; where it was proposed, that they should raise their Shaving from 8 to 10s. per Quarter, and that they should advance 5s. on the Price of making common Wiggs and 10s. on their Tye ones. It was also propos'd, that no one of their Faculty should shave or dress Wiggs on Sunday Mornings for the future, on Penalty of forfeiting 10 pounds for every such Offense: From whence it may fairly be concluded, that in times past such a Practice has been too common among them.

Collective action by journeymen workmen in colonial towns, as distinguished from combinations by licensed trades, guild groups, or employers' trade associations, was comparatively rare, but manifestations in the form of strikes, slowdowns, and conspiracies to desert go back to the earliest days of settlement. John Winter, who was constantly struggling to keep his bound workmen and fishermen at work on Richmond Island, off the coast of Maine, in the interests of his employer, Robert Trelawny, reported in 1636 that they "fell into a mutany" against him for withholding the previous year's wages. Under the leadership of one of their number named Lander, who later successfully recovered his wages due in court, a "Consort ship" to run away was entered into and mass desertions took place. Winter issued an "order along the Cost [coast] that no man shall entertaine them," but in order to be freed from their contracts other workmen made "stryfe" to compel the overseer to "turne them away." Winter advised his employer that in the future he bind his fishermen by "a sumsion"—doubtless he meant an agreement stipulating a penalty for nonfulfillment. Again he complained that "they ar all gathered in a head togeather heare," and found it necessary to send home a brewer named Thomas Samson lest he "poyson som of men on[e] tyme or other yff he had stayed heare with vs." On a still later occasion in 1641 the workers stopped work in the afternoon in protest against inadequate food, and the carpenters engaged in one of the earliest slowdowns on record in the colonies. When rebuked, they answered: "Yf you do not like vs we will be gon, the[y]

[8] See *supra*, pp. 142–145.

knowing our worke must be donn and no other to be gotten." [9] The first lock out in American labor history took place in 1643 at the Gloucester yards, when a group of obstreperous shipwrights were forbidden by the authorities "to worke a stroke of worke more" upon a certain ship without further orders from the governor.[10]

In 1741 the Boston caulkers, one of the earliest well-knit occupational groups and traditionally radical in sympathy, entered into an agreement to refuse to accept notes from their "Employer or Employers" on shops for goods or money in payment of their labor, specifying penalties for breach thereof. The newspaper, in its account of the agreement, expressed the opinion that "this good and commendable Example will soon be follow'd by Numbers of other Artificers and Tradesmen," desirous of protecting themselves against paper money inflation.[11]

A few strikes of journeymen are recorded prior to the rise of more permanent trade unions. Because of a "late Reduction of the Wages of journeymen Taylors" in New York some twenty tailors decided in 1768 to go on strike. They offered to work in families at "three Shillings and Six Pence per Day" with "Diet." Their "House of Call" was at the "Sign of the Fox and Hounds," in Moravian (now Fulton) Street. They were careful in their public announcement to make no direct statement that they had refused to work, and merely asserted that they could no longer support themselves and their families "by working as Journeymen." This appears to have been a concert of workers to compete directly with their former masters in retaliation for a wage cut.[12]

In 1778 the journeymen printers of New York City demanded a substantial increase in wages on the ground of the exorbitant wartime increase in the cost of living. The Tory James Rivington gave space to this important labor incident in his *Royal Gazette* of November 14, 1778.

New-York, Nov. 9, 1778.

Gentlemen,

As the necessaries of life are raised to such an enormous price, it cannot be

[9] "Trelawny Papers," Me. Hist. Soc., *Coll.*, III, 92, 93n. (1636), 108, 113, 114 (1637), 172, 173, 205 (1639), 258 (1641). For a strike at Pemaquid in 1702, see *CSPA, 1702*, No. 810, p. 501.

[10] A breach of public order appears to have been involved rather than an economic conflict. E. Hazard, *Historical Collections, Consisting of State Papers and Other Authentic Documents* (Philadelphia, 1792–94), I, 516, 517.

[11] *Boston Weekly Post-Boy*, Feb. 23, 1741. R. F. Seyboldt, "Trade Agreements," *N.E.Q.*, II, 307–309, places this in the same category as the previously mentioned agreement of tanners not to pay above a stated price for leather. The latter is clearly a trade agreement of master artisans, however; whereas it seems highly probable that journeymen made up the bulk of the caulkers entering into the agreement not to work for notes.

[12] *N.Y.J.*, April 7, 1768.

expected that we should continue to work at the wages now given; and therefore request an addition of Three Dollars per week to our present small pit-
tance; It may be objected that this requisition is founded upon the result of a
combination to distress the Master Printers at this time, on account of the
scarcity of hands; but this is far from being the case; it being really the high
price of every article of life, added to the approaching dreary season. There is
not one among us, we trust, that would take an ungenerous advantage of
the times—we only wish barely to exist, which it is impossible to do with our
present stipend.

There is scarcely a common Labourer but gets a Dollar per day and provisions, and the lowest mechanics from 12 to 16s. per Day.

We wait the result of your determination.

The Journeymen Printers

To the Master Printers, New-York.

I do consent to the above Requisition.

James Rivington

The demands of the journeymen printers were made as a group against
the master printers of the city. Beginning in May of that year Rivington
and other printers established a mutual daily gazette, first for five and
later for six days a week, an arrangement that produced in effect the
first daily in America. The protest of the printers was a threat against
the continued publication of this daily, but a threat couched in courte-
ous language. The hesitancy of the journeymen to be labeled "a combination to distress the Master Printers" is readily understandable in
view of the occupation of the city at that time by the British army,
which they might very well have feared would have been all too willing to introduce some of the methods used at home in dealing with
labor combinations.[13]

Strikes and slowdowns marred production in the iron industry in
the middle of the eighteenth century. That indefatigable promoter,
Peter Hasenclever, was harassed by labor trouble. When the artisans and
laborers induced to migrate by his agents in Germany arrived at the
ironworks, they demanded higher wages, despite the contracts they had
made abroad, and when Hasenclever refused to accede, they proceeded
to give a good colonial version of the twentieth-century "slowdown."

[13] Pasko refers to the strike, without mentioning the date, in *American Dictionary of Printing*
(New York, 1894), p. 390. D. J. Saposs was unable to verify the incident, probably because he
assumed Pasko meant 1776. J. R. Commons *et al., History of Labor in the United States* (New
York, 1936), I, 25. This date is also accepted without substantiation by G. A. Tracy, *History of
the Typographical Union* (Indianapolis, 1913), pp. 17, 18, and by N. J. Ware, *Labor in Modern
Indust. Soc.*, p. 128. Lee calls the strike "in all probability . . . the first strike of printers in
America." J. M. Lee, *History of American Journalism* (Boston, 1917), p. 96.

Because of his inability to obtain competent replacements, Hasenclever
was forced to yield, and their wages were raised.[14] When their wages
were not paid them promptly, the carpenters at the Hibernia Iron Works
in New Jersey struck in 1774.[15]

The only type of permanent or semipermanent organization of workers to take root in the pre-Revolutionary period was the association of
craftsmen for philanthropic ends. Organized on craft lines, these
"friendly societies" included masters as well as journeymen; among
mariners their membership seems to have been confined to masters.
The Friendly Society of Tradesmen House Carpenters, organized in
New York City in 1767, was a typical mutual aid society restricted to a
single trade. According to its twenty articles, membership was limited
to house carpenters, "free from all bodily Distempers," and within the
ages of twenty-one and forty. An initiation fee of 4s. and a monthly
payment of 1s. 6d. went to a general fund which assured sick benefits
for members. After the first six days of illness the member was entitled
to 10s. a week during the reminder of his indisposition.[16] Friendly societies, also known as "box clubs," had during this period spread rapidly
in the mother country. Such organizations were often a mask for illegal
combinations, and the boundary line between the friendly society and
the trade union came to be extremely shadowy.[17] Whether the New
York society engaged in activities other than those announced at its
formation cannot be determined, as no records of the organization are

[14] Peter Hasenclever, *The Remarkable Case of Peter Hasenclever, Merchant* . . . (London,
1773), pp. 5, 6, 9. In an earlier strike of 1711 some 300 or 400 Palatines engaged in the naval-
stores project took up arms to gain their demands for lands in the Schoharie Valley. Governor
Hunter called out the troops and had them disarmed. Though they went back to work under
military surveillance, they worked indifferently and with repugnance. See *Doc. Hist. of N.Y.*, III,
664, 669–671; W. A. Knittle, *Early Eighteenth Century Palatine Emigration* (Philadelphia, 1937),
pp. 163–165, 175.

[15] Stirling MSS, lib. IV, fols. 10, 13 (March 8, April 2, 1774).

[16] There were social features as well as benefits. One of the articles provided that "If any
Member calls for Liquor without the approbation of the stewards, he shall pay for the same
himself"; another, "If any member presumes to curse or swear, or cometh disguised in Liquor
and breed Disturbance . . . or promoteth Gaming at Club Hours," he shall pay to the "Common
stock" 6d. for each violation. "Articles and Regulations of the Friendly Society of Tradesmen
House Carpenters," March 10, 1767, Broadside, Evans Coll., No. 24,606, N.Y. Pub. Lib.

[17] For examples as early as 1688, see Wadsworth and Mann, *Cotton Trade and Indust. Lancashire*, pp. 341, 375; also P. Mantoux, *The Industrial Revolution of the Eighteenth Century*, pp.
78–84; Heaton, *Yorkshire Woollen and Worsted Industries*, pp. 317, 318; Webb, *Trade Unionism*,
p. 24, and *Industrial Democracy*, pp. 153, 154. The worsted smallware weavers of Manchester,
acting under the guise of a friendly society, were prosecuted in 1760 as a combination to raise
wages. G. W. Daniels, *The Early English Cotton Industry* (Manchester, 1920), p. 44. An important motive for the Friendly Societies Act of 1793, which provided for the registration of such
societies, was the desire to confine them to specific approved activities. See Bowden, *Indust. Soc.
in Eng.*, pp. 297, 298. For a general survey, see Sir Frederick Eden, *Observations on Friendly
Societies* (London, 1801), pp. 5–7, and *The State of the Poor* (London, 1797), I, 461; II, 58, 310;
III, 873, 874.

extant today, although its articles provided for the recording of minutes in a "Book of Transactions." However, in 1771 an organization calling itself The Society of House Carpenters announced that it was using Mr. David Philips's establishment as a house of call, where workmen could be secured "on reasonable Terms." [18] While it is by no means clear that the two societies were by that time one and the same, it is apparent that by the eve of the Revolution the house carpenters did find it necessary to act together for certain economic ends. [19]

A more permanent type of organization of master workmen was afforded by the marine societies which were especially strong in New England. These societies do not appear to have been formed to regulate wages or prices or to control the labor market, but rather for the relief of distressed shipmasters and their widows and children. The first of these was the "Marine Society of Boston in New England," organized in 1742. [20] The "Fellowship Club" of Rhode Island, established in 1752, was of the same nature. [21] Salem, New York, [22] Philadelphia, [23] and Newburyport soon followed suit. But combinations of mariners for higher wages were not tolerated. When, in the winter of 1779, 150 mariners went on strike for higher wages at the port of Philadelphia, the state authorities had the magistrates arrest the ringleaders and the Board of War ordered the troops out to support the officials. [24]

[18] *N.Y. Gazette and Weekly Mercury,* Nov. 18, 1771.

[19] The host of societies which sprang up in colonial towns to assist immigrants, such as the Scots' Box of Boston, the Welsh Society, and the Hibernian Club in Philadelphia, were principally immigrant aid groups and were not organized along vocational lines. Erna Risch, "Immigrant Aid Societies before 1820," *Pa. Mag. of Hist. and Biog.,* LX, 15–33; Mass. Hist. Soc., *Proceedings,* LVI, 48; also *N.Y. Gazette or Weekly Post-Boy,* Feb. 18, 1762, for the economic activities of the St. Andrew's Society.

[20] *Constitution and Laws of the Boston Marine Society* (Boston, 1792), Harvard Coll. Lib.

[21] *R.I. Col. Rec.,* X, 113.

[22] In New York the Marine Society is still actively functioning. Its original incorporators included leading merchants active in marine insurance as well as shipmasters. *The Marine Society of the City of New York* (New York, 1933). A New York Mariners' Friendly Society was founded in 1792 for benevolent purposes. *N.Y. Directory, 1795.*

[23] *Pa. Stat. at Large,* VII, 341–346 (1770). The hope was expressed that through the distribution of relief benefits men would be encouraged to become skilful mariners. See also *ibid.,* pp. 387–392. A Ship Masters' Society is listed in the *Phila. Directory, 1793,* p. 207.

[24] While originally the membership of the New England marine societies was confined to masters, the ranks were soon opened to owners of vessels, merchants, and persons of other professions, either as regular or honorary members. The East India Marine Society at Salem (1808), however, confined membership to masters, commanders, owners, or supercargo. The earlier Salem Marine Society provided that each member pay into the box for the use of the society, 20s. at the time of entry, and 8d. per month. A number of these New England societies still survive. See L. W. Jenkins, "The Marine Society at Salem in New England," *Essex Inst. Hist. Coll.,* LXXVI, 201 *et seq.* For the dates of incorporation of these marine societies, see J. S. Davis, *Essays in the Earlier History of American Corporations* (Cambridge, 1917), p. 101. For the Charleston, S.C., Marine Anti-Britannick Society, see *infra,* p. 204 n. Riot rather than conspiracy was the basis of the strike prosecution of 1779. *Pa. Col. Rec.,* XI, 664, 665; *Pa. Packet,* Jan. 16, 1779.

With the close of the American Revolution a sharp cleavage between groups on economic or regional lines becomes apparent. Highly complex conservative-rural, radical-urban groupings were now taking on a political character,[25] with the journeymen giving their support to the urban group, which also included the mercantile interests. In most towns, mechanics' tickets were set up [26] and on a number of occasions craftsmen were sent to the state legislatures.[27]

In this period employers continued to enter into trade associations to protect their economic interests, but labor for the first time turns to the more permanent type of trade-union organization. The rise of the factory, the transition from custom work to wholesale order work, and the concentration of workers in certain expanding industries served to bring about more distinct class stratifications. This period was marked by the decline of the apprenticeship system; inexpert workmen now came into direct competition with skilled journeymen, as middlemen now pitted master against master, giving their orders to the lowest cost producer and forcing masters to increase sharply the ratio of apprentices (now called "green hands") to skilled journeymen. As the vast majority of workers came to abandon hope of ever being admitted into the ranks of the employers, they turned increasingly to the strike as the best economic weapon to advance their interests and to the trade union as the most suitable form of trade organization.

Among the early strikes of the post-Revolutionary era one of the most notable was that of the New York shoemakers in 1785 for higher wages.[28] The masters quickly retaliated by entering into an employer

[25] The concept of a basic social cleavage after 1783 is pressed by Merrill Jensen, *The Articles of Confederation: an Interpretation of Social-Constitutional History of the American Revolution, 1774–1781* (Madison, 1940). Oscar and Mary F. Handlin properly object to a unitary and over-simplified interpretation of the politics of this period, and give due emphasis to urban v. rural, new social groupings, etc., in "Radicals and Conservatives in Massachusetts after Independence," *N.E.Q.*, XVII (1944), 343–355. Cf. also R. A. East, "Massachusetts Conservatives in the Critical Period," in *Era of the American Revolution*, ed. R. B. Morris, pp. 349–391; O. G. Libby, *Geographical Distribution of the Vote of the Thirteen States on the Federal Constitution, 1787–88* (Madison, Wis., 1894); R. L. Brunhouse, *The Counter-Revolution in Pennsylvania* (Philadelphia, 1942).

[26] See *Mass. Centinel*, July 10, 1784; *Mass. Spy* (*Worcester Gazette*), June 24, 1784. For New York City, see broadsides for Dec. 23, 26, 27, 29, 1783, N.Y. Hist. Soc.

[27] *N.Y. Packet*, April 4, 7, 14, 21, 24; *N.Y. Gazette*, April 15, 1785; *N.Y. Morning Post*, April 21, 1785. In 1789 the "Mechanics" of Montgomery Ward protested that the polls had been closed before their working day had ended, but their request for another day's polling was rejected by the council. N.Y.C.C. Rec., File Box 11, Bundle 1, Board of Aldermen and City Clerk's Library; *M.C.C., 1784–1831*, I, 460. The Tammany Society recruited its strength heavily from the artisan ranks. *N.Y. Daily Advertiser*, April 28, 1800; *American Citizen*, May 7, 1800. But it was not until well along in the nineties that the allegiance of the journeymen to the anti-Federalist party became clear-cut, with occasional exceptions.

[28] A number of students of labor history call the printer's strike in Philadelphia in 1786 the first strike of wage earners in this country. D. J. Saposs in Commons, *op. cit.*, I, 27; S. Perlman,

combination, and demanded that the workers agree to work for no one who sold English shoes, having specifically in mind a certain low-cost manufacturer named Smith. After a strike lasting three weeks, both sides withdrew their demands when Smith advertised that he needed more good workmen for his shoe factory and adroitly coupled this announcement with a low scale of prices for his shoes.[29] More permanent manifestations of union activity did not arise until the next decade, but before the close of the century the New York typographers, carpenters, masons, and coopers had set up effective trade unions.[30]

Labor union activity in Philadelphia in this period surpassed that in New York. In 1786 the journeymen printers went on strike to protest a reduction of wages and passed a resolution of joint support for the duration of the strike—probably the first instance on record in this country of a union strike-benefit fund.[31] But permanent organization of this craft does not appear to have been effected in that city until 1802.[32] Following the organization in 1789 of the Philadelphia Society of Master Cordwainers, the journeymen in the same trade formed in 1794 a union known as the "Federal Society," to protect themselves from "scab labor." On at least three occasions before the end of the century they went on strike for higher wages.[33]

Employers were equally aggressive and alert in setting up trade associations in the post-Revolutionary period. The objectives of these associations were threefold: 1) control of the labor market and curtailment of labor union activity; 2) political aid for commerce and manufactures; and 3) broad philanthropic or educational ends.

A History of Trade Unionism in the United States (New York, 1922), p. 3; W. M. Leiserson, "Labor Relations and the War," ed. Herman Feldman, *Annals of the American Academy of Political and Social Science* (Philadelphia, Nov., 1942), p. 1. It is clear, however, that the New York printers' strike of 1778, the Salem, N.C., strike of the same year, the Philadelphia seamen's strike of 1779, and the shoemakers' strike of 1785 take precedence.

[29] *N.Y. Packet,* March 21, 1785. The *Packet,* March 31, 1785, carried a reprint of an article from the *Pa. Gazette* detailing a meeting of the cordwainers of Philadelphia, who agreed not to buy or sell any European manufactures nor to work directly or indirectly for any one who bought or sold such goods.

[30] For successful strikes brought by typographical unions in this period (1794–1800), see *N.Y. Diary or Evening Register,* July 3, 1794; E. Stewart, *A Documentary History of the Early Organization of Printers,* Bureau of Labor Statistics, *Bull.,* No. 61 (Washington, 1905), p. 863; R. H. Cressingham, *The Official Annual of Typographical Union No. 6* (March, 1892); Stevens, *op. cit.,* pp. 38–40. The call for the union was issued by "A number of journeymen." Greenleaf's *N.Y. Daily Advertiser,* Nov. 24, 1798. For the coopers, see Stevens, *op. cit.,* p. 36; for the building trades, *N.Y. Daily Advertiser,* March 30, April 1, 1795. See also Commons, *op. cit.,* I, 108–110; *Doc. Hist. of Amer. Indust. Soc.,* III, 26, 27.

[31] Stewart, *loc. cit.,* p. 860; Commons, *op. cit.,* I, 25; Perlman, *op. cit.,* p. 3.

[32] The constitution of this society, believed to be the oldest constitution of a labor organization extant in the United States, is published in Stewart, *loc. cit.,* pp. 941–945. Provision was made for a strike-benefit fund.

[33] C. D. Wright, *The Battles of Labor* (Philadelphia, 1906), pp. 77, 78.

1. In the first category were various associations of masters along craft lines. In New York, for example, the Gold and Silver Smiths' Society was functioning as early as 1786, under the chairmanship of that distinguished craftsman Myer Myers.[34] In the same year a "Society of Peruke Makers Hair Dressers, etc.," numbering twenty-three members, was listed in the *New York Directory*. A New York Coopers' Society, under the chairmanship of John Utt, was listed in the *Directories* of 1795 and 1796, and in the latter year reference is made to an organization of masters known as "The Associated Body of House Carpenters of the City of New-York."[35] The Society of Master Sail Makers appears to have been a far more democratic body than other associations of masters. Among other libertarian toasts, it offered one "To the societies of America as nurseries of Republicanism."[36]

The master shoemakers, as has already been pointed out, combined in 1785 to lay down conditions of employment to their striking journeymen.[37] In 1795 the master masons and house carpenters appear to have been behind a move to get the public to resist a wage rise demanded by the building trades journeymen, who also sought to root out the kick-back system, then well-entrenched in that industry.[38] In 1786 the Philadelphia employing printers joined together in efforts to reduce the wages of their journeymen.[39] This combination was given more formal organization in 1794.[40] In this same period the master cordwainers of Philadelphia entered into an agreement not to engage in wholesale business. The enterprising firm of Peter Gordon, Prentice and Company struck back at "the envious combination" by advertising an improved patented boot and offering higher wages to workmen.[41] In this struggle the masters had the wholehearted support of the jour-

---

[34] Other members and officers of this society were master workmen in that trade. See *N.Y. Directory, 1786, 1787;* Stephen G. C. Ensko, *American Silversmiths and Their Marks* (New York, 1927), pp. 77, 84, 87, 90, 99.

[35] At least one of the objectives of this organization was philanthropy, as its roster contains a list of "Members who visit and relieve the sick or afflicted," two being named for each two-month period. A bar association and a medical society appear well-entrenched by this date. See *N.Y. Directory, 1789.*

[36] *N.Y.J.,* Nov. 14, 1795.   [37] See *supra,* pp. 200, 201.

[38] See *N.Y. Daily Advertiser,* March 30, April 1, 1795.   [39] Commons, *op. cit.,* I, 25.

[40] This organization has at times been mistakenly designated a labor union, but it is clear from its constitution that it was in fact a combination of employers. Article 14 empowered the society "to regulate the prices which its members shall execute printing work; to determine the terms of employing journeymen; to fix penalties for the violation of their regulations; and, in general, to adopt such rules as may be considered conducive to the prosperity of the printing business." The document is signed by nine individuals who were the heads of printing and publishing firms. Stewart, *loc. cit.,* pp. 861–863.

[41] *Doc. Hist. Amer. Indust. Soc.,* III, 128; IV, 44; Dunlap's *Amer. Daily Advertiser,* June 25, 30, 1791, and repeated from time to time.

neymen cordwainers, naturally opposed to wholesale methods and to competition with "green hands." [42] In the nineties the master cordwainers agreed upon a scale of piece-work wages for their journeymen,[43] and the master cabinet- and chairmakers took steps to fight union recognition in their industry by distributing handbills in which they stated that they would not employ any journeymen "as society men, but as individuals." The journeymen in that trade then called upon labor to form "an union of the respective mechanical branches in this city, and throughout America." [44] They followed up a strike for higher wages by setting up their own shop and issuing a call to the unions of hatters, shoemakers, house carpenters, tailors, goldsmiths, saddlers, coopers, painters, printers, and others to meet together "to digest a plan of union, for the protection of their mutual independence." [45] Master house carpenters in 1791 successfully fought a strike of their journeymen for shorter hours. The journeymen in this trade, as in the cabinet and carpentry fields, in self-defense started their own cooperative shop and offered to work for the public below the prevailing scale set by the masters.[46]

2. Manufacturers and merchants joined forces in the "critical period" for political action in matters relating to business. When, in the summer of 1785, the Tradesmen and Manufacturers' Association of Boston called upon similar groups in other cities to organize to obtain adequate laws for the encouragement of home industries and to cooperate in the exchange of American products, New York, Philadelphia, Baltimore, and Charleston rallied to the call.[47] The provisions of the Federal Constitution regarding the regulation of commerce and the imposition of import duties attest to the influence of the mercantile and manufacturing interests in the drafting of that document. The Tariff of 1789 was in response to petitions from organizations of mechanics and manu-

[42] See Dunlap's *Amer. Daily Advertiser*, May 16, 1791. Other employer combinations with price- and wage-fixing objectives are known to have been in existence in Philadelphia before 1800. Among them was the Stone Cutters' Company, founded in 1790. James Mease, *The Picture of Philadelphia: Its Origin, Increase, and Improvement in Arts, Sciences, and Manufactures* (Philadelphia, 1811), pp. 270, 271. The Master Bricklayers' Society was established in 1809 after the plan of the Stone Cutters' Society. Mease, *op. cit.*, pp. 271, 272; Commons, *op. cit.*, I, 69.

[43] *Federal Gazette*, May 19, 1791.

[44] *Pa. Packet*, July 16, 1795; Feb. 17, 1796.

[45] *Aurora*, April 7, 1796.

[46] Commons, *op. cit.*, I, 110. The master cordwainers of Pittsburgh somewhat later entered into secret agreement to fix prices. *Doc. Hist. Amer. Indust. Soc.*, IV, 55. In 1793 the Baltimore Mechanical Society cautioned its members not to increase prices of goods of their own or others' manufacture, so as not to take advantage of the numerous French refugees coming into town. *Md. J.* (Baltimore), July 26, 1793.

[47] See, e.g., *Gazette of the State of S.C.*, Nov. 24, 1785.

facturers who demanded protection as well as aid for domestic manufactures.[48]

3. The "friendly societies" of the earlier period were suspected in the mother country of secretly nurturing labor ends. In the Confederation period the American public viewed with a certain suspicion associations of employers ostensibly for philanthropic purposes. A law of 1785 chartering a Mechanics' Society in New York City was vetoed by the Council of Revision on the ground that such a corporate group might keep emigrants from gaining entry into trades and occupations.[49] Finally a loophole was found whereby the General Society of Mechanics and Tradesmen was set up as a charitable organization and incorporated as such a few years later.[50] While in theory all mechanics and tradesmen resident in the city were eligible for admission, the membership in fact appears to have been largely confined to master craftsmen from the chief trades of the city.[51] Similar mechanics' associations arose in this period at Albany, Portsmouth, Providence, Baltimore, Norfolk, and Savannah.[52]

[48] See *Amer. Museum*, I, 19; IV, 347–348; *Amer. State Papers, Finance*, I, 89; S. Rezneck, "The Rise and Early Development of Industrial Consciousness, 1760–1830," *J. Econ. and Bus. Hist.*, IV, 788, 789.

[49] See Morris, "Criminal Conspiracy and Early Labor Combinations," *loc. cit.*, pp. 83, 84; C. Z. Lincoln, *Messages from the Governors* (Albany, 1909), II, 228 *et seq.*; *N.Y. Assembly Proceedings*, 8 Sess., Feb. 3, 9, 15, March 9, 1785, pp. 13, 27–28, 39, 77–78; A. B. Street, *Council of Revision of the State of New York* (Albany, 1859), pp. 261–264.

[50] N.Y. State Laws, 15th Sess., March 14, 1792, c. 26.

[51] By 1798 there were 488 members compared with 47 in 1786. *N.Y. Directory, 1786*. Represented were the hatters, potters, carpenters, butchers, tobacconists, masons, tallow chandlers, sailmakers, coachmakers, staymakers, coopers, blacksmiths, stonecutters, ropemakers, tailors, blockmakers, cutlers, tanners, pewterers and plumbers, combmakers, bookbinders, shipjoiners, brewers, skinners, saddlers, bolters, ship carpenters, hairdressers, and bakers. A smith named Robert Boyd, who also served in the Assembly, was the first chairman. Some journeymen were later admitted to the society, but the bulk of the membership remained employer-craftsmen. *Annals of the General Society of Mechanics and Tradesmen of the City of New-York from 1785 to 1880*, ed. T. Earle and C. T. Congdon (New York, 1882), pp. 10–11, 16; Pomerantz, *op. cit.*, pp. 95–97, 214, 215.

[52] In addition, there was an Association of Mechanics of the Commonwealth of Massachusetts and a Maine Charitable Mechanic Association. The Albany Mechanics Society was founded in 1793, "for the laudable purpose of protecting and supporting such of their brethren as by sickness or accident may stand in need of assistance, and of relieving the widows and orphans of those who 'may die in indigent circumstances, and also providing the means of instruction for their children." Over 150 mechanics and tradesmen were the founding members. Crafts represented included those of printer, gold- and silversmith, hatter, tailor, brass founder, carpenter, stonecutter, brewer, cordwainer, baker, and bricklayer. Unfortunately, there is no available record of the proceedings of the society, so that it is by no means clear that it had other than charitable ends. It was incorporated by the legislature in 1801 and dissolved by act of Nov. 25, 1824. See MS Mechanics Society Record Book and Proceedings of the Board of Trustees set up by the legislative act of 1824 dissolving the Society. N.Y. State Lib., Albany. See also Munsell, *Annals*, VII, 240–244; Ensko, *op. cit.*, p. 68, for silversmiths among its membership. Cf. also Norfolk, Va., Common Council Mins., f. 239 (May, 1790).

Charleston employers in this period organized in such trades as tailors and carpenters, as well as among master mechanics generally. See J. Brevard, *An Alphabetical Digest of the Public Statute*

It is significant that, with the possible exception of the master bakers' strike of 1741 and the prosecutions of certain licensed trades for refusal to work, associations of employers were never prosecuted either in the colonial or post-Revolutionary periods. According to the law-on-the-books, strikes and concerted action by journeymen workers were illegal activities. They were contrary to the spirit of colonial statutes setting criminal penalties for the refusal of workmen in stated occupations to work [53] and the practice of the courts of specifically enforcing contracts of employment.[54] However, save in one instance, the colonial authorities never met the problem squarely. Georgia, in attempting to crush a strike by putting relevant British statutes into effect, was that notable exception. When, in 1746, a number of Savannah carpenters went on strike, the trustees considered such action to be outlawed by parliamentary statute. The all-too-brief report of their action follows:

Present
Earl of Shaftesbury President
Earl of Egmont
Mr Vernon
Sr William Heathcote
Mr L'apostre
An Advertisement being read, sign'd by several Carpenters at Savannah and stuck up at several Places in the said Town, whereby they have combin'd and resolved not to work below particular Prices Specified therein
Ordered
That the Act of Parliament Intitled —— [*sic*] be sent over to the President and Assistants, with orders for them to apprize the People of the Consequences of the said Act, and to put the same in force.[55]

It is undoubtedly significant that this action was taken by the trustees back in England, where labor combinations were frequently prosecuted at that time, and that the initiative was not taken by the colonial authorities. Aside from this instance, masters and journeymen, except in the licensed trades, were virtually unmolested if they sought to combine,

---

Law of S.C. (Charleston, 1814), III, 17, 31, 74, 213, 214, 216. These societies were primarily operated to provide relief to indigent families of members. In the case of the Master Taylors' Society, the funds were transferred in 1808 to charitable institutions and the society was dissolved. Cooper and McCord, *S.C. Stat.*, VIII, 132 (1785), 247 (1808). See also *ibid.*, V, 329, 460; VIII, 200, 201. Another such organization which had philanthropic as well as trade aims was the Marine Anti-Britannick Society. The preamble to the bylaws of that society was reprinted in the *Mass. Spy* (Worcester), May 24, 1784. Occasionally individual trades seem to have organized for relief purposes, among them the Cartmen's Society, founded in New York in 1792. Pomerantz, *op. cit.*, p. 212.
[53] See pp. 6–8, 223.   [54] See pp. 221–224.   [55] *Ga. Col. Rec.*, I, 495 (Dec. 29, 1746).

whereas instances of concerted action by white bound servants were systematically suppressed.

In the Confederation interlude the authorities took no legal steps against combinations of either masters or workmen, whereas in contemporary Britain the courts were ruthlessly consistent in punishing combinations of labor and were just as consistent, if less logical, in their partiality toward antilabor combinations of masters, which were tolerated at law.[56] However, as labor organizations became more persistent and permanent in character and the strike weapon increasingly effective, American employers shortly turned to the criminal machinery to stamp out the trade-union movement. In Philadelphia a series of strikes by journeymen cordwainers in the very early years of the nineteenth century culminated in a successful criminal prosecution. The issue in this case was sharply drawn between the Federalists, who were antilabor, and the Jeffersonian Republicans, who favored trade unions.[57] A few years later the *New York Cordwainers' Case,* 1809–10 (reported as *People v. Melvin*) followed the Philadelphia decision.[58] In denying that the crime of conspiracy at common law embraced the acts of workers in concert, counsel for the defense, Cadwallader D. Colden, subsequently mayor of the city, and that brilliant Dublin barrister William Sampson raised issues which were soon to be vital to the very continuance of the trade-union movement in both Britain and America.[59] The

[56] Adam Smith, *The Wealth of Nations* (London, 1826), p. 89; Lipson, *Woollen and Worsted Industry,* p. 122; Webb, *Trade Unionism,* pp. 72, 73; J. L. and Barbara Hammond, *The Town Labourer, 1760–1832* (London, 1917), pp. 60–66. Lipson (*Econ. Hist. of Eng.,* III, 386–392) cites an instance of an injunction having been issued in 1696 to prosecute employers who had entered into combinations directed against their workmen, "as it is said to be done at Colchester." *Cal. State Papers, Dom., 1696,* p. 205.

[57] When the celebrated trial was pending, a bill was introduced in the state legislature "to supersede the operation of the common law," but it was defeated by a vote of 44 to 32. *U.S. Gazette,* March 18, 1806. For the report of this case, see *Trial of the Boot and Shoemakers of Philadelphia* (Philadelphia, 1806); *Doc. Hist. Amer. Indust. Soc.,* III, 59, 233. The cordwainers were found "guilty of a combination to raise their wages," and were each fined $8, as the masters were merely concerned with the establishment of the principle rather than with punishing the journeymen. See also Walter Nelles, "The First American Labor Case," *Yale Law J.,* XLI (1931), 165–200.

[58] For a fuller treatment, see Morris, "Criminal Conspiracy and Early Labor Combinations," *loc. cit.* This case is reported in condensed form in 2 Wheeler Cr. Cas. 262 (New York, 1810), and more extensively by William Sampson, an attorney for the defense, in a pamphlet, entitled *Trial of the Journeymen Cordwainers of the City of New York for a Conspiracy to Raise Their Wages* (New York, 1810), reprinted in *Doc. Hist. Amer. Indust. Soc.,* III, 251. See also N.Y.G.S. Mins., 1810, fols. 210–215. It is perhaps significant that in this case the prosecution denied that the masters' association had ever sought to control the workers.

[59] The repeal by Parliament in 1824 of the Combination Act of 1800 was followed the next year by a statute which, while repealing the statutory penalties against labor combinations, left conspiracies to commit any of the acts prohibited to be dealt with at common law. The English courts then held such conspiracies to be offenses at common law. Stats. 5 Geo. IV, c. 96; 6 Geo.

bakers' strike of 1741, adduced by Thomas Addis Emmet for the prosecution as a supporting colonial precedent to justify the prosecution of labor combinations, was dismissed by them as inconclusive, as there was no evidence of a conviction having been obtained.[60] Sampson very courageously denied the relevance of English common-law precedents to American legal problems.[61]

Whether or not English common law provided historical justification for these convictions of American labor combinations must remain a debatable issue. The attitude of the colonial and Revolutionary courts toward combinations by employers or journeymen is too obscure to furnish satisfactory precedents from which the judiciary might induce the principle of an American "common law of criminal conspiracy." From the employers' point of view, statutes authorizing compulsory labor and setting heavy penalties for absenteeism and desertion and the judicial practice of specifically enforcing labor contracts were, in the absence of any common-law principle, sufficiently potent weapons against strikes and union activity.

IV, c. 129. G. Howell, *Labour Legislation, Labour Movements, and Labour Leaders* (London, 1902), p. 57; Sir James Stephen, *History of the Criminal Law of England* (London, 1883), III, 210–211, 218, 219, 223, 224. See *contra* A. V. Dicey, *Law and Public Opinion in England* (London, 1905), pp. 190–200; Sir William Erle, *The Law relating to Trade Unions* (London, 1869), p. 58.

Similarly, in New York, when an indictment was brought under a provision of the N.Y. Revised Statutes of 1829, including among criminal conspiracies "Conspiracy to injure trade or commerce," the court considered the act as continuing the common-law crime, not as creating a new one. People v. Fisher, 14 Wend. (N.Y.) 2 (1835). It should be noted that the earlier New York statute of 1801 dealing with criminal conspiracy did not go beyond acts to obstruct or defeat justice. Laws of New York, 24 Sess., c. 87. For the line of cases culminating in Commonwealth v. Hunt (1840), see A. Lenhoff, "A Century of American Unionism," *Boston Law Rev.*, XXII (1942), 357–374; Walter Nelles, "Commonwealth v. Hunt," *Columbia Law Rev.*, XXXII, 1128 at pp. 1166–1169; also Felix Frankfurter and Nathan Greene, *The Labor Injunction* (New York, 1930), pp. 2 *et seq.*

[60] See *supra*, pp. 162–163.

[61] "When is it," he declaimed, "that in search of a rule for our conduct, we shall no longer be bandied from Coke to Croke, from Plowden to the Year Books, from thence to the dome books, from *ignotum* to *ignotius*, in the inverse ratio of philosophy and reason. . . . How long shall this superstitious idolatry endure?" His arguments have been considered "penetrating as well as monumental" by the late Walter Nelles. Perhaps the quondam Dublin barrister shines more brilliantly than his distinguished colleague because Colden's rebuttal was not published by the reporter (Sampson), who accidentally mislaid it and destroyed his transcribed notes. *Trial of the Journeymen Cordwainers*, p. 141. Sampson was a pioneer in this country in advocating law reform, codification, and a break with the common law. His most widely published statement was *An Anniversary Discourse Delivered before the Historical Society of New York . . .* (Dec. 6, 1823), reprinted in *Sampson's Discourse upon the History of the Law*, comp. P. Thompson (Washington, 1826), which also contains (pp. 131–150) an extract of his defense of the journeymen cordwainers. His writings possess a verse, wit, and emotional quality unusual for the day and subject. Cf. also Natl. Protective Assn. v. Cumming, 170 N.Y. 315, 332 (1902).

IV. THE TERMS AND CONDITIONS OF EMPLOYMENT

THE SYSTEM OF WAGE PAYMENT

THE SYSTEM of wage payment, whether time rates or piece rates or whether fixed in money or goods, is generally recognized today as the most important element in the employment contract.[1] It effects not only the earnings of workers, but also the costs, volume, and quantity of production. Hence, it has an ultimate bearing upon prices.[2] This held true in the colonial period as well as in the modern industrial era.

In colonial times, in areas or during periods in which the regulation of wages was not a matter of public concern, the wage rate was determined by a bargain between employer and employee. For example, the Newport general sessions in 1687 empowered three officials "to Bargaine and Agree to and with Such and Soe many Workemen Artists and Others for the Materials, Building and Erecting" of court houses in Newport and Rochester.[3] In such cases wages were determined by a legally free labor contract between the employer and the employee.

If the wage contract did not specify payment in pound sterling or "silver money,"[4] the courts normally considered that such payments were to be made in current money of the colony. Wages were often payable in commodities in lieu of or in addition to money.[5] This was particularly true of New England and New York in the seventeenth century, as well as in the tobacco colonies. Wages might be payable in corn, wheat, oats, feathers, whale oil, codfish, wool, wood, beavers, dry goods, tobacco, or even in cattle and land.[6] In colonies such as Maryland

[1] See L. S. Lyon, M. W. Watkins, and V. Abramson, *Government and Economic Life* (Washington, 1939), I, 467.

[2] National Industrial Conference Board, *Systems of Wage Payment* (New York, 1930), p. 1.

[3] Newport G. S., lib. I, f. 92; *R.I. Col. Rec.*, III, 237 (1687).

[4] See *Md. Arch.*, X, 268 (1653); Ulster Dutch Transcripts, lib. III, 168, 169 (1683).

[5] Commodity money was frequently legalized by colonial assemblies for the payment of taxes and all other public debts. See C. P. Nettels, *Money Supply of the American Colonies before 1720* (Madison, Wis., 1934), p. 209.

[6] Land: *Md. Arch.*, X, 267 (1653); articles of agreement between Philip Wagenaer of Duanesburgh, miller, and James Duane, to serve as miller, millwright, and carpenter, for 2 yrs. 6 mos.; Duane to convey to him 100 acres of land, working clothes, and at the end of the term tools, in addition to 10s. pocket money and 6 gallons of rum each year (1770). Duane MSS, N.Y. Hist. Soc.

Corn: The Massachusetts General Court provided in 1641 that workmen's wages might be paid in corn. If the parties could not agree upon the price to be set for the corn, the master and the servant were each to choose an arbiter; when the two arbiters could not agree a third man was to be chosen by the nearest magistrate or constable. *Mass. Bay Rec.*, I, 340. See also *Brook-*

and Virginia, where the staple was legal tender, crop or transfer notes payable in the staple were customarily accepted in payment of wages. The Kingston, New York, court ruled in 1668 that grain should be accepted in payment at the market price, and that "every body is at liberty to employ a man and have the work inspected." [7] The same court ruled a few years earlier that for mason work three schepels of oats were "to be reckoned equal to one schepel of wheat." [8] Occasionally the employer gave the employee the choice of accepting payment either in "money or in Goods." [9] Where the employer was in the import trade and likely to have a variety of foodstuffs and dry goods on hand, it was not infrequent for him to arrange for part payment out of the stock in his warehouse. Thus, Aaron Lopez of Rhode Island paid his workmen part in cash and part in piece goods, hardware, sugar, rum, and "eatables." [10] A not infrequent complaint was that masters sought to pay their workmen in "goods at a dear rate." [11] Hence at times workmen refused to work for commodities.[12]

Where the rate of wages was not specified in the contract, the workman could sue to recover the reasonable value of his services, as the

---

haven, L.I., Rec., 1662–79, I, 54 (1678, corn and feathers), 161 (1670); Plymouth Col. Rec., II, 6 (1641); Ulster Dutch Transcripts, lib. II, 26 (1675); Cape May, N.J., County Court, 1699–1712 (March 12, 1700).

Whale Oil: Brookhaven, L.I. Rec., I, 50 (1677), 105 (1673).

Dry goods: Ibid., p. 44 (1677).

Fish: Essex, IV, 254 (1670), V, 8 (1671), 11 (1672).

Wool: Newtown, L.I., Court Rec., f. 137 (1682).

Boards: Essex, III, 347 (1666), if employee did not like the wool. See also Kingston Town Court Mins., 1724–46 (Nov. 3, 1742).

Wheat: Ulster Dutch Transcripts, lib. II, fol. 54 (1675), 249 (1676), 508 (1681); III, f. 133 (1683).

Oats: Ulster Dutch Transcripts, lib. II, f. 31 (1675).

Beavers: "Kingston Dutch Rec.," N.Y. State Hist. Assn., Proceedings, XI, 19 (1662); R.N.A., III, 175 (1660), 356, 357 (1661); Early Records of the City and County of Albany and Colony of Rensselaerswyck, III (Notarial Papers, 1660–1696), trans. J. Pearson, in N.Y. State Lib., History Bull., No. 10 (Albany, 1918), pp. 122, 138 (1661), 143 (1662).

Cattle: Md. Arch., X, 466 (1656); Northumberland, Va., O.B., 1699–1713, Pt. I, f. 218 (1702 Essex, V, 443 (1674), a steer.

Tobacco: Accomac O.B., I, f. 95 (1637); Northampton, Va., O.B., 1655–56, f. 9 (1655); Westmoreland, Va., O.B., 1675/6–88/9, f. 432 (1685).

See also Nettels, op. cit., pp. 209 et seq.; Gray, op. cit., I, 227, 229.

[7] Ulster Dutch Transcripts, lib. II, f. 526 (1668).

[8] "Kingston Dutch Rec.," loc. cit., p. 13 (1662). [9] Md. Arch., X, 269, 389, 390 (1654).

[10] Agreements of Lopez with Ebenezer Dunson for joiner's work (1765), with Caleb Childs et al. for ship carpentry (1772), with Elisha Green to ship as a cooper (1767), with Sylvester Child to build a ship (1774), with Nath. Miller for ship carpentry (1775)—Lopez MSS, Newport Hist. Soc. See also Hempstead, Diary, p. 56 (1716), where a monthly rate is stipulated, payable half in salt and rum.

[11] CSPA, 1704–5, No. 606, p. 290 (1704); Ga. Col. Rec., XXI, 272 (1736).

[12] CSPA, 1693–96, p. 243 (1694).

courts saw to it that masters were not unjustly enriched from their employee's labor.[13] In determining compensation, the courts had to hear evidence as to the prevailing wage for like work.[14] Very rarely such evidence might induce the court to award wages "above the bargain." [15] In the determination of the rate of wages where none was specified in advance, or in appraisal of work done, the courts not infrequently resorted to arbitration by "indifferent" men, frequently chosen from the same trade. This was especially true of seventeenth-century New England, of the early courts on Long Island, and of the Dutch language courts.[16] At a church meeting at Wareham on Buzzard's Bay, held in 1761, a complaint was lodged by Benjamin Norris against Benjamin Fearing, in which Norris contended that both parties had agreed to submit a dispute regarding compensation for a fishing voyage to the Reverend Ruggles of Rochester and to "stand by his judgment." Fearing later reneged, refusing to settle unless a court judgment were procured against him. Accordingly he was suspended by the church meeting "till he should give Christian Satisfaction." [17] Under the Dutch in New Amsterdam a vast amount of litigation, involving wage suits among other matters, was referred by the court of burgomasters and schepens to "good men" or arbitrators, appointed by the bench or selected by the litigants. This practice was perpetuated under English rule by the mayor's court of New York City.[18]

In addition to money wages, the employment contract often included diet and rum. Liquor was an invariable part of the wage contract in

[13] Riles v. Sidwell, Bucks County, Pa., C.P., 1684–1730, f. 8 (1684); Vaughan v. Trafford, *Md. Arch.*, IV, 201 (1643); Godfrey v. Cox, Burlington, West Jersey, Court Book, f. 91 (1690). For suits at common law on a *quantum meruit* for services actually rendered, see F. R. Batt, *The Law of Master and Servant* (London, 1929), pp. 39, 162, 163.

[14] Ariaensen v. Pels, "Dutch Rec. of Kingston," *loc. cit.*, p. 16 (1662); Clasen de Wit v. Lammersen, *ibid.*, p. 39 (1662). Crupel v. Doorn, Ulster Dutch Transcripts, I, f. 219 (1664); Crupel v. Gerritsen, *ibid.*, f. 225 (1664). Hofman v. Teunisse, Kingston Town Court Mins., 1688–98 (1698). See also Onckelbagh v. Flipzen, where, in a dispute as to the amount to be paid for stringing sewan, the court ordered payment "according to the custom heretofore." *R.N.A.*, V, 176 (1665).

[15] *Plymouth Col. Rec.*, II, 24 (1641).

[16] See Lechford's *Note-Book*, pp. 331, 342, 343, 358 (1640); *Essex*, IV, 223 (1670); Newtown, L.I., Court Rec., fols. 220, 222 (1669); *R.N.A.*, II, 20 (1656); III, 211 (1660); IV, 327 (1663); *Albany, Rensselaerswyck, and Schenectady Court Mins.*, I, 82 (1669); Ulster Dutch Transcripts, II, f. 43 (1674); Kingston Town Court Mins., 1688–98 (1690); *Vestry Book of Kingston Parish, Mathews County, Va., 1679–1796*, ed. G. C. Chamberlayne (Richmond, Va., 1929), p. 62 (1757).

[17] Wareham, Mass., Church Rec., Bk. I, f. 22 (1761).

[18] See Morris, ed., *Sel. Cases, Mayor's Court*, pp. 44, 551–565. See also *R.N.A.*, V, 124 (1664); V, 246 (1665). For the arbitration of mercantile disputes by the Committee on Arbitration of the New York Chamber of Commerce, see *Earliest Arbitration Records of the Chamber of Commerce of the State of New York, founded in 1768—Committee Minutes, 1779–1792* (New York, 1913).

such out-of-doors occupations as farming, fishing and other types of maritime employment, in the building trades, and among ironworkers.[19] Cider was carted out to the hands in the hay fields and rum dispensed to building-trades workers or money in lieu thereof.[20] To forbid workers beer and rum, as did the manager of the state ironworks run by Virginia during the Revolution [21] was indeed a radical innovation for that period. A contract made in 1682 between a master tailor and a journeyman in Ulster County, New York, provided for a daily wage of four guilders in wheat to be paid by "the best customers"; during the period when there was no work, free board and lodging was to be provided by the master.[22] When, in 1662, Hester Douwens of Kingston accused Hey Olfersen of the theft of some flour and meat, the defendant contended that he took the food to satisfy his hunger. "As she would not give me food and I was working for her, I tried to procure it, since there was little or no food for sale here." [23] As a matter of fact the practice of working for one's victuals was carried on far beyond the colonial period.[24] Dick and Lewis, managers of Virginia's government-operated arms plant, laid out a vegetable garden adjacent to the factory to provide food for the strictly-disciplined workmen.[25] In addition to money wages, Washington provided his miller with a dwelling house and a garden, "sufficient to raise vegetables and garden roots for his family." [26]

[19] *Essex*, III, 347 (1666); Aquidneck Quarter Court Rec. in H. M. Chapin, *Documentary History of Rhode Island* (Providence, 1916–19), II, 161, 162 (1646); Gravesend, L.I., Town Rec., IV, 1662–99, f. 4 (1663); Ulster Dutch Transcripts, II, fols. 584, 585 (1687), free board and a half pint of rum daily; Riker, *Harlem*, p. 418, an allowance of a gallon of rum was made for the carpenter working on the Harlem town house; Stokes, *Iconography of Manhattan Island*, IV, 505 (1727), 538 (1734), where allowance is given to building-trades workers for drink in addition to wages. See also *Md. Arch.*, XIX, 201, 265 (1695); N. V. Russell, *The British Régime in Michigan and the Old Northwest, 1760–1796* (Northfield, 1939), p. 252; J. S. Bassett, *The Writings of "Colonel William Byrd of Westover in Virginia Esquire"* (New York, 1901), p. 354; Kathleen Bruce, *Virginia Iron Manufacture in the Slave Era* (New York, 1931), p. 34.

[20] "*Mechanicks* and low-liv'd *Labourers* drink Rum like *Fountain-Water*, and they can infinitely better endure it than the idle, unactive, and sedentary part of Mankind." Ames, *Almanac!* 1752, in Briggs, *op. cit.*, p. 238.

[21] *Cal. Va. State Pap.*, III, 355. Washington saw to it that the army artificers were provided with rum or paid an equivalent in money when rum was not furnished. *Writings* (Fitzpatrick ed.), XVII, 102 (1779).

[22] Ulster Dutch Transcripts, lib. II, f. 634 (1682). See also Heays v. Chambers, Court of Oyer and Terminer at Kingston Rec. (June 4–7, 1684), where a year's contract of service was alleged for which cash, a fat hog, beer, bread, corn, and house room for the employee and his wife were to be furnished. See also Westchester Co. Hist. Soc., *Coll.*, II, 52 (1687).

[23] Schout v. Douwens and Olfersen, "Dutch Rec. of Kingston," *loc. cit.*, pp. 30, 31 (1662). See also Olfersen v. Gerritsen, *ibid.*, pp. 33, 34 (1662).

[24] See agreement of Thomas Harkness with Aaron Lopez (Jan. 11, 1765), Lopez MSS, Newport Hist. Soc.; Selden Warner's Account Book, *c*. 1815, Conn. State Lib.

[25] K. Bruce, *op. cit.*, p. 34.   [26] Bathe, *Oliver Evans*, pp. 30, 31.

In agricultural areas, particularly in the South, the farmhand was occasionally given a share of the crop—generally 50 per cent—as wages. On the tobacco plantations it was customary to give overseers a share of the surplus produce remaining after the entire expenses of operating the plantation had been deducted. This system, while designed to encourage overseers to produce to the utmost, might also, unless controlled, lead to overtaxing both the soil and the laborers. The overseer's share varied from one fifth to one tenth of the produce remaining after all costs for the year had been met. In addition, they received certain specified commodities or wages.[27] While this system was more popular in the South than elsewhere, it was not confined to that area. The Buzzard's Bay justice of the peace, Israel Fearing, recorded the following memorandum of such a bargain:

A bargen with Jonathan Chechbuck—hee is to clear a peace of ground of mine at the River for one pound and one Shilling And hold plow for 6 Shillings and hee is to plant the ground and how 3 times and I am to plow the ground and find the seed and I am to have one half And hee is to gather the corn and cut the Stocks and wee are to devid In the heap And Shock and hee Is to how in the Rie and Reep and Shock the rie and wee are to devid in the Shock and hee to find the rie and I to put in my creaters as I ues to dow.[28]

Occasionally such arrangements were found in industry as well as in agriculture. An advertisement in the *Pennsylvania Packet* of February 22, 1780, for a master workman to serve as a foreman in a glass factory offered to the prospect a "share in the Works if he should choose it." Such contracts were enforceable in the courts.[29]

[27] See S. M. Kingsbury, *Records of the Va. Company of London: the Court Book*, I (Washington, D.C., 1906), pp. 304–307; Morton, *Robert Carter*, pp. 92–94; *Amer. Husbandry*, I, 246; Gray, *op. cit.*, I, 545. Unlike the overseers, the stewards were paid in cash and received no shares of the produce. George Washington agreed to pay one overseer "two clear shares" of all the tobacco, corn, and other grain raised under his direction, and, to encourage his care of the stock, 400 lbs. of pork, one young steer not above two years of age, and four shoats under twelve months. On other occasions he offered his overseers a seventh or an eighth of the produce. *Diaries*, II, 36 (1771), 81 (1772). W. C. Ford, *Washington as an Employer and Importer of Labor* (Brooklyn, 1889), pp. 28–32 (1762). See also Henrico Co. O.B., I, f. 10 (1677). For the view that share-croppers in the tobacco region generally received one-third at the close of the eighteenth century, see Gray, *op. cit.*, I, 407.

[28] Bliss, *Buzzard's Bay*, pp. 60, 61. See also *Va. Gen. Court Mins.*, pp. 84 (1626), 154 (1627), 178 (1628); Accomac O.B., I, 105 (1638); *Brookhaven, L.I., Rec.*, 1662–79, I, 113 (1675); Westchester Co. Hist Soc., *Coll.*, II, 52 (1687).

[29] Suit was brought in August, 1691, in the Cecil County court in Maryland by Hugh Douch against Charles James, merchant and one of the justices of the peace of the county, on a contract entered into between the parties in 1688 whereby Douch had agreed to work on the tobacco and corn crop the ensuing year with two of James's servants on James's plantation, for which he was to be allowed one whole share of tobacco and corn. Defendant pleaded his privileges as justice of the peace, but the court held him liable to pay plaintiff the agreed shares of tobacco and corn. Cecil, 1683–92 (August, 1691).

The time of payment of wages was frequently a subject of litigation. At times contracts provided that the journeyman's daily wages were to be paid literally every day.[30] More frequently such payments were made monthly,[31] at three or six month intervals,[32] or by the year. Where materials were to be provided by the workman, it was not unusual to require a part payment as an advance, the remainder to be paid when the work was completed.[33] Where the employer was a governmental body, collection of wages might involve considerable difficulties. Thus, one Connecticut town ruled that those working for the town should "stay" their pay "till the next year." [34]

While the time wage was widely used in colonial America, alternative methods of wage payment were employed to stimulate the worker to his best effort. The "incentive system" of wage payments was employed, as has already been shown, on the plantations, particularly to encourage overseers. However, the chief alternative to the time wage was the piece-wage system, the principal characteristic of which is a uniformity in the basic rate but diversity in time earnings.[35] Time rates were the normal form of wages for journeymen, but many workers were paid on a piecework basis.[36] Piecework is more effective with productive labor than with "non-productive." Therefore, it is principally in the former field that we find its employment in the colonial period. As indicated in the section on the regulation of wages, piece rates were common, although not an invariable practice, in such trades as those of coopers, sawyers, smiths, glaziers, tanners, shoemakers, hatters, sailmakers, and goldsmiths.[37] Artificers engaged in the forge and furnace industries often worked on a piecework basis,[38] although the bulk of the laborers

[30] Ulster Dutch Transcripts, II, f. 634 (1682).

[31] *R.N.A.*, V, 218 (1665); Ulster Dutch Transcripts, lib. I, f. 517 (1668); III, fols. 168, 169 (1683); *Albany Notarial Papers*, p. 423 (1674).

[32] Ulster Dutch Transcripts, lib. II, f. 623 (1683). Cf. HMC, *Rep.*, XIII, 297, for the English practice of paying servant's wages quarterly. For a half year's payment, see *Letter Book of John Watts of New York*, p. 220 (1764).

[33] *Pa. Col. Rec.*, XIV, 597 (1785).

[34] *Derby, Conn., Rec., 1655–1710*, p. 241 (1706).

[35] Nat. Indust. Conf. Bd., *Systems of Wage Payment*, pp. 11, 34, 35, 52, 123.

[36] The assertion that the piece-rate system followed the Industrial Revolution (Daugherty, *Labor Problems in Amer. Ind.*, pp. 573–574) is not strictly accurate, although there is no question that the division of labor and the introduction of power-driven machinery encouraged the practice of rewarding workers according to output.

[37] See, e.g., Grindlay's Executrix v. Roulain, carpenter and joiner, Charleston C.P., Feb.–Aug., 1767, f. 88; also *supra*, pp. 65–69, 79, 80, 82, 96, 109, 110; but cf. p. 87. Farm hands were at times employed on this basis,—for example, mowers at a stipulated rate per acre. Hempstead, *Diary*, p. 368 (1740); also Ulster Dutch Transcripts, lib. I, 346 (1667).

[38] J. S. Bassett, ed., *The Writings of "Colonel William Byrd of Westover in Virginia Esqr"* (New York, 1901), pp. 371, 372.

employed in such occupations worked by the day.[39] Piecework rather than time rates seems to have prevailed in the woolen and linen trades. John Watts, the New York merchant, in a letter to Moses Franks in 1765, described in these words "the Rates of Labour" and terms of employment in those trades:

I dont imagine there is or can be any stated Terms, most Familys during a long idle Winter go thro' most of the Business themselves and Casually employ supernumerarys as their productions may be more or less prosperous and their family of Children and Servants more or less numerous. A Weaver may be paid by the yard as they can agree and then he sticks to his Loom more or less as he may be calld off by other Avocations.[40]

During the Revolution the manager of Virginia's arms plant encouraged piecework, both as an incentive to the workmen and on grounds of economy.[41]

In the enforcement of the wage contract the courts occasionally had to deal with the problem of gratuities and the "kick-back" system. In 1658 Pieter Roode brought suit in the Dutch court of Fort Orange and Beverwyck for tips received while employed by the defendant as an assistant waiter to draw grain. He demanded that these tips be turned over to him, but the court obliged him to accept his employer's offer to release him from service on condition that he turn over any money he had received over and above his wages.[42] Tips were customary to employees at inns and lodging houses and to other attendants.[43] The working of the "kick-back" system is disclosed in the proceedings of a committee of the common council of New York City in 1763 which made a contract with a master builder to alter and repair the City Hall, for which he was to be allowed, "as being the principal Carpenter or Master workman," the sum of sixteen shillings a day for every day in actual service, but he was "to Receive no benefit from those who he shall Imploy under him," and was to "keep the accts which Immediately Relate to his Business etc."[44]

[39] See *Remarkable Case of Peter Hasenclever* (London, 1773), pp. 81, 82, 88–89; Boyer, *Early Forges and Furnaces in New Jersey*, p. 24.

[40] *Letter Book of John Watts of New York*, p. 348 (1765); *Moravian Rec.*, I, 264; II, 705; IV, 1738.

[41] K. Bruce, *op. cit.*, p. 35. See also Washington, *Diaries*, I, 380 (1770).

[42] Roode v. Janssen, *Ft. Orange and Beverwyck Court Mins.*, II, 115.

[43] County court members customarily voted tips to servants attending them in the houses where they sat. One mistress, testifying before the Essex quarterly court concerning her maidservant, stated that "as for money she had of lodgers at my house, she layd it out so needlessly that I have blamed her for it." *Essex*, VII, 144. See also E. S. Morgan, "Masters and Servants in Early New England," *More Books* (Sept., 1942), p. 325; Washington, *Writings* (Sparks ed.), X, 48n.

[44] *M.C.C.*, VI, 314 (1763).

Before the introduction of the mechanic's lien in America, the machinery for which was not set up in this country prior to 1791,[45] some measure of protection was afforded the worker in the collection of his wages by the attachment procedure. This procedure was available to workmen for recovery of their wages.[46] A crop might be assigned or attached, or execution levied on goods and cattle.[47] In addition, statutes were enacted in a number of the colonies permitting the levy of execution on the lands as well as the goods of debtors.[48] In order to ensure the speedy recovery of wages the Gravesend sessions ordered that the inhabitants of Staten Island pay their workmen their wages for digging ditches "forthwith according to the Agreemt if not Execution to issue forth within a month." [49] The procedure of foreign attachment, or garnishment, was widely adopted by colonial courts. Such attachment preceded a formal adjudication of the issues between the principals. The procedure was speedy and cheap, and especially efficacious where the defendant debtor had removed himself from the jurisdiction of the court. By this means goods in the hands of a garnishee belonging to an employer in default for nonpayment of wages could be attached as well as wages owing to a workman in default on a debt.[50]

[45] See Farnam, *Chapters in the History of Social Legislation in the United States to 1860*, pp. 152–156. In Wormell v. Dotey the Plymouth court in 1672 allowed the mechanic to attach and sell the frame of a house he had constructed in the event that he was not paid for his labor. *Plymouth Col. Rec.*, V, 87, 88 (1672).

[46] However, cf. the curious decision in the Dutch language court at Kingston in 1666 indicating that in that jurisdiction such wages were payable "pro rata" and "after the preferred creditors." Ulster Dutch Transcripts, lib. I, f. 245 (1666). This procedure was ignored in other decisions of upstate courts. Only five years later the court at Albany gave a plaintiff preference over other creditors because the money was "due him for wages." Cornelisz v. Jansz, *Court of Albany, Rensselaerswyck, and Schenectady Mins.*, I, 217 (1671). See also Tyssen v. Tack, "Dutch Rec. of Kingston," *loc. cit.*, p. 162 (1664), *contra* the decision of that court two years later.

[47] See will of John Farra, Henrico O.B., I, f. 298 (1685). The New York mayor's court in 1668 attached grain in the hands of a defendant baker in a suit for wages and ordered that "defendant shall not alienate any of it" until further order of the court. *R.N.A.*, VI, 108 (1668).

[48] *N.H. Prov. Laws*, II, 293; *Mass. Acts and Resolves*, I, 68, 69 (1692), II, 42, 43 (1716), 150, 151 (1719); *Mass. Charters and General Laws* (Boston, 1814), pp. 292, 293 (1696); W. Brigham, *New Plymouth Colony, the Compact with the Charter and Laws* (Boston, 1836), pp. 33, 282. In explaining the differences between the North Carolina act of 1716, § 12 (subjecting the lands of fugitive debtors to the payment of their debts) and the English rule, Governor Burrington stated "that Lands in England being improved to a great yearly value may by the annual income on an extent pay the Debt but Lands here are generally of little yearly rent and the Benefit of them is the accruing Improvements of the Occupyer which on extent in the end he must loose the Benefit off would be too hard." *N.C. Col. Rec.*, III, 182. See also R. B. Morris, *Studies in the History of American Law* (New York, 1930), pp. 123, 124.

[49] Gravesend Court and Road Rec., lib. II, 1668–1766, f. 58 (1675).

[50] For the development of this procedure in England and its adoption in the colonies, see Morris, ed., *Sel. Cases, Mayor's Court*, pp. 14–21, and cases cited; *Letter Book of John Watts*, pp. 14, 15 (1672). See also *New Haven Col. Rec., 1638–49*, p. 28; *Assistants*, II, 9 (1630); Flatbush Court Rec., f. 22 (1681); *Md. Arch.*, XLIX, 291, 326, 327, 343, 385, 403 (1664, 1665). For an interesting antigarnishee ordinance passed to protect the employees of the Dutch West

In suits for the recovery of wages workmen on the average fared very well in colonial courts. Between 1665 and 1668 twenty-three suits for wages were brought in the court held at Kingston, New York, in which judgments were awarded plaintiffs in eighteen actions, a measure of relief in one other, and two were submitted to arbitration.[51] Wage earners had little cause to complain of their treatment in such tribunals as the mayor's court of New York City.[52] From early times the court frowned upon the practice of withholding wages due. When it was brought to the attention of the New Netherland authorities that local inhabitants had dismissed the Indians they had employed without paying them, "thereby inspiring a threat of summary vengeance from these Indians," Stuyvesant and the Council warned the delinquents "to pay them without contradiction" and to reimburse them for any future employment.[53] When the pay of employees at an ironworks was withheld, they procured an order from a special court at Boston in 1673 for the payment of their wages.[54] A master who was served by the constable with the justices' warrant in a wage suit was found guilty of disorderly behavior when he refused to obey, and the Burlington justices committed him to prison until he gave security for his good behavior.[55] If a worker was dismissed contrary to agreement, the court might award him damages in addition to wages due.[56]

Among the favorite defenses pleaded by masters in suits for wages were the pleas that the employee had left before the expiration of his contracted term of service, frequently during the harvest or at the "height of the crop," or that his work was incomplete,[57] or badly done

---

India Company from "some self-interested persons" who got assignments "on the Company's books of account" against the employees for debts contracted for "trifles," for which they charged more than 50 per cent above the price in beaver, see *Laws and Ord. N. Neth.,* pp. 410–411 (1661).

A legacy in a will, written and duly attested, bequeathing wages due the testator was upheld by the New Haven authorities in preference to a nuncupative will made by the decedent in Virginia, witnessed by one witness, an interested party, in which the same sum of wages due was bequeathed to another person. Galpine's case, *New Haven Col. Rec., 1638–49,* pp. 366, 450–452 (1647–49).

[51] Ulster Dutch Transcripts, lib. I, fols. 342, 347, 348, 352, 379, 380, 382, 387, 390, 391, 393, 403–405, 427, 431, 466, 475, 490.

[52] See Morris, ed., *Sel. Cases, Mayor's Court,* pp. 472, 478.

[53] *R.N.A.,* I, 11; *Laws and Ord. N. Neth.,* p. 103.   [54] *Essex,* V, 194 (1673).

[55] Brown v. Beck, Burlington, West Jersey, Court Bk., f. 157 (1698).

[56] Peares v. Heathcote, *ibid.,* f. 121 (1693).

[57] Gravesend Town Rec., Bk. I, Town Meetings, f. 60 (1651); *R.N.A.,* IV, 164 (1662); "Dutch Rec. of Kingston," *loc. cit.,* p. 17 (1662); Ulster Dutch Transcripts, lib. I, f. 325 (1665), 346 (1666), 517 (1668); lib. II, f. 383 (1666). Employment contracts in the Dutch language areas occasionally contained express stipulations that the workman was to have deducted from his wages damages attributable to his negligence or that in case of sickness he work extra time (e.g., three days for every day lost). *Albany Notarial Papers,* pp. 308 (1664), 399 (1762). An overseer forfeited his wages or share of the crop for absenteeism. J. Davis, *The Office and Authority of a Justice of Peace* (New Bern, N.C., 1774), p. 313.

and therefore he was entitled to counterclaim for damages [58] or to secure extra service without compensation.[59] Back in 1640 carpenter Timothy Hawkins built a defective house. As he was unable to eliminate the defects, the Massachusetts General Court held that he "hath nothing due to him in justice, so nothing is to be allowed to him, but if he will put in security to pay £45, hee is granted the house to take away and dispose of it, provided he give his answer within a month." [60] If an employee could prove that he was fully competent to harvest a crop, the court ordered that he receive the same wages as any other harvest hand.[61] However, where a master was able to prove to the satisfaction of the court that the artificer had misrepresented his skill and was in fact "not a master of his trade," the court generally ordered a substantial reduction in the amount of his yearly wages [62] or otherwise ruled that he be considered an ordinary servant and reimbursed according to custom.[63] One of the most interesting colonial cases in this category arose in Pennsylvania in 1685 when Joshua Titterie sued Benjamin Chambers, President of the Society of Free Traders, for a sum of £163 15s. 7d. due as salary under contract from 1683 to 1686 for work and disbursements. Plaintiff produced the original articles, an account of disbursements, and witnesses. In his defense the defendant introduced depositions of workmen who had worked with the plaintiff in England to show that he never made a "bitt of broadglass" and was "accompted no workman," and had been dismissed as an apprentice from an English glassworks. Nonetheless, the jury awarded plaintiff the heavy damages of £131 15s.[64]

Where one workman proved that, although he had covenanted to serve some ten months for wages of eighty pounds of tobacco and cask, he was "pressed by the Govrs warrant to serve in the Garrison at Pascatoway," the Maryland provincial court granted an attachment against the employer for 600 lbs. of tobacco and cask "for neare 5 months service

[58] See Davis, *op. cit.*, p. 312; also *Albany, Rensselaerswyck, and Schenectady Court Mins.*, I, 165, 166 (1670); Newtown, L.I. Court Rec., f. 141 (1682); Horse v. Hardenbroeck, *R.N.A.*, VI, 142 (1668), neglect of tan vats pleaded in defense.

[59] George Webb, *The Office and Authority of a Justice of Peace* (Williamsburg, Va., 1736), p. 292.

[60] Lechford, *Note-Book*, p. 303 (1640–41).

[61] Ulster Dutch Transcripts, lib. II, f. 44 (1688).

[62] Mosely's case (joiner, wages reduced from £17 to £5 and board if "anything of a workman," otherwise to receive "nothing more than a Common Servant"), Prince George, 1720–22 (1722). Pausey's case (mason, wages reduced from £12 per annum to £4), Spotsylvania, Va., O.B., 1724–30, f. 147; Wallor's case (carpenter, wages reduced by £3 yearly), *ibid.*, f. 287 (1729).

[63] Harrison's case, Ann Arundel, lib. 1720–21, f. 74 (1721).

[64] Defendant appealed to the provincial court. Pennypacker, *Pa. Col. Cases*, pp. 86–88 (1685).

the Principall pt of the yeare." [65] On another occasion a Maryland master contested an employee's suit for wages on the ground that the workman had taken Saturday afternoons off.[66] Occasionally, masters' defenses rested on alleged trial clauses whereby they had reserved the right to discontinue the servants' services after six weeks or a quarter of a year as in England. In such cases the court would award wages for the period the employee actually served.[67] A misunderstanding might arise as to the actual meaning of conversations between master and servant. Where one master shouted, "Where have you been during the day, go there also at night," the court construed such language as tantamount to dismissal, and ordered payment of wages for the period served up to that time.[68] On the other hand, where the plaintiff had fallen sick a short time after entering upon the contracted work and had ordered the contract torn up, the court denied his claim for wages.[69] Where an executor pleaded the statute of limitations to an account due, plaintiffs asserted that the amount sued for was for servant's wages which "ought not to be barred by the said Statute." The North Carolina General Court sustained plaintiffs in such actions.[70]

THE PERIOD OF EMPLOYMENT

NEXT TO WAGES, the most important issue in labor contracts upon which colonial courts were frequently obliged to rule was the period of employment. Numerous contracts, particularly in farming occupations, were for such relatively indefinite periods as a "season" or "during the height of the crop." Occasionally a formal guarantee of employment, while not specifying the period of time, assured the worker that he would be kept for a stated period provided there was work, or in preference to other employees. One such contract incorporating the principle of seniority rights was filed in the Augusta County court [1] in Virginia in 1768:

[65] *Md. Arch.*, IV, 286 (1644).　　　　[66] *Ibid.*, p. 306 (1655).

[67] *R.N.A.*, II, 362 (1658); IV, 226 (1663).

[68] "Dutch Rec. of Kingston," *loc. cit.*, p. 4 (1661).

[69] *Md. Arch.*, IV, 472 (1648). Deductions were normally made for the time lost through illness or otherwise. Israel Fearing agreed with Samuel Barns in 1763 "to worck with me six mounth for 22 pounds and if he loos Any time to abate accordingly and If I se cause to have him make up the los of time after he hath made his Salt hay he is to du it." At times the issue as to whether the lost time was to be made up at once or upon the expiration of the contracted period of service was ruled upon by the court. Ulster Dutch Transcripts, lib. II, f. 486 (1668). Cf. also *R.N.A.*, V, 153 (1664), where the court ordered the payment of the second year's wages of two children on condition that they serve out the lost days in full.

[70] Jennings and wife exx [executrix] v. Goddin exr, N.C. Gen. Court Mins., 1695–1712, f. 84 (1697); Charleston v. Goddin exr, *ibid.* (1697).

[1] Augusta Co. Court Rec. (May, 1768).

This, my note, shall oblige me to pay unto Mr. W. Mann, at the rate of fifty pounds a year for whatever time he shall be by me employed to assist in Indian trade, hunting, or whatever service he shall be by me directed to perform.— given by my Hand 19 Feb. 1762, signed I. Christian I promise if I keep any hands employed in the above service the whole year; William Mann shall be preferred and Kept as long as any other in said service he complying as well as he can with my direction.

[Signed] Israel Christian

Feb. 19, 1762

In England the Tudor statutes had provided for long instead of short hirings. The Statute of Artificers required that in a large number of specified employments the hiring be for one year and that a quarter's notice be given to terminate the contract by either employer or workman.[2] Contracts for annual employment were widely but by no means universally used in the colonies.[3] Annual employment was customary in such occupations as domestic service and husbandry,[4] but in others the custom of annual hiring does not appear to have gained a foothold.[5] Artisans were frequently hired by the day [6] or month.[7] A West Jersey

---

[2] 2, 3 Edw. VI, c. 15; 5 Eliz. 4 §§ 2, 4. These rules did not apply in the case of workmen hired by the day or week, or to do a particular piece of work. 5 Eliz. c. 4 §§ 9, 10. There grew up a presumption at common law that an indefinite hiring was a yearly hiring. Cf. J. C. Atkinson, ed., *North Riding Quarter Sessions* (London, 1884), I, 148; Fitzherbert, *New Natura Brevium* (London, 1730), p. 391; Co. Litt. 42b; Fawcett v. Cast, 5 B. and Ad. 904 (1834). See also Graydon, *Justice of the Peace*, p. 281. Under the Law of Settlement the overseers warned inhabitants not to hire workmen by the year in order to avoid giving them a settlement. Where the hiring was for a year the employers were counseled "to pick a quarrel with them before the year's end, and to get rid of them." Richard Burn, *The History of the Poor Laws: with Observations* (London, 1764), p. 211; Adam Smith, *Wealth of Nations*, Bk. I, ch. x, Pt. ii. However, it must be borne in mind that the presumption of a yearly hiring could be displaced by custom. Batt, *Master and Servant*, p. 44.

[3] See Lechford, *Note-Book*, p. 153 (1639); *Essex*, V, 151, 220 (1673); *Plymouth Col. Rec.*, II, 6 (1641); *Albany Notarial Papers*, pp. 122 (1661), 307, 308 (1664), 379, 386 (1671), 527, 528 (1682); Philadelphia Supreme Court Docket, lib. 1772-76 (March, 1776); *Va. Gen. Court Mins.*, p. 197 (1629); *Doc. Hist. Amer. Indust. Soc.*, I, 354 (1767); Lower Norfolk, Va., lib. II, fols. 34, 35 (1644); Washington, *Diaries*, I, 214n. (joiner, 1759), 282 (carpenter, 1768), II, 46 (1771).

[4] See Graydon, *op. cit.*, p. 281; Carman, ed., *Amer. Husbandry*, p. 121; Hempstead, *Diary*, p. 93 (1719).

[5] For Connecticut, see Tapping Reeve, *The Law of Baron and Femme; of Parent and Child; of Guardian and Ward; of Master and Servant; and of the Powers of Courts of Chancery* (New Haven, 1816), p. 347.

[6] Kingston, N.Y., Town Court Mins., lib. 1724-46 (1724); Peter Van Schaick and Peter Silvester, Receipt Book, 1785-1812 (1785), Van Schaick MSS, Box IV, Gansevoort-Lansing Coll. (N.Y. Pub. Lib.); Uriah Woolman's Ledger, 1786-1805, farm labor (N.Y. Pub. Lib.). Hempstead, *Diary*, pp. 38 (1714), shipbuilding; 549 (1750), farm labor; 590 (1752), tailor. *S.C. Hist. and Gen. Mag.*, XXVII, 191 (1722); weekly wages were less frequent, Hempstead, *Diary*, p. 99 (1720), housekeeper. Cf. James Gowen's Ledger, 1781-1813; *Moravian Rec.*, I, 264.

[7] Gray v. Pinhorne, Rec. of Wills, lib. XIXB, f. 361 (1680), Surrogate, N.Y. Co.; *S.C. Gazette*, Oct. 25, 1773; *Gazette of State of S.C.*, July 30, 1783.

millowner advertised in 1771 for a fuller, offering "good encouragement by the year, month, or to work in shares, or have the mills rented to him. There is always plenty of work." [8]

The requirement that three months' notice be given before discharge was widely observed in the colonies, although, as with other labor customs, there was no uniform adherence. [9] A typical agreement incorporating this practice entered into between a tobacco planter and an artisan was that made by George Washington [10] with a carpenter in 1771:

Articles of Agreement entered into this 25th day of February Anno Domini One Thousand seven hundred and seventy one, between Benjamin Buckler (late of the Province of Maryland but now) of Fairfax County in Virginia Carpenter of the one part and George Washington of the said County and Colony Gent'n of the other part Witnesseth that the said Benjamin Buckler for the Considerations hereinafter mentioned doth by these presents oblige himself to work true and faithfully at his trade as a Carpenter for the said George Washington from the date hereof until the 25th day of December next ensuing; that is to say, he shall be constant and diligent at his business from day break till dark; and if the weather is such that he cannot work out of Doors or is unfit for him to do so that he shall in these cases keep himself closely employed in making of shoes for the said George Washington or at any other business he may be set about; and more over is to reap, or otherwise to employ himself at harvest as the exigency of business may require. The said Benja Buckler doth further agree not to absent himself from the service of the said George Washington without leave, and if it should happen, that by sickness, or any other cause whatsoever he should lose any time the same shall be allowed for or made up at the years end. And whereas the said George Washington hath several Negro Carpenters which he proposes to put under the said Benjamin in order that they may work together and thereby be properly attended to the said Benjamin Buckler doth oblige himself to use his utmost endeavours to hurry and drive them on to the performance of so much work as they ought to render and for this purpose he the said Benjamin is hereby invested with sufficient power and authority which he is to make use of and to exercise with prudence and discretion. And Lastly, as the said Benja Buckler is in a manner a stranger to the said Geo. Washington and is received

---

[8] *N.J. Arch.*, 1st ser., XXVII, 646 (Nov. 15, 1771). For other advertisements for artisans wanted by the month, see *Boston Gazette*, Nov. 3, 1760; *S.C. Gazette*, Nov. 15, 1773; *Gazette of the State of S.C.*, July 30, 1783. For an earlier period, see also *R.N.A.*, VII, 160, 161 (1657), six months' contract payable monthly; *Albany, Rensselaerswyck, and Schenectady Court Mins.*, I, 206, 207, 211 (1670).

[9] See *R.N.A.*, V, 77, 78 (1664); HMC, *Rep.*, LIX, Pt. I, 104 (1777).

[10] Ford, *Washington as an Employer*, pp. 41–43 (1771). For other contracts made by Washington with artisans for one year, see *ibid.*, pp. 25, 26, 43, 44.

into his Service without a proper Recommendation, he the said Benja doth
hereby agree that it shall and may be lawfull for the said George Washington
if he should hear anything disadvantageous of his Character, or find him the
said Benja in any respect dishonest or unfaithful or if upon trial he should
prove idle, or negligent, either in his own work or in his looking after those
who may be put under his charge to turn him the said Benja of[f] at any
time between this and the 25th of December next upon paying him for the
time he has worked in proportion to the number of days and season he has
been in the said Washington's service.

In consideration of these things well and truely performed and done by the
said Benj. Buckler the said George Washington doth promise and engage on
his part to let the said Benj. Buckler have a house for himself wife and children
to stay in during the aforementioned term, that he will find the said Benjamin
with Three hundred pounds of Porke and three Barrels of Corn and will
moreover at the experation of the above term fully compleated and ended
according to the true intent and meaning hereof pay or cause to be paid unto
the said Benja Buckler the sum of Twenty-five pounds curr'y For the true and
faithful performance of all and singular these Articles the Parties each to the
other do bind themselves in the full and just sum of Fifty Pounds the day and
year first written   **His**
                                          Benj ✕ Buckler
                                          G° Washington

ENFORCEMENT OF THE CONTRACT

THE principal objective of workmen suing on contracts of employment
was the recovery of wages. The masters, on the other hand, sought
specific fulfillment of agreements or damages for failure or unsatisfactory performance of the contract where the task was not done in a
"workmanlike manner." Colonial courts frequently granted both types
of remedies.[1] Typical of the informal decrees for specific performance
awarded by seventeenth-century courts was the following action taken
by the Maine court sitting at Casco in 1666:

In answer to John Budizerts petition about James Michimore, by mutuall consent of both persons referring the difference to this Court, This Court ordereth
that James Michimore shall within two Moenths tyme finish that house which
by Contract hee is bound to doe and should have done long before this tyme
for John Budizerts, or upon not doeing thereof within the tyme aforesaid the

---

[1] See, e.g., Eden v. Davis, special assumpsit on a promise to work as a drayman in a brewery
(1774), Kempe C–F, N.Y. Hist. Soc. When Thomas Grant refused to work for Nicholas Weekes,
that master brought an action on the case in York Co. Court in Maine in 1673, "for declyneing
his Imployment." But the court awarded defendant costs of 8*s.* 2*d.* Weekes v. Grant, *Me. Prov.
and Court Rec.*, II, 465, 466 (1673).

sayd Michimore is to forfitt the some of Tenn pounds to the said Budizerts, which by execution is forthwith to be Leavied upon his person or estate.[2]

Even more informal was the decree of the Plymouth court two years later:

In reference unto the complaint of an Indian called Powas against Peter Pitts, of Taunton, for detaining of his gun from him on pretence of none performance of bargaine about breaking up of ground, the court have ordered, that the said Indian shall break up twenty rodd of ground for the said Peter Pitts; and when that is done, he shall haue his gun returned to him againe in good condition.[3]

A house carpenter promised the Dutch court at Kingston in 1662 that he would complete the building of a house according to contract within two weeks, and in case of failure agreed to pay a fine of fifty guilders to the poor.[4] In 1669 Edmund Scarburgh, an important planter and businessman of Virginia's Eastern Shore, brought suit in the Accomac court against Martin Moore, currier, on a breach of contract for the nonperformance of a promise to curry leather. While no final action is recorded in this case, Scarburgh's complaint as entered in the order book [5] is worth studying in full both for its legal as well as its economic implications.

January the 5th A Domini 1668

Edmund Scarburgh maketh protest against Martin Moore Currier wch is prosecuted to the Worppll Court to take Cognizance thereof and to be put on Record for his more Legall proceedings agt the sd Martin Moore In Manner and forme as followeth

That the sd Martin Moore Currier haveing by Agreemt to and wth the sd Edm: Scarburgh firmly obleiged himselfe as a Workman and Currier of Leather at a Certaine price agreed on well and Sufficiently to Curry all hides Cipps [6] and Skins that the sd Edm: Scarburgh Shall have to be Curried and that wthout delay nor to intend any other worke untill all hides Cipps and skins that are Ready for his Curring be compleatly well done and finished Now so it Is that Notwithstanding the sd Martin Moore is in the Manner as abovesd Obliged as also by the Statute in Such Cases provided hath not Continewed in his worke but contrary to Condition and Legall injunction hath departed from his worke when there was One hundred hides ready for him and more, all

[2] *Me. Prov. and Court Rec.*, I, 320 (1666).   [3] *Plymouth Col. Rec.*, IV, 183 (1668).

[4] "Dutch Rec. of Kingston," *loc. cit.*, p. 23 (1662). For other instances in the Dutch language courts of specific performance of a contract to work, see case of the workman on the Ditch (Broad St.), *R.N.A.*, VII, 173 (1658); Duyckingh v. Reintje the mason, *ibid.*, p. 202 (1658); Connick v. Lodowyckzen, *ibid.*, V, 54 (1664).

[5] Accomac O.B., lib. 1666–70, fols. 98–99 (1669).   [6] "Kips" is meant.

wch are now needed and the want so great that fourteen Shoemakers are Idle and out of theire imploy for makeing of Shoes by reason of want of upper Leather Curried wch the sd Martin Moore was often admonished to prevent when the Weather was good and hath received great paymt before hand for his worke so Obliged to bee done

Therefore the sd Edm: Scarburgh doth protest Against the sd Martin Moore for all his Damages that now is or shall bee for want of the Curried Leather in any tyme to Come and prayeth for Judgmt against the sd Martin Moore as Damadges shall be made Evident and farther processe proceed

Edm: Scarburgh

As Moore had disobeyed a "Legall injunction" to proceed with his contract, there was no recourse left to Scarburgh but to bring suit for damages.[7] In 1672 the Grand Council of South Carolina remanded a certain smith to the marshal's custody until he completed repairs on firearms.[8] A decree of specific performance entered against a group of workmen who refused to work would in reality discourage strikes or combinations either by journeymen or master craftsmen.[9]

At times penalties were set for nonperformance of a labor contract on the part of a workman. A Maryland statute of 1671 provided that any cooper who agreed to make tobacco hogsheads or casks would be expected to furnish one half of the quantity contracted by October 10 of any year and the other half by December 10 in any year. For failure, neglect, or refusal to do so, the cooper was to forfeit one hundred lbs. of tobacco for every ton of cask or hogshead left unfinished, unless the cooper could convince the county commissioner that he had been hindered in the performance of his agreement by sickness "or some other lawful impediment to be adjudged and approved" by the commissioner.[10] More frequently, however, such penalties were set by con-

---

[7] This case affords interesting comparison with one brought in the New York City mayor's court in 1670 by the shoemakers against Arian and Stoffel Van Laer for failing to "grind or pound their tan" according to agreement. The Van Laers told the court that it was impossible for them to crush the tan for the prices established in the contract and renounced the work in accordance with the contract, "first giving the shoemakers a year's notice." *R.N.A.*, VI, 273 (1670).

[8] *S.C. Grand Council J.*, pp. 46, 51, 52. In 1697 complaint was brought against Richard Lewis, one of the carpenters employed at the State House, that he was negligent and usually drunk, and in general retarded the work. The sheriff of Ann Arundel County was directed by the authorities to put him in prison if he failed to behave and obey instructions. *Md. Arch.*, XXIII, 130 (1697).

[9] For example, in 1658 the court in New Amsterdam ordered three workmen on the Ditch to get back to work, although they had remonstrated that the weather was not seasonable. *R.N.A.*, VII, 173.

[10] *Md. Arch.*, II, 288 (1671), 529 (1676). Workmen "imported on wages" could be required by the courts of North Carolina to make up their lost time, "and without wages." In such cases the law imposed a double service penalty as in the case of absentee servants in general. J. Davis, *The Office and Authority of a Justice of Peace* (New Bern, 1774), p. 312.

tract between the parties. In the case of an overseer engaged by George Washington in 1762, the employee agreed to the penalty "of being turned of[f] at any season . . . and of forfeiting his wages, in cases of failure or neglect, to observe and fulfil all, and each of these several articles."[11] Aside from the exaction of penalties, the master, in a suit for wages, could counterclaim for damages accruing by reason of the nonperformance of the contract within an agreed time.[12]

Judgments for damages were not infrequently recorded against workmen for poor workmanship.[13] Where a workman was paid 20s. wages and agreed that "hee would not leave the worke untill it was finished," but went off and got drunk, a jury awarded the employer 41s. damages and costs of suit.[14] In *Green v. Duncan* suit was brought in the mayor's court of New York City in 1721 against a tailor for cutting and making a suit of clothes "inartificially" out of broadcloth, London shalloon, and white ozenbrigs which the plaintiff had provided. The parties had attempted to effect a concord before resorting to the law courts. The mediators brought about an agreement that the defendant "Should Spend upon him the said Arthur [plaintiff] and their friends Aforesaid four shillings Currant Money of New York in Beer" and be thereof discharged of liability for ruining the suit of clothes by poor tailoring. After the brief hour of good cheer the plaintiff brought suit in the mayor's court, denying any such agreement. But the jury was reasonably certain that there had been "such Concord" and rendered a verdict for the defendant with costs.[15]

---

[11] Ford, *op. cit.*, pp. 27, 28 (1767).   [12] Cooke v. Rhine, 1 Bay, S.C., 16 (1784).

[13] For typical suits by masters for damages, see *Me. Prov. and Court Rec.*, II, 347 (1679); Old Norfolk Co., Mass., Rec., I, fols. 1 (1648), 31 (1665); *Plymouth Col. Rec.*, VII, 177 (1673); Plymouth C.P., I, f. 25 (1713); *New Haven Col. Rec., 1638–49*, p. 75 (1642); Aquidneck Quarter Court Rec., in Chapin, *loc. cit.*, II, 158–160 (1646); Newtown, L.I., Court Rec., fols. 223–229 (1669); Somerset, Md., Rec., 1671–75, f. 138 (1672); Cecil, Md., Rec., 1683–92 (Aug., 1692); *Md. Arch.*, XLIX, 461, 462 (1663).

[14] Righton v. Sheepey, Burlington, West Jersey, Court Book, f. 105 (1691). In a previous action (f. 97), defendant workman recovered his wages for work done.

[15] Morris, ed., *Sel. Cases, Mayor's Court*, pp. 44, 45, 510–512 (1721).

V. MARITIME LABOR RELATIONS

MARITIME OCCUPATIONS were a principal source of labor's income in colonial times. On the eve of the Revolution it was estimated that the average number of seamen employed in the American colonies was 33,000.[1] The maritime industries were given a great stimulus by the sharp rise of domestic shipbuilding from an average annual output of 4,000 gross tons in 1700 to 35,000 tons by the eve of the Revolution.[2] Colonial shipping was employed both in the coastwise and direct overseas carrying trade of the colonies as well as in the fisheries off the Grand Banks.[3] In the economic thinking of the day the fisheries played a role of the first importance. Petty placed the seaman "in the highest place in the scale of labor," and considered the labor of seamen as well as the freight of ships in the nature of an exported commodity which brought wealth to the mother country.[4] It was estimated that in the decade from 1765 to 1775 there was an average of 665 ships, of 25,630 tons, employing 4,405 men in the Massachusetts fishery.[5]

At the outset it must be understood that labor relations in this important branch of colonial economic enterprise must be distinguished from the usual type of master-servant relationship. On the high seas the relations of master and servant were largely determined by a venerable tradition which antedated the common law and found its roots in continental rather than English practices. The essence of these relations was the principle of obedience. A strike which might have been treated as an illegal combination at common law would, if committed by mariners, be deemed a mutiny. In maintaining his authority, the cap-

---

[1] In the port of New York the number of seamen employed rose from 755 in 1747 to 3,552 in 1762. *Amer. Husbandry*, pp. 494, 495; Dr. Mitchell, *The Present State of Great Britain and North America with Regard to Agriculture, Population, Trade, and Manufactures* (London, 1767); Writers' Program, W.P.A., *A Maritime History of New York* (New York, 1941), p. 60.

[2] J. G. B. Hutchins, *The American Maritime Industries and Public Policy, 1789–1914* (Cambridge, 1941), pp. 150, 152, increases by 50 per cent the estimates contained in *An Account of the Number and Tonnage of Vessels Built in the Provinces, 1769, 1770, 1771, Journal of the House of Commons, 1792*, p. 356.

[3] G. F. Dow, "Shipping and Trade in Early New England," Mass. Hist. Soc., *Proceedings*, LXIV (1930–32), 186–191. See also R. McFarland, *A History of the New England Fisheries* (Philadelphia, 1911); S. E. Morison, *Maritime History of Massachusetts* (Boston, 1921); J. Robinson and G. F. Dow, *The Sailing Ships of New England* (3d ser., Salem, 1921–28).

[4] See E. A. J. Johnson, *Predecessors of Adam Smith* (New York, 1937), pp. 240–242, and ch. xv; H. A. Innis, *The Cod Fisheries: the History of an International Economy* (New Haven, 1940).

[5] McFarland, *op. cit.*, pp. 104 *et seq.*; Innis, *op. cit.*, p. 200.

tain or master was allowed to correct physically or confine disobedient mariners. The wage contract of the mariner was a far more complex matter than that of other workers.

In addition to contracts at fixed rates of wages, mariners frequently shared in the risk of an enterprise and were compensated, not as wage earners, but as fellow entrepreneurs. The best examples of this are found in the fields of fishing, whaling, and privateering, where the financial return to the seaman took the form of a "lay," or a fractional share in the net proceeds of an entire voyage. In fishing voyages the master and men customarily received a third of the fish, and the remaining two thirds went to the owners. This arrangement was considered a better incentive than monthly wages as it "made every man careful for the good of the voyage." [6] Readers of Moby Dick are familiar with the complicated arrangements worked out in whaling expeditions, where a green hand commonly started with a lay of $\frac{1}{200}$, an able seaman secured about $\frac{1}{150}$, a boat steerer often obtained $\frac{1}{75}$, and captains occasionally as much as $\frac{1}{10}$ or $\frac{1}{12}$.[7] As Hohman points out, the lay bore no resemblance to the familiar time wage or piece wage or to the numerous variants of the task and bonus system. There was truly no cooperation in management, as the foremast hands had no part whatever in the functions of ownership or management. Under such a plan of reimbursement, seamen shared to the full the risks of enterprise without being allowed the slightest part in the determination of those risks.[8] In privateering the prize was divided among the owner, the captain, and the crew, the size of each share being determined by rank. The crews on men-of-war were also entitled to share in prizes.[9] During the

[6] "Trelawny Papers," Me. Hist. Soc., *Coll.*, III, 281 (1641); *CSPA, 1714–15*, No. 289, p. 123 (1715); *A.P.C., Col., Unbound Papers*, No. 277, p. 110 (1718).

[7] An apprentice or "cut-tail" who served for three or four years received no money save for the fish he caught, each of which was marked for him by snipping a piece from the tail. For agreements with Indians to engage in whaling on shares, see *Southampton Town Rec.*, II, 68, 69, 72, 246, 247 (1673–78).

[8] E. P. Hohman, *The American Whaleman* (New York, 1928), pp. 15, 217, 221; Weeden, *Econ. . . . Hist. of N.E.*, II, 831; McFarland, *op. cit.*, pp. 68, 69, 151. In England before the passage in the 19th century of acts restoring admiralty jurisdiction, none but contracts in the usual form were allowed to be prosecuted in the admiralty, and a fixed rate of pecuniary wages was held to be the usual form. E. C. Benedict, *The American Admiralty: Its Jurisdiction and Practice* (New York, 1870), I, 129. However, colonial vice-admiralty does not appear to have been restricted in this regard.

[9] The prize act of 13 Geo. II, c. 4 (1739) provided that prizes captured by privateers should, after condemnation, go entirely to the owners, officers, and crew of the privateer, in such proportions as should be specified in the articles of agreement. For examples of the division of shares among privateersmen, see J. F. Jameson, *Privateering and Piracy in the Colonial Period* (New York, 1923), pp. 394–396, 581–585. For the shares of the captain, officers, and crew of a man-of-war during the early Intercolonial Wars, see Ruth Bourne, *Queen Anne's Navy in the West Indies* (New Haven, 1939), pp. 219, 220n. For unusual agreements among pirates to shares

Revolution a captain might retain six shares, the mate, gunner, and boatswain, one and one-half shares each, and privates one share apiece.[10] A fourteen-year-old lad on the Continental cruiser *Ranger* received as his share of a million-dollar prize haul in 1779 a ton of sugar, from thirty to forty gallons of Jamaica rum, twenty pounds of cotton, and a like amount of ginger, logwood, and allspice, beside $700 in cash.[11]

These facts set early American maritime labor relations quite apart from other labor categories which are considered in this volume. By the term mariner as used in this study is meant all persons employed aboard ship during the voyage, including masters, mates, sailors, carpenters, cooks, and cabin boys.

EUROPEAN ORIGINS OF AMERICAN MARITIME LABOR LAW

THE MARITIME LAW adopted in the colonies fully reflected the indebtedness of English admiralty and maritime law to classical and continental origins. The ancient Rhodian code, the later imperial codifications known as the Rhodian Sea Law, the early Decisions of Trani, the *Consulado del Mare* of Barcelona, the Pisan Code, and the Laws of Visby, all influenced the formulation of English sea law and administration. Perhaps most of all, the laws of Oléron, which were widely recognized in the English coastal towns and were incorporated in the *Liber Memorandum* of the City of London, in the Little Red Book of Bristol, in the Oak Book of Southampton, and by the Admiralty itself. As with commercial law, patterned by local and borough custumals and the practices of piepoudre and mayor's courts,[1] the maritime law spread

---

in the loot, see Captain Charles Johnson, *A General History of the Pyrates* (2d ed., London, 1724), pp. 230–232, 397–398; Jameson, *op. cit.,* pp. 141, 142.

[10] See Washington's commission to Capt. Cort for naval service, Conn. Hist. Soc., *Coll.,* VII, 94 (1775). The size of the share reserved for the public varied according to Congressional legislation passed in the course of the American Revolution. See "Memorandum respecting division of prize money," Osgood MSS, N.Y. Hist. Soc. See also *Extracts from the Journals of Congress Relative to Prizes and Privateers* (Philadelphia, 1777); *Naval Records of the American Revolution, 1775–1788* (Washington, 1906), pp. 35, 36 (1777), 64, 67, 68 (1778), 104, 129 (1779), 132, 144, 145 (1780), 190, 191 (1782); G. W. Allen, *Naval History of the Revolution* (Boston and New York, 1913), I, 24, II, 686 *et seq.;* E. S. Maclay, *A History of American Privateers* (New York, 1924), pp. 8–10. A typical prize agreement in the Revolutionary period was made between the commander and company of the privateer *Rover* in 1776, according to which one half of the prize went to the owner, the other half to the sloop's company. The captain was to have eight shares, first lieutenant five, second lieutenant and master four, and so on in proportion. *Essex Instit. Hist. Coll.,* LXXV (1939), 15.

[11] Maclay, *op. cit.,* p. 11.

[1] See R. B. Morris, *Select Cases of the Mayor's Court of New York City, 1674–1784* (*American Legal Records,* Vol. II, Washington, 1935), Introduction; Sir Travis Twiss, *The Black Book of the Admiralty, Rolls Series* (London, 1871–76), I, lviii, lxi.

largely by means of borough custumals. The colonists were actually more familiar with the maritime practices of English local courts than with the rules enforced by the High Court of Admiralty.[2] They were also well acquainted with the continental origins of the maritime law as well as with the English modifications thereof, and frequent references, in statute and decision, to such codes are found in early American law.

In 1650 a committee was appointed by the Massachusetts Bay General Court to read Malynes' *Lex mercatoria,* and extract from it such laws as might be applied to advantage in the maritime cases before the courts of Massachusetts.[3] There is no evidence that an admiralty code was adopted at that time, but in 1668 a set of maritime laws was enacted. The Code of Maritime Affairs of that year provided that masters of vessels should furnish food and drink for seamen and passengers "according to the laudable custom of our English Nation, as the custome and capacity of the places they sail from will admit." [4] In Rhode Island the General Court of Trials was authorized in 1653 to hear prize cases and to proceeed according to the "law of Alleroone." [5] The continuity of the Oléronic tradition is seen in the Virginia statute of 1779 which provided that the court of admiralty should be governed by the regulations of Congress, the acts of the General Assembly, "the Laws of Oléron and the Rhodian and Imperial Laws, so far as they have been heretofore observed in the English courts of admiralty, and by the laws of nature and of nations." [6] The Federal act of 1790 expressly declared that the "forms and modes of proceeding in cases of admiralty and maritime jurisdiction, should be according to the course of the civil law." But the subsequent act of 1793 substituted for the civil-law practice that of the English admiralty courts as modified by the usages of our own courts.[7]

Numerous parallels may be drawn between the provisions of the

[2] For the background of maritime law, see F. R. Sanborn, *Origins of the Early English Maritime and Commercial Law* (New York, 1930); L. Goldschmidt, *Handbuch des Handelsrechts,* 3d ed., Vol. I (Stuttgart, 1891), A. Desjardins, *Introduction historique à l'étude des droit commercial maritime* (Paris, 1890); W. Ashburner, *The Rhodian Sea Law* (Oxford, 1909); Twiss, *Black Book of the Admiralty;* R. Wagner and M. Pappenheim, *Handbuch des Seerechts* (Leipzig, 1884, 1906). In early modern times many English seaport towns exercised admiralty jurisdiction. All such local admiralty jurisdiction, however, with the exception of the Cinque Ports, was abolished in 1835 by the Municipal Corporations Act (5, 6 Gul. IV, c. 76).

[3] *Mass. Bay Rec.,* II, 193; *ibid.,* IV, Pt. I, 10. Gerard Malynes' *Lex mercatoria* was published in 1622 and reprinted several times in the course of the seventeenth century.

[4] *Mass. Col. Laws, 1660,* p. 253.   [5] *R.I. Col. Rec.,* I, 266. Obviously Oléron is meant.

[6] Hening, X, 98 (1779).

[7] S. R. Betts, *A Summary of Practice in Instance, Revenue and Prize Causes in the Admiralty Courts of the United States, for the Southern District of New York* (New York, 1838), p. x.

Massachusetts code of 1668 and continental maritime custumals, especially in the field of maritime labor relations. In the first place, seamen's contracts of employment were to be entered in a register.[8] Secondly, the ship was liable for the wages.[9] Thirdly, food and drink were to be provided for seamen in accordance with "the custom of the English nation." [10] Penalties were set for enticing or hiring seamen who had signed previously with another master.[11] While the Hanse law required the consent of the mariners to a deviation in the voyage, the Massachusetts code forbade mariners from interfering unless they had stipulated to the contrary in their contracts, had stayed out above a year, or were to be carried to a place where they were liable to be pressed into service.[12] In accord with maritime custom, the Massachusetts code provided a penalty for every unauthorized absence by the mariner,[13] a fine or corporal punishment for insubordination aboard ship,[14] and forfeiture of wages of deserters.[15] Finally, in case of distress at sea mariners were to assist in salvage and were to be specially compensated out of the goods salvaged.[16] Attorneys in maritime cases before common law courts as well as proctors in vice-admiralty had more than a mere familiarity with Molloy's *De jure maritimo,* the *Sea Laws,* and Burchett's *Articles.*[17]

[8] Mass. Code, § 5; Marine Ordinances of France, Bk. II, tit. ix, art. x; Bk. III, tit. iv, art. i.

[9] Mass. Code, § 5; Marine Ord. of France, Bk. III, tit. iv, art. xix.

[10] Mass. Code, § 6; but cf. Visby, art. xxix; Oléron, art. xvii.

[11] Mass. Code, § 7; Visby, art. i; Laws of the Hanse Towns, art. xlviii; Marine Ord. of France, Bk. vii.

[12] Mass. Code, § 9.

[13] Mass. Code, § 18; Oléron, art. v; Visby, art. iv; Hanse Towns, art. xix.

[14] Mass. Code, §§ 19, 25; Oléron, art. xii; Visby, art. xxiv; Marine Ord. of France; *De jur. mar.,* art. iii.

[15] Under the Mass. Code a mariner who had received a considerable part of his wages before deserting would be prosecuted and punished as a disobedient runaway servant. Mass. Code, §§ 22, 23; Visby, art. lxv; Hanse, art. xliii; Marine Ord. of France; *De jur. mar.,* art. iii.

[16] Mass. Code, § 26; Oléron, art. iii; Hanse, art. xliv; *De jur. mar.*

[17] Cocx and Co. v. ketch *Hoopwell,* which cites "Custom of Sea and Lawes of Oulleron," for priority of wage claims. Morris, *Mayor's Court,* p. 694 (1669). See also Cook v. Geddes, *ibid.,* p. 716, citing "*Jur. Marit.* 244; *Lex mercatoria* 68; *Sea Laws,* 295, 308, 309." "*Sea Laws* 139" was cited as authority for lawful correction. Morris, *op. cit.,* p. 661. Cook v. Geddes involved the question of forfeiture of wages for desertion, both *Sea Laws* and *Lex Mercatoria* being cited. *Ibid.,* p. 716 (1729) at p. 722. See also Kery v. Briggs, Kempe J–L, N.Y. Hist. Soc.; Blackleach's agreement in S.C. Court of Ordinary, lib. 1672–92 (1675). See also N.C. Vice-Admiralty Rec., lib. III (Nov. 14, 1747); King v. Tickle, N.Y. Vice-Admiralty Mins., lib. I, f. 39 (1724); C. M. Andrews, introd. to D. S. Towle, *Records of the Rhode Island Vice-Admiralty Court (American Legal Records,* Washington, 1937), III, 15n.

COLONIAL LEGISLATION DEALING WITH MARITIME LABOR RELATIONS

IN ADDITION TO borrowing from English and continental maritime usages, the colonists enacted a good deal of legislation of their own dealing with maritime labor relations. These statutes fell into certain main categories: 1. Restraints were imposed upon the arrest for debt of seamen who had not completed their voyages. The end sought was to assure the master an adequate supply of maritime labor.[1] Innkeepers or other vendors of liquors, at times even other tradesmen, were not permitted to extend credit to seamen.[2] 2. Penalties were laid down for shipping a seaman who had previously signed on another ship and for entertaining or harboring seamen without the consent of their masters.[3] 3. Legislation was enacted against deserting seamen similar in character to the statutes against fugitive servants.[4] 4. Some colonies provided that the seaman's contract be in writing.[5] 5. The mariner was required by statute to obey the commands of his master.[6] 6. The latter in turn was admonished to refrain from immoderate correction and to provide his seamen aboard ship with good food and living conditions.[7]

THE SEAMEN IN THE COURTS OF COMMON LAW

BEFORE THE ESTABLISHMENT of courts of vice-admiralty in the American colonies at the end of the seventeenth century, maritime matters were dealt with both in the regular courts of common law and in special courts set up for that purpose. Examples of the latter are furnished by Massachusetts Bay and Rhode Island. In 1639 provision was made in

[1] Compare the Federal act of March 4, 1915 (Seamen's Act, § 12) providing that no wages due or accruing to any seaman or apprentice shall be subject to attachment or arrestment from any court.

[2] *CSPA*, 1702, No. 221, p. 148; *Acts and Laws of N.H.*, I, 19 (1701); *Conn. Pub. Rec.*, 1678–89, p. 54 (1680); *N.Y. Col. Laws*, I, 345 (1695), 866 (1715); IV, 483 (1760); *S.C. Stat.*, II, 54 (1691), 127, 219 (1696), III, 735 (1751).

[3] *Acts and Laws of New Hampshire*, I, 19 (1701); *N.Y. Col. Laws*, I, 866, 867 (1715); Hening, III, 486–489 (1710), VI, 24–28 (1748); Starke, *Office of a Justice of the Peace*, p. 318.

[4] *N.Y. Col. Laws*, IV, 483 (1760); Hening, VI, 24–28 (1748); Starke, *op. cit.*, p. 318.

[5] *N.Y. Col. Laws*, IV, 483 (1760); *S.C. Stat.*, III, 735 (1751). Cf. the Federal act of 1790, which provided that, if a master proceeded to any foreign port without executing an agreement with his seaman, he could be required to pay the highest wages paid at the port of starting for a similar voyage within three months next preceding the time of shipment, and, in addition, would forfeit $20 for each seaman. A seaman who had not signed was not bound by the regulations, nor subject to the penalties of the act. *U.S. Stat. at Large*, I, 131–135, c. xxix. These colonial acts did not bar seamen from suing on parol agreements. A study of the testimony in many of the colonial cases reveals that this requirement was by no means universally observed. But cf. *R.N.A.*, V, 69, 70. For illuminating early recorded agreements, see *Essex*, II, 391 (1662). Cf. also the draft convention on seamen's articles, Geneva, 1926. Natl. Ind. Conference Bd., *The Work of the International Labor Organization* (New York, 1928), pp. 91–94.

[6] Hening, I, 107 (1722); VI, 24–28 (1748).   [7] Hening, VI, 24–28 (1748).

Massachusetts for special courts, consisting of the governor or his deputy, two magistrates, and a jury, to try cases involving strangers.[1] In 1674 the General Court ordered "all Cases of Admiralty" to be heard by the Court of Assistants without a jury unless otherwise thought best; however, other courts were expressly permitted to entertain suits by mariners and merchants "upon any matter or Cause that depends upon Contract, Covenant, or other matter of common Equity in Maritime Affaires" in accordance with "the known Lawes of this Colony." [2] As a result of this exception, county courts continued to handle the bulk of maritime causes, including seamen's wage suits and other types of maritime labor litigation.[3] Rhode Island had a maritime court as far back as 1653 when the General Court of Trials was authorized to hear prize cases and employ a jury.[4] Again, in 1694, that colony authorized the Governor and Council to act as a maritime court. They are known to have adjudged prizes, and, in addition, were given jurisdiction over "other seafaring activity as occasion shall require." The court was finally abolished by an order in Council in 1704, when the act under which it functioned was disallowed.[5] Elsewhere during this early period all maritime actions, including labor cases, were entertained in the mainland colonies in their courts of common law. Throughout this section illustrations of colonial common-law practice will be cited for this period.

Aside from statute, between 1660 and 1697, colonial governors exercised by virtue of their commissions either as governors or vice-admirals, whatever admiralty authority existed in the plantations.[6] The governors' commissions were limited to marine matters and it is doubtful whether they were regarded as having jurisdiction over the acts of trade. As a result of the act of 1696[7] and the representation of Edward Randolph to the British authorities at home, commissions were duly issued in 1697 for the appointment of vice-admiralty officials in the colonies.

Notwithstanding the establishment of the vice-admiralty courts, maritime causes, and particularly disputes involving seamen, continued to be heard in the courts of common law between 1697 and the American Revolution. While the vice-admiralty courts were at variance in remedies and procedure with traditional common-law tribunals, there was less real objection on the part of the American colonists to their deal-

---

[1] *Mass. Bay Rec.*, I, 264.   [2] Whitmore, *Mass. Col. Laws, 1672–86*, p. 213.
[3] Chafee, *Suffolk Court*, p. lxxiii.   [4] *R.I. Col. Rec.*, I, 266.
[5] Marguerite Appleton, "Rhode Island's First Court of Admiralty," *N.E.Q.*, V, 148–158.
[6] Helen J. Crump, *Colonial Admiralty Jurisdiction in the Seventeenth Century* (London, 1931); Andrews in Towle, *op. cit.*, p. 8; *CSPA*, No. 810, *1661–68*, p. 238 (1664); *1689–92*, Nos. 2636, 2705, pp. 739, 740, 749 (1692); *1702*, No. 743, p. 462; *1702–3*, No. 748, p. 461 (1703).
[7] 7, 8 Gul. III, c. 22.

ing with marine causes than to the enforcement of the acts of trade. According to Dr. Andrews, the vice-admiralty courts performed "a work of inestimable value to the colonists themselves" in their handling of marine causes.[8] In the first place, admiralty permitted suits *in rem* —of great advantage to seamen suing for wages, as their ship could be attached to satisfy the judgment. Secondly, in admiralty procedure all seamen on a vessel could unite in one action for wages, whereas common law courts insisted on separate actions. Furthermore, the admiralty had much freer rules of evidence than the common law.[9] Lastly, vice-admiralty did not provide for jury trials.[10] The absence of juries did not appear to work to the disadvantage of mariners, who were about as successful in their actions to recover wages in admiralty as were plaintiffs in similar causes at common law. In general, it will be shown that the vice-admiralty courts were more vigilant guardians of the rights of seamen than were the courts of common law.

From the rise of the courts of vice-admiralty to the close of the colonial period the common-law courts exercised what was tantamount to concurrent jurisdiction in maritime labor causes. Both in the proprietary and the royal colonies the jurisdiction of the vice-admiralty was frequently challenged. Of its own accord vice-admiralty turned over to the common-law tribunals certain types of actions, such as were involved when the libeled master or mate was fined for assault or injury to a seaman, who then brought suit for damages.[11] Judges of superior courts and, at times, governors and councils issued writs of prohibition on the ground that the cause of action lay outside the competence of the vice-admiralty court and was concerned with the land rather than the sea. With certain exceptions these writs were obeyed and the common-law court proved the more powerful and independent of the two.[12] In Massachusetts the conflict was most acute and involved political considerations, but maritime labor as such was not directly involved.

Out of twenty-nine cases of seamen's wages litigated between 1675 and 1681 before the Massachusetts Bay Court of Assistants sitting as a

---

[8] Andrews in Towle, *op. cit.*, p. 16.

[9] See Richard Zouche, *The Jurisdiction of the Admiralty of England Asserted* (London, 1663), p. 130.

[10] It is interesting to note that the General Court of Trials which sat in seventeenth-century Rhode Island to condemn prizes used a jury. The most striking feature of the state admiralty court of Rhode Island was the presence of a jury to determine issues of fact. *R.I. Col. Rec.*, VII, 481, 484 (1776); *R.I. Acts and Resolves*, July, 1780, 2d Sess., p. 9. For a warrant to draw jurors and a verdict, see F. B. Wiener, "Notes on the Rhode Island Admiralty," *Harvard Law Rev.*, XLVI, 89, 90.

[11] Andrews in Towle, *op. cit.*, p. 68.

[12] See Noble in Col. Soc. of Mass., *Transactions*, VIII, 167n.

special court of admiralty only eight were decided in favor of defendants. All awards were made by the court without jury trials.[13] Between 1671 and 1680 twenty-nine suits for mariners' wages came up in the Suffolk County court, of which only six were decided for defendants. In all the other cases, the juries awarded the verdict to plaintiffs. Hence, during the same period seamen coming up before juries in Suffolk County court did even better than mariners bringing suits before the Assistants without juries. Again, out of twelve suits for mariners wages brought before the Suffolk County court between 1680 and 1692, only four were lost by plaintiffs. Jury trials were granted in all cases.[14]

Although judgments in common law actions were *in personam*,[15] Massachusetts law made the ship liable for the contract of employment. The Assistants frequently levied execution on vessels in judgments for wages,[16] but in some instances the courts of that colony levied execution on the person of the master as well as upon the ship.[17] The practice of attaching the ship in suits for maritime wages was by no means confined to the courts of Massachusetts. In 1649 the governor of New Haven had to decide on the validity of an attachment of a ship which had been seized in Virginia in execution of a judgment for wages and turned over to the mariners. In order to put the ship into condition to continue on her voyage, she had subsequently been pledged to the outfitter. The court held that the "marriners wages have eatton out" the value of the vessel, and, since they had "the first cheife right to their wages," the outfitter's only recourse was "to secure his debt from the owners by the shipp and her furniture, not from the marriners out of the wages which should grow due from hence to the Barbadoes or any other port." Possession of the ship by the mariners and a claimant from them was accordingly upheld.[18]

Under the Roman-Dutch procedure in force in the court of burgo-

---

[13] *Assistants*, I, 43, 62, 63 (2 cases), 76, 92, 93, 106, 117 (2 cases), 119, 128, 130, 131, 132, 148 (2 cases), 150, 159, 172 (2 cases), 173 (2 cases), 175, 177, 178, 179, 372, 373.

[14] *Suffolk, 1671–80*, p. 64, 127, 134, 140 143, 270, 275, 384 (2 cases), 385, 462, 612, 613, 651, 744, 822, 855, 858, 863, 874, 930 (2 cases), 931, 1050, 1059, 1077 (3 cases), 1092; Suffolk, lib. 1680–92, I, fols. 23, 59 (2 cases); II, fols. 239, 248, 322 (2 cases), 323 (2 cases), 353, 410, 434. Plaintiff mariners were equally successful in jury trials in the Mayor's Court of New York City. See, e.g., Morris, *Sel. Cases, Mayor's Court*, pp. 694, 695, 698, 700, 701, 705, 708, 710, 714, 716, 722, 732; Rec. of Wills, lib. XIX B, f. 637.

[15] See, e.g., Blushott v. Wills, *Essex*, II, 385 (1662).

[16] For a good example, see *Assistants*, I, 391.

[17] *Ibid.*, pp. 373, 374. Cf. also Blushott *et al*. v. Wills, *Essex*, II, 385 (1662), where the writs in seven actions against the master for wages were served by the marshal of Salem by attachment of the ship; Cook v. Stretton, *ibid.*, VI, 78 (1675), sails and rigging attached.

[18] Evans's case, *New Haven Col. Rec., 1638–49*, pp. 467–469 (1649); but cf. Pollett v. Manning, *ibid., 1653–65*, p. 74 (1654).

masters and schepens in New Amsterdam ships were regularly attached for wages.[19] For a brief period the same practice was continued in the successor court of mayor and aldermen,[20] and almost until the end of the century occasional instances of such attachments were found,[21] but by the time the rival vice-admiralty court was set up in New York the mayor's court confined itself to hearing only actions *in personam* for mariner's wages, in which the individual defendant and not the ship was liable.[22]

Generally speaking, the common-law courts of the Southern colonies gave judgments *in personam* for mariners' wages. In 1684 the commanders of three ships petitioned the Maryland provincial court on behalf of their seamen, asking that, in view of the fact that their ships had been forfeited at a special court held for that purpose, seamen's wages might be allowed out of the appraisal of the ships. They conceived such relief "to be Consonant both to reason law and several presedents in this province." The court, however, contrary to later decisions in vice-admiralty, held that, although the seamen "ought to have their wages," the sum "ought not to be allowed out of the Appraisement of the ship." [23]

THE MARITIME CONTRACT OF EMPLOYMENT IN VICE-ADMIRALTY

ALTHOUGH in eighteenth-century England the jurisdiction of admiralty over suits to recover for mariner's wages was restricted to ordinary mariner's contracts and considered an excepted case,[1] in the American

[19] See, e.g., *R.N.A.*, II, 428, 429 (1658).

[20] *R.N.A.*, VI, 45 (1666); Cocx and Co. v. ketch *Hoopwell*, Morris, ed., *Sel. Cases, Mayor's Court*, p. 694 (1669), in accord with "the Custome of Sea and Lawes of Oulleron."

[21] Wilkinson v. bark *Samuell*, Salzer Papers (1694–[9]); N.Y.M.C.M., 1682–95, fols. 396, 397 (1695); Stephenson and Hardy v. sloop *Endeavour*, Salzer Papers, (1697–[5,7)]; N.Y.M.C.M., 1695–1704, fols. 64–67 (1697).

[22] In addition to cases cited *supra*, n. 14, the Salzer Papers have the following actions *in personam* for mariners' wages: Ogall v. Wake (1688–[2]); Anderson v. Wake (1688–[3]); Bondghe v. de Harte (1692–[3]); Hicks v. Glover (1692–[14]); Wilkinson v. Same (1694–[2]); Hill v. Stevenson (1694–[6]); Dolling v. Shelly (1694–[10]); Vanderpoel v. Evertse (1697–[4], Supreme Court); Cross v. Watson (1699–[9]); Varick v. Van Brugh (1711–[45]); Foster v. King (1714–[1711–45]); Carswell v. Smith (1760–[5, 5a]); Newport v. Smith (1760–[6]); Losk v. Moore (1760–[11]); Daly v. Williams (1761–[22]); Flanagan v. Same (1761–[23]); Bell v. Winn (1761–[25]). In 1770 George Johnson petitioned the attorney general that he had been confined to the city gaol upon warrants and execution against him issued in suits for wages due by four French sailors belonging to his vessel. "New Goal," Aug. 2, 1770, Kempe J–L, N.Y. Hist. Soc.

[23] Md. Prov. Court Rec., lib. 1684–87, f. 138 (1684); *J. Grand Council of S.C., 1692*, ed. A.S. Salley, Jr. (Columbia, S.C., 1907), pp. 17, 21, 25. Cf. Bully *et al.* v. Gard, *Md. Arch.*, LVII, 174, 175 (1667); appraisal of ship *Ann* of New Castle, *ibid.*, VIII, 445 (1692 ?).

[1] See Charles Abbott, *A Treatise of the Law Relative to Merchant Ships and Seamen*, 14th ed.

colonies suits involving breaches of a mariner's contract of employment were held to come within the jurisdiction of the courts of vice-admiralty from the establishment of these courts at the end of the seventeenth century.[2] A plea to the jurisdiction of the vice-admiralty was interposed in a libel for wages brought in the Rhode Island court in 1743. Respondent's proctor pleaded that the contract "was made at Land within the Town of Newport in the County of Newport" and therefore "was cognizable in the Kings Court only." But the court overruled it as trifling and evasive.[3] Again in 1748, in the case of Edward Howard v. the ship *Duke,* the Rhode Island court rejected the plea that the suit for wages was based upon a contract made within the colony and therefore triable only at common law.[4]

Terms and Conditions. Unlike most labor contracts in colonial times involving free artisans ashore, the mariner's contract of employment was generally in writing in accord with traditional maritime law or specific colonial statutes. Nevertheless, where the contract was verbal the seaman could, according to maritime law, recover his wages at the highest rate given at the port of shipment in the previous three months.[5] Sometimes the written agreement might be a collective one between all the mariners and the master. A typical example of the terms and conditions stated in such ship's articles is that entered in the records of the court of vice-admiralty in Philadelphia in 1776:

It is agreed between the Master Seamen and Mariners of the Ship *Juno* Saml Marsom Master now bound for the Port of Bristol to Cork and Jamaica and from thence to Bristol That in Consideration of the Monthly or other Wages against each respective Seaman and Mariner's Name hereunder set They severally shall perform the abovementioned Voyage and the said Master doth hereby agree with and hire the said Seamen and Mariners for the said Voyage at such Monthly Wages to be paid pursuant to the Laws of Great Britain And the said Seamen and Mariners do hereby promise and oblige themselves to do their Duty and obey the lawful Command of their Officers on board the said

---

(London, 1901), pp. 281 *et seq.;* Bruce, Jemmett, and Phillimore, *Admiralty Acts and Appeals* (London, 1902), p. 200; Ragg v. King, 2 Stra. 858; 1 Barn. K.B. 297 (1730), and King v. Players, therein cited; Clay v. Sudgrave or Snellgrave, 1 Salk. 33; 1 Ld. Raym. 576 (1701); Read v. Chapman, 2 Stra. 937 (1732); *The Favourite,* 2 C. Rob. 232 (1799). Cf. also *Select Pleas of the Admiralty* (S.S.), II, lxxix.

[2] In the New York court of vice-admiralty, libels for wages appear as early as 1716 (Hough, *op. cit.,* p. 5); in Rhode Island the first case recorded by Mrs. Towle is in 1742 (Towle, *op. cit.,* p. 150).

[3] Shilcock v. Banister, Towle, *op. cit.,* pp. 243–245 (1743).   [4] *Ibid.,* p. 478.

[5] See Jameson v. ship *Regulus,* Richard Peters, *Admiralty Decisions in the District Court of the United States for the Pennsylvania District, Comprising Also Some Decisions in the Same Court by the Late Francis Hopkinson, Esq.* (2 vols., Philadelphia, 1807), I, 212 (1800). Hereafter cited as Peters.

Ship on the Boats thereunto belonging as becomes good and faithful Seamen and Mariners and that all places where the said Ship shall put in or anchor at during the said Voyage to do their best Endeavours for the preservation of the said Ship and Cargoe and do not neglect or refuse doing their Duty by Day or Night nor go out of the said Ship on board any other Vessel or on Shore under any Pretense whatsoever without Leave first obtained of the Captain or Commanding Officer on board that in Default thereof they will not only be liable to the Penalties mentioned in an Act of Parliament made in the second Year of the Reign of King George the second &: Intitled An Act for the better Regulation and Government of Seamen and Merchants but will further in Case they should on any Account whatsoever leave or desert the said Ship discharged of her Loading be liable to forfeit and lose what Wages may at such Time of their Desertion be due to them together with every their Goods and Chattels etc: on board renouncing by their presents to all Right Title Demand and Pretension thereunto forever, for them their Heirs Executors and Administrators And it is further agreed by both Parties that eight and forty hours absence without Leave shall be deemed a total Desertion and render such Seamen and Mariners liable to the penalties above mentioned That each and every lawful Command which the said Master shall think necessary hereafter to issue for the effectual Government of the said Vessel suppressing Vice and Immorality of all Kinds be strictly complied with under penalty of the Person or persons disobeying forfeiting his or their whole Wages or Hire together with everything belonging to him or them on board the said Vessel And it is further agreed that no Officer or Seaman belonging to the said Ship shall demand or be intitled to his Wages or any part thereof until the Arrival of the said Ship at the above mentioned port of Discharge in Bristol That each Seaman and Mariner who shall well and truly perform the abovementioned Voyage (Provided always that there be no Plunderage Embezzlement or other unlawful Acts committed on said Vessels Cargoes and Stores) be entitled to the Wages or Hire that may become due to him pursuant to this Agreement That for the due performance of each and every the above mentioned Articles Agreements and Acknowledgment of their being voluntary and without Compulsion or any cladestine [*sic*] Means being used agreed to and signed by us In Testimony whereof we have each and every of us under affixed our Hands the Month and Day against our Names affixed and in the Year of our Lord one thousand seven hundred and seventy-five. . . .[6]

These agreements usually specified in detail the amount of wages the seaman was to receive, the scale of the provisions to be supplied, the nature and length of the voyage, the ship on which he was to be em-

---

[6] There follows a list of the names of the mariners and their respective monthly wages, including first mate £3 5s., second mate £2 5s., boatswain, £2 10s., carpenter £3 5s.; seaman £1 10s.; cook £1 15s. Philadelphia Vice-Admiralty Minutes, lib. III (1776). Ships' articles signed in other countries also contained provisions that deserters should forfeit their wages. See Noorbeck *et al.* v. *De Jugste Elias* (1785) 10CH–646M, Clerk of the Superior Court, Baltimore Co.

ployed, the time when he was to commence duty, and the capacity under which he was engaged to serve.[7] The rate of wages was generally specified in money either for a stated period or term or for a particular voyage. Some litigation arose in the colonial courts of vice-admiralty when masters or owners sought to pay off their seamen in depreciated currency rather than specie. In 1717 the sailors of the *Ludlow* galley sued the master in the court of vice-admiralty at Charleston because the latter insisted on paying them in the colony's money of which "twenty five shillings paper [was] of no more value than a piece of eight." The master pleaded that the seamen had signed ship's articles which contained the phrase "pound for pound Carolina money," and disclaimed responsibility for the "great depreciation" which had taken place "only during the last three or four months." Judge Trott decided for the sailors on the ground that "to pay in depreciated currency was neither just nor impartial." The master was condemned to pay in pieces of eight at six shillings the piece.[8] The court in a later case was less generous to the seamen. In *Dawcey v. Smith* (1736) the seamen had signed an agreement to accept proclamation money for wages, but refused payment. The judge, in dismissing their libel for wages, held that the libelant's ignorance of the difference between proclamation and sterling money was not to be so far presumed as to overthrow the intention of the defendant as expressed in the contract.[9]

Less frequently than with contracts for work ashore, agreements might be made for payment in commodities or cattle. Thus, when Timothy O'Brien libeled the sloop *Somerset* for wages in 1752, evidence was introduced of an agreement between the captain and O'Brien to pay the libelant's first month's wages by the delivery of four sheep. According to testimony, he had received a barrel of sugar on account of wages. But the court in its decree in the libelant's favor made no mention of the sheep and granted him £51 in bills of credit of the "Old Tenor."[10]

Where the rate of wages of a mariner was not definitely agreed upon before sailing, the amount due would be determined by maritime custom, which enforced the prevailing rate.[11] Where the rate of wages was

---

[7] A. W. Lindsay, *History of Merchant Shipping and Ancient Commerce* (4 vols., London, 1874–76), III, 301.

[8] S.C. Admiralty Rec., lib. A–B, fols. 62–78. See also Andrews in Towle, *op. cit.*, pp. 27, 28, citing Bodleian, Rawlinson, c. 385.

[9] S.C. Admiralty Rec., lib. C–D (1736).

[10] O'Brien v. sloop *Somerset*, Towle, *op. cit.*, pp. 549–553.

[11] Durfee v. Salter, Towle, *op. cit.*, p. 541 (1751). In Belsworth v. Norton (Mass. Vice-Admiralty Rec., Box II, f. 98 [1731]), Judge Byfield found that the wages claimed were "something less than what is commonly given" a mariner per month.

deemed exorbitant by the court, judgment was entered for such seamen at the customary rate.[12] The Navigation Acts are believed responsible, in part at least, for a rise in the prevailing wages of seamen during the latter half of the seventeenth century.[13]

The change from the practice of sharing in the profits and risks of a voyage to straight monthly wages doubtless benefited seamen materially. In 1716 the Board of Trade reported to the king that

the high demand for wages by all persons imploy'd in the fishery is represented to us as a great obstruction to it. A boat master's wages about six or seven years ago was from £12 to £14 for the season and now it is from £20 to £30, and that of the other seamen and fishermen in proportion. This is attended with two evil consequences. It makes the fish dearer in foreign markets, and the men negligent and lazy, being sure of their wages whether a good voyage is made or not, whereas formerly when that trade flourished most, that part of the management was (and is still in some places) as follows: The owners found the ship, wear, tear, and craft, and the commander with his men had for their labour one third part of the fish taken and cured. Thus every man made it his business, and took more care for the good of the voyage, having a more particular interest therein; for the more fish was taken, the greater was his share; if this method could be again reestablished it would undoubtedly be of considerable advantage.[14]

In addition to his stipulated wages and food, the sailor customarily had the right to ship on board a small amount of cargo for himself, both outgoing and returning, or in lieu thereof the freight payable to the

[12] Chadwick v. Clark, Towle, *op. cit.*, p. 539 (1751).

[13] For prevailing wages, see Harper, *Navigation Laws*, p. 367n.; Andrews in Towle, *op. cit.*, p. 25. In this wage rise, seamen on merchant vessels shared more generously than did sailors in the Royal Navy. The latter averaged about £1 7s. monthly in 1676. *CSPA, 1675–76*, No. 1035, pp. 450–455 (1676–77). In New England, seamen's wages in 1681 averaged at least £1 15s. monthly. Kent v. Dole, *Essex*, VIII, 77 (1681). But wages might vary considerably. According to Weeden, a seaman in 1694 received from £3 to £3 15s. per month, as against £1 15s. for a gunner, carpenter, or boatswain in 1707. In 1713 wages of seamen ranged from £2 2s. to £2 15s. per month, but generally averaged £2 10s. Mates received £3 5s. and captains £4 10s. Weeden, *Econ. . . . . Hist. of N.E.*, II, 577, 887, 889. Wages of £4 sterling per month were paid the first mate and carpenter, £3 10s. went to the second mate, £3 to the boatswain and four seamen; six other seamen, including a cook, received from 15s. to £1 5s. aboard the ship *Ann*, Liverpool to New York, in 1763. Hough, *op. cit.*, p. 215n. Monthly wages of £1 10s. for a similar trip were paid on the ship *Glasgow* in 1774. Kempe W-Y (1774). Sailors received from £3 to £3 6s. on the brig *Nancy* which sailed from Rhode Island to the Salt Islands in 1776. Weeden, *op. cit.*, II, 911. Wages of officers and crew of the ship *Union* in 1777 ranged from an average of £12 per month to as high as £20. *Essex Inst. Hist. Coll.*, LXXV (1939), 21, 22. Where a pilot of the port of New York was unable to get off a vessel at Sandy Hook owing to tempestuous weather and was carried to London, the court reimbursed him under the statute of 1763 at the rate of £6 per month for his absence from port. Smith v. Hyatt, Salzer Papers (1770). The plaintiff was the clerk of the port who sued on the bond.

[14] *CSPA, 1716–17*, No. 70, pp. 35–37 (1716). Cf. W. T. Baxter, *The House of Hancock* (Cambridge, Mass., 1945), p. 127.

ship in the amount of cargo which they might have embarked.[15] Furthermore, the mariner was entitled to a share of the prize[16] or to a share in salvage as part of wages.[17] By an act of Parliament passed in 1740, officers, seamen, and soldiers were given sole property in such prizes as were adjudged lawfully taken by them.[18] Under maritime law, sailors were allowed salvage if they had assisted in saving a ship that had stranded or had gone on the rocks or if they succeeded in re-taking a ship captured by pirates or the enemy. The reward was made to seamen of the rescuing vessel who were not bound to render such assistance; it was denied to those under some contractual or binding obligation.[19]

The vice-admiralty courts occasionally wrestled with the concept of consideration to support a contract for wages. Where a passenger had agreed to do some work aboard ship over and above the payment of five guineas for his passage, and a subsequent promise was made to him on

[15] Laws of Oléron, § 12; Holdsworth, *HEL*, V, 121; Weeden, *Econ. . . . Hist. of N.E.*, II, 590; Andrews in Towle, *op. cit.*, p. 25. "A mariner may either keep his portage in his own hand or put forth the same for freight." William Welwood, *An Abridgement of All Sea-Lawes* (London, 1613), tit. xi. See also Mumford v. *Wheel of Fortune*, Towle, *op. cit.*, pp. 520–522, where "a Draught of Logwood" free of freight was included in the employment contract.

[16] For prize jurisdiction, see E. S. Roscoe, *A History of the English Prize Court* (London, 1924); R. G. Marsden, *Documents Relating to Law and Custom of the Sea* (Naval Records Society, 1915–16), II, 199 *et seq.*

[17] As early as 1679 several seamen recovered in the Suffolk, Mass., County court the unusually large verdict of £5,000 as their shares of prize money. White *et al.* v. Lemoigne, *Suffolk*, p. 988 (1679); but cf. Jackson v. White *et al., ibid.*, p. 982 (1679). See also Rand *et al.* v. Smith, *Essex*, VI, 36 (1675).

[18] Stat. 13 Geo. II, c. 4 § 1 (1740). During the colonial period many captains of the Royal Navy were prosecuted for embezzlement. Bourne, *op. cit.*, p. 219n. For typical cases in which the crew recovered their share of the prize (there were a great many instances during the third and fourth intercolonial wars), see N.Y. Vice-Admiralty Mins., lib. I, 1715–46, fols. 124 (1741), 140 (1743), 165, 167 (1744); lib. II, 1746–57, fols. 123–132 (1748), 224, 225 (1755); III, 1758–74, fols. 29–32 (1758), 155 (1761), 180 (1762). For the question as to whether the captain was accountable to the crew for their share of prize which had not come into his own hand, but was in the hands of his agent or factors, see Wigder v. Johnson, Kempe W–Y (1760). Where seamen had shipped on board an American privateer and had been turned off by the master when only fifteen miles from Philadelphia, the court ordered payment to them of a proportionate share of a prize captured subsequent to their dismissal. The decree of the admiralty was affirmed by the court of appeals. Mahoon *et al.* v. *The Gloucester*, Peters, p. 403 (1780).

[19] While the crew of the distressed vessel could not claim salvage, they could, if, after the ship had gone aground, they had been discharged by the master, and subsequently salvaged some of the stores. R. M. Hughes, *Handbook of Admiralty Law*, 2d ed. (St. Paul, Minn., 1920), pp. 137, 138; *The Warrior*, Lush. 476 (1862); Taylor *et al.* v. Goods saved from the *Cato*, Peters, p. 48 (1806). Judge Menzies barred the mariners' claims to salvage on the basis of the owner's expenditures in maintaining and transporting them after the wreck. Clark v. Belvin, Mass. Vice-Admiralty Rec., Box II, f. 15 (1727). On a number of occasions the vice-admiralty courts awarded out of the salvage the wages of seamen working for a salvor. Wickham v. *Jolly Batchellor*, Towle, *op. cit.*, p. 234 (1743); Coventry v. snow *Doddington* and White, C. M. Hough, *Reports of Cases in the Vice Admiralty of the Province of New York and in the Court of Admiralty in the State of New York, 1715–1788* (New Haven, 1925), pp. 32–35 (1749).

the high seas by the captain that, if he would serve in the place of one of the mariners who was disabled, "he should be paid for it," Judge Wickham held that he was entitled to be paid from the date of the captain's promise to the time of landing.[20] On the other hand, the New York court held that a definite agreement to work on board ship for passage was not converted into a contract for wages by subsequent statements of the captain that he would "make an acknowledgment" to such passage workers. As regards the alleged promise of the captain in New York that he would pay the libelants their wages, the court held that a promise to pay wages after the service was performed "was a promise without a Consideration."[21]

Time of Payment of Wages. Considerable litigation arose in the colonial courts of vice-admiralty over the issue of time of payment of seamen's wages. Under the venerable Oléronic code mariners were not entitled to the whole of their wages until the ship reached her destination, and the master was permitted to retain some part as security that they would finish the voyage.[22] Agreements to sailors for the fishing voyage to Newfoundland customarily included a clause providing that their wages were not to be paid until their return to England.[23] Parliamentary statutes aimed at discouraging desertion by seamen put teeth into this maritime custom. Thus, the act of 1721 provided that the master who advanced any seaman above one half his wages while he was abroad would forfeit double the sum advanced, which could be recovered in the admiralty by the informer.[24] The original Federal act of 1790 required the captain to pay, at every port at which cargo was discharged, one third of the wages then due and the balance at the end of the voyage.[25] It is interesting to note that the English practice prevalent in colonial times whereby seamen could demand half their wages prior to the termination of the voyage was reestablished in this country in 1898.[26]

[20] Johnson v. Scarr, Towle, *op. cit.*, pp. 523–525 (1750).

[21] The decision also implied that the libelants were not entitled to be paid for unloading the ship, as such work was part of a seaman's duty, which they had agreed to perform for their passage. Benson *et al.* v. sloop *Polly*, Hough, *op. cit.*, pp. 235–239 (1770).

[22] Art. 19, *Black Book of the Admiralty*, III, 24, 25.

[23] This deterred them from staying abroad, although it was reported that 120 stayed in Newfoundland in 1683. *CSPA, 1681–85*, No. 1907, p. 708 (1684).

[24] Stat. 8 Geo. I, c. 24 (1721–22); 12 Geo. II, c. 30, § 12 (1739).   [25] 1 Stat. at L. 133.

[26] 30 Stat. at L. 756. See also Benedict, *op. cit.*, I, 711. However, the intent of the law was defeated by stipulations to the contrary in the contract. The La Follette Act, § 4, provided that "all stipulations in the contract to the contrary shall be void." Under this law failure of the master to comply with the proper demand of a seaman for wages due constituted a violation of the contract, entitling the seaman to full payment of wages earned.

The question as to when wages were due was occasionally agitated in the colonial courts prior to the establishment of the vice-admiralty. In 1644 the master of the ship *Gillyflower* sued for wages in the courts of Massachusetts, lost the verdict, and appealed to the General Court, where the majority decided that the wages were not due until the ship reached London again.[27] A group of mariners libeled the master of the ship *Providence* in the Massachusetts Court of Assistants sitting in admiralty in 1675. They alleged that they had been shipped from Lyme to Virginia and return. The master and supercargo decided that insufficient tobacco had been obtained in Virginia and therefore headed the ship for New England. On arrival at Boston the crew sued for wages due on the ground that that town was the second delivery port. Therefore, they requested that they be freed or be given security that their wages would be paid on arrival at the port of discharge. The court favored the latter proposal, and ordered the master to give the crew a certificate under his own hand declaring that their wages were due. Upon his compliance, the seamen were ordered to proceed on their voyage.[28]

On numerous occasions the vice-admiralty courts ordered part of the wages paid to the crews at the second port of delivery, but generally required the seamen in return to give security to proceed on the voyage.[29] It was proper defense to a libel for wages that the suit was instituted in the first delivery port.[30]

Judge Michie in the vice-admiralty court of South Carolina justified the rule that a seaman was not entitled to more than half his wages before completing the voyage with the argument that, otherwise "no longer wou'd Freight be the Mother of Wages" nor would owners be relieved from wage payments when no freight was payable to them or

[27] Winthrop, *Journal*, ed. J. K. Hosmer (New York, 1908), II, 199, 202; *Mass. Bay Rec.*, II, 84, 90; Helen J. Crump, *Colonial Admiralty Jurisdiction in the Seventeenth Century* (London, 1931), pp. 48 *et seq.* A jury in the Court of Assistants sustained the findings in the previous courts.

[28] Bacon *et al.* v. Bull, *Assistants*, I, 40, 41 (1675). For other early cases upholding the rule of payment at second port of delivery, see *ibid.*, pp. 172, 173 (1680); New Haven Co. Court, lib. I, f. 109 (1678). For the provision in 1680 that masters and mariners were to receive half pay when reaching port, see Mass. Arch., LXI, 214. But see Zeeman *et al.* v. Capps, *R.N.A.*, V, 91 (1664), where suit was brought on a specific promise to pay wages at the first port of call.

[29] See Sailors v. Tudar, Mass. Vice-Admiralty, Box I, 1718–26, f. 36 (1719), *John and Ann*, *ibid.*, f. 52 (1720); Shillicorne v. Sailors, *ibid.*, f. 158 (1723).

[30] See Boswell and Gascoigne v. *Noble James*, Towle, *op. cit.*, p. 450 (1747), where the case was compromised by the parties. Where articles signed in Holland provided that a crew were not entitled to receive any wages until the voyage was completed, the court dismissed the mariner's libel. Norbeck *et al.* v. ship *De Jugste Elias* (1785), Maryland Court of Admiralty, 10 CH646A–H, Clerk of the Superior Court, Baltimore City. Barratry and refusal to obey orders were additional defenses to this libel for wages.

when they had lost their vessels. This would have the "most hurtful
. . . Consequences to Commerce in General." [31]

There was at least one exception to this rule. Masters were not justified in lingering in a port for an unreasonable length of time without
paying at least part of wages due. Judge Byfield maintained that the rule
related to "Voyages regularly perform'd." [32]

Sailors seemed well posted on their rights on this point, for, as John
Watts, the New York merchant, grudgingly admitted, "a Number of
Pettifoggers were always ready to disturb the Minds of Seamen and puz-
zell the Laws." If their wage claims were not satisfied they "would not
stir" out of port. [33]

Procedure in Wage Suits. The admiralty courts permitted the crew to
join in suit for their wages, whereas common law courts insisted upon
separate actions. [34] The rights of the various seamen joining in the suit
were nonetheless separate and independent. [35] Suit for wages was commenced by the filing of a libel. Admiralty law provided for simplified
pleading, but the libel was supposed to allege the rate of wages stipulated in the contract, the performance of the services, or a lawful discharge. [36]

[31] Brown v. Thompson, S.C. Vice-Admiralty Mins., E–F (1757); appealed to the Court of
Admiralty of Great Britain.

[32] When seamen were detained in port for nine or ten months on salt provision and without
beer contrary to custom, he decreed that half wages were due and payable within 48 hours by the
master or owner. The seamen were obligated to sail with the ship provided it left by a specified
date; otherwise they were to be discharged. Harris v. Tuder, Mass. Vice-Admiralty Rec., Box I,
1718–26, f. 36 (1719). Where a deviation had been agreed upon by the crew or they had failed
to protest at the time when the master changed his course, then recovery of part wages at the
second port was not justifiable. Brown et al. v. *Dolphin*, Towle, *op. cit.*, pp. 408, 409 (1747);
but cf. Sailors v. Burnett, Mass. Vice-Admiralty Rec., Box I, f. 94 (1721).

[33] Watts pointed out that in one controversy it was possible to induce the mariners to go
aboard ship by paying half their wages before the vessel put to sea. The statute of 1760, c. 1132,
disallowed by the Crown in 1762—*Laws of New York, 1691–1773* (New York, 1774), I, 385—
was, in his opinion, "the only proper one the Legislature ever past to remedy the Evil." *Letter
Book*, pp. 62 (1762), 112 (1764).

[34] *Sel. Pleas of the Admiralty* (S.S.), II, lxxxvii; Holdsworth, *H.E.L.*, I, 555. See also U.S. Stat.,
July 20, 1790, § 6.

[35] In the modern American admiralty law they are considered co-libelants rather than joint
libelants and as such are competent witnesses for one another. In the colonial vice-admiralty
members of the crew were sworn in court in wage claims—Brown et al. v. *Dolphin*, Towle,
op. cit., pp. 408, 409 (1747); Crandall v. *Mermaid*, *ibid.*, pp. 383, 384 (1746)—but it is not
at all clear that they were permitted to testify for each other if the witness and the party suing
had a common interest in the contest. In the early Federal courts each man's case had to be separately proved and separately passed upon and the decree was supposed to be separate for each.
Oliver v. Alexander, 31 U.S. (6 Pet.) 143; Benedict, *op. cit.*, I, 710, 711.

[36] For a typical colonial vice-admiralty libel, see Towle, *op. cit.*, pp. 561, 562; for a libel in
the early 19th-century Federal courts, see Hall, *op. cit.*, pp. 130–132. Where libelant failed to
allege performance or discharge, respondent pleaded that the libel was defective. It was later
withdrawn. Bilby v. Bannister, Towle, *op. cit.*, p. 532 (1751). Where the suit was brought at
common law, it was generally instituted by a declaration in special assumpsit which contained
the traditional fictitious allegations of fraud and deceit. See Morris, *Mayor's Court*, pp. 695–736.

In admiralty law the ship was pledged for the payment of wages to the last plank and the last nail. As the arrest of the ship provided far more effective security for those employed upon her, the seaman in colonial times normally libeled *in rem* for wages. Where the crew were to be reimbursed by fractional shares of the net proceeds of the voyage, they had a lien for their respective shares upon the vessel and the catch on board. Since the seaman might choose to sue the owner or the master instead or besides the vessel, it is important to distinguish such suits *in personam* from the usual libels against the ship. In proceeding *in rem,* notice was not served on the owner, as it was presumed that the seizure of his property would soon come to his knowledge and cause him to take steps to defend it. When he appeared, it was rather as claimant or intervenor than as defendant. In the foreign attachment procedure frequently used in the colonies against absentee debtors and, therefore, applicable to absentee owners of vessels, the debtor was the defendant by name, and, if he appeared, a personal judgment might be rendered against him. In other words, the attachment of the property was for the purpose of compelling the appearance of the defendant.[37] The ship was seized as a result of the issuance of a process of arrest. Upon failure of any person to appear and answer when libel was read in open court, decree for wages was entered, and the vice-admiralty courts ordered the sale of the vessel if payment was not forthcoming within ten days from the date of the decree.[38] This procedure was especially efficacious where the master had died in the course of the voyage,[39] or had absconded,[40] and it has been substantially retained in the modern British and American admiralty law.[41]

In the early, informal, period of colonial justice pleadings were simple. See, e.g., Lechford *Note-Book,* pp. 214, 215, declaration in Witherle v. Heale, which would have satisfied the requirements of an admiralty libel.

[37] See Morris, ed., *Sel. Cases, Mayor's Court,* pp. 14–21, 102–106; Hughes, *op. cit.,* p. 401; Hall, *op. cit.,* p. ix. But see Betts, *op. cit.,* pp. 59 *et seq.,* who points out that in the 19th century it was lawful for the judge of the district court to summon the master to show cause why process should not issue. Other uses of *in rem* procedure in admiralty are in suits on bottomry bond or for salvage.

[38] Baker v. brigantine *Little Betty,* Towle, *op. cit.,* pp. 298–300 (1744); Henderson and Almy v. sloop *Kingston, ibid.,* p. 479 (1748); Humphreys v. sloop *Venus, ibid.,* p. 522 (1750); Gorham v. sloop *Jupiter, ibid.,* p. 525 (1750); Pincken et al. v. sloop *Mary Ann, ibid.,* p. 526 (1750); Phillips v. sloop *Jupiter, ibid.,* p. 529 (1750)—twenty days allowed; Wells v. sloop *Lydia, ibid.,* p. 548 (1752); Stanley v. *Hopewell, ibid.,* p. 553 (1752). See also Sailors v. ship *Elizabeth,* Mass. Vice-Admiralty Rec., Box I, f. 38 (1719); Martin v. ship *Aurora,* N.Y. Vice-Admiralty Mins., I, 1715–46, f. 135 (1742); Fishley *et al.* v. brigantine *Milborough, ibid.,* fols. 142, 143, 151 (1743); Mate and Mariners v. ship *Albany, ibid.,* fols. 151, 157 (1743). Boyd *et al.* v. ship *Friendship,* S.C. Vice-Admiralty Rec., A–B (1719).

[39] *Flying Brigantine,* S.C. Vice-Admiralty Mins., lib. A–B (1717).

[40] Sloop *Elizabeth, loc. cit.* (1717).

[41] See Jud. (Cons.) Act, 1925, §§ 22, 33 (2); U.S.R.S. 4546.

An interesting case illustrating the *in rem* procedure for wages, the priority of wage claims, and the jurisdictional conflicts between common law and vice-admiralty in the colonies arose in the New York vice-admiralty court in 1763, when the crew of the ship *Ann* libeled for wages. Shortly after the arrival of the ship in New York from Liverpool the master was arrested and the ship attached by process issued out of the Supreme Court of the province. Under this attachment the *Ann* was advertised for "Sale at Publick Outcry for the Benefit of the Creditors of the Owner or Owners of the said Ship," such sale to be held at the Merchant's Coffee House. Although the ship was in custody of a common-law court, vice-admiralty authorized seizure of the *res*. From the sale of the ship £680 was derived, of which £511 16s. ½d. was paid by court order for wages, £67 2s. 1d. was deducted for costs, and the remained turned over to the claimants.[42] Where a ship was the property of several owners who had fractional shares in her and some of the owners had paid their proportional share of the wages and others had not, vice-admiralty ordered that the fractional share representing the defaulting owner or owners be sold to satisfy the unpaid balance of wages.[43] In *Williamson v. The Hampton* a two thirds owner appeared in the New York state admiralty court and admitted liability for wages. According to Judge Hough, this was a plain instance of using a small claim to procure a judicial sale and probably get rid of a minority owner.[44] Even where the mariner was hired by the master without the consent of the owners, the vice-admiralty court entered a decree for wages against the ship.[45]

Alone of the crew, the master in admiralty law was not permitted to libel the ship for wages. The courts justified this discrimination on the ground that the mariners contracted on the credit of the ship, but the master contracted on the credit of the owner.[46] While the rule is different in England in modern times,[47] American admiralty law has continued the distinction in remedies available.[48] It must be borne in mind that in colonial times many masters owned their ships or were part-owners. Out of 329 ships in the port of New York during the years 1763 and 1764 26.7 per cent of those of New York registry were owned by the master in whole or in part as against 20.4 per cent of those in Port

[42] Johnson *et al.* v. ship *Ann*, Hough, *op. cit.*, p. 214 (1763).
[43] Mate and Mariners v. ship *Albany*, ibid., p. 22 (1743). [44] *Ibid.*, p. 254 (1786).
[45] Kyley v. sloop *Hopewell*, Towle, *op. cit.*, p. 538 (1751).
[46] Molloy, *De jur. mar.*, bk. ii, c. iii, § 8. See also *A.P.C., Col., Unbound Papers*, VI, No. 433, p. 218 (1731), sustaining a prohibition issued in Lupton's case in Pennsylvania.
[47] Covert v. *The Wexford*, 3 Fed. 577.
[48] Drinkwater v. *The Spartan*, 1 Ware 149; Benedict, *op. cit.*, I, 127, 128.

Hampton, Virginia, for the same period, 23.4 per cent of British ships in New York, and a general average of 25.8 per cent.[49]

Both in earlier times and in the modern law the seaman had a right of action either *in rem* against the ship or he could recover wages *in personam* against the owner or the master.[50] The Massachusetts vice-admiralty ruled in 1719 that both ship and master were liable for wages.[51] In colonial times seamen, when instituting suits in vice-admiralty, quite naturally preferred to proceed *in rem* because of the greater security offered. Actions against the master for wages were rare in vice-admiralty, but they were by no means infrequent in the colonial and early state courts of common law.[52] At times the mariners sought relief in vice-admiralty against the owners [53] instead of pursuing their remedy at common law. Part owners of a vessel were liable for mariner's wages in proportion to their share of ownership.[54] In one such case the respondent pleaded that he was only a part owner and that the libel should also have included the other joint owner, a London merchant; that the libel did not state the place whence the ship sailed; and that, since libelant had been paid wages in advance, he should have sued on the contract itself. Judge Gridley rejected this plea, asserting that he always would so overrule "all Manner of Triffling Evasions to throw the Charges on any poor man when I think his Case is Just as to the Merits of the Cause." [55]

When seamen were involved, both the common-law courts and the vice-admiralty liberalized their rules of evidence. The New York Supreme Court in 1759 ruled that seamen "must of necessity be witnesses" in their own suits for wages, as it was often not feasible to transport witnesses from abroad.[56] Of genuine advantage to the seamen suing in vice-admiralty on wage claims was the practice of such courts in issuing commissions to examine witnesses outside the jurisdiction of the

---

[49] I am indebted to Professor Lawrence A. Harper of the University of California for these statistics which were compiled under his direction.

[50] See Brevoor *et al.* v. ship *Fair American* and Dutilh and Gourjon, Peters, p. 87 (1800), at pp. 94, 95.

[51] Sailors v. Tuder, Mass. Vice-Admiralty Rec., Box I, 1718–26 (1719).

[52] See above for colonial common-law cases; see also Farrel v. McClea, 1 Dallas 393 (1788).

[53] Williams *et al.* v. Cornel *et al.*, Towle, *op. cit.*, p. 519 (1749), where Wickham ruled that owners were jointly liable for the payment of wages.

[54] McLeod v. sloop *Triton*, Towle, *op. cit.*, p. 527 (1750), in which the court rejected the plea of the respondents that, as they owned only thirteen-sixteenths of the vessel, they were not liable.

[55] Shilcock v. Banister, Towle, *op. cit.*, pp. 243–245 (1743). For court order to pay mariner's wages to the minor's guardian, see Mumford v. *Jolly Batchelor*, *ibid.*, pp. 337, 338 (1746).

[56] Meyer v. Lindeboom, N.Y. Supreme Court (April term, 1759), William Smith MSS, lib. V, N.Y. Pub. Lib.

court or abroad. The authority to take depositions *de bene esse*—very similar to the liberal evidence procedure of the New England common-law courts in the seventeenth century—has been continued by modern Federal legislation.[57] The New York court of vice-admiralty held in 1745 that the witnesses' intention of departing to sea was sufficient reason for examining them *de bene esse*. The register had made copies of depositions taken by William Smith, Junior, proctor for the libelant, but Smith refused to pay the fees as he did not have any of his client's money in his hand. The court nonetheless insisted upon perusing all the depositions to help in reaching a judgment.[58] In a libel for wages against the sloop *Somerset* brought in 1752 before the vice-admiralty court at Newport the testimony of a number of witnesses was obtained by commission issued to an examining officer in Bristol County, Massachusetts, where these witnesses resided.[59]

Many wage cases were left to a reference and settled out of court.[60] Arbitration was frequently proposed by the court. A great many others were settled out of court by agreement and in order to obviate delays and excessive costs.[61] When the owners of a vessel failed to make an offer prior to the decree of the full amount of wages due, the vice-admiralty court imposed full costs.[62]

Charles M. Andrews, in his definitive study of the vice-admiralty court, has pointed out that suits for wages were rarely, if ever, appealed to England. In the first place, such appeals had to involve amounts of at least £300. Secondly, the time for appeal was limited to ten months. For failure to prosecute an appeal within this period—either because of delay in finding security or for some other reason—the appellant had to pay treble costs. The appeal, whether to the High Court of Admiralty or to the Privy Council, was too long and expensive a process for the average seaman to contemplate.[63]

Grounds Barring Full Recovery of Wages. Matters which formed the ground for defenses to an action for wages were nearly all based on the nonperformance or improper performance of the seaman's duties. Desertion and willful disobedience or refusal to work were the leading defenses.[64] English statutes and colonial enactments, following closely

[57] 27 Stat. 7; U.S. Comp. Stat., § 1476. [58] McFarlin v. White, Hough, *op. cit.,* p. 25 (1745).
[59] O'Brien v. sloop *Somerset,* Towle, *op. cit.,* pp. 549–553 (1752).
[60] See, e.g., Lock and Gould v. Marshall, S.C. Vice-Admiralty E–F (1760).
[61] Andrews in Towle, *op. cit.,* p. 27.
[62] Perry v. *Providence,* Towle, *op. cit.,* pp. 544–547 (1752).
[63] Andrews in Towle, *op. cit.,* pp. 21, 22.
[64] E. S. Roscoe, *The Admiralty Jurisdiction and Practice of the High Court of Justice* (5th ed., London, 1931), pp. 218, 219.

the maritime law, provided that in the event of desertion the seaman was to forfeit all wages due him for the voyage.[65] The colonial laws regarding desertion paralleled the statutes relating to fugitive servants. In addition, the mariner could be held liable for breach of contract, was subject to punishment as a runaway by the criminal machinery, and could be ordered by the court to return to his ship. For example, the Massachusetts code of 1668 provided, in addition to the forfeiture of all wages, imprisonment of the seaman or other punishment to be adjudged by the magistrates unless he justified "his so leaving the voyage" (§ 22).[66] A mariner absconding after receiving a considerable part of his wages was to be punished as a "disobedient runaway servant" (§ 23). In addition to forfeiture, the New York statute of 1760 provided for the commitment of the absconding seaman at hard labor until he was ready to go to sea.[67] Under a Virginia act of 1748 a fine could be recovered before any justice of the peace out of the wages of seamen absent without leave.[68] Imprisonment, although the term was gradually modified, remained a basic penalty for desertion in our Federal legislation from the original act of 1790 down to the passage of the White Act in 1898, which still retained a one-month imprisonment term for desertion in a foreign port, and the La Follette Act of 1915, which abolished imprisonment for desertion entirely.[69]

Colonial statutes attest the fact that desertion was one of the most serious problems in the merchant marine.[70] In the Royal Navy the problem was even more acute. Several factors encouraged seamen to desert His Majesty's men-of-war: the higher wages prevailing in colonial

[65] Molloy, *De jur. mar.,* Bk. I, ch. 4, § 24; Bk. II, ch. 3, § 10; Stat. 11–12 *Gul.* III, c. 7 § xvii (1700).

[66] *Mass. Col. Laws, 1660–72,* p. 256.

[67] *N.Y. Col. Laws,* IV, 483 (1760). See warrant of Alderman Waddell against John Wilson and other sailors of the ship *Glasgow,* who had signed for a trip from Liverpool to New York and return and then jumped ship in New York. The constables or marshals of the latter city were ordered to apprehend them and put them in the House of Correction to labor not exceeding 30 days nor less than 14. Kempe W–Y (1774). See also Spey v. Cobins *et al.,* where the deserting seamen broke gaol. Salzer Papers (1698–[16]);N.Y.M.C.M., 1695–1704, fols. 107, 110 (1699).

[68] Hening, VI, 24–28 (1748).

[69] See *U.S.Stat. at Large,* I, 134 (1790); IV, 359 (1829); XII, 273 (1872); XXVIII, 667 (1895). The Federal act of 1872 was modeled largely on the British act of 1854. See also act of Dec. 21, 1898 (§ 19) and Robertson v. Baldwin, 165 U.S. 275 (1897); also International Seamen's Union of America, *Proceedings* (1915), pp. 28, 29, 83, 84; A. E. Albrecht, "International Seamen's Union of America: A Study of Its History and Problems," U.S. Bureau of Labor Statistics, *Bull.,* No. 342, pp. 37 *et seq.* See also Walter Macarthur, *The Seaman's Contract, 1790–1918* (San Francisco, 1919), pp. xviii, xix.

[70] See *Acts and Laws of New Hampshire,* I, 19 (1701); *N.Y. Col. Laws,* IV, 483 (1760). For typical newspaper notices of deserting seamen, see *Md. Gazette,* March 17, June 16, July 21, Dec. 2, 1747; Jan. 20, Feb. 10, 17, March 30, April 6, 20, 27, 1748; July 26, Aug. 9, Sept. 6, 9, 1759; May 15, 1760.

ports, both in the merchant service and among artificers and laborers ashore; the unpopularity of life aboard naval vessels in those days; and the practice of lending out crews from two to four months to work ashore. When voluntary enlistments were insufficient, the admiralty resorted to the press gang and the press boat to fill quotas.[71] Fearing impressment, sailors from merchantmen were prone to desert in droves when rumors of European war spread in colonial ports.[72] The fighting effectiveness of the Royal Navy was seriously impaired during the American Revolution. It has been estimated that some 42,000 seamen deserted from the British navy between 1774 and 1780.[73] A similar problem confronted the Continental navy, as the greater rewards offered by privateers induced substantial desertions from ships of war.[74] In short, as the old sea chantey pithily sums it up, the temptation to quit the sea was ever present:

> O, the times are hard and the wages low,
> Leave her, John-ny, leave her;
> I'll pack my bag and go be-low;
> It's time for us to leave her.

Vice-admiralty customarily decreed that the wages of deserting seamen were forfeited.[75] Where the seamen were within the jurisdiction of the court, they might be subject to an order to proceed on the voyage, merely suffering deductions of wages for the period of the desertion.[76]

[71] See J. R. Hutchinson, *The Press-Gang Afloat and Ashore* (New York, 1914). For the complaint of the Lords of Admiralty about desertions in South Carolina owing to the high wages currently offered by captains of merchant ships as well as by landsmen, see S.C. Commons Journal, 1742–43, fols. 399–402 (1743), 8 seamen listed as deserters.

[72] *CSPA, 1702,* No. 537, p. 354. A comparatively small vessel often lost from 40 to 60 of her crew. *Docs. Rel. to Col. Hist. of N.Y.,* V, 194; Weeden, *op. cit.,* I, 369; Andrews in Towle, *op. cit.,* p. 25.

[73] See "Letter-Books and Order-Book of George, Lord Rodney," N.Y. Hist. Soc., *Coll.* 1932, pp. 8, 169, 214, 446, 626; "Kemble Papers," *ibid.,* 1883, I, 556; H. M. Lydenberg, ed., *Archibald Robertson, Lieutenant-General Royal Engineers: His Diaries and Sketches in America, 1762–1780* (New York, 1930), p. 151 (1777); *Orderly Books of the Three Battalions of Loyalists Commanded by Brigadier General Oliver De Lancey, 1776–1778* (New York, 1917), p. 103 (1778); Allen, *op. cit.,* I, 56.

[74] Allen, *op. cit.,* I, 49. Continental naval regulations provided the death penalty "or such other punishment as a court-martial shall inflict" for officers or crew who deserted their duty or station in time of action or who should entice others so to do. *Ibid.,* II, 691.

[75] See, e.g., Pomroy v. Sailors, Mass. Vice-Admiralty Rec., Box I, f. 168 (1724); Henderson v. Cullock, *ibid.,* f. 187 (1724); Shepherd v. Sailors, *ibid.,* Box II, f. 16 (1727); Clark v. *Phenix, ibid.,* f. 17 (1727); Condon v. Pitkin, S.C. Vice-Admiralty Mins., E–F (1759). However, a seaman deserting to join a royal warship was permitted to get his chest and clothes. Markey v. Sailors, Mass. Vice-Admiralty Rec., Box I, f. 98 (1721); Watt v. Archer, *ibid.,* f. 195 (1725). For forfeiture of wages in the common law courts, see *Suffolk,* p. 620 (1675). Some leniency appears to have been shown deserters in New Amsterdam. See *R.N.A.,* VI, 126 (1664). For forfeiture under the early Federal statutes, see Peters, p. 162n.

[76] Foster v. Sailors, Mass. Vice-Admiralty Rec., Box I, f. 207 (1726).

In order to prevent seamen from deserting to the Royal Navy, only to quit as soon as "a profitable Voyage Offers," Byfield ordered them to resume their original voyage and to receive no further wages until its completion.[77] At times the courts were strict in their construction of desertion, holding that if a master had failed to apply to the authorities at the port where the boat was docked to compel libelant to proceed on the voyage, his failure precluded forfeiture of wages;[78] and that there was no breach of contract if a mariner left the vessel temporarily with the consent of the owners in order to find employment elsewhere.[79] Furthermore, where the absentee had been permitted to return to duty within a reasonable period of time, his wages would not be forfeited.[80]

In addition to suffering forfeiture of wages, deserting seamen were liable either at common law[81] or in vice-admiralty for damages for breach of contract. In 1720 the owners of the schooner *King Fisher* brought suit in the Massachusetts vice-admiralty court against a group of mariners for desertion. Menzies found that one member of the crew named Holmes, who had bound himself to sail to Cape Sable as a fisherman upon shares until the end of the fishing season, had deserted and "was Instrumental to Cause others of the Crew to relinquish the Vessel." As a result, the owners lost the fishing season and the court decreed against Holmes and another seaman damages to the amount of £250 bills current and costs.[82]

Another principal ground for defense to an action for wages was the willful disobedience of the seaman or his refusal to work.[83] Under the discussion below of the discipline of the sea the criminal consequences of mutiny and combinations aboard ship will be taken up, but at this

[77] Guy v. Sailors, Mass. Vice-Admiralty Rec., Box II, f. 93 *et seq.* (1731). For an example of forfeiture of wages for desertion to his Majesty's service, see Sailors v. Rushton, *ibid.*, Box II, f. 136 *et seq.* (1733).

[78] Mariner was required, however, to pay costs for contempt. Holton v. Bulenceau, Mass. Vice-Admiralty Rec., Box I, 1718–26 (1718).

[79] It was brought out in evidence that another mariner had been procured in place of the libelant and without holding up the sloop. Hoxsea v. Polock and Levy, Towle, *op. cit.*, pp. 542, 543 (1752).

[80] This was in accord with Oléronic law. Art. 13. In Whitton *et al.* v. Master and Owners of the brig *Commerce*, Peters, pp. 160–164 (1798), the seamen had been subsequently received on board unconditionally. In Dixon *et al.* v. ship *Cyrus*, *ibid.*, pp. 407–414 (1789), the mariners had repeatedly left and returned to their ship without demur on the part of the captain. Where the deserter was not the libelant but his servant whom he had hired out to the captain of another vessel, the Rhode Island court awarded the libelant wages for the servant's time up to the date of the latter's desertion. Johnson v. Dyre, Towle, *op. cit.*, p. 248 (1744).

[81] See Stuyvesant v. van Deventer, *R.N.A.*, VII, 87 (1674).

[82] Belcher and Ingersoll v. Holmes *et al.*, Mass. Vice-Admiralty Rec., Box I, f. 66 (1720).

[83] For a clear statement of this rule see the undated opinion handed down by the Maryland state court of admiralty (*c.* 1787) in Harrison v. schooner *Phenix*, 12CH–1220, Clerk of the Superior Court, Baltimore City.

point emphasis is placed on the effect of such conduct on the contractual rights of the insubordinate seaman. The Massachusetts maritime code of 1668 (§ 25) provided: "If any officers or mariners, shall combine against the Master, whereby the voyage shall be diverted or hindred, or that damage shall accrue to the ship and goods, they shall be punished with loss of wages, or otherwise as mutiniers." Admiralty claimed the right to forfeit wages for persistent mutinous conduct.[84] Colonial vice-admiralty exercised this power on occasion. For example, in 1716 Captain Thomas Beck libeled nine of his crew in the vice-admiralty court of South Carolina for refusing to remove some barrels of pitch on board ship. Depositions were submitted that when the mate sought to prevent their going ashore they assaulted him and had acted mutinously on several occasions. Trott justified the forfeiture of their wages on the ground that, were the court to compel them to go aboard again, the master could not with safety receive them.[85] The libel for wages of the mariners of the *Loyal George* was rejected by Judge Whitaker of the same court when it appeared that they had been guilty of mutiny and disobedience, of refusing to pump when commanded, or, when coming into Charleston, of refusing to moor the vessel until the master got hands from some other ship, and of barratry of sugar. One of the seamen, when ordered to look out for land, took a keg of rum to the masthead. Their wages were accordingly forfeited.[86] In a Massachusetts vice-admiralty suit brought in 1725 the court found a seaman guilty of mutiny. In the court's opinion his commission of disorderly acts on board ship, including insolence to the master whom he dangerously wounded in the arm, tended "in all probability to Open pyracy if he had been in a Capacity to Accomplish it." The forfeited wages, therefore, were awarded to the master for reparation *pro tanto*. In addition, the defendant was required to pay the doctor's bill of £3 10s., a fine of £5 6s. to the king, and a further fine of £5 to the captain, with costs taxed at £5 17s. 4d., and to remain in prison until these sums were paid.[87]

Participation in a mutiny was held a legal defense to a claim for a

---

[84] Relf *et al*. v. ship *Maria*, Peters, p. 186 (1805).

[85] Beck v. Champion *et al*., S.C. Vice-Admiralty Mins., A–B (1716). The libel as to Wharton, one of the mariners, was withdrawn.

[86] S.C. Vice-Admiralty Mins., A–B (1730).

[87] Booker v. Grey, Mass. Vice-Admiralty Rec., Box I, 199 (1725). For deductions from wages for insubordination, see Hopkins v. Kirby, *Assistants,* I, 92, 93 (1677); Mackie v. Powell, Mass. Vice-Admiralty Rec., Box II, f. 129 (1732). Cf. also Constable v. Petel *et al., R.N.A.,* VI, 54 (1667). The master had the right to deduct costs of imprisonment for mutiny from wages. Astell's motion, Mass. Vice-Admiralty Rec., Box I, 1718–26 (1718).

share of prize money as well as for wages. In 1744 two seamen, John Austin and Henry Clark, libeled in the Rhode Island vice-admiralty court for their share of prize money resulting from the capture of a Spanish ship. Their captains refused to allow them shares on the ground that they had taken part in a mutiny, and that, according to articles of agreement among the captors, such conduct constituted forfeiture of their shares. The mutiny aboard the sloop *Prince Frederick* appears to have been started by the quartermaster, but the captain squelched it by distributing cutlasses to his loyal following. The mutineers were set ashore on an uninhabited spot known as Norman's Key. Judge Lockman, after reviewing a good many depositions, found that Clark had participated in the mutiny and upheld the forfeiture of his share; but cleared Austin of any complicity in the affair.[88]

Other grounds existed in maritime law for barring the seaman from the full recovery of his wages or for justifying legal deductions from the stipulated wage rate. By the laws of Oléron (§ 3) if the ship was lost, the mariner's right to wages was also lost.[89] The historical basis for the rule that "freight is the mother of wages" was the custom of seamen to take shares in the adventure and was justified in admiralty on the ground that laborers and servants did not have a fund "peculiarly appropriated for payment of wages."[90] Although by colonial times such risk sharing was pretty generally confined to fishing and whaling voyages and prize expeditions, the rule was retained when the practice became obsolete in order to induce men to do their best for the ship.[91] The approach was in sharp contrast to that of the common law regarding the responsibility of masters for the payment of wages contracted in ordinary trades on land. Where some of the freight had been salvaged

---

[88] Austin and Clark v. Dennis and Calder, Towle, *op. cit.*, pp. 250–259 (1744). Cf. articles agreed upon between Captain Abijah Boder, commander of the privateer sloop *Rover*, and his company, according to which the ring-leader in any mutiny or disobedient action was to forfeit one half of his share of the prize money. *Essex Inst. Hist. Coll.*, LXXV (1939), 15 (1776). Later courts were reluctant to declare insubordinate acts to be in effect mutiny, leading to wage forfeiture. Broils, assaults upon or resistance to masters were regarded as "merely the intemperate effects of personal animosities." Thorne v. White, Peters, p. 168 at pp. 170, 171 (1806).

[89] This rule was accepted in the common law (Molloy, *De jur. mar.*, Bk. II, c. 3 § 7), and was in effect in English admiralty law at the time of the passage of the Merchant Shipping Act of 1854. 17, 18 Vict. c. 104 § 183. See Holdsworth, *H.E.L.*, VIII, 253, 254. However the rule no longer prevails in the United States as a result of Federal statutes. U.S. Rev. Stats. § 4525; Benedict, *op. cit.*, I, 714.

[90] See Howland v. brig *Lavinia*, Peters, p. 123 at p. 125 (1801). See also Hart v. ship *Littlejohn*, *ibid.*, pp. 115, 121 (1800).

[91] Jonson v. Bannister, *Sel. Pleas of the Admiralty* (S.S.), II, 25 (1550). This rule applied to a loss through "mysadventure of the seas or tempest." Where the voyage was abandoned, half wages were due. Tye v. Springham, *ibid.*, II, 122–123 (1561); Thornton v. the *Elizabeth Bonaventure* and Jobson, *ibid.*, II, 131–132 (1565).

through the subsequent efforts of the crew, the courts allowed wages out of such of the ship and cargo as had been saved.[92] Since, by the custom of merchants, freight was due at every port where an outward cargo was delivered in safety, every such port was, as regards claims of seamen, deemed a port of delivery and wages to that time were earned.[93]

Deductible from wages due were freight charges over and above the amount customarily allowed mariners of specified ranks.[94] According to the "ancient Marine Laws and the present Usuage," the Massachusetts court allowed deductions from wages for the master's advances in money, clothes, and stores.[95]

The master might also legally deduct doctor's fees, medicines, and other items advanced for the seaman on account of illness and at his request.[96] According to law all seamen were required to pay a small sum known as hospital money for the maintenance of the seaman's hospital at Greenwich. This sum was legally deductible from wages.[97] Where the seaman's illness was attributed by the court to his "Sin and Folly" or where he had by his own actions disabled himself from performing his contract, deductions were made for the period of the illness.[98] Otherwise wages were not deductible for illness contracted in the performance of duty.[99]

The owners of a ship had the right to deduct from wages such

[92] See petition of sailors, *Exec. J., Va.,* II, 267, 268 (1702); Taylor *et al.* v. Goods saved from the *Cato,* Peters, p. 48 at p. 58 (1806).

[93] Luke v. Lyde, 2 Burr. 882; 1 Black. 190. See the interesting opinion of Judge Winchester in Peters, pp. 186–196n; also Giles *et al.* v. brig *Cynthia, ibid.,* pp. 203–209 (1801). Even where the merchant had recovered insurance on the freight, wages were denied by the court. McQuirk v. ship *Penelope, ibid.,* p. 276 (1806).

[94] Yeoman v. *Charming Molly,* Towle, *op. cit.,* p. 557 (1752).

[95] Collins v. Lillie, Mass. Vice-Admiralty Rec., Box I, f. 110 (1722).

[96] Trapier v. Banister, Towle, *op. cit.,* p. 500 (1749); Folger v. brigantine *Swansey, ibid.,* pp. 513, 514 (1749). See also Clarke v. Ashby, *Essex,* VIII, 254 (1679); *Conn. Pub. Rec.,* VI, 135, 136.

[97] Caswell v. brigantine *Swansey,* Towle, *op. cit.,* p. 516 (1749); Martin v. ship *Aurora,* N.Y. Vice-Admiralty Mins., I, 1715–46, f. 135 (1742); Fishley *et al.* v. brigantine *Milborough, ibid.,* fols. 142, 143, 151 (1743). The original act passed in 1696 imposing a tax of 6*d.* per month to be deducted from the seaman's wages was extended by subsequent legislation. In 1729 the tax was extended to vessels belonging to subjects living in the Channel Islands, the Isle of Man, and America, and in 1761 this was made perpetual. *Stat. at Large, 1 Jas. 1–10 Wm. III,* III, c. xxi, 608; *1 Geo. 1–3 Geo. II,* V, c. vii, 676; *30 Geo. II–2 Geo. III,* VIII, c. xxxi, 662–663. Instructions were sent to the governors of the plantations to assist the receivers in collecting this money. *N.J. Col. Docs.,* V, 144 (1729). See also *J. Commrs. Trade and Plantations, 1728/9–34,* pp. 67, 76, 83 (1729), 121 (1730).

[98] Camel v. Turner, Mass. Vice-Admiralty Rec., Box III, f. 6 (1740).

[99] If the sailor died on the voyage, his heirs were to have full wages. Hart v. ship *Littlejohn,* Peters, p. 115 at pp. 118, 119, 123 (1800). Cf. Tindell v. Moynes, where the seaman had come aboard sick and continued sick most of the time. Rec. of Wills, lib. XIXB, f. 336 (1680), Surrogate, N.Y. Co.

damages as were attributable to the barratry of master or mariners.[100] By barratry the courts meant an act committed for some unlawful or fraudulent purpose,[101] not mere negligence, although gross negligence might be evidence of such intention. In the libel brought by William Skinner for wages in 1751, respondent, John Banister, pleaded that the libelant had neglected his duty by failing to save as much goods as possible from a vessel shipwrecked off Long Island, and, on the contrary, had converted some Irish linen to his own use. Judge Wickham entered the decree for the libelant for his wages less the value of the goods he had converted.[102] When, in 1752, mariner Samuel Powers libeled the ship *Providence* for wages, evidence was introduced by the owners that the libelant had, with seven others, consumed the contents of four quarter casks of wine while the vessel was in the bay of Honduras. The court deducted from his claim for wages one eighth of the value of the wine.[103] The Massachusetts court in 1722 deducted from mariner's wages "the Proportion of Damages Sustained by" neglect of the mariners, probably, although the facts are not clear, because of the crew's gross negligence.[104] Where the barratry was not wholly chargeable to the libelant but apparently was participated in by the whole crew, the Massachusetts court in 1718 held that the damages "ought to be made up by contribution and Average common." The shortage was accordingly made up by proportionate deductions from the wages of the crew and the master was permitted to withhold the cook's entire wages, as it appeared that he had carried away the goods.[105]

Deductions from the rate of wages specified in the ship's articles were also permitted where it could be shown that the mariner was incompetent. Seamen who were capable before the mast often proved grossly incompetent on the quarter-deck; and such litigation generally involved officers or those shipping for specialized duties. Generally the incompetent mariner would be reduced to the grade for which he was fitted and paid wages accordingly; but occasionally an additional sum was deducted for the mariner's deception and the consequent damage to the owner.[106] In 1719 the Massachusetts court found that the libelant had signed on shipboard as a splitter but proved unqualified and there-

[100] Molloy, *De jur. mar.*, Bk. II, c. 3, § 9.
[101] Marcardier v. Chesapeake Ins. Co., 8 Cranch 39 (1814).
[102] Skinner v. Banister, Towle, *op. cit.*, p. 533 (1751). Cf. Jones v. Barnerd, *Essex*, II, 391 (1662).
[103] Powers v. *Providence*, Towle, *op. cit.*, p. 547 (1752). Cf. also *Md. Arch.*, X, 350 (1654).
[104] Collins v. Lillie, Mass. Vice-Admiralty Rec., Box I, 110 (1722).
[105] Dudley v. Gates, Mass. Vice-Admiralty Rec., Box I, 1718–25 (1718).
[106] Lindsay, *op. cit.*, II, 527.

fore was set to work as a sailor. The court allowed the defendant to retain one half the amount of wages due for his services as a sailor.[107]

The fortunes of the sea provided a number of situations where, despite
the owner's losses, the mariners' wages were held not deductible. Where
a ship was seized for debt, the mariner received his wages nonetheless.[108]
He was considered a privileged creditor, and his wages were preferred
to all other claims on the theory that it was through the labors of the
crew "that the common pledge of all these debts has been preserved and
brought to a place of safety." [109] The mariner's wages were held to rank
a bottomry bond executed for the necessities of that very voyage.[110]

A moot question in colonial vice-admiralty law was the status of seamen's wage claims where the ship had been seized for violation of the
Acts of Trade. In the old maritime law such a forfeiture "disables not
the Mariner of his Wages, for the Mariners having honestly perform'd
their Parts, the Ship is tacitly obliged for their Wages." [111] The New
York court in 1711 took under advisement the question whether a libel
for mariner's wages could be filed after condemnation of a pink for a
revenue violation, but we do not have the record of its decision.[112] In
a Philadelphia libel brought in 1735 against the brigantine *John* for
wages, the defendants, according to Judge Read, pleaded "no Custom
or Usage . . . to shew that it was in my power legally and equitably
to dismiss the said Libel, and leave the said Mariners to recover the
Wages due to them, for the Service done on board the said Brigantine,
from the Owner or Master." Only one argument appeared to him
"plausible," and that was

That if the Sailors were allowed to take the method these have done, it might
encourage ill designing owners and Merchants to bring in considerable quantities of prohibited or contraband Goods in rotten or unsound Vessels, and
when they had clandestinely put on Shore what they saw fit, leave just as much
on board as might subject the Ship to be seized and forfeited, and then in order
to defraud his Majesty and others concerned, of the benefit of the forfeiture,
get the Mariners to Libel the Ship for their Wages.

[107] The rate was £3 a month and allowance. Slaughter v. Cunningham, Mass. Vice-Admiralty
Rec., Box I, 1718–26 (1719). See also Mitchell v. the ship *Orozimbo*, Peters, pp. 250–252 (1806),
where the court found that the master was acquainted with the qualifications of the mate and
that no deception had been exercised. Hence, wages were awarded.

[108] Molloy, *De jur. mar.*, Bk. II, c. 3, § 7; Bell v. Byrde, *Sel. Pleas of the Admiralty* (S.S.), II,
84 (1553).

[109] See the *Paragon*, 1 Ware 326.

[110] However, salvage ranked seamen's wages incurred prior to the salvage services. See *Fort
Wayne*, 1 Bond 476; Hughes, *op. cit.*, p. 380.

[111] Molloy, *De jur. mar.*, Bk. II, c. 3, § 7.

[112] Harison *qui tam.* v. pink *Good Intent* and European goods, Hough, *op. cit.*, pp. 4, 5
(1716–17).

In the case of such a manifest fraud, Read pledged that the malefactors would not go unpunished. However, the case at hand appeared to him "in a very different Light." The owner enjoyed the reputation of "fair Trader," and seems to have been ignorant of the illegal acts his master had committed. Furthermore, the judge declared, it was customary for the "Judges of the Courts of Vice Admiralty in the neighbouring Provinces to, without any Motion made for that purpose, insert a Saving Clause for Mariners Wages in their Decrees." Such a practice was justified on the ground that it was "unequitable that innocent Mariners be deprived of any one Means the Law entitles them to for the recovery of what they earned. . . . I think a Mariner after he has honestly done his Duty, ought not to be set a scrambling or worse for his Reward." He therefore ruled that the collector should have paid the wages when he seized the ship, that such wages should come out of the sale, with costs paid to the mariners, as in this case costs had cut the wages nearly in half.[113]

There was no doubt whatsoever as to the fate of wage claims of mariners engaged in trading with the enemy. That they were clearly not entitled to wages is borne out by the libel brought in the Rhode Island court in 1747 against the brigantine *Victory,* seized as a prize for trading with the French. The vessel was brought to Boston and acquitted in the vice-admiralty court of that port. The captor then appealed to the Lords Commissioners of Appeals in causes of prize. The appeal pending, the vice-admiralty at Newport entered an interlocutory decree, directing the owner to pay the wages due the libelants, but requiring the latter to post a bond to restore sums paid as wages in the event that the Lords Commissioners finally condemned the vessel. The court thus recognized that seamen on a vessel found to have been trading with the enemy were considered guilty of a criminal offense, and therefore could not demand compensation for work aboard such ship.[114]

In maritime law where a seaman was carried off by a pirate as a hostage for the release of the ship and crew, his wages and ransom had to be paid. There was considerable difference of opinion, however, among jurists

[113] Peel *et al.* v. brigantine *John*, Philadelphia Vice-Admiralty Rec., I, 1735–47, fols. 16–19 (1735). See also Andrews in Towle, *op. cit.,* pp. 26, 27n. In support of his contention that mariners were likely to lose their wages where the ship was forfeited, Professor L. A. Harper cites a Virginia case, *The Catherine*, C.O. 5:1405, pp. 753–754; *CSPA, 1689–92*, No. 2388. The Council of Virginia in this case stated that "noe wages [were] to be paid them by TM Govt. or Informer."

[114] Thurston *et al.* v. brigantine *Victory*, Towle, *op. cit.,* pp. 418–420 (1747). But see Bordman *et al.* v. brig *Elizabeth*, Peters, p. 128 at p. 130 (1798), in which the court ruled that, where a vessel is condemned in the lower court of admiralty and an appeal is entered, the claim for wages must be suspended until the appeal is known.

as to the seaman's right to wages where he was forcibly and unconditionally seized.[115] Charles M. Andrews reports the libel in 1720 in the vice-admiralty court at Barbados of the crew of the *Callahan* galley. The master pleaded that the crew had been hired for the triangular voyage to Guinea for slaves, thence to Carolina, and thence to London, but that the ship was captured before completing the first leg of the voyage. The pirates gave them a brigantine in exchange for the galley, and they were able to save a considerable part of the cargo which they exchanged on the African coast for one hundred and ten slaves. These they sold at Barbados. The master contended that the voyage had not been completed, but the court, in view of the circumstances, ordered that the men be paid in proportion to their merits, those who had been drunk and did not work to be docked accordingly.[116]

Where ship and crew were captured by a privateer, the mariner was entitled to his wages performed on board up to the time of the return of the ship to her owners without deduction either for the period during which she was in the privateer's possession or for the subsequent period when she was held by captors retaking her.[117] While the law was sympathetic to seamen seized by pirates or privateers, it did not look with favor upon the claims for wages against ships or owners brought by seamen who were impressed.[118]

Grounds for Discharge or Relief on the Part of the Mariner. While upholding the traditional discipline of the quarter-deck, vice-admiralty managed to maintain the principle that seamen were entitled to special protection in somewhat the same sense as minors, and were truly the "wards of admiralty." The following were some of the principal grounds for discharge or relief on the part of the mariner: 1) immoderate cor-

[115] Peters, p. 133n.
[116] Andrews in Towle, *op. cit.,* p. 28, citing Rawlinson MSS, A, 289, fols. 264–269, Bodleian.
[117] Brown v. snow, *Diligence,* Towle, *op. cit.,* pp. 508–510 (1749). In this case the owners claimed that, as one-half salvage had been paid to the captors, they should be held liable for only one half of libelant's wages after restoration of the vessel to the owners, and for no wages during the time of detention by the enemy captor. As regards the latter contention, the court held that it seemed "to carry Some Show of Reason," yet could find no law or precedent to support it. The Continental Congress, by a resolution of March 23, 1776, made provision for paying such captured seamen out of the prize money. Cf. also *N.H. Acts and Laws,* IV, 32, 84, 113 (1776–77), later repealed on the ground that the safeguarding of wages of mariners aboard prize ships might "have a Tendency to discourage the fitting out of Armed Vessels for the purposes" of the act. As regards a mariner of a neutral vessel carried off by captors, admiralty law provided that, on the arrest of the ship for adjudication, he shared the ship's fate. If ship and cargo were discharged by the court of the captor, he saved his wages. Watson v. brig *Rose,* Peters, p. 132 at p. 133 (1806); Singstrom *et al.* v. schooner *Hazard, ibid.,* p. 384 (1807). See also Hart v. ship *Littlejohn, ibid.,* p. 115 (1800).
[118] Watson v. brig *Rose, ibid.,* p. 132 at p. 134 (1806).

rection; 2) improper food; 3) illness; 4) unsafe condition of the ship; 5) deviation from a stipulated course; 6) wrongful dismissal.

The master's right to administer corporal punishment was subject to the restriction that the punishment be moderate. The courts were vigilant in seeing that excesses did not go unpunished. The judicial records are replete with instances where the court granted seamen relief from cruel and inhuman treatment. Generally, on proof of such misconduct, the seamen were discharged by the court and awarded their wages, but they also had their right to seek damages at common law.[119] In addition, the master was subject to criminal prosecution for such gross misconduct. Numerous instances of judicial intervention will be cited in examining the discipline enforced at sea.[120]

In addition to abuses of discipline for which the mariner might prosecute the ship's captain and seek his discharge, there were a number of other grounds for discharge or relief. First in order of such complaints were those charging bad food and unfit living conditions aboard ship. The long continuance of a salt-pork diet and the corresponding lack of fresh provisions led to scurvy, the peculiar curse of seamen.[121] It is perhaps significant that complaints on the score of food seem to have occurred most frequently when the master of a vessel was also a part owner.[122] In view of the fact that a sizable proportion of masters of colonial vessels were part owners,[123] it is unlikely that food on colonial ships could have been better than the prevailing fare on the British marine. Living conditions were generally poor; the forecastle was small, ill-ventilated, dirty, and likely to be vermin-infested. An officer of the Guards summed up life aboard the transports which brought British troops to America during the Revolution in these words: "There was constant destruction in the foretops, the pox above-board, the plague

[119] Andrews in Towle, *op. cit.,* p. 68.   [120] See *infra,* pp. 262–268.

[121] While it was to be many long years before mariners as well as landsmen were to be versed in the properties of vitamin C, a good deal of empirical knowledge of antidotes for scurvy was put to common use in the British merchant marine and among the naval and military forces. Lime or lemon juice was in particular favor, but hemlock, spruce, sauerkraut, malt, and vinegar were also used as antiscorbutics. E. C. Curtis, *The Organization of the British Army in the American Revolution* (New Haven, 1926), pp. 88, 89. "Limeys," a term synonymous with British tars, stems from a British Admiralty ruling in 1795 that an ounce of lime juice be a daily part of seamen's rations. See also Ames, *Almanack,* 1759, in Briggs, *op. cit.,* p. 300; R. H. Shryock, *The Development of Modern Medicine* (Philadelphia, 1936), pp. 73, 74, 301. In the rules for the regulation of the Continental navy as laid down by Congress, daily menus were specified for the crews, providing in substance for rations of bread, beef or pork, potatoes, turnips, or peas, or, instead, cheese and rice, and an occasional pudding. Allen, *op. cit.,* pp. 690, 694.

[122] For later corroboration, see Charles Wilkes, *Narratives of the United States Exploring Expedition during the Years 1838–42* (6 vols., Philadelphia, 1845), V, ch. xii; Hohman, *op. cit.,* p. 130.

[123] See *supra,* pp. 244, 245.

between decks, hell in the forecastle, the devil at the helm." [124] Hospital facilities in colonial ports were generally completely inadequate and crews were often decimated by serious epidemics.[125] While the colonial vice-admiralty courts were reluctant to grant seamen their discharge because of bad provisions [126] and to award damages against the master, they would on occasion set certain minimum standards as regards food supplies,[127] and award seamen their wages when their desertion had been caused by inadequate provisions.[128]

Liquor was generally considered a regular part of the mariner's provisions. The New England sea chantey went:

> I thought I heard the old man say,
> Whisky Johnnie,
> I'll treat my crew in a decent way,
> Whisky for my Johnnie.

A fishing journey would have been dismal indeed without its quota of rum. Rum was a basic provision for the seamen of the Royal Navy during the American Revolution, although wine was preferred by the authorities.[129] In the Continental navy during the Revolution a half pint of rum was the daily allowance, with an additional amount permitted "on extra duty and in time of engagement." [130] Experience aboard naval vessels during that conflict showed that "seamen are creatures that must have it" and were "much Dissatisfied" when it was not served.[131]

Early maritime law recognized the mariner's right to maintenance

[124] Henry Belcher, *The First American Civil War* (2 vols., London, 1911), I, 255.

[125] Bad provisions account for the loss of a shocking proportion of the crew under Commodore William Kerr in the West Indies in 1707. During Queen Anne's War troops left on transports in the West Indies in the hot season died like flies. Bourne, *op. cit.*, pp. 88, 89, 94, 95, 196. It has been estimated that, in the period 1774 to 1780, 18,000 men in the British navy died of disease as a result of bad medical attention and improper food. Allen, *op. cit.*, I, 56.

[126] For example, in Sailors v. Vincent, Mass. Vice-Admiralty Rec., Box I, f. 46 (1719), Menzies dismissed the libel, held the sailors accountable for costs which the master could deduct from their wages, and remanded them back to prison, where they had been committed by virtue of a warrant from a justice of the peace. In Patridge v. Bennett, *ibid.*, f. 59 (1720), the court granted the wages sued for, but as regards the libel for discharge "for being pinched in his Provisions," ordered the mariner to proceed on his voyage in accord with a new agreement made with the master. But cf. Gray v. Travisa, *ibid.*, II, f. 56 (1728), where libelant was given the wages due him and was discharged.

[127] Sailors v. Cumberland, *ibid.*, I, 1718–26 (1718).

[128] Ship *Ann of New Castle*, Md. *Arch.*, VIII, 445 (1692). See also Swift v. *The Happy Return*, 1 Peters 253 (1799).

[129] "Letter-Book of Admiral Lord Rodney," *loc. cit.*, pp. 154–155, 342, 651. In one case a physician and three surgeons were asked to "taste the wretched mixture issued as Wine," and unanimously reported, the captains concurring, "that it is by no means fit for Men to drink." *Ibid.*, p. 439 (1782). On postwar American ships domestic whisky supplanted West India rum.

[130] Allen, *op. cit.*, II, 694.   [131] *Cal. Va. State Papers*, I, 572, 573 (1781).

and cure when he contracted illness on the voyage.[132] In modern law the disabled seaman has a right to maintenance and cure whether the injury was occasioned by negligence, his own or another's, or by simple accident.[133] Under an act of 1696 the Royal Hospital at Greenwich, for the support of which monthly deductions were made from seaman's wages, provided for seamen disabled by virtue of age, wounds, or accident, and extended the relief to their widows and children. This system was maintained by some of the American states, notably Virginia [134] and North Carolina [135] during and after the American Revolution. In 1798 Congress adopted what was virtually compulsory sickness insurance for seamen.[136] Provision was made for the collection of a direct tax and the establishment of hospitals and other agencies for the care of sick mariners.[137] During the period of the Intercolonial Wars and the Revolution contracts were not infrequently entered into which protected the seaman's right to a share in the prize where he had been injured in an engagement of his privateer.[138]

Where the ship had become unsafe to continue on her voyage, seamen were entitled to apply to the vice-admiralty court for a discharge,[139] and their refusal to proceed on the voyage until repairs were made would not constitute desertion. In 1724 the crew of the ship *Granvill* complained to the Boston vice-admiralty court that their ship had sprung a leak and was not safe to proceed on the voyage. The court sustained their contention, ordered the master to repair the ship, and ruled that, until such repairs were made, there was no breach of petitioners' engagement in their refusal to go to sea. On the other hand, the court required them to continue in the service, and ordered the master to maintain them and allow them their wages while the ship was being

[132] Oléronic code, art. vii; also Swift v. *The Happy Return*, 1 Peters 253 (1799).

[133] The *Osceola*, 189 U.S. 158 (1903). Both vessel and owner are liable in the sailor's action to recover such maintenance and cure. Benedict, *op. cit.*, I, 131. By the Seamen's Act of 1915, those in command of a vessel were not held to be fellow servantts with those serving under them who sustained injuries.

[134] Hening, X, 385; XI, 161; XII, 494–495.

[135] Haywood, *Manual of the Laws of North Carolina* (1801), p. 350; Iredell, *Laws of the State of North Carolina* (1791), p. 704.

[136] *U.S. Stat. at Large*, I, 605–606, c. lxxvii.

[137] For the administration and extension of this act, see Farnam, *op. cit.*, ch. xviii.

[138] Dillon v. Sears, Kempe C–F (1759); *Essex Instit. Hist. Coll.*, LXXV (1939), 15 (1776). The "extraordinary" share for being wounded, was, in accordance with the articles, to come from the prize money of the privateer's owners and company rather than from the captain's third. Holborne v. Reade; Same v. Axtell, N.Y. Vice-Admiralty Mins., II, 1746–57, fols. 224, 225 (1755).

[139] To be on the safe side, master and seamen might hasten to register their protest against their ship's condition at the first port at which they were forced to put in. See protest against the *Hopewell*, Plymouth Col. Rec., IV, 171 (1667).

repaired. If he failed to do so, the sailors were to be freed from their services and their past wages paid them.[140] A master brought a libel in the Charleston court in 1719 against the mate and six other mariners, asking that their wages be forfeited for desertion. He alleged that, during a hurricane, the mariners wanted to hoist a distress signal and did not wish to continue on the voyage because of leaks in the ship. On this point there are some fifty pages of depositions and interrogatories in the court minutes, but no record of a final decree. According to the gist of the evidence, the captain declared that he would shoot through the head the first man that would carry up the distress ensign. Thereupon the mate drew up a paper of protest which most of the mariners signed.[141] It may be worth noting here that under the White Act of 1898 the majority of a vessel's crew, exclusive of the officers, was given the power to compel a survey of any vessel believed to be unseaworthy.[142]

The ship's articles usually specified the course of the voyage, to alter which the crew's consent was necessary in maritime law.[143] It was not uncommon to have the agreement of the major part of the crew to such a deviation committed to writing.[144] Where there was a serious deviation without their consent the seamen were entitled to their discharge, but in practice the vice-admiralty courts were reluctant to enforce the letter of the law and did not construe shipping articles too strictly. However, gross and unnecessary deviation would be ground for freeing a mariner from his contract.[145] Where the crew divided on the question of agreeing to a deviation, the court might refuse to discharge one of the dissenters on the ground that it would be detrimental to trade in general as well as to the owner of the ship.[146]

Frequently seamen complained that they had been wrongfully dis-

140 The master was to pay costs. Sailors v. ship *Granvill*, Mass. Vice-Admiralty Rec., Box I, f. 185 (1724). See also Vans v. Stuart, *ibid.*, II, f. 35 (1727)—mariner freed.

141 Clipperton v. Key *et al.*, S.C. Vice-Admiralty Mins., A–B (1719).

142 See A. E. Albrecht, "International Seamen's Union of America: A Study of its History and Problems," U.S. Bureau of Labor Statistics, *Bull.*, No. 342, p. 33.

143 But see *contra*: Mass. Code of 1668, § 9.

144 See Fielding v. Cleavland, Mass. Vice-Admiralty Rec., Box II, f. 70 (1729).

145 Gibbs v. Hazelwood, R.N.A., VI, 371 (1672); Smith's case, Middlesex, N.J., Co. Court Mins., lib. I, f. 32 (1685); Dawson v. Legard, Mass. Vice-Admiralty Rec., Box I, f. 208 (1726); Moran v. Baudin, Peters, p. 415 at pp. 417, 418.

146 Fielding v. Cleavland, Mass. Vice-Admiralty Rec., Box II, f. 70 (1729). A subsequent agreement modifying the ship's articles as regards the course of the voyage would be carefully scrutinized by the authorities for evidence of coercion. One such complaint brought by a Portuguese seaman resulted in the captain and mate being ordered to appear before an alderman of New York City, who referred the issue to attorney-general Kempe for his opinion. Unfortunately it is not among his papers. Joseph's case, Kempe J–L (1765).

missed and claimed full wages for the voyage. A parliamentary act passed in 1710 provided that a master who forced seamen ashore, willfully abandoned them in any of the plantations, or refused to take them home when they were ready to proceed on the homeward voyage would be liable to suffer three months' imprisonment without bail or mainprize.[147] However, the courts in the colonies usually let the master go unpunished, merely requiring him to pay full wages or to continue the mariner in his service.[148] When some mariners libeled their master in 1721 in the Boston vice-admiralty court for their chests, clothes, and wages, and asked for a discharge, the court, on reviewing the evidence, found that they had not really been discharged, but that the master "in Passion" had ordered them "to be gone out of Town." As they were bound in writing, such removal on their part, according to the court, did not constitute a discharge. They were therefore ordered to return to their service, but the master was required to pay their wages "as tho no Such Mistake had happened." [149] In the suit of *Care v. Condy* in the same tribunal the vice-admiralty judge upheld the libelant's claim to wages and ruled that the master

could not legally dismiss the plaintiff for refuseing to accept the wages as offered at Leghorn, and that upon the plaintiff's offering to perform the Voyage hee ought to have been continued therein; and also find the Master turning him out of the Vessel without allowing him to take out his clothes or time to shift was unwarrantable.[150]

Similarly, where the seaman had been found by the court to have behaved well and to have discharged his duties properly, the court held his dismissal overseas to have been "wrong and unwarrantable" and contrary to the "Law marine" which "allows a Sailor (who has been left on Shoar or dismist without sufficient Cause) to follow the Ship." The court ordered the master to pay him his full wages and turn over to him his clothes.[151] Furthermore, even where the court conceded that

---

[147] Stat. 11–12 Gul. III, c. 7 § xviii. See also 4 Ann, c. 34; 1 Geo. I, c. 25; 9 Geo. I, c. 8; 6 Geo. I, c. 19.

[148] When the master was able to show that he had dismissed the mariner because of the latter's habit of getting drunk on shore leave, the burgomasters and schepens of New Amsterdam upheld the dismissal, but required that the mariner be paid his earned wages less three days' pay. Van Scherman v. Bestevaar, *R.N.A.*, III, 322 (1661). Similarly, see Dandy *et al.* v. Tudar, Mass. Vice-Admiralty Rec., Box I, 1718–26.

[149] Defendant was adjudged to pay costs. Levermore v. Stafford, Mass. Vice-Admiralty Rec., Box I, f. 99 (1721).

[150] Decree was entered for the remaining wages of £5 17s. 6d., and, in view of the fact that the libelant was idle at Leghorn before getting another passage to Boston, the master was sentenced to pay costs of £5 8s. 6d. Care v. Condy, Mass. Vice-Admiralty Rec., Box I, f. 132 (1723).

[151] Dennis v. Armstrong, *ibid.*, I, 190 (1725).

a mate "had not been exact in his business," Menzies held that his dismissal was unjustifiable on the ground that the alleged incompetence should have been "made appear before a Judge Competent before dismission which is not done." [152]

The New York vice-admiralty court held in 1750 that a seaman who engages for a voyage under a certain captain may leave the ship and collect wages to the date of his leaving if the owner discharges the captain without cause. Under such circumstances mariners were not bound to proceed on the voyage with the new master unless they had made a new agreement with him. As to whether the owner had the power to turn the master out and appoint another, the court sustained the owner's right to do so "if he thinks he does not do his Duty," but added that "it is Customary when a Master is shipped to perform a voyage, that he is seldom removed till the voyage be performed." [153]

Enforcement of the Contract. Seamen's contracts of employment were specifically enforced by the courts. Early Massachusetts law required fishermen shipping for the winter and spring "to attend," and those engaged for the whole summer "shall not presume to break off before the last of October without the consent of the Owner, Master, and Shoreman." [154] The New Haven town court committed a recalcitrant seaman to prison because "he was stubborne and gave vncomely answers and would not promise to goe the voyage and doe his service." [155]

THE DISCIPLINE OF THE SEA

The Master's Right of Correction aboard Ship. The master, by a venerable tradition of the sea, was authorized to administer to his crew "moderate and due Correction." [1] This disciplinary authority was up-

---

[152] Winde v. Ward, *ibid.*, I, 190 (1725).

[153] Flood v. snow *Hector*, Hough, *op. cit.*, p. 71; N.Y. Vice-Admiralty Mins., II, 1746–57, fols. 173, 174 (1750).

[154] Mass. Arch., lib. LX, f. 184.

[155] Fenn v. Edward, *New Haven Town Rec.*, I, 84, 85 (1651); similarly Hutson v. Gysbert, *R.N.A.*, VI, 211 (1663); but *contra* in Weit v. Pieckehingh, *ibid.*, III, 220 (1660), where defendant had previously been given a lawful discharge. For other cases of specific enforcement by the common law courts of the mariner's contract of service, see, e.g., Emory v. Jackson, Elizabeth City, Va., O.B., 1684–99, f. 121 (1697); Trotter v. Smith, Chowan Precinct Court files, Edenton Court House (n.d.). For instances in Vice-Admiralty, see, e.g., McNamara v. Sailors, Mass. Vice-Admiralty Rec., Box I, f. 145 (1723); Childerstone v. Call, *ibid.*, Box II, f. 22 (1727).

[1] Molloy, *De jur. mar.*, Bk. II, ch. iii, § 12. The limits to such correction were indicated by Judge Peters in an opinion in which he paid tribute to the medieval maritime codes: "When the crime of a sailor is too great for the master's authority to punish (which should be evident on the trial, to justify severe measures) the master and his officers are to seize the criminal, put him in irons, and not take the law into their own hands, but bring him to justice on their return." Thorne v. White, Peters, pp. 168 *et seq.* at pp. 172, 173 (1806). See also Sampson v. Smith, 15 Mass. 365 (1819); Brown v. Howard, 14 Johns. (N.Y.) 119 (1817).

held by colonial courts. In fact, under certain circumstances the colonial vice-admiralty might choose to emphasize the reasonableness of the punishment rather than its moderation. In 1750 a seaman named Mc-Farlin libeled the master of the snow *Doddington* for assault on the high seas. The court found that, after the capture of the *Doddington* by the French, she was turned over to the defendant master. The depositions agreed that there was a plot on the part of Read and Dickey, two of the mariners on board the snow, to murder the defendant, throw him overboard, and then proceed to the gold coast with the ship. By his subsequent conduct the libelant, so the court held,

was Concerned with these mutiniers (or Pyrates more properly) for they ran away together in the Snows boat, and Read and Dickey endeavoured to rob the tent on Shoar, and Seize the Peoples arms; and by the Depositions it appears the Deserters sent on Board a message to the Defendant to come on Shoar, and they would beat him, Nay cut him into pound pieces.

The defendant pursued them with the assistance of some officers belonging to a Boston ship then at the Isle of May. The libelant was taken, brought on board, and punished. According to the court,

the Punishment was far from being either Cruel or Inhumane; it is proved the Defendant fired a Pistol at the Lybellant and like to have killed him; as to that, I think the Case was Justifiable, if he had shot all these, who had formed a Design to kill him, and only wanted an Opportunity to put in execution; and that from the first Law of Nature which is self preservation.[2]

The most frequently administered form of correction aboard ship was flogging. It was traditional in the British navy.[3] As many as a thousand lashes were administered for insubordination.[4] The vice-admiralty courts also upheld the master's right to flog disobedient merchant seamen. Indeed, short-tempered captains had quick recourse to flogging even for relatively minor lapses on a seaman's part. In 1727 a mariner brought suit against his captain in the Massachusetts vice-admiralty for

---

[2] McFarlin v. White, Hough, *op cit.*, pp. 25–27; N.Y. Vice-Admiralty Mins., II, 1746–57, fols. 159, 160 (1746–50).

[3] The practice of flogging seamen in the Royal Navy was brought out in the investigation in 1704 of Admiral Graydon's conduct. He went so far as to have masters of merchant ships in his convoy beaten and laid in irons. See Stock, *Proc. Brit. Parl.*, III, iv, v, 50n., 55–57, 59.

[4] On occasion disorderly sailors were severely flogged during the American Revolution. For mutiny and disobedience Nicholas Burn, boatswain's mate, and George McNeil, seaman, were sentenced by a court martial to receive respectively 500 and 300 lashes on their bare backs with a cat of nine tails, alongside their ship. Orders were given to start the flogging with ten lashes alongside the ten ships nearest their own. Sentences of one hundred and two hundred lashes were more in the normal course of events. *Letter-Book of Admiral Lord Rodney*, pp. 836, 837 (1782); also pp. 144, 647, 648. See also G. R. Scott, *The History of Corporal Punishment* (London, 1938), pp. 92, 93. For the British army, see "The Kemble Papers," N.Y. Hist. Soc., *Coll., 1883* (New York, 1884), p. 289.

damages for assault, alleging that the captain had beaten him on the back with a rope an inch and a half in thickness. The court found that the captain "had Lawful provocation to Correct the Complainant and had not Exceeded the bounds of Humanity." Apparently he had taken these measures in order to discourage the use of profanity on the voyage.[5] It would be interesting to learn whether or not he was successful, for profanity was an integral part of the routine of the forecastle,[6] though doubtless illustrations of choicer forms could be overheard on the quarter-deck. During the Revolution the Continental navy limited the amount of corporal punishment to be administered by a commander to twelve lashes. Only a court martial could authorize a greater penalty.[7] This set a precedent for later Federal legislation.[8]

Lawful correction, as the McFarlin case indicated, included, in addition to flogging, other kinds of punishment, most favored being the confinement of an insubordinate mariner aboard ship. The vice-admiralty court of New York in 1754 upheld the legality of the confinement by the captain of a ship's officer who had unreasonably chastized a number of mariners.[9]

In addition to the master's right to administer moderate correction to an incorrigible seaman, confine him in the brig, or dock him of provisions, he was also empowered to discharge him, although this right was severely restricted in the Oléronic code, which provided (art. xiv) that upon the submission of an incorrigible mariner his service must be accepted.[10]

Under admiralty law seamen were not permitted to interfere when

[5] Broughton v. Atkins, Mass. Vice-Admiralty Rec., Box II, f. 25 (1727). See also Hall, *op. cit.*, pp. 207–210, for an answer to a libel for assault and battery (1801), in which the respondent alleged that the libelant had refused to do as he was told during a storm and therefore the respondent struck him to insure the performance of his duty and for the safety of the vessel.

[6] See, e.g., Kenard *et al.* v. Dring, *Essex*, IV, 33 (1668), where the seamen were subjected to profanity and constant threats.

[7] Allen, *op. cit.*, II, 687. For sentences in the Continental army, see H. Whiting, ed., *Revolutionary Orders of General Washington, 1778–82* (New York, 1844), p. 64; *Pa. Arch.*, 6th ser., XIV, 92; W. C. Ford, ed., *General Orders Issued by Major-General William Heath* (Brooklyn, 1890), pp. 12, 22, 56, 108.

[8] The act of March 3, 1835, § 3, provided a fine of not more than $1,000 or imprisonment for five years, or both, for maltreatment of the crew by officers of vessels. These penalties were continued in the acts of March 3, 1897, § 18, and of March 4, 1909, § 291. As to the difficulties involved in successfully prosecuting an officer and the widespread disregard of the enactments, see Hohman, *op. cit.*, pp. 76 *et seq.* Flogging was abolished by act of Congress in 1850; but in Marion v. Moody, tried in the court of common pleas at Boston in June, 1854, the court, in a questionable interpretation of this act, stated that it did not prohibit the use of force in any form as a means of coercion and authorized chastisement intended to induce a return to duty.

[9] White v. Hall, Hough, *op. cit.*, pp. 80, 81 (1754). For the view that a confinement in irons of two disobedient seamen was justifiable and necessary and that wages be deducted from that part of the voyage during which they were confined, see Peters, p. 173n.

[10] Cf. Thorne v. White, Peters, p. 68 at p. 175 (1806).

ships' officers confined or otherwise punished one of the crew for dis-orderly conduct. Actually they were bound to assist the master "to constrain, imprison, and bring to justice, any disobedient, mutinous and rebellious mariner." [11] At times colonial seamen upheld their master in disciplining one of their number, particularly when it was to their advantage. In a dispute over the ownership of certain articles left aboard the privateer *Prince Frederick* by a mariner who had deserted, depositions relate that "the People said you dont know Which is yr own, and you shall have none and for that was whipt, by A Vote of the whole Company." [12]

In addition to physical correction, docking of provisions, and the threat of discharge, masters frequently drove their crews to the limit of endurance by bullying, profane threats, and the unsavory practice of hazing or "working up," which consisted of assigning dirty, disagree-able, and dangerous tasks to a particular seaman, too often as a means of settling personal grudges. Despite well-known abuses of the disciplinary authority, it must be admitted that strict discipline was imperative to assure the safety and success of the voyage. The population of the forecastle often comprised criminal and degenerate elements, un-willing impressed hands, and men who recognized no authority other than force. [13] The morals of colonial seamen were doubtless no higher than later generations. Not alone were they lacking in *"Serious Piety,"* according to Cotton Mather, but on their return from the voyage they would rush to the harlot and the bottle. [14]

[11] Relf *et al.* v. the ship *Maria, ibid.,* p. 188 at p. 192 (1805).

[12] Austin v. Calder, Towle, *op. cit.,* p. 250 at p. 252 (1744). However, the practice of whipping seamen on board this very same ship led to a mutiny, as a result of which the quartermaster and several followers were set ashore on an uninhabited West Indian key.

[13] Hohman, *op. cit.,* pp. 14, 59.

[14] See C. Mather, *The Sailours Companion and Counsellour* (Boston, 1709); W. M. Davis, *Nimrod of the Sea, or, The American Whaleman* (New York, 1874), p. 92. A typical illustration of the roustabout character of crews in the late eighteenth century is taken from the "Transactions on Board the Brig *Betsy*," on a coastal voyage in the winter of 1796–97:

"This day thick weather and fine snow. Now laying in Tarpaulin Cove waiting for a fair wind. At 6 o'clock this afternoon Mr. Harris came aboard to Pilot the brig to New London. All hans gone ashore today. No work dun aboard. At 5 o'clock this afternoon they came aboard all drunk and got a fiting with clubs and A hammer. And bruise themselves varry bad. The pilot wanted to heve up the Anchor but we could not get no work out of them. . . . December 7th 1796. Last night all hands left the brig without aney live. And went with Number more ships chru [crew] to A hore Hous Pon the hill. And at 10 o'clock begun to fit with some Frenshman. And the Marakin sailors had nothing to fit with and the Frenshman had sords and pistols and they killed on Marakin and wounded 2. And the Marakins most killed on Frenshman and wounded 3. And this morning 6 frenshman taken up and put into jail and this day fine plesen weather."

For the discipline inflicted in a rough-and-tumble voyage on the ship *Providence* around the Cape of Good Hope to Batavia, Canton, Hong Kong, and Manila, 1838–40, see J. W. Snyder, "Discipline at Sea 100 Years Ago," *Fair Winds,* I, no. 3 (1939).

While the colonial courts recognized the disciplinary authority of the master at sea, they were vigilant in restraining immoderate correction and cruelty. Just what constituted unlawful conduct toward the crew on the master's part may be ascertained by reviewing the decisions both of common-law tribunals and of vice-admiralty courts on this point.

In the first place, excessive corporal punishment was unlawful. The classic case is that of Captain Kidd, a New York settler, who was seized in Massachusetts and sent to England, where he was tried and condemned at the Old Bailey for the murder of an insubordinate gunner as well as for piracy, and was hanged at Execution Dock in 1701. A ballad which had wide currency in the colonies faithfully follows the evidence at the trial:

> Because a word he spoke,
> I with a bucket broke
> His scull at one sad stroke,
> While I sail'd.[15]

Menzies fined one captain who had beaten a mariner "to the Effusion of his blood and with such Weapons no ways warrantable by Law to Correct a Common Sailor."[16] Even where the seaman had given the captain the lie, the captain was not justified, according to the court, in administering "so Extraordinary a Punishment," involving the drawing of blood.[17] In other cases the court freed the libelant and awarded him his wages.[18] The Massachusetts Court of Assistants freed a ship's chirurgeon in 1680 because he had been whipped by his master "for no other reason but because he would not do the office of a cooke not being bound thereto."[19] The Maryland vice-admiralty declared in

---

[15] The more popular version of the ballad, included in the collections of John and Alan Lomax, Eloise H. Linscott, and Olin Downes and Elie Siegmeister, differs somewhat:
"I murdered William Moore, and left him in his gore,
Not many leagues from shore, as I sailed, as I sailed."
The notoriously unfair trial is printed in *The Trial of Captain Kidd*, ed. Graham Brooks (Edinburgh, 1930); also in Jameson, *Privateering and Piracy*, pp. 190–257. Under Massachusetts law Kidd could not have been condemned to death for piracy. For a recent emphasis upon the murder conviction, see Morton Pennypacker, "Captain Kidd," *N.Y. Hist.* (Oct., 1944), pp. 482–531.

[16] In addition to a fine of £5 to the king, he was also sentenced to pay £10 damages to the injured mariner and costs exceeding £6. Hooper v. Harris, Mass. Vice-Admiralty Rec., Box I, fols. 197, 198 (1725). In Virginia the seaman's right of action against the master for immoderate correction was founded in statute, Hening, VI, 24–28 (1748); Starke, *Office of a Justice of the Peace*, p. 318.

[17] In this case while the master was fined, the seaman was referred to the common-law courts to recover damages. Fall v. Smith, *ibid.*, Box II, f. 62 (1729).

[18] Wills v. Legall, *ibid.*, fols. 29, 30 (1727); Woollinson v. Hooper, *ibid.*, f. 86 (1730).

[19] He was also awarded six weeks' wages and defendant was assessed costs. Kelso v. Branson,

1763 upon the occasion of releasing members of a crew from service on grounds of cruel and barbarous usage that "by the Marine and Civil Law and every other Law violent and Inhuman Treatment is a legal discharge of Whatever Covenants of time of Service Mariners or other set of Men may have entered into." [20] The courts pursued their own investigations when excessive punishments administered by captains on the high seas were suspected of having directly caused the seaman's death.[21]

The master had no legal right to administer corporal punishment to a sick mariner. While it was justifiable to put in irons a mutinous seaman who raved "like a Madman," the South Carolina court held that the immoderate correction to which he had been subjected was unlawful, as he was sick at the time.[22] Improper food was not alone a ground for discharge but also considered a form of unlawful discipline, subjecting the master responsible to a fine. Thus, one might discipline a quarrelsome and abusive seaman by confining him, but it was improper to limit his rations to bread and water.[23]

Assistants, I, 174 (1680). But cf. March *et al.* v. Kilner, where the master was merely reprimanded for striking both a seaman and a passenger. Pennypacker, *Pa. Col. Cases*, pp. 29 *et seq.* (1683).

[20] The commander was found to have beaten his crew black and blue with a "Reef tackle ball" on a rope two and a half inches thick. Edwards *et al.* v. snow *Hannah*, Maryland Vice-Admiralty Rec., 1754–73 (1763). Moderate correction, the courts later held, did not justify the use of such deadly weapons as a cutlass or a hot iron poker. Fleming v. Ball, 1 Bay (S.C.) 3 (1784); Jarvis v. *The Claiborne*, 3 Fed. Cas. No. 7225 (Bee 248) (U.S., 1808). See also Avery v. McGillicuddy, Kempe A–B (1761), a suit for assault and battery in which an officer aboard a privateersman accused the captain of beating and kicking him and rupturing his abdomen. Defendant was held by Judge Horsmanden in lieu of bail of £200. Other forms of punishment, such as tying up a mariner's hands and feet and gagging him might be actionable if unprovoked. Kery's complaint, Kempe J–L. "As a Stranger to the Laws," the complainant hoped "to be directed by a Gentn Acquainted with Oleron." See also Austin v. Dennis and Calder, Towle, *op. cit.*, pp. 250–259 (1744); also Gordon v. Blake *et al.*, Hough, *op. cit.*, p. 84 (1755), master not excused of striking seamen even where he was apparently overexcited by the heat of Curaçao; but cf. De Quitteville v. Woodbury, Mass. Vice-Admiralty Rec., Box III, f. 5 (1740), where the court mitigated the damages when the master mistakenly took the libelant for a mutineer. A pilot was not lawfully one of the crew and therefore not subject to the master's correction. Hopkin v. Fennel, S.C. Vice-Admiralty Mins., C–D (1737), appealed to the High Court of Admiralty.

[21] *S.C. Gazette*, Dec. 2–9, 1732, verdict of the coroner's inquest: manslaughter; *ibid.*, June 16, 1733, where Edward Little was acquitted by a special court of admiralty of the murder of his cabin boy by caning him. Medical testimony was admitted that the boy had died of a malignant fever.

[22] Littman v. Bostock, S.C. Vice-Admiralty Mins., E–F (1753). An impressed mariner who accused the chief mate of having beaten him when he was ill appealed to the attorney-general of New York for relief on the ground that such correction and ill usage were "Contrary to Any law it being an inhuman Behaviour." King v. Garlin, Kempe G–J (1762–63). See also libel of Peter Collis, Hough, *op. cit.*, pp. 262–264, alleging that he had been belabored at a time when he was injured and unable to carry out orders which involved communicating with the enemy.

[23] In one case the court felt that the mate deserved to be beaten and confined for refusing to alter his course contrary to the captain's orders, but that the manner in which the punishment was administered was not lawful. The captain was fined 5*s.* and costs of prosecution. White v.

Lest this stress upon complaints of ill-usage at sea paint a highly distorted picture of the rigors and barbarous usages to which seamen were exposed in the seventeenth and eighteenth centuries, let us remember that contented mariners did not go into court. On the other hand, the fear of being treated as insubordinate deterred many a seaman from registering his complaint with the authorities ashore. Still others accepted such treatment as the usual lot of mariners and chose not to air their grievances in court. For a seaman's life in those days was a hard and hazardous one. Service under a cruel and abusive master was, perhaps, less perilous than the risks of scurvy, pestilence, storms, piracy, and impressment. Were the seamen to be spared any of these experiences he was certain to face continual exposure to bad food, cramped and insanitary living conditions aboard ship, and the monotony of the long voyage. Withal, the colonial seaman was probably a happier man than his nineteenth-century successor. The crews in colonial times, particularly on New England ships, were made up of more homogeneous elements than in the later period, promotion was rapid, and officers' berths were not class preserves as they were abroad.[24]

Legal Punishment for Mutiny and Insubordination on the High Seas. In addition to the right to administer correction aboard ship to mutinous or incorrigible seaman—whether corporal punishment, confinement in the brig, or being docked of provisions, or perhaps all three —and the right to discharge such a seaman, the master had the further right at law to prosecute him for mutiny and insubordination in the vice-admiralty court on his return to port.[25] The punishment under the Oléronic code for an assault on a master aboard ship was very severe. The offender's hand was to be cut off unless he redeemed it by payment of a fine.[26] But by the colonial period a fine or imprisonment were the penalties usually imposed.[27]

Hall, King v. White, Hough, *op. cit.,* pp. 80, 81; N.Y. Vice-Admiralty Mins., II, 1746–57, f. 219 (1754). See also Lawler v. Forrest, Mass. Vice-Admiralty Rec., Box I, f. 198 (1725). An early common-law court admonished a master to provide seamen with "sufficient allowance of meat drink and such like necessaries." Garret *et al.* v. Claybourne, *R.N.A.,* VI, 367 (1672).

[24] See S. E. Morison, *The Maritime History of Massachusetts, 1783–1860* (Boston and New York, 1921), p. 106.

[25] The mutineers believed responsible for Henry Hudson's tragic end on his fourth expedition were acquitted by a jury at Southwark in 1618. See T. A. Janvier, *Henry Hudson* (New York and London, 1909); Llewellyn Powys, *Henry Hudson* (New York, 1928), pp. 143 *et seq.*

[26] Art. 13; Molloy, *De jur. mar.,* Bk. II, ch. 3, § 6.

[27] The colonial practice has been preserved in the modern law. By an act of April 30, 1799,. § 12, a fine of not more than $1,000 was to be imposed for inciting a revolt or mutiny on shipboard or a term of imprisonment of not more than 5 years, or both. The act of March 4, 1909, § 292, preserved this penalty unchanged. For revolt and mutiny the 1790 act (§ 8) doubled the fine. This was retained in the act of 1909 (§ 293). Combining with any of the crew to disobey

Instances of prosecutions for mutiny before special commissions or the common-law courts are found going back as far as 1657, when Governor D'Oyley of Jamaica appointed a commission to inquire into "the difference that had lately happened betwixt Captain Wm. Swanley commander of the *Susanna* of London And the Shipps company." The finding was that the mate and company were guilty of "absolute rebellion against the said Master contrary to the lawes and Customes of the sea." [28] For failing to substantiate his accusation that his mariner had struck him, one master named Samuel Leeck was fined by the burgomasters and schepens of New Amsterdam fifty guilders. For abusive language to their captain and offering him resistance, the General Court of Virginia in 1675 ordered that

Capt Newham Tye [tie] them to the Capstone and Give them such Punishment as he shall thinke fitt and if the said Gilbert and Gudeford shall Resist him, then a Magistrate is to procure him Assistance from the Shore for the Execution of this Order but uppon their Submission and promises of their future Dilligence, then it is Left to the Discretion of the Said Capt Newham." [29]

In the same year the Suffolk County court in Massachusetts sentenced an incorrigible seaman who had struck his master and threatened to stab him to be whipped twenty stripes or to pay £5 as a fine to the county.[30] In 1675 the New York authorities investigated the complaint of Andrew Ball, master of the *Susannah* of Jamaica, charging that there had been a mutiny on board his vessel. According to his deposition, he had sailed from New York with a cargo of pipe staves and anchored off New Utrecht awaiting wind and tide to go out to sea. After three days "the Mate Mutinyed and quarreling with the Mast'r drew his Knife upon and forced him to deliver up his Lett' passe from Jamaica and cleering at the Custome house here with all other papers

---

lawful commands or to neglect duty or impede the progress of the voyage was punishable by act of June 7, 1872, § 57, by a term of imprisonment for not more than twelve months. Two years was the term set by this act for assaulting a master or mate. Early 19th century cases construed mutiny somewhat more narrowly than in the colonial period. The courts held that an assault and battery by the seaman upon the master did not of itself constitute an attempt to excite a revolt. U.S. v. Lawrence, Fed. Cas. No. 15, 575, 1 Cranch C.C. 94, U.S., 1802. Nor was a mere act of disobedience a revolt within the meaning of the act of 1790, unless it was combined with an attempt to incite others of the crew to resist or disobey orders. U.S. v. Smith, Fed. Cas. No. 16, 337, 1 Mason 147, U.S., 1816.

[28] British Museum, Add. MSS 12423, f. 38; cited by Crump, *Colonial Admiralty Jurisdiction*, pp. 97–99.

[29] Schout v. Hatkes, *R.N.A.*, IV, 197, 198 (1663); cases of Gilbert and Guidiford, *Va. Gen. Court Mins.*, p. 404 (1675).

[30] Evans' case, *Suffolk*, II, 628 (1675).

that hee had, whereupon being affrighted hee made a shift to get ashore in a small Canoe belonging to a sloope thereby apprehending he was in danger of his life by the steerman or Mate and other seamen." He accused the mate of mutiny and charged that he and his accomplices were "Robbers and Sea Rovers," planning to dispose of the ketch. In reply, Gerritz denied that Ball was the master, but asserted he was merely the cook, and that he had bought the ketch at Curaçao with his own money.[31] The disposition of this case is unknown, but this was not the last example of an alleged mutiny in or near the waters of New York.

During the month of June, 1717, the *Mary Anne,* a pirate sloop, lay off Sandy Hook preying upon peaceful commerce. Among the motley crew of thirty-seven, "two whereof were Artists, and fifteen or sixteen, Negroes and Mulattoes," were some twenty-eight men who had been impressed against their will. They planned to mutiny and "cut off the rest of the pirates belonging" to the sloop, and arranged to have the ship piloted into New York harbor. One of them, when under the influence of liquor, is reported to have told John Kelsall, a New York physician who happened to be a passenger aboard a near-by vessel, that "he would see such a thing done that night with a Hurah as he had never seen done before." According to depositions in the archives of the vice-admiralty court of New York, the mutiny took place on schedule. Incoming shipmasters reported that the impressed members of the crew, who insisted on heading the ship into the harbor and going ashore, mutinied against the pirates as planned, but were put down after five or six were dangerously wounded. But fortunately "none dyed of their wounds." Williams, the pirate commander, then hanged three of the mutineers, and, having quelled the rebellion, weighed anchor.[32]

---

[31] N.Y. State Historian, *Ann. Rep., 1897, Col. Ser.,* II (Albany, 1898), pp. 350–353 (1675).

[32] This information comes from a study of the examinations of pirate master Richard Caverley and boatswain Richard Huggins and the depositions of many witnesses in the files of the Federal district court, southern district of New York. For the provenance of this material, see R. B. Morris, "The Ghost of Captain Kidd," *N.Y. Hist.,* XIX, 280–297. For a successful mutiny against pirates in 1724, see Johnson, *Hist. of the Pyrates,* pp. 396–410; Jameson, *Privateering and Piracy,* pp. 323–345. Seven of the mutineers probably murdered the captain of the Boston brigantine *Charles* in 1703 and entered upon a career of piracy. They were convicted in the vice-admiralty court in Massachusetts and executed the following year. *The Arraignment, Tryal, and Condemnation of Capt. John Quelch, and Others of His Company* . . . (London, 1705). See also G. F. Dow and J. H. Edmonds, *The Pirates of the New England Coast, 1630–1730* (Salem, 1923). For other mutinies in which the crews turned to piracy, see Jameson, *op. cit.,* pp. 68–71 (1673), 165 (1696); Bourne, *op. cit.,* pp. 68, 69 (1704). The notorious failure of Captain Richard Kirby of the Royal Navy to join the attack against the French fleet in the West Indies in 1702 resulted in his being convicted of mutiny and shot. *Ibid.,* pp. 155–158.

For later mutiny prosecutions in colonial vice-admiralty courts, see Franklin v. Midwinter, Mass. Vice-Admiralty Rec., Box I, 1718–26 (1718). See also Wingfield v. Lobb and Norton, *ibid.,* Box II, f. 68 (1729), where defendants, found guilty of assaulting the master and going ashore

In 1722 three shipmasters—Isham Randolph, Constantine Cane, and William Halladay—petitioned Lieutenant-Governor Spotswood for relief from the consequences of want of discipline among seamen. The problem of order aboard ship in those days was set forth in some detail:

it is frequently the misfortune of Masters of Ships at their fitting out in England, to be obliged to ship men for forreign Voyages of whose disposition and character they have no knowledge; whereby it happens that the turbulent and refractory Tempers of Some of their sailors comes too late to be discovered, and proves often of very bad example to the rest of the Crew, and of Evil consequence to their Voyages, more especially in This Country, where the nature of the trade obliges us to send our men in Sloops and Boats, far remote from our Ships, and only under the direction of Some of our Under Officers. In these short voyages it is, that quarrells arise between the officers and men, wch are greatly promoted, by the opportunitys they then have of getting drunk That as no Society can be long kept in Order, without discipline, so it is but too well known that common sailors are of all men least Capable of Submitting to the authority of their Commanders, when they find themselves under no fear of correction. And indeed, such has of late years, been the pernicious practice of some persons at home, pretending to be Sollicitors and Attorneys for Sailors, that many Masters of Ships have been prosecuted and put to great trouble and Expense for giving their Sailors moderate Correction, even less than their offences deserved, besides the far greater hazard, which we run, in case of meeting with Pyrates, where we are sure to suffer all the tortures wch such an abandoned Crew can invent, upon the least intimation of our striking any of our men.

The petitioners expressed concern not only for the setting up in Virginia of a definite procedure for punishing mutinous and disobedient seamen, but also for provision that the complaints of seamen against their masters, whether as to allowance, labor, or other "unjust usage," be redressed in the speediest possible manner. To this end they urged that the governor see to it that complaints of masters against seamen be

---

contrary to his orders, were fined £5 to the king in bills of credit and an additional £4 11s. 6d. in silver at 8s. per ounce or in bills of credit of double that amount. In Cumberland v. Sailors, *ibid.*, Box I, 1718–26 (1718), the mutineers were sentenced to pay costs, and one of them was imprisoned for wounding his master, pending payment of costs, when he would be released at the court's discretion. Again, Menzies jailed mutinous seamen, subject to later release by court order. Astell v. White *et al.*, *ibid.* (1718). In Rex v. Moor, *ibid.*, Box II, f. 148 (1733), the court found that the mutinous behavior of a sailor had been punished in a previous action and therefore dismissed the suit. For a mutiny culminating in the murder of the captain, for which the ringleader, Matthew Turner, was convicted in 1769 by the Charleston Vice-Admiralty court and hanged on Hangman's Point, see *S.C. Gazette*, May 4, 1769; cf. prosecution of eight mariners of the brigantine *Two Brothers*, acquitted by Judge Drayton of the S.C. state court of admiralty, who found that the captain had been insane and had thrown himself overboard. *Gazette of the State of S.C.*, May 18, 1786.

legally determined and such punishment decreed "as may Serve to keep their Ships Companys in due obedience." Such a course, they shrewdly added, would not only benefit the owners of merchant ships, but the inhabitants of Virginia as well, since tobacco shipments would be facilitated "if such wholesome discipline were once established amongst those employed in that service." [33]

Operations of the Continental navy during the American Revolution were frequently hampered by mutinies, often provoked by English and Irish sailors on board Continental ships.[34] John Paul Jones found it necessary to quell a number of mutinies against his iron rule. A naval lieutenant named Thomas Simpson was arrested by Jones for having "held up to the crew that being Americans fighting for liberty, the voice of the people should be taken before the Captain's orders were obeyed." [35] Although the Continental Congress authorized the death penalty for mutiny, floggings and confinement in irons seem to have been adequate to maintain discipline in emergencies.[36]

Impressment. The right to compel seamen to fulfill their contracts is quite another matter from the impressment of seamen for the Royal Navy.[37] Owing to a constant stream of desertions from the Royal Navy,[38] voluntary enlistments were never sufficient to complete the quota of his Majesty's ships of war. The admiralty, in spite of opposition, con-

---

[33] *Cal. Va. State Papers*, I, 202, 203 (1722). For the authority of the justice of the peace to mete out corporal punishment to insubordinate seamen, see Starke, *Office of a Justice of the Peace*, p. 318. For the widespread fear of mutiny at an earlier period, see *CSPA, 1681–85*, No. 2067, p. 765 (1685).

Much rarer than mutinies by seamen were mutinies staged by passengers, chiefly redemptioners protesting atrocious conditions aboard ship. For a few such instances, see "Journey of Francis Louis Michel, January, 1702," *VMH*, XXIV, 6—ringleaders locked up in irons for the duration of the voyage; *Pa. Gazette*, Oct. 19, 1732; *S.C. Gazette*, Dec. 9–16, 1732—leaders committed to prison upon landing. Risings on slaving voyages were not unknown. See Gipson, *op. cit.*, I, 320, 321. At least three serious risings of convict servants against their ships' officers en route to America are on record, in one of which the captain was murdered. HMC, *Rep.*, XXXVIII, 77 (1741); *Pa. Gazette*, April 11, 1751; *Va. Gazette*, Dec. 5, 1751; Sept. 22, 1768. See also S. P. Dom, Geo. II (undated).

[34] See Allen, *op. cit.*, I, 198, 199; II, 439–441, 449.

[35] *Ibid.*, p. 351; also pp. 527, 534. For Jones's pre-Revolutionary career, in the course of which he was accused of having been the cause of the death of an incompetent and lazy ship carpenter by too diligent an application of the cat-o'-nine tails and of slaying a mutineer in self-defense, see L. Lorenz, *John Paul Jones* (Annapolis, 1943), pp. 192, 240–241; Emma Repplier, "How many Mutineers Did Paul Jones Kill?" *The Independent*, April 12, 1906.

[36] Allen, *op. cit.*, I, 355; II, 691, 692. Three principals in a mutiny on the *Alliance* in the winter of 1781 were sentenced to death, but this penalty was not exacted. *Ibid.*, II, 548–550. See also *Naval Records of the American Revolution, 1775–1788* (Washington, 1906), p. 190.

[37] See Molloy, *De jur. mar.*, Bk. I, ch. vi. Only the impressment of mariners is considered in this section. Impressing servants, apprentices, and other landsmen for military service is taken up elsewhere. See *infra*, pp. 294, 295.

[38] See Bourne, *op. cit.*, pp. 86, 87.

tinued throughout the period under review to resort to impressment to force men into the service.[39] The history of impressment in England runs from medieval times down to 1815. Under Elizabeth, local justices of the peace were required to return a specified number of able-bodied men for the navy.[40] The legal authority to impress was supported by the courts, although Lord Mansfield deplored the practice, which he justified as necessary for the safety of the state, and Blackstone regarded as "only defensible from public necessity."[41]

By authorization of an order in council the Admiralty would issue press warrants to naval officers.[42] Equipped with these warrants, press gangs forcibly seized able-bodied men in streets and taverns, and carried off sailors, watermen, and dock-side laborers, and mariners from merchantmen. In 1776 and again in 1779 a general press of rogues and vagabonds in London and other English cities was found necessary because of the great difficulty in recruiting sailors for the war with the colonies.[43]

No practice was better calculated than impressment to arouse the working classes in the colonies to take concerted action with the seamen against its enforcement. Because of constant complaints from the colonies of the irregularity of the impressment procedure,[44] the sole power of impressing was given in 1696 to the governors of the plantations in their capacity as vice-admirals on application of naval commanders. It was their duty to see that ships-of-war were supplied with the number of seamen the commander of the vessel might specify as needed for service on board.[45]

[39] See J. K. Hutchinson, *The Press-Gang Afloat and Ashore* (New York, 1914). See also HMC, *Rep.*, XV, 111 (1624), XXII, 183 (1624, 1625), XXIX, Pt. IV, 475, 476, (1708), Pt. VIII, 209–212 (1706); *A.P.C. Col., 1613–80*, No. 1183, p. 749 (1677).

[40] 5 Eliz., c. 5.

[41] Broadfoot's Case, Foster's Crown Cases, 154 (1743); Rex v. Tubbs, 2 Cowp. 512 (1776); 1 Bl. Comm. 267–268 (Cooley ed., Chicago, 1872). See also Sir Michael Foster, *A Report of Some Proceedings on the Commission of Oyer and Terminer and Gaol Delivery* (Oxford, 1762), p. 156.

[42] For a typical press warrant of the colonial period, see J. F. Zimmerman, *Impressment of American Seamen* (New York, 1925), p. 12n. See also S.C. Council Journal, 1742–43, fols. 122, 123, 409, 410 (1743).

[43] Admiral Rodney endeavored to recruit seamen for his ships without having recourse to the "disagreeable mode of pressing." He generally called upon the civil authorities to assist in manning the fleet and offered officers employed in this service 40s. plus expenses for every seaman brought to the navy. "Letter-Book," *loc. cit.*, pp. 85, 299, 455. However, he did resort to "a general Press" when absolutely necessary. *Ibid.*, p. 465. See also Curtis, *op. cit.*, p. 128.

[44] See, e.g., *CSPA, 1696–97*, No. 1207, p. 568 (1697); *A.P.C., Col., Unbound*, VI, 190 (1727); HMC, *Rep.*, XXXIX, 215 (1712); Stock, *Proc. Brit. Parl.*, II, 11–13 (1689), 136n. (1695).

[45] L. W. Labaree, *Royal Instructions*, pp. 442, 443; *Acts and Laws of New Hampshire*, II, 23, 24 (1702); *Md. Arch.*, XX, 287. See also *CSPA, 1696–97*, Nos. 455, 458, p. 236; No. 333, p. 183

As a further method of curbing reckless impressments which were detrimental to trade, the British authorities granted passes to vessels bound for the colonies to proceed without further molestation or without suffering impressment in his Majesty's navy.[46] In addition, at times colonial governors called on officials in adjacent provinces for protection of crews from impressment.[47]

Despite the transfer of impressment authority from the naval commanders to the provincial governors serious complaints of violations continued to be forthcoming, especially during the War of the Spanish Succession.[48] In at least two instances a press gang under Captain Jackson of His Majesty's sloop the *Swift* seized the entire crew of vessels in Boston harbor.[49] In New York City the lessee of a ferry complained "that the officers of the Man of warr now rideing in this harbour, wanting hands, have for some time last past been about with their press warrants wch: hath prevented many persons from Comeing to the said Citty as Usuall wch: has and daily doth Lessen the proffits wch: would arise to yor Petitioner from the said Ferry."[50] In 1707 one hundred and fifty merchants petitioned Parliament describing the disastrous commercial situation resulting from impressment in America, especially in the West Indies, and praying for relief.[51] The fear of the mercantilist government that merchants would begin to trade directly with the Dutch and Danish West Indies to avoid the press gang led to the passage in 1708 of an Act for the Encouragement of Trade to America,[52] which contained the following provision regarding impressment:

that no mariner or other person who shall serve on board or be retained to serve on board any privateer, or trading ship or vessel, that shall be employed in any part of America, nor any mariner or other person, being on shore in

---

(1696); *ibid., 1702*, p. 348 (1702); *VMH*, XXI, 393 (1701). At times colonial governments initiated the impressment procedure, as in the case of Plymouth during King William's War. *Plymouth Col. Rec.*, VI, 233 (1690).

[46] See *VMH*, XVII, 286 (1652); XV, 276 (1666). See also *CSPA, 1696–97*, No. 663, p. 345 (1697); No. 739, p. 377 (1697); No. 751, p. 381 (1697); No. 755, p. 382 (1697); No. 758, p. 382. For the later period, see "Letter-Book of Admiral Lord Rodney," *loc. cit.*, pp. 612, 697 (1782).

[47] *VMH*, XXIV, 76 (1703).   [48] See Stock, *Proc. Brit. Parl.*, III, 27, 28 (1703).

[49] See Dora Mae Clark, "The Impressment of Seamen in the American Colonies," in *Essays in Colonial History Presented to Charles McLean Andrews by his Students* (New Haven, 1931).

[50] Benson's petition for rent abatement, N.Y.C. Board of Aldermen and City Clerk's Records, File Box No. 2, Bundle 1. See also *M.C.C.*, II, 252.

[51] For protests against brutal impressment measures in the West Indies during Queen Anne's War, see Bourne, *op. cit.*, pp. 89–92, 96; also Stock, *Proc. Brit. Parl.*, III, 157–159 (1707), 167, 182 (1708); Clark, *loc. cit.*, p. 205, citing, *H. of L.MSS, 1706–1708*, New Ser., VII, pp. 99 *et seq.*

[52] 6 Anne, c. 37, § 9; *Statutes*, VIII, 804–809.

any part thereof, shall be liable to be impressed or taken away by any officer or officers of or belonging to any of her Majesty's ships of war impowered by the Lord High Admiral, or any other person whatsoever, unless such mariner shall have before deserted from such ship of war belonging to her Majesty at any time after the fourteenth day of February one thousand seven hundred and seven.

The act also provided in Section 13 that trading ships and packet boats should take extra seamen to America for the use of the Royal Navy there.

Did this act restrain provincial governors as well as ships' officers from impressing seamen in America? Dora Mae Clark in a valuable and suggestive study of the enforcement of this statute has traced the course of the controversy which this question evoked. The law officers of the crown answered this question in the negative, and asserted that officers of the Royal Navy were the only persons specifically prohibited in the act from impressing seamen.[53] Nevertheless, beginning in 1709, instructions to the royal governors omitted a grant of authority for impressment.[54] As a result, when the British fleet was at Boston in 1711 in preparation for an attack on Quebec, great numbers of the crew deserted and neither the governor nor the ships' commanders had authority to impress seamen, a dangerous situation in wartime.[55]

The termination of the War of the Spanish Succession raised a further question. Was the act of Anne perpetual or intended merely to operate during the period of the war. The latter view was held by the law officers of the crown.[56] In 1723 instructions to commanders in American waters omitted any further reference to the statutory prohibition against impressment. Hence, from that date ships' commanders made use of press warrants in colonial ports. On the other hand, the royal instructions to the governors still required those officials to take an oath to observe certain Parliamentary statutes, among them the sixth of Anne.[57]

This confusion as to whether or not the parliamentary exemption was still in force led to numerous protests by merchants and seamen. The British West Indies sharply criticized the renewal of impressment.[58] To provide that area with relief, Parliament in 1746 passed a statute similar

---

[53] *Docs. Rel. to Col. Hist. of N.Y.*, V, 99–100; Admiralty Papers, Secretary's Dept., 3667, fols. 207, 228, 229, 305; British Museum, Add. MSS, No. 21947, fols. 108, 158b.

[54] See, e.g., *ibid.*, pp. 124 *et seq.*   [55] Clark, *loc. cit.*, p. 210.

[56] *Pa. Arch.*, I, 638; C. H. Lincoln, ed., *The Correspondence of William Shirley* (New York, 1912), I, 418.

[57] See *Shirley Corr.*, I, 75.

[58] Sir John Barnard warned Parliament "that by manning our navy in this manner, we shall put an end to our power and our commerce." Cobbett, XI, 417–418. See also Stock, *Proc. Brit. Parl.*, V, 121, 127, 129 (1742).

in scope to the act of the sixth of Anne.[59] Thus, Parliament showed consistent partiality to the sugar colonies and slighted the mainland plantations which had the same grievances.

Despite the unpopularity of impressment, the colonial governors in the course of the later Intercolonial Wars repeatedly authorized the press of seamen as well as ships for expeditions and provincial legislatures voted wages due to such impressed crews.[60] When, in the forties, captains attempted to impress seamen in the mainland ports, they were mobbed, imprisoned, and held in high bail pending trial.[61] Governor Shirley was far more zealous in pressing men in Boston than were the authorities in New York and Rhode Island, and an exodus of seamen to the safer ports resulted. As early as 1741 the Boston selectmen declared that impressment procedure carried out by Captain Edward Hawkes "greatly Terrifyes the Coasters and other vessels bringing Grain, Wood, etc. to this Town." [62] In 1746 Captain Forrest of the *Wager* began a press in which two sailors were killed. Riots were now inevitable whenever a press was threatened in the harbor.[63] When, the following year, Commander Knowles undertook the wholesale impressment of "sailors, ship-carpenters and labouring land-men" in the port of Boston, three days of rioting followed. A barge thought to belong to the royal squadron was burned, Governor Shirley was forced to quit Boston for his own safety, and had to call upon the militia of neighboring counties when the Boston militia were slow in responding. According to Hutchinson, "most if not all" of those impressed were afterward released.[64]

Despite colonial demands that the act of 1708 be made perpetual and that the discrimination in favor of the sugar islands implicit in the act of 1746 be ended, the practice of impressment was renewed during the Seven Years' War and continued after the close of the war. Complaints were general along the Atlantic coast.[65] In 1764 mob violence and the destruction of a navy tender marked the impressment of four fishermen in New York.[66] When, in 1768, the commander of the man-of-

[59] 19 Geo. II, c. 30; Ruffhead, VI, 680; Pickering, XVIII, 472.

[60] See, e.g., *Mass. Acts and Resolves*, X, 108, 119, 139 (1722), 234, 252, 265 (1723), 304, 309, 328, 351, 372, 380, 386, 388, 417 (1724), 440, 489, 490, 492, 523 (1725), 588, 651, 660, 745 (1726); XI, 10, 31, 61, 87, 179 (1727), 222 (1728); XII, 707, 708 (1741); XIII, 613, 621, 624, 632, 642 (747).

[61] *Pa. Arch.*, I, 638 et seq.   [62] *Boston Selectmen Mins., 1736–42*, p. 315 (1741).

[63] *Shirley Corr.*, I, 421, 422.   [64] *Hist. of Mass. Bay*, II, 386–390; *Shirley Corr.*, I, 413 et seq.

[65] Mass. Hist. Soc., *Proceedings*, LV, 250 et seq.; Clark, *loc. cit.*, p. 219. Even where the authorities cooperated, it was at times "absolutely impossible to get a Number of Seamen here at this time by any means whatever for his Majesty's Navy." *Md. Arch.*, IX, 137 (1758).

[66] Stokes, *Iconography*, IV, 742, 749. A few years earlier four sailors of the H.M.S. *Winchester*

war *Romney* ordered a press in Boston harbor, the infuriated mob, unable to locate the *Romney's* press boat, burned a boat belonging to a customs collector. Hutchinson pointed out that the fear of impressment "prevents coasters as well as other vessels coming in freely; and it adds more fewel to the great stock among us before." [67] At the behest of the citizens of Boston, John Adams drafted special instructions to their representatives asserting that impressment was in direct contravention of the statute of 1708. [68] The following year Michael Corbet was charged with the murder with a harpoon of Lieutenant Panton of the British frigate *Rose* while Panton was trying to impress Corbet and his companions from on board a brigantine belonging to a Marblehead resident as she was coming in from Europe some six or seven leagues from land. In defense of Corbet and three other sailors, Adams again contended that the act of the sixth of Anne was still in force. After an adjournment by Hutchinson, the court pronounced "that the killing Lieutenant Panton was justifiable homicide in necessary self-defence," thus evading the real issue of the operative effect of the statute. [69]

This question was settled by Parliament in 1775 by the repeal of the sixth of Anne. If that statute had expired in 1713, the repeal would seem to have been unnecessary. Despite the repeal of the statute, it must be borne in mind that by the time of the American Revolution there was considerable opposition in Great Britain to impressment on the part of some leading naval officers, [70] and its legality was vigorously contested. [71] Nevertheless the British did not abandon the practice during the Revolution and on numerous occasions instituted "hot presses" of sailors in those towns in which the fleet was anchored. [72] In the American states, however, impressment was the exception rather than the rule. For a

were killed outside New York harbor by the crew of a privateer, who mistook the sailors for a press gang. *Docs. Rel. to Col. Hist. of N.Y.*, VII, 446, 454 (1760). The grand jury refused to indict them, but the governor, on the advice of the council, turned them over to the Royal Navy for service. J. Goebel and T. R. Naughton, *Law Enforcement in Colonial New York* (New York, 1944), pp. 306–309.

[67] Mass. Hist. Soc., *Proceedings*, LV, 250 *et seq.*

[68] *Works,* ed. C. F. Adams (Boston, 1850–56), III, 503 *et seq.*

[69] *Ibid.,* II, 225–226, 526–534.

[70] See Frederick Hervey, *Naval History of Great Britain* (London, 1779), III, 18; Zimmerman, *op. cit.,* p. 13.

[71] J. Almon, *An Enquiry into the Practice and Legality of Pressing by the Kings' Commission* (London, 1770); *An Enquiry into the Nature and Legality of Press-Warrants* (London, 1770). Many of these arguments were later embodied by John Adams in his *Inadmissible Principles of the King's Proclamation* (Boston, 1809). For the support of the legality of impressment, see Charles Butler, *Legality of Impressing Seamen* (London, 1777). See also Admiralty Papers: 298–300 (Law Officers' Opinions, 1733–83); *ibid.,* Secretary's Dept., 3676.

[72] See, e.g., *Diary of Frederick Mackenzie* (Cambridge, Mass., 1930), II, 406 (1778).

brief period it was authorized in Rhode Island in 1777,[73] and, in 1780, when the coast of Virginia was harassed by enemy vessels, the legislature authorized the issuance of impressment warrants, specifically excepting crews of foreign vessels or of other states.[74] In the post-Revolutionary period impressment once more served as a serious source of friction between Great Britain and the merchants and seamen of the Atlantic seaboard, an issue which the War of 1812 failed to settle.[75]

[73] *R.I. Session Laws, May, 1777*, p. 29; *July, 1777*, p. 8.

[74] Hening, X, 379–386. See also Elizabeth Cometti, "Impressment during the American Revolution," in *The Walter Clinton Jackson Essays in the Social Sciences*, ed. Vera Largent (Chapel Hill, N.C., 1942), pp. 99 *et seq.*

[75] For a directive by the Continental Congress to the commander of a frigate to dismiss all men he had impressed in defiance of the governor of Maryland, see *Pa. Arch.*, 1st ser., V, 328 (1777).

VI. LABOR AND THE ARMED SERVICES

EXEMPTIONS AND DEFERMENTS
FROM MILITARY SERVICE

THE ENLISTMENT or impressment of servants and laborers in the militia, their conscription in the military forces for service as artificers, and their impressment in the Royal Navy posed legal and economic problems similar to those resulting from the enticement of servants and laborers in civilian fields of employment.[1] Conscription was universal in the colonies.[2] However, in order to assure a satisfactory labor supply some of the colonies exempted workers in certain essential or favored industries from military service. This was similar to the exemptions from the payment of taxes over stated periods of years occasionally granted to entrepreneurs or artisans in favored industries.[3]

As early as 1639 Massachusetts Bay exempted from military training fishermen while abroad during fishing seasons, ship carpenters who followed their calling, and millers, but provided that they were to be furnished with arms.[4] In 1645 the Maine General Court ruled "that all labourers that constantly worke upon the [iron] worke shalbe free from watching and trayning." [5] Plymouth in 1655 exempted the Taunton ironworkers from training during their working season.[6] The Connecticut Council in 1675 exempted schoolmasters, physicians, and millers from watch and ward.[7] During the Intercolonial Wars millers were

---

[1] See *infra*, pp. 414–434.

[2] Implementing the Massachusetts order of 1631 establishing universal military service (*Assistants*, II, 12), an order of the Assistants the following year provided that those who did not furnish themselves with sufficient arms should be "compelled to serve by the yeare with any maister that will retaine him with such wages as the Court shall thinke meet to appoynte." *Ibid.*, p. 21 (1631). This was really a work-or-fight law. See also H. L. Osgood, *American Colonies in the Seventeenth Century* (New York, 1904), I, 506, 508, 511; *Plymouth Col. Rec.*, II, 64 (1643), III, 173 (1659), V, 198 (1676); Jerman's case, *Essex*, VII, 333 (1680). See, e.g., *Md. Arch.*, XIII, 555–559 (1692), for impressment of males between 16 and 60.

[3] See, e.g., *New Haven Col. Rec.*, I, 149, 175 (1655–56); *Conn. Pub. Rec., 1665–78*, p. 108.

[4] *Mass. Bay Rec.*, I, 258 (1639). See also, M. Sharp, "Leadership and Democracy in the Early New England System of Defense," *Amer. Hist. Rev.*, L (1945), 252.

[5] *Me. Prov. and Court Rec.*, II, 91 (1645).   [6] *Plymouth Col. Rec.*, III, 89 (1655).

[7] *Conn. Pub. Rec., 1665–78*, p. 361. Individuals in strategic industries—for example, a cloth and serge worker and his servant or the "chief workman" in the iron works at Saybrooke—were at times specifically exempted. *Ibid., 1678–89*, pp. 196 (1686), 390 (1702). In Maryland white men working in the iron industry were exempted in 1732 from attending the muster or performing road duty. Ten years later an undertaker of a copper works successfully petitioned the legislature to exempt such experienced workers as he should bring to the colony from payment of taxes, road duty, and militia service. *Md. Arch.*, XXXVII, 540–541; XLII, 430–431.

occasionally exempted from military service in other colonies,[8] and in Virginia seamen, when in service, could not be compelled to serve in the militia.[9]

During the Revolution the exemption of workmen and skilled artificers employed in essential war industries was quite common, but these exemptions or deferments were parceled out as necessity dictated. War workers were not given blanket deferments.[10] Under the plan worked out late in 1776 to raise eighty-eight battalions, a portion of the workers employed in the powder mills were exempt.[11] On the recommendation of the Board of War the Continental Congress on occasion found it expedient to exempt workmen in essential industries, and Washington gave specific exemptions to munitions workers in order to expedite the fulfillment of war contracts.[12]

New York, which was typical of state governments in its handling of exemptions and deferments, exempted workers in industries closely related to the war effort. State regiments enrolled all able-bodied men between sixteen and sixty, but exemptions were provided for one miller to each grist mill, three powder makers to each powder mill, five men to each furnace, three journeymen in each printing office, and one ferryman to each public ferry.[13] Still further exemptions in specific war industries were dictated by labor shortages. A complaint to the authorities from Fishkill late in 1776 revealed that

Our militia constantly employed in the field are drawn from their ordinary business; the inhabitants themselves are destitute. We have few manufacturers, and cloth of every kind is scarce and dear beyond description.[14]

[8] Leon de Valinger, Jr., *Colonial Military Organization in Delaware, 1638–1776* (Wilmington, 1938), pp. 36, 37.

[9] Hening, V, 81, 82 (1738); Starke, *Office of a Justice of the Peace*, p. 317.

[10] A similar policy was adopted by the Union during the Civil War. For a discussion of occupational deferments under the Militia Act of July 17, 1862 and the Enrollment Act of 1863, see F. A. Shannon, *The Organization and Administration of the Union Army, 1861–65* (Cleveland, 1928), I, 279, 285, 307; II, 120.

[11] *Amer. Arch.*, 5th ser., II, 763.

[12] See letter of the Board of War, June 23, 1777, relative to 11 workmen employed by Col. Mark Bud at his Cannon and Nail Rod Works in Berks County, Pa., and letters of Charles Hoff, Jr., to Gov. Livingston, 1777, specifically asking exemptions for 25 workers at the Hibernia Furnace, or, as an alternative, proposing that 30 or 40 Hessian deserters be sent to him and "I would do my endeavor to make 'em serviceable." Morristown, N.J., National Historical Park. Where artificers were employed by the Continental army, regimental commanders were enjoined "on no acct whatsoever [to] take away those Artificers whose Times of Enlistment are not expir'd till the Public Works are compleated and then they will be paid and Discharged agreeable to a former Gen. Order." *Orderly Book of Brig. Gen. Anthony Wayne, Oct. 17, 1776–Jan. 8, 1777, at Ticonderoga and Mt. Independence* (Albany, 1859), pp. 79, 95 (1776).

[13] J. A. Roberts, comp., *New York in the Revolution as Colony and State* (2d ed., Albany, 1898), p. 11.

[14] "Journal of the Committee of Safety," *J.N.Y. Prov. Cong.*, I, 782.

Local committees of correspondence as well as the Provincial Congress granted specific exemptions to shoemakers, their journeymen and apprentices, to masters and journeymen employed at nailmaking, to blacksmiths and to those engaged in servicing the blacksmiths, to linen workers, and to flaxseed mill operatives.[15] The problem of exemptions was also exigent in Virginia, where, as early as July, 1775, the convention had exempted from military service "all persons concerned in iron works." This policy was reversed for a short period in 1780, when skilled workmen were conscripted into the army. Hunter's ironworks was so hard hit that the legislature was forced once more to return to its original policy of exempting workers in the private iron industry.[16] The legislature of that state also specifically exempted from military duty "of every kind" workmen if employed in the public shipyards, foundry, rope walks, or other public works, provided they had signed to serve for six months.[17] Were it not for these exemptions from military duty workmen could not have been procured for such state war-production enterprises as the gun factory, despite the high rate of wages prevailing.[18]

[15] *Mins. Albany Comm. Corr.,* I, 584, 586 (1776), 942, 943 (1773); *Cal. Hist. MSS Relating to the War of the Revolution* (Albany, N.Y., 1868), I, 310 (May 29, 1776); *N.Y. Prov. Cong. J.,* I, 548, 589 (1776); C. C. Knight, comp., *New York in the Revolution as Colony and State* (Albany, 1901), p. 73. Compare the request of two paper manufacturers of Milton, Mass., that four enlisted soldiers, formerly their apprentices, be released from the army on the ground that they had "attained so great a knowledge in the art of paper making, that their attendance on that business is absolutely necessary to its being carried on." Force, *Amer. Arch.,* 4th ser., II, 609 (1775). The *N.J. Gazette,* Jan. 7, 1778 carried an advertisement by Nathaniel Pettit, offering "Extraordinary Wages and an exemption from serving in the militia" to a few "choice" woodcutters and laborers to be employed at the "independent salt works." For the exemption in Pennsylvania of tailors and shoemakers working on government contracts, see *Pa. Stat. at Large,* IX, 192 (1778). Cf. *Moravian Rec.* III, 1186 (1777).

[16] Hening, IX, 28, 267 (1777); X, 262 (1780), 397, 425, 444. See also Kathleen Bruce, *Virginia Iron Manufacture in the Slave Era* (New York, 1931), p. 75.

[17] Hening, X, 384 (1780). Cf. *Cal. Va. State Papers,* I, 464 (1781); *VMH,* LIII, 163–171.

[18] Charles Dick to the governor of Virginia, April 5, 1781. *Cal. Va. State Papers,* II, 13. At that time wages ran from £15 to £35 per day.

Similar manpower problems confronted the British at home. The British conscription law of 1778, which authorized the justices of the peace to levy and deliver to the recruiting officers "all able-bodied idle and disorderly Persons, who could not, upon Examination, prove themselves to Exercise and industriously follow some lawful Trade or Employment, or to have Substance sufficient for their Support and Maintenance," specifically exempted harvest laborers between May 25th and Oct. 25th. *Stat. at Large* (Ruffhead), XIII, 273–280. The second press act of 1779 was suspended by order in Council in certain areas of Britain in order not to interfere with the harvest. *Ibid.,* pp. 316–317; E. E. Curtis, *The Organization of the British Army in the American Revolution* (New Haven, 1926), p. 59.

Even in the post-Revolutionary period manufacturing interests found occasion to complain that state military-service laws providing that all able-bodied male citizens answer the call for training and assembly involved the loss of productive time of mechanics and were thus a hindrance to industry. For a contemporary comment on the Connecticut law (*Acts and Laws of Conn., 1784,* pp. 151, 381), see Cole, *Hamilton,* pp. 13–14. Workmen also protested compulsory military service. See Commons, *Hist. of Labor,* III, 281.

THE MILITARY SERVICE OF SERVANTS

BECAUSE of the master's property interest in the services of his servant, some colonies imposed greater restrictions upon the enlistment in the armed services of apprentices or other indentured servants than upon the recruiting and conscription of free laborers. In certain areas, notably in New England, the military service of servants was obligatory.[1] Massachusetts, for example, specifically included servants in its conscription law.[2] Early New Haven regulations also required servants and laborers to do military service,[3] but in 1648 that colony freed from watch "farmers and covenant servants wch have no estate in the towne."[4] While specifically requiring servants to train, an order of the following year exempted one servant belonging to every magistrate or teaching elder, as well as servants of families in remote localities.[5] In Connecticut and Rhode Island, servants and field workers served in the militia.[6] In general, the enlistment of bound servants and their impressment into the armed service were sanctioned by the New England colonies during the Intercolonial Wars,[7] and provision was made for the payment of their wages either to their master, as in Massachusetts or Rhode Island,[8] or, in the latter colony, for dividing such wages between master and servant.[9]

[1] The agents for the New England colonies made specific objection in 1693 to a provision of a joint stock company charter given to Sir Matthew Dudley and others which exempted the company's servants from service in the militia. In deference to the wishes of the Massachusetts authorities this clause was waived. *CSPA, 1693–96*, No. 55, p. 158 (1693).

[2] *Mass. Bay Rec.*, I, 84, 93, II, 222; *Assistants*, II, 12 (1631); *Mass. Col. Laws* (ed., 1889), p. 177. One master was fined 10s. "for wanting armes for his man" and for his own absence from training. *Mass. Bay Rec.*, I, 102 (1632). Servants were not included in categories later exempted from training. *Mass. Bay Rec.*, II, 31, 221, IV, Pt. I, 87. In King Philip's War one volunteer company serving under Captain Samuel Moseley included apprentices and servants along with strangers and jailbirds. G. M. Bodge, *Soldiers in King Philip's War* (Boston, 1906), pp. 59, 64, 65 *et seq*. For the charge that a servant was "pressed for the war," see *Essex*, VI, 189 (1676). Plymouth as an independent colony did not admit servants to training. *Plymouth Col. Rec.*, II, 61 (1643).

[3] *New Haven Col. Rec., 1638–49*, pp. 40 (1640), 85 (1643).   [4] *Ibid.*, p. 382.

[5] However, seamen and ship carpenters were required to "watch as others doe" and train twice a year. *Ibid.*, pp. 457, 464.

[6] If a deserter from the militia was a servant he was "to make reparation to his" master "by longer and farther service." *Conn. Pub. Rec., 1689–1706*, p. 41. By Rhode Island law the fine against absentee servants was recoverable by distraint on the master's goods. *R.I. Col. Rec.*, II, 111–115 (1665); *ibid.*, p. 50 (1677).

[7] *Mass. Acts and Resolves*, XII, 192 (1736), 712 (1741); Col. Soc. of Mass., *Publications*, IV, 423 (1756). For instructions to arm and train "Christian Servants" antedating these wars by a number of years, see Labaree, *Royal Instructions*, I, 392, 393. See also *Acts and Laws of N.H.*, II, 231 (1761), 575, 576 (1740); *Laws of N.H.* (ed. 1771), p. 148.

[8] *Mass. Acts and Resolves*, I, 532 (1704), 559 (1705), X, 197 (1723); *R.I. Col. Rec.*, V, 470 (1755).

[9] *R.I. Col. Rec.*, V, 480 (1756). Cf. also *ibid.*, VI, 23 (1757), 145 (1758), 448 (1765), involving request for recovery of a servant, discharged from the army, or compensation therefor.

In Pennsylvania and the tobacco provinces, where there was a substantial number of white servants, a serious issue was raised during the Intercolonial Wars over the question of servant enlistments and compensation to masters. The initial approach was to protect property interests by forbidding such enlistments, or, as with the Pennsylvania statute of 1711, to provide compensation to masters of servants who enlisted without securing consent.[10] This act was prompted by the "great inequality and hardship which appears to fall upon such masters" as "lose their servants and yet pay proportionately their rates."

The question came up in New Jersey and again in Pennsylvania at the time of the war with Spain in 1740. Governor Lewis Morris of New Jersey, confronted with a Quaker pacifist element in his province, stoutly contended, in an opinion drafted to expedite enlistments for the Cuban expedition, that the king's right to military support transcended the contract rights of any of his subjects. Hence, apprentices, persons hired for a year, and laborers who contracted to do piecework had the right to enlist without incurring any penalties for breach of contract. He denied that a redemptioner who had signed articles in Great Britain or Ireland to serve in America had become "so absolutely the Property of the Person with whom he engaged, or of him to whom his Service was transferred, as to incapac[i]tate him from enlisting in the King's Service as a Soldier."[11]

While Goveror Thomas of Pennsylvania was as eager as was Morris to aid in recruiting and actually urged servants to join the armed forces,[12] he found it expedient to conciliate the Assembly, which was controlled by the colony's Quaker minority, hostile to military cooperation, and ardent in affirming the property interests of masters in their servants. When the Quakers charged that the secret muster rolls contained the names of indentured servants who had enlisted, Thomas agreed to dismiss from the service only those who consented to return to their masters, but opposed wholesale discharges, which, he felt, would "breed such a Mutiny as will not be easy for me to quell." He cited

[10] Masters were entitled to 10s. for every month's absence, the total sum recoverable not to exceed £20 unless the servant returned "whole and unmaimed" by Dec. 1, 1711. *Pa. Stat. at Large*, II 399.

[11] As the legal authorities he cited showed that even impressing was not unlawful, he argued, *a fortiori*, that "Entertaining Volunteers must be quite Legal." By analogy to 2 and 3 Ann., c. 6, § 4, providing that seamen apprentices over 18 could be impressed but their masters were entitled to their wages, he argued that the wages of apprentices or contracted servants by right also belonged to their masters. See William Smith MSS, lib. II, fols. 269–283, N.Y. Pub. Lib. Morris also defended the enlistment of debtors not taken in execution or against whom judgments had not been secured. N.J. Hist. Soc., *Coll.*, IV, 87–89, 96, 97 (1740).

[12] *Pa. Col. Rec.*, IV, 453; *Pa. Gazette*, April 24, 1740.

one instance in which enlisted servants were returned to their masters, whereupon both freemen and servants laid down their arms in protest, declaring that they would go to colonies where the king's soldiers were better used.[13] As a result of the deadlock the Assembly never appropriated money for the troops and held up Thomas's salary, but voted substantial compensation to masters whose servants had left for the wars.[14]

The issue was fought out even more bitterly in the French and Indian War, when a much higher quota of recruits was set for the province than in any previous conflict. Yet between 1755 and 1763 the Assembly repeatedly passed legislation forbidding the enlistment in the militia of "any bought servant or indentured apprentice" without the written consent of his master.[15] General Shirley, then in command of the British armies in America, at first cautioned the recruiting officer in Pennsylvania against enlisting apprentices or indentured servants, but soon found it necessary to countermand this order. The Assembly memorialized Lieutenant Governor Robert Hunter Morris that the enlistment of servants "drained" the province of "hired Labourers" and caused those remaining in the service to grow mutinous, disorderly, and idle, and requested that enlisted servants be restored to their masters. Morris, while confessing to grave doubts as to the legality of servant enlistments, felt that any action taken by him would be "extrajudicial" and not binding on the parties concerned, and left the issue to be finally determined by the courts.[16] Shirley stood his ground, but the Assembly, pacifist in doctrine and sympathetic with property interests, failed to co-

[13] *Pa. Col. Rec.*, IV, 456. See also de Valinger, *op. cit.*, pp. 32, 33. For complaints of masters during this period, see, e.g., representation of the owners of ironworks at Coventry that the enlistment of ten of their servants, among them colliers, had stopped production and caused the petitioners several hundred pounds damages. Geiser, *Redemptioners and Indentured Servants*, p. 97. For an instance where a captain in the Royal Navy refused to transport enlisted servants to Jamaica for fear that he might be sued by their masters, see *Pa. Gazette*, April 22, 1742. An opinion rendered by William Smith, Advocate General, in Captain Cosby's case (1752) deals with the steps which might be taken by a master to recover an apprentice who had voluntarily enlisted in the navy. Kempe C–F. The master was not justified in using force.

[14] Throughout the controversy the legislature represented the point of view of farmer and tradesman, who "very much depend on the Labor of their Servants, purchased, perhaps, at the Expence of most they are worth, deprived of that Assistance and put under the greatest difficulties." The blame was assigned both to "the Caprice of the Servant and Will of an Officer, under Pretence of serving the Crown." *Pa. Col. Rec.*, IV, 437, 438. Out of some 800 recruits, 276 were found to have been enlisted servants. C. A. Herrick, *White Servitude in Pennsylvania* (Philadelphia, 1926), p. 242. Compensation in the amount of £2,588 was voted to the masters. Robert Proud, *History of Pennsylvania* (2 vols., Philadelphia, 1797, 1798), II, 221, 230.

[15] *Pa. Stat. at Large*, V, 200, 201 (1756), 268, 282 (1757), 336 (1758), 426 (1759); VI, 52 (1760), 246–252 (1763). This clause originally appears in the Militia Law of 1741, where it was inserted because of the alleged Negro conspiracy to burn New York City in that year.

[16] *Pa. Col. Rec.*, VII, 37–40; *Pa. Gazette*, Feb. 19, 1756.

operate with the military authorities in the French and Indian War and repeatedly passed acts curtailing the enlistment of servants without their masters' consent.[17]

The intransigent attitude of the Pennsylvania legislature on this question forced Parliament to act, and in 1756 it specifically authorized officers to enlist any indentured servant regardless of any existing colonial law or practice.[18] In 1757 Franklin made representations to London against the enlistment of servants by Shirley and Braddock and the failure of the British government to provide compensation.[19] Finally, in 1763, the Pennsylvania Assembly passed acts for the relief of masters whose servants had enlisted.[20]

A similar controversy between civilians and the military over the enlistment of servants occurred in Maryland. Universal conscription of males from sixteen to sixty years of age, both freemen and servants, was provided for by seventeenth-century legislation.[21] In the early Intercolonial Wars a good many members of the servant and laboring classes served in the Maryland militia. Upon the advice of Governor Blackiston the Maryland legislature provided that servants be given guns in order that they might be an effective part of the militia, not a mere "rabble" with clubs.[22] The Maryland House of Delegates stated in 1702 that only the laborers who were the best off in the province could be sent to fill the militia quota,[23] leaving the poorer inhabitants to shoulder the onerous tax burden. From the census reports of that period it is clear that servants were included in the numbers of persons listed as "fit to bear arms." [24]

After the second Intercolonial War came a decided change in atti-

---

[17] *Pa. Stat. at Large*, V, 197–201, 268, 282, 336. See also Herrick, *op. cit.*, p. 248. The original act of 1755 was disallowed. *Pa. Stat. at Large*, V, 532.

[18] Under this act, if the master objected within six months after the enlistment, the servant was to be released or the master recompensed, the choice resting with two justices of the peace. 29 Geo. II, c. 35, §§ 1, 2. For the operation of this act, see Herrick, *op. cit.*, p. 249. For a disturbance in connection with the recruiting of servants, see *Pa. Gazette*, Feb. 26, 1756.

[19] *Works* (Bigelow ed.), II, 512, 513; *Writings* (Smyth ed.), III, 391, 396.

[20] The Assembly had considered such remedial legislation much earlier. *Pa. Gazette*, Nov. 11, 1756. *Pa. Col. Rec.*, IX, 17, 24. The Delaware Assembly on two occasions in 1762 defeated an attempt to reimburse the masters of enlisted servants. De Valinger, *op. cit.*, p. 51. As late as 1772 Abraham Hasselby petitioned the Philadelphia quarter sessions that a bound servant named Henry Beafort had run away on three occasions and had enlisted at the barracks. The court granted his petition that the boy be discharged of his indenture and bound to the man with whom he had expressed a desire to stay. Philadelphia County Court Papers (Jan. 21, 1772).

[21] Under acts of 1678 and 1692 a master who prevented a servant from attending muster was subject to a fine of 100 lbs. of tobacco to go to the company to buy a drum or colors. *Md. Arch.*, VIII, 54 (1678); XIII, 555–559 (1692).

[22] *Ibid.*, XXII, 343 (1699).   [23] *CSPA, 1702*, No. 242, p. 161.

[24] *Ibid., 1704–5*, No. 1,210, p. 553 (1705).

tude. Between the second and third wars Maryland enacted legislation forbidding the enlistment of servants "unless upon such an Emergency as may be judged necessary and proper by the Field Officers of the respective County or the major Part of them." [25] It is clear that local sentiment was opposed to sending servants on distant military expeditions. In the third war the legislature protested against the enlistment of servants in the Canadian campaigns. Governor Bladen, in a conciliatory reply, stated that he had already ordered the discharge of enlisted servants upon specific application, but that in carrying out this policy he had to be "Careful to avoid giving any obstruction to his Majestys service." [26]

The enlistment of servants in the French and Indian War brought Marylanders into conflict with both Braddock and Shirley.[27] Governor Sharpe vainly sought to dissuade Braddock from ordering such enlistments, reporting that "the Servants immediately flocked in to enlist, convicts not excepted, and their masters made innumerable applications to me for Relief which I was sorry to be unable to grant." Sharpe's sympathies were clearly with the planters whose fortunes consisted "in the number of their Servants who are purchased at high rates as the estates of an English Farmer do in the Multitude of Cattle." This tragic campaign served to bring out the fact that the proprietors were more worried about protecting their property interests than in defeating the French.

Shirley found it necessary, as in Pennsylvania, to countermand his original order forbidding the enlistment of servants.[28] The arrest of a recruiting officer for enlisting servants brought the issue to a head. The governor referred the following questions to two members of his council:

(1) Whether an indentured servant has a right to Enlist in his Majesty's Service?
(2) Whether a Military Officer enlisting such servant is liable to an Action?
(3) Whether the Governor can discharge such action?

They flatly controverted the position adopted earlier by Governor Lewis Morris of New Jersey and maintained:

(1) A Master has property in an indentured servant, therefore he has no right to enlist.

[25] *Md. Arch.*, XXXIX, 118 (1732).   [26] *Ibid.*, XLIV, 367, 385.
[27] See *Pa. Gazette*, Feb. 26, 1756.
[28] Under his order servants wishing to return to their masters would be permitted to do so provided their masters furnished able-bodied substitutes for them. *Md. Arch.*, XXXI, 106 (1756).

(2) A recruiting officer, enlisting an indentured Servant, is liable to Action.

(3) The Governor cannot discharge a civil action, commenced by a man for the recovery of his property.

Therefore it is the opinion of the Board, that as Mr. Sterling is arrested on a civil action for damages, the Governor cannot discharge the arrest.[29]

In a separate opinion Daniel Dulany concurred in all three points; but, as regards the second, he differentiated between an officer who enlisted a servant knowing him to be such and one who did so without knowledge of his true status. In the former situation he felt that the officer would be liable to an action brought by the master; in the latter he would not, in Dulany's opinion, be liable "unless after Notice of Masters Right or property in Such Servant the Officer should detain the servant against the Will and Consent of his master." From the correspondence of Shirley with the governors of Maryland and Pennsylvania it would appear that the recruiting officers were permitted to continue to enlist servants, but that the masters had a right to sue for civil damages. It was felt in both colonies that the courts would uphold this right.[30]

Sentiment in Virginia veered from supporting universal conscription in the early years of settlement to advocating exemptions of servants from military service during the Intercolonial Wars. The acts of 1639 and 1640 imposed military obligations upon all males of legal age, and made the master responsible for the performance of military duties by each member of his family, including servants.[31] In 1645, after an Indian massacre, the Assembly permitted servants to enlist in the militia to march against the Indians.[32] In order to reduce Virginia to obedience to the regime of Cromwell, the Parliamentary Commissioners were instructed in 1651 to raise forces for the reduction of the colony and to set free from their masters "such persons as shall serve as soldiers if their Masters stand in opposition to the present Government."[33] By 1672 class and sectional divisions were more pronounced than in the earlier decades. A militia act of that year admitted into the armed services only those white servants whose terms had nearly expired, and who would therefore have little incentive to turn their weapons against their masters. When the militia left their plantations to defend the coast against the Dutch the following year they were genuinely apprehensive

[29] *Ibid.*, p. 112 (1756). Cf. also Merriam v. Bissel, 2 Root (Conn.) 378 (1796), where a master was granted recovery against a recruiting officer who enlisted his apprentice without his consent.

[30] H. L. Osgood, *American Colonies in the 18th Century* (New York, 1924), IV, 409.

[31] See P. A. Bruce, *Institutional History of Virginia in the 17th Century* (New York, 1910), II, 5. Slaves were excluded because of fear of arming Negroes.

[32] Hening, I, 292.   [33] *VMH*, XVII, 283.

of the likelihood of an insurrection of servants working in collaboration with the smaller landowners.[34] At the time of Bacon's Rebellion many servants flocked to the insurrectionary cause.[35] Bacon issued commissions of impressment which did not discriminate between servants and planters.[36] Among Bacon's laws, later repealed, was the provision that, where a master was willing, a servant could be admitted to the militia, the master to have the pay allowed to soldiers under the act "and the servant the plunder to his owne proper use." [37]

As a result of the rebellion and of a number of conspiracies fomented by servants, the planters were loathe to allow them to serve in the militia, although as late as 1688 the authorities ordered that Christian servants be provided with arms and trained for the defense of the colony.[38] In 1699 the House of Burgesses opposed Governor Nicholson's proposal to train servants in the militia on the ground that this would burden both large and small planters, but more especially the latter who would be inconvenienced if militia officers summoned their servants at the time of the year when the tobacco crop required greatest attention to protect it from the worms and weeds in the field or to cure it properly in the barns. Furthermore, it was maintained that the arming of white servants would endanger the safety of the community, as "for the most part" they numbered "the worser sort of people of Europe," including Irish soldiers and "soldiers in the late wars," recently transported to Virginia. These immigrants were found to be a sullen and unruly addition to the laboring class. It was hard enough, the burgesses protested, to control their white laborers when unarmed, but if armed and permitted to attend musters, they might be encouraged to "rise upon us." Furthermore, the fear was expressed that in a war with a foreign enemy, such servants as the Irish were more likely to desert than to assist the colonists.[39] Notwithstanding this opposition by the Lower House and the recorded objection of the Council in 1701 to the effect that in its "opinion . . . Christian servants should be exempt from military duty," [40] the Board of Trade the following year urged the governor to follow the example of a recent Maryland statute by which all masters were obliged to furnish their servants with a gun at the ex-

[34] See Bruce, *op. cit.*, II, 199, 200.   [35] See also *supra*, pp. 175–177.

[36] See commissions for impressing 20 men with horses and arms in Lancaster County, July 26, 1676. *VMH*, XVI, 212.

[37] Hening, II, 346 (1676).   [38] *Exec. J. Council of Va.*, I, 516 (1688).

[39] *CSPA*, 1699, No. 473, pp. 260, 261 (May 30, 31, 1699); Bruce, *op. cit.*, II, 6, 7.

[40] *Exec. J. Council of Va.*, II, 184 (1701).

piration of their servitude, "wch seems to us one very good means to keep them armed, and in a condition to defend themselves when there may be occasion."[41]

With the outbreak of the third Intercolonial War, the Virginia Council issued an order specifically forbidding the enlistment of servants in the king's service.[42] This prohibition was continued on the eve of the French and Indian War, when provision was made for the enlistment of "such able bodied men, as do not follow or exercise any lawful calling or employment, or have not some other lawful and sufficient support and maintenance, to serve his majesty, as soldiers in the present expedition."[43] Notwithstanding this prohibition, Washington urged upon Loudon the enlistment of servants in the Virginia volunteers. If no provision was made for such enlistments, they would run off and enlist in the regular army, he realistically warned. He himself recruited numerous servants for his regiment, and called upon Governor Dinwiddie to arrange for compensation to their masters under the act of Parliament.[44] A statute of 1756 empowered the courts to draft soldiers from among "all such able-bodied persons, within their respective jurisdictions, as shall be found loitering and neglecting to labor for reasonable wages," including the idle, vagrant, and dissolute.[45] This threat of impressment was clearly calculated to depress the wage scale of laborers and forestall combinations and strikes without any impairment in the masters' property interest in their bound servants.

In the Carolinas, legislation dealing with the enlistment and conscription of servants was motivated in large measure by fear of Negro insurrections. From early settlement, masters were required by law to send their servants to the watch.[46] However, in consequence of the escape from the province of an armed band of servants,[47] the Commons House of Assembly in 1741, in reply to a message from the governor respecting the purchase of white servants to serve in the garrison,

[41] *VMH*, XXIII, 392. See also the specific instructions to the Earl of Orkney, 1714, that all Christian servants be armed and available for military service when needed. *Ibid.*, XXI, 229.

[42] *Ibid.*, XIV, 351 (1740). Governor Gooch did not see eye to eye with Governor Lewis Morris of New Jersey on this question. See N.J. Hist. Soc. *Coll.*, IV, 97 (1740).

[43] Hening, VI, 438, 439 (1754). Masters might petition for relief where servants had enlisted and had not returned to their service owing to death or other reasons. See Wright's petition, Prince William O.B., 1754–55, f. 220 (April 14, 1755). It is clear that servants on the frontier especially sought to enlist. In 1756 Richard Mihills agreed not to enlist in the king's service, in return for which his master, William Preston, remitted one year's service due. Augusta Co. Court Rec. (Nov. 22, 1756).

[44] Washington, *Writings* (Sparks ed.), II, 169, 199.   [45] Hening, VII, 70 (1756).
[46] *S.C. Grand Council J.*, p. 12 (1671).   [47] *S.C. Gazette*, Feb. 12, 1737.

expressed the "Opinion it might be of dangerous Consequence to in-
trust white servants in the service."[48] Nevertheless, the law still required them to bear arms during military emergencies and to attend
muster, an obligation which continued into the early Federal period.[49]
Georgia also conscripted servants for the militia and provided compensation for poor freemen and white servants injured in war.[50]

The British West Indies generally favored using their white servants
for military purposes in order to guard against Negro insurrections,[51]
but the planters were by no means enthusiastic about the prospect of losing them entirely by enlistments in the regular army.[52] In fact, the
Attorney General in 1701 reported to the Board of Trade adversely on
an act passed in Nevis requiring the militia to meet and drill every
month on the ground that the training of servants would be "inconvenient and prejudicial" to their masters, who were not allowed
compensation. He also regarded as "unreasonable" a provision freeing
servants who had behaved bravely under arms.[53] In recommending disallowance, the Board of Trade raised certain constitutional objections
to provisions of the law setting severe penalties for servants absent from
training on the ground that the lives of the offenders could be taken
away "by Martiall Law in times of peace which we conceive to be
contrary to the law of England."[54] Where available, white servants
were generally included in estimates of numbers of men in the British
West Indies fit to bear arms.[55]

[48] S.C. Council J., lib. 1737–41, f. 379. For earlier requirements that Negroes be enrolled in the
militia and separately trained, see *S.C. Stat.*, II, 254 (1704). For occasional use of Negro troops
in the West Indies owing to the shortage of white men, see *CSPA, 1701*, No. 941, p. 573; *1702*,
Nos. 25, 1150, pp. 16, 721; *1708–09*, No. 739, p. 466 (1709).

[49] For the effect of the militia act of 1747, see Simpson, *Practical Justice of the Peace*, p. 237.
The master was held responsible for furnishing his servant with arms. *S.C. Stat.*, VIII, 489 (1794).

[50] One act specifically provided that all servants who fought in the militia would be set free.
Ga. Col. Rec., XVIII, 42 (1755). The master was liable to a penalty if his servant failed to
attend muster. *Ibid.*, p. 18 (1755).

[51] *CSPA, 1681–85*, No. 768, p. 317 (1682). Barbadian planters reported in 1685 that, owing to
hard times, they had "been obliged to discharge our hired servants, who were a great safety to the
Island, since they formed most part of the Militia and curbed our negroes and white servants,
which last, being the sweepings of the jails, will be a danger for England if they return." *Ibid.*,
1685–88, No. 367, p. 93 (1685). See also *ibid., 1696–97*, No. 49, p. 23 (1696). In 1702 Barbadians
stated that "the present militia are but few and consist of servants." *Ibid., 1702*, No. 804, p. 507.
One of the West Indian commanders reported in 1712 that in one island there were "but seven
men to do duty in the Fort, and but now six of which four are my servants." *Ibid., 1711–12*,
No. 392, p. 270. As in South Carolina, West Indian masters were required by law to equip their
servants in the militia. *Laws of Antigua* (London, 1805), II, 150 (1793).

[52] *CSPA., 1706–8*, No. 322, p. 135.

[53] *Ibid., 1701*, No. 919, p. 565 (1701). Cf. also Jamaica act of 1693, Baskett, *Laws of Jamaica,
1681–1737*, p. 66 (1693).

[54] *CSPA, 1701*, Nos. 707, 816, pp. 404, 495 (1701).

[55] For example, a report of Governor Hamilton to the Board of Trade in 1720 listed the total

Owing to the difficulties in raising an army during the American Revolution, the Continental Congress and a number of the states encouraged the recruiting of servants.[56] In Rhode Island, Maryland, and New Jersey, servants were declared eligible for enlistment without requiring their masters' consent, and, for a time, all three states provided compensation for masters.[57] Other states, following the lead of the Continental Congress, permitted the enlistment of servants only when their masters consented, but provided no compensation for the masters.[58] In the second group of states was New York, which nonetheless definitely discouraged such enlistments. In the summer of 1775 the Provincial Congress directed General Wooster to restore to their masters those apprentices and indentured servants who had enlisted with the Continental troops in Connecticut.[59]

Pennsylvania and Virginia specifically exempted servants from the militia.[60] The recommendation of the Continental Congress that servants be permitted to enlist aroused a good deal of apprehension in Pennsylvania, the state with the largest white servant population. In September, 1776, the Council of Safety passed a resolution against enlisting servants and apprentices for the "Flying Camp" without the con-

---

free adult white male population of the Leeward Islands as 2,467 and the total number of men servants, both free and unfree, as 731. Yet 2,948 men were listed as "fit to bear arms." *Ibid., 1720-21,* No. 204, p. 115 (1720).

[56] While a resolution permitting enlistment of servants and apprentices was carried in April, 1777, a clause requiring compensation to be made to masters was defeated by a close vote. *J. Continental Cong.,* VII, 262, 369. In a suggestive paper William Miller has pointed out the error of J. C. Hurd's assertion (*The Law of Freedom and Bondage in the United States* [Boston, 1858], I, 220-221) that "servants enlisted in the Continental army were to be deemed freemen." "The Effects of the American Revolution on Indentured Servitude," *Pennsylvania History* (July, 1940).

[57] Early Rhode Island legislation gave the servant his bounty but split his wages with the master. *R.I. Col. Rec.,* VII, 319, 386 (1775). But by 1777 apprentices were given their entire bounty and wages. *Ibid.,* VIII, 243 (1777). The early laws in Maryland and New Jersey made no provision for compensation for masters. *Md. Laws,* June Session, 1777, ch. VIII; *N.J. Laws,* March 15, 1777, ch. XX § 14. Later both states legislated compensation, although the Maryland law, enacted in Feb., 1777, was repealed in June of that year. *Md. Laws,* Feb., 1777, ch. iii; *N.J. Laws,* Session 1777 (May 28, 1777); *Pa. Laws,* Session 1778 (March 11, 1778).

[58] *Cal. of Hist. MSS Relating to the War of the Revol.* (Albany, 1868), II, 11 (Oct. 23, 1776). This position was also taken by the Continental Congress as regards enlistments in both the army and the navy of the "United Colonies," as early as Jan., 1776. See *J. Continental Cong.,* IV, 56.

[59] Their masters were to reimburse him for any expenses he had incurred. *J. Prov. Cong.,* I, 68; *Amer. Arch.,* 4th ser., II, 1345. For treatment of such cases by the Albany Committee of Correspondence, see *Mins. Albany Comm. Corr.,* I, 379, 381; II, 1071, 1072 (1776). At a later time the New York courts held that the relation of master and apprentice was dissolved by the latter's voluntary enlistment, as the government's right to the services of its citizens is paramount to indentures sanctioned by local law. Johnson v. Dodd, 56 N.Y. 76 (1874).

[60] Pennsylvania exempted "servants purchased bona fide and for a valuable consideration." *Pa. Laws,* 1780 (March 20, 1780); *Va. Laws,* May, 1777, Session ch. II. See also A. V. Alexander, "Pennsylvania's Revolutionary Militia," *Pa. Mag.* (Jan., 1945), pp. 15-25.

sent of their masters in writing, and declaring that all servants previously enlisted should be discharged on application to their masters.[61] Nevertheless an act passed in February, 1777, set a fine for masters who prevented their apprentices from joining the "associators." [62] A statute enacted two months later provided that the master should be liable for the cost of providing a substitute where his apprentice neglected or refused to attend the militia as well as for all fines imposed on a delinquent apprentice.[63] The issue was epitomized in a memorial drawn up by the County Committee of Cumberland, meeting at Shippensburgh, May 15, 1777, which is expressive of an attitude toward property that doubtless would have won high favor among Southern planters during the fugitive-slave crisis of a later generation.

Resolved, that all Apprentices and servants are the Property of their masters and mistresses, and every mode of depriving such masters and mistresses of their Property is a Violation of the Rights of mankind, contrary to the Continental Congress, and an offence against the Peace of the good People of this State, except the consent of the masters and mistresses, in their proper persons, or by their Representatives in Genl. Assembly met, shall be first had and obtained.

The County Committee requested that servants or apprentices who had enlisted be returned to their masters on application, there to remain until the legislature had decided the issue. They appealed to the freemen of the county to assist in returning such persons to their "owners" or in bringing them before the next justice of the peace or the next township committee to be committed to prison.[64] Moved by these sentiments, the legislature refused to concur in the recommendation of the Supreme Executive Council that servants be permitted to enlist and proceeded to issue a proclamation forbidding the recruiting officers from enlisting servants or apprentices within the state "on pain of being prosecuted with the utmost rigour of the Law." [65] When servants disregarded this proclamation and enlisted in large numbers, the legis-

[61] *Pa. Arch.*, 1st ser., V, 340. The Board of War in April, 1777 directed that an indentured servant boy belonging to a member of the 9th Virginia Regiment be dismissed, "as the Hon'ble Continental Congress have directed the quotas which shall be raised by each State, and as it would be extremely oppressive and unjust should a servant be taken from the inhabitants of one state to make up the quotas of another state." *Ibid.*, pp. 328, 329. See also *Pa. Col. Rec.*, X, 470.

[62] *Pa. Stat. at Large*, IX, 52, 53.

[63] *Ibid.*, p. 87 (March 17, 1777). Apprentices or servants not subject to the militia law could, according to an act passed later in the year, substitute for their masters. *Ibid.*, p. 186.

[64] *Pa. Arch.*, 1st ser., V, 340.

[65] Such enlistments were declared to be "distressing to the Masters" without promoting "the General Service to any proportionable degree." *Ibid.*, 4th ser., III, 656–657.

lature was forced in 1778 to enact a law providing compensation for masters.[66]

Virginia, whose record in the Intercolonial Wars was one of hostility to the enlistment of apprentices, made provision in 1775 to restrict such enlistments unless the servant were an apprentice "bound under the laws of this colony" who had first obtained his master's consent in writing.[67] The exigencies of war caused Virginia to modify her policy, and in 1777 a statute was enacted requiring all free males, including hired servants and apprentices, from sixteen to fifty to be enrolled in the militia.[68]

The British naturally encouraged defections of servants and slaves to their armed forces as effective blows at disloyal subjects. In 1774 Governor Gage flirted with a plan to arm the Negroes.[69] At the outbreak of the war Governor Dunmore of Virginia proclaimed that all indentured servants and Negroes belonging to the rebels who joined His Majesty's troops would have their freedom.[70] As a result of this proclamation a considerable number joined the British armed forces.[71] The greatest losses took place during the invasion of the South in the late years of the war. It is estimated that Virginia lost 30,000 slaves and

[66] Bioren, *Laws*, I, p. xlvii; *Pa. Stat. at Large*, IX, 216, 217. As a matter of fact, so many servants enlisted from Lancaster County that the county treasurer refused in 1781 to pay masters for the time of their enlisted servants "since it will take more stale money than we will receive in taxes." He had already paid out £415 10s. *Pa. Arch.*, 1st ser., VIII, 730. For advertisements warning recruiting officers not to enlist a runaway servant of Tory sympathies, see *Pa. J.*, March 12, 1777.

[67] Hening, IX, 12, 81 (1775). To stop the practice among tradesmen of enticing their apprentices to enlist as soldiers and of selling them as substitutes for large sums of money, a penalty of double the sum of the gratuity to be recovered by an action of debt was set by law; but where the offender was an able-bodied man under 50 he was to be impressed under the state's quota of Continental troops. *Ibid.*, X, 335, 336 (1780).

[68] *Ibid.*, IX, 267. An act passed shortly thereafter permitted the enlistment of servants or apprentices, except "hired servants, under written contracts," and apprentices at any ironworks or public firearms factory during the period of such contracts without written permission of the owner or manager of such works. Exception was likewise made for "every imported servant." This statute was reenacted in Oct., 1777, and again in May, 1778. *Ibid.*, pp. 342, 346, 452.

[69] See G. H. Moore, *Notes on the History of Slavery in Massachusetts* (New York, 1866), p. 129; C. F. Adams, ed., *Letters of Mrs. Adams, the Wife of John Adams* (3d ed., Boston, 1841), I, 24.

[70] *Amer. Arch.*, 4th ser. III, 1385–1387 (1775). Governor Martin of North Carolina saw fit to deny that he had offered encouragement to the Negroes to revolt against their masters. *Ibid.*, pp. 8, 9, 40 (1775).

[71] Cf. Force, *Amer. Arch.*, 4th ser., III, 256; *VMH*, XIV, 136; *Md. Arch.*, XVI, 5; *Pa. Gazette*, Aug. 21, 1776; *Pa. Evening Post*, Aug. 17, 1776; March 4, 1777. For charges against Governor Eden of enticing servants to board ships of the Royal Navy, see Red Book, IV, f. 2, XII, fols. 42, 43; Rainbow Papers, Hall of Records, Annapolis; *Md. Arch.*, XI, 511–517, XII, 98 (1776). Colonel Landon Carter criticized a Scotch renegade to the side of Governors Eden and Dunmore "who carried off all the slaves and servants almost out of Maryland." *WMCQ*, 1st ser., XX, 180 (July 4, 1776).

South Carolina at least 25,000, carried off or victims of disease.[72] As far as the home country was concerned, the British opposed the impressment of servants. Under the press act of 1779 apprentices in Great Britain were surrendered on the master's demand in accordance with an opinion rendered in 1760 by Attorney General Sir Charles Pratt.[73]

IMPRESSMENT AND ENLISTMENT OF SERVANTS, FREE WORKERS, AND OTHER LANDSMEN IN THE NAVY

IN ADDITION TO seamen, whose impressment for ships of the British navy we have previously considered,[1] servants, apprentices, slaves, and other landsmen were not infrequently seized for duty on ships of war. Occasionally the colonies cooperated and issued orders for impressing young men and vagrants as seamen,[2] but dissents were by no means infrequent. During the French and Indian War the Rhode Island Assembly appointed a committee to "prepare a bill to prevent soldiers, servants, apprentices, and so forth, being carried off to sea." [3] The main attack against the impressment of landsmen was launched in the West Indies, which appear to have been more heavily hit than the Continental colonies.[4] Representations were made in 1702 that "the pressing of Landmen is the greatest grievance imaginable in this country which is almost undone for want of white men." [5]

The Continental Congress at the beginning of the Revolution was compelled to resort to the expedient used by the British government during the Intercolonial Wars. A set of instructions issued by Congress to commanders of privateers in April, 1776, required that one third of their companies be landsmen.[6] Recruiting officers exhorted throngs

---

[72] Gray, *op. cit.*, II, 596. For Negro slaves owned by Loyalists and seized by the Revolutionary authorities, see Egerton, *op. cit.*, pp. 172, 307, 330.

[73] The authorities found by experience that "Fraudulent Claims of Apprentices are so frequent and so detrimental to the Service that they ought to be guarded against with Caution." Curtis, *op. cit.*, p. 63, citing the War Office papers.

[1] See *supra*, pp. 272–278.

[2] *Exec. J. Council of Va.*, I, 49 (1683), II, 362 (1704), III, 215 (1709), 531 (1720); *VMH*, XV, 128 (1741). When a commander was short of hands owing to sickness and desertion, the Norfolk authorities in 1757 ordered that 50 Negroes be hired to work on board ship for a brief period. Norfolk Common Council Mins., f. 70 (1757). Cf. also *Mass. Acts and Resolves*, VII, 169, 579 (1697).

[3] *R.I. Col. Rec.*, VI, 13 (1757). Cf. also *ibid.*, p. 64 (1757), setting a fine for the carrying away of a slave by a privateer.

[4] See *CSPA, 1696–97*, No. 234, p. 123 (1696); No. 458, p. 236; No. 519, p. 264; No. 1166, p. 543 (1697); *1699*, pp. 517, 519; *VMH*, XXII, 34, 35 (1699).

[5] *CSPA, 1702*, pp. 402, 599. In the same year the Barbadian Assembly resolved that servants receiving wages on board men-of-war be returned to their masters or otherwise secured. *Ibid.*, pp. 647, 651. For Newfoundland, cf. *ibid., 1704–5*, p. 558 (1705).

[6] Allen, *op. cit.*, II, 697.

of workmen in seaport towns to sign aboard privateers, and sang a persuasive tune:

> All you that have bad masters,
> And cannot get your due,
> Come, come, my brave boys,
> And join our ship's crew.[7]

NONMILITARY SERVICES OF ARTIFICERS, LABORERS, AND SERVANTS IN THE ARMY

DURING THE COURSE of the seventeenth century laborers and artificers were at times impressed for nonmilitary services with the armed forces and on other occasions were recruited by means of voluntary enlistments or by regular labor contracts. Men and carts were impressed by the Massachusetts authorities for work on the fort at Castle Island in Boston harbor; both in New Haven colony and in Carolina gunsmiths and certain other artificers were conscripted to repair firearms; and Connecticut impressed shoemakers to make shoes for the soldiers.[1]

With the advent of the Intercolonial Wars impressment of artificers and laborers for nonmilitary duties with the armed forces became more frequent. Virginia and Maryland impressed carpenters and laborers,[2] and most colonies were obliged to impress drivers, together with their horses and carts, for military duties.[3] New York and Bermuda impressed all inhabitants for work on fortifications. In New York the citizens and freeholders were given the option of appearing in person with spades, shovels, or pickaxes, or of having laborers serve for them.[4]

[7] C. K. Bolton, *The Private Soldier under Washington* (New York, 1902), p. 38.

[1] The Massachusetts order of 1634 provided that the impressed laborers be paid ordinary wages to make carriages and wheels needed for the ordnance. *Mass. Bay Rec.*, I, 125, 147 (1634, 1635). Impressment for work about the castle served as one defendant's plea to a suit for breach of contract. Lechford, *Note-Book*, pp. 215, 216 (1639). For impressment a quarter century later, see *Mass. Bay Rec.*, IV, 42, 43, 332; V, 105. In 1633 "the whole strength of men able to labour in the colony" was impressed for the building of a fort at Plymouth. *Plymouth Col. Rec.*, I, 6 (1633). See also *New Haven Col. Rec.*, *1658-65*, p. 298 (1659); *Conn. Pub. Rec.*, *1665-78*, p. 449 (1676); Osgood, *op. cit.*, II, 383.

[2] *Md. Arch.*, VIII, 461 (1693); *Exec. J. of the Council of State of Va.*, I, 248 (1692). Jamaica authorized a contractor to impress workmen 'if he cannot hire them." *CSPA, 1693-96*, No. 473, p. 133 (1693). See also Baskett, *Acts of Jamaica* (London, 1756), p. 163 (1728). Negroes were also impressed in the West Indies for defense work. *CSPA, 1702*, Nos. 132, 457, pp. 94, 305. While the governor of Pennsylvania was urged "to use compulsion" to impress workmen for road work, instead he resorted to advertisements "inviting" laborers to enter upon this service. *Pa. Arch.*, II, 320, 325. For New York, see Stokes, *Iconography*, IV, 600 (1746), 677 (1756), 689 (1757), 696 (1758). *N.Y. Col. Laws*, III, 1093 (1755); IV, 343 (1749).

[3] *Pa. Stat. at Large*, V, 330 (1758), 373, 420, 421 (1759); Cooper, *S.C. Stat.*, IV, 104, 148 (1760, 1761).

[4] *M.C.C.*, II, 303-305. *CSPA, 1701*, No. 847, p. 511, *1704-5*, No. 455, p. 217 (1704), *1711-12*, No. 164, pp. 139, 140 (1711); in Massachusetts carpenters, smiths, and other artificers in towns adjacent to Boston were impressed, *ibid.*, pp. 139, 140 (1711).

According to a newspaper account, all persons were forbidden "all manner of Labour, and all shops shut up until the Fortifications of the City be finished, so that we have near 1000 men at work every day." [5] This practice was not without effect upon the prevailing wage scale. In 1712 the Massachusetts legislature called upon the governor to empower the Commissary General to impress certain specified foodstuffs and "all Bakers, Brewers, etca. who will or can not Supply the Publick in their way at the stated price and to impress all artificers and Labourers necessary." [6] The New York impressment law of 1746 provided that the "usual Rates" were to be paid carpenters for work on bateaux for military expeditions.[7]

In addition to impressment, military authorities secured the services of artificers and laborers by voluntary enlistments or short-term contracts at wages attractive to labor. Carpenters, bricklayers, armourers, and smiths were designated by the authorities to do work for the army and to render an account to the colony.[8] However, there was a constant scarcity of artificers working on military projects,[9] and in order to keep them on the job it was necessary to pay them promptly [10] and to offer them higher wages than the soldiers received.[11] At times artificers were discouraged by the difficult specifications set by the

[5] *Boston News-Letter*, Aug. 5, 1706.

[6] *Mass. Acts and Resolves*, IX, 185 (1712).

[7] All persons neglecting or refusing upon such impress to work were subject to one month's imprisonment. Special provision was made that artificers, servants, and laborers from New York, Richmond, Westchester, and the counties of Long Island would not be required to perform work outside the counties to which they belonged. *N.Y. Col. Laws*, III, 593; *N.Y. Post-Boy*, July 21, 1746; *Cal. Council Mins.*, p. 356.

[8] *CSPA, 1681–85*, No. 1051, p. 421 (1683), *1700*, Nos. 575, 686, 702, 953, pp. 353, 459, 470, 687, *1702*, Nos. 28, 186, 292, 387, 424, 666, 819, pp. 21, 123, 190, 271, 295, 427, 511, *1702–3*, No. 13, p. 8 (1702), Nos. 652, 948, 954, pp. 396, 570, 575 (1703). *Exec. J. of the Council of State of Va.*, I, 215 (1691); *Mass. Acts and Resolves*, VII, 226 (1700), VIII, 168, 582 (1707), XIII, 442 (1745); *Acts and Laws of N.H.*, II, 107, 108 (1711); III, 161 (1757). The authorities had frequent recourse to advertisements. *S.C. Gazette*, April 3–10, 1742; *Pa. Col. Rec.*, VI, 402–403 (1755).

[9] "Armourers are greatly wanted, there not being One in the Garrison belonging to the Army," it was reported from Mobile just after the termination of the French and Indian War. *Mississippi Provincial Archives: English Dominion* (Nashville, Tenn., 1911), p. 109.

[10] For complaints on this score, see *CSPA, 1689–92*, No. 999, p. 301 (1690); *Md. Arch.*, IX, 158, 162; *R.I. Col. Rec.*, VI, 504 (1766).

[11] *Pa. Col. Rec.*, VI, 434 (1755). While a private received 1s. per diem and a lieutenant 5s., a smith received 5s., a wheelwright and carpenter each 3s., and a waterman 1s. 6d. Hening, VII, 28 (1756). Boat builders engaged to construct a flotilla to carry the British army across Lake Ontario were offered "half extra wages" to join General Shirley's Company of Pioneers. "Journal of Stephen Cross of Newburyport, entitled 'Up to Ontario,' " *Essex Inst. Hist. Coll.*, LXXV (1939), 334 *et seq.* (1756). "The Pay of a Common Carpenter at Pensacola," Gage reported only a few years after the close of the war, "is nearly equal to that of a Field Officer." *Gage Corr.*, II, 434 (1767).

army.[12] Then, too, they were often required to perform their tasks on the front lines under extremely hazardous conditions.[13]

A typical regiment in the French and Indian War included an impressive number of craftsmen and laborers.[14] In addition to outside artificers especially engaged for particular tasks, important construction work was undertaken by the corps of engineers, which did not have military status until 1757.[15]

ARTIFICERS AND LABORERS IN THE CONTINENTAL AND BRITISH ARMIES DURING THE AMERICAN REVOLUTION

THE EFFECTIVE MOBILIZATION of manpower for civilian as well as military tasks was never brought about during the American Revolution.[1] Manpower problems similar to those confronting military and civilian administrative agencies in this country in the first and second World Wars were dealt with *ad hoc* without any serious attempt at over-all planning. Actually the impressment of property, particularly of supplies and provisions and of transportation facilities, was resorted to far more frequently than the impressment of labor.[2] But even in this field the authorities were reluctant to antagonize civilians or jeopardize property rights, and therefore trod softly. Washington told the Continental Congress in December, 1777: "I confess I have felt myself greatly embarrassed with respect to a vigorous exercise of military power. An Ill

---

12 See Mass. Arch., lib. 303 (Petitions, 1659–1786), f. 85a, wherein it appears that the smiths "grew discouraged" because of the complexity of making different sized bayonets for various guns used and stopped work (1758).

13 See "Journal of Stephen Cross, *loc. cit.,* pp. 334 *et seq.* For the hazardous position of the workmen at Ninety-Six during the battle there in the American Revolution, see M. Haiman, *Kosciuszko in the American Revolution* (New York, 1943), p. 112. See also "Journal of Joseph Joslin, Jr., of South Killingly, Conn.," *Conn. Hist. Soc., Coll.,* VII, 368 (1778).

14 See the return of Col. Clapham's regiment stationed at Ft. Augusta, Oct. 18, 1756. *Pa. Arch.,* III, 15. For a return of the companies of artificers among the Maryland, Virginia, and North Carolina troops encamped at Will's Creek in 1755, see S. M. Pargellis, ed., *Military Affairs in North America, 1746–1765* (New York, 1936), pp. 88–89.

15 W. Porter, *History of the Corps of Royal Engineers* (London, 1889), I, 180.

1 The result was critical in civilian occupations, especially farming, and women often had to shoulder the farm duties of their absent husbands. There is also evidence that less farm acreage was planted in certain areas owing to a shortage of hands. See letter of John Ormsby to General Hand, Pittsburgh, Jan. 20, 1778. Misc. MSS, N.Y. Pub. Lib.

2 See Elizabeth Cometti, "Impressment during the American Revolution," *Walter Clinton Jackson Essays in the Social Sciences,* pp. 100 *et seq.;* V. R. Johnson, *The Administration of the American Commissariat during the Revolutionary War* (Philadelphia, 1941), pp. 83, 100, 160, 186, 190, *passim.* When, in January, 1781, 9 out of 16 wagoners who had agreed to terms for transporting stores and arms for the Southern army refused to perform their duties, the deputy quartermaster, George Elliot, reported his intention of seizing their wagons. *Cal. Va. State Papers,* I, 466.

placed humanity perhaps and a reluctance to give distress may have restrained me too far." [3] In 1780 he justified impressment on the ground that "Our Affairs are in so deplorable a condition (on the score of provisions) as to fill the Mind with the most anxious and alarming fears. . . . Men half starved, imperfectly Cloathed, riotous, and robbing the Country people of their subsistence from shear necessity." [4]

The Continental army employed a wide variety of artisans, ranging from construction gangs working with the military engineers to blacksmiths, tailors, and even laundresses. [5] These artificers were often formed into companies, and there was at least one regiment in the army. [6] One such company of artificers, organized in 1776, comprised a captain paid at the rate of a dollar a day, a lieutenant, at seventy-five cents a day, and twenty-five able house carpenters, boatbuilders, and wheelwrights, receiving daily wages of half a dollar. They were to find their own tools, blankets, and clothing, "and when occasion requires it, are [to] act the part of Soldiers in either attack or defence as well as Artificers." [7]

[3] E. C. Burnett, *The Continental Congress* (New York, 1941), p. 271. For widespread opposition to the impressment of food and teams, see *Writings of Washington* (Fitzpatrick ed.), X, 175 (1777), 267 (1778). Actually the impressment of property for military purposes goes back to the early colonial period. See, e.g., *Plymouth Col. Rec.*, VI, 65 (1681).

[4] Burnett, *op. cit.*, p. 402. See also *Writings* (Fitzpatrick ed.), XVII, 351, 368 (1780). But in May, 1781, he wrote: "We are daily and hourly oppressing the people—souring their tempers—and alienating their affections." *Diaries*, II, 207.

[5] See, e.g., *Orderly Book of Brig. Gen. Anthony Wayne*, pp. 104, 111, 125, 128, 133; *Pa. Arch.*, 1st ser., VII, 652. In 1779 blacksmiths were paid $8 a day and rations. For companies of artificers working under Kosciuszko, see Haiman, *op. cit.*, pp. 19, 22, 35, 51 *et seq.*

[6] A corps of artillery artificers was raised at Washington's direction in the summer of 1777. Benjamin Flowers was made colonel. Companies were stationed at Carlisle and Philadelphia; their duties were to cast cannon, bore guns, and prepare ammunition for the army. *Pa. Arch.*, 2d ser., XI, 249; 5th ser., III, 1083–1145. For distribution of trades in typical companies in this corps, the muster rolls prove illuminating.

Capt. Wylie's Company of Artillery Artificers, April, 1780: carpenters, 5; armorers, 4; blacksmiths, 8; file cutters, 3; nailors, 3; lock filers, 2; grinders, 2; shoemakers, 2; and one each of the following trades: cooper, tailor, wheelwright, lock forger, foundry boy. Of this company ten were listed as deserters. *Ibid.*, pp. 1091–1093. Capt. Parkes' Company employed at the leather accoutrements factory in Philadelphia included: 3 curriers; 5 whitesmiths; 31 shoemakers; 3 sadlers; 5 sewers. *Ibid.*, p. 1119. A return of the Pennsylvania Corps of Artillery Artificers showed that the men were stationed at 1) New London, Va.; 2) Southern Army; 3) Philadelphia; 4) Fort Pitt. Of these 12 were employed at "Laboratory" work, 7 were harnessmakers, 5 carpenters, 4 armorers, 3 blacksmiths, 2 tinmen, 2 nailors, and a scattering number of tailors, turners, file cutters, curriers, wheelwrights, and waiters. *Ibid.*, pp. 1095–1096. See also return of artificers at Saratoga under Col. Baldwin. Emmett MSS, No. 4295, N.Y. Pub. Lib. For other references to companies of artificers, see Orderly Book of Col. James Chambers of the 1st Pa. Regiment, *Pa. Arch.*, 2d ser., XI, 304 (July 29, 1778); Journal of Capt. Joseph McClellan of the 9th Pa., *ibid.*, p. 609 (1780); Orderly Book of the 1st Pa., *ibid.*, p. 643 (1780); H. Whiting, ed., *Revolutionary Orders of General Washington, 1778–82* (New York, 1844), p. 116 (1780). For references to detachments of woodcutters and ship carpenters, see W. C. Ford, comp., *General Orders Issued by Major-General William Heath* (Brooklyn, N.Y., 1890), pp. 66, 86 (1777); Gen. Glover's Orders, *Essex Inst. Hist. Coll.*, V, 119 (1778).

[7] Warrant to Joseph Lindsley for a company of artificers, March 4, 1776. Stirling MSS, lib. IV, f. 62, N.Y. Hist. Soc.

General Lee proposed and the New York Provincial Congress adopted in 1776 a typical plan: a company of some sixty men was headed by a captain who was a carpenter and drew the pay of a captain of a marching regiment; both of his associates, a blacksmith and a carpenter, drew lieutenants' pay; the privates had the same pay as prevailed at the company of artificers encamped near Cambridge, which was ten dollars per month. General Lee urged that

the works to be erected will require the assistance of carpenters and blacksmiths without delay, and unless this company is embodied, the General will be obliged to employ a number of tradesmen at daily wages, which will incur a greater expense to the public than would be created by the company above mentioned.[8]

The Continental authorities and state officials preferred to rely upon voluntary enlistment of mechanics and laborers rather than resort to impressment. Jefferson was willing to order tailors and shoemakers to report to the shoe factory,[9] but he turned down Steuben's request for help in obtaining militia labor for building defense works in Virginia. The Council had expressed the view that they "had no right to call out the militia to do fatigue duty." They went even further and declared that they had "not by the Laws of this State any power to call a freeman to labor even for the public without his consent, nor a Slave without that of his Master." Jefferson conceded that the work was essential, and admitted that the Council "may possibly be disappointed in their expectations of engaging voluntary laborers, the only means in their power." [10] Shortly after Bunker Hill a number of gunsmiths and locksmiths were brought over from Great Britain by the New York Provincial Congress.[11] Advertisements for forgemen, nailers, iron- and steelworkers, smiths, armorers and carpenters, and carters and wagoners for the Continental army were commonplace in the war years.[12]

Artificers among enlisted men were not infrequently transferred from regular duty and set to work at their own trades. Those so engaged

---

[8] *J.N.Y. Prov. Cong.*, I, 299, 302 (Feb. 14, 1776). For artificers in the New York Line, see J. A. Roberts, ed., *New York in the Revolution as Colony and State* (2d ed., Albany, 1898), p. 67.

[9] *Cal. Va. State Papers*, I, 414 (Jan. 3, 1781). Complaints were made at this time of the poor quality of shoes delivered, "so mean as to be useless."

[10] *Official Letters of the Governors of the State of Virginia*, ed. H. R. McIlwaine (3 vols., Richmond, 1926–29), II, 333–334. But cf. *ibid.*, III, 17 (1781).

[11] *Amer. Arch.*, 4th ser., II, 1791 (1775).

[12] See *N.J. Arch.*, I, 78 (1776), 385, 409, 544 (1777); II, 80, 199, 202 (1778). For typical wages paid artificers and laborers in the armed services, see "Journal of Joslin," Conn. Hist. Soc., *Coll.*, VII, 319 (1777); *R.I. Col. Rec.*, VII, 356 (1776); *Mins. Albany Comm. Corr.*, II, 1048–1050, 1056 (1776).

were given extra compensation.[13] But perhaps an even larger share of the nonmilitary tasks were performed by regular troops as fatigue duty. This was particularly true of unskilled or semiskilled tasks, such as building earthworks, cutting wood, repairing huts, clearing roads, hunting, and making cartridges and flour bags.[14]

The working conditions, wages, and hours of laborers working on military tasks were not infrequently regulated by the military authorities,[15] and were more rigidly enforced than in peacetime. Such artificers and laborers were under military orders to stay at work,[16] and were subject to court-martial for absenteeism or refractory conduct.[17] Generally speaking, artificers in the armed services, out of devotion to the cause, accepted lower wages than they could have obtained had they resigned and gone to work on their own account. "Grating comparisons" were drawn by the privates in the regiment of artificers between their scanty pay and the higher wages prevailing in the open market and paid to hired workmen. The Board of War pointed out to Congress that these workmen could only be replaced at higher wages, since workers outside the service, "having for some time past attended only to their private affairs," had "contracted more avaricious inclinations." [18] As late as 1781 the distress of laboring men in the military service was attested by a number of authorities.[19]

The control exercised by the army over laborers working for contractors engaged in the production of military supplies was much more

[13] See Gen. Glover's Orders, *Essex Inst. Hist. Coll.*, V, 117 (Ft. Arnold, June 29, 1778); *Heath Orders*, p. 108 (Lancaster, Jan. 3, 1778); Orderly Book, 1st Pa. Regiment, *Pa. Arch.*, 2d ser., XI, 469, 484 (1779); Orderly Book, 7th Pa. Regiment, *ibid.*, p. 530 (1779). See also *Pa. Arch.*, 1st ser., II, 439 (1777); 5th ser., III, 1127; Bolton, *op. cit.*, p. 154; Washington, *Writings* (Fitzpatrick ed.), XVII, 159 (1778) and *Diaries*, II, 226 (1781).

[14] Bolton, *op. cit.*, pp. 151-153; Journal of Simeon Lyman of Sharon, Conn. Hist. Soc., *Coll.*, VII, 121, 122 (1775); *Md. Arch.*, XII, 53 (1776); *Heath Orders*, p. 55 (1777); Whiting, *op. cit.*, pp. 40, 41 (1778), 241 (1782); *Pa. Arch.*, 2d ser., XI, 24, 499-501 (1779); Charles Martyn, *The Life of Artemas Ward* (New York, 1921), pp. 203-204 (1776).

[15] See also *supra*, pp. 125-127.

[16] See *Orderly Book of Brig. Gen. Wayne*, p. 114 (Dec. 7, 1776). In the same month Wayne ordered that "any woman belonging to the Reg't who shall refuse to wash for the Men, shall be immediately drumm'd out of the Reg't." *Ibid.*, p. 116.

[17] Orderly Book, 1st Pa. Regiment, *Pa. Arch.*, 2d ser., XI, 318, 385 (1778).

[18] Board of War to Congress, May 1, June 4, 1779, Board of War Papers, III, 365-371, 385-386, cited by L. C. Hatch, *The Administration of the American Revolutionary Army* (New York, 1904), p. 102.

[19] See *Md. Arch.*, XLVII, 126. For the difficulty in securing coopers to work at the canteens, see *ibid.*, XII, 188 (1776). Reed reported to Congress how hard it was to secure teams and drivers for the army at prevailing rates of compensation—6s. 8d. specie per diem. Previously, when the supply of wagons and labor had been more abundant and forage much cheaper, the rate had been $2.00 per day. "The Manifest Injustice of the Price," he affirmed, "will also be more striking as the agents under Monsr de Cornay now offer one third more than the stated Price allowed by Congress, and yet have made little Progress." *Ibid.*, p. 351 (1780).

indirect. Actually a substantial amount of the munitions and other articles required by the Continental army was procured from civilian manufacturers or contractors reimbursed by public authority. Ironmasters of New Jersey and Pennsylvania such as John J. Faesch were engaged in important armament work. The Maryland authorities procured a number of laborers to work on the fortifications and breastworks at Annapolis, and authorized them "to engage and employ such others as they shall apprehend necessary, upon such Terms as they may agree." [20] One gunsmith reported in 1776 that he had nine hands employed and expected two more to report shortly for work.[21] A clothing contractor reported that he was setting up a factory with sixteen.looms and that he had hired journeymen and apprentices, and also set up a mill for processing flax and had engaged enough spinners to produce one hundred yards of linen a day in order to fill the needs of the Maryland Council of Safety for coarse linen for tents and sheeting. He claimed to have "brought manufacturing of linen to greater perfection than has ever been done in the province." [22] Virginia offered even better examples of private plants operating on war contracts. Perhaps the best known were James Hunter's ironworks near Fredericksburg, the Albemarle Iron Company, the Providence Forge, and the Oxford, Neabsco, and Redwell Furnaces.[23]

Contracts with such private manufacturers might stipulate the rate of wages to be paid to artisans. John Michaelson, a gunsmith, agreed with the Pennsylvania Committee of Safety to manufacture on the following terms: £300 per year for himself and a dwelling for his family; £5 per one hundred guns made in the factory under his supervision, and £8 per month for each of the two apprentices and three servants he planned to engage as workmen.[24] In addition to these cost-plus-fixed fee contracts, which have enjoyed a great deal of vitality in wartime, the cost-plus-a fixed commission contract was strongly favored by the army commissariat.[25]

A third method of producing military stores was the setting up by the states or the Federal government of agencies under their own control to engage in manufacturing. The Continental authorities produced armaments at Springfield, Massachusetts, operated a "leather accouterment factory," an ordnance yard, a "drum maker shop," a foundry, and a paint shop in Philadelphia, and established a gun factory at Lancaster

[20] *Md. Arch.*, XII, 53, 211, 216, 223, 271 (1776); *Pa. Arch.*, 1st ser., IV, 696, 709.
[21] *Md. Arch.*, XII, 271.   [22] *Ibid.*, p. 278 (1776).
[23] K. Bruce, *Va. Iron Manufacture*, pp. 63 *et seq.*   [24] *Pa. Arch.*, 1st ser., IV, 768 (1776).
[25] See Johnson, *op. cit.*, pp. 65, 71, 73, *passim.*

and a gunlock factory at Trenton.[26] The state of Virginia set up a gun factory at Fredericksburg under the management of Fielding Lewis and Charles Dick. The legislature authorized the management in 1777 to increase the number of "artists" needed in the plant by taking in a group of white youths to be trained there. These apprentices were to be provided with adequate clothing, bedding, and provisions, and, at the expiration of their terms of service were to receive such wages as were deemed reasonable, not exceeding £30 each. All complaints of immoderate correction, insufficient clothing, or other grievances were to be heard in the county court, "as in the case of other apprentices." [27] Dick, who was both disciplinarian and efficiency expert, discovered that the workers would work at a lower rate of wages in the government plant than in private industry provided that they were paid promptly. He maintained that they worked for him "at a cheaper rate and much greater despatch than private shops, where they hardly know what it is to do a Day's work." [28] Another government-operated industry was the Westham Foundry near Richmond, which was largely destroyed by a British raid in 1781.[29]

In 1778 General Gates ordered several officers of the Pennsylvania State Regiment of Artillery to study the manufacturing processes at the Carlisle arsenal with a view to attaining a greater familiarity with their matériel. They were urged to engage in manual labor, the general holding up to them the example of "Czar Peter, who was not satisfied with seeing a ship built, but employed himself as a common labourer in the lowest and most laborious Parts of the Business." He further declared:

No Person, in our Opinion, by merely viewing a complex Machine, altho' he should attend to its Parts never so minutely, either in the whole or by Detail, could at once produce of his own Manufacture, a similar one. Practice must complete what Speculation only begins.[30]

Manufacturers of war materials were affected by conditions in the labor market. A linen manufacturer reported that production was curtailed

[26] Muster roll of Capt. John Jordan's Company, *Pa. Arch.*, 5th ser., III, 1107, 1114, 1115 (April, 1780); Bolton, *op. cit.*, p. 107. When it was planned to discontinue the gun factory in Pennsylvania run at government expense, two entrepreneurs proposed that it be turned over to them in copartnership on condition that materials on hand be sold to them at cost and that they be given preference in further ordnance contracts. They justified their terms on the ground that the factory workers would not have to be thrown out of work "in this inclement season." *Pa. Arch.*, 1st ser., VII, 133 (1776). Unpaid workers quit. *Official Letters, Va. Govs.*, III, 230, 242 (1782).
[27] Hening, IX, 426, 427. See also *Cal. Va. State Papers*, III, 17–18, 305 (1782).
[28] *Ibid.*, p. 305 (1782).
[29] At Westham a considerable body of white artificers were employed, but the bulk of the labor appears to have been slave. Bruce, *op. cit.*, pp. 18, 34, 36, 37, 45 *et seq.*, 54, 55, 61, 62.
[30] *Pa. Arch.*, 2d ser., XI, 198 (1778).

by the "difficulties in procuring weavers as great numbers in our parts have enlisted in the Flying Camp and those that remain have advanced their prices." [31] A tent manufacturer complained that he was unable to purchase a quantity of coarse linen "owing to the scarcity of Hands to manufacture" as well as to the rising demand for various articles of clothing which advanced the price of linen.[32] Thomas Savadge, the proprietor of a saltworks in Pennsylvania, reported that his workmen had "decamped in haste" on the approach of the British army and that he had not been able to get them back to work "by reason of having nothing but continental money to pay them with." He described his workers as "chiefly poor men with large families," who "must have their wages every Saturday" and were unable to purchase provisions for their families with Continental money. The proprietor sought not only a cash advance from the authorities in old money but a restraint upon General Putnam from impressing his employees for the militia under threat of gaol.[33]

To relieve labor shortages in war industries regular troops were at times employed. When a shoe manufacturer complained to the authorities that, while he had a sufficient supply of leather on hand, workmen were "very scarce," an artillery lieutenant agreed to send him several shoemakers for the emergency, and the manufacturer sought permission to employ them.[34] On one occasion Commodore Hazelwood refused as improper a request that he assign seamen in the Continental service to work as guards at saltworks or to do such other work on the premises as might be needed, because the contractor had the right to use available artisans among the enlisted men.[35] In New Jersey the operator of a saltworks, a former officer in the Continental army, was allowed to use Continental troops to guard his property. When an investigation by the New Jersey Council in 1778 disclosed that the soldiers had actually "been employed in collecting Materials and erecting Buildings to promote the private Interest of Individuals," Washington transferred them to regular duty "to avoid the imputation of impartiality." [36] State governors generally objected to keeping the militia on duty during the harvest and planting seasons.[37] In fact, the practice of short enlistments, which seri-

[31] *Md. Arch.*, XII, 193 (1776).   [32] *Ibid.*, p. 218 (1776).

[33] *Pa. Arch.*, 1st ser., V, 194 (1777). Savadge's labor difficulties did not end at this time. The following year he notified President Reed that a number of workmen left him because their wages remained unpaid. *Ibid.*, VII, 109 (1778).

[34] *Md. Arch.*, XII, 389 (1776).   [35] *Pa. Arch.*, 1st ser., VI, 182, 236 (1778).

[36] Washington, *Writings*, X, 412; XI, 148–149; L. Lundin, *Cockpit of the Revolution* (Princeton, 1940), p. 290.

[37] See Margaret B. Macmillan, *The War Governors in the American Revolution* (New York, 1943), p. 167.

ously interfered with military operations, was largely dictated by agricultural manpower requirements.

The Continental authorities were sharply criticized by the British for their failure to live up to the Saratoga Convention and for farming out prisoners of war to military contractors. David Franks, who had been authorized to act as agent to the contractors responsible for victualing the prisoners, was directed to sell bills of exchange drawn by the captive officers and to encourage the prisoners to earn money by plying their trades among the inhabitants in the neighborhood of their quarters.[38] In 1777 permission was requested of the Pennsylvania Supreme Executive Council to employ Hessian prisoners in a nail factory about to be set up under private management.[39] Depositions were taken before British officers in New York early in 1783 to the effect that the German prisoners of the Saratoga Convention, when taken to Lancaster or Reading, were visited by American clergymen who read them the following proclamation:

The King of Great Britain refused to pay for their maintenance, their Tyrant princes also had abandoned and sold them. Congress did therefore leave it to their choice, either to enlist in the American Service, or pay 30 *l.* currency of Pennsylvania for their past maintenance in hard money, which sum, if they could not afford to pay, the farmers would advance for them on binding themselves to serve them for three years, in both of which cases they must take the Oath of Allegiance to the United States.

They were advised by the clergymen to accept the first alternative rather than to be disposed of by the farmers.[40] One of the most notorious instances of farming out was that of thirty-five prisoners of war bound out to the ironmaster John Jacob Faesch, at Mount Hope. These prisoners wrote Lieutenant General de Lossberg that Faesch had procured their liberation from the Philadelphia gaol in April, 1782. They attempted to escape to New York, but were again put in gaol at Newark, whereupon Faesch again procured their freedom, paying the sum of twenty dollars for each of them and deducting this sum from their wages. Again they were seized, this time for the Continental army, but once more Faesch bought them off and put them to work to repay the debt. In one instance the runaways complained that, upon their recapture, they

---

[38] *J. Continental Cong.*, IV, 115, 369.

[39] *Pa. Arch.*, 1st ser., V, 206 (1777). For a proposal to employ German workmen among the Convention troops at Charlottesville in making wagon harnesses, as such workers were available "upon reasonable Terms," see *Cal. Va. State Papers*, I, 483 (Feb. 2, 1781).

[40] HMC, *Rep.*, LIX, Pt. III, 314, 315. Actually the enlistment of deserters and prisoners was prohibited by a resolve of Congress of May 22, 1778. E. J. Lowell, *The Hessians and the Other German Auxiliaries of Great Britain in the Revolutionary War* (New York, 1884), pp. 288, 289.

were cruelly whipped. General de Lossberg reported to Sir Guy Carleton in June, 1783, that these and other German prisoners who had been indentured as servants or made to enlist in the Continental army were reduced "to this condition by compulsion and other devices," and that "many of them are strongly desirous of returning to their duty," but "are detained against their inclination." He urged Carleton to issue a public proclamation protesting against this "unprecedented" and "illegal" procedure, declaring their liberty to return to their respective corps and forbidding all inhabitants from detaining them further.[41] The development of the woolen and worsted industries in this country was aided both by British military prisoners who remained in the country after the war and by deserters from the British army. From these men, one manufacturer later testified, "we have acquired some useful Knowledge, tho at a dear rate." [42]

In their conduct of the war the British also had to face complex labor-relations problems. The army employed large numbers of civilian workers, notably in the shipyards, on baggage trains, and in the commissary department. Carpenters were employed for building barracks, making and repairing tools, and in many other ways. Carters and laborers were quite generally used, and miners at times worked "by relief day and night" for the army, which had charge of the operations of a colliery on Cape Breton Island and shipped the coal to Halifax. Ship carpenters, joiners, caulkers, and sawyers were employed in building and repairing boats, and the services of wheelwrights, blacksmiths, and harnessmakers were frequently enlisted.[43] Two hundred civilian artificers were engaged

[41] HMC, *Rep.*, LIX, Pt. III, 407; Pt. IV, 153, 167. A slightly different set of facts was incorporated in the petition of William Conrad, a deserter from the Hessian regiment of Knyphausen in the retreat of the British army from Philadelphia in 1778. Conrad alleged that he was persuaded by "some of his Workfellows (Germans by Birth)" to hire himself to John Mifflin for a four-year term. After acknowledging the indentures before a justice he discovered that he had been bound out to Mifflin by the overseers of the poor, although he denied ever having applied to them for relief. He asked for his freedom and compensation for his labor. The court voided his indentures and discharged him, but made no provision for payment of wages. Philadelphia Q.S., 1779–82 (April, 1780). Hessians appear to have been employed particularly in the paper mills during the Revolutionary years. M. Keir, *Manufacturing* (New York, 1928), pp. 475, 476. Art. viii of Burgoyne's capitulation specifically included artificers. It must be remembered that Burgoyne himself was not too scrupulous in interpreting the terms of the Convention. See J. Winsor, ed., *Narrative and Critical History of America* (Boston and New York, 1887), VI, 317.

[42] Elisha Colt to John Chester, Hartford, Conn., Aug. 20, 1790. Cole, *Hamilton*, pp. 7–8. Faust, on the basis of Kapp's figures, conservatively estimates that over six thousand Hessian soldiers remained in the United States at the end of the war. A. B. Faust, *The German Element in the United States* (New York, 1927), I, 356; Friedrich Kapp, *Der Soldatenhandel deutscher Fürsten nach Amerika* (Berlin, 1874), pp. 209–210; T. Anbury, *Travels* (1789), II, 440–441.

[43] HMC, *Rep.*, LIX, Pt. I, 122 (1777), Pt. II, 145, 208 (1780), 236, 263, 294, 323–325 (1781), Pt. IV, 117 (1783); *General Sir William Howe's Orderly Book at Charlestown, Boston and Halifax, June 17, 1775 to May 26, 1776*, ed. E. E. Hale (Boston, 1890), pp. 129, 135, 182, 197, 207,

for Burgoyne's expedition.[44] The British army in New York saved the government considerable sums over the market price by employing artisans to cut and saw timber and provide fuel for the encamped troops.[45]

As in the Continental army, companies of artificers were organized, generally comprising fifty men each, including separate companies of Negro laborers. Muster rolls of artificers and laborers employed by the British army in New York testify to the importance and extent of labor's services with the armed forces.[46] Special companies of military artificers like the one that is the ancestor of the Royal Sappers and Miners do not seem to have been dispatched to America from Great Britain, although a recommendation was made that a corps of military artificers be formed for American service.[47] Apparently the artificers' companies, recruited in America and supplemented by civilians, appear to have been adequate for military requirements.[48] At times material and labor were hired from contractors and paid by the day,[49] as in the Continental army. On occasion explicit orders had to be given that artificers were not to be taken off their tasks for military service until such tasks were completed.[50]

Labor shortages and high wages were the bane of the military works program. In May, 1779, Brigadier General Campbell wrote Sir Henry Clinton that he was unable to construct a post on the Mississippi owing

216, 251, 252, 275; *Orderly Book of Sir John Johnson during the Oriskany Campaign, 1776–1777* (New York, 1887), pp. 42, 43, 82, 83, 406; carpenter's work done for 2d Battalion of British Grenadiers, Emmet MSS, No. 5975, N.Y. Pub. Lib.

[44] John Burgoyne, *A State of the Expedition from Canada* (London, 1780), p. 93.

[45] "Proceedings of a Board of General Officers of the British Army at New York, 1781," N.Y. Hist. Soc., *Coll.* (1916), p. 199.

[46] The staff of Engineers at New York in 1774 included a wheeler, a collarmaker, three smiths, one cooper, and one armorer; similarly, the Engineers' staff in Canada, 1776–78, which also had five carpenters. Curtis, *op. cit.,* p. 153. In the Quartermaster General's shipyards there were employed in August, 1781, 3 foremen, 14 ship carpenters, 3 caulkers, 2 joiners, 6 sawyers, 3 blacksmiths, and, in addition to these 31 artificers, there was a "working party" of the 22d Regiment comprising a sergeant, and corporal, and 12 men constantly employed there. "Proceedings, Board of General Officers," *loc. cit.,* pp. 50, 51, 176, 177. An additional group employed in the yards comprised 43 carpenters and sawyers, 34 blacksmiths, 7 harness makers, 49 laborers, and 45 wagon masters and conductors. The Commissary General's Provision Department employed for the same period 17 carpenters, 8 coopers, 6 butchers, 106 laborers, and 2 masons, in addition to numerous others employed at different provision magazines in New York and Brooklyn, at Harlem Heights, and on Staten Island. *Ibid.,* pp. 120 *et seq.,* 126–137. The Barrack Master General returned the following muster roll for the same period: 19 carpenters, 58 laborers and carmen, and 63 Negro laborers. The Commanding Engineer employed 155 workmen, including foremen, carpenters, sawyers, masons, smiths, and laborers. *Ibid.,* pp. 146–157. During the same period there were employed at Fort Knyphausen 4 conductors, 10 carpenters, 4 blacksmiths, and 85 drivers. *Ibid.,* pp. 182–189.

[47] Curtis, *op. cit.,* pp. 8, 9.

[48] Some drivers were contracted in England for employment in the transport services in America. *Ibid.,* pp. 138, 139.

[49] HMC, *Rep.,* LIX, Pt. II, 73 (1779).   [50] *Howe's Orderly Book,* p. 180 (1775).

to the lack of carpenters. Only seven such craftsmen could be procured at Pensacola and at very high wages. The military artificers were of little or no use. He accordingly requested Clinton to send him fifty carpenters from New York,[51] but Clinton was unable to do so.[52] In view of the fact that the shipwrights at the New York dockyard were not working "with any great spirit" on ships of the Royal Navy, one officer suggested that every shipwright in town be rounded up and compelled to work on the ships.[53] As late as September 23, 1783, shortages of artificers and laborers were reported to the British military authorities in New York.[54]

Owing to necessity or prejudice, the military authorities often turned to their own soldiers who were experienced as artificers instead of calling upon local workmen. To supply wood for the garrison at Boston Howe was forced to call upon enlisted men in December, 1775, "particularly those who understand the use of the axe." [55] Each corps was ordered to send one man to the ordnance office to be constantly employed at making cartridges. Later, when in Halifax, Howe ordered a soldier who had been a tinsmith by trade to work at the deputy quartermaster general's office and eight sawyers to report to Captain Montresor, army engineer.[56] One officer at St. Augustine preferred Negroes and artificers already in the regiment to other labor, having "resolved to have nothing to say to your town people who are all Jews." [57]

Toward strikes on the part of military artificers the British army

---

[51] HMC, *Rep.*, LIX, Pt. I, 431 (1779).

[52] *Ibid.*, Pt. II, 8 (1779). For Campbell's previous complaint to Clinton, Feb. 10, 1779, of lack of artificers and equipment, see C.O. 5:597, pp. 41–98, Lib. of Cong.

[53] Mackenzie, *Diary*, II, 507 (1781).

[54] HMC, *Rep.*, LIX, Pt. IV, 295, 370 (1783). The British authorities at times regulated wartime wages. See *supra*, pp. 125 f. Provisions for a daily allotment of rum were also made. See, e.g., *Howe's Orderly Book*, pp. 174 (1775), 234 (1776). Nevertheless the military authorities constantly complained that materials, tools, and lumber had advanced, and the wages of artificers proportionally, by June, 1780, "many hundred per cent." HMC, *Rep.*, LIX, Pt. II, 145 (1780), 313, 314 (1781). The Purveyor's Office in New York conceded that the "exhorbitant increase of price of mason's and carpenter's work and materials, and the extra supernumerary mates, servants, etc." was brought about by "the dearness of living." *Ibid.*, p. 148 (1780).

[55] For each cord cut and piled the soldiers were allowed 5s. sterling and the officer acting as overseer 5s. per diem, and the men were to be allowed a gill of rum a day and required to "do no other duty." "Kemble Papers," I, N.Y. Hist. Soc., *Coll., 1883* (New York, 1884), pp. 276, 277.

[56] *Ibid.*, p. 352. For other instances of British soldiers working on nonmilitary duties, see H. M. Lydenberg, ed., *Archibald Robertson, Lieutenant-General Royal Engineers; His Diaries and Sketches in America, 1762–1780* (New York, 1930), p. 78 (carpenters, 1776); Mackenzie, *Diary*, I, 13 (cartridge-making, 1778); *Orderly Book, De Lancey Brigade*, p. 74 (tailors, 1778).

[57] HMC, *Rep.*, LIX, Pt. II, 37 (1779). For the use of slaves in West Florida and the West Indies to cut wood, build redoubts, and assist in transporting foodstuffs, see *Gage Corr.*, II, 405 (1767); HMC, *Rep.*, LIX, Pt. I, 261 (1778), Pt. II, 37 (1779), Pt. III, 2, 3 (1782); W. H. Siebert, "Slavery and White Servitude in East Florida, 1726–1776," *Fla. Hist. Soc. Q.*, X (1931), 3–32, 138–161; *Loyalists in East Florida, 1774–1785* (2 vols., De Land, Fla., 1929), I, 63, 79, 88, 94, 96, 99.

authorities adopted an opportunistic policy.[58] On at least one occasion the army gave in to the strikers. This happened when the artificers at Pensacola went out on strike in 1779. According to the report of Brigadier General John Campbell to Sir Henry Clinton, fourteen carpenters of the Waldeck regiment struck for higher wages at the King's Works. They refused to continue working at the wage scale then set for military artificers in North America, which was 15*d*. "York currency" per diem. Such wages, they claimed, were insufficient to cover wear and tear of clothing, purchase of necessaries, and the "extraordinary" amount of bread they consumed.[59] When the colonel in charge proposed to punish the strikers for mutiny, General Campbell restrained him on the ground that "punishment would not answer to the forwarding of the Public Works." Accordingly, he sent a message to the strikers that, although he was without power to raise their wages, he would submit their demands to Sir Henry. He agreed to "pardon their present Unmilitary Behaviour, on condition that they resumed working immediately." They accepted these terms and went back to work. The crux of the trouble seems to have been that, before Campbell's arrival, the artificers at the King's Works got the 15*d*. York wages, and their provisions for nothing, besides. Campbell put an end to this practice, in effect reducing their wages. He also ended payments of 10*d*. York currency per diem to soldiers employed as laborers. When the native carpenters made "exorbitant demands," he dismissed them and was obliged to import a corps of skilled carpenters. Having provoked the serious labor situation by these high-handed methods, Campbell was then forced to eat humble pie and to support the workers' demand for an increase in wages, expressing the fear that "unless some satisfaction is given to the Waldeckers they will refuse to work." [60] The impasse was thus ended in an extraordinary way: a British general, instead of prosecuting his striking artificers for mutiny, was virtually forced to act as an intermediary for them in their demands for higher wages! The Pensacola incident provides thoughtful comparison with the manner in which the government handled the demands of the coal miners during the second World War.

On another occasion the very same year artificers were threatened

---

[58] When, back in 1771, General Gage, from his headquarters in New York, instructed the military authorities in Newfoundland to reduce the rate of wages for common labor employed on military works from 9*d*. to 6*d*. per diem, there was "much Murmur and Discontent." Gage admitted that the workmen were able "to impede the carrying on the Works with the alacrity to be wished." *Gage Corr.,* I, 313.

[59] One of the officers stated that "a German Soldier to satisfy him would eat at least two pounds of Bread per day, and as Bread here is at the extravagant Price of 4 sh. 4½d. York currency for four pounds he reckoned they spent their whole artificers pay in that article only."

[60] *Ibid.,* pp. 412–413.

with prosecution by martial law for desertion if they went on strike. "A general discontent" prevailed among the artificers employed in the ordnance service in New York because their wages were considerably below those of similar craftsmen in other branches of the service. For example, the carpenters at the shipyards were receiving four or five times the wages paid the ordnance workers. The remarks of Major General Pattison, Commandant of the Garrison of New York, are illuminating:

I have receiv'd two Memorials in the Name of the Artificers, setting forth their Grievances and praying for an Augmentation of Pay, to be upon the same Footing at least, as those in other Branches of the Public Service. I have pacified their Minds for the present, by giving them to understand that I wou'd lay their complaints before the Hon'ble Board, and would cause them to be inform'd whenever I shou'd know the Determination you shall be pleas'd to take thereupon. We are now in great Want of more Artificers, but none will enter on the present Wages, and nothing prevents those we have from leaving the Service, but the Fear of being tried by Martial Law, as Deserters, which they are threatened with, in case they Abscond.[61]

Pattison's attitude was much more comparable to that of certain Union generals during the Civil War [62] than to that of our War Department in the two World Wars.

[61] "Letters of General Pattison," N.Y. Hist. Soc., *Coll.*, *1875*, pp. 67, 68.

[62] See Jonathan Grossman, "Government and Labor in Wartime under the Lincoln Administration," *International Molders' and Foundry Workers' J.*, LXXX (1944), 72–73.

PART II: BOUND LABOR

VII. THE NATURE OF BOUND LABOR

BOUND LABOR or indentured servitude was an institution which evolved out of the circumstances of colonial emigration and settlement and along lines quite original and distinct from the common law. The word "servant" was used in the seventeenth and eighteenth centuries as a general term to include all types of employers working for wages or commissions,[1] but the only person bound by contract to labor for a period of years in English law was the apprentice, who was bound for instruction in a trade. In the colonies, however, apprenticeship was merely a highly specialized and favored form of bound labor.[2] The more comprehensive colonial institution included all persons bound to labor for periods of years as determined either by agreement or by law, both minors and adults, and Indians and Negroes as well as whites.

Where the binding was effected by written agreement of the parties, articles of indenture were prepared in duplicate on a sheet of parchment or paper. The two copies were then cut apart so as to leave each with a jagged or indented edge.[3] Even in the seventeenth century printed forms were frequently employed,[4] and as time went on attorneys came

---

[1] "Apprentices, laborers, stewards, factors, and bailiffs, are considered by law as servants." William Graydon, *The Justice's and Constable's Assistant* (Harrisburg, Pa., 1803), p. 281. For the view that an apprentice is not a servant, see Batt, *Master and Servant*, p. 10.

[2] In colonial times the term "apprentice" was often used loosely to designate servants not receiving special training along craft lines. But these are really ordinary bound servants. *Plymouth Col. Rec.*, I, 110 (1639); *York, Me., Deeds*, Bk. F, Pt. I, f. 115 (1661); *Va. Gen. Court Mins.*, p. 124 (1626); *Md. Arch.*, LIV, 543 (1672). For the misuse of the term "apprentice" in indentures of servitude for debt, see New Hampshire Co. Court Papers, lib. I, f. 571 (1672); lib. II, f. 417 (1673); lib. V, f. 187 (1679), New Hampshire Hist. Soc.

[3] In England prior to stat. 31 Geo. II, c. 11, the deed had to be indented. After that time a deed legally stamped was declared sufficient. J. Chitty, *Treatise on the Law of Apprenticeship* (London, 1812), p. 27; O. J. Dunlop, *English Apprenticeship and Child Labour* (New York, 1912). By the early Federal period actual indenting of the deed was regarded as a "useless formality," and its omission would not invalidate the contract. Liver v. McFarland, Chatham, Ga., Court Mins., lib., 1782–90, f. 143 (1785); Tapping Reeve, *The Law of Baron and Femme; of Parent and Child; of Guardian and Ward; of Master and Servant; and of the Powers of Courts of Chancery* (New Haven, 1816), p. 343; *New Conductor Generalis* (Albany, 1819), p. 30.

[4] In the first half of the 17th century Nicholas Bourne, a London stationer, printed indentures for binding servants to the plantations and registered his forms in the Stationers' Company. His executrix petitioned Parliament that the right to reprint them be denied to others. L. F. Stock, ed., *Proceedings and Debates of British Parliaments Respecting North America, 1542–1783* (Washington, 1924–), I, 291 (1661).

to rely upon them more and more. Colonial courts required that the indentures be sealed, and where this requirement was not observed, the servant might be bound to serve according to custom rather than by specific agreement [5] or else entirely discharged from his contract.[6] The courts would not tolerate "obliterations" in the indentures [7] nor consider them valid without proof.[8]

Contracts of employment entered into under duress were voided by the court. In point of fact this rule applied strictly to redemptioners and apprentices. It would be unrealistic to consider as voluntary the binding of convicts transported from Britain, persons convicted in the colonies of certain crimes, and delinquent debtors, even though theoretically such persons had voluntarily accepted bound labor in lieu of a more drastic alternative. In one suit for freedom on grounds of coercion, a Maryland master argued that it would be a dangerous precedent to allow servants to plead *"non est factum."* [9] A servant induced to sign indentures after he had been deliberately plied with liquor by his prospective employer had not done so voluntarily, a Henrico County court held. In order to get at the facts the court put the following six interrogatories to witnesses:

1. What Liquors was drank on Xmas day at Mr. Reeves and Company.
2. What was the occation of that Drinking.
3. What Condition was the def't in that Night by reason of the drink.
4. Was the def't perfectly recovered in his Sence the next morning.
5. Whether they or Some one of them did not hear the Sd def't Martin Say once and ofener that [he] would not hire himself to the pl'tf.
6. And whether the def't did not utterly refuse to accept of the Shoes as Earnest or to Sign any covenants that the sd Reeves being then prepared and offered to him.[10]

[5] See Somerset, Md., lib. 1689–90, f. 47 (1690).

[6] Hunterdon, N.J., C.P. and Q.S., lib. 1773–82 (Feb. term, 1779). A seal was necessary in an indenture of apprenticeship under the Pennsylvania act of 1770. Comm. v. Wilbank, 10 Serg. and R. 416 (1823).

[7] Ann Arundel, Md., lib. 1702–4, f. 277 (1704).

[8] Under Virginia law blank indentures and office certificates of servants coming to Virginia, signed by the. official keeper or register and sealed with his seal, could not "reasonably" be accounted valid without "better testimony." Hening, II, 488 (1680). See also Somerset, Md., lib. 1670–71, f. 206 (1671); *Md. Arch.,* LIII, 428.

[9] Stitt v. Starrett, Somerset AW, 1690–91, f. 66 (1691). Defendant pleaded in bar to the judgment on the ground that the verdict of the jury was "Contrary to positive evidence." See also Talbott NN, No. 6 (March 19, 1689). For other instances, see N.Y.G.S., lib. 1732–62 (1757); *Md. Arch.,* XLIX, 387, 388 (1665); Accomac, Va., lib. 1710–14 (Nov. 4, 1713).

[10] Reeves v. Martin, Henrico, lib. V, fols. 409 *et seq.* (1693). See also Gaynor's petition, Philadelphia Mayor's Court Papers (*c.* 1740).

In the case of dependent children, the binding was, of course, involuntary; the articles generally cited the approbation of the parent or were executed before a magistrate.[11]

Fraud would also vitiate such a contract, when, for example a servant was told that the articles bound him for a four-year term and in reality he had signed for five years,[12] or when he had been fraudulently assured that he would be discharged on redemption of a debt.[13] As emigrants not well versed in the English language were not infrequently induced by false representations to sign such agreements, complaints to the authorities on the score of fraud were by no means unexceptional.[14]

To secure their freedom or to obtain a modification of the terms to which they had placed their signatures, servants were not infrequently tempted to steal, mutilate, burn, or even forge their articles of indenture.[15] Unscrupulous masters or ship captains destroyed indentures when they felt that it would be to their advantage if the servant were bound by the custom of the country rather than by contract.[16] Where the servant had lost the counterpart of his indentures, he might be denied his freedom dues.[17] On the other hand, masters in such a predicament would generally find the court willing to order the servant to finish out his term or to sign new articles.[18] Where a sloop upon which the servants were trans-

[11] In such case it was not essential for parent or guardian to sign the indentures. Liver v. McFarland, Chatham, Ga., lib. 1782–90, f. 143 (1785). An indenture binding a minor by his mother without his father's consent was void. Lancaster, Pa., Road and Sess. Docket, No. 3, 1760–68 (1764); West Chester, Pa., Q.S., lib. A (Nov. 29, 1768). In the absence of parents the consent of a grandparent was held essential. Suffolk G.S., lib. III, f. 237 (1723).

[12] *Ibid.*, f. 90 (1715).   [13] *Ibid.*, lib. II, f. 102 (1715).

[14] See Petition to the Rhode Island General Assembly, lib. 1748–50 (Feb. 27, 1749); also *infra*, pp. 400, 401.

[15] Freeman's case, York G.S., lib. VII (April 7, 1719), stripes remitted at the request of the master provided that the master administer due correction in the presence of the constable of York forthwith; Lane's case, Suffolk G.S., lib. II, f. 135 (1716); Anne Hutchins' case, *ibid.*, lib. III, f. 125 (1722), ordered to serve out term and to sign a new indenture; Collins v. Heming, New Haven Co. Court, lib. II, f. 92 (1702); Hodgkin's case, Burlington, West Jersey, Court Book, f. 209 (1705). Virginia statutes provided that servants stealing their indentures were to be stood in the pillory for two hours on a court day. *VMH*, X, 156, 157. See Henrico, lib. V, fols. 262, 263 (1692). The Maryland provincial court sentenced two servants to receive 20 lashes, but the punishment of one of them was remitted on condition that he whip the other. *Md. Arch.*, X, 516 (1657). In Jamaica servants forging their certificates were to be proceeded against according to the laws and statutes of England against forgery. C.O. 139:1, f. 126b (1672). The *N.Y.J.*, July 13, 1741, recounts that a maidservant, accused of stealing her indentures out of the pocket of her master, "a Country Man," pleaded that "her Master had given them to her for a Favour." A bystander who observed that he had "spoilt the Price" was mobbed.

[16] Allen's case, Ann Arundel, lib. 1692–93, f. 331 (1693); cf. Damer's case, *Md. Arch.*, LX, 492 (1673); also Pasternell's and Swillivant's cases, Northumberland, Va., lib. 1699–1713, Pt. I, f. 94 (1700).

[17] Ford's petition, *Chester Co., Pa., Court Rec., 1681–97*, p. 312 (1694).

[18] Lock's case, Suffolk G.S., lib. 1718–20 (Athenaeum), f. 8 (1718); Grafton's petition, *ibid.*, lib. IV, f. 45 (1726). Cf. also Thorne v. Perry, *ibid.*, lib. II, f. 90 (1715), where the master had mistakenly surrendered the indentures to the servant.

ported had been taken by pirates, who destroyed the indentures, the New York general sessions committed the servants to gaol until they bound themselves again for the terms stated in the original contract.[19]

Those entering the country without formal articles of indentures were bound by colony custom, in most cases restated by statutory enactment.[20] The tobacco colonies required masters to bring into open court all servants arriving without indentures so that the age of each and the remaining time of service could be adjudged; these facts were recorded and the servant was formally bound over by the authorities.[21] However, valid indentures would, if produced, supersede obligations to serve by custom, which generally required minors to serve for longer periods than did the usual contract of redemption.[22]

In considering the problems raised by the institution of indentured servitude we shall, wherever necessary, distinguish the following areas: 1) the New England group of colonies, consisting of small farm holdings worked by intensive agriculture, requiring few servants and having a relatively low percentage of non-English stock and comparatively few redemptioners or transported convicts; 2) the Middle colonies, with a larger proportion of non-English stock and of foreign immigrant servants, many of whom came as redemptioners; 3) the tobacco colonies, with a sizable white servant population in both the seventeenth and eighteenth centuries, despite the influx of Negro slaves who proved too costly for the frontier and marginal planters; 4) the rice and sugar colonies (including the remaining South Atlantic provinces and the British West Indian possessions), in which slaves greatly outnumbered whites and special efforts were directed toward inducing white servants to establish themselves in trades and agriculture. In the West Indies white servants were in demand for guarding the Negro slaves rather than for performing labor services. For convenience, North Carolina will be considered with this fourth group owing to similarities in her labor law, although in respect to her socioeconomic structure she differed rather sharply from her Southern neighbors. Convict servants were a greater factor in master-servant relations in the tobacco colonies than elsewhere on the mainland. As the tobacco, rice, and sugar colonies produced staples for an export market, they soon entered upon a stage of agricultural

[19] Ellis's complaint, N.Y.G.S., lib. 1694–1731/2, f. 338 (1717).
[20] See *infra*, pp. 390, 391.   [21] See *infra*, pp. 391, 392.
[22] Churnell v. Butler, Westmoreland, Va., lib. 1675/6–88/9, f. 516 (1686); Northumberland, Va., lib. 1699–1713, Pt. I, f. 94 (1700). In the absence of indentures proof of such formal contracts could be made by oral testimony or sworn depositions. See Tiddeman v. Obe *et al.*, *R.N.A.*, VI, 152, 153 (1668); Goffe's case, York, Va., lib. 1657–62, f. 85 (1658).

capitalism. In these areas of extensive agriculture it was profitable to supplant the relatively more expensive and more volatile white contract-labor system by Negro slavery, particularly since servants were not procurable in sufficient quantities to replace those who had served their terms.[23]

[23] See Eric Williams, *Capitalism and Slavery* (Chapel Hill, N.C., 1944), pp. 4–19; L. C. Gray, *History of Agriculture in the Southern United States to 1860* (2 vols., reprinted, New York, 1941), I, 301–372.

VIII. THE SOURCES OF BOUND LABOR

IMMIGRATION

REDEMPTIONERS OR "FREE-WILLERS." Redemptioners, often called "free-willers," were white immigrants who, in return for their passage to America, bound themselves as servants for a varying period of years. The institution of the redemptioner provided the principal means of populating the American colonies by European settlers and was accepted by contemporaries as the obvious way of "peopleing a Country," and "the greatest step to its Growth and improvement." [1] It has been estimated by John R. Commons, Carter Goodrich, and other students of emigration that nearly half of the total white immigration to the Thirteen Colonies came over as bound labor. This figure must be considered very conservative.[2] In the seventeenth century such immigra-

---

[1] *Md. Arch.*, XXIV, 394 (1701).

[2] Of the 6,000 emigrants leaving England between Dec. 11, 1773, and Oct. 30, 1775, approximately 4,000 left from the port of London for the colonies; 87 per cent of these went over as indentured servants. Transcribed in part from the Treasury Papers 47, Bundles 9-11, in the Public Record Office and published in the *N.E. Hist. and Gen. Register*, LXII, 1908-11, 242-253, 320-332; LXIII, 16-31, 134-136, 234-244, 342-354; LXIV, 18-25, 106-115, 214-227, 314-326; LXV, 20-35, 116-132, 232-251. It must be borne in mind that a large number of emigrants during the period were leaving from Irish and Scottish ports, in addition. See Treasury Papers I:500, fols, 231-235. One estimate gives the figure from the five Irish ports for the years 1769-1774 as 43,720 people. *Gentleman's Mag.*, XLIV (1774), 332; S. C. Johnson, *A History of Emigration from the United Kingdom to North America, 1763-1912* (London, 1913), pp. 1, 2. For the list of more than 10,000 servants who sailed from Bristol to the colonies in an earlier period, see *Bristol and America; a Record of the First Settlers in the Colonies of North America, 1654-1685* ... (London, 1929).

The incomplete Naval Office lists show the relative significance of redemptioner immigration as compared with slave importations in the Middle Colonies and the South, Pennsylvania excepted. The following statistics have been compiled, as available, for certain years between 1683 and 1769: Entering the port of New York (1732-54, with gaps from 1743-48, 1748-53, 1755-63) were the following: 1,469 Palatines, 362 "other" servants, 170 "passengers," and 1,138 Negroes. For Virginia, Accomac (1733-69, with gaps from 1734-59, 1764-66, 1767-69) listed 37 Negroes and 2 passengers; Rappahannock (1726-69, with gaps from 1746-49, 1764-68), 7,156 Negroes, 793 servants, 448 felons, and 1,494 "passengers"; South Potomac, Virginia (1733-68, with gaps from 1743-46, 1747-49, 1757-58), 1,256 Negroes, 251 servants, 769 convicts (also included "passengers"), and 1,712 "passengers." Entering South Carolina (1718-67, with gaps from 1719-23, 1724-26, 1727-30, 1732-34, 1739-52, 1753-57), were 31,445 Negroes and in excess of 2,600 "passengers," including 536 Palatines, 193 Swiss, about 750 Irish, 300 other Germans, and 132 French. Jamaica, 1683-92, listed 11,774 Negroes, 798 "passengers," 922 servants, 249 convicts, and 106 convicted rebels; and Kingston reported for the period 1718-69 (with gaps from 1720-28, 1729-43, 1749-51, 1757-61), 164,592 Negroes, and a dozen shipments of unspecified numbers, 236 prisoners, 10 Frenchmen, and 6 Indians, clearly showing the virtual disappearance of redemptioner immigration to the West Indies in the 18th century in striking contrast to the Middle colonies. All "passengers" were by no means redemptioners, but a considerable proportion of immigrants listed in this category probably were, notably the Palatines. The Entry Books for the Patuxent District, Port of Annapolis (Md. Hist. Soc. and Hall of Records) for the years 1746-1775 include 2,142 German and Irish passengers,

tion was primarily of English stock. But in the course of the following century Germans, Swiss, Scots, Scotch-Irish, Irish, and people of other national and linguistic stocks came to this country in such considerable numbers that, by the advent of the American Revolution, fully 50 per cent of the population south of New England was of non-English stock.[3] Before the expansion of the Southern slave economy at the end of the seventeenth century there was a brisk demand for redemptioners in the tobacco provinces. Thereafter Pennsylvania was the chief reception center for bound immigrants, who often moved to other colonies after completing their terms of service.

The period of labor service for which the redemptioners bound themselves varied from two to seven years, with four years as the average length of service.[4]

9,035 indentured servants, 8,846 convicts, and 3,324 Negroes. Not including any of the passengers, though many were doubtless bound for their passage, 77 per cent of the immigrants were bound to service in the colony.

[3] This was an acute judgment of the late J. Franklin Jameson in an unpublished lecture, "American Blood in 1779," which differed sharply from the estimate of W. S. Rossiter, Bureau of the Census, *A Century of Population Growth* (Washington, 1909). Jameson's estimate of a total English and Welsh population of 60 per cent for all the colonies in 1775 as against three governmental estimate of 82.1 per cent in 1790 has been substantiated by the "Report of the Committee on Linguistic and National Stocks in the Population of the United States," Amer. Hist. Assn., *Proceedings, 1931*, I, 103–408. This valuable and suggestive investigation gives the following percentage classification of the English stock in the population by 1790: Maine 60; New Hampshire 61; Vermont 76; Massachusetts 82; Rhode Island 71; Connecticut 67; New York 52; New Jersey 47; Pennsylvania 35.3; Delaware 60; Maryland and District of Columbia 64.5; Virginia 68.5; North Carolina 66; South Carolina 60.2; Georgia 57.4; Kentucky and Tennessee 57.9; Northwest Territory 29.8. It has been estimated that between 1702 and 1727 some forty to fifty thousand Germans left their homeland for the colonies. I. D. Rupp, *Collection of Thirty Thousand Names of Immigrants in Pennsylvania* (Philadelphia, 1876), p. 2. For other non-English immigrant passenger lists compiled by O'Brien, Donovan, Evjen, Bergen, Faust, Gerber, Roberts, Strassburger, Jordan, and others, see A. H. Lancourt, comp., "Passenger Lists of Ships coming to North America, 1607–1825," N.Y. Pub. Lib., *Bulletin*, XLI (1937), 389–398.

[4] A vast majority of the redemptioners emigrating from the port of London, 1773–76, were specifically bound for four-year terms. A minority were bound for longer terms running to as much as seven years, but the bulk of the latter appear to have been emigrants under nineteen years of age. *N.E. Hist. and Gen. Register*, LXII–LXV, *passim*.

These emigrants were bound to individual masters rather than to the government. The early Virginia settlers were an exception. The Palatines who came over to New York in 1710 contracted to obey the governor and to work for the government until their settlement costs had been paid. This was an unusual arrangement, as the immigrants were bound to the government rather than to a private individual. See W. A. Knittle, *Early Eighteenth Century Palatine Emigration* (Philadelphia, 1937). Comparable were the Georgia servants bound to the trustees for long terms. See *Ga. Col. Rec.*, II, 101, 102. For a proposal that the king pay the transportation of ex-soldiers, see *CSPA, 1696–97*, No. 1407, p. 670 (1697).

The same system was found in the French colonies. G. Debien, in his recent suggestive study, *Le peuplement des Antilles françaises au XVIIe siècle: les Engagés partis de la Rochelle* (Cairo, Egypt, 1942), distinguishes between ordinary emigrants, who were similar to the British colonial redemptioners, and contract laborers, who were generally skilled workers, bound customarily for three years to planters who paid for their transportation and were required to provide them lodging, food, and clothing, and pay them wages or allow them a share (one third to one half) of the profits.

The obligations of 127 redemptioners sailing from the port of London in January, 1775, were recorded on the emigration lists as follows:

N.B. All these People that have shipped themselves on Board the *Jane,* are going to settle abroad and by an agreement with the Captn are to pay him so much for their passage to Maryland, on their arrival, but if they cannot then the Captn is to dispose of them for a number of years to defray the expences of their passage.

Before embarking, the individual emigrant usually signed articles of indentures such as the following:

Citie of Bristol

This indentur [5] maid the 31th of July Ao [Anno] 1662 in the 14th year of the Raigne of our Souveraigne Lord King Charles the Second etc. between Mathew Browne of the one party and William foxe of the Cittie of Bristol of the other party witnesseth that the sayd Mathew Browne doth Couenant Promis and grant to and with the sayd William fox his Executors Assignes from the day of the daet hearof untill his first and next Arrivall at the port of Verginia and after for and during the tearme of four years to sarue in such saruice and imployments as he the sayd William fox or his assignes shall thear imploy him according to the Custom of the County in the licke kind in Consideration whearof the sayd William fox doth hearby Couenant and grant to and with the sayd Mathew Browne to pay for his Passing and to allow him meat drincke apparrel and Lodging with other necessarys during the sayd tearm and at the end of the sayd tearme to haue 1 axe 1 how 1 years Prouision the Custom of the County in witness whearof the Partys aboue named to thees indenturs haue Inter Changably set thair hands and seales the day and year aboue written Nathaniell Cole mayor and Thomas Steephens and John Hix Sheriffs

Sealed and delivered   William fox
  in presence of us
    Anne Hayes

This Indenture,[6] made the Fourteenth Day of November in the Fifteenth Year of the Reign of our Sovereign Lord George the third King of Great Britain, etc. And in the Year of our Lord One Thousand Seven Hundred and seventy four between Charles Bush of Southwark in the County of Surrey Labourer of the one Part, and Frederick Baker of London Mariner of the other

---

[5] Brought into court in Maryland and recorded; a notation was made to the effect that Browne arrived in Virginia on the ship *Alexander* on Nov. 17, 1662. *Md. Arch.,* LIII, 579. See also *ibid.,* p. 510 (1661); *York, Me., Deeds,* Bk. I, Pt. I, f. 148 (1662). It should be noted that the nature of the employment was generally at the employer's discretion, subject to "the custom of the country." For redemptioner indentures specifying three years' service "in planting, fyshing, and to other labour," see "Trelawny Papers," *Doc. Hist. of Maine,* III, 336–343 (1642).

[6] W. C. Ford, *Washington as an Employer and Importer of Labor,* pp. 76, 77.

Part. Witnesseth That the said Charles Bush for the Consideration hereinafter mentioned, hath, and by these Presents doth Covenant, Grant and Agree to, and with the said Frederick Baker, his Executors, Administrators and Assigns, That he the said Charles Bush shall and will, as a Faithful Covenant Servant, well and truly serve Frederick Baker his Executors, Administrators or Assigns in the Plantation of Virginia and Maryland beyond the Seas, for the space of Five Years next ensuing his arrival in the said Plantation, in the Employment of a Servant. And the said Charles Bush doth hereby Covenant and declare him self, now to be the Age of eighteen Years and no Covenant or Contracted Servant to any Person or Persons. And the said Frederick Baker for himself his Executors, and Administrators, that he the said Fred. Baker his Executors, Administrators or Assigns, shall and will at his or there proper Cost and Charges with what Convenient Speed they may, carry and convey or cause to be carried and conveyed over unto the said Plantation, the said Charles Bush and from Henceforth and during the said voyage, and also during the said Term, shall and will at the like Cost and Charges, provide and allow the said Charles Bush all necessary Cloaths, Meat, Drink, Washing, and Lodging, Fitting and convenient for him as Covenant Servants in such Cases are usually provided for and allowed and for the true Performance of the Premises, the said Parties to these Presents bind themselves, their Executors and Administrators, the either to the other, in the Penal Sum of Thirty pounds Sterling, firmly by these Presents, In Witness whereof they have hereunto interchangeably set their Hands and Seals, the Day and year above written.

The mark of
Charles X Bush [seal]

Sealed and delivered
in the Presence of
    J. Pattinson
    C. Capon

These are to Certify, that the above named Charles Bush came before me Thomas Pattison Deputy to the Patentee at Gravesend the Day and year above written and declared himself to be no covenant nor Contracted Servant to any Person or Persons, to be of the age of eighteen Years, not Kidnapped nor enticed, but desirous to serve the above-named or his assigns, five Years, According to the Tenor of his Indenture above written, All of which is Registered in the office for that Purpose appointed by the Letters Patents. In Witness whearof I have affixed the Common Seal of the said office.
Ths Pattinson
      D.P.

Endorsement: Jan. 22nd 1775
The ship Elizabeth arrived at her Moorings
Fred. Baker

Once having signed the indentures, the servant was obligated to go to the ship's port of destination.[7] Such indentures were usually assigned

[7] Fyfield's case, Henrico O.B., I, f. 428 (1692).

over by the merchant or recruiting agent to the ship's captain who would sell the passenger on his arrival at a colonial port and in this way recover the passage money. The following is a typical assignment:

This Indenture made the 15th day of the 3rd moneth . . . 1639 betweene George Richardson, mariner, and Michael Gabilloe, Frenchman, of the one parte, and Edmund James of Watertowne in New England, planter, of the other parte, Witnesseth that the said George Richardson for the summe of eight pounds to him in hand payd for the passage of the said Michael, by the said Edmund James, doth assigne and put over the said Michael, and the said Michael Doth put himselfe a servant unto the said Edmund James, him his executors administrators and assignes truly and faithfully to serve from the day of the Date of these presents for and During the space of seaven yeares thenceforth next ensuing fully to be compleat and ended. And the said Edmund James shall finde and provide to and for his said servant sufficient and reasonable meate drinke lodging and apparell during the said terme, and in the end of the said terme shall give his said servant double apparell and five pounds in money.[8]

While in the case of emigrants leaving Great Britain, the terms of service were generally fixed by indentures which were required to be witnessed before a magistrate, German servants, on the other hand, usually came over without signed articles, bringing instead signed notes in which they agreed to pay a certain sum on arrival in America or within a reasonable time thereafter.[9] But in most cases they were without money or friends and had to sell themselves to pay off the debt.[10] During most of the seventeenth century the average cost of transportation varied from £5 to £6 sterling. Where it was necessary to furnish clothing and pay middlemen's commissions, the cost was closer to £10 or £12. The higher figure approximated costs in the eighteenth century, although by the eve of the Revolution sundry extra charges could run them up to £20.[11] Such costs in no unimportant part determined the price of a servant,

---

[8] Lechford, *Note-Book*, p. 76; cf. also *Md. Arch.*, X, 121 (1650). In general, cash payments at the end of the term were uncommon. See *infra*, p. 397.

[9] At times English redemptioners made similar arrangements. See Paterson v. Gordon, Morris, *Sel. Cases, Mayor's Court*, pp. 684–687 (1718), £5 sterl. to be paid 15 days after arriving at an American port. The court would void an indenture wrongfully obtained after the arrival of a servant who could prove that she had paid her passage. Margaret Moffett's petition, West Chester, Pa., Q.S., lib. 1723–33, f. 244 (1731).

[10] For early cases in which the court enforced this obligation, see Middlesex, N.J., Court Mins., lib. I, f. 123 (1689); also Herrick, *White Servitude in Pa.*, pp. 195, 196. Christopher Saur repeatedly urged the necessity of securing written contracts. J. O. Knauss, "Social Conditions among the Pennsylvania Germans," Pa.-German Soc., *Publications*, XXIX (1918), p. 62.

[11] See *The Records of the Virginia Company*, ed. Susan M. Kingsbury (4 vols., Washington, D.C., 1904–35), III, 618, 619; *Essex*, I, 27 (1641), 381, 382 (1655); *R.N.A.*, II, 75 (1656); Philadelphia Co. Court. lib. 1785–87, f. 206 (1787). For payment in cattle see *Md. Arch.*, XLIX, 7 (1663). See also *Winthrop Papers*, III, IV, *passim*.

which, because of the shorter term of service, was invariably less than that of a slave.[12]

The underwriting of transportation was assumed either directly by the planter, as in Virginia and Maryland (where he received a head-right or land grant for each immigrant), or indirectly by merchants specializing in the sale of servants' indentures. Recruiting agents employed by the merchants and called "Crimps" in England and "New-landers" on the Continent, hired drummers to go through various inland towns in England or along the Rhineland areas devastated by years of warfare publicly crying the voyage to America. They also arranged for the distribution of extravagant literature at annual fairs with the help of a piper to draw the crowd. The bulk of the contemporary descriptive material relating to the colonies may be viewed as optimistic sales propaganda to be placed in the hands of credulous prospects.[13]

The evils of the system constituted one of the major scandals of the colonial period. Fraudulent practices were commonplace in binding servants in England or in selling or assigning them in America. Agents persuaded the ignorant, the idle, and the credulous that they would be taken to a place "where food shall drop into their mouthes," [14] assured the laborer of good wages and free land, and the craftsman of an incomparable income.[15]

[12] Bruce has compiled a price list from 17th-century inventories of estates which shows that male servants usually commanded from 40 to 50 per cent higher prices than females. The sale of the unexpired term of a servant beyond two years would more than compensate for passage money. *Econ. Hist. of Va.,* II, 51. In the 18th century, prices ranged from £2 to £4 per year, when contractors sold redemptioners for from £8 to £20 apiece to cover actual transportation costs averaging £6. *Md. Arch.,* VI, 295, 300; Gray, *Hist. of Agriculture in Southern U.S.,* I, 370. Skilled artisans brought from £5 to £25. W. C. Ford, *op. cit.,* p. 15; Cheyney, "Conditions of Labor in Early Pennsylvania," *The Manufacturer* (March 16, 1891). £15 was the average price of a female servant on the eve of the Revolution. *Pa. Gazette,* Jan. 11, 1770. By this time the premium for slaves was only slightly higher, but their expectation of years of service considerably greater. See Gray, *op. cit.,* I, 371; II, 664. For the advantages, to the Carolina planter, of Negro slavery over white labor, see *American Husbandry,* ed. H. J. Carman (New York, 1939), p. 302.

[13] William Byrd was the "Wilhelm Vogel" of Samuel Jenner's German tract, *Newly-Found Eden,* published in 1737, which described Byrd's holdings as an earthly paradise. See L. B. Wright and Marion Tinling, eds., *The Secret Diary of William Byrd of Westover, 1709–1712* (Richmond, 1941), pp. xii, xiii. For early Pennsylvania promotional literature, see J. F. Sachse, "The Fatherland," Pa. German Society, *Proceedings,* VII, 177, 178, 197, 198; K. F. Geiser, *Redemptioners and Indentured Servants in the Colony and Commonwealth of Pennsylvania* (New Haven, 1901), pp. 12, 13. William Eddis observed in 1770: "In your frequent excursions about the great metropolis you cannot but observe numerous advertisements, offering the most seducing encouragement to adventurers under every possible description." *Letters from America, Historical and Descriptive, Comprising Occurrences from 1769 to 1777* (London, 1792). For comparable promotional methods used to send laborers to the French colonies, see É. Levasseur, *Recherches historiques sur le système de Law* (Paris, 1854), pp. 153–154.

[14] William Bullock, *Virginia Impartially Examined* (London, 1649), p. 14.

[15] For an investigation conducted by a committee of the Irish Commons in 1736, see Stock,

Ships were overcrowded; passengers were at times packed like herrings in a box.[16] Insanitary conditions prevailed. A mortality of more than 50 per cent of the passengers was not an unusual experience on the "White Guineamen," as the ships engaged in this trade were called.[17] Typhus contracted on shipboard by the German emigrants to New York in 1710 came to be known as "Palatine fever." [18] Insufficient and poor rations left the servants in a seriously weakened condition on their arrival in America.[19] Remedial legislation was cautiously adopted in Pennsylvania, whose commerce depended in no unimportant measure upon the importation of servants.[20]

One of the greatest criticisms leveled at the redemptioner system was that it led to the break-up of families.[21] Husbands and wives were sold to different masters and parents not infrequently were forced to sell their children. The separation of many of the young Palatines from their families constituted a major cause of discontent among those who settled in New York.[22] Children and young people were in great demand, as they could be purchased for a longer term than adults. As chil-

Proc. Brit. Parl., IV, 851 *et seq.* Redemptioners were not easily dissuaded from going to America even when a more realistic picture was given them. See HMC., *Rep.*, XXXVIII, 302 (1768).

[16] Vessels from the continent averaging less than 200 tons' burden carried an average of 300 passengers for a series of years. F. R. Diffenderffer, *German Immigration into Pennsylvania Through the Port of Philadelphia (1700–1775), Part II: The Redemptioners* (Lancaster, Pa., 1900), p. 51.

[17] Mittelberger charged that children from one to seven years of age rarely survived the voyage, but the lists of Palatine emigrants to New York reveal a goodly proportion of youngsters. Compare Pa. German Soc., *Proceedings*, VIII, 93–96, with W. A. Knittle, *op. cit.*, pp. 282–291.

[18] Such conditions were by no means confined to German emigrants sailing from Dutch ports. The Irish Commons' investigation of 1736 brought to light a number of instances of overcrowding, insufficient provisions, and abusive treatment of passengers on the part of ships' captains. Stock, *Proc. Brit. Parl.*, IV, xix, 848–857. See also Knittle, *op. cit.*, p. 147; Geiser, *Redemptioners . . . in Pa.*, pp. 46–51; L. P. Hennighausen, *History of the German Society of Maryland* (Baltimore, 1909), pp. 17, 22; Herrick, *op. cit.*, pp. 161–165; T. G. Morton and F. Woodbury, *The History of the Pennsylvania Hospital, 1751–1895* (Philadelphia, 1895). There are many references to the heavy casualties on these crossings in Christopher Saur's paper, *Der Hoch-Deutsch Pennsylvanische Geschicht-Schreiber Oder: Sammlung Urchtigen Nachrichten aus dem Natur- und-Kirchen Reut,* especially for the years 1749 and 1752. See also Paterson v. Gordon, Morris, *Sel. Cases, Mayor's Court*, pp. 684–687 (1718).

[19] See M. G. St. Jean de Crèvecoeur, *Letters from an American Farmer* (London, 1782), p. 95. A New York jury awarded one passenger £30 damages and £6 8s. 10½d. costs in a suit against a master for poor rations which incapacitated him on arrival in this country. Paterson v. Gordon, Morris, *op. cit.*, pp. 684–687 (1718).

[20] Minimum deck space per passenger was set by law. *Pa. Stat. at Large*, V, 94–97; *Pa. Col. Rec.*, V, 427, 428; VI, 225, 226, 243. For evasions, see Diffenderffer, *op. cit.*, Pt. II, pp. 211, 212.

[21] More considerate employers, such as George Washington, sought to buy the time of a whole family. Washington, *Diaries*, III, 140 (1786).

[22] *Ecclesiastical Rec. of N.Y.*, III, 2168; *Doc. Hist. of N.Y.*, III, 425. The Barbadian code of 1661 provided that "Man and Wife brought out as Servants in one Ship, shall not be severed; but sold together." Hall, *Acts of Barbados*, No. 30, cl. xiv. In Saur's paper for Nov. 16, 1745, there were two advertisements by persons desiring to know the whereabouts of their children who had been sold without their consent or knowledge. Knauss, *loc. cit.*, p. 61.

dren over four went for half fare, their sale was more profitable to the ship captain.[23] Another serious evil of the redemptioner system was that young girls were at times bound out ostensibly for trades or housework, but actually for immoral purposes.[24] Courts and public officials endeavored to prevent the trade in white servants from degenerating into a form of white slavery.

Of all phases of indentured servitude the redemptioner system aroused the sharpest criticism in the post-Revolutionary period.[25] Greater safeguards were now provided for the registry of newly arrived foreign passengers.[26] Other restrictions on the flow of immigration were imposed abroad. Some of the German states had already prohibited the emigration of their subjects, thus forcing the recruiting agents to go further inland in Germany to obtain redemptioners.[27] Britain in 1785 prohibited the transportation of persons on English ships for the purpose of servitude for debt.[28] Nevertheless, business enterprises required emigrant labor. A New York statute of 1788 reaffirmed the legality of the redemptioner system in order to remove all doubts, and the system lingered on in such states as Pennsylvania and Maryland until the third decade of the nineteenth century, although both states reduced the time for which the redemptioner might be bound, required registration, and provided greater official supervision of the contract.[29]

[23] One correspondent of Mittelberger stated that most of the 22,000 people who had arrived in Philadelphia in the fall of 1754 had to sell their children. Gottlieb Mittelberger, *Journey to Pennsylvania,* trans. C. T. Eben (Philadelphia, 1898), p. 37.

[24] See Warren v. Mitchell, *Md. Arch.,* X, 161 (1652); also *infra,* pp. 350 ff. In addition, the transportation system provided planters with wives. See *Va. Gen. Court Mins.,* p. 154 (1627), where a woman servant was bound out for a term of two years because of a "dislike" arising between master and servant which resulted in a mutual breach of the contract to marry.

[25] See, e.g., the statement in the *N.Y. Independent Gazette,* Jan. 24, 1784, that "the traffick of White People was contrary to the feelings of a number of respectable Citizens, and to the idea of liberty this country has so happily established." Public subscriptions were solicited to pay the passage of a shipload of servants just arrived in New York. The sum advanced was to be recovered "by a small rateable deduction out of the wages of such Servants." McKee, *Labor in Col. N.Y.,* p. 176.

[26] Such legislation reflected the activities of German societies founded as far back as 1764 to reform or abolish this institution. See Hennighausen, *op. cit.,* p. 5.

[27] See Sartorius von Waltershausen, *Die Arbeits-Verfassung der Englischen Kolonien in Nord-Amerika* (Strassburg, 1894), p. 66; Geiser, *op. cit.,* p. 40; Gray, *op. cit.,* I, 350.

[28] Stat. 25 Geo. III, c. 67.

[29] On the basis of entries in the registry of redemptioners, Geiser (*op. cit.,* p. 41) computed that two thirds of all immigrants entering Pennsylvania between 1786 and 1804 came as bound servants. See also Herrick, *op. cit.,* pp. 265, 266; E. I. McCormac, *White Servitude in Maryland* (Baltimore, 1904), p. 111; Guido Kisch, "German Jews in White Labor Servitude in America," Amer. Jewish Hist. Soc., *Publications,* No. 34 (1937). One writer asserts that the redemptioner arrangement was "constantly practiced" in the United States and Canada until 1805. S. C. Johnson, *Hist. of Emigration,* pp. 71, 72. The records of the registry of redemptioners in Pennsylvania end in 1831, but by that time the entries had grown fewer and fewer.

British Convict Servants. As a result of the researches of a number of historians of the colonial period we now have a more accurate picture of the role of the British convict in the plantations than was available in the days of Bancroft.[30] A relatively small amount of convict dumping in the continental colonies took place in the first half of the seventeenth century. At first the Virginia Company was definitely antagonistic to the program. The *True and Sincere Declaration,* issued in 1609, opposed receiving in Virginia the "weeds of their native country . . . who would act as a poison in the body of a tender, feeble, and yet unformed colony."[31] The Company announced that it would not receive any man who could not show "a character for religion and considerate conduct in his relations with his neighbors" or who was not trained in certain specified callings.[32] But the Company did not remain steadfast to this policy. In 1611 Dale, who advocated martial law and had no illusions about the character of the population of the colony, proposed that, in emulation of methods pursued by the Spanish government in peopling her colonies, felons be sent over to add to the labor forces of Virginia.[33] In 1615 James I issued a commission which inaugurated the transportation of convicted felons, except those found guilty of murder, rape, witchcraft, or burglary. They were to be transported for unspecified lengths of service at the discretion of the commissioners. This commission was renewed from time to time.[34] A goodly portion of these felons were sent to Virginia; the rest to the West Indies.[35]

In the latter half of the seventeenth century, the program of convict transportation was stepped up. In England the Civil Wars and the London plague had caused heavy population losses at a time when the nation was making bold strides as a commercial and industrial power. Skilled artisans could not be spared for the colonies, so the English

[30] See P. A. Bruce, *Economic History of Virginia in the 17th Century* (New York, 1895), I, 590 *et seq.;* James D. Butler, "British Convicts Shipped to American Colonies," *Amer. Hist. Rev.,* II (1896), 12–33; Abbot E. Smith, "The Transportation of Convicts in the American Colonies in the Seventeenth Century," *Amer. Hist. Rev.,* XXXIX (1934), 232–249. For an earlier analysis, see A. Sartorius von Waltershausen, *Die Arbeits-Verfassung der Englischen Kolonien in Nord-Amerika* (Strassburg, 1894), pp. 74–78.
[31] Brown, *Genesis of the United States,* p. 352.   [32] *Ibid.,* p. 355.
[33] *Ibid.,* p. 506; CSPA, *1574–1660,* No. 26, p. 12.
[34] *A.P.C., Col., 1613–80,* pp. 10 (1616), 12, 19, 21 (1617), 22 (1618), 52, 55 (1622), 56 (1623); *Cal. State Papers, Dom., 1619–23,* pp. 306, 307 (1621), 439 (1622), *1631–33,* p. 547 (1633). The commission of 1621 excluded from reprieve criminals guilty of arson or highway robbery in addition to other felonies previously singled out.
[35] *Cal. State Papers, Dom., 1634–35,* p. 166 (1634); *1635,* pp. 265, 535; *1635–36,* p. 437 (1636); *1639–40,* pp. 183 (1639), 349, 486 (1640). For petition to Parliament in 1646 to transport several prisoners convicted of petty misdemeanors to Barbados, see Stock, *Proc. Brit. Parl.,* I, 175, 176.

authorities encouraged the slave trade by establishing the Royal African Company in the 1660s, and commuted with increasing frequency the death sentences of convicts to transportation to the colonies for terms of service. Beginning in 1655, convicts who had been granted conditional pardons were turned over by the sheriffs to merchants for transportation and the merchants were required to give security for their safe conveyance. A study of the Patent Rolls made by Abbot Emerson Smith for the years 1655–99 reveals that approximately 4,500 persons were pardoned for transportation during that period.[36] There is however, considerable doubt whether all these convicts were actually shipped.[37]

In 1661 the period of exile was fixed at ten years, but in 1684 the term of seven years was set [38] in accordance with an act of 1662 empowering country justices to sentence such "rogues, vagabonds, and sturdy beggars" as might be adjudged to be "incorrigible" to transportation to "any of the English plantations beyond the seas" for a term not exceeding seven years.[39]

This was but one of many similar statutes, for, with the Restoration, a long series of specific crimes were made punishable by transportation to the colonies.[40] In 1718 Parliament authorized the transportation for

[36] *Amer. Hist. Rev.*, XXXIX, 238, 243.

[37] In 1682 the Commissioners of Trade and Plantations ordered that no felon be shipped unless he furnished security in £100 that he would not return within four years. See *CSPA, 1681–85*, No. 800, pp. 336, 337. This large amount might well have discouraged plans for transportation during that period.

[38] Smith, *loc. cit.*, p. 240. The act of 1657 provided a 7-year transportation term for irresponsible persons who failed to give security for their good behavior. Firth and Rait, *Acts and Ordinances*, II, 1263–1264.

[39] 13, 14 Car. II, c. 12 (*Stat.*, V, 401).

[40] Among these may be mentioned the following: 1) 14 Car. II, c. 1 (1661), against Quakers refusing to take an oath; third offense (*Stat.*, V, 350); 2) 14 Car. II, c. 12 (1662), the most sweeping, cited *supra;* 3) 14 Car. II, c. 22; 18 Car. II, c. 3, 29; 30 Car. II, c. 2; 7, 8 Gul. III, c. 17, against border outlaws (*Stat.*, VII, 86; Ruffhead, V, 499); 4) 16 Car. II, c. 4 (1664), five or more persons assembling under pretense of religion; third offense, 7 yrs. to any of the plantations except Virginia and New England (*Stat.*, V, 516); 5) 22 Car. II, c. 5 (1670), stealing cloth or embezzling his majesty's stores to the value of 20s. (*Stat.*, V, 657); 6) 22 Car. II, c. 10 (1670), arson of corn stacks and malicious killing of cattle; 7) 8, 9 Gul. III, c. 27 (1697), rescuers of prisoners taken by any officers (7 yrs.) or harboring or concealing a rescue (*Stat.*, VII, 274); 8) 4 Geo. I, c. 11, crimes within benefit of clergy (7 yrs.), outside, 14 yrs., discussed *infra;* extended in 12 Geo. II, c. 21 (1739) to abettors of exporters of wool (Ruffhead, VI, 340); 9) 1 Geo. II, stat. 2, c. 19 (1728), destruction of turnpike gates, docks, or floodgates; amended 5 Geo. II, c. 33 (Ruffhead, V, 665; VI, 110; Pickering, *Stat.*, XVI, 362); 10) 2 Geo. II, c. 25 (1729), perjury or subornation of perjury (Ruffhead, V, 699); 11) 4 Geo. II, c. 6 (1731), theft of linen, fustian, cotton goods, etc. (Pickering, *Stat.*, XVI, 239); 12) 4 Geo. II, c. 32 (1731), stealing of lead or iron bars from houses or fences (Pickering, *Stat.*, XVI, 260); 13) 7 Geo. II, c. 34 (1734), smuggling tea, brandy, or other spirits (Ruffhead, VI, 232); 14) 10 Geo. II, c. 32 (1737), certain offenses concerning deer stealing (Ruffhead, VI, 285; Pickering, XVII, 159); 15) 11 Geo. II, c. 26 (1738), rescue of violators of act laying duties upon retailers of spirituous liquors or the assault of informers (Ruffhead, VI, 395), etc. Later acts extended transportation to such offenses as robbing lead mines, the rescue of any person convicted of murder, the assault of an officer while

seven-year terms of those convicted of lesser crimes within the benefit of clergy, and fourteen years of servitude for those guilty of offenses punishable by death. The former came to be referred to as "His Majesty's Seven-Year Passengers"[41] or "Seven-Year Servants."[42]

In addition to this motley company of vagabonds, unemployed poor, and felons, of whom the convicted felons comprised the lion's share, some, but not a great many, political prisoners were transported to the continental colonies, the bulk of them going to the West Indies. Cromwell's Scottish prisoners were sent to Barbados rather than to the mainland of North America.[43] Those convicted of participation in the Monmouth rebellion and sentenced to transportation by Jeffries were shipped principally to Jamaica and Barbados.[44] In the eighteenth cen-

---

salvaging a vessel or its goods, and the solemnizing of marriage without proclamation of bans, etc. See Stock, *op. cit.*, V, xx, xxi.

[41] *Md. Gazette*, July 17, 1755.   [42] *Md. Arch.*, LV, 378, 379, 763 (1757).

[43] In the Protectorate Parliament of 1659 a petition was submitted by Marcellus Rivers and Oxenbridge Foyle in behalf of themselves and some seventy others transported to Barbados for alleged complicity in the Salisbury rising in 1654, without legal conviction. They charged that the aged, ministers, officers, and gentlemen were forced to labor at "grinding at the mills and attending at the furnaces, or digging in this scorching island; having nought to feed on (notwithstanding their hard labour) but potatoe roots, nor to drink, but water with such roots washed in it . . . being whipped at the whipping-posts (as rogues) for their master's pleasure, and sleeping in sties worse than hogs in England." One of the agents engaged in procuring convicts refuted their charges of hard labor, contending that the terms were for five years at "the yearly salary of the island," the hours of labor from six to six, and the work not near as hard "as the common husbandman here." Stock, *Proc. Brit. Parl.*, I, 248, 251 *et seq.* For Scottish prisoners sent to Massachusetts at this time, see *N.E. Hist. and Gen. Register*, I (1847), 377–380.

[44] Butler, "British Convicts," *Amer. Hist. Rev.* II, 14, 15; S. R. Gardiner, *History of the Great Civil War* (3 vols., London, 1886–89), III, 448; Stillé, *Pa. Mag. of Hist. and Biog.* (Jan., 1889). See also *A.P.C., Col. 1613–80*, p. 788 (1678); HMC, *Rep.*, XLIV, Pt. I, 81–82 (1685); *CSPA, 1685–88*, Nos. 380, 381, 402–404, 420, 421, 422, 424, 441, 442, pp. 98, 105, 109, 110, 114 (1685). But cf. *Acts of the Parliaments of Scotland* (Edinburgh, 1814–24), VI, Pt. II, 745 (1650) for order to transport Scots to Virginia and New England.

The position of these political convicts was that of "conditional servitude." They were afterwards pardoned and many returned from exile. In Virginia the Preston rebels demanded their freedom after five years under the laws of the colony on the ground that they had come in without indentures, but the home authorities ruled that they had by their consent waived the benefit of the law and should serve out their seven-year terms. *CSPA, 1722–23*, No. 58, pp. 22, 23 (1722).

Some masters put their own economic interests ahead of their servants' liberty and openly opposed the granting of pardons to this group of convicts. A spokesman for the planters' point of view was Governor Kendall, who wrote the Earl of Shrewsbury:

"There has also been great mortality among the white servants here, and by reason of the war the planters have been unable to supply themselves with white servants. For this reason I have not announced the repeal of the act concerning the Monmouth rebels to the Council and Assembly. It seems that, when they arrived, the Lieutenant-Governor received positive orders from King James that their servitude should be fixed by act to ten years. The planters accordingly bought them and, thinking themselves secure of them during that time taught them to be their boilers, distillers, and refiners, and neglected to teach any others as they would otherwise have done. If these men are freed the loss to the planters will be great, and since we are at war and so thinly manned I think it would be a great kindness to the Island if the King ordered an Act to reduce their servitude to seven years. But if the King adhere to his original orders, no injustice

tury a somewhat larger proportion of convicts in this category were sent to the continental colonies. Some 135 political prisoners were shipped to Maryland after the uprising of 1715,[45] and again after the ill-advised attempt in 1745 of the Highlanders to place Bonnie Prince Charley, the Young Pretender, upon the throne, when possibly a thousand rebels were transported.[46]

Estimates of the total number of British convicts shipped to America must remain approximate, as immigrant and convict rosters, such as those available for certain Maryland counties, are partial and incomplete. Further partial assistance in making such compilations is offered by the accounts and lists in the *Historical Register, Gentleman's Magazine,* and the *London Magazine.*[47] It has been estimated that some fifty thousand convicts were shipped to America—to at least nine of the continental colonies. Butler places the total number of convicts sent from Old Bailey alone between 1717 and 1775 as not less than 10,000.[48] In Maryland, which, according to one authority,[49] received 20,000 (about half of them after 1750), the convicts comprised almost one half of all the indentured servants during the eighteenth century. In addition, large numbers went to Virginia and the West Indies. In fact the Caribbean colonies seemed more willing than the mainland to receive these convicts, because of the extreme shortage of white labor. New England's share was smallest of all.[50]

---

will be done to these rebels, for by law of the country if they come without indentures they must serve for five years, which period will expire next Christmas. . . ." *CSPA, 1689–92,* No. 968, pp. 288, 348 (1690).

[45] J. T. Scharf, *History of Maryland from the Earliest Period to the Present Day* (Baltimore, 1879), I, 385. See also *CSPA, 1716–17,* Nos. 128, 144, pp. 63, 73 (1716), No. 543, p. 291 (1717), *1720–21,* No. 214, p. 130 (1720); *WMCQ,* 1st ser., V, 267, 268 (1716). See also 1 Geo. I, stat. 2, c. 54 (Ruffhead, V, 90).

[46] See J. P. MacLean, *An Historical Account of the Settlement of Scotch Highlanders in America* (Cleveland, 1900); Butler, *loc. cit.,* p. 16.

[47] For the seven years ending in 1743 2,000 names of felons and vagabonds were listed as having been ordered for transportation from Ireland. Stock, *op. cit.,* V, 594n–604n.

[48] Butler, *loc. cit.,* p. 25.

[49] Scharf, *op. cit.,* I, 371. According to the compilation of Basil Sollers ("Transported Convict Laborers in Maryland during the Colonial Period," *Md. Hist. Mag.,* II [1907], 17–47), Scharf's estimate overshot the mark by 30 to 40 per cent. Sollers put the average annual influx of convicts in the province at 300 as against Scharf's figure of 400 to 500. Cf. also Sartorius von Waltershausen, *op. cit.,* p. 75.

[50] For the occasional transportation of convicts to New York, see *Calendar of Hist. MSS in the Office of the Secretary of State: Part II: English MSS* (Albany, 1866), pp. 525, 527. In the West Indies there was less disposition to receive women convicts than men, as English women were not put to work in the fields in the Caribbean colonies; in Virginia and the Carolinas, European servants, both men and women, worked at husbandry. *CSPA, 1574–1660,* No. 125, p. 281 (1638), No. 13, p. 410 (1653); *1661–68,* Nos. 292, 394, pp. 88, 117 (1662), No. 872, p. 259 (1664); *1681–85,* Nos. 1668, 1729, 1826, pp. 628, 648, 673 (1684); *1685–88,* Nos. 380, 402–404, 453, pp. 98, 105, 116 (1685); *1696–97,* Nos. 657, 1134, 1156, 1172, 1189, 1190, 1194,

There is some evidence that even after the American Revolution the British authorities attempted to dump convicts in this country. In 1783 Governor Paca of Maryland informed the Assembly of "information of a Fraudulent Plan which British subjects are adopting to introduce British and Irish Convicts into the United States." [51] Hancock protested to the Continental Congress in August, 1787, that convicts had been landed on the shores of Massachusetts by a brig bound from Ireland.[52] In September of that year Congress adopted a resolution calling upon the states to pass suitable laws "for preventing the transportation of convicted malefactors from foreign countries into the United States,[53] and several states speedily incorporated this recommendation into law.[54] The tax levied by the first Federal Congress on "the importation of certain persons" was held to apply to convicts as well as to slaves.[55] The British were thus forced to turn to Botany Bay.[56]

Who was the typical transported convict? A cross-section of an average convict shipment can be obtained from the records filed in accordance with the Maryland act of 1728, requiring shipmasters to file with the clerk of the county court a "testimonial" stating the offense and term of service of each convict passenger.[57] The Kent County court records reveal that in the years 1732–34 some sixty-five convicts were transported to that county. Of these one third had been convicted in Eng-

---

1195, 1205, 1216, pp. 341, 530, 541, 544, 559, 560, 567, 570 (1697); *A.P.C., Col. 1613–80*, pp. 64, 310, 314 (1661); *1680–1720*, p. 314 (1697); *WMCQ*, 1st ser., VII, 273; XXVII, 209.

[51] *Md. Arch.*, XLVIII, 484 (1783).

[52] *J. Continental Cong.*, XXXIII, 511. Some 140 convicts were reported to have landed at Fisher's Island in the summer of 1788. *Salem [Mass.] Mercury*, July 15, 1788. Still others were landed at Baltimore. Jay proposed that "a gentle Remonstrance on this Subject" be sent to the "Court of London." *J. Continental Cong.*, XXXIV, 494, 528–530.

[53] *Ibid.*, p. 528 (Sept. 16, 1788).

[54] See Sartorius von Waltershausen, *op. cit.*, pp. 77–78; Bioren, *Laws of Pa.*, II, 485, 486; Collinson Read, *An Abridgment of the Laws of Pennsylvania* (Philadelphia, 1801), pp. 50, 51; Hening, XII, 668 (1788).

[55] McCormac, *White Servitude in Maryland*, p. 106. Some Americans appear to have wanted the British to continue transporting convicts after the Revolution. *Mass. Centinel*, Oct. 16, 1784.

[56] James Maria Matra's plan to colonize convicts in Australia was favored over James De Lancey's proposal to settle the Nova Scotia Loyalist refugees in New South Wales. The hostility of Lord Howe at the Admiralty was apparently decisive. See R. B. Morris, *James De Lancey of New York* (New York, 1940) and *Historical Records of New South Wales*, I, Pt. II (1783–92).

[57] The penalty was £5 current for nonobservance. *Md. Arch.*, XXXVI, 298, 389 (1728–29). By a supplementary act this procedure was limited to a mere declaration upon oath stating whether the servant was then under sentence of transportation, for what offense, and the length of the term he had to serve. *Ibid.*, p. 492 (1729). For a typical transportation agreement, filed in Kent Co. court in 1732, see contract between two justices of Dorset Co., England, and George Burk of Bideford, merchant, for the transportation of George Batt, convicted of felony at the sessions and barred from benefit of clergy. He was sentenced to be transported for 14 years. The named justices were authorized to contract for his transportation, and the convict was then made over to a ship's captain for transportation to Maryland.

land and sentenced to serve fourteen-year terms for offenses as serious as murder.[58] The more extensive Baltimore County records for the years 1770–74 listed 655 imported convicts, of whom women amounted to 111, or about one sixth of the total. A surprisingly high number had been convicted of nonclergyable felonies—murder, rape, highway robbery, burglary, horse stealing and sheep stealing, and grand larceny; others were sentenced for shoplifting and petit larceny of as little as 6*d.;* only a few were classified as rogues or vagabonds. Fourteen-year terms had been meted out to 123, or slightly less than one fifth of the total; the remainder received seven-year terms, with the exception of eleven convicts who were sentenced to life servitude for such serious felonies as murder, rape, and burglary.[59] A very small proportion of these convicts were skilled workers.[60] It is certain that not all of them remained in Baltimore County. Of 43 transported in the *Hercules* from Dublin, 17 went to Virginia, 16 to Augusta County; 15 others went out to Frederick County in Maryland; and only six were listed as remaining in Baltimore. It is thus apparent that by the eve of the Revolution a large proportion of the convicts were settling along the frontier,[61] where slave labor proved more expensive and less practicable than in the Tidewater and Piedmont regions. Because of their longer terms of service convicts were more profitable purchases than ordinary indentured servants.[62]

A review of these all too fragmentary entries should serve to modify the contention of Bancroft and Bruce that the bulk of the convicts coming to this country were really political prisoners. Actually, they were

[58] Kent, lib. JS, No. 17, fols. 55, 58, 61, 62, 64, 67, 69, 91, 104, 105, 107, 108, 110, 111, 149, 155.

[59] Baltimore, lib. AL, "Convicts, 1770–74," fols. 1–388, *passim*. The Charleston, S.C., Probate Court, lib. 1727–29, f. 253, contains a list of convicts imported on the ship *Expedition* from Bristol in 1729. Of the 24 convicts, one had been convicted of petit larceny, three of "Felony 14 Years," and the rest of "Felony 7 Years." A list of convicts transported from 13 Irish counties, 1736–42, contains the names of 243 transported as vagabonds, 143 for grand larceny, 14 for petit larceny, one each for forgery and perjury, and 9 who had been found guilty of felony punishable by death. Stock, *op. cit.*, V, 594, 595n. Vagabondage was the principal offense of transported convicts from Cork Co. *Ibid.*, p. 601n.

[60] One was a serge weaver who had stolen 68 yards of woolen cloth. The bulk of the transported felons were unskilled workmen. For health certificates made out by the surgeon and apothecary who attended the gaol, see Baltimore, lib. AL, "Convicts, 1770–74," f. 335 (1773).

[61] 13 convicts who arrived in 1773 in the brig *Dublin*, however, indicated Baltimore Co. as their final destination. *Ibid.*, fols. 140, 368.

[62] In his 1722 edition of the *Hist. of Va.*, Beverly conceded that "the greedy planter will always buy them." See also Eddis, *Letters from America*, pp. 63–75, 109–110; M. S. Morriss, *Colonial Trade of Maryland, 1689–1715*, p. 77; Gipson, *Brit. Empire before the Amer. Revol.*, II, 95–97, 99–101. The frontier's demand for convicts continued unabated down to the Revolution. See Ford, *Washington as an Employer of Labor*, pp. 16, 17.

criminals, and many had been convicted for serious offenses.[63] The colonists themselves generally recognized the kinship between the convict servants and crime in the colonies. Convicts were more prone to mutiny or desert than other immigrants.[64] They were unquestionably responsible for an increase in crime, particularly in Maryland and Virginia. Among their motley ranks were women of the Moll Flanders type,[65] men out of Hogarth's sketches, characters like the university book thief Henry Justice, barrister and bookseller, and the "Princess Susanna Carolina Matilda, Marchioness of Waldegrave," who doubtless caused Philadelphia society some embarrassing moments when she was revealed to be plain Sarah Wilson, transported for the theft of some of the royal jewels.[66]

The convict problem first seems to have become acute in Maryland in the 1720s. An increase in criminal prosecutions and felony trials, "as well as Common Trespasses breaches of the peace and Other Misdemeanors Since the Late Importation of Convicts from Great Britain into this province" was observed in 1721, and there was a feeling of widespread insecurity on the plantations.[67] Long-protracted litigation was brought against Jonathan Forward, a well-known merchant under contract with the British government to ship convicts to Maryland,[68] by Gilbert Powlson, the master of a ship which had brought convicts as well as slaves to the province. Powlson's attorney, Thomas Bordley, later superseded him and carried on the contest in his own interest as a purchaser of bills of exchange drawn on Forward. The Maryland courts supported Powlson and Bordley throughout. Forward's agents were prevented from selling convict servants in the colonies without posting bond, and even the governor fought with Dulany, Forward's attorney. Opposition to the importation of convict servants doubtless had a large

[63] See Smith, "Transportation of Convicts, *Amer. Hist. Rev.*, XXXIX, 248. This controversy still engages the attention of genealogists. See *VMH*, LII (1944), 180–182; LIII (1945), 37–41.

[64] Convicts sentenced for relatively minor offenses proved far less refractory than the more dangerous felons and assumed useful roles upon completion of their terms of service. See *Md. Gazette*, July 9, 1767.

[65] The "Sot-Weed Factor" overheard one member of "a jolly female crew" charge another:

"You'd blush (if one cou'd blush) for shame,
Who from Bridewell or Newgate came."

Ebenezer Cook, *Sot-Weed Factor, or, A Voyage to Maryland* (London, 1807).

[66] Anent the convict record of some of these emigrants, see *Gentleman's Mag.*, *1767*, p. 92, for an account of one of the passengers, a notorious army deserter, who had "been confined in 73 jails," though but 32 years of age. See also *ibid.*, May 17, 1736; *London Mag.*, May 10, 1736.

[67] Md. Prov. Court Proceedings, lib. 1719–22, f. 362 (1721).

[68] See *Md. Arch.*, XXV, 435.

part in the hostility to the defendant; [69] but the convict servant plot of 1721 (discussed under concerted action among workers) and during these years the aggressive practices of Forward's cordially detested agents, Cockey and Moale, had created in Maryland a general aversion, not alone to the convicts, but also to the merchants who shipped them. In an action brought in 1722 to recover a servant who had run away to England, only to be transported to Maryland as a convict, the court, besides ordering the master to give recognizance in the amount of £5 current for his servant's good behavior, ruled "that Security be given in the penaltie of fifteen pounds Curr't Money for the good behavior of Every Convict already Imported or to be into this Province during the time of their Service or Continuance therein which shall first Determine." [70]

Because of mounting evidence of crime the Baltimore County court in August, 1723, issued a warrant to the sheriff to take any convicts found in his bailiwick and oblige them to give security in the amount of £15 sterling for keeping the peace—a greater sum in fact than that required by the Provincial Court order of the previous year. Even more direct action was dictated by the course of events. In September, 1723, Charles Hammond of Ann Arundel County made oath in the Provincial Court that "a parcell of Reputed Convicts," fourscore in number, were banded together at the near-by plantation of Robert Jubbs. James Baldwin, who corroborated this testimony, pointed out that when he asked John Moale what he intended to do with the convicts lately imported, the latter replied that he would sell them and dared any one to take them up. He further threatened that if a certain convict then detained in the Ann Arundel County gaol were to die, he would not even be satisfied with £50. Mary Owerard of Annapolis reported a conversation she had had with Moale in which she had told him that her husband was unwilling to put up security for a servant woman of hers. To this Moale was alleged to have declared that "it was only a silly Notion that Some People had for that he would put a Ships load of Convicts on Shore if he had them here and see who dare touch them." In view of this testimony and the further complaint of John Beale of the

---

[69] The Privy Council, on appeal, reversed the Maryland judgment in favor of Bordley. The late Chief Judge Carroll T. Bond, in his illuminating analysis of this intricate litigation, suggested that the royal instructions of 1727 for stay or suspension of execution during appeals from the colonies were to some extent induced by Bordley's aggressive conduct. *Proceedings of the Md. Court of Appeals, 1695–1729 (American Legal Records,* I, Washington, 1933), pp. xli–xliv. For this litigation, instituted in 1723, see *ibid.,* pp. 288, 303–305, 334, 336, 346–357, 402–409, 436–438, 445–447, 471, 490–516, 519–521, 526, 527.

[70] Jones v. Brinley, Md. Prov. Court, lib. 1719–22, f. 639 (1722).

same county that "Six persons Deemed to be Convicts runaway whom he hath reason to Suspect are now Lurking on or near his Plantation" and whom he feared, would do injury to his person or estate, the court ordered the sheriff "to Raise a Sufft Number of persons and to go with Such persons in pursuit of the Runaways afd." [71] Long after this date the provincial press carried very frequent references to runaway convict servants.[72]

Virginia charged that convicts were involved in the conspiracies of 1663.[73] Writing in 1724 of the convicts transported to Virginia, Hugh Jones asserted that "abundance of them do great Mischiefs, commit Robbery and Murder, and spoil Servants, that were before very good: But they frequently there meet with the End that they deserved at Home, though indeed some of them prove indifferent good." [74] Governor Gooch, in a message to the Assembly in 1731, attributed the increase in robberies to the convict servants, who were also believed responsible for a wave of arson.[75] The editor of the *Virginia Gazette* was moved to indict the whole system in stirring language:

When we see our papers filled continually with accounts of the most audacious Robberies, the most cruel Murders, and infinite other Villanies perpetrated by Convicts transported from Europe, what melancholy and what terrible Reflections must it occasion. . . . These are some of the Favours Britain, Thou art called Mother Country; but what good Mother ever sent thieves and villains to accompany her children; to corrupt with their infectious vices and to murder the rest.[76]

Many of the runaway servants listed in the *Virginia Gazette* proved to be recently imported convicts with bad records, which they further blackened by misconduct in America.[77] When Charles Bush ran away, his master, in advertising a reward of 40s. for his return, was careful to

[71] *Ibid.*, lib. 1722–24, fols. 271, 272 (1723).
[72] See, e.g., *Md. Gazette,* June 14, July 5, 12, Aug. 23, Sept. 16, Dec. 31, 1745; April 1, June 17, June 24, July 15, August 19, 26, Sept. 16, 30, Oct. 14, 1746; May 24, 31, June 30, Sept. 15, Oct. 17, 21, 1747; April 6, 20, May 11, 18, June 15, 29, Aug. 17, Sept. 14, 21, Nov. 9, 30, Dec. 28, 1748; Aug. 5, Sept. 16, 23, Oct. 7, 21, Nov. 11, 1756; March 17, April 7, June 30, July 7, Aug. 11, 18, Sept. 1, 8, 15, 22, 29, Oct. 6, 1757; Jan. 5, March 9, April 27, May 11, July 27, Aug. 17, Dec. 21, 1758; Feb. 15, April 12, 26, May 15, 24, June 7, July 12, 19, 26, Aug. 9, 16, Sept. 6, 20, Oct. 18, Nov. 29, 1759; Feb. 28, March 27, April 10, 1760.
[73] See *supra,* p. 173.
[74] *Present State of Virginia* (Sabin's reprint, New York, 1865), pp. 53, 54.
[75] See A. P. Scott, *Criminal Law in Colonial Virginia* (Chicago, 1930), pp. 214–215; also *VMH,* XXX, 253–254; LIII, 38, 39; *Va. Gazette,* March 23, 1739.
[76] *Va. Gazette,* May 24, 1751. See also *ibid.,* Dec. 5, 1751.
[77] See *infra,* p. 469. Joshua Dean, counterfeiter, *Va. Gazette,* Aug. 11, 1738; Edward Daniels, blacksmith, *ibid.,* Feb. 16, 1769.

warn: "Any person so doing, I caution them to be careful, for he is of a bloody mind and made many threats a few days before he went off." [78] Perhaps the most notorious of these escaped convict servants was William Mann, who had run away from his master, Colonel John Chiswell of Hanover County, in the spring of 1737, joining three other servants of Captain Avery of Prince William County, and then proceeding to shoot Eliphalet Larby, a frontier hunter, in the back and beat out his brains lest he inform on them. Mann's arrest and published confession led to the apprehension of two of the others who had gone into business in Pennsylvania. They were extradited to Virginia and tried in the General Court. Mann was permitted to testify against them and they were convicted and promptly executed.[79] The murder of a coachman named Evans the following year by a convict runaway named Anthony Francis Dutton, found guilty upon circumstantial evidence and executed, also created great uneasiness over the convict servant problem.[80]

Robberies and larcenies attributed to Virginia's convict servants surpassed in number murders for which they were believed responsible.[81] Landon Carter had ground to suspect a former servant named George Keele, "a Convict who some years ago served his Time with me, and has since his Freedom" plotted with another to hire Negroes as accessories to steal a copper still and a "fine noble worm," conveyed by cart out of the plantation.[82] Convict runaways usually took such property along with them as would help in their escape, especially boats.[83] When they ran away to the woods, they added to their crimes by catching and kill-

[78] *Ibid.*, May 12, 1768.
[79] *Va. Gazette*, June 10, 1737; Marion Dargan, *Crime and the Virginia Gazette, 1736–1775* (Albuquerque, N.M., 1934), pp. 10, 11.
[80] *Va. Gazette*, Aug. 18, 25, Oct. 20, Nov. 3, 24, 1738. Hue and cry was raised by Governor Gooch in 1745 against two servants of David Galloway of Northumberland alleged to have barbarously murdered Tobias Horton, their skipper, en route from Norfolk in a small schooner. They were described as a Scotch weaver and an Englishman pretending to be a baker, who would pass muster for sailors and seek to escape by ship. *Ibid.*, Sept. 26, 1745; Dargan, *op. cit.*, pp. 15, 16. When the snow *Fortune* was wrecked off Chesapeake Bay in 1769, her cargo of indentured servants escaped and scattered, the men dressed in sailors' habit. As distinguished from the run-of-the-mill convict importations, this boatload comprised mostly skilled craftsmen, including a shipwright, plasterer, surgeon, sailor, farmer, turner, tailor, and wheelwright, and two carpenters, drawers, and weavers. In addition, the list included one female mantua-maker and three convict women whose trades were unspecified. *Va. Gazette*, Oct. 5, 1769.
[81] *Va. Gazette*, Sept. 5, Oct. 17, 1755; Scott, *Criminal Law in Col. Va.*, p. 220; High Court of Admiralty Papers, Misc. 1066 (1756).
[82] Keele was described as "a tall lusty Fellow, with the Ploughman's lounging forward Gait, and as much of the drab Gallows in his Face as is common to be seen in noted Villains. It is reported that he carries on a thievish Traffic from Virginia into the Upper Parts of Maryland." *Va. Gazette*, March 12, 1767; Dargan, *op. cit.*, pp. 26, 27.
[83] See *supra*, pp. 171, 177n.; *infra*, p. 511n.

ing hogs that had been allowed to roam at large.[84] Counterfeiting [85] and arson [86] were also frequently attributed to them.

Though fewer convicts were transported to Pennsylvania than to the tobacco colonies, her residents were equally appalled at the extent of their criminal activities.[87] Franklin charged that the British practice of "emptying their jails into our settlements is an insult and contempt, the cruellest, that ever one people offered to another." [88] To him is generally attributed the famous proposal that rattlesnakes should be sent in return for the "human serpents" that England shipped to America.[89] A writer in a Pennsylvania newspaper in the same year ironically referred to "that good and wise act of Parliament by virtue of which all the Newgates and Dungeons are emptied into the Colonies." Continuing in the same vein, he declared:

Our Mother knows what is best for us. What is a little House-breaking, Shoplifting, or Highway-robbing; what is a son now and then corrupted and hanged, a Daughter debauched, and Pox'd, a wife stabbed, a Husband's throat cut, or a child's brains beat out with an Axe, compared with this "Improvement and Well peopling of the Colonies.[90]

Owing to the widespread apprehension of convict dumping, the Middle and Southern colonies from 1670 onwards passed acts placing prohibitive duties on imported convicts or requiring ship captains to give bond for their good behavior.[91] Virginia took the initiative in the passage of such legislation. As a result of the influx of convicts after 1660 and their participation in the plot of September, 1663,[92] the Virginia General Court in April, 1670, was impelled to issue its famous "order about Jayle birds." Importers of persons guilty of offenses for which they "deserved to dye in England" were forbidden to land them in Virginia. The order declared further that

[84] Dargan, *op. cit.*, p. 34.

[85] *Va. Gazette*, Aug. 11, 1738, contained "A Caution to the Paper Money Colonies" to beware of Joshua Dean, transported to the plantations for life for counterfeiting, and now runaway from Col. Alexander Spotswood. See also *ibid.*, Oct. 12, 1752.

[86] *Ibid.*, March 17, 1738.

[87] See *Pa. Gazette*, June 28, 1750; April 11, June 27, Sept. 5, 1751.

[88] *Works* (Bigelow ed.), IV, 255.

[89] *Ibid.*, May 9, 1751; Franklin, *Writings* (Smyth ed.), III, 45–48. See also L. H. Gipson, "Crime and Its Punishment in Provincial Pennsylvania," *Pennsylvania History* (Jan., 1935); J. F. Watson, *Annals of Philadelphia* (Philadelphia, 1830), pp. 485–486.

[90] *Pa. Gazette*, May 9, 1751.

[91] For recognizances of good behavior of convicts imported into Baltimore County, see Baltimore, lib. "AL, Convicts, 1770–74," fols. 24–29, 31–37, 86–90, 191–203, 239, 241, 280, 362–367, 369.

[92] See *supra*, p. 173.

We have been the more induced to make this ordr by the horror yet remaining amongst us of the barbarous designe of such villaines in September 1663 who attempted at once the Subversion of our Religion laws libertyes rights and proprietyes the sad effect of which desperate Conspiracy we have undoubtedly felt to the ruin or at least the very great hazard of the peace and welfare of this Collony and neighbour plantations.[93]

The Privy Council confirmed the order, only to set it aside in 1678 when Ralph Williamson was authorized to carry fifty-two Scottish convicts to Virginia.[94] A Maryland act of 1676 forbade the importation of convicts under penalty of 2,000 lbs. of tobacco.[95] In general, the West Indies, with the exception of Barbados, showed far less inclination to accept convicts by the end of the seventeenth century.[96] Governors were instructed to withhold their approval from such legislation, which the British government disallowed.[97] Nevertheless, it does appear that the duties, although high, were paid at times by importers.[98]

Pennsylvania appears to have been more successful in curbing the trade. Her opposition was first expressed in 1683, when it was proposed that "no felons be brought into this country." [99] In 1722 a duty of £5 was placed on every convict imported; the importer was also to post a bond of £50 for the servant's good behavior for one year.[100] This law was repealed in 1729 on the ground that ship masters then brought their

[93] *Va. Gen. Court Mins.*, pp. 209, 210 (1670); *VMH*, XIX, 355, 356. See also order of 1671, *Va. Gen. Court Mins.*, p. 252, and Nevett's case, p. 288 (1671). See also Hening, II, 509–511: "Nor hath it been a small motive to us to hinder and prohibite the importation of such dangerous and scandalous people since we thereby apparently loose our reputation whilst we are believed to be a place only fitt to receive such base and lewd persons."

[94] For later restrictions and the reaction of the home authorities, see *A.P.C., Col., 1720–45*, pp. 54, 57; *J. Commrs. Trade and Plantations, 1722/3–1728*, pp. 30, 34; *CSPA, 1722–23*, Nos. 613, 629, 637, 698, pp. 293, 301, 303, 335 (1723). The question of a possible conflict between the laws of Virginia obliging servants not bound by indentures to maximum terms of five years and the usual seven-year term of service for imported felons was raised in 1722. The Attorney General ruled that since these confessed felons had petitioned for transportation, they could not claim the benefit of Virginia laws, since "a person by consent may waive benefit of the Law." *CSPA, 1722–23*, No. 58, p. 22 (1722).

[95] *Md. Arch.*, II, 540; XV, 136, 137 (1676). This act was revived down to 1692 (*ibid.*, XIII, 539) and considered in force in 1699, when it was disallowed (*ibid.*, XXV, 82). The act was considered in force by the legislature, nonetheless (*ibid.*, XXIV, 104). As a result of the Parliamentary act of 1717 the legislature in 1723 passed an act requiring the purchasers of convicts to give security in the amount of £30 for the good behavior of the imported servant for one year. This act received the dissent of the Proprietary on the ground that it was in contravention of an act of Parliament by authority of which certain contractors had the right to offer these convicts for sale. See *ibid.*, XXXV, preface; XXXVIII, 320 (1723).

[96] See Smith, *loc. cit.*, pp. 242, 243.

[97] See *Pa. Arch.*, I, 306 (1731); Labaree, *Royal Instructions*, pp. 673, 674.

[98] *Md. Arch.*, IX, 5 (1752).

[99] *Pa. Col. Rec.*, I, 72. For expressions of opposition in the press of the colony, see *Amer. Weekly Mercury*, Feb. 14, April 13, 1721.

[100] *Pa. Stat. at Large*, III, 265–267.

passengers to adjacent provinces, whence they were smuggled into Pennsylvania.[101] The bond feature, however, was reaffirmed in the session of 1729–30.[102] Exclusion acts continued to be passed down to 1742 without being sent to the home government for approval.[103] When these acts were finally submitted to the King in Council they were disallowed.[104]

In England opposition to such laws was led by the contractors of convicts. Generally the home authorities heeded their own merchants and ignored the clamor from beyond the seas. In 1754 the Maryland Assembly imposed a duty of 20s. on each servant having seven years or longer to serve.[105] Reinforced by the opinion of William Murray, then Attorney General of the Crown and later to become Lord Mansfield, that such a tax was "in direct opposition to the authority of the parliament of Great Britain," [106] John Stewart, the London merchant who was the principal contractor shipping convicts to Maryland at this period, had refused to pay the duty. He claimed that seven-year servants were in reality convicts, and that the rights of the Crown to support convicts were infringed. The issue came to a head in 1757 when it was brought out that naval officers, in instances where captains had refused to pay duties on convict servants on the ground that the impost was contrary to the laws of England, had allowed them to be landed upon posting of sufficient bond by the captains. This action was condemned by the Lower House, which chose to regard convicts in the light of servants, and in this way circumvent the issue of the Crown's prerogative.[107] Lord Baltimore called on Sir Robert Henley, the Attorney General, for a legal opinion. While that official declined to give a categorical answer, he stated that as far as he could see the act was not repugnant to the laws of England nor an improper exercise of the legislative power of the colony. Furthermore he advised the proprietor not to change the

---

[101] *Votes of Assembly*, III, 66.

[102] *Pa. Stat. at Large*, IV, 164–171. See also *Pa. Arch.*, 1st ser., I, 306 (1731); *Pa. Stat. at Large*, IV, 360, 361, 366 (1743). Similarly, the New Jersey act of 1730. Allinson, *N.J. Acts*, pp. 84–88 (1730), disallowed. *J. Commrs. Trade and Plantations, 1728/9–34*, p. 314 (1732).

[103] In 1740 Governor Thomas informed the Assembly that inasmuch as that body had excluded felons from coming into the colony as servants, it was a fair presumption that Pennsylvania had no servants under indentures. Hence, masters would be unjustified in their complaints about servants enlisting. *Pa. Col. Rec.*, III, 442; Herrick, *op. cit.*, pp. 125, 126.

[104] *Pa. Stat. at Large*, IV, 501–513. However, the earlier act of 1729–30 fixing a duty of £5 and the supplementary act for collecting duties were continued and administered as the law of Pennsylvania until the legislation of 1789. *Ibid.*, V, 131, 132; Herrick, *op. cit.*, p. 127.

[105] *Md. Arch.*, L, 550.

[106] *Ibid.*, LV, 763–771; George Chalmers, *Opinions of Eminent Lawyers on Various Points of English Jurisprudence Chiefly Concerning the Colonies* (London, 1858), I, 344–348.

[107] *Md. Arch.*, LV, 89–90.

law "after so long an Acquiescence," and not to refund the duties to Stewart. In effect, this was a reversal of the Murray opinion.[108] Perhaps it is significant that the initiative in protesting the Maryland impost was taken at this time by the contractor rather than by the British government.

In addition to the passage of laws imposing duties and requiring bonds for good behavior, some consideration was given in Virginia to a proposal to give convict servants less ample freedom dues [109] than were allowed other servants. In 1748 the burgesses from the Northern Neck opposed reenacting the act of 1705, which was in effect the servant code of the province. Their position was that the code recognized only two kinds of labor, providing one rule for servants and another for slaves, and that a separate rule should be made for convict servants who had been transported as a means of punishment. To treat them as well as the honest redemptioners would encourage the home government to send more convicts. It was argued that such action might "confirm an Odium on this Country that we are like those we encourage, and honest Men will not chuse to live in such Company." Fairfax Harrison suggests that the prevailing majority were motivated by a desire to use the convicts to man and garrison the frontier against the French and the Indians.

The traffic in convict servants was a profitable one to the contractors. The proceedings of the parliament of Ireland for the session 1739–40 record that rival merchants petitioned for this business at £3 for each felon or vagabond transported. This rate, one half the previous charge, was fixed by law. Some of the convicts were sold by the shippers for sums ranging from £9 10s. each for unskilled workers to £25 for trained artificers. Sheriffs of the Irish counties received £5 a head for convicts sentenced to transportation, but only paid out on an average £3 to the merchant transporters. One particular contractor, over a period of seven years, had transported on an average of 473 convicts annually. Even allowing for transportation costs, it is clear that both sheriffs and contractors made handsome profits.[110] As long as there was a demand the contractors continued to ship convicts.

No serious attempt was ever made to set convict servants to work on

---

[108] *Ibid.*, p. 771.

[109] The law increasing freedom dues to £3 10s. was disallowed after further protests from the Northern Neck in which the governor joined. Later the bill was reenacted and permitted to remain in force. Hening, V, 550, 568; VI, 356; *Legislative Journals of the Council*, II, 1034; C.O. 5:1327, p. 143; *VMH*, XXX, 250–260.

[110] Stock, *op. cit.*, V, xx, xxi, 591–607; Ford, *op. cit.*, pp. 15, 16. For charges that John Stewart, London contractor, made exorbitant profits, see *Md. Arch.*, IX, 4–5 (1757).

public works projects, nor was any comprehensive program ever instituted to give them suitable training. In 1724 the Virginia Assembly rejected after debate a plan to seat all the convicts in a county by themselves where they were to cultivate hemp and flax under the supervision of overseers who were to "keep them to their labour by such methods as are used in Bridewell."[111] The Earl of Halifax suggested some such plan to the Board of Trade in 1763, but was told that no such projects were being carried on, except, perhaps, under the military department, which did not come within the Board's jurisdiction.[112]

Victims of Kidnaping. In traditional treatments of early American history kidnaping has generally been emphasized as a significant source of British labor in the colonies.[113] Credence is generally given to the charge of Morgan Godwyn in his *The Negro's and Indian's Advocate* that wholesale kidnaping took place in England, as many as ten thousand persons being annually spirited out of the kingdom. However, in a recent study of this subject, Abbot Emerson Smith has flatly controverted the charges, and contends that actually there never was any great amount of kidnaping at all. The figure ten thousand is in his opinion twice the maximum number of servants sent to the colonies in any one year; usually the number was very much lower. The word "kidnabber" was invented in the 1670s to blacken the character of recruiting agents. Whether deservedly or not, the agents, nicknamed "Spirits," engaged in recruiting English servants, gained for themselves a reputation for unscrupulous behavior rivaling that of the German Newlanders. Their job was to persuade people to sign up for emigration. Doubtless they painted a rosier picture of conditions of service and general prospects than was warranted. After the recruiting agent had obtained the necessary signatures, he often had the prospective emigrants confined in "cookes houses" to prevent their escape. He operated purely under the profit motive, and yet it was primarily through the activities of such agents that the colonies south of New England were supplied with British and Irish workingmen.[114]

[111] Fairfax Harrison, "When the Convicts Came," *VMH*, XXX, 250–260.

[112] C.O. 5:65, p. 281 (transcript, Lib. of Congress). Halifax made the point that, by employing the transported convicts "in some publick Works," their labor might "turn to the Advantage of the Community." See also *N.J. Col. Docs.*, V, 374.

[113] For kidnaping as a method of settling the French colonies, see A. de Boislisle, ed., *Mémoires de Saint-Simon*, XXXVII (Paris, 1925), pp. 257–258. For the work of the press gangs, see Jean Buvat, *Journal de la régence* (Paris, 1865), II, 78, 87–88. See also Dorothy M. Quynn, "Recruiting in Old Orleans for New Orleans," *Amer. Hist. Rev.*, XLVI (1941), 832–836.

[114] A. E. Smith, "Indentured Servants: New Light on Some of America's 'First' Families," *J. Econ. Hist.*, II, 40–53 (May, 1942).

Doubtless one basis for the charge of duress in connection with the transportation of servants was their detention in these "cookes houses," where, according to a contemporary account, "being once entred, [they] are kept as Prisoners until a Master fetches them off; and they lye at charges in these places a moneth or more, before they are taken away." To get a servant from one of these depots in the seventeenth century generally involved a cash payment of £3 to cover the agent's fees and expenses of detention.[115] This detention may have been legitimate on the basis of contract, but the technique was crude.

Another ground for complaint was the practice of false kidnaping. Runaway bound servants and children, wife deserters, and even escaped criminals signed up for passage to America, leaving the "spirit" to face the wrath of master, wife, or constable.[116] Others signed up for the passage, and then, after they had been bound in the registry office, placed on shipboard, and provided with clothes, members of their gang would search for them and threaten to denounce the agent or master as a kidnaper. Agents were prosecuted and others threatened even in cases where the servants had voluntarily declared at the registry that they were going of their own free will.[117] This was in effect an extortion racket, although in the notorious prosecution of the London merchant John Wilmore it would appear that he was the victim of a political frame-up.[118]

On the other hand, there were legitimate and numerous cases of the kidnaping of minors and the shanghaing of adults. The methods employed were similar to those of the press gang. The victim was plied with liquor or knocked insensible—or otherwise beguiled or "trepanned"[119]—and then hastily conveyed on board ship. The fear of spiriting was widespread in England. Accusations were by no means infrequent, even though convictions were relatively few. Certainly the

---

[115] William Bullock, *Virginia Impartially Examined* (London, 1649), p. 14.

[116] *CSPA, 1661–68*, No. 331, p. 98 (1662). Cf. the testimony of Micajah Perry, a prominent colonial merchant of London. Stock, *Proc. Brit. Parl.*, II, 453–455 (1702); also *ibid.*, pp. 36 (1690), 390 (1701).

[117] *CSPA, 1681–85*, No. 768, p. 317 (1682).

[118] See Smith, *loc. cit.*, pp. 48–50. See also Joshua Gee's report, *CSPA, 1716–17*, No. 505, p. 272 (1717). In 1724 Thomas Ludwell of Bruton, England, wrote Philip Ludwell of Virginia that he was afraid to get involved in procuring servants for him lest he "be accounted a Kidnapper. Not but there are enough gardeners and other workmen to spare here, but they will live meanly and send their Families to the Parish to be relieved, rather than hear of such a long journey to mend their condition." *WMCQ*, 1st ser., III, 198.

[119]   "In better times e'er to this Land
                    I was unhappily trapann'd,"
lamented the maidservant in Ebenezer Cook's *Sot-Weed Factor, or, A Voyage to Maryland* (London, 1807).

unfortunates and their families are entitled to as much credence as the agents and merchants engaged in the traffic.[120] Magistrates and town officials were frequently in cahoots with recruiting agents. They would round up vagrants and unemployed workmen and others accused of petty offenses, and illegally threaten them with hanging. On advice the ignorant prisoner would ask for transportation as the only alternative.[121]

Most impressive testimony as to the existence of kidnaping comes, however, not from the injured parties and their families, but from English officials themselves. For example, in 1619 the Privy Council, learning that the city of London had by act of the Common Council "appointed one hundred Children out of the swarms that swarme in the place, to be sent to Virginia to be bound as apprentices for certain years," commended the city authorities "for redeeminge so many poore Soules from misery and ruyne, and putting them in a condition of use and Service to the State." Nevertheless, it came to the attention of the Privy Council that "among that number there are divers unwilling to be carried thither"; and that the city and the Virginia Company were without authority to transport persons against their wills. The Privy Council therefore ordered that if any of the children "shalbe found obstinat to resist or otherwise to disobey such directions as shall be given in this behalf," those in charge of the transportation were authorized to "imprison, punish and dispose of any of those children upon any disorder by them committed, as cause shall require; and so to Shipp them out for Virginia, with as much expedition as may stand for convenience." [122] An ordinance of 1647 legalizing the transportation of persons for employment in the plantations contained the proviso that the names of those transported be first registered in the custom houses "and that neither force be used to take up any such servants, nor any Apprentises entised to desert their Masters, nor any Children under age admitted without express consent of their Parents." [123]

In the summer of 1660 a ship called the *Seven Brothers* lying off Gravesend and two others in the Thames were known to have children and servants "deceived and inticed away Cryinge and Mourning for Redemption from their Slavery." The boats were bound for Virginia and the West Indies. The Privy Council considered the refusal of the

---

[120] *CSPA, 1661–68*, No. 771, p. 221 (1664); No. 909, p. 269 (1665). See also J. C. Jeaffreson, ed., *Middlesex County Rec.* (4 vols., London, 1886–92), III, 181, 182.
[121] See *WMCQ*, 1st ser., III, 135, 136.   [122] *A.P.C., Col., 1613–80*, No. 42, p. 28 (1619).
[123] C. H. Firth and R. S. Rait, eds., *Acts and Ordinances of the Interregnum, 1642–1660* (3 vols., London, 1911), I, 912–913.

agents to return the children or servants to their parents or masters without substantial compensation as "a thinge so barbarous and inhumane, that Nature itself much more Christians cannot but abhorr." The searchers and other officers at Gravesend and in the Thames were ordered to board the vessels, check on the complaints, and discharge any persons found forcibly detained. In case of resistance, the ships were to be placed under arrest and the masters brought before the Council.[124]

The attorney general and the solicitor general had frequent occasion to voice objections to various acts passed in the West Indies for the encouragement of the importation of white servants. Recommendations for disallowance were frequently made on the ground that such laws gave "encouragement to the spiriting away of Englishmen without their consent and selling them for slaves, which hath been a practice very frequent and known by the name of kidnapping." [125] Legislation in aid of the victims was also enacted. Barbados in 1661 provided that persons enticed aboard ship and transported to that island could sue for their freedom and recover damages provided that they instituted their complaint within thirty days after landing. Servants under fourteen years of age entering the colony were required to have a certificate from the parish stating that they had emigrated with their own consent or at their own request.[126]

Those who sought to stamp out the practice attempted unsuccessfully in 1670 to have Parliament impose the death penalty on persons found guilty. The traders in servants, on the other hand, endeavored to have Parliament set up a registry office where servants could signify their willingness to depart and declare upon oath that they were not deserting either masters or wives. Such registration was to provide legal exemption for merchants and agents from responsibility—either to the servant or to any one else who might raise objections. But Parliament resisted the merchants' lobby. In 1664 the crown set up a registry office by letters patent, and later instructed magistrates to record the names and indentures of such departing servants as should be brought before them.[127]

---

[124] *A.P.C., Col., 1613–80*, No. 486, p. 296 (1660). See also petition of John Baker, Stock, *Proc. Brit. Parl.*, I, 269 (1660); order to search Joseph Strutt's vessel for victims of kidnaping. *Ibid.*, II, 61n. (1692).

[125] *CSPA, 1701*, No. 919, p. 565 (1701). See also *ibid., 1693–96*, No. 622, p. 182 (1693), *1696–97*, No. 381, pp. 200–201 (1696); *A.P.C., Col., Unbound Papers*, No. 151, p. 47 (1706).

[126] Hall, *Acts of Barbados*, p. 35 (1661).

[127] See C.O. 380, pp. 185–187; 389:2, pp. 6–13; *A.P.C. Col.*, II, 41–43 (1682); *CSPA, 1661–68*, Nos. 769, 798, 802, pp. 220, 232, 333 (1664); *1681–85*, No. 846, p. 350 (1682); *1689–92*, Nos. 63, 154, pp. 29, 48 (1689); *1701*, No. 322, p. 156. In a suit for freedom brought by Margaret Devorge in a Virginia County court in 1693 the following certification from an English official was introduced (*VMH*, XII, 191–194. See also *supra*, p. 318):

"These are to Certifie that the above named Margrett Devorage Came before me Denis Russeli,

The crown constantly encouraged the agents in the recruiting of un-skilled labor, as long as they did not go as far as kidnaping. It was the official view that "the generality of volunteers for transportation are the scum of the world, brought to volunteer by their own prodigality; if they do not go to the colonies, they will probably go to Tyburn." [128] But legal exemption was not secured until Parliament in 1717 validated the transportation of servants when registered in proper form before a magistrate.[129]

Some of the earliest complaints of kidnaping were made in New England. In 1661 William Downing and Philip Welch pleaded that "We were brought out of o'r owne country, contrary to our owne Wills and minds, and sold here unto Mr. Symonds by the master of the ship yet notwithstanding we have indeavoured to do him the best service wee could these seaven compleat yeeres, which is 3 yeeres more than they used to sell them for at Barbadoes, wn they are stollen in England." In his bill of sale the captain had described the defendants as "two Irish youthes I brought over by order of the State of England." A witness de-posed that he

with divers others were stolen in Ireland, by some of the English soldiers, in the night out of their beds, and brought to Mr. Dills ship where the boat lay ready to receiue them, and in the way as they went some others they took with them without their consents, and brought them aboard the said ship, where there were divers others of ther Countrymen because they were stolen from their freynds, weeping and crying, they all declaring the same, and amongst the rest were these two men, William Downeing and Philip Welch, with several of their countrymen, and there they were kept until on a Lords day morning the master set sail and left some of his water and vessells behind for hast.[130]

Maior of the Town of Falmouth in the County of Cornewall, this fowerth day of April, 1689, and declared herselfe to be of the age of nineteene years and to be single and unmarried and noe Covenant or Contract servant to any person or persons whatsoever and also by Voluntary Consent and desire to Serve the above named James Trewolle According to the Tennor of the Indenture above Written.

"In Wittness whereof I have hereunto putt my hand the day and year above Written.
Recordat.   D. Russell, Maior of Falm:
     Test: Edwin Thacker
         Cl. Cur. Comt Middlx"

[128] *CSPA, 1681–85*, No. 768, p. 317 (1682).

[129] Bills to strengthen the powers of the office for registering servants offered on a number of occasions after the establishment of the registry office in 1664 were proposed but failed to pass. Stock, *Proc. Brit. Parl.*, I, 400, 401 (1673); II, vii, 46–50 (1691). Cf. also *ibid.*, III, 9 (1703), 402 (1718).

[130] *Essex*, II, 293 (1661). The court upheld the legality of the indentures for nine-year terms and ordered them to serve their terms. The servants appealed to the Assistants, but the frag-mentary records of that court for this period shed no further light on the course of this litigation.

In the same year another Irish youth named William Hiferney petitioned the Plymouth court that he had been "stolen away out of his own countrey" and asked relief from a contract of service for the long term of twelve years, to which he had agreed "when hee was vnacquainted with the English tongue." The court induced the master to remit two years of his term.[131]

In a suit brought in the Suffolk County court in 1671 by the master of the *Arabella* for nonpayment of passage from London to New England, in lieu of which the defendant Collins had bound himself when he came on board ship to serve four years, the defendant answered by denying that he had ever seen the shipowner or agreed to become his servant and described the circumstances of his going on board as follows:

a suttle Fellow . . . Mett with him in London . . . sayd he was a Botswaine of the ship Arrebella, . . . And then he Asked the sayd defendant if he would goe to sea: telling him that he the sayd defendant should haue 18s in money as soune as he Came on bord the sayd ship and also 18s a moneth otherwise untill he Came to new England, and sayd otherwise that he would be a friend to him all the sayd voyage, the wch made the sayd defendant through ignorance Condecend: But this pretended Botswaine would not leue the sayd defendant but provoked him . . . to goe on borde, and haled the Ships boat for that end; and promised emediently to Follow himself vpon which this sayd defendant went one bord; expected the sd pretended Boatswaine would sodenly follow (at which time it is possible that he might say he was willing to be a servant to New England for his 18s per moneth answerable to this sayd pretended boatswaine's agreement; and then this sayd defendant waited several days for the sayd pretended Boatswaine to come on borde but he not Coming of many dayes (for he Came not at all), he then inquired of the seamen for this sayd pretended Boatswaine: that Came not a bord; then the seamen one bord laughed at this defendant, and told him that he was catched by the Kidnapper; But they tould him also that when the serchers Came on borde he might gaine a release.

The defendant admitted going ashore at Gravesend, but asserted that he was with three or four others "to looke after him and that in blind Corners, and uncoth places that he knew not which way to goe if he had binn at liberty." He further charged that the kidnaper had been paid forty shillings for luring him on board. There was also a supporting deposition to the effect that the defendant had declared to the searchers that he was unwilling to ship to New England, whereupon

131 Hiferney v. Hollot, *Plymouth Col. Rec.*, III, 221 (1661).

he was told that he would be stripped naked and turned ashore, which actually was done. The jury brought in a special verdict as follows:

That if a person inticed or perswaded aboard a ship by a Kidnapper and there to declare his willingnesse to be transported as a servant and such person afterward but before the shipp sayle or leave the land shall desire Dismicion and manifest his unwillingnesse to proceed or be transported and shall notwithstanding be brought away and transported be by Law Liable to pay passage and necessary supplyes then we finde for the plaintiffe fiue shillings in money with Costs of Court otherwise wee finde for the Defendt costs of Court, The Magistrates in perusall of this Verdict declar for the Defendt.[132]

Less favorable treatment was accorded the victims of kidnaping in the Charles County court in Maryland in 1690, when it was held that the indentures of seven servants of four different masters which were made out aboard ship at Gravesend were "kidnappers Indentures." As there was no proof that the indentures had been acknowledged before any justice of the peace, the court held them invalid, but ordered the servants to return to their respective masters and serve according to the custom of the country.[133]

The courts of the Middle colonies appear to have manifested greater repugnance to the institution of kidnaping than did the justices of the tobacco provinces. The Philadelphia quarter sessions in 1753 freed a girl from her indentures when she had proven that she had been brought from Ireland against her consent and "Cruelly used on the Voyage."[134] In the case of a servant who had been bound as an infant by indenture executed before the mayor of Philadelphia, the Burlington, New Jersey, court in 1769 discharged him from his indentures when it was established that he had been "clandestinely" brought from Ireland to Philadelphia five years earlier, even though the master appeared to have purchased him "for a Consideration, Bona Fide paid."[135]

While the bulk of the kidnaped persons were doubtless vagrants and poor people from off the streets of London and Bristol, occasionally celebrities were spirited away who lived to return and write books about their adventures. Such a person was James Annesley, son and heir of Lord Altham. Twelve years after his arrival in Philadelphia his claim

[132] Lidgett v. Collins, *Suffolk Court*, pp. 18–20, 43, 44 (1671). There is no record of an appeal to the Assistants. The master had previously failed to recover damages from Collins for his absenting himself from his service.

[133] Cases of Hall *et al.*, Charles, lib. 1690–92, fols. 2, 3 (1690).

[134] Ann Dempsey's petition, Philadelphia Q.S., lib. 1753–60, f. 3 (1753).

[135] White's case, Burlington, N.J., Q.S., lib. 1764–87, f. 85 (1769). White was twenty-one the year before.

to noble lineage was authenticated and he returned to England where he attained considerable notoriety. Another was Peter Williams of Aberdeen, who later returned and filed a protracted suit against the magistrates of his home town as well as his alleged abductors.[136] There was a family tradition that George Eskridge, for many years a member of the House of Burgesses and the legal guardian of George Washington's mother, had also been kidnaped in Wales and sold in Virginia as an indentured servant.[137] Whether fact or fiction, such stories inspired Smollett, Goldsmith, and Richardson, not to mention Walter Scott and Robert Louis Stevenson of a later generation, all of whom accepted kidnaping as a traditional method of procuring servants for transportation to the colonies.

The practice was not exclusive to old England. In the labor traffic between the colonies charges of kidnaping were occasionally raised. In 1707 Nathaniel Wilson told the Hartford County court that, while at Boston five years previously, he had been plied with liquor by his two brothers-in-law, conveyed on a ship to Virginia, and there sold by the ship captain as a servant for several years.[138] In 1710 two Indians complained to the Suffolk sessions magistrates in Boston that they had been forced aboard ship and sent to sea against their will. The court held that their indentures were not "executed according to law" and freed them from their service.[139] A few years previously the Kent County court in Delaware sent one lad, aged fourteen, back to his mother in Annapolis upon finding that he had been "enticed" to board a brigantine from Annapolis to Philadelphia and then to bind himself as a servant.[140]

Considering the thousands of servants who came to the colonies annually and the vast number of servants' contracts which were litigated in colonial courts, it must be conceded that the relatively few petitions for freedom founded on grounds of kidnaping or duress and the infrequency with which servants pleaded kidnaping as a defense to a suit by a master for enforcement of the labor contract bespeak the minor role which kidnaping played in servant emigration. Nevertheless, it must be recognized that, while forcible abduction may well have been the exception, a great many emigrants never would have set food on board

---

[136] See *The Life and Adventures of Peter Williamson* (Liverpool, 1807).
[137] *VMH*, XXII, p. xiii; Herrick, *op. cit.*, pp. 147–156.
[138] Hartford, Conn., Co. Court, lib. 1706/7–18, f. 27 (1707).
[139] Cases of Heicom and Eleazer, Suffolk G.S., lib. I, f. 203 (1710).
[140] Kent Co., Del., Court Rec., lib. 1699–1703, f. 81a (1703).

ship were it not for the false or over-optimistic representations which were made to them by the importers or their agents.[141]

SERVITUDE IN SATISFACTION OF CRIMINAL SENTENCES IMPOSED BY COLONIAL COURTS

A SUBSTANTIAL source of bound labor was provided by persons sentenced to servitude in satisfaction of other penalties. The two principal crimes for which persons were regularly bound out were absenteeism and larceny. The former is treated in detail in the section dealing with the fugitive servant problem.[1] In regard to larceny, it must be remembered that in many of the colonies corporal punishment plus multiple restitution was the usual penalty—a punishment far more humane than prevailed in contemporary England. If the prisoner was unable to make restitution he was normally bound out to service by the court. He therefore falls into the same category as the judgment debtor.[2]

Let us consider a few of the colonial regulations and laws on this subject. Instructions to Governor Wyatt of Virginia in 1621 provided that all servants were "to fare alike in the colony, and their punishment for any offences" was "to serve the colony in publike works." [3] The Plymouth law of 1645 provided

That whatsoeuer servant or apprentice or labourer that shall purloyne or steale or ymbessell his Masters goods shall make double restitution either by payment or servitude as the Court shall judg meete for the first default, and for the second default of the labourer to make double restitution, and either fynd sureties for his good behauior or be whipt." [4]

New Haven extended this to arson committed by servants or others. Where the offense was "heynous" the penalty was death, but otherwise it was corporal punishment or double or treble damages. If the prisoner could not pay the sum imposed, he could be sold as a servant "either into these English colonies or abroad" to make proper satisfaction.[5] Some seven years later Barbados provided that servants who stole cattle or fowl belonging to their masters could, upon conviction, be sentenced to serve an extra three-year term. It is important to note that the law is

---

[141] See Abbé Raynal, *Philosophical and Political History of the British Settlements and Trade in North America* (Edinburgh, 1776), II, 167.

[1] See *infra*, pp. 434–461.

[2] For restraints upon condemnation to service as a punishment for crime in the Spanish colonies, see Carney, "Legal Theory of Forced Labor." Univ. of Miami, *Hispanic-American Studies*, No. 3, p. 30.

[3] Hening, I, 115–118 (1621). [4] *Plymouth Col. Rec.*, XI, 47, 48 (1645); also pp. 96, 173.

[5] *New Haven Col. Rec.*, pp. 175, 176 (1656).

specifically restricted to servants, hired men, overseers, and such.[6]

While in the main these early laws were confined to those already in the status of servitude, later legislation covered convicts of every stripe. Statutes in Pennsylvania provided that convicts incapable of making the required fourfold satisfaction for burglary or arson were to be sold into servitude;[7] seven years was the maximum term for those convicted of forging, counterfeiting, or raising bills of credit, and who were unable to pay the fine.[8] New Jersey authorized the justices of the courts of general quarter sessions to sell into servitude for reasonable terms not exceeding five years criminal offenders who were unable to satisfy their fines and fees.[9] Aside from sentences to servitude in lieu of satisfaction for fines, Pennsylvania from the earliest period stressed programs for the employment of convicts at hard labor.[10]

While examples of servitude in lieu of criminal sentence can be cited from virtually every colony, the bulk of such cases come from New England and Pennsylvania. The Massachusetts Court of Assistants recorded cases as far back as 1633,[11] when a man convicted of stealing corn, fish, and clapboards was not only whipped and required to pay double restitution, but was also bound out as a servant for three years and his daughter was bound out along with him for fourteen years. In 1638 the records of that court tell us that Gyles Player, who was found guilty of thefts and housebreaking, was sentenced to be severely whipped "and delivered up for a slave to whom the Court shall appoint."[12] Sentences of slavery were also imposed on Thomas Dickerson in 1639 and on Thomas Savory and Jonathan Hatch the following year. But, after one year, Dickerson was "discharged from his slavery."[13] On the other

---

[6] John Jennings, *Acts and Statutes of the Island of Barbados* (1654), p. 18.

[7] *Pa. Stat. at Large*, II, 11, 12 (1700), 173 (1706). The act of 1700 was repealed by the Queen in Council, but the later act was allowed to become law by lapse of time.

[8] *Ibid.*, III, 331, 332, 404 (1723); IV, 113, 359 (1729, 1739); V, 248 (1756), 300, 307 (1757), 443 (1759); VII, 104 (1767), 201, 208 (1769). See also *Md. Arch.*, XLIV, 115.

[9] Allinson, *N.J. Acts.*, p. 491 (1775).

[10] "The Great Law" of 1682 punished crimes of violence against the person by imprisonment at hard labor in the "house of correction." *Pa. Charter and Laws* (Harrisburg, 1879), p. 113. Profanity and drunkenness were punishable by a fine or imprisonment for five days at hard labor on bread and water. *Ibid.*, p. 111. In the pre-Revolutionary period the gaol rather than the workhouse was the typical penal institution of the colony. In the latter, vagrants, paupers, and disorderly servants were employed at spinning, weaving, and cobbling in addition to heavy labor. *Pa. Stat. at Large*, VI, 167–171 (1718); H. E. Barnes, *The Repression of Crime* (New York, 1926), p. 57; G. Ives, *A History of Penal Methods* (London, 1914), pp. 188 *et seq.*

[11] Sayle's case, *Assistants*, II, 32 (1633). For cases in which extra service was exacted of servants convicted of larceny, see *infra*, pp. 466 *et seq.*

[12] *Ibid.*, II, 79 (1638).

[13] *Ibid.*, II, 90 (1639), 94, 97 (1640). See also cases of Barton and Allen, *Essex*, I, 35 (1641); Shoreman's case, *ibid.*, p. 205 (1650); Godwin *et al.*, *ibid.*, III, 143 (1664), where the extra

hand, during the same period Richard Wilson was put to service for several years in lieu of a fine of £10 for theft.[14]

Regardless of what the Assistants may have meant by imposing slavery as a criminal sentence,[15] it is clear that regular indentured servitude supplanted the earlier vague status. As a matter of fact, the commutation of a criminal sentence by servitude was far more frequent and matter-of-course in the last quarter of the seventeenth century and in the eighteenth century in Massachusetts than in the earlier decades.[16] In virtually every instance in Suffolk sessions between 1680 and 1780 the convicted person was unable to pay the fine and was accordingly sold into service. Servitude was imposed for larceny in sixty cases, for robbery in two, for assault and battery in one, for bastardy in three,[17] and for illicit sexual relations and for having contracted "Morbus Gallicus" in only one case. After the year 1707 no crime other than larceny was punished by servitude. Considerable inequities appear in the sentences. Indians, Negroes, and white servants in general received heavier sentences to servitude than the rank-and-file of convicts. An Indian was required by the court to serve four years in lieu of a 15*s.* fine in 1685, whereas two years earlier the same term was imposed on a settler in place of a fine of £15 13*s.* In 1705 the illegitimate child of a mulatto and a Negro servant was bound out for the exceptionally long term of twenty-five years. A Negro servant named Prince was sentenced to fifty years of servitude in 1746 to satisfy a fine of £181 10*s.*, whereas a white man received only seven years in 1730 in lieu of £174, which, in view of the rapid depreciation of the currency in the forties, was actually a much higher fine. Women convicts received somewhat harsher sentences than men. Jane Campbell and James Keatting were both fined £18 for

---

service was allowed the master for loss of his servant's time; Laycrosse's case, *ibid.*, V, 312 (1674); Grant's case, *ibid.*, VI, 223, year and a quarter extra for arson; Bettes' case, *ibid.*, VIII, 302 (1682). For Plymouth colony, see the Indian Partrich's case, *Plymouth Col. Rec.*, VI, 104 (1683).

[14] *Assistants*, II, 86. See also Fairfax's case, *ibid.*, I, 200 (1681).

[15] "Perpetual servitude" was meted out to the Indian leaders and their families captured in King Philip's War. See, e.g., *Plymouth Col. Rec.*, V, 245 (1676).

[16] The libers of the Suffolk court of general sessions give us a detailed picture of the frequent application of this penalty. Suffolk G.S., lib. I, fols. 64 (1680), 107 (1681), 169 (1683); lib. II, fols. 255, 263, 265 (1685), 290, 300 (1686), 364 (1689), 423 (1691); lib. I, fols. 4, 26 (1702), 103 (1704), 116, 124 (2 cases) (1705), 152 (1707, 2 cases); lib. II, fols. 35 (1713), 118, 142 (1716), 176 (1717, 2 cases), 237 (1719); lib. 1718–20, Athenaeum, fols. 16 (1719, 2 cases), 25 (1720); lib. III, 66 (1720), 90, 111 (1721), 173 (1722, 2 cases), 293, 299 (1724), 327 (1725); lib. IV, fols. 90 (1727, 2 cases), 207, 213, 247 (1729), 290, 301, 307, 310, 322 (1730), 350, 371, 377, 389 (2 cases) (1731); MS 1737–39 (1738, 2 cases); lib. 1743–49 (1746); lib. 1754–58 (1755); lib. 1764–68 (1767), (1768); lib. 1769–73 (1769, 3 cases), (1770), (1772), (1773, 2 cases), (1777, 2 cases), (1779), (1780).

[17] In one such case the charge was having a Negro child by a mulatto.

larceny in 1738. The former had to serve two years in lieu thereof; the latter, one. The rapid currency depreciation of the Revolutionary period explains the relatively short terms of servitude imposed during those years for heavy fines. [18]

The practice of giving the prisoner convicted in a larceny case the alternative of paying a fine or serving a term was well entrenched in New England, and seems to have been especially favored by the courts of New Hampshire in the post-Revolutionary period.[19] In a few exceptional cases, expulsion from the colony or sale outside it (a practice reminiscent of the sale in the West Indies of Indians captured in the Pequot War and in the conflict with King Philip) were substituted for servitude within the jurisdiction of the court.[20]

In the Middle colonies and the tobacco provinces servitude was occasionally imposed in lieu of or in addition to other penalties for criminal acts.[21] In addition, short-term labor sentences were at times meted

[18] For other Massachusetts cases, see Mass. Arch., lib. CV (1722); *Plymouth Col. Rec.,* VII, 308, 309 (1690); Plymouth G.S., lib. 1723–30, fols. 85, 91 (1728), lib. 1730–49, fols. 1 (1730), 28 (1731), 142 (6 yrs.), 181 (1745); Middlesex G.S., lib. 1686–88, 1692–1723, I, f. 163 (1705), lib. 1771–90, VI, f. 18 (1771); Hampshire G.S., and C.P., lib. 1741–44, fols. 203, 204 (1745), lib. 1746–57, fols. 52 (1748), 301 (1757); lib. 1758–62, f. 20 (1758); John Fearing's Justice of the Peace Book (1771), cited by Bliss, *Buzzard's Bay,* pp. 74, 75. In Berkshire County, servitude for theft in lieu of treble damages was in effect down into the Federal period. Berkshire G.S., lib. I, fols. 46, 70 (1763), 74 (1764); lib. B, fols. 473 (1787, 7 yrs. in lieu of treble damages for horse-stealing amounting to £150), 486 (1787, Negro, 15 yrs. for two thefts), 522 (1789, 10 yrs., larceny), 547 (1790, 18 mos. larceny). A number of these cases involved Indians, who were not infrequently sentenced to servitude for drunkenness. This policy served to encourage corrupt settlers to furnish Indians with rum toward the end of the specified term (or to pay them their wages in rum) in order that the term of service might be lengthened by court order. See Daniel's case, Plymouth G.S., lib. 1730–49, f. 143 (1741), 20 stripes and six months term imposed for assaulting children while under influence of liquor. See A. W. Lauber, *Indian Slavery in Colonial Times within the Present Limits of the United States* (New York, 1913), pp. 203, 204. The Indians also sold members of their tribes for terms of years as punishment for certain offenses. *Ibid.,* p. 196.

[19] See Cheshire, N.H., Supreme Court of Judicature, lib. I (1784), 3 yrs. in lieu of twofold damages for theft of a gelding, horse, and bridle. See also New Hampshire G.S., lib. 1734–39 (1737); *R.I. Col. Rec.,* III, 15, 16 (1678); Providence, R.I., Court Rec., lib. 1747–69, fols. 452, 454, 455 (1766); lib. 1769–90, fols. 190–193 (1733); Conn. Particular Court Rec., 1639–63, p. 11 (1640); New London, Conn., Co. Court, lib. 1724–25, XV, fols. 28, 47 (1724); New Haven Co. Court, lib. III, f. 298 (1729); IV, f. 719 (1755); Hartford Co. Court, lib. 1706/7–18, f. 192 (1711).

[20] *New Haven Col. Rec., 1653–65,* pp. 187–189 (1656), expulsion for rebellious conduct toward master and mistress, "lying and atheisticall miscariages," and filing off the marks of stolen spoons. The court justified its sentence by remarking that any one of these "would haue bine death in some other place." See also New Haven Co. Court, lib. I, f. 145 (1683).

[21] Examples are rare in New York. Robert Bowman, convicted of the theft of some lining, a mulatto slave, and a cannon (!) was sentenced by the mayor's court to receive 39 stripes and to serve his master 5½ years extra in consideration of the loss and damage of the master, who evidently reimbursed the injured party. N.Y.M.C.M., lib. 1674–75, f. 63 (1675). Elizabeth Robinson was ordered to stay with her mistress until she had served out the amount of her fine imposed for stealing wine and sugar. *Ibid.,* lib. 1677–82, f. 244 (1680). See also Burlington, West Jersey, Court Bk., f. 101 (1691); *Records of the Courts of Chester Co., Pa., 1681–97* (Phila-

out for lesser crimes and misdemeanors, the general public becoming the beneficiary rather than a particular wronged individual. An Eastern Shore county court in Virginia in 1638 sentenced Samuel Powell to "pay Fower dayes worke" for stealing a pair of breeches and some other articles.[22] A neighboring court on the Maryland side of the boundary line sentenced Thomas Oxford for assault with intent to commit rape to "40 dayes work and tools with diet." [23] This was the origin of the practice of sending convicts "to the wheelbarrow"—the real beginning of the chain gang, which still operates in the Southern states. A Pennsylvania statute passed in 1751 provided that servants incurring any fine or penalty upon conviction under the act regulating the nightly watch were to be given twenty-one lashes and put at hard labor in the public workhouse for a term of three days during which time they were to have a diet of bread and water. For the second offense thirty-one lashes were to be given and a sentence of six days at hard labor imposed.[24]

In addition to exacting servitude in lieu of damages or fines for crimes against property, the colonies generally provided that certain criminal offenses of servants, primarily to the detriment of their own masters, should be compensated for by extra service. Foremost among such offenses was unlawful absence, punishable by as much as tenfold extra service for the period of the unauthorized absence.[25] Furthermore, the servant might be required to serve additional time for having an illegitimate child, for marrying without the master's consent, or even for fornication. Thus, the law recognized that the master's property interest in his servant entitled him to compensation for any interruption or impairment of the servant's ability to work or for any expenses beyond those stipulated in the contract of indentures which the master might incur through the servant's fault. In the case of bastardy, the community expected the master to maintain the servant's child, thus saving the public the expense of maintenance.[26]

At the core of the problem of bastardy and fornication by servants

---

delphia, 1910), p. 206 (1690); *Pa. Gazette*, April 16, 1748; Cumberland, Pa., Q.S., lib. 1765–72, f. 102 (1767); Newcastle Q.S., lib. 1780–83 (1782), 6 yrs. for fourfold restitution; *Md. Arch.*, LI, 214, 215 (1677); Md. Prov. Court, lib. 1719–22, fols. 254, 255 (1720); Baltimore, lib. 1772–80 (1772, 2 cases), (1773); Ann Arundel, lib. 1702–4, f. 2 (1703); lib. 1745–47 (1746); Somerset, lib. 1722–24, f. 256 (1724); Prince George, lib. 1775–77, f. 431 (1775); Charles, lib. 1775–78, f. 570 (1777); *Va. Gen. Court Mins.*, p. 382 (1674); Middlesex, Va., O.B., 1673–80, f. 23 (1674), 36 (1675); Westmoreland, lib. 1675/6–1688/9, f. 476 (1685).

[22] Accomac, lib. I, f. 107 (1638).   [23] Somerset, lib. AW, 1690–91, fols. 38, 39 (1691).

[24] *Pa. Stat. at Large*, V, 126 (1751), 241 (1756).

[25] For a detailed discussion, see *infra*, pp. 434–461.

[26] For the general problem, see A. W. Calhoun, *A Social History of the American Family* (Cleveland, 1917), I, 313–329.

was the refusal of the authorities, particularly in the Southern colonies, to permit a servant to marry without his master's consent.[27] The masters were thus given virtually complete control over their servants' private lives.[28] In order to avoid the penalties of the law servants wishing to marry often entered into written agreements with their respective masters.[29]

It was to the master's economic interest to keep his women servants from marriage and to prevent their having illicit sexual relations, very likely to result in childbearing with consequent interruption of work and impairment of health and stamina. As a practical matter the guarding of this interest was most difficult. Work in the fields brought women into intimate contact with the menservants. Household duties exposed them to the advances of members of the master's household, perhaps even the master himself. Poor Richard's advice to his readers in 1736 was doubtless well founded. "Let thy maidservant be faithful, strong, and homely," he cautioned. Children born out of wedlock were an all-too-common occurrence in the servant ranks.

In many of the colonies a servant guilty of bastardy was required to pay the fines and fees usually exacted from free unmarried mothers and,

[27] The first General Assembly of Virginia enacted such a prohibition, providing damages amounting to double the value of the service and a fine of 500 lbs. tobacco to the parish. L. G. Tyler, ed., *Narratives of Early Virginia* (New York, 1907), p. 273; *VMH*, I, 102; Hening, I, 252, 253 (1643), 438 (1658), II, 114 (1662), freemen liable to pay the master 1,500 lbs. tobacco or a year's service in addition to the servant's extra year. Subsequently it was made a penal offense for ministers to marry servants without a certificate of authorization from their masters. Hening, III, 444 (1705); VI, 83, 84; *Exec. J. Council of State of Va.*, III, 106 (1706). The British West Indies followed Virginia's lead. Barbados set 4 yrs. extra service for a manservant, double the value of a maidservant's time to be paid by the freeman marrying her; a manservant marrying a woman servant was required to serve double her time remaining time. Hall, *Acts of Barbados* (London, 1764), No. 30, cl. viii (1661). £100 was the penalty fixed for marrying a servant in Antigua. Baskett, *Acts of the Charibbee Leeward Islands* (London, 1734), No. 153, cl. 16; *Laws of the Island of Antigua, 1690–1798* (London, 1805), I, 186 (1716). British law officers approved such legislation on the ground that the absence of such curbs would "create great confusion in the colony, and no one person would purchase servants on these terms." *CSPA, 1706–8*, No. 922, p. 434 (1707). Pennsylvania imposed one year's extra service as well as a heavy penalty upon the performers of such marriages. *Pa. Stat. at Large*, II, 22, 161 (1700); *Acts of the Assembly of the Province of Pa.* (Philadelphia, 1775), p. 18. See also West Chester, Pa., Q.S., lib. 1733–42, f. 7 (1737); also *Md. Arch.*, I, 73 (1639).

[28] Exceptional was the Plymouth Colony act of 1638 which set a penalty of £5 or corporal punishment or both for the marriage of daughters or maidservants without the consent of their parents or masters. Where the master, through sinister end "or Covetous desire," refused his consent, the magistrates were authorized to investigate and make such order as they deemed equitable. *Plymouth Col. Rec.*, XI, 108 (1638), 190, 191. Cf. also *Winthrop Papers*, IV, 167 (1640).

[29] See agreements of John Jones and Sarah Garnett to serve four years from date, the master to maintain such children as might be born of the marriage. Lancaster Co., Nov. 14, 1666, *VMH*, XII, 292; also Accomac O.B., lib. I, f. 148 (1639); Augusta O.B. (1761, 1766). For agreement of George Haddock to work out the remainder of his wife's term of servitude to her master, see Barbados Deeds, lib. I, f. 746 (1740), Davis Coll., Box No. 4, cited by V. T. Harlow, *A History of Barbados, 1625–1685* (Oxford, 1926), p. 294.

in addition, was obliged to indemnify her master for the loss of services he had suffered through her pregnancy and confinement. Few maid-servants had funds of their own or sufficiently prosperous friends or relations to pay these charges. Extra service was the only alternative.[30] While both Maryland and Virginia imposed some measure of responsibility upon the putative father,[31] later Virginia statues merely required him to give bond for the maintenance of the child, but the obligation of extra service was solely the mother's.[32] Pennsylvania and North Carolina followed Virginia in imposing extra service upon female servants guilty of bastardy.[33] South Carolina, on the other hand, placed the responsibility of reimbursing the master upon the putative father. He was either to pay the master £5 current or serve double the time the mother had left to serve at the time the offense was committed, such penalty not to exceed one year.[34] The plentitude of illustrations of extra service imposed upon maidservants for bastardy by the courts from Pennsylvania down to the Carolinas point to the inescapable conclusion that in those areas the master was often enriched far beyond his actual

---

[30] The New England courts held the putative father responsible for the maintenance of the child (*Essex*, V, 298 [1674]), but the child might be bound to the master until 21, when the father was expected to "redeem" him and to satisfy the master for the costs of his education. *Ibid.*, p. 103 (1672). Not all masters sought to profit from the sexual lapses or marital misfortunes of their servants. John Woodbridge petitioned the Essex sessions in 1704 for an adjournment of his maidservant's trial for fornication, asserting that she had been married Dec. 1, 1703, and her child was born March 12, 1704. As her husband was reported drowned, "she has no Relations In this world that will take care of her." Essex Clerk of Court, Drawer 1, Bundle 7 (3).

[31] In Maryland, if the maidservant could prove that a certain person was the father of her child, he was required, if a freeman, to pay the whole damages to her master for the loss of her services; if a servant, the father was obliged to pay only half. *Md. Arch.*, II, 396–397 (1674); *Laws of Md.* (ed. Maxey), I, 1102. See Marsh v. Utie, *Md. Arch.*, LI, 460, 461 (1671). The Virginia statute of 1658 obliged the putative father to pay the master 1,500 lbs. tobacco or serve him one year, besides giving security to defray the charges of the child. Hening, I, 438–439.

[32] By act of 1662 the woman servant was required to serve an extra two years in return for the "losse and trouble" sustained by her master, or pay him 2,000 lbs. of tobacco in addition to her fine. The putative father was merely required to give bond to "save the parish harmless." If he were a servant, the parish was required to support the child until the expiration of his term, at which time he was required to make satisfaction. By later statutes the amount of damages to which the master was entitled for the loss of service was reduced from 2 yrs. or 2,000 lbs. tobacco to 1 yr. or 1,000 lbs. Hening, II, 115, 167, 168 (1662); III, 139–140 (1696), 453; VI, 361.

[33] In Pennsylvania the reputed father was required to give security for the care of the mother as well as the child. Originally an extra year of service was imposed upon female servants, but subsequently the courts of quarter sessions were given the power to fix the amount of additional time to be served. *Pa. Stat. at Large*, II, 6 (1700), 182 (1706). See also *N.C. Col. Rec.*, XXIII, 64, 65, 195. Cf. Pennypacker, *Pa. Col. Cases*, p. 88 (1686).

[34] *S.C. Stat.*, II, 226–227; *Public Laws of S.C.* (ed. Grimké), pp. 5–7. See also Mrs. Julia C. Spruill, *Women's Life and Work in the Southern Colonies* (Chapel Hill, N.C., 1938), pp. 317, 318. This law was closer to the Barbadian act of 1661 providing that the putative father should serve the master of the woman servant 3 yrs; the offending maidservant, 2 yrs. Where the male offender was a servant, he was obliged to serve the owner double the time the woman had left to serve. Hall, *Acts of Barbados*, p. 35 (1661). See also *Md. Arch.*, XIII, 501 (1692), providing servitude on the part of the putative father in lieu of damages.

losses. They also demonstrate the direct relationship between illicit unions and the prohibition against the marriages of indentured servants without their masters' consent.[35]

To illustrate the amount of extra service thus imposed, let us consider the case of Ann Hardie, brought into the Ann Arundel court by her master in 1747. She was sentenced to serve six months (for an expenditure of 614 lbs. of tobacco for costs of suit), an additional year (for having a mulatto bastard "to the trouble of his house"), and six months or £3 current for a second child. In addition, the second child's father was required to serve six months or pay £3 currency, and to serve an additional nine months for the child's maintenance.[36] As late as 1780 an extra term of seven years was imposed by the Frederick County court upon Fanny Dreaden for having a "base born child." [37] The bastardy prosecutions of servants Nicholas Millethopp and Mary Barton also illustrate the master's interest in keeping his servants from marrying. The servants pleaded marriage in England, were unable to furnish proof by witness or certificate, and were found by the Virginia county court not to have come into the country as man and wife nor to have declared themselves until some months after their arrival. They had concealed their marriage upon the advice of their importer, who sold them into servitude without revealing their status. They were condemned for fornication and enjoined from living together as man and wife until they had served their terms. "Such presidents [prece-

[35] For examples of extra service imposed upon mothers of illegitimate children:

Pennsylvania: Chester Co. Court Rec., pp. 166, 167 (1689). Bucks C.P. and Q.S., lib. 1684–1730 (1727). Lancaster Road and Sess. Docket, 1729–42, No. 1, f. 74 (1733); lib. 1760–68, No. 3 (1763), (1764), (1767); lib. 1768–76, No. 4 (1770); lib. 1776–82 (1777). Philadelphia Q.S., lib. 1773–80 (1779). York Q.S., lib. XI, f. 28 (1778).

Delaware: Kent Q.S., lib. 1703–17 (1708); lib. 1712–16 (1712); lib. 1753–56 (1753).

Maryland: Charles, lib. 1682–84, f. 224 (1683); lib. 1685–86. Somerset, lib. AW, 1690–91, f. 35 (1691). Baltimore, lib. F. 1, 1691–93, f. 131 (1691); lib. IS, No. C, 1718–21 (1719). Talbot, lib. AB, No. 8 (1697); lib. 1703–4 (1704). Prince George, lib. A, 1696–1702, fols. 169, 170 (1697), 339 (1698); lib. 1708–10 (1709), (1710). Ann Arundel, lib. 1702–4, fols. 47 (1703), 303 (1704); lib. 1745–47, f. 553 (1747). Queen Ann, lib. 1709–16 (1712), (1716); lib. 1728–30 (1728). Cecil, lib. 1723–30 (1724); Frederick, lib. 1748–50, f. 144 (1749).

Virginia: Va. Gen. Court Mins., pp. 238 (1670), 469 (1640). Accomac, lib. 1666–70, f. 46 (1667); lib. 1671–73 (1671). Charles City, lib. 1655–65, f. 58 (1658). Fairfax, lib. 1768–70, f. 90 (1769), Lib. of Cong. Fincastle, lib. 1773–77 (1773). Henrico, lib. III, f. 77 (1695); lib. 1710–14, f. 122 (1712). Lancaster, lib. 1656–66, f. 346 (1665). Middlesex, lib. 1673–80, f. 89 (1678). Northumberland, lib. 1699–1713, fols. 91 (1700), 393 (1706). Rappahannock, lib. 1686–92, f. 147 (1689). Richmond, lib. 1692–94, f. 16 (1694). Spotsylvania, lib. 1730–38, f. 217 (1733). Westmoreland, lib. 1675/6–1688/9, fols. 90 (1677), 113 (1678); lib. 1698–1705, f. 160 (1702). York, lib. 1690–94, f. 17 (1691).

[36] Ann Arundel, lib. 1745–47, f. 674 (1747).

[37] She was sentenced to be sold at public vendue to the highest bidder. Frederick, lib. 1780–81, f. 54 (1780).

dents] being allowed," the court concluded, "All whores and Rooges might say the like." [38]

Where the putative father of the illegitimate child happened to be the master, there was a danger that he would brazenly assert his rights at law to extra service from his maidservant. A Virginia statute of 1672 confessed that "late experiments shew that some dissolute masters have gotten their maides with child, and yet claime the benefitt of their service." To prevent such scandalous conduct, the legislature deprived such masters of their legal claims to extra service. Instead, the maidservant was to be sold for the extra term by the church wardens or required to pay 1,000 lbs. of tobacco to the parish.[39] However, the determination of the authorities that the master should gain no extra advantage from his own wrongdoing did not preclude their ordering the maidservant to return to her master and serve out her term. Other than an occasional admonition and the requirement that he post security for the maintenance of the child, no punishment was accorded the master under these acts.[40] One maidservant on a Maryland plantation preferred whipping to marriage with her master, the father of her child, on the ground that "he was a lustful, very lustful man." [41] Under Virginia law, if the unmarried mother happened to have had a criminal record, her master was entitled not only to an extra year of service but to the service of the illegitimate child as well, and it must be borne in mind that the services of a minor between the ages of twelve and eighteen had very considerable economic value on a plantation.[42]

Finally, some of the colonies provided servitude for fornication committed by a servant, male or female, and for miscegenation. A Virginia statute fixed a penalty of a year extra whenever a manservant was convicted of having had illicit relations with a maidservant. A freeman convicted of having relations with a woman servant was liable to serve the master a year.[43] This penalty was later reduced to one-half year

[38] Accomac, lib. 1666–70, f. 38 (1667).

[39] Hening, I, 438; II, 167 (1672); III, 140, 447 *et seq.* See also Moon's petition, *Pa. Col. Rec.,* I, 189 (1686), master fined; *Exec. J. Council of State of Va.,* II, 35. Similar provisions were found in the North Carolina acts of 1715 and 1741. *N.C. Col. Rec.,* XXIII, 64–65.

[40] Mary Minchall's case, York, lib. 1657–62, f. 454 (1662), admonition that "she is Carefully looked after and that he does not abuse her at his peril." See *Ga. Col. Rec.,* XX, Pt. II, 53 (1738): "Three of the women servants are his [Mr. Bradley's] or his sons concubines. One of them lately delivered of, another big with child."

[41] *Md. Arch.,* LIII, xxviii–xxix.

[42] Hening, VIII, 376 (1769). For the binding out of illegitimate children, see *supra,* pp. 384 f.

[43] Hening, I, 252, 253 (1643). See also *ibid.,* p. 438 (1658), where the servant was given the option of paying the master 1,500 lbs. of tobacco. See also Allinson, *N.J. Acts,* pp. 84–88 (1730), justices to require servants to serve as much longer as they in their discretion deemed reasonable.

extra.[44] The penalty was applied to women servants as well as to men.[45] A Maryland act of 1692 provided that any white woman marrying a Negro would become a servant for seven years; if the Negro were free, he was to become a servant for the remainder of his life.[46]

The reformation of the penal code, which was initiated in Pennsylvania,[47] resulted in the supplanting of this practice of permitting convicted persons to work off their sentence by binding themselves as indentured servants to private employers [48] by the penitentiary system and prison contract labor.[49] The three systems had one point in common. All stressed the utilization of the labor services of the convict rather than mere incarceration or corporal punishment—an emphasis which was urged by such advanced legal reformers as Benjamin Franklin and Thomas Jefferson.

SERVITUDE FOR DEBT

THE JUDGMENT DEBTOR was an important source of bound labor in the American colonies. While the practice of having a defaulting debtor turned over to a creditor to perform compulsory service goes back to ancient times, the English law substituted imprisonment for debt.

[44] Hening, II, 115, 168 (1662); III, 139, 140 (1696). If the master did not pay a fine of 500 lbs. for his servant's fornication or adultery, the servant was to receive 25 lashes. Prior to the statute of 1643 the Virginia courts meted out penalties ranging from seven years extra, to being sentenced to build a ferry boat across a creek, or to be lashed and do penance fortnightly at the chapel. *Va. Co. Rec.*, I, 311 (1619); *Va. Gen. Court Mins.*, p. 117 (1626); Accomac, lib. 1632–40, f. 123 (1642); Lower Norfolk, lib. I, f. 122 (1641).

[45] See, e.g., Lancaster, lib. 1656–66, f. 109 (1660); York, lib. 1675–84, f. 77 (1678), lib. 1697–1702, f. 187 (1695). See also order of the Fincastle court: "on the motion of Rogert Oats it is ordered that Eleanor Thomas his Servant do serve him Eighteen months to pay him for his expences in getting her cured of the Veneral [*sic*] Disease." Fincastle, lib. 1773–77 (1773). For extra service for fornication in other colonies, see *Assistants*, II, 107 (1641); Conn. *Particular Court Rec., 1639–63*, p. 20 (1643), to be kept "to hard labor and course dyet during the pleasure of the court"; New Haven Co. Court, lib. I, f. 88 (1675); Kent, Del., lib. 1699–1703, fols. 79a, 80, 80a (1703); Queen Ann, Md., lib. 1728–30 (1728), an additional seven years and six mos. for fornication and having a mulatto bastard, lib. 1716–40 (1740).

[46] *Md. Arch.*, XIII, 546–549 (1692); also *ibid.*, XXII, 546–553 (1699), extending the same penalty to white men as to white women. For enforcement, see Queen Ann, lib. 1759–66 (1760).

[47] See Pennsylvania Constitution of 1776. *Pa. Arch.*, 4th ser., III, 644; *Pa. Stat. at Large*, XII, 280–281. For the variety of products manufactured at the Philadelphia gaol at the end of the 18th century, see *Pa. Packet*, Jan. 3, 1798. Cf. *Mass. Centinel*, Sept. 22, Oct. 20, 1784, for a recommendation of a nail-making establishment employing convict labor to be jointly maintained by Massachusetts and New Hampshire.

[48] For instances of the persistence of servitude in lieu of fines for criminal convictions, see T. C. Pease, "The Laws of the Northwest Territory, 1788–1800," Ill. Hist. Lib., *Coll.*, XVII, 18 (1788), 250 (1807).

[49] Prison contract labor was used at least as early as 1780 at Newgate prison in Connecticut and even earlier in Pennsylvania and Virginia. By 1791 it was estimated that the Newgate prisoners were manufacturing from 15 to 20 tons of nails a year. Cole, *Hamilton*, p. 31. See also "Cumberland Proceedings," *loc. cit.*, p. 38 (1776); Clark, *Hist. of Mfrs.*, pp. 219–221.

Readers of Dickens will recall the vivid accounts of the operations of this system which came from the pen of that very competent legal historian.[1] The colonies also at times chose to incarcerate debtors in gaol as in contemporary Britain.[2]

However, in a country where labor was scarce, imprisonment for this cause was a waste of manpower. Hence, very early in colonial history laws were enacted releasing the debtor from prison to serve the creditor or his assigns for a period of time deemed sufficient to satisfy the debt. In 1642 the Maryland Assembly provided that, if his goods were insufficient to satisfy the judgment, the debtor himself or any of his servants could be attached and either "sold at an outcry, or otherwise his service valued and appraised by the month . . . and delivered in execution to the party or parties recovering . . . until the execution be satisfied." [3] A Barbadian law of 1653 authorized the release of poor debtors from prison provided that they served their creditors at a rate of eighty lbs. of sugar per month until the debt was satisfied. Where the debtor was an artificer, his wages were to be increased in proportion.[4] The general policy expressed in this act was widely observed in the British West Indies.[5]

The course of Pennsylvania legislation on the subject is typical. An act of 1700 provided for servitude in satisfaction of debt to be made on demand of the creditor.[6] When this law was repealed by the Queen in Council in 1706, another statute was passed that very same year providing that debtors in foreign attachment could make satisfaction by servitude. For unmarried debtors under fifty-three years of age a term not exceeding seven years was set; but if the debtor was married and under forty-six, his term of service was not to exceed five years. This enactment was allowed to become law by lapse of time.[7] An act passed early in 1731 provided that debts under forty shillings could be satisfied

---

[1] Imprisonment of the debtor to insure his appearance—arrest in mesne process—was abolished in 1838, but it was not until 1869 that imprisonment for debt was entirely abolished as part of a general bankruptcy act. While in modern times an ordinary contract debt may not be enforced by threat of imprisonment, a debt involving fraud or willful disobedience of court order may be so enforced. This is substantially the case in American as well as in English law as a result of state constitutional provisions and 19th-century legislation. See Holdsworth, *HEL*, I, 470–473.

[2] A Virginia act for the punishment of persons aiding or assisting prisoners for debt to escape or attempt to escape was disallowed as arbitrary and superfluous in view of available common-law remedies. *A.P.C., Col., 1766–83*, No. 83, pp. 161–164. For imprisonment in New Jersey for small debts, see N.J. Hist. Soc., *Coll.*, IV, 96 (1740).

[3] *Md. Arch.*, I, 9 (1647).   [4] Jennings, *Acts of Barbados*, pp. 136, 137, cl. 82 (1653).

[5] Jamaica set a maximum service term of 4 yrs. in payment of debts. C.O. 139:1, fols. 11–12.

[6] *Pa. Stat. at Large*, II, 129.

[7] *Ibid.*, pp. 250, 251 (1706); *Pa. Col. Rec.*, II, 231, 522. Masters of vessels trading to the province were exempt from the operation of this law.

by servitude with the consent of the debtor.[8] This was defended by the Pennsylvania Council on the following grounds:

That altho' in Britain they are wholly Strangers to Servitude as practised amongst us, or binding of persons otherwise than as Apprentices, and therefore none of their Acts have ever Directed Satisfaction to be made for Debts by any such means, yet in these Countries (and) nothing is more common than for Husbandmen and others to lay out their money in Purchases of this Sort, 'tis highly reasonable that People fitt for Labour, or performing any Service by which they can earn Money, should by the same Method make Satisfaction for their just Debts.[9]

Mittelberger, in the middle of the century, gave a popular but significant exposition of the debt law as follows:

If any one contracts debts, and does not or cannot pay them at the appointed time, the best that he has, is taken away from him; but if he has nothing, or not enough, he must go immediately to prison and remain there till some one vouches for him, or till he is sold. This is done whether he has children or not. But if he wishes to be released and has children, such a one is frequently compelled to sell a child. If such a debtor owes only five pounds, or thirty florins, he must serve for it a year or longer, and so in proportion to his debt, but if a child of 8, 10, or 12 years of age is given for it, said child must serve until he or she is 21 years old.[10]

The New England practice of exacting service for debt led to charges in the latter part of the seventeenth century against unscrupulous Yankees who, in exchange for fish brought to Madeira, returned to Newfoundland with brandy, duty free, or with New England rum. The thirst of the Newfoundland fishermen often led them into indebtedness for sums as much as £4 in a season for brandy, "which obliges the man to stay there a year around and so to free his debt."[11] These charges were frequently revived.[12]

The debtor legislation was translated into action by administrative and judicial practice. As early as 1634 the Massachusetts Court of As-

---

[8] *Ibid.*, IV, 213 (1731). Cf. the New York act of 1732. *N.Y. Col. Laws*, II, 753 (1732). A Bermuda act which empowered a justice of the peace to hire out to service a debtor unable to satisfy a debt of 20*s.* was disallowed on the ground that there was "no provision to determine how the defendant shall obtain his liberty. *A.P.C., Col., Unbound*, No. 178, p. 58 (1707).

[9] *Pa. Col. Rec.*, III, 376 (1730). This law was not repealed until 1810.

[10] Mittelberger, *Journey to Pennsylvania*, p. 91; also quoted in Sartorius von Waltershausen, *Die Arbeits-Verfassung*, p. 78. Cf. petition of Sarah Stansell that she had bound her son in consideration of her husband's debt, since satisfied. Accordingly the court freed the boy. Queen Ann, Md., 1709–16, f. 143 (1711).

[11] *CSPA, 1675–76*, No. 405, p. 154.

[12] *Ibid.*, No. 38, p. 21 (1720); H. A. Innis, *The Cod Fisheries: the History of an International Economy* (New Haven, 1940), p. 103.

sistants ordered one Robert Way to serve William Almy "till he hath satisfied the somme of" £4.[13] In his appeal against a judgment in the Suffolk County court in favor of the defendant Abraham Briggs, William Rawson assigned among other reasons the argument that Briggs had no right to trade with Rawson's servant Hukeley, an action in violation of a law of the colony, or to have him (Rawson) put in prison for a period over five weeks as a result of a controversy ensuing. Rawson asserted **that**

William Hukely was his Servant by an execution legally extended upon his person by vertue of a Judgment acknowledged by the sd Hukely for forty pounds in mony, and thereupon the sd Hukely voluntarily and freely surrendred himself to serve out the Debt wth the Appellant.

He challenged the power of the Suffolk jury to deprive him of his servant for a space of time and before his debt was "Satisfyed by Service as that law directs." Further, he contended that the law entitled "Direction to Marshalls and other officers about executions" [14] provided that the debtor should satisfy his debt by service if the creditor required it, the latter being privileged to sell the judgment debtor; and, further, that lands and property taken on execution and delivered to the person and duly recorded, as was the case with Hukeley, "shall bee a legall assurance." [15]

The period of Rawson's appeal marks the real beginning in Massachusetts and Plymouth of the practice of having judgment debtors engage in court to serve their creditors.[16] Terms from six months to as much as seven years were ordered to satisfy judgments. The General Court in 1683, in order to eliminate abusive practices in the binding out of debtors, enacted that the enforcement of the service obligation was to be supervised by the proper legal authorities.[17] A striking instance of servitude for debt was found in Hampshire County court, which in 1690 assigned to Colonel John Pynchon a son of Thomas Barber, deceased, as an apprentice in satisfaction of a debt of £4 due from Barber's estate to Pynchon. The boy was to serve until twenty-one (he was ten years old at the time of the binding out) and to receive 40s. and apparel at the expiration of his term. Here the court was killing two birds with one stone—carrying out its regular duty of binding out orphan children

[13] *Assistants*, II, 61 (1635).   [14] *Mass. Col. Laws, Suppl. of 1675*, p. 220.
[15] *Suffolk*, pp. 713–715 (1676). Rawson lost the appeal. *Assistants*, I, 65 (1676).
[16] See *Essex*, V, 23, 50, 116 (1672), 264 (1673), 383 (1674), VI, 394 (1678), VII, 333, VIII, 62 (1680); *Plymouth Col. Rec.*, VI, 32 (1680).
[17] *Mass. Bay Rec.*, V, 415 (1683).

and providing satisfaction by personal service for an unsatisfied debt.[18]

In eighteenth-century Boston it was the practice of the gaol-keepers to petition the sessions court for the power to dispose of prisoners in service for failure to pay for their "keep." In the case of a servant whose master failed to pay her gaol costs, the court authorized the keeper to dispose of the prisoner for the remainder of her term of service to her master, first satisfying himself for her keep from the proceeds and then turning the surplus over to the master. Her maintenance was charged at the rate of five shillings a week.[19] Where no person appeared to take the prisoner into service in accordance with the provisions of the law, the Essex sessions ordered him committed to the Salem gaol until he either paid or was disposed of in service—a rather gloomy prospect for the judgment debtor.[20]

Elsewhere in New England judgment debtors were put to service.[21] When Robert Westcot brought two actions of debt in the Rhode Island Court of Trials in 1658 against Samuel Crooke, the debtor defiantly declared that "he would work it out, But Sayth he in the Court who-so-ever takeith me Servant I will be the Death of him or he shall be the Death of me!" The court ordered a lock put back on his leg and proceeded to trial, at which judgments were awarded the plaintiff.[22] In *Dewey v. Huntington* the Connecticut Superior Court upheld the principle that creditors could not keep their debtors in jail after refusing to allow them to work out their debt in service.[23]

Servitude for debt was customary in the Middle colonies. One early sessions court ordered the body of the judgment debtor to be taken in execution in the event that he did not have sufficient estate to satisfy

---

[18] Hampshire Co. Court, lib. 1677–78, fols. 119, 129 (1690).

[19] Cornwall's case, Suffolk G.S., lib. III, f. 136 (1722). See also Allen's case, *ibid.*, f. 312 (1724).

[20] Estate of English, Essex G.S., lib. 1692–1709 (1704).

[21] See, e.g., Knight's Case, *New Haven Col. Rec., 1638–49*, p. 403 (1648); Edgecomb v. Charles, an Indian, New London Co. Court, lib. 1724–25, XIV, f. 29 (1724); Factor v. Negus, New Haven Co. Court, lib. IV, f. 673 (1754). See also *Records of the Court of Trials of the Town of Warwick, 1659–74*, ed. Helen Capwell (Providence, R.I., n.d.), p. 118 (1660), where service was imposed to satisfy the cost of medical attention.

[22] *R.I. Court Rec.*, I, 41 (1658).

[23] Superior Court Files, Hartford (March, 1750), cited by J. T. Farrell, *The Superior Court Diary of William Samuel Johnson, 1772–73 (American Legal Records*, IV [Washington, 1942]), pp. xxvii, xxviii. This decision was based upon Connecticut remedial legislation which provided that when the debtor had no estate "he shall satisfy the debt by service if the creditor shall require it, in which case he shall not be disposed of in service to any but the English nation." Timothy Green, *Acts and Laws of His Majesties Colony of Connecticut in New England, 1715–47*, p. 5. In Huntington v. Jones, Kirby 33 (1786), a Connecticut court held that the assignment of a poor debtor is limited to the person of the master named, and does not extend to his heirs and assigns, on the ground that the practice of assigning debtors in service constituted "an abridgment of personal liberty" and should "not be enlarged by implication."

the judgment, "and to Imploy, untill by his labour hee have Defrayed the Same: And if hee refuses So to labour; then to lay him in Prison, unlesse hee produce Suffitient Security for the payment thereof according to the verdict and Judgemt thereupon aforesd." [24] The town of Brookhaven, Long Island, provided in 1674 that where a man could not pay the smith once a year in wheat, pork, or Indian pay for work he had performed, the smith could "choose whether he will work for him till it be satisfyed." [25] A petition of Mary Van der Ripe to the common council of New York City in 1726 asking that two years' indentured servitude might be considered adequate satisfaction for a debt of a few pounds reveals some of the evils inherent in this system of exploitation of unfortunate debtors. While working for Joost Sooy, a cooper, and his wife, she fell sick. Her master bought her "a few odd Necessarys" to the amount of 46s. 6d. "and Engaged for to pay the Doctor," but failed to do so. In order to show her gratitude, the petitioner in 1724 "willingly Sign'd an Indenture," acknowledging an indebtedness in the sum of £15 lawful money of New York. "Having noe other way to pay or Satisfy the same than by Servitude," she agreed to serve the Sooys and their assigns for a term of four years. The first of these years she claimed to have served faithfully, "(tho' under the greatest hardships that ever poor Soul Labour'd) as it can be proved by most of the Neighbors, for with Submission" she "went allmost Naked and Sildome a Stockinges or Shoes to her feet either winter or Summer . . . besides the other bitter usage which she has received from their hands." After a year her master and mistress moved out of town and "hired her out to Mr. John Garra . . . a Victualler" for £9 a year ("which is not out") paid to Sooy. According to the terms of the contract for hire, Garra was "to find your petitioner in Such apparel as was Suteable to her Imployment." Notwithstanding, she charged that he had "found her Nothing so that yr Petitioner must undoubtly perisht" but for "well Dispos'd persons" and her "present Mistress." To cap it all, she was now being "Dun'd by the Doctor for to pay him for his Medicine and Attendance," which she felt she was "not oblig'd to pay lest she was free." She accordingly prayed that "Yr Honours in your great Wisdome may deem Two Years Servitude not to[o] Small requite for Soe Small a summe" as 46s. 6d. and "beggs to be reliev'd in the premisses and made a free woman." [26]

[24] Cooper v. Diment, Southampton Sessions, fols. 1, 2 (1667).
[25] *Brookhaven Rec., 1662–79,* I, 113 (1674). Cf. also Manuel's case, Ulster Dutch Transcripts, II, f. 338 (1672).
[26] Original Records of the Common Council, File Box No. 2, Bundle 2, Board of Aldermen

Debtors frequently petitioned the Philadelphia courts asking to be sold to satisfy their debts.[27] In 1754 Robert Rea, a shoemaker, petitioned the Philadelphia justices from prison, stating that he had been confined to gaol for debt at the suit of Abraham De Haven. To satisfy this judgment he had indentured himself for a two-year term to a man named Singleton to work at shoemaking. Singleton turned him over to another creditor, who gaoled him for ten shillings. Afterward Singleton visited the petitioner in gaol and "balanced accounts." As he had a "helpless child" to provide for, Rea asked that he be adjudged to serve a reasonable time to pay his debts or else be granted a weekly allowance during the period of his confinement as he had no property to satisfy creditors.[28] In order to effect a sale of their persons to satisfy creditors debtors sometimes resorted to advertisements.[29]

In the Southern colonies debtors were also bound out to service to satisfy their debts.[30] In the case of planters, they generally were able to assign one or more of their own servants to work out the judgment debt.[31] Harlow has selected a typical debtor's agreement of servitude in Barbados made by Richard Atkinson in 1640 for a debt of 2,000 lbs. of cotton. For failure to pay on the date specified, Atkinson agreed to allow John Batt or his assigns "to take the body of me Richard Atkinson,

---

and City Clerk's Records. Her indentures were acknowledged before Philip Cortlandt, a justice of the peace. N.Y. Hist. Soc., *Coll.*, XLII (1909), 179 (1725). For servitude for judgment debt in New Jersey, see Jenning's case, Middlesex Court Rec., lib. I (1687); Hollinshead v. Thrumbell, Burlington Court Book (1684); case of Anne Stevens sold at public vendue to discharge a debt, *ibid.* (1704); Nowland's case, Monmouth C.P. and Q.S., lib. 1735–44 (1735)—where he was to serve his creditors a year and a half, "they finding him in Cloathes and taking Care of his Children."

[27] See Phila. Court Papers, 1732–44, Hist. Soc. of Pa.

[28] Phila. Co. Court MSS (1754). For petition of debtors in the Philadelphia gaol to be sold for their debts, see MS Court Papers, 1732–44, Pa. Hist. Soc. See also Rawlins v. Chandler, *Chester, Pa., Court Rec., 1681–97*, p. 196 (1690); McCoy's petition, York, Pa., Q.S., lib. I, f. 13 (1756); McDonald's petition, *ibid.*, f. 18 (1757). For Delaware, see Mary Blocq's petition, *Newcastle Court Rec.*, I, 320 (1679); Edwards' petition, *Some Court Records of Sussex Co., Del.*, p. 113 (1684); Peason's case, Kent Co. Court Rec., lib. 1699–1703; Vassell's case, *ibid.*, 1703–17, f. 4 (1704); Butcher's case, Sussex C.P. Docket, 1770; King's petition, Sussex Q.S. and C.P., lib. 1736–38 (1738).

[29] See, e.g., *Pa. Gazette*, Oct. 10, 1759.

[30] See Blumfeild's petition, *Md. Arch.*, XLIX, 509, 510 (1665); Vincent's case, *ibid.*, LVII, 254 (1670), bound to sheriff for a year to work out fees, 601–603 (1669), but cf. *ibid.*, p. 117; Bertha Cunningham's indenture, Somerset, lib. AW, 1690–91, f. 96 (1691); Hayes v. Hobbs, *ibid.*, f. 170 (1691), Hayes bound to Hobbs to pay for the cure of a scald on his head, an ulcer on the left leg, and the "King's evil" in his right leg; Martha Wakeling (Prince George, lib. B, 1699–1705, f. 50 [1700]), and Thomas Barber (*ibid.*, f. 404 [1705]), both bound for a cure; Parish's case, Ann Arundel, lib. 1720–21, f. 76 (1721); Ramshaw's case, *Va. Gen. Court Mins.*, p. 124 (1626); Perry's case, Prince George, Va., Co. Rec., 1737/8–40, lib. II (April term, 1738); Richard Day and Thomas Forest, both bound for cures. Westmoreland O.B., 1675/6–88/9, f. 691 (1688); Fincastle O.B., 1773–77 (1775). For West Florida, see Cecil Johnson, *British West Florida, 1763–1783* (New Haven, 1943), p. 162.

[31] Cf. also *infra*, pp. 409, 414.

servant for the terms of sixe years, without any further trouble or suite of law." [32]

In alleviation of the debtor's status an important body of colonial statutes were enacted. One type of statute provided that debts might be paid in commodities or manufactured products at rates fixed by the legislature.[33] Another type of statute, aimed at encouraging immigration, granted newcomers exemption from arrest at least for a specified period of time for debts previously contracted. Laws of this type were generally disallowed by the British authorities on the ground that the establishment of an asylum for the protection of debtors against lawful creditors appeared "inconsistent with the principles of justice, as well as of good policy." [34] A third group set comparatively brief time limits on the bringing of actions for debts. Such legislation was also regarded with disfavor by the Board of Trade.[35]

Numerous bankruptcy acts were passed in the colonies releasing from prison debtors who voluntarily confessed themselves insolvent and surrendered their assets; these acts reflected a growing leniency in the mother country toward the unfortunate debtor. When the Council ceased to arrange or enforce compositions with creditors, Parliament stepped in. By an act passed in 1671 [36] it was provided that a prisoner for debt was to be discharged, if he swore that he had no estate above the value of £10 and that he had not conveyed his estate to defraud his creditors, and his oath could not be disproved at quarter sessions. A creditor who insisted upon keeping his debtor in prison, was required to pay a weekly sum for his maintenance.[37] In reviewing statutes along

---

[32] Harlow, *Barbados,* p. 294, citing Deeds of Barbados, Dec. 14, 1640, in Davis Collection, III, 359, Box No. 1. Cf. *Southampton, L.I., Town Rec.,* I, 137 (1653); *Easthampton, L.I., Town Rec.,* II, 86 (1679), 94, 97 (1681).

[33] See, e.g., *Mass. Charters and Gen. Laws,* p. 173 (1640); Hening, II, 506, 507 (1682). The home authorities might well consider such acts detrimental to the interests of English creditors. *A.P.C., Col.,* IV, 389. See also E. B. Russell, *The Review of American Colonial Legislation by the King in Council* (New York, 1915), pp. 128, 129.

[34] *A.P.C., Col.,* IV, 408; *1766–83,* pp. 311–312, 315–316, 320, 321 (1771), 329–330 (1772); Russell, *op. cit.,* p. 129.

[35] Russell, *op. cit.,* p. 131.   [36] 22, 23 Car. II, c. 20.

[37] Typical of such bankruptcy laws were the statutes passed in New York. An act of 1730 provided that a debtor was discharged from custody if he had delivered all his effects to his creditors and filed a statement of his assets, excepting wearing apparel and bedding for himself and family and the tools of his trade not exceeding £10, and certifying that he had not sold or concealed any assets in defraud of creditors. If the creditor was not satisfied with the truth of the statement, further time might be granted by the court, during which the debtor was to remain in prison. If the creditor could discover no omissions of property from the debtor's statement, the prisoner was then to be discharged unless the creditor insisted upon his detention, in which event the creditor had to agree in writing to pay the debtor in prison such weekly sum as should be fixed by the court. *N.Y. Col. Laws,* II, 1669 (1730). Cf. also *ibid.,* III, 312 (1743), 693 (1748), 822 (1750), 866 (1751), 924 (1753), 1099 (1755); IV, 10 (1755), 103 (1756), 526 (1761); V, 120 (1770). For petitions for relief under these statutes, see Bernhart's petition,

this line passed in Massachusetts in 1757 and in Virginia in 1762 the Board of Trade acknowledged the beneficial intent of these laws, but recommended their disallowance nonetheless because of fear that their operation would work injustice to absent British creditors. The Board's reasoning reveals how watchful the home government was of the economic interests of English merchants and creditors:

Upon . . . the whole . . . a Bankrupt Law though it be just and equitable in its abstract Principle, has always been found in its Execution to afford such opportunities for fraudulent Practices, that even in this Country, where, in most Cases, the whole number of Creditors are resident on the spot, it may well be doubted whether the Fair Trader does not receive more Detriment than Benefit from such Law. But if a like Law should take place in a Colony, where . . . not above a Tenth part of its Creditors are resident, and where that small proportion of the whole, both in Number and Value, might (as under the present Act they might) upon a Commission being issued, get possession of the Bankrupt's Effects, and proceed to make a Dividend before the Merchants in England, who make the other Nine Tenths of the Bankrupts Creditors could even be informed of such Bankruptcy, it is easy to foresee that such a Law can be beneficial to the very small part of the Creditors resident in the Colony only . . .[38]

Notwithstanding the Board of Trade's reaction to this colonial legislation, similar legislation was enacted in eighteenth-century England by which honest, as distinguished from fraudulent, debtors were entitled to a discharge from prison with the consent of their creditors. Thus, both in England and the colonies the groundwork was laid for the bankruptcy legislation of the nineteenth century, which recognized that insolvency was not necessarily traceable to wrongful or punishable conduct but might well be the result of cyclical factors and other economic and social conditions and which introduced the principle of

---

Dutchess C.P., D, 1766-70 (1770); petition of Fry *et al.*, Kempe C–F (1771). See also Stokes, *Iconography*, IV, 451 (1704). The humane operation of such statutes is illustrated in *Letter Book of John Watts*, p. 312; *Select Cases of the Mayor's Court of New York City, 1674–1784*, ed. R. B. Morris, pp. 179, 190–194 (for the discharge of seamen debtors from imprisonment, see *ibid.*, p. 194). For post-Revolutionary remedial legislation, see D. M. Schneider, *The History of Public Welfare in New York State, 1609–1866* (Chicago, 1938), pp. 142–148.

An act similar to the New York statute of 1730 was enacted the previous year in Pennsylvania, but as a result of complaints of its operation, the legislature provided that unmarried persons under 40 without dependent children were subject to arrest as before the act of 1729 if unable to satisfy judgments for not more than £20. Persons imprisoned for less than 40*s.*, willing to make satisfaction by servitude, could be sentenced to service by two magistrates. *Votes of Assembly,* III, 132, 147; *Pa. Stat. at Large*, IV, 211–213.

[38] *A.P.C., Col.,* IV, 388, 389 (1758); IV, 563 (1763); Russell, *op. cit.,* pp. 125, 126. For Massachusetts, see petition for release of Joshua Edwards, laborer, of York, Me., a prisoner for debt. Mass. Arch., Vol. 105 (Petitions, 1643–1775), f. 289 (1746).

voluntary bankruptcy. Zephaniah Swift, writing toward the close of the eighteenth century, defended this differentiation in the treatment of the honest and the fraudulent debtor, but made a further distinction between laboring men and persons of substantial property that few would be willing to accept as valid in modern times:

In the case of a dishonest debtor, there is the greatest propriety in compelling him to pay his debts by service, for the purpose of punishing him and holding him up as a public example. So where, from the character and rank of a man in life, labour is a proper business, he cannot complain of injustice to be compelled to work to pay his debts. But where a man has lived in affluence, and by some unforeseen misfortune and unexpected accident, is reduced to poverty, it would be cruel to aggravate his wretchedness, by subjecting him to servitude. Between these extremes there are a great variety of grades in which courts must exercise a discretion tempered with humanity, in designating the proper objects of this law.[39]

Since Swift's day the bankruptcy power in this country has expanded from the regulation of traders for commercial purposes into a national policy of relief for debtors of all classes.[40]

The legislation for the relief of poor debtors passed in the late colonial and post-Revolutionary periods contributed to the gradual decline of indentured servitude. With the abolition of imprisonment for small sums and the elimination of the most glaring abuses of the system, service in lieu of prison terms for debt disappears.[41]

APPRENTICESHIP AND CHILD LABOR

APPRENTICESHIP [1] was a medieval guild institution transplanted to a land where guilds failed to thrive and industrial labor monopolies faced ever-

[39] Zephaniah Swift, *A System of the Laws of the State of Connecticut* (2 vols., Windham, Conn., 1795, 1796), I, 219.

[40] See Charles Warren, *Bankruptcy in United States History* (Cambridge, Mass., 1935), pp. 7, 8, 56–79; F. R. Noel, *A History of the Bankruptcy Clause of the Constitution of the United States of America* (Gettysburg, 1918).

[41] The Pennsylvania Constitution of 1776 provided for the abolition of imprisonment for debt. See also, e.g., *Laws of N.Y., 1789*, c. 24, *Laws of 1817*, c. 260; Geiser, *op. cit.*, pp. 42, 75. The effective reform, however, did not come until two or three decades after 1820. As late as 1830 the ratio between the aggregate number of debtors and criminals confined in 17 prisons located in the Northern and Eastern states was nearly 5 to 1. Prison Discipline Society, *5th Ann. Rep.* (1830). See also F. T. Carlton, "Abolition of Imprisonment for Debt in the United States," *Yale Review*, XVII (1908), 339–344.

[1] Many aspects of colonial apprenticeship have been competently treated by Seybolt, Douglas, Jernegan, and McKee. These phases need not detain us long. Some valuable illustrative documents implement these monographic studies. See Grace Abbott, *The Child and the State* (Chicago, 1938), I, 195–213; N.Y. Hist. Soc., *Collections, 1885, 1909*, and town and vestry records listed in E. B. Greene and R. B. Morris, *A Guide to the Principal Sources for Early American History (1600–1800) in the City of New York* (New York, 1929).

increasing laissez faire opposition. It differed from other forms of indentured service in that it was only open to minors and invariably provided training in return for their services in specified trades. If the articles of indenture contain no provision for trade education, we are dealing with the regular form of indentured servitude regardless of the label. Conversely, "servants" whose articles of indenture provided such education were in fact apprentices even though the title was not given them.[2] In England apprenticeship was traditionally confined to the skilled trades, but the Statute of Artificers (c. 25) permitted householders having a minimum of half a ploughland in tillage to receive apprentices in husbandry between the ages of ten and eighteen to serve until twenty-one minimum and twenty-four maximum. Hence, indentures to learn the "art and mysteries of husbandry" are considered as forms of apprenticeship even though less technical training may have been provided than in the industrial trades.[3] Furthermore, as a general rule apprenticeships were not assignable without the consent of both parties, whereas assignability was a characteristic of other forms of bound labor.[4]

The system had a twofold objective: 1) to provide skilled labor; 2) to relieve the community of the burden of supporting poor orphans and other dependent children. In the case of the first group the form may be considered voluntary, as its validity depended upon the consent of the parent or guardian. The second form was truly involuntary, as the binding out was done by local officials. Since the latter type generally involved binding out until twenty-one years of age, the term of service of pauper apprentices frequently exceeded the usual maximum term of voluntary apprenticeship, which was seven years.

In England apprenticeship as a national system stems from the Statute of Artificers of 1562.[5] The statute imposed a minimum seven-year term of service upon all entering any industrial calling, such term not to ex-

---

[2] P. H. Douglas, *American Apprenticeship and Industrial Education* (New York, 1921), cites the apprenticeship of John Sherman who bound himself out as "a servant to be taught in the art, trade, and mystery of a spinning wheelmaker and have three quarters schooling." Records of Indentures of Individuals Bound out as Apprentices, Servants, etc. in Philadelphia (1771–73), f. 5. According to the letter of the law, however, the apprentice had to be expressly bound as an apprentice; otherwise the binding was invalid. R. Burn, *Justice of the Peace Abridgment* (Boston, 1773); J. F. Grimké, *The South-Carolina Justice of Peace* (Charleston, 1788), p. 7, both citing Dalton, c. 58.

[3] See Tapping Reeve, *The Law of Baron and Femme* . . . (New Haven, 1816), p. 341. See *contra* Douglas, *op. cit.*, p. 29; Hill v. Spencer, 61 N.Y. 274 (1874). For apprenticeship to husbandry in England, see Mildred Campbell, *The English Yeoman* (New Haven, 1942), p. 214. For early instances in the colonies, see *Va. Co. Rec.*, I, 306 (1620); III, 115 (1619).

[4] See *infra*, pp. 401–412. [5] 5 Eliz. c. 4, §§ 25-35.

pire until the apprentice reached the age of twenty-four (c. 26). It further imposed restrictions on the taking of apprentices. Merchants in foreign trade, mercers, drapers, goldsmiths, ironmongers, embroiderers or clothiers [6] could not take any apprentice except their own sons, unless the parents of the apprentice were possessed of a freehold worth forty shillings (cc. 27, 29); if the parents had no such estate it was lawful for them to apprentice their sons to certain specified trades (c. 30). By this act, local custom was officially superseded by the custom of London, whose chief features were: 1) the apprentice was bound by articles of indenture; 2) the articles were duly recorded; 3) the minimum term was seven years; and 4) the apprentice was to live with his master who, during the period of the indentures, was to stand *in loco parentis.*

By the time the colonial settlements were well under way this national system of apprenticeship was no longer uniformly enforced in England. It was breaking down at the beginning of the eighteenth century and, at the close, the seven-year period of training required by the act—in many cases far longer than was actually needed to learn a trade—was enforced only in trades still operating under the old guild system. In such trades the employer continued to enjoy the benefits of cheap labor for an unduly long period. Laissez faire, which sought to break the monopolies of the guilds, thereby removed certain valuable safeguards to child welfare in industry, for, with the transition in the eighteenth century from the guild system to the larger-scale industrial economy, the exploitation of child labor was manifest in its most repulsive phases.[7]

The national system of apprenticeship as established by the Statute of Artificers was in general transplanted to the American colonies, but there was no uniformity of observance and some of the provisions of the statute were never embodied in the colonial labor codes.

The Legal Formalities of Apprenticeship. In accord with common law practice colonial courts held that parol contracts of apprenticeship were not binding,[8] and that one could not be bound an apprentice without a deed.[9] Colonial indentures of apprenticeship were in the

---

[6] § 32 also included woolen-cloth weavers (except in the counties of Cumberland, Westmoreland, Lancaster, and Wales), who wove friezes, cotton, or household cloths.

[7] See Morris, *Sel. Cases, Mayor's Court,* pp. 27 *et seq.;* O. J. Dunlop, *English Apprenticeship and Child Labour* (New York, 1912), pp. 21, 22, 48, 118, 119. In 1814 the system of national apprenticeship was brought to an end in Great Britain with the repeal of the Statute of Artificers, 54 Geo., III, c. 96.

[8] See also Hall v. Rowley, 2 Root (Conn.) 161 (1791); but cf. Huntington v. Oxford, 4 Day (Conn.) 189 (1810).

[9] See Burn, *op. cit.,* p. 18; Grimké, *op. cit.,* p. 7; *New Conductor Generalis* (Albany, 1819), p. 30; Reeve, *op. cit.,* p. 341; also Short v. Millechop, D. J. Boorstin, ed., *Delaware Cases, 1792–1830* (3 vols., St. Paul, Minn., 1943), I, 618.

main formal in character, and incorporated English legal phraseology as well as content. By the end of the seventeenth century, printed forms were generally employed.[10] From the Deed Books of York County, Maine,[11] a typical set of articles is reproduced:

This Indenture witnesseth that I John Maisters of Wells, In the County of Yorke, with the Consent of my father Nathall Masters doe bind my selfe an apprentice to William Partridg of Wells Carpenter, in the same County, to continew with, abide and faithfully serve him my maister as a faithfull apprentice out to doe, the full and Just tearme of four years, to bee fully ended from the date hereof; The sayd apprentice his sd Maister faithfully to serue, his lawfull secrets keepe, hee shall not play at unlawfull games, nor vnseasonably absent him selfe from his sayd Maisters busines, hee shall not frequent Tavernes, nor lend, nor spend the goods or victualls of his sd Maister, without his leaue, hee shall not Contract Matrimony, or Committ fornication, but truely and trustily obserue his sd Maisters lawful Comands as a faithfull servant out to due. The sd Maister his sd apprentice shall teach, and Instruct in the Trade of a Carpenter, to the best of his skill, according to what his sayd apprentice is Capable of, and alsoe doe promiss to teach him to write and siffer, If hee bee Capable, and to giue him a set of Tools at the end of his tyme, and to prouide him dureing the sd apprentishipe, Convenjent Meate drinke, lodging and washing, and seaven pounds per Ann: for to bind him aparell, and provided his Maister shall goe out of the County, hee shall not haue him his sayd servant to goe along with him, without his sd apprentice Consent. In witness wr of [whereof] Wee haue here unto set our hands and seales interChangeably this sixteenth day of Septembr, one thousand six hundred seaventy foure, 1674:

John Maisters his marke   [his seale]

William Partridg   [his seale]

Slight elaboration and better English characterizes eighteenth-century indentures, such as the following, registered in New York City [12] in 1718:

This Indenture Wittnesseth that I, William Mathews, son of Marrat of the City of New York, Widdow, hath put himself and by these Presents doth voluntarily and of his own free Will and Accord and by the Consent of his said Mother put himself Apprentice to Thomas Windover of the City aforesaid Cordwiner with him to live and (after the Manner of an Apprentice) to serve from the fifteenth day of August last Anno Dom one thousand and seven

[10] For printers' advertisements of apprentice's indentures for sale, see *N.Y. Weekly J.*, Jan. 25, 1748; *S.C. Gazette*, Sept. 9–16, 1732; July 28, August 11, 1733. The New England schools of the eighteenth century taught boys to copy these forms and at the same time familiarized them with the terms of apprenticeship. B. E. Hazard, *The Organization of the Boot and Shoe Industry in Massachusetts before 1875* (Cambridge, 1921), pp. 9, 10, citing Ebenezer Belcher's Exercise Book, 1793, Harvard University Archives.   [11] Bk. II, f. 159.

[12] N.Y. Hist. Soc., *Coll., 1909*, pp. 113, 114.

hundred and Eighteen untill the full Term of seven years be Compleat and Ended. During all which Term the said Apprentice his said Master Thomas Windover faithfully shall serve his secrets keep, his lawfull Commands gladly every where Obey, he shall do no damage to his said Master nor see to be done by Others without letting or giving Notice to his said Master, he shall not waste his said Masters Goods, nor lend them unlawfully to any, he shall not Committ fornication nor Contract Matrimony within the said Term. At Cards, Dice or any Other unlawfull Game he shall not play whereby his said Master may have Damage with his Own Goods or the Goods of those during the said Term without Lycense from his said Master he shall neither buy nor sell. He shall not absent himself day or night from his Masters service without his leave, nor haunt Alehouses, Taverns or Playhouses, but in all things as a faithfull apprentice he shall behave himself towards his said Master and all his during the said Term. And the said Master during the said Term shall, by the best means or Method that he can Teach or Cause the said Apprentice to be taught the Art or Mystery of a Cordwiner, and shall find and provide unto the said Apprentice sufficient Meat, Drink, Apparel, Lodging and washing fitting for an Apprentice, and shall during the said Term every winter at Nights give him one Quarters schooling, and at the Expiration of the said Term to provide for the said Apprentice a sufficient New Suit of Apparell four shirts and two Necletts, for the true Performance of all and every the said Covenants and agreements Either of the said parties bind themselves unto the Other by these Presents.

In Witness whereof they have hereunto Interchangeably put their hands and seals this twenty fifth day of September in the fifth year of his Majesties Reign, Annoque Domini One thousand seven hundred and Eighteen. The Marke of William Mathews (seal) sealed and delivered in the Presence of John Rushton, H. D. Meyer, New York Sept. 26th Ao 1718 then appeared before me Jacobus Kip one of his Majties Justis of the Peace for the City and County of New York the within Named Apprentice and acknowledge the signing and sealing of this Indenture to be his Voluntary Act and Deed.

Jacobus Kip, Justice of the Peace

These indentures had to be in written or in printed form,[13] were generally signed by the apprentice in the presence of witnesses, and acknowledged before public authority.[14] Occasionally the apprentice's father or mother signed in his stead.

Except in the case of orphan and pauper apprentices, the approval of the minor's parent or guardian was necessary, although the indenture

[13] But see case of Gilbert's servant, where the New Haven colony court ordered that the servant must stay with the master for another year even though the master had "nothing to show in writing." *New Haven Col. Rec., 1638–49*, p. 163 (1645).

[14] See Howard v. Robinson, Boorstin, 1 Del. Cas. 164 (1797), where the apprentice was discharged on the ground that the magistrate had not signed and certified the indenture.

need not state in express words that the binding was of the minor's own free will and consent. There was no uniform rule in the colonies as to the necessity of the parent's or guardian's consent. Where an orphan apprentice bound himself before a guardian had been chosen for him, his signature, according to an opinion of William Henry Smith to Henry Lloyd of Long Island in 1761, was valid.[15] A Suffolk, Massachusetts, general sessions' decision in 1765 ruled that an indenture was invalid where neither parents nor guardian had signed it. In other words, if signed by an infant alone, it could not be enforced in that court.[16]

Not infrequently the courts went behind the indentures to ascertain whether the lad had bound himself freely and willingly. One Maryland witness to the signing of articles of indenture testified in 1690 that when a master, shortly after having freed a servant from his indentures, produced articles of apprenticeship with the same servant, the witness called the lad before him and stated:

Sweet hart the binding of apprentiship is and ought to be a tender thing, Thou hast heard thy late Master declare thou to be a freeman before me and these other people present, If thou art in the place of Justice and shall have Justice, Thy Master hath declared thee to be a freeman and thou art a freeman, and if at any time thy Master should say the same to me, and I will appear as an Evidence against him upon this I Bid him consider. . . . [The witness added] in Justice if his Master or no other had ordered him by fair words pretended to make him give his consent he said no, I demanded his reason for binding himself again, he said a desire he had to learn the trade of a Cooper and

---

[15] "Honored Sir with respect to the poor Lad that is to be bound Out An Apprentice I am of Oppinion there is no Manner of Occasion to be at the trouble and Expence of Choosing a Guardian for binding him. his Own Indenture will most Certainly Secure his Service to his Master as fully as if he had been bound by his Father and all the Difference between Binding himself and being bound by A Guardian is that the Master may have Some person to come upon for the Apprentices breach of Covenant. The Law is quite Clear for Infants binding themselves Apprentices Especially After fourteen years of age for By the statute of the fifth of Elizabeth Apprentices Are bound by their Indentures notwithstanding their nonage." "Papers of the Lloyd Family of Lloyd's Neck, 1654–1826," N.Y. Hist. Soc., *Coll.* (1927), II, 620, 621. At common law such an indenture of apprenticeship was not void, but only voidable. See Bacon, *Abridgement*, V, 341, 342. For an indenture of apprenticeship reciting the grandfather's consent, see Emmett MSS, No. 11025 (1777), N.Y. Pub. Lib.

[16] Dehon v. Edes, Suffolk G.S., lib. 1764–68 (1765). However, cf. petition of Todd and his wife that their son be bound out to some one else, as his indentures to a glazier were made without their knowledge. Petition dismissed. Suffolk G.S., III, f. 237 (1719). Where the father was away at sea and the mother outside the jurisdiction of the court, the New York court of general sessions permitted a grandfather to bind his grandson as apprentice. N.Y.G.S., lib. 1694–1731/2, f. 529 (1730). For the Pennsylvania rule that the infant had to consent and be a party to the contract, see *Pa. Stat. at Large*, VII, 360, 361 (1770). Cf. also 1 Ashmead 123–126; 6 Sergeant and Rawle 340–342; 5 Wharton 128–131. Cf. also In re McDowle, 8 Johns. (N.Y) 253 (1811); Ivins v. Norcross, 3 N.J. Law (2 Penning.) 977 (1812). The father's consent was also required. 8 Watts and Sargent, 339–340. Cf. also People v. Gates, 57 Barb. (N.Y.) 291 (1869).

like wise that his master had been a good master to him and therefore he had rather trust him than any one else. I immediatly signed the Indenture to which I swore before your Worship.[17]

Throughout the colonies indentures of apprenticeship had to be entered in some public record office, such as the town clerk's records or the records of the county court, in accordance with English law and practice.[18] The apprentice could be discharged by the court for the master's failure to register the indentures.[19] Generally this requirement held true also of other forms of indentured servitude.[20]

Premiums for Apprenticeship. The property restrictions of the Statute of Artificers upon entering certain trades were never in force in the colonies. However, the master might wish to assure himself that the apprentice came of a "responsible family," [21] in order to give preference to boys from more prosperous homes. Possibly the same results were obtained in the colonies as under the English statute by the practice of demanding premiums. As in England, such premiums were frequently paid masters for taking apprentices. In the mother country such fees might be very substantial and effectually preclude the possibility of poor children entering certain trades.[22] This was especially true of professions like law and medicine and in the field of commerce,[23] but even in the industrial trades it was not out of the ordinary.[24] Benjamin Frank-

[17] Somerset, lib. 1690–91, fols. 67, 68 (1690).

[18] See R. F. Seybolt, *Apprenticeship and Apprenticeship Education in Colonial New England* (New York, 1917), pp. 9, 10.

[19] Aspinwall's case, Morris, ed., *Sel. Cases, Mayor's Court*, p. 185 (1725).

[20] See, e.g., *R.I. Col. Rec.*, I, 177 (1647); *N.Y. Col. Laws*, I, 18 (1665); also *supra*, p. 322.

[21] See advertisement in *Rivington's N.Y. Gazetteer*, May 18, 1775, for an "apprentice of credible parents." See also *Freeman's J.* (Philadelphia) June 1–15, 1785.

[22] For example, "a very ingenious chemist" demanded £50 in 1692, while a ship surgeon was willing to take an apprentice for £10. HMC, *Rep.*, XXIX, Pt. III, 510 (1692). Premiums of from £200 to £800 were given in London. High premiums were never found in the poorer trades, but were common in the wealthier ones. Strype's *Stow* (London, 1720), II, 329; Defoe, *Complete English Tradesman* (London, 1738), p. 147; Dunlop, *op. cit.*, pp. 199–212. See also *Va. Co. Rec.*, I, 424 (1620).

[23] In the *New-York Mercury*, May 17, 1766, there was an advertisement for "an Apprentice to the Doctor's Business." The advertisement stated that "An Apprentice Fee will be expected." For merchant apprenticeship a fee of £100 sterling was not unusual. See *Lloyd Papers*, I, 245; II, 520–521, 527–528, 565. Dr. Charles Carroll arranged to have his second son, John Henry, work in a Philadelphia counting house, and agreed to pay for his son's maintenance and instruction £30 sterling per annum for three years. In addition, Carroll agreed to pay for instruction in writing and arithmetic and provide his son's clothing. *Md. Hist. Mag.*, XXXVII (1942), 295.

[24] "An apprentice is wanted for Carving and Gilding; none need apply but those who have a lad of a sober and promising genius, and are willing to give a Premium." *N.Y. Journal or General Advertiser*, March 16, 1775. See also *Pa. Packet*, Dec. 17, 1772; *Pa. J.*, April 6, 1758; Feb. 28, 1776. Bonnis and Morris, proprietors of a china factory in Philadelphia, advertised that they would accept a few more apprentices "without a fee," indicating that this was the exception rather than the rule. *Pa. Gazette*, July 26, 1770.

lin's father was deterred from apprenticing the lad to the cutler's trade because of the high fee that was demanded. In fact, the absence of positive evidence in the records is no proof that such premiums were not often paid in the colonies. In England until the Stamp Act of 1709 [25] their payment was purely a private transaction between the parent and the master and entries were not made in the enrollments or on the indentures. After that date, however, the sum given with an apprentice had to be stated in the indentures. No parallel legislation was enacted, however, in the American colonies.

Litigation over fees generally arose when for one reason or another the apprenticeship was terminated before the expiration of the stipulated period. In England it was a by no means infrequent practice for masters on the verge of insolvency to take an apprentice for the sake of the fee, and then so ill-treat the child that he would run away or become rebellious, in other words, give the master legal grounds for obtaining from the magistrates a cancellation of the indentures without requiring a return of the fee.[26] In such cases the apprentice or his parents might sue for restitution of at least part of the fees paid. The New York general sessions in 1733 returned to the parents £8 current money of the province, part of the £20 paid to a New York chirurgeon. In turn the parents delivered to the master their counterpart of the articles of indenture.[27]

The Minimum Term of Service. While the seven-year minimum had considerable vogue,[28] it was not uniformly adopted in the colonies. There, apprenticeship usually terminated when the apprentice reached the age of twenty-one.[29] In New York in the early years of English rule

[25] 8 Anne, c. 9, i. 35. This act imposed a duty of 6*d.* in the pound upon services of £50 or under, and 1*s.* upon services over £50 paid as premiums to learn a trade; it provided the government with a profitable source of revenue.

[26] See Morris, *Sel. Cases, Mayors Court,* p. 36, and London cases cited *infra,* p. 377n.; M. Dorothy George, *London Life in the XVIIIth Century* (New York, 1930), p. 229. Chancery ruled that on the master's death before the apprentice had learned his trade, part of the premium paid was to be restored. Reeve, *op. cit.,* p. 346.

[27] Munroe's case, N.Y.G.S., lib. 1732–62, f. 21; 1722–42/3, f. 169 (1733). In 1751 a New York cordwainer named Woodhouse agreed to discharge an apprentice provided that the boy's father reimbursed him for his expenses in apprehending and committing the apprentice after he had run away. Shearer's case, *ibid.,* lib. 1743–60 (August 8, 1751). In a similar case in New Jersey in 1764 referees reported that the master had sustained damages amounting to £7 5*s.* current and costs and ordered the indentures delivered up whenever damages and costs were paid. The court rendered judgment accordingly. Vanderpool v. Potter, Essex, N.J., lib. D, 1752–64 (Sept. 15, 1763).

[28] In England municipal and craft regulations generally required a seven-year term. Seybolt, *op. cit.,* pp. 11, 12.

[29] See indenture between Michael Hawkins, aged 19, and Abraham Rapley, to learn coach and chair-making, to serve one year and four months (1796). Easthampton, N.Y., Free Library.

there was no uniform term of service. In 1695 the common council per-mitted four-year terms,[30] which Albany had adopted nine years earlier.[31] However, out of ninety-seven New York City indentures of apprentice-ship available for the period 1694–1707, twenty were for the seven-year period, sixteen (in most cases indentures of paupers and orphans) were for more than seven years, and sixty-one were for periods under seven years, the majority being for four and five year terms.[32] The four-year term was found in 1711 to be too brief a time to master a craft and there-fore the period was extended to seven years.[33] Common council ordi-nances of 1763, 1773, 1784, 1786, 1797, 1801, and 1815 "to regulate the admission of freemen in the City of New York" prescribe "a regular apprenticeship of seven years" as a prerequisite to becoming a citizen through apprenticeship,[34] although back in 1731 the council dropped the stipulated term from the requirement for binding apprentices before the mayor, recorder, or one of the aldermen.[35] The provision of 1695 seems to have been generally observed prior to 1731. Paul H. Douglas [36] has estimated that in the years 1718–27, 60.6 per cent of the published in-dentures of apprenticeship were for terms of seven years, whereas 34.8 per cent were for a longer period and only 4.6 per cent for a shorter one. From the failure of the city after 1731 to stipulate the term of apprentice-ship, it might be reasonable to infer that the seven-year term was no longer uniformly observed. This inference is supported by the apprentice-ship papers extant at the Hall of Records for the years 1748–86. Out of thirty-one articles of apprenticeship examined, fifteen were for periods under seven years (the bulk of these for five- and six-year terms), seven for seven years, and nine for more than seven years.[37] On Long Island, communities paid little heed to the seven-year tradition and indentures were recorded ranging from as little as one year to as high as eleven years.[38] In general, the customary minimum term was not observed north of the city limits.[39] To clear away any doubts a New York act of

[30] *M.C.C.*, I, 373, 374. [31] Munsell, *Annals*, VII, 175.

[32] N.Y. Hist. Soc., *Coll., 1885*, pp. 567–622. [33] *M.C.C.*, II, 454, 455, 467, 475; III, 392.

[34] N.Y. Hist. Soc., *Coll., 1885*, pp. 239, 274–275, 294–295, 298–299, 399, 532, 556.

[35] *M.C.C.*, IV, 97.

[36] *Amer. Apprenticeship*, p. 40; N.Y. Hist. Soc., *Coll., 1909*. See also N.Y.G.S., lib. 1694–1731/2, f. 529 (1730).

[37] See Pl A–304–314, 316–329, 364–367, 430, Hall of Records, New York City.

[38] *Southold Rec.*, II, 105 (1707, 5 yrs.); *Huntington Rec.*, I, 275 (1680, 1 yr.), 444 (1686, until 21); II, 488 (1767, 11 yrs.), 494 (1768, 11 yrs.); *Oyster Bay Town Rec.*, I, 145 (1682, until 21); *Southampton Town Rec.*, II, 244–246 (1672, 6 yrs.).

[39] Westchester Deeds, lib. 1665–96, fols. 160 (1686, 5½ yrs.), 161 (1686, 10 yrs., 7 mos.), 165, 166 (1697, 5½ yrs.), lib. 1707–20, f. 252 (1718, 5 yrs., 3 mos.), Comptroller's Office, New York City; Book of Supervisors, Dutchess County, f. 19 (1720, 7 yrs.); Old Misc. Rec., Dutchess County, Bk. II, f. 151 (1731, 6 yrs.); Ulster Dutch Transcripts (1682, 2 yrs.).

1788 upheld the validity of apprenticeships to serve until twenty-one.[40]

Elsewhere in the colonies longer terms were the rule in pauper and orphan apprenticeships but terms somewhat shorter than seven years seem to have been the practice in voluntary apprenticeships. Both in New England and in the South it was quite customary to apprentice boys until twenty-one and girls until sixteen or eighteen years of age, and the English statutory provision confining apprenticeship to those who had attained the age of fourteen was consistently ignored. Thomas Lechford recorded indentures of apprenticeship ranging from four to eight years.[41] During its first decade the Massachusetts Court of Assistants actually recorded more indentures of less than seven years than for seven years or longer.[42] However, of twenty-four indentures tabulated in the Essex quarterly court files between 1644 and 1681, six were for a period below seven years, five for the seven-year term, four for more than seven years, seven until twenty-one, one until twenty, and one, a girl apprentice, until eighteen.[43] This would indicate a gradual trend in the direction of longer terms. During the corresponding period the town of Boston recorded apprenticeships for terms ranging from six to fourteen years,[44] as the result of the "sad experience" of Boston tradesmen with shorter terms. According to an ordinance passed in 1660, the practice had grown up of apprenticing youths for a mere three or four years. Such youths had shown themselves "uncapable of being artists in their trades, besides their unmeetness at the expiration of their Apprenticeship to take charge of others for government and manual instruction in their occupations." Furthermore, the practice was asserted to be "contrary to the customes of all well Governed places." Therefore, the Boston authorities required apprenticeship until twenty-one, with

---

[40] *Laws of the State of New York,* 11th Sess., 1788, ch. xiii.

[41] Lechford, *Note-Book,* pp. 316, 362, 363, 437 (1640–41). The one-year "apprenticeship" of a blacksmith named John Edwards to Harman Garret, gunsmith, was apparently contracted by an established craftsman rather than a minor and was really a wage contract in which the employee was to get one half the profits of his work and agreed not to set up the trade of a gunsmith in Charlestown unless he bought the employer's house at the price set by four arbiters to be chosen by both parties. *Ibid.,* pp. 316, 317 (1640). Richard Handy, a Sandwich woolcomber, who apprenticed himself to James Skiffe of the same town, cooper, until "hee judge in himselfe that hee hath fully attained the skill and craft of a cooper," was in all probability a parallel case. Handy made à similar agreement not to set himself up or instruct anyone else in the cooper's craft in Sandwich. *Plymouth Col. Rec.,* IV, 194 (1668). Cf. also covenant of Perkins, *Essex,* VII, 259–261 (1679).

[42] *Assistants,* II, 17, 22, 25, 26, 41, 104, 117.

[43] *Essex,* I, 25, 72, 90, 132, 143, 201, 206, 231, 246, 380; II, 163, 311; III, 117, 296; IV, 256; V, 37, 300, 335; VI, 18; VIII, 205. For indentures of apprenticeship in Hampshire County until age twenty-one, see Hampshire County Court Rec., 1677–1728, fols. 12 (1678), 51 (1681), 154 (1692).

[44] *Boston Town Rec.,* II, 87, 88; VII, 6, 7, 37.

a minimum term of seven years.[45] The majority of apprenticeship indentures recorded for the same period among the deeds of York County in Maine or in the records of the courts sitting in that area were for terms exceeding seven years, one, involving a three-year-old child, for a period as long as eighteen years.[46]

Apprenticeship articles for eighteenth-century Massachusetts show little consistency as regards length of term.[47] Of twelve indentures in a Plymouth notary book between 1733 and 1762, mostly involving the occupation of mariner, eight were for less than seven years, one for seven years, and three for more than seven years. In one case an Indian apprenticed his son to a Pembroke resident for sixteen years, nine months, and six days to be taught to cast accounts as well as to read and write in the English language.[48] On the other hand, by the middle of the eighteenth century Boston tradesmen customarily accepted apprentices to serve until twenty-one or twenty-two years of age. Such apprentices were customarily bound to the trade at the ages of fourteen or fifteen.[49]

An interesting case involving an interpretation of the term of service came up in Essex general sessions in 1697. Charles Attwood of Ipswich had been indentured to William Baker of the same town to serve until 1699, a period of thirteen years, when he would be twenty-one years of age. The final "nine" was inadvertently omitted from the date. Charles took advantage of the error and quit before his term was up. The master prosecuted the lad for stealing, but when he failed to prove his case, he brought another suit for running away. One deponent testified that when she asked the father "why he wold bind a child so yong for so long time to a Glover, he said he had several Children and that he did like sd Baker and was sattisfied." Other evidence was introduced to show that it was the honest intent of the parties that the lad be bound for the full thirteen-year term, and that the year of expiration had been incorrectly stated in the contract. When the widow Attwood

---

[45] *Boston Town Rec.*, II, 156, 157 (1660); Seybolt, *Apprenticeship*, p. 26.

[46] *York Deeds*, Bk. I, Pt. I, fols. 66, 148; Bk. II, f. 159; Bk. III, f. 73; *Maine Province and Court Rec.*, I, 90; II, 431, 517. Long-term apprenticeships were also favored in seventeenth-century New Hampshire. N.H. Co. Court Papers, lib. I, f. 271 (1667, 8 yrs.), lib. IV, f. 113 (1669, until 21); Chesley's indenture, New Hampshire Q.S., 1683–88 (1686, 8 yrs.), N.H. Hist. Soc.

[47] See, e.g., Bishop's indentures, Dr. 1, Bundle 11 (20), Clerk of Court, Essex Co. (1700, 7 yrs.); Publick Notary Book, II, 1724–68, Essex Co., fols. 13 (1725, 7 yrs.), 22 (1723, 11 yrs.), 55 (1744, 3 yrs.), 56 (1739, 6 yrs.). See also Hampshire G.S. and C.P., lib. 1735–40/41, fols. 385, 386 (1738, 3 yrs.); Suffolk G.S., lib. III, f. 83 (1721, 5½ yrs.); IV, 113 (1727, 9 yrs.).

[48] Winslow's Notary Book, fols. 4 (1742), 7 (1733), 11 (1738), 16, 22, 24, 25 (1743), 28, 42, 45 (1744), 63 (1747), 94 (1752), 183 (1762).

[49] See *Papers of the Lloyd Family*, II, 520 (1754), 527 (1755), 564, 565 (1769).

had been told: "You know in your Conscience that the nine was forgettfully omitted and that Charles time is not out till the year 1699," she replied that "whatever was the Intent, that which is writ must stand, and she had discovered several vnderstanding men about it, that said what was written must stand" despite the oral evidence to the contrary. The court, surprisingly enough, upheld her contention, and ruled that the "apprentice is not obliged to serve any longer by said Indenture." [50]

In seventeenth-century Connecticut and New Haven colony the customary seven-year term was normally honored in the breach.[51] The town records of Providence contain numerous entries for the colonial period; the minimum term was six years and the bulk of the indentures ranged from ten to fifteen years. In one instance a two month's old baby girl was apprenticed until eighteen to learn the "Trade and art of a Tailor in making Apparrill." [52] Other Rhode Island towns completely ignored the seven-year term.[53] The attempt on the part of the New York City authorities to enforce observance of the English tradition was not paralleled in New Jersey, Pennsylvania, or Delaware, where terms of less or more than seven years were preferred.[54] According to Douglas's computations of Philadelphia indentures for the years 1771–73, 55 per cent of the apprenticeships were for periods of less than seven years. Only 9.4 per cent were for seven years, and approximately 35 per cent for longer terms. The bulk of the shorter terms ranged from three to six years.[55] However, the seven-year period was popular in early West Jersey indentures.[56] As late as 1772 we find a Pennsylvania firm advertising as follows:

[50] Baker v. Attwood, *Essex Inst. Hist. Coll.*, XI (1872), 74–80, 235–238 (1697).

[51] *Conn. Particular Court Rec., 1639–63*, pp. 243 (1661, 7 yrs. and 10 yrs.), 262 (1662, until 21, 2 cases); *New Haven Col. Rec.*, 1638–49, pp. 30 (1639, 9 yrs.), 77 (1642, 9 yrs. and 3 yrs. to another master), 135 (1644, 5 yrs.), 279 (1646, 8 yrs.).

[52] *Early Records of the Town of Providence*, II, 37 (1658, 7 yrs., 2 cases); IV, 132 (1769, 10 yrs.), 156 (1704, 14 yrs.); V, 17–19 (1708, until 18), 146 (1703, 14 yrs.), 292 (1674, 15 yrs.); IX, 5, 6 (1713, 6 yrs.), 12–14 (1716, until 21). See also Providence Court Papers, lib. IX, f. 229 (1670, 12 yrs., 5 mos.); X, f. 297 (1697, until 21).

[53] See *Portsmouth, R.I., Rec.*, pp. 409 (1668, 5 yrs.), 412, 413 (1668, 14 yrs., 2 mos.), 415 (1668, 6 yrs.); *Warwick Rec.*, pp. 253 (165[?], until 21), 265 (1665, 8 yrs.), 273 (1661, 5 yrs.), 289 (1660, 3 yrs., 11 mos.).

[54] Hunterdon, N.J., C.P. and Q.S., lib. 1714–21, f. 58 (1719, until 21), 1721–28, f. 68 (1725, 3 yrs.); Phila. Misc. Co. Court Papers, lib. 1738–67 (1753, 11 yrs.), (1760, 13 yrs., 9 mos., 5 days); Bucks C.P., lib. 1684–1730 (1684, until 21, 7 and 9 yrs. respectively, 2 cases); *Newcastle, Del., Court Rec.*, I, 287, 288 (1679, 12 yrs.); Kent Co., Del., Court Rec., lib. 1699–1703, fols. 28a (1701, two girls, until 18), 32 (1701, boy until 21), 1712–16 (Orphan's Court [1714], two boys to serve until 21, two girls until 18, and one girl until 16).

[55] Douglas, *op. cit.*, p. 41, based upon Records of Indentures of Apprentices, Servants, etc., 1771–73, filed in the Office of the Mayor of Philadelphia.

[56] See Burlington, West Jersey, Court Book, fols. 177, 180 (1700).

Wanted, by the Proprietors of the China Manufactory in Southwark, Several apprentices to the painting branch, a proper person being engaged to instruct them: The advantage resulting to poor people by embracing such an opportunity of bringing up their children creditably, are too obvious to be overlooked.—Wanted Also, several apprentices to the other branches, of equal utility and benefit to children. None will be received under indentures for less than seven years, and will be found during that term in every necessary, befitting apprentices.[57]

In the tobacco provinces boys were generally bound out until twenty-one and girls until sixteen or eighteen, and in most cases the children appear to have been under fourteen.[58] With very few exceptions indentures entered on the court records of North Carolina stipulated service until twenty-one in the case of boys and eighteen in the case of girls. Of thirty-five apprentices indentured by the Craven County court between 1748 and 1799 all except three were bound until majority. Of these thirty-two, twenty-four were under fourteen years of age.[59] Fifteen different trades were represented in the articles of indenture. However, the bulk of the indentures passed upon by the Southern courts appear to have involved paupers and orphans. Other instances of trade-education apprenticeships for somewhat shorter terms are found in the Southern colonies.[60] At Charleston the seven-year term appears to have prevailed

[57] *Pa. J.*, April 16, 1772.

[58] See, e.g., Ann Arundel, lib. 1708-12 (1709, 2 cases). Baltimore, lib. D., 1682-86, 2 cases, lib. 1772-80, 2 cases. Cecil, lib. 1708-16 (1713, 3 cases, 1715); 1746-69, f. 103 (1769); 1770-71, lib. B.Y. No. 1 (1771). Charles, lib. 1704-10 (1704); 1775-78, f. 439 (1775, 2 cases). Prince George, lib. A., 1696-1702, f. 162 (1697). Queen Ann, lib. 1728-30 (1729). Somerset, lib. AW, 1690-91, f. 87vso. (1688); 1690-92, f. 153 (1691); 1692-93, f. 175 (1693); 1740-42, fols. 32 (1740), 98, 99 (1741). Occasionally the 7-year term or even shorter periods were specified in Maryland indentures. *Md. Arch.*, LIII, 462 (1662); Ann Arundel, lib. 1721-22 (1722); Somerset, lib. 1690-92, fols. 39 (1690), 163 (1691).

For apprenticeship until majority in Virginia, see Caroline O.B., 1732-40, Pt. II, fols. 392, 451 (1737), 501 (1738); Lancaster O.B., 1778-83, fols. 15, 21, 22, 31 (1778); York O.B., 1684-87, f. 60 (1685), 1702-6, f. 289 (1705), 1706-10, fols. 242, 243. For other terms ranging from three to eight years, see Augusta O.B., (1758, 1767); Rappahannock, lib. 1656-64, f. 174 (1659); Caroline O.B., 1732-40, f. 282; *WMCQ*, 1st ser., XXVII, 139; York O.B., 1694-97, fols. 71 (1694), 390 (1697).

[59] Craven Co. Court Rec., 1748-79. For other North Carolina indentures until age 21 or, in the case of girls, 16 or 18, see Beaufort, lib. 1756-61 (1759); Bertie, lib. 1724-69 (1759, 1763, girl until 21); Cartaret, lib. 1723-47, f. 9 (1727), lib. 1764-77, f. 44 (1770); Chatham, lib. 1774-79 (1776); Craven, lib. 1730-46, fols. 10, 11 (1731), 58 (1740); Edgecombe, lib. 1764-72 (1767); Granville, lib. 1786-89 (1786); Guilford, lib. 1781-88, f. 75 (1783); Hyde, lib. 1764-97 (1786); Martin, Indentures of Apprenticeship (1774); Onslow, lib. 1734-37, f. 3 (1734), lib. 1765-78, f. 66 (1778); Pasquotank, lib. 1737-55 (1750, 1754), lib. 1765-68, lib. 1777-81, Pt. II, fols. 4, 6 (1777), 8, 17 (1728), 21, 25 (1779); Perquimans, lib. 1698-1706 (1701); Rutherford, lib. 1783 (1783); Tyrell, lib. 1718-1829 (1715, 1782, 1783); N.C. Gen. Court Mins., 1695-1712, fols. 201, 202, 205 (1698).

[60] See *N.C. Col. Rec.*, II, 42 (1713, 5 yrs.); Craven, lib. 1767-75; S.C. Court of Ordinary, 1672-92, f. 123 (1682, 7 yrs.).

in apprenticeships to trades. A South Carolina law of 1740 required all apprentices to serve the full seven-year period even though they had come of age before the expiration of their indentured terms.[61]

A Dutch language indenture of apprenticeship, signed in Albany in 1670, contained an unusual stipulation. An apprentice to the millwright's trade agreed to serve his master two years "on the express condition that the servant may try the first six weeks how he likes it and if he does not like it, he may give up his service and be free and shall then receive for the six weeks' service not more than free fare with a horse from Sprinckvielt[62] to Albany." [63] In the absence of such an express stipulation no trial period was recognized at law for apprentices.

The Master in Loco Parentis. The apprentice came under the discipline of the master and his household.[64] In addition to working in the shop, he had to help the mistress in household chores.

> However things do frame,
> Please well they Master, but chiefly they Dame

was the refrain of the English apprentice, as well suited to colonial life as to conditions in the mother country. By agreeing to obey the master's "Lawful Comaundes" the apprentice recognized the master's right to discipline him. One mother who had bound out her daughter agreed that the new master and mistress "shall be to her as a father and a mother and have the right to properly punish her from wrongdoing and disobedience, giving them full power to do so and trusting them to do all that is good." [65] When Jacob Clarke, the son of a Bristol, Rhode Island, tailor, was apprenticed to William Harris of Providence, the master agreed to instruct the lad "in the Art Trade or Calling of a Planter which hee useth in new England after the best manner he may or Cann, useing resonable Chastisement." [66] Standing in the parent's place, the master customarily obligated himself to find the apprentice "sufficient Meat, Drink, Apparel, Lodging and washing fitting for an Apprentice." [67]

When the master absconded or failed in business and abandoned his apprentice, the courts normally discharged the lad from his indentures. Such complaints were common to sessions in both England and the colonies. Unscrupulous employers would accept considerable sums for

[61] *S.C. Session Laws*, 1740, p. 84; Carl Bridenbaugh, *Cities in the Wilderness* (New York, 1938), pp. 356, 357.

[62] Springfield, Mass.

[63] *Albany Notarial Papers*, pp. 372, 373 (1670).

[64] See *infra*, pp. 461, 462.

[65] *Albany Notarial Papers*, p. 415 (1674).

[66] *Providence Town Rec.*, IV, 132 (1769).

[67] For the enforcement of this provision, see *infra*, pp. 470–483, *passim*, 490, 491, 497.

taking apprentices and then abscond with the money or so ill-treat their apprentices that they were forced to petition the court to annul their articles. If, as a result of the master's abuse, the servant was incited to commit some insubordinate act or to run away, the master would then go into court and ask for cancellation of the indentures without having to return any part of the fee. This evil was particularly widespread in contemporary British towns.[68]

Out of eight petitions for relief on the ground of abandonment brought by apprentices to the Suffolk, Massachusetts, sessions, the court discharged the apprentices in two cases, bound one over to another master plying the same craft, ordered two masters to take their apprentices back, required one master's attorney to keep the apprentice one month, after which he was to be discharged if the master had not returned by then, and dismissed the petition in two cases.[69] The New York court of general sessions entertained twenty-nine such complaints. In every case, with one doubtful exception, the servant was freed from his indentures, even when the master actually appeared in court to answer the summons. In a number of cases the master had left for parts unknown—for Montreal, Boston, or regions beyond the seas; sometimes, as in the case of perukemaker Richman, he was "Reputed to be Broke." These cases constitute a roll-call of craftsmen who did not find success in New York City and were forced by circumstances to try their luck elsewhere.[70] Numerous complaints came up before the Pennsylvania and Delaware justices that masters had not carried out the terms of indentures, sometimes because they had absconded to avoid arrest by creditors,[71] or were confined in gaol,[72] or were forced to bind themselves for a long term to satisfy their debts.[73] Still others charged that the master was ill [74]

---

[68] See Morris, *Sel. Cases, Mayor's Court*, p. 36; George, *London Life*, p. 229. The mayor's court of London, sitting on its equity side, entertained suits by apprentices who had been discharged by their masters before the expiration of their terms and who sought to recover part of the fees. William Bohun, *Privilegia Londoni* (3d ed., London, 1723), p. 295; Daniel v. Chapman, London Mayor's Court Equity Papers, 1700–1701; Burford v. Appleford, Anderton v. Hancock, Stevenson v. Houldith, Jennings v. Chamberlain, *ibid.*, 1701–2; Prouting v. Lawford, Tonis v. Coatsworth, Abingdon v. Peacocke, Banington v. Hanbury, *ibid.*, 1702–3.

[69] Suffolk Sess., lib. 1712–19, fol. 12 (1713), 58 (1714), 120 (1716); lib. II, 1718–20 (Athenaeum), fols. 28, 261 (1719); lib. III, fols. 49, 57 (1720); lib. IV, fols. 329 (1731), 436 (1732).

[70] N.Y.G.S., lib. 1732–62 (1737), (1745), (1751, 3 cases), (1752, 2 cases), (1754), (1755), (1757), (1760), (1761, 3 cases), (1762); lib. 1760–72, (1763, 2 cases), (1764), (1765), (1766), (1769); lib. 1772–89, (1773), (1775, 5 cases), (1776, 3 cases). See also Albany G.S., lib. 1717–23 (Feb. 7, 1722); lib. 1763–82 (Oct. 5, 1763).

[71] Clayton's case, Newcastle Q.S., 1764–65 (May, 1765).

[72] McClean's case, *ibid.* (May, 1764), apprentice discharged; Dawes's case, Philadelphia City Court, lib. 1785–87, fols. 205, 206 (1787), bound to another in same trade.

[73] Longhman's case, Lancaster Road and Sess. Docket, No. 2, 1742–60 (Aug., 1757).

[74] Duncan's case, Kent, lib. 1703–17, f. 12 (1704), apprentice discharged.

or that the deceased master's widow had married a tavernkeeper, thereby providing "a very improper place" to rear an apprentice.[75] The apprentice could also obtain his discharge where he could show that the master was a lunatic.[76]

The Provision for Trade Education. The indentures of apprenticeship obligated the master to employ the apprentice in his trade, generally narrowly construed,[77] and to teach him its "mysteries." In turn the apprentice promised not to reveal his master's trade secrets. Occasionally the court fixed penalties in advance for failure to give such trade instruction.[78] Nevertheless suits for damages brought under this provision of the articles are the exception rather than the rule. In the overwhelming majority of cases the court discharged the apprentice if the master failed to teach him his trade or turned him over to another trade.[79]

[75] Vanhorne's case, Philadelphia Q.S., lib. 1753–60 (1758), apprentice discharged, master to be paid £10. Other Philadelphia Q.S. cases: Lowry's case, lib. 1759–62 (1764); January's case, lib. 1779–82 (1781); petition of Joseph and Thomas Butcher, lib. 1780–85 (1783). See also Waner's case, Philadelphia City Court Papers (July 3, 1770); Mary Nash's petition, Lancaster Road and Sess. Docket, No. 4, 1768–76 (1770); Catherwood's case, Newcastle, Del., Q.S., lib. 1778–93 (1781), no final action recorded.

[76] Wally's case, Bucks Q.S., lib. 1715–39, f. 230 (1741). The tobacco colonies were likewise concerned that abandoned apprentices should not become a charge upon the locality. See, e.g., Elizabeth Lane's case, Ann Arundel, lib. 1720–21, fols. 400, 401 (1721), to be allowed 300 lbs. tobacco for her support and to be entertained or employed by any charitable person in Annapolis. Rather than have the servant become a public charge a Maryland court ordered that she be shipped back to Great Britain at the expense of the county. Ann Arundel, lib. 1721–22 (1722).

[77] Testimony was offered in the Essex quarterly court in 1670 that ivory combmaking and horn combmaking were distinct trades. Perkins v. Cooke, *Essex*, VII, 259–261 (1679). But on the frontier combinations of trades were not infrequently taught. For example, John Steward was bound as an apprentice in Kentucky in 1782 to Michael Humble to learn the art and mystery of the trades of blacksmith and gunsmith "and every other mechanical art, that he the said Michael Humble is acquainted with." Jefferson County Court Rec., *Filson Club Hist. Q.*, III, 134 (1782).

[78] *Conn. Particular Court Rec., 1639–63*, Bk. II, pp. 258, 259 (1662).

[79] This remedy was in accordance with the Statute of Artificers, 5 Eliz. c. 4, which authorized the justices to cancel apprenticeship indentures when the conditions of the agreement as to trade instruction were broken. The Statute required four justices for the canceling, but later acts cut the requirement to two if the indenture was returned at the next session with the reason for canceling. Dunlop, *Amer. Apprenticeship*, p. 173. See also Comm. v. Hemperly, 3 Amer. Law J. (N.S.) 17.

Massachusetts courts seemed reluctant to comply with this practice. See e.g., *Essex*, VIII, 249 (1681); Suffolk G.S., lib. II, 1712–19, fols. 12 (1713), 56 (1714), 120 (1716), 261 (1719); lib. 1718–20 (Athenaeum), f. 28 (1719); lib. III, fols. 49, 57 (1720); lib. IV, fols. 329 (1731), 436 (1732). But cf. *Assistants*, I, 19 (1674); *Essex*, IV, 218 (1670). Connecticut courts at times awarded the apprentice damages: Davis's case, New Haven Co. Court, lib. I, f. 115 (1679), also complaint that extra service was demanded. See also Linch v. Sanford, *Conn. Particular Court Rec.*, p. 202.

In 19 cases in the New York court of general sessions, the court ordered the apprentice to return to his master in only four; in 11 cases he was discharged; in four the judgment is not recorded. N.Y.G.S., lib. 1732–62 (1759); lib. 1760–72 (1766), (1769), (1771, 2 cases), (1772); lib. 1772–89 (1773), (1774, 4 cases), (1775, 2 cases), (1785), (1786), (1787), (1788, 2 cases). See also Trotter's case, Albany G.S., lib. 1763–82 (1765); Mill's case, Dutchess G.S., lib. C,

A favorite complaint was that the master had hired out his apprentice to husbandry despite the obligation in the indentures to teach some such trade as felt- and castor-making or had employed the apprentice in "servile work" instead of in the trade of a turner.[80] At what point was the obligation of the master fulfilled? In a New Haven suit, where it appeared that the master had promised to make his apprentice "a perfect workeman" at the trade of a currier, the employer introduced evidence to show that such a trade could be adequately taught within two years. One witness who controverted the master's evidence pointed out that his father "had a man at the trade four yeares in England, who was insufficient for the trade, though he had constant employmènt, and that he hath heard his father say that there are but few that can dress leather for the good of the country." The court held that it was too "great a hazzard" to let the master train his servant in the short space of two years.[81] Where the master had abandoned his trade, for instance, had turned from carpentry to tavernkeeping,[82] or had died and the mistress's second husband was deemed ill-fitted to instruct others,[83] the courts might properly intervene on behalf of the apprentice. When the Philadelphia sessions learned that Frederick Stillman had failed to

---

1758–66, f. 82 (1765), discharged in both; English's case, Ulster G.S., lib. 1711/12–20 (1719), left "to a private Result of the Justices of the peace in the afternoon." For New Jersey, see Wetherill v. Wills, Burlington Court Book, f. 173 (1699). Cf. also Alcot's complaint, *ibid.*, f. 229 (1705).

The normal procedure in Pennsylvania was to discharge the apprentice or bind him to another trade. Philadelphia Q.S., lib. 1759–62 (Nov., 1763); lib. 1773–80 (1774); lib. 1779–82 (1780), (1781); lib. 1780–85 (Sept., 1781, 2 cases), (June, 1784), (March, 1785). Patten's petition, Philadelphia City Court Papers, *c.*1747. Cf. also Bucks Q.S., lib. 1754–82, f. 104 (1758), 295, 296 (1765), 426 (1770); Chester Q.S., lib. 1742–59, f. 294 (1757); Creigher v. Wilfling, Philadelphia Supreme Court Docket, 1772–76 (Dec. term, 1773). Following the discharge the court might bind the lad over to another master deemed qualified to teach the craft. Scot's case, Philadelphia City Court, lib. 1785–87, fols. 71, 100, 101, 198 (1786, 1787). At times, however, the master was specifically instructed by the court to provide the necessary instruction, to teach the boy the cooper's trade instead of hiring him out to work on a farm, or to have him properly instructed in the coppersmith's business. Field's case, Bucks Q.S., lib. 1715–53 (1753); Harbison's case, Philadelphia Q.S., lib. 1759–64 (1762).

For Maryland cases, see Egerton's petition, Ann Arundel, lib. 1702–4, f. 278 (1704); Butler's case, Prince George, lib. B, 1699–1705, f. 352 (1704); Chamberlain's case, Baltimore, lib. I.S., 1718–21 (Nov., 1718); Davis's case, lib. H.S. No. 7, 1730–32 (March, 1730).

For Virginia: Townsend's case, *Va. Gen. Court Mins.*, p. 117 (1626); Stott's petition, Northumberland O.B., 1699–1713, Pt. ii, fols. 669, 678 (1710). See also Cotton's case, Augusta Co. Rec., Nov. 21, 1768; Mathews's case, *ibid.*, Nov. 29, 1770.

For North Carolina, see Averett's petition, Onslow, lib. 1741–49, f. 43 (1745); Hall's petition, Craven, lib. 1747–56 (1753).

[80] See, e.g., Smith v. Carrington, *Suffolk*, p. 155 (1672); Newman's complaint, Queen Ann, Md., lib. 1709–16, f. 189 (1712). Cf. T. Boyd, *Poor John Fitch* (New York, 1935), pp. 14–27.

[81] This case also involved the question of the assignment of an apprentice and the inducing him to sign articles by false promises. Wheadon v. Meiggs, *New Haven Col. Rec.*, II, 250–253 (1658).

[82] Hough's case, Bucks Q.S., lib. 1754–82, f. 21 (1755).

[83] Harnes' petition, Philadelphia Q.S., lib. 1780–85 (1784).

teach his apprentice the "mystery of a Bisquit Baker" or reading, writing, and ciphering "to the rule of Three," but instead had turned the lad over to his son-in-law for work as a kitchen boy, had neglected to furnish him with necessaries, and "in every respect" had acted "as if the Boy had been a Brute and not a human Creature, often without Shoe or Stocking in the Coldest Weather, locking him in a Cold out House in the Winter Time without Bed Cloaths, only some Straw so that the Boy became lousy," the lad was promptly discharged by the justices from his indentures.[84]

Provision for General Education. In making provisions for rudimentary education for apprentices the colonial indentures generally went considerably beyond the normal educational obligations of English apprenticeship articles, according to which stipulations for the schooling of apprentices were considered exceptional.[85] Beyond the requirement of reading [86] and writing set by some of the English companies, colonial articles of apprenticeship normally bound the master to have the apprentice instructed in ciphering at least "as far as the Rule of three." [87] Schooling was not infrequently provided for in the articles.[88] Seybolt has demonstrated that such provisions were largely responsible for the early development of evening schools in colonial America, as many of the masters were illiterate themselves and incapable of teaching their apprentices even such rudimentary learning. Still others sent their apprentices to evening schools to avoid using valuable working time. In agreeing to furnish one quarter's schooling every year, masters generally specified night schooling.[89] The Philadelphia quarter sessions

[84] Moses' case, Philadelphia Q.S., lib. 1779–82 (1780).

[85] This colonial tradition was recognized in such 19th-century decisions as Comm. v. Penott, Brightly N.P. (Pa.) 189 (1849); Comm. v. Bowen, 5 Phila. (Pa.) 220 (1863), which held that an indenture which does not contain a covenant to give the apprentice a reasonable education is void.

[86] For the enforcement of the reading obligation, see Mary Atkins' case, Suffolk Sess., lib. III, f. 132 (1722).

[87] *M.C.C.*, IV, 309; Taylor's case, Morris, *Sel. Cases, Mayor's Court*, p..188 (1733). In a New York indenture of 1720 the master agreed to provide instruction in "writing and cyphering So far as Addition Subtraction and Multiplication." In some instances the apprentice was to be taught "to Cypher so as to keep his Own accounts," or "so far as he be able to keep his Booke." Seybolt, *op. cit.*, p. 98.

[88] See, e.g., *New Haven Col. Rec.*, I, 30 (1639); *Essex*, II, 135 (1658); *Plymouth Col. Rec.*, I, 36, 37.

[89] See, e.g., the following indentures of apprenticeship in the Hall of Records, New York City: Pl A-304 (1767); A-307 (1749); A-308 (1751); A-309 (1765); A-311 (1754); A-314 (1750); A-317 (1748); A-319 (1759); A-320 (1759); A-321 (1762); A-322 (1750); A-326 (1770); A-328 (1774); A-365 (1765). For provisions of six months' or even three quarters' schooling during the first three years or during the entire term, see Pl A-327 (1768); A-329 (1761); A-364 (1772). Seybolt found 108 indentures which contained provisions for sending apprentices to evening schools. R. F. Seyboldt, "The Evening School in Colonial America," University of Illi-

considered lack of formal schooling sufficient ground for discharge, as is demonstrated in the handling of the complaint against the merchant William Cross for not giving his apprentice even "one Hours Schooling" in the course of two years,[90] or in the case of William Booth, who, according to the court, ought to have been sent to school for nine months.[91]

South of Philadelphia less stress was placed upon general education for apprentices. A Delaware indenture, for example, provided that the master and mistress were "not to learn" the apprentice "further than the Sd servant is cappable to learn." [92] Occasional provisions were inserted to teach the apprentice to write a legible hand as well as a knowledge of arithmetic up to division, or to the rule of three, or merely to read the Bible.[93] Provisions for schooling are exceptional.[94]

Aside from obligations under the articles of apprenticeship, parents and masters in the New England colonies were required by law to see that their children and servants could read and write the English language. For failure to teach their children "to read and understand the principles of religion and the capital lawes of the country," the Massa-

nois, *Bulletin*, XXII, No. 31 (Urbana, 1925) and *Apprenticeship*, ch. vii. See also N.Y. Hist. Soc., *Coll., 1885*, pp. 578, 581, 590, 593, 600; *1909*, pp. 113–115, 118, 122, 130, 132, 135. For evening school provisions in upstate New York indentures, see Ulster Dutch Transcripts, lib. II, fols. 257 (1679), 637 (1682). For the stipulation that the father pay the tuition: *Early Records of the City and County of Albany and Colony of Rensselaerswyck*, III (*Notarial Papers, 1660–1696*), trans. J. Pearson (N.Y. State Library, *Hist. Bull.*, No. 10, Albany, N.Y., 1918), pp. 422 (1674), 524 (1681), 544 (1682), 561 (1683). Master to pay the tuition: *ibid.*, pp. 485 (1680), 530, 532, 547 (1682). Provisions for evening school education are frequent among apprenticeship indentures to Philadelphia craftsmen. In most such cases the master paid for the instruction, but occasionally the apprentice's relatives or friends agreed to pay. See Servants' and Apprentices' Indentures, 1745–46, 1772–73, Hist. Soc. of Pa. For instances of tuition paid for evening schooling for apprentices, 1803–8, by Jacob Sanderson, Salem cabinetmaker, see *Essex Inst. Hist. Coll.*, LXX (1934), 335.

[90] Philadelphia Q.S., lib. 1780–85 (Sept., 1781).

[91] Booth's petition, *ibid.* (March, 1784). A Maryland county court ordered one master to give his apprentice six months' additional schooling or forfeit 5,000 lbs. of tobacco. Granger's case, Queen Ann, lib. 1709–16, f. 195 (1712). The court referred to the "Record in Lib: A folio 22." In 1715 the North Carolina Council reversed a judgment of the Craven precinct court which had set two apprentices at liberty for not being able to read and write. Bell's case, *N.C. Col. Rec.*, II, 172 (1715).

[92] Kent, Md., lib. 1703–17, f. 48 (1705).

[93] Kent, Md., lib. J.S., No. 17, fols. 4 (1731), 35, 45, 46 (1732), 76, 78 (1733), 122 (1734); Somerset, Md., lib. 1740–42, f. 98 (1741); Frederick, Md., lib. 1748–50, f. 394 (1749); Surry, Va., lib. 1684–86, f. 28 (1685); *WMCQ*, 1st ser. IV, 41 (1655); Cartaret, N.C., lib. 1778–89, f. 45 (1783). For the enforcement by the courts of these general educational provisions, see Jernegan, *Laboring and Dependent Classes*, pp. 162–164.

[94] See indentures to teach an apprentice to be a "tight Cooper" and to provide him with one year's schooling, clothing, and the tools of his trade. Somerset, Md., lib. 1740–42, f. 32 (1740). See also L. G. Tyler, "Education in Colonial Virginia," *WMCQ*, 1st ser., V, 220. For provisions for at least two years' schooling in early Tennessee, see Washington County court rec., *Amer. Hist. Mag.*, I, 265 (1783); II, 142 (1789).

chusetts act of 1642 penalized the parents by apprenticing their children to others, boys until twenty-one, girls until eighteen. In order to make certain that the youth of the land were brought up to be God-fearing and law observing, the celebrated Massachusetts act of 1647 made the establishment of schools compulsory for all towns of a certain population.[95] Selectmen were required to go the rounds to see that these provisions were enforced,[96] and towns were presented for failure to carry out these enactments.[97]

The provision in the Duke's Laws, obviously borrowed from the New England codes, requiring the inhabitants to instruct their children and servants "in matters of Religion, and the Lawes of the Country," and parents and masters to bring up their children and apprentices "in some honest Lawfull calling Labour or Employment,"[98] was not implemented by legislation prescribing compulsory education and fixing penalties for noncompliance.[99] In the South the education laws were principally concerned with safeguarding the education of orphans and pauper apprentices. In Virginia an act of 1632 required parents and masters to teach their children and apprentices the catechism.[100] Seventeenth-century laws merely provided for trade education for orphans and pauper apprentices,[101] and it was not until 1705 that book education was specifically prescribed.[102] However, the labor code of 1748 was

[95] *Laws and Liberties, 1648*, pp. 11, 47; *Mass. Col. Laws, 1660–72*, pp. 136, 190, 191; *Mass. Charter and General Laws*, pp. 186, 187, 245; *Mass. Acts and Resolves*, II, 756 (1735), children not able to distinguish the alphabet at the age of six were to be bound out; IV, 179 (1758), servants and apprentices not taught reading, writing, and ciphering could be freed; but if under twenty-one for males and eighteen for females, could be bound out by the court to other masters. Cf. also Scant's case, *Suffolk Court*, p. 599 (1675); *Conn. Pub. Rec.*, I, 520–521 (1650); *1689–1706*, pp. 30, 31 (1690); *New Haven Col. Rec., 1653–65*, pp. 583–584 (1655); Brigham, *Compact and Charter of New Plymouth*, pp. 270–271 (1671). Rhode Island was the exception to the New England system of compulsory education. See also Jernegan, *op. cit.*, pp. 69–128.

[96] *Watertown Rec.*, I, 102–105, 107, *passim*.

[97] See, e.g., *Essex*, V, 378 (1674); and cf. *ibid.*, p. 427 (1674). There were numerous prosecutions of Massachusetts towns for violations of these laws in the eighteenth century. See also Jernegan, *op. cit.*, p. 127.

[98] *N.Y. Col. Laws*, I, 26.

[99] The New York mayor's court in 1681 authorized the church deacons to bind out John White's children and left "it to the sd Deacons to make Such terms and Conditions for them as they shall thinke fitt." N.Y.M.C.M., 1677–82, f. 263a (1681). In New York City the common council in 1736 required that parish children bound out "be religiously educated and taught to read, write, and cast accounts." M.C.C., IV, 309. The important post-Revolutionary statute of 1788 provided that poor children bound out be instructed to read and write. *Laws of N.Y., 11th Sess.*, 1788, 130. Seybolt maintains that in actual practice the New York apprentice received an education equal to that of the New Englander. *Op. cit.*, p. 92. See also *New Conductor Generalis* (Albany, 1819), p. 30.

[100] Hening, I, 290. An act of 1646 made delinquents subject to a penalty of 500 lbs. of tobacco for the use of the parish "unless sufficient cause be shewn to the contrary." *Ibid.*, pp. 311–312.

[101] *Ibid.*, I, 260–261 (1643), relating to orphans; 416 (1656).

[102] *Ibid.*, III, 375.

more general in scope and made provision for orphan apprentices to be taught "to read and write." [103]

Wages or Other Forms of Compensation. Traditionally apprentices received no wages. At common law the master was entitled to all the earnings of the apprentice, either in his own service or in the employment of another.[104] However, in the colonies monetary payments to an apprentice are occasionally found. As early as 1632 Joshua Barnes of Massachusetts agreed to pay his apprentice annual wages of £4 and an additional £5 at the end of his term.[105] Andrew Burn, New York cabinet- and chairmaker, covenanted to pay John Vernon four shillings daily for every day he should work during the last year of his apprenticeship,[106] and Franklin's apprenticeship terms granted him journeyman's wages during the last year of his term.[107] Somewhat more frequent was the practice of giving the apprentice a sum of money at the end of his term. This sum might range from £4 to £20 or more.[108] A Virginia law of 1705 provided that at the expiration of the term of a poor orphan apprentice the master should "pay and allow him in like manner as is appointed for servants by indenture or custom." [109] In 1727 this provision was made applicable to other poor children bound

---

[103] *Ibid.*, V, 450–452. The legal requirement for inserting in the indentures a provision for book education was fairly generally observed in orphan and pauper apprenticeships. A study of parish indentures of apprenticeships of orphans, poor children, illegitimate children, and mulattos for the eighteenth century reveals that in at least twenty-five per cent of the cases no educational requirement was included. Only three out of 163 required ciphering in addition to reading and writing. Jernegan, *op. cit.*, p. 167. The Petsworth Parish vestry book ordered in 1724 that "all Orphant children, bound out by the Parish hereafter, that if they cannot Read at thirteen years old that they shall be set free from theire sd Mastrs and Missrs or be taken from them." *WMCQ*, 1st ser., V, 219, 220. See also Rachel v. Emerson, 45 Ky. 280 (1845), interpreting the state statute of 1843 relieving masters of the duty of teaching free Negro apprentices to read and spell.

[104] J. Chitty, *Treatise on the Law of Apprenticeship* (London, 1812), p. 67; cf. Austin, *Law of Apprenticeship*, p. 61. See also Dunlop, *op. cit.*, pp. 177, 178. It was not material that the wages were earned without the consent of the master or in another trade. Reeve, *op. cit.*, p. 343.

[105] *Assistants*, II, 26 (1632). See also *Albany Notarial Papers*, pp. 372, 373 (1670), 524 (1681).

[106] An unusually generous treatment of an apprentice was provided for in the indenture of Salomon Morache to Isaac Hays, merchant (1749), by the terms of which he was to receive £3 New York money at the end of the second year; £5 the third year; £7 the fourth year, and £12 the last year, as well as a consignment of merchandise on the master's account if he shipped to the West Indies at the end of his term. Pl A-307 (1749). See also indenture between Michael Hawkins, aged 19, and Abraham Rapley, to learn coach- and chairmaking. He was to receive £20 for the first year and £8 6s. 8d. for the remaining four months he was bound to serve, the latter sum to be paid in four payments (1796), Easthampton Free Library.

[107] *Autobiography* (Philadelphia, 1895), p. 36. Cf. *Moravian Rec.*, III, 1083 (1776).

[108] *Essex*, I, 113 (1647); III, 362 (1664); *Plymouth Col. Rec.*, VI, 25 (1679); *Conn. Particular Court Rec., 1639–63*, Bk. II, p. 81 (1650); N.Y. Hist. Soc., *Coll., 1885*, p. 622 (1707); Pl A-364 (1772), Hall of Records, New York City; Flatlands Town Rec., Misc., 1661–1831, f. 211 (1681); Burlington, West Jersey, Court Book, f. 245 (1707).

[109] Hening, II, 375.

out.[110] While monetary compensation was exceptional, the provision that the apprentice be given two suitable suits of clothing, one for working days and one for holidays, at the expiration of his term was universally applied.[111] During their term of service apprentices and servants were expected to wear apparel not "exceeding the quality and condition of their Persons or Estate." [112] The phraseology of the Massachusetts law was an amplification of an earlier act forbidding "men or women of mean condition" from dressing themselves in "the garb of Gentlemen by wearing gold or silver lace, or buttons, or points at their knees, or to walk in great boots, or women of the same ranke, to wear silk or tyffany hoods, or scarfes." [113] These regulations were in accord with contemporary English rules suppressing with an iron hand extravagance in dress and personal adornment of apprentices.[114]

Apprenticeship of Poor Children. Apprenticeship was not only a method of trade education; it was also an institution utilized by the community for the welfare of poor children, orphans, and illegitimate offspring. Just as trade apprenticeship as a national system rested upon the Statute of Artificers, so the system of apprenticeship of poor children was determined by the English Poor Law of 1601,[115] which authorized the overseers of the poor of the parish to bind out to apprenticeship "the children of all such whose parents shall not . . . be thought able to keep and maintain their children," boys until twenty-four, girls until twenty-one or marriage, "the same to be as effectual to all purposes, as if such child were of full age, and by indenture of covenant bound him or her self." Parish apprenticeship, then, differed from ordinary trade apprenticeship in its longer term of servitude and its compulsory character.[116] Parish apprentices ordinarily came from a lower social class than trade apprentices and were less likely to be

---

[110] *Ibid.*, IV, 212. For the freedom dues of indentured servants, see *infra*, pp. 393 ff. For other payments to parish apprentices, see Wells, *Parish Education in Colonial Virginia*, pp. 88, 89.

[111] "One new suit, convenient for publick occasions, the other suit convenient for common wear and service." Robbins Family Papers, Middlesex County, Mass., MSS (1774), N.Y. Pub. Lib. At times more elaborate outfits were provided, including shirts, shoes, stockings, and a hat. See N.Y. Hist. Soc., *Coll., 1909*, p. 115 (1718); *Albany Notarial Papers*, p. 211 (1663)—provision for an *innocent*—or Dutch dressing gown; *Providence Town Rec.*, IX, 12–13 (1716).

[112] See *Mass. Col. Laws, 1660–72*, pp. 220, 221 (1662).

[113] *Ibid.*, p. 123 (1651).   [114] See Dunlop, *op. cit.*, pp. 190–193.   [115] 43 Eliz., c. 2 (1601).

[116] See Sidney and Beatrice Webb, *English Local Government: English Poor Law History: Pt. I: The Old Poor Law* (London, 1927), I, 200, 201; J. F. Scott, *Historical Essays on Apprenticeship and Vocational Education* (Ann Arbor, 1914), pp. 62, 63; M. D. George, *London Life in the 18th Cent.*, pp. 215–225; E. Lipson, *The Economic History of England* (London, 1920, 1931), I, 435. For the activities of the English quarter sessions in the supervision of poor relief, see Eleanor Trotter, *Seventeenth Century Life in the Country Parish* (Cambridge, 1919), p. 51; J. D. Chambers, *Nottinghamshire in the Eighteenth Century* (London, 1932), p. 227.

received in their master's household as members of his family. As an educational device the English poor law apprenticeship system was rather ineffective. Its failure to provide adequate instruction in the trades led to the establishment in the eighteenth century of workhouses and charity schools.[117] It was less a system of apprenticeship than a system of compulsory support and guardianship under public supervision, in which parish funds were used to compensate masters in part for taking young children during their unproductive years.

The system of pauper apprenticeship was literally transplanted from the mother country, for in 1619 the city of London sent out to Virginia one hundred homeless London children to serve as apprentices in the colony. The Virginia Company was so gratified with the results that it petitioned the mayor and aldermen to send another hundred in the spring of 1620. The company specified that the children were to be twelve years old or above and were to be apprenticed for minimum terms of seven years, boys until twenty-one, girls until twenty-one or marriage,[118] and "brought vpp in some good Craftes, Trades, or Husbandry," upon completion of which they were to be placed as tenants on the land to work for shares.[119]

The binding out of children as a method of poor relief and guardianship was universally established by colonial legislation and local ordinances, and carried out by town officials or the vestry under the supervision of the courts. Three classes of children were customarily bound out in this way: 1) poor children;[120] 2) orphans, in some cases with property; and 3) illegitimate children.[121]

---

[117] See Dunlop, *op. cit.*, p. 249. That author makes the point that "apprenticeship in the usual sense of the term was not an essential part" of this contract. *Ibid.*, p. 251.

[118] Children coming over on the first shipment were apprenticed until twenty-four.

[119] *Records of the Virginia Company of London: the Court Book*, ed. by Susan M. Kingsbury (Washington, 1906), I, 270–271, 304–307.

[120] In 1725 John Boreman sued Luke Gibbins "for absenting himself," alleging that defendant had been bound as an apprentice by the selectmen of Boston. Defendant pleaded in abatement. Plaintiff was then permitted to amend his writ, and issue was joined on the question of whether defendant's family were actually in such want as would justify the Boston selectmen in binding out the lad. The jury upheld the indentures on the ground that the lad's parents, having failed to provide for him, had exposed him "to Want and Extremity." New London, Conn., County Court Rec., lib. XIV, f. 284 (1725).

[121] For New England, see, e.g., *Essex*, V, 103 (1672); *Mass. Acts and Resolves*, I, 538 (1704); II, 182 (1721), 579, 580 (1731), 1067 (1742); V, 161, 325; *Acts and Laws of New Hampshire*, I, 136 (1719); IV, 16, 17 (1776); *R.I. Col. Rec.*, V, 40 (1741), 378 (1753). See also *Plymouth Col. Rec.*, II, 112, 113 (1647); *Boston Town Rec.*, VII, 67 (1672); *Suffolk Court*, p. 599 (1675); petition of Esther Harrison, Suffolk G.S., III, f. 133 (1722); *Essex Inst. Hist. Coll.*, II (1860), 90 (1757), Ezra Very bound out by overseers of Danvers for 16 yrs., 3 mos., and 16 days to learn trade of a wheelwright; indenture of John Wing, Falmouth Hist. Soc. (1807). When the overseers of the poor of Boston placed a pauper girl with a family in Plymouth, the selectmen of the latter town certified that the master was "a Man of sober Life and Conversation and in such

Female Apprenticeship. The colonial child-labor system included girls as well as boys in its program. Female children were generally bound until sixteen or eighteen or until marriage.[122] Orphan girls were usually apprenticed to receive instruction in plain sewing and "housewifery," and reading and writing. However, certain limitations were placed upon the general educational requirements for female apprentices. A Massachusetts act of 1710, modifying a previous law which

Circumstances that we can recommend him as a fit Person to bind an apprentice to." Indenture of Bassano Shaw (1718), Plymouth County Courthouse. See also *Maine Province and Court Rec.,* I, 177 (1651), II, 4, 5 (1655), 422 (1671); New Hampshire G.S., 1692–1704, f. 53 (1697); *Warwick, R.I., Rec.,* p. 317 (1666); *Providence Town Rec.,* III, 30 (1662), 120 (1667), X, 28–31 (1695), 35 (1696), 53–54 (1700); New Haven County Court Rec., III, 1713–39, f. 6 (1713), term of 20 yrs., 9 mos.; indentures of Cook (1767), Champon (1774), and Crossman (1775), New London Apprenticeship Bundles, Conn. State Library. See also Reeve, *op. cit.,* p. 343.

In New Amsterdam the orphanmasters occasionally bound out children. *Minutes of the Orphanmasters,* I, 13. The conclusion of A. E. Peterson (*New York as an Eighteenth Century Municipality,* p. 23) that "we are glad to find no records to indicate that this practice (i.e., binding out of paupers) prevailed in New York" is contrary to fact. Cf. D. M. Schneider, *The History of Public Welfare in New York State, 1609–1866* (Chicago, 1938), pp. 76, 77. See also *R.N.A.,* VI, 288, 289 (1671); *M.C.C.,* I, 348 (1694); Morris, *Sel. Cases, Mayor's Court,* pp. 184–188 (1714, 1715, 1730, 1731, 1733); Stokes, *Iconography,* IV, 470 (1710), regarding the apprenticeship of the orphan children of the Palatine immigrants and *ibid.,* IV, 620 (1750); Westchester Sessions, Westchester Co. Hist. Soc., *Coll.,* II, 42 (1687); Kingston Sess., lib. 1737–50 (Sept. 16, 1746); *Huntington Rec.,* II, 518 (1772), 534 (1774); *Southampton Town Rec.,* III, 316 (1787), 322 (1788), 332 (1790), V, 67 (1794). In virtually the same status as a pauper orphan was Joseph Johnson, a six-year old lad whose father, a convicted felon, had "fled from Justice." He was apprenticed to William Bradford, the printer. N.Y.Q.S., lib. 1732–61, f. 5 (1735). For the Pennsylvania statutes, see *Pa. Stat. at Large,* II, 253 (1706). See also for the Middle colonies, Hunterdon, N.J., C.P. and Q.S., lib. 1729–33, f. 254 (1731); Monmouth C.P. and Q.S., lib. 1688–1721, fols. 317 (1712), 322 (1713), 372 (1716); *Newcastle, Del., Court Rec.,* I, 32 (1676); Kent Co., Del., Court Rec., lib. 1703–17, f. 3 (1703); *ibid.,* 1712–16 (1714).

For Virginia, see Hening, I, 336 (1646), II, 168 (1662), VI, 32 (1748), VIII, 374–377. On the basis of an examination of vestry books of 27 Virginia parishes one investigator concludes that an inconsiderable number of poor children were apprenticed, although in many cases it is likely that the wardens apprenticed the children without intervention of the vestry and the indentures were not preserved or recorded. Wells, *op. cit.,* pp. 74, 75, 77, 78, 86–89. Cf. Jernegan, *op. cit.,* pp. 143–152; *WMCQ,* 1st ser., V, 219, 220. For supervision by the courts in Virginia, see Middlesex O.B., 1673–80, f. 3 (1673); Fairfax O.B., 1772–74, fols. 83, 90; Jefferson Co., Ky., Court Rec., *Filson Club Hist. Q.,* III, 61 (1781). For Maryland, see Somerset, 1754–57, f. 144 (1756). Cf. also *supra,* p. 15n.

For the management of the orphan house in Georgia, see *S.C. Gazette,* July 4, 1743 (Supp.).

In Pennsylvania, Maryland, Virginia, and North Carolina the binding out of illegitimate children was normal procedure. See Bucks, Pa., C.P. and Q.S., lib. 1648–1730 (1727); Lancaster, Pa., Road and Sess. Docket, No. 3, 1760–68 (1770); Queen Ann, Md., lib. 1709–16 (1715); lib. 1728–30 (1728). *Bristol Co., Va., Vestry Book,* pp. 2, 6, 36; Cumberland, Va., lib. 1774–79, f. 68 (1775); York, lib. 1706–10, f. 19 (1706). North Carolina: Bertie, lib. 1767–72 (1770); Bute, lib. 1767–76, fols. 109, 136, 172, 177; lib. 1774–78, f. 50; Caswell, lib. 1770–80 (1777); lib. 1777–81 (1779); Cumberland, lib. 1777–78, f. 75; Edgecombe, lib. 1772–76 (1774), (1775); lib. 1778–84 (1779), (1783); Gates, lib. 1779–84, f. 28 (1780); Guilford, lib. 1781–88 (1782); Nash, lib. 1779–85, f. 13 (1779); Tryon, lib. 1769–79 (1774).

122 Douglas, *op. cit.,* pp. 48, 49, states, on the basis of an examination of Philadelphia apprenticeships, that they generally served longer terms than men.

specified that girls as well as boys were to be taught to read and write, provided that henceforth girls were to be taught merely to read "as they respectively may be capable." [123] This law was in force throughout the remainder of the colonial period. On the other hand, in Virginia after 1751 orphan girl apprentices were to be taught reading and writing, a provision which was extended in 1769 to the indentures of illegitimate children of both sexes.[124]

Somewhat less emphasis was placed on education in the trades in girls' indentures than in boys'. In England, spinning, cleaning, and carding were traditionally performed by women and children. In America, instruction in spinning was frequently provided for in girls' indentures, but weaving also seemed to be a not uncommon occupation of colonial women.[125] In addition to these normal occupations for women, the indentures generally provided for instruction in "Sewing, Knitting or any other manner of housewifery." [126] Girls were also apprenticed to such trades as dress, stay, and mantua-making, millinery, laundering, dyeing, glazing, pastry cooking, and confectionery.[127] Occasionally, too, women were engaged in less traditionally feminine occupations, such as the trades of butchers, upholsterers, silversmiths, tanners and leatherdressers, gunsmiths, and operators of blacksmith shops, fulling mills, tanyards, and shipyards. But the overwhelming majority of such instances are those of widows who took over their husbands' establishments, and it is doubtful whether girls were ever accepted as apprentices in such fields.[128]

[123] *Mass. Acts and Resolves*, I, 654 (1710); *Acts and Laws, 1788*, ch. lxi; *Public Laws of R.I.* (1798), p. 351 § 4; Seybolt, *op. cit.*, pp. 47, 61, 93. At times no provision for general education was made. See York, Va., O.B., 1687–91, f. 515 (1690); *Plymouth Col. Rec.*, II, 38 (1642).

[124] See Mary S. Benson, *Women in Eighteenth-Century America* (New York, 1935), pp. 224, 225.

[125] Edith Abbott, *Women in Industry* (New York, 1924), pp. 28, 29.

[126] N.Y. Hist. Soc., *Coll., 1885*, p. 578 (1698).

[127] This is a wider field than in modern times, where apprenticeships of girls seem to have been confined chiefly to dressmaking and millinery shops. See "Sex and Industry," Mass. Bureau of Labor, *Bull., 1903*, p. 210.

[128] See, e.g., *Plymouth Col. Rec.*, II, 67 (1644); N.Y. Hist. Soc., *Coll., 1885*, pp. 582 (1699), 590 (1700), 598 (1702), *1909*, pp. 120 (1718), 130 (1720), where a girl, a "sempster," is apprenticed to a painter (apparently she was to learn her trade elsewhere), 141 (1721), 158 (1723), 167 (1724), 179, 180 (1725); *S.C. Gazette*, Nov. 12, 1739, Aug. 23, 1742, Dec. 14, 1747, Sept. 26, Nov. 10, 1766, Aug. 29, 1769; *Pa. J.*, May 17, 1775; *Mass. Centinel*, June 29, 1785; Albany, N.Y., G.S., lib. 1763–82 (1773), where a boy was apprenticed to a widow, Mary Hugar, "to learn the Art and Mystery of a Blacksmith while she continues to Keep up said Business of a Smith and during the term of his Indenture." See also Abbott, *op. cit.*, pp. 13–171; Spruill, *Women's Life and Work in the Southern Colonies*, pp. 284–291; R. B. Morris, *Studies in the History of American Law*, pp. 173–184, for the contractual capacity of married women in colonial law; Morris, ed., *Sel. Cases, Mayor's Court*, pp. 21–26.

Apprenticeship of Negroes and Indians. Both Indians and Negroes were often apprenticed to agriculture and the trades in New England and New York. To make sure, as one petitioner to the Essex quarterly court put it, that "an Indian may have the same distribution of Justice with our selves," [129] a number of the colonies required that a justice of the peace give his consent in order validly to bind an Indian apprentice.[130] In effect, however, a good deal of discrimination existed, and Indian and Negro minors were often in the same category at law as orphans and pauper children, and were not infrequently bound out to very long terms as apprentices, sometimes until twenty-four or even thirty-one years of age, and without reference to the parents' ability to support them.[131]

Apprenticeship often served as a step toward freedom for the Negro. On the Southern plantations masters at times put out their trained Negroes as "apprentices" to master tradesmen, not infrequently allowing them to retain a portion of their hire. By saving the fraction of the wages allotted them, many slaves were enabled to purchase their freedom. Free Negroes were frequently apprenticed by their parents or by the county justices. Apprenticeship was an important factor in the economic life of the free Negro in the ante-bellum South.[132] In the

[129] *Essex,* II, 240 (1660).

[130] *Mass. Acts and Resolves,* I, 436 (1701); II, 104 (1718), 364 (1725). Cf. Hening, I, 410 (1655); *Laws of the State of New York,* 11th Sess., 1788, c. xiii. For the insistence that the Indian apprentice's father agree, see *Essex,* III, 366 (1666).

[131] *Boston Town Rec.,* VIII, 173, 174 (1723); *Boston Gazette or Weekly Advertiser,* Feb. 12, 19, 26; March 5, 1754; *Boston Gazette and County J.,* Sept. 14, 1767; *Portsmouth, R.I. Rec.,* pp. 430–433 (1678); Conn. Apprenticeship Bundles, Conn. State Lib. (1766); New London Apprenticeship Indentures, 3 bundles, *loc. cit.;* N.Y. Hist. Soc., *Coll., 1885,* pp. 581 (1699, 7 yrs.), 601 (1702, 18 yrs.); *Southold Rec.,* I, 154 (1665, until 21); Burlington, West Jersey, Court Book, f. 151 (1697, 8 yrs.); L. J. Greene, *The Negro in Colonial New England, 1620–1776* (New York, 1942). In the Southern colonies a mulatto, born of a white mother, was bound out in the same manner as an illegitimate child born of a free white woman. The length of service until 30 yrs. of age in the case of mulattos under the Virginia act of 1705 was reduced to 21 in the case of males and 18 in the case of females by the act of 1765. Hening, III, 86–87 (1691), 457 (1705); VI, 361 (1753); VIII, 133–134 (1765), 450 (1769). For Maryland, cf. *Md. Arch.,* I, 534 (until age 30). For binding out of mulattos by the courts until 31, see Charles, Md., lib. Q, No. 2, fols. 518, 520; Somerset, Md., lib. 1752–54, fols. 205–206, lib. 1767–70, f. 335; Accomac, Va., O.B., lib. 1777–80, f. 41 (1777); Craven, N.C., lib. 1765–75 (1767, freeborn Negress). See also J. M. Wright, *The Free Negro in Maryland* (New York, 1921), pp. 28, 29, and cases cited.

[132] See *The Negro in Virginia,* comp. by the Writers' Program, Works Projects Administration, State of Virginia (New York, 1940), pp. 34, 35; J. M. Wright, *op. cit.,* pp. 34, 35; J. H. Franklin, *The Free Negro in North Carolina, 1790–1860* (Chapel Hill, 1943), Appendix, p. 227, for the number of free Negro apprentices by counties in 1860. For instances of Negro apprenticeships to trades in the ante-bellum South, see Helen T. Catterall, *Judicial Cases Concerning American Slavery and the Negro,* II (Washington, D.C., 1929), 309, 324, 407, 427, 435–436; also Phælon v. M'Bride, 1 Bay (S.C.) 170 (1791). Indentures frequently specified that the Negro apprentice was to be taught to read and write. The North Carolina law of 1762 made this compulsory, but the master was relieved of that obligation in 1838. Franklin, *op. cit.,* p. 130.

Northern states apprenticeship for the Negro became a transitional stage to complete emancipation at law.[133]

[133] See, e.g., *Laws of Pa.*, March Sess., 1780, c. 146; E. R. Turner, *The Negro in Pennsylvania, 1639–1861* (Washington, D.C., 1911), pp. 78, 92, 106; P. H. Douglas, *op. cit.*, p. 21; H. S. Cooley, *A Study of Slavery in New Jersey* (Baltimore, 1896), pp. 28–31; N. D. Harris, *The History of Negro Servitude in Illinois*, pp. 6–103. For a parallel development in the British West Indies and Cuba, see R. L. Schuyler, *Parliament and the British Empire* (New York, 1929), ch. iv (Abolition Act of 1834); W. Bevan, *Operation of the Apprenticeship System of the British Colonies* (London, 1838), pp. 35 *et seq.*; L. J. Ragatz, *A Guide for the Study of British Caribbean History, 1763–1834* (Washington, 1932), pp. 41, 465, 515, 544, *passim;* Williams, *Capitalism and Slavery*, pp. 158, 159; H. H. S. Aimes, "Transition from Slave to Free Labor in Cuba," *Yale Review*, XV, 68–84. Despite the provision of the Northwest Ordinance of 1787 prohibiting slavery and involuntary servitude, slaves were brought into the Indiana Territory and registered as indentured servants. The long-term indentures to which the Negroes agreed were a transparent subterfuge. See F. S. Philbrick, ed., "The Laws of the Indiana Territory, 1801–1809," Ill. State Hist. Lib., *Coll.*, XXI (*Law Series*, II) (Springfield, Ill., 1930), pp. cxxxviii–cxli.

IX. THE LEGAL STATUS OF SERVITUDE

TERMS AND CONDITIONS OF EMPLOYMENT

ERM OF SERVICE. Unlike the slave the indentured servant was bound to labor for his master merely for the period of time expressly stated in his contract or, in the absence of a formal contract, as laid down by custom or statute. At the expiration of his service he was a free man.[1] The term of service of bound servants ranged, in the case of adults, from one to seven years or more, although the bulk of such indentures averaged from three to five years.[2] A Massachusetts order of 1631 forbade the hiring of any person as a servant for less than a year "unless hee be a settled housekeeper." [3] In the seventeenth century the colony fined masters for freeing servants before the end of their terms or for selling them their time. The government doubtless wished to prevent unemployed workmen from becoming public charges.[4]

Servants coming to the colonies without indentures were bound according to the custom of the country. In the tobacco provinces legislation provided in substance, despite variations and modifications, that servants twenty years of age or over were to serve four years, those between sixteen and twenty from six to eight years, and those under sixteen, usually, until they reached twenty-one.[5] Under these statutes very considerable numbers of servants were brought before the courts

[1] See Hurd, *Law of Freedom and Bondage*, I, 220.

[2] In the indentures registered before the Philadelphia mayors for the two years, 1745, 1746, 707 out of a total of 1,904 indentures recorded were for four years, 211 for five years, and a scattering remnant from two years up to nineteen years. See "Register before James Hamilton, Mayor," *Pa. Mag. of Hist. and Biog.*, XXXII, 358; "Record of Indentures before Mayors," Pa. German Society, *Publications* (Lancaster, 1907); Herrick, *op. cit.*, pp. 200, 201.

[3] *Assistants*, II, 15 (1631). For examples of one-year indentures, see Ulster Dutch Transcripts, II, f. 303 (1666); II, f. 432 (1679); III, f. 9 (1683). Typical terms of service of six years or more: Lechford, *Note-Book*, p. 93 (1639); *Plymouth Col. Rec.*, II, 69 (1644); *Essex*, I, 381, 382 (1655), II, 293 (1661); Israel Fearing's Book, cited by Bliss, *Buzzard's Bay*, pp. 71, 72 (1729); Essex, Va., O.B., 1695–99, fols. 248, 269 (1699); Henrico, Va., O.B., I, f. 337 (1685); Surry, Va., O.B., 1645–72, f. 282 (1664).

[4] See *Assistants*, II, 84, 88 (1639), 100 (1640), 105 (1641), 106 (1641), 135 (1643).

[5] Pennsylvania. Those over 17, 5 yrs.; under 17, until 22. *Duke of York's Book of Laws*, p. 153. Minors, male until 21; female until 18. *Pa. Stat. at Large*, VII, 361–363 (1770).

Maryland. *Md. Arch.*, I, 80 (1639), 352, 353 (1654), 409, 433-434, 453-454 (1661). The act of 1666 provided service of five years for those over 22. By the act of 1704 servants between 15 and 18 were to serve 7 yrs.; between 18 and 22, 6 yrs., and under 15 until 22. *Ibid.*, II, 147 (1666), 335 (1671); XXVI, 254 (1704).

Virginia. 1643: over 20, 4 yrs.; between 12 and 20, 5 yrs., under 12, 7 yrs., Hening, I, 257. 1653: above 16, 4 yrs.; under 15 until 21, *ibid.*, p. 257. 1662: above 16, 5 yrs.; under 16, until 25, *ibid.*, II, 113. 1666: under 19, until 24; 19 or above, 5 yrs., *ibid.*, II, 240. Similarly in 1705 and 1745: *ibid.*, III, 447, V, 457, VI, 357-369 (1753). For a brief period Virginia discriminated against Irish servants and other aliens who were required to serve somewhat longer terms.

to have their ages adjudged and the length of service determined.[6] In this way their service was made a matter of record. The Virginia labor code of 1705 provided that, where a servant had been sold by the custom but pretended to have indentures, he was to be allowed two months in which to produce the articles, failing which he was to be permanently estopped from making any claim under such a covenant.[7]

A study of this important activity of the colonial court discloses the relative youthfulness of the typical emigrant servant. Of the 392 servants in Virginia whose ages were given in the census of 1624–25, the average age was twenty-three. Only thirteen were forty or over, and 154 were under twenty-one.[8] An examination of the county court records reveals that the overwhelming majority of emigrant servants coming in without indentures were adjudged to be under nineteen. The average age was between fourteen and sixteen and the average terms assigned by the courts ran from six to eight years. Some servants coming to the colonies were as young as six years.[9] Whether or not county justices were as

Hening, I, 411 (1655), 471 (1658). As this served to discourage emigration, it was soon repealed. *Ibid.*, pp. 538, 539 (1660).

South Carolina. 1687: under 10, until 21; between 10 and 15, 7 yrs.; above 15, 5 yrs., *S.C. Stat.*, II, 30. 1698: 12 to 14, until 21; 14 to 16, 7 yrs.; above 16, 5 yrs., *ibid.*, p. 153. Repealed, 1700, p. 165. The original of the act of 1683 listed by title in Trott's *Laws of S.C.*, pp. 1–3, has not been located.

Barbados. 1661: under 18, 7 yrs.; above 18, 5 yrs. Hall, *Acts of Barbados* (London, 1764), No. 30, cl. xiv.

Jamaica. 1681: under 18, 7 yrs.; above 18, 4 yrs. Baskett, *Acts of Jamaica* (London, 1738), pp. 2–5.

Antigua. 1716: under 17, until 21; 7 yrs. maximum term for indentured servant; without indenture and age certificate from JP, 4 yrs. *Laws of the Island of Antigua* (London, 1805), I, 184; Baskett, *Acts of Charibee Leeward Islands, 1690–1730* (London, 1734), p. 160.

[6] The Virginia General Court freed a servant because his age had not been adjudged in court. *Va. Gen. Court Mins.*, p. 385 (1674). Eighteenth century statutes did not go that far, but provided that the servant be brought into court within six months after his arrival or else be required to serve no longer than five years. Hening, III, 447 (1705); V, 547 (1748); VI, 357–369 (1753). Under Maryland law a master failing to bring his servant into court within three months after arrival was to lose a year of the servant's term. *Md. Arch.*, I, 443 (1662). A penalty of 1,000 lbs. of tobacco was fixed in the act of 1666. *Ibid.*, II, 147.

[7] Hening, III, 447 (1705).

[8] See J. C. Hotten, *The Original Lists of Persons of Quality: Emigrants; Religious Exiles; Political Rebels; Serving Men Sold for a Term of Years; Apprentices, etc., Who Went from Great Britain to the American Plantations, 1600–1700* . . . (London, 1874), pp. 201–265; Bruce, *Econ. Hist. of Va.*, I, 600, 601. See also *Va. Gen. Court Mins.*, p. 430 (1676).

[9] Typical instances follow:

New Jersey. Burlington, West Jersey, Court Book, fols. 56 (1686, age 12), 172 (1699).

Pennsylvania. Pennypacker, *Pa. Col. Cases*, p. 115 (1686, age 26); *Chester Co. Court Rec., 1681–97*, pp. 300, 355, 361, 374, 393 (1693–1696), average age 14; Bucks C.P., lib. 1684–1730, f. 341 (1699), age 10.

Delaware. Kent Co. Court, lib. 1697–98, fols. 13a, 18a, 32a; 1699–1703, fols. 1, 4a, 14a, 21, 24, average age 14.

Maryland. In 249 cases studied in the *Md. Arch.*, LIII, LIV, only 10 servants were adjudged 21 yrs. of age or over; 51 were under 15; 12 were under 10, and the remainder between the ages

acute as modern railroad conductors in judging children's ages must remain a matter of speculation. The economic and social interests of the justices might well have subjectively influenced them at times to adjudge such youngsters somewhat below their true ages in order to provide longer terms for their fellow planters, just as the conductor, identifying his interest with his company, might be at times impelled to regard a child as older than he or his parent says he is. The Virginia Assembly in 1666 frankly admitted that it was "Sensible that no infallible Judgement of Age can be given." [10] Those coming in without indentures, especially by the eve of the Revolution, were somewhat more mature. The average age of bound labor coming to Maryland or Virginia between 1773 and 1776 from Great Britain was the early or middle twenties. Relatively few redemptioners as young as fourteen or fifteen are found in the passenger lists for this period; the few in their late forties were generally skilled workers.[11]

Child labor was as basic to the colonial labor system as it was to the industrial system of contemporary England. The children of the Palatines who had been shipped to New York to manufacture naval stores were expected by the authorities to help the adults in the project by gathering wood and boiling pitch and rosin, in which task, "the children from eight years and upwards" were expected to be "usefully imploy'd." [12]

---

of 15 and 20. The average period of service was 6 to 7 yrs. Of 11 cases noted in Baltimore Co., lib. 1683–84, the average age adjudged was 15 (Baltimore, lib. D., 1682–86). This was the average also in 65 instances noted in Charles Co. court records, 1665–76 (Charles, lib. 1665–68, 1668–70, 1670–74, 1674–76, *passim*); and of the 19 cases noted in Prince George (lib. A., 1696–1702, lib. B, 1699–1705, *passim*), a slightly lower average was noted in the scattering instances in the 18th century Queen Ann records (Queen Ann, lib. 1709–16, 1728–30, 1735–39, *passim*). The average was between 14 and 15 in the 84 instances noted in Talbot Co., 1685–1705 (Talbot, lib. NN, No. 6; AB, No. 8; RF, No. 10, *passim*). The average is close to 14 yrs. of age in the 84 instances noted in Somerset Co. between 1671 and 1701, with one lad as young as 7 (Somerset, lib. 1671–75; lib. LO–7, 1689–90; 1690–91; 1692–93; 1693–94; 1698–1701, *passim*).

Virginia. Out of 43 cases adjudged in the Henrico court between 1677 and 1692 the average age was about 12; some of the children adjudged were Indians (Henrico, lib. I, II, *passim*). The average was closer to 14 in Lancaster (lib. 1656–66, *passim*), and to 15 in Middlesex (lib. 1673–80, 1680–94, *passim*) and in Rappahannock (lib. 1686–92, *passim*). Of 32 servants adjudged in Northumberland in the years 1668–1670, the average age was 13; 48 youngsters adjudged in 1675 ran from 13 to 18, and the average age of 16 servants adjudged in 1699 was 15 (Northumberland, lib. 1666–78, fols. 19, 49, 125; 1699–1713, Pt. I, f. 1). The average age was close to 14 in York County between 1657 and 1704 (see York, lib. 1657–62, 1664–72, 1671–94, 1675–84, 1684–87, 1697–1704, *passim*).

North Carolina. N.C. Gen. Court Mins. (1684), 15 yrs. old.

[10] Randolph MSS, *VMH*, XVII, 233, 234 (1666).

[11] *N.E. Hist. and Gen. Register*, LXII–LXV, *passim*. The average age of the 85 servants in the years 1772–74 at "Northampton," a plantation in Baltimore Co., was estimated at 25.27 years. W. D. Hoyt, Jr., "The White Servants at 'Northampton,' " *Md. Hist. Mag.* (June, 1938), p. 129.

[12] *CSPA, 1710–11*, No. 872 (1711); *1711–12*, No. 210, p. 175 (1711). For lists of children

Compensation. Aside from food, clothing, and lodging, the indentured servant normally did not receive compensation during his period of service, although occasionally annual wages were specified in the articles. Such cases are, however, hardly distinguishable from free laborers working for annual wages.[13]

Hebraic law as well as English custom may well have influenced some of the colonies in the matter of compensation to servants. Under the Biblical law the servant was to serve six years and in the seventh "go out free for nothing," but the master was enjoined to provide liberally for his servant at the end of his term.[14] The Massachusetts codes provided that "all servants that have served diligently and faithfully to the benefit of their Masters Seven years shall not be sent away emptie," [15] an injunction also incorporated in the later Duke's Laws.[16]

In most colonies at the expiration of his term of service the servant was entitled by custom or statute to receive his "freedom dues." These dues universally included clothing for one year, and often tools, seed, arms, and some provisions as well. Thus, the Maryland act of 1639 provided that the servant was to receive

3 barrels of corn, a hilling hoe, and a weeding hoe and a felling axe and to a man servant one new cloth suit, one new shirt, one pair of new shoes, one pair of new stockings, and a new monmouth cap, and to a maid servant, one new petty coat and wastcoat, one new smock, one pair of new shoes, one pair of new stockings and the clothes formerly belonging to the servant.[17]

Specifications changed from time to time.[18]

---

brought over in the Palatine emigration to New York, see Knittle, *Early Palatine Emigration,* pp. 243–299. As many as nine children were brought over by individual families. Emigrant families with seven children were by no means unusual. Childless couples were in a distinct minority.

[13] Lechford, *Note-Book,* p. 251 (1639); *Plymouth Col. Rec.,* II, 6 (1641); *New Haven Col. Rec., 1638–49,* p. 321 (1647); *WMCQ,* 1st ser., XIII, 224 (1772), £ 10 a year the two last years. An unusual arrangement permitted the servant two days a week to work for himself. Lechford, *Note-Book,* pp. 307, 308 (1640). Wages at the rate of 10s. per week were allowed in one Maryland contract in consideration of the servant's former service. *Md. Gazette* (Annapolis), Dec. 16, 1773.

[14] Exod. 21:2; Deut. 15:12–14.

[15] *Laws and Liberties, 1648,* p. 39; *Mass. Col. Laws, 1660–72,* p. 175.

[16] *N.Y. Col. Laws,* I, 47.   [17] *Md. Arch.,* I, 80 (1639).

[18] Cf. *Duke of York's Laws and Laws of Pa.,* p. 153; *Pa. Stat. at Large,* II, 54–56; J. C. Ballagh, *White Servitude in the Colony of Virginia* (Baltimore, 1895), p. 62; *N.C. Col. Rec.,* XXIII, 63 (1715), 196 (1741); Cooper, *S.C. Stat.,* II, 30 (1687), III, 621–629 (1744); Simpson, *Practical Justice of the Peace,* p. 236. *Laws of the Island of Antigua* (London, 1805), I, 84; Baskett, *Acts of the Charibbee Leeward Islands* (London, 1734), p. 160 (1716).

Deerskin, leather, or homespun breeches, a drugget or fustian coat, and a dimity jacket were the characteristic apparel of the servant class. See *Boston Gazette,* June 17–24, 1728, August 17–24, 1737; *Boston News-Letter,* Dec. 30–Jan. 6, 1737. An unsuccessful attempt was made in Parliament in 1699 on behalf of the feltmakers' trade to require all women servants in England and the

The assertion is not infrequently made that freedom dues included a grant of land to the servant. Plymouth was noteworthy for her emphasis upon such land grants. The authorities ordered in 1634 that "whereas by indenture many are bound to give their servts land at the expiration of theire terme, it is ordered, that they haue it at Scituate, or some other convenient place, where it may be usefull." [19] But only two years later the colony enacted that masters make good their covenants to give servants land "out of theire proper lands, the countrey being free from any such engagement." [20] However, there is some evidence to show that land grants continued to be given by the towns in which servants lived and were received as inhabitants.[21] This early practice died out in New England. The author of a currency tract in 1716 suggested that, in order to attract good men to come over as indentured servants, a homestead policy be adopted of giving immigrants fifty- or sixty-acre tracts, but this suggestion was not carried out in Massachusetts.[22] In Pennsylvania, Penn proposed that servants be allotted fifty acres at the end of their term, for which they were to pay a quitrent of 2s. annually and the masters an additional fifty at a rental of 4s. If the master were obliged to allot the servant the fifty acres out of his own lands by reason of indentures, he was then to receive the entire one hundred acres at a rental of 6s. per annum.[23] This practice appears to have been discontinued by the proprietor around 1700.[24]

---

plantations whose wages did not exceed £5 a year to wear felt hats. The decline of the hat industry was attributed to the disuse of such hats "among women of inferior quality." Stock, *Proc. Brit. Parl.*, II, viii.

[19] *Plymouth Col. Rec.*, I, 23 (1634).

[20] *Ibid.*, XI, 188 (1636). The amount of land to be granted was limited to 5 acres per servant. *Ibid.*, I, 44 (1636).

[21] *Ibid.*, II, 16 (1641), 69 (1644); III, 216 (1661); IV, 19 (1662), 75 (1664), 128 (1666); V, 125, 126 (1673); VI, 18 (1679), 55 (1680). Apparently in some cases some nominal payment was expected of the old servants. Sometimes the master agreed to give 50 acres. *Ibid.*, VI, 4 (1679). Such rights of servants to land could be assigned for a consideration, *ibid.*, I, 43 (1636); as punishment, an unruly servant might be deprived of his right to land "except hee manefest better desert." *Ibid.*, p. 64 (1637).

[22] A. McF. Davis, *Colonial Currency Reprints, 1682–1751* (4 vols., Boston, 1910–11), I, 335–349; F. J. Turner, "Frontier of Massachusetts," Col. Soc. of Mass., *Publications*, XVII, 266. However, see indentures of redemptioners, Elizabeth McMeans and her son, dated June 15, 1730. *Essex Inst. Hist. Coll.*, LVIII, 264.

[23] *Pa. Arch.*, 4th ser., I, 20 (1681).

[24] Herrick, *op. cit.*, p. 33. Under the original warrants of surveys whole townships were set apart as "Servants or headland." Approximately 4,500 acres were surveyed and granted "to sundry servants of the first purchasers and adventurers into Pennsylvania." Geiser estimates on the basis of the available records that the bound servants were one sixth as numerous as the first purchasers. Geiser, *op. cit.*, pp. 25, 26. Seventy-five acres were offered in New Jersey in 1665 to every Christian servant at the expiration of his or her term of service. N.J. Hist. Soc., *Coll.*, I, 38. For a land grant at the expiration of articles of indenture, see Newtown, L.I., *Rec.*, 1653–1720, f. 159, which appears to be a case of servitude for debt.

In Maryland for a time servants were also entitled to receive as freedom dues fifty acres of corn.[25] However, by the terms of the act passed in 1663 the allowance of land ceased to be obligatory, and in the course of events relatively few servants appear to have taken out patents upon completing their service.[26] It was reported in 1698 that servants, upon finishing their terms, received "all necessities sufficient for one year." Those that were industrious were expected to purchase land; no provision was to be made for the improvident.[27]

In the early years of settlement in Virginia servants coming over were given land as well as tools and clothing.[28] However, by 1627 it seems apparent that no land was given to servants at the end of their terms.[29] Instead, leases for years were proposed.[30] Instructions were given to the governors from time to time to issue patents to servants for fifty acres of land at the end of their terms;[31] but, as Bruce points out, there is no evidence that these instructions were ever translated into established procedure or that the General Assembly ever passed any legislation to carry them out.[32] George Cabell Greer has collected the names of some 25,000 immigrants brought over to Virginia by patentees, and, on the basis of his examination of the Land Office records at Richmond, asserted that the great majority of these immigrants do not appear as patentees.[33]

The Carolina Concessions of 1665 offered to every Christian servant

[25] See *Md. Arch.*, I, 97 (1640); IV, 464 (1647). In 1648 the Provincial Court found that the custom of the country for servants' wages required: "one cap or hatt, one new cloath or frize suite, one shirt one pr shoes and stockins one axe one broad and one narrow hoe, *50 Acres Land,* and 3 barrels Corne." *Ibid.*, IV, 361 (1648). Fifty acres "according to the custom of the country" were considered to be part of the freedom dues by the Talbot County court as late as 1683. See Hughes' case, Talbot NN, No. 6, f. 1 (1683). But cf. Jane Robinson's petition, *Md. Arch.*, XIII, 337 (1692).

[26] See A. E. Smith, "The Indentured Servant and Land Speculation in Seventeenth Century Maryland," *Amer. Hist. Rev.*, XL (1935), 467–472. See also *Md. Arch.*, I, 97; II, 523 (1676); IX, 404–407 (1760); Kilty, *Land-Holders' Assistant and Law-Office Guide*, pp. 38–40, 55.

[27] *Md. Arch.*, XXII, 120 (1698).   [28] *Va. Gen. Court Mins.*, p. 138 (1626).

[29] But see indentures of Thomas Titterton, a redemptioner (1649), *Essex Inst. Hist. Coll.*, LVIII, 263.

[30] *Ibid.*, p. 135 (1627).

[31] See instructions to Lord Culpeper, 1681–82, *VMH*, XXVIII, 45; also Hening, III, 304 (1705); *VMH*, XXI, 232 (1715).

[32] Bruce, *Econ. Hist. of Va.*, II, 42, 43; but see *contra* Ballagh, *White Servitude in Va.*, pp. 85–87, who contends that servants were entitled to enter a legal claim to the land on the basis of the instructions. In exceptional cases land might be offered by the master to induce the servant to agree to an extension of his term, as was the case in an agreement made by Colonel Alexander Spotswood with his servant to serve him two years extra in return for "land to marry" and £5 in goods at a store "in money rates" as well as clothing. Spotsylvania O.B., 1730–38, f. 271 (1733).

[33] G. C. Greer, *Early Virginia Immigrants* (Richmond, 1912). For instances of convict servants acquiring estates, see Tyler, *Mag.*, VIII, 6; *WMCQ*, 2d ser., II, 157–161.

already in the colony forty acres at the expiration of his or her period of service. Those coming in later were to have smaller amounts. Two years later the acreage was raised to fifty, and to one hundred in 1699. This offer is not mentioned in later instructions.[34] The situation in Georgia must be considered as exceptional, as the bulk of the indentured servants coming over in the early years were bound to the trustees. From twenty- to fifty-acre lots were laid out for servants "newly out of their times," depending on the period. In addition, they were to receive a cash allowance, cattle, and working tools. Such allowances also seem to have been made to parish apprentices and German redemptioners, and, finally, to all servants.[35]

In Florida such leading importers of labor as Denys Rolle and Dr. Turnbull added very substantially to their holdings through the headright system. Although the latter transported some fourteen hundred bound servants from the Mediterranean region to British East Florida, promising them half of the produce they raised and ultimately plots of land, Governor Tonyn's agents made it clear to them that, as they were Catholics, they would not get title deeds to their lands, Protestant settlers being specified in the grants.[36]

In at least 90 per cent of the cases which arose in the colonial courts involving freedom dues, clothes and tools were awarded, but a grant of land was neither regarded as an obligation under the contract nor required by custom.[37]

[34] For "industrious and usefull" service to the colony, two servants were awarded 10 acres each in 1671. *S.C. Grand Council J.*, p. 7; also *N.C. Col. Rec.*, I, 334; A. F. McKinley, *The Suffrage Franchise in the Thirteen English Colonies in America* (Philadelphia, 1905), p. 123. However, J. S. Bassett, *Slavery and Servitude in the Colony of North Carolina* (Baltimore, 1896), pp. 78, 79, claims that it was allowed as late as 1737 and perhaps later, although actually such instances must have been exceptional.

[35] *Ga. Col. Rec.*, I, 405 (1742), 535 (1749), II, 14, 16, 18, 24, 35, V, 479, VI, 54 (1742); Stock, *Proc. Brit. Parl.*, V, 86, 87 (1741). For an instance where land does not appear to have been granted to servants of the trustees, see *Ga. Col. Rec.*, VI, 13 (1741).

[36] C.O. 5:552, pp. 111–112; W. H. Siebert, "Slavery and White Servitude in East Florida, 1726–1776," *Fla. Hist. Soc. Q.*, X (1931), 8, 18, 19.

[37] In New England merely double or "necessary" apparel was customarily awarded. See *Plymouth Col. Rec.*, I, 20 (1633); *Essex*, IV, 112 (1669), 261 (1670), VII, 73 (1678); Mass. Arch., Vol. 105 (Petitions, 1643–1775), fols. 81, 82 (1722); Washburne v. Washburne, Plymouth C.P., I, f. 387, double apparel and tools; *R.I. Col. Rec.*, III, 202 (1686); *Warwick, R.I., Rec.*, p. 318 (1666).

For early New York see *R.N.A.*, V, 171 (1664), 191, 192 (1665); *Albany, Rensselaerswyck, and Schenectady Court Mins.*, II, 321, 322 (1678); Gravesend Town Rec., IV, 1662–99, f. 8 (1663), in addition to double apparel, "a cowe calfe." Clothing and occasionally provisions were customarily allowed in Pennsylvania. See, e.g., *Chester Co. Court Rec.*, pp. 293, 294 (1693). Lancaster Road and Sess. Docket, No. 2, 1742–60 (1753). Dillworth v. Anthony, Philadelphia Co. Court Papers (*c.* 1715). Philadelphia Q.S., lib. 1773–80 (1774); 1779–82 (1780); 1780–85 (1780). West Chester Q.S., lib. 1742–59, f. 19 (1743). For emphasis on working tools, see

The freedom dues might be commuted by money payments ranging generally from £4 to £6 in cash.[38] In the Northern and Middle colonies the indentures at times provided for cash payments at the end of the servant's term.[39]

As the weight of the evidence proves conclusively that freedom dues did not as a general rule include land, they should be carefully distinguished from headrights, generally fifty-acre land grants to importers or masters for the transportation of an emigrant. The extensive use of the headright system to encourage the emigration of white labor proved a boon to the Southern landed proprietors, who through this

---

Burlington, West Jersey, Court Book, f. 52 (1686); Turner, *Some Records of Sussex County, Del.,* p. 66 (1682); Kent Co., Del., Court Rec., lib. 1699–1703, f. 1 (1699).

In Maryland corn, clothes, and tools rather than land were invariably dispensed. By act of 1699 a gun was substituted for the three barrels of Indian corn. See *Md. Arch.,* XXII, 445, 546–553 (1699); *CSPA, 1699,* No. 655, p. 349; *1702,* No. 1117, p. 701. See also *Md. Arch.,* X, 247, 255 (1652), 334 (1653), 565, 566 (1665); LIII, 185. Ann Arundel, lib. 1702–4, fols. 44 (1703); 1704–8, fols. 301 (1706), 734 (1708). Charles, lib. 1670–74, f. 47 (1671); 1678–80, fols. 43, 44, 214; 1688–89, f. 195 (1690). Frederick, lib. 1750–51, f. 294 (1751). Prince George, lib. A., 1696–1702, f. 58 (1696); lib. B, 1699–1705, f. 152 (1702); lib. C, 1702–8, f. 77 (1706); Queen Ann, lib. 1709–16, fols. 82, 114 (1710), 157 (1711), 170 (1712). Somerset, lib. 1690–92, f. 1 (1688), 1692–93, f. 49 (1692), 1730–33, f. 27 (1730). Talbot, lib. NN, No. 6 (1689); 1703–4 (1704).

Virginia generally gave merely apparel and provisions. See, e.g., *Va. Gen. Court Mins.,* pp. 75, 98 (1625), 214 (1670), 294 (1672), 349 (1673), 367, 377 (1674), 432 (1676), 466 (1640). In 1672 the General Court set one servant free "provided that when he comes to demand his Corn and Clothes, he be whipt and receive 39 lashes." *Ibid.,* p. 297. See also Accomac O.B., I, fols. 33 (1636), 315 (1644), 1671–73 (1671, *passim*). Charles City O.B., 1655–65, fols. 81 (1657), 390 (1663). Elizabeth O.B., 1684–99, f. 247 (1692). Henrico O.B., II, f. 229 (1689); III, f. 134 (1697). Lancaster O.B., 1656–66, fols. 111 (1660), 251 (1663). Northampton, lib. I (1661). Prince George, lib. 1737/8–40 (1738); *VMH,* V, 278. Rappahannock, lib. 1683–86, fols. 11 (1684), 69 (1685). Richmond, lib. 1692–94, fols. 67 (1693), 127 (1694). Spotsylvania, lib. 1730–38, f. 423 (1735). York O.B., 1657–62, f. 48 (1658), in addition to clothes, the bed, rug, and blankets which he used during his term; *ibid.,* 1671–94, fols. 219 (1675); 1675–84, f. 146 (1679); 1690–94, f. 144 (1692); 1697–1702, f. 1 (1697). Westmoreland, lib. 1675/6–88/9, f. 219 (1681).

In North Carolina corn and clothes were invariably awarded. N.C. Gen. Court Mins., lib. 1695–1721, f. 314 (1705); New Hanover, lib. 1740–1814, f. 101 (1740); Perquimans, lib. 1689–1693 (1689).

[38] *Chester, Pa., Court Rec., 1681–97,* p. 348 (1695); Lancaster, Pa., Road and Sess. Docket, No. 4, 1768–76 (August, 1772); Philadelphia Q.S., lib. 1773–80 (June, 1779), 1780–85 (Sept., 1781); West Chester Q.S., lib. B (1771–1776); York, Pa., Q.S., lib. XII, 1779–81, f. 228 (1781); *Md. Arch.,* IV, 271 (1644); Prince George, Md., Co. Court, lib. 1782–84 (August, 1783); Hening, VI, 357–369 (1753), VIII, 547–558 (1748), £3 10s. current; Bruce, *Econ. Hist. of Va.,* II, 42; Cartaret, N.C., 1747–64, f. 11 (1749); Onslow, N.C., lib. 1749–65, f. 27 (1754); Pasquotank, N.C., Mins., 1737–55 (1746). See also Gray, *op. cit.,* I, 365, 366. During the currency depreciation of the Revolutionary period freedom dues were occasionally valued as high as £30. See also Geiser, *op. cit.,* p. 72.

[39] *Plymouth Col. Rec.,* I, 35 (1635), 103 (1638), II, 82, 83, 89 (1645), VI, 25 (1679); *Warwick, R.I., Rec.,* pp. 310 (1665), 334 (1667); Stokes, *Iconography,* IV, 262 (1667). Under West Florida law a servant who had served at least four years was to be given a new suit of apparel and 30s. sterling at the end of his term. Johnson, *op. cit.,* p. 179.

means were able to add to their holdings materially.[40] Actually, how-ever, the headright system fostered speculation in land warrants and often raised the price of land beyond the means of servants who had worked out their time. Owing to the fraudulent and haphazard work-ings of the system, it was finally abolished in Maryland and Virginia. This action had the effect of separating land policy from labor policy in the tobacco provinces.[41]

Behind the colonial custom of freedom dues was the determination that servants should not become a public charge when dismissed. Mas-ters had a responsibility to the community to see that their servants were in fit condition to support themselves at the expiration of their term. The South Carolina Code of 1744 in emulation of West Indian legisla-tion, went even further, and provided that, where a sick servant was dismissed by a master under pretense of freedom and died for want of relief, the master was subject to a penalty of £20 proclamation money for the use of the parish.[42]

Generally it was stipulated in covenants of indenture that in con-sideration of the agreement to be bound for a stated term of years mas-ters would pay their servants' passage or give them food and clothing. Seldom was the issue of consideration raised by litigants to annul such a contract. The Maryland courts were the scene of protracted litigation over the articles of indenture of Hester Nichols, bound in 1659 at the age of ten or eleven by her father, an impoverished planter, to Thomas Cornwallis, a leading settler. A few months later Cornwallis went to England and, instead of taking the girl with him, sold her before his departure to a certain Thomas Nuthall. Upon petition of the father that Cornwallis, in so doing, had violated his agreement to care for the child as if she were his own, a jury ordered the girl released.[43] Corn-wallis then appealed the case on the ground of error to the Upper House of the General Assembly in 1663, claiming that the girl had been bound by ordinary indentures. The Upper House sent the case to the Court of Chancery on the ground that, as it involved an interpretation of a contract, it should not have been tried before a jury.[44] Before Chancery the girl's father urged that the indenture be declared invalid because no consideration was named in it. By a vote of three to two the court

---

[40] See Gray, *op. cit.*, I, 386–391. The Virginia order books are replete with instances of sub-stantial grants to planters for importing servants.

[41] E. I. McCormac, *White Servitude in Maryland, 1634–1820* (Baltimore, 1904), pp. 22, 26; Hansen, *The Atlantic Migration, 1607–1860* (Cambridge, 1940), p. 44.

[42] *S.C. Stat.*, III, 621–629 (1744). See also *supra*, pp. 17, 18. However, a servant recovering on a judgment for freedom dues was not necessarily treated as a preferred creditor. See *Va. Gen. Court Mins.*, p. 300 (1672).

[43] *Md. Arch.*, XLI, 515–516.   [44] *Ibid.*, I, 463–466, 481.

upheld the indenture and required Hester to serve out her seven-year term. The minority held it invalid for want of consideration allowed at the expiration of the term and also because Hester had not been bound before a magistrate.[45]

Enforcement of the Contract. The master's quasi-proprietary interest in the contract with his indentured servant was more substantial than with a free laborer. Hence, the courts readily decreed specific performance of such contracts on the part of the servant. Masters were concerned with seeing that redemptioners fulfilled contracts signed abroad and that servants in the colonies remained at their tasks until the end of their contracted terms. The first Assembly of Virginia enacted in 1619 that

whatsoeuer servant hath heretofore or shall hereafter contracte himselfe in England, either by way of Indenture or otherwise, to serve any Master here in Virginia and shall afterward, against his said former contracte depart from his Mr without leave, or, being once imbarked shall abandon the ship he is appointed to come on, and so, being left behind, shall putt himselfe in the service of any other man that shall bring him hither, that then at the same servant's arrival here, he shall first serve out his time with his former Mr according to his covenant.[46]

If a servant quit without legal grounds before the expiration of his term, the court generally ordered him to serve out the remainder of his term, although the master might be cautioned to provide suitable living conditions.[47] Failure to obey such an order might involve a substantial penalty.[48] The court might choose to require the servant to

---

[45] *Ibid.*, XLIX, 137 (1664). For cases where the courts voided indentures without formal or token consideration, see *Va. Gen. Court Mins.*, p. 103 (1626); Henrico O.B., lib. V, fols. 409 *et seq.* (1693).

[46] L. G. Tyler, ed., *Narr. of Early Va.* (New York, 1907), pp. 273, 274.

[47] *Me. Prov. and Court Rec.*, II, 66 (1658), 372 (1661); *Assistants*, I, 221 (1682), II, 100 (1640); *Essex*, I, 197 (1650); R.N.A., V, 217 (1665); *Rensselaerswyck Court Mins., 1648–52*, p. 24 (1648); Newtown, L.I., Court Rec., f. 49 (1665); *Chester Co., Pa., Court Rec., 1681–97*, pp. 211, 212 (1690); Md. Prov. Court Rec., lib. 1684–87, f. 68 (1684), 1692–93, f. 329 (1692); Ann Arundel, lib. 1704–8, f. 401 (1706); Charles, lib. 1682–84, f. 128 (1683); Queen Ann, lib. 1709–16, f. 252 (1713); Somerset, lib. 1671–75, fols. 42–45 (1671–72), 1692–93, f. 7 (1692); Talbot, lib. RF, No. 10 (1705); *Va. Gen. Court Mins.*, p. 413 (1675); Accomac O.B., I, f. 319 (1644), 1663–66, f. 73 (1664), 1666–70, f. 12 (1666), 1671–73 (1671); Henrico O.B., I, 1677–92, f. 209 (1688), 1710–14, fols. 12 (1710), 89 (1711), 184 (1712); Spotsylvania O.B., 1724–30 (1730); Westmoreland O.B., 1675/6–88/9, f. 391 (1685); York O.B., 1697–1704, f. 134 (1699); Craven, N.C., lib. 1757–62 (1759), *S.C. Grand Council J.*, 1692, pp. 34, 35.

[48] The Plymouth court ordered a servant to serve out the remaining three years of his term under penalty of a public whipping and of "being forced to returne to his said master." Bartlett v. Cooper, *Plymouth Col. Rec.*, IV, 154 (1667). See also *Rensselaerswyck Court Mins., 1648–52*, p. 29 (1648). Under New York law the apprentice or servant refusing to serve could be committed to bridewell or the county gaol, there to remain until he agreed to serve. 1 R.L. 137 § 6; *New Conductor Generalis* (Albany, 1819), p. 30.

post bond for the nonperformance of the court order.[49] Suits for damages were rarely brought against servants for nonperformance of their covenants, for servants were likely to be judgment-proof.[50] Specific performance, in fact extra service, might be exacted of servants for nonperformance of their contracts under an early Massachusetts law which provided that

if any [servants] have been unfaithfull, negligent or unprofitable in their service, nothwithstanding the good usage of their masters, they shall not be dismissed, till they have made satisfaction according to the judgement of authority.[51]

Modification of the Terms of the Contract of Employment. The articles of indenture might be modified by mutual consent.[52] But as many servants were minors, illiterates, or ignorant of the English language, the authorities sought to prevent ship captains from fraudulently inducing redemptioners to agree to a modification of their indentures once they were aboard ship [53] and to prevent masters from exercising undue influence in modifying an original contract or from making a second contract with their servants before the first term had been completed by providing that any indentures made after the original term of service had been entered upon would require the approval of the court.[54] This applied also to releases, and to transfers of the servant or

[49] £5 sterling security in *Va. Gen. Court Mins.*, p. 466 (1640). The employer was permitted to keep an Indian's gun until the Indian had broken up twenty rods of land in accord with his contract. Powas v. Potts, *Plymouth Col. Rec.*, IV, 183 (1668).

[50] However, in 1626, in lieu of a year's service due him by indentures, one master was awarded 360 lbs. of tobacco and the servant's corn crop, except for a small amount "to be allowed for his victualls." In addition, the servant was ordered either to deliver up his indentures "or to come in lieu a tenant uppon his land." *Va. Gen. Court Mins.*, p. 131 (1626). See also Rochford v. Hickman, *Chester, Pa., Court Rec., 1681-97*, pp. 52, 53 (1685), where judgment was awarded against a third party who had in his possession some goods belonging to the delinquent servant. As to whether actions of covenant could be brought against minor apprentices at common law, see Burn, *Justice of the Peace Abridgment* (Boston, 1773), p. 18.

[51] *Mass. Col. Laws, 1660-72*, p. 175.

[52] See Lechford, *Note-Book*, p. 393 (1641).

[53] See Petition of Wimpy *et al.*, Queen Ann, Md., lib. 1718-19 (1718), where a group of redemptioners were induced to give up their indentures in return for a promise to pay each of them 40s. While the court voided their second indentures, it ordered them to serve their respective masters five years each instead of four years as they had originally agreed. A 13-year-old lad was ordered to serve according to the act of Assembly. See also York, Va., lib. 1664-72, f. 455, contract held void; Lancaster, Pa., Road and Sess. Docket, No. 1, 1729-42, f. 12 (1730), referred to 3 arbiters. See also *Va. Gen. Court Mins.*, p. 12 (1623); *New Haven Col. Rec., 1638-49*, p. 58 (1741).

[54] See Hill v. Whitehead, New Haven Co. Court Rec., lib. I, f. 99 (1677). Cf. also *Md. Arch.*, XLIX, 220, 221, 237-238, 265, 380 (1664). In Virginia in the early years a release, if properly attested, need not have the court's approval to be valid. *Va. Gen. Court Mins.*, p. 131 (1626); Coleman's case, Accomac O.B., II, f. 221. In the later period, however, such modifications of

apprentice [55] to other trades on the ground, for instance, that the one to which he had bound himself was detrimental to his health.[56] If a second contract had been made without the approval of the court, it was held void.[57] A Maryland county court held it to be "Contrary to the Lawe of this Province, that any Master should make any bargain With any servant for any time Longer not Untill his first time of servitude be fully Expired." [58] In Maryland masters were subject to criminal prosecution for forcing their servants to sign indentures before they had gained their freedom.[59] In South Carolina contracts made with servants during the period of their original indentures were declared void.[60] In West Florida a bargain made with a servant during the period of his indenture to increase his term of service was not binding.[61]

THE MASTER'S QUASI-PROPRIETARY INTEREST IN THE SERVICES OF HIS SERVANT

The Sale and Assignment of Servants. Visitors to the old slave marts in Southern towns little appreciate, perhaps, the extent of the traffic in white indentured servants and bound apprentices during colonial times. William Byrd wrote in 1739 to a correspondent in Rotterdam the following with reference to the trade in servants:

I know not how long the Palatines are sold for, who do not Pay Passage to Philadelphia, but here they are sold for Four years and fetch from 6 to 9 Pounds and perhaps good Tradesmen may go for Ten. If these Prices would answer, I am pretty Confident I could dispose of two Shipsload every year in this River: and I myself would undertake it for Eight [per] cent on the Sales, and make you as few bad Debts as possible. This is the Allowance our Negro Sellers have, which sell for more than Double these People will, and consequently afford twice the Profet." [1]

---

the original terms required the court's approval. Hening, II, 388 (1677). See Accomac O.B., 1666–70, f. 47 (1670); Botetourt O.B., 1770–71, Pt. II, f. 490 (1771); Goochland O.B., *WMCQ*, 1st ser., V, 109, 110 (1737, 1738). See also Lancaster O.B., 1656–66, f. 110 (1660), extra service of one year for lacking in skill as a cooper; 1666–80 (Sept. 11, 1667). *VMH*, XII, 294 (1684), extra service in consideration of servant's being permitted to work at the corn crop instead of in the tobacco fields. Northumberland O.B., 1699–1713, Pt. II (1703).

[55] Ryder's case, Gravesend Sess., Gravesend Court Rec., II, f. 143 (1681).

[56] New Haven Co. Court Rec., I, f. 117 (1697).

[57] Wheadon v. Meiggs, *New Haven Col. Rec.*, II, 250–253; Hughes's case, Westmoreland O.B., 1662–64.

[58] Charles Co., Md., lib. 1678–80, f. 247 (1680). See also Prince George, Md., lib. 1696–1702, f. 469 (1699).

[59] Cases of Sterrett and Alexander, Somerset, 1689–90, f. 87 (1690).

[60] *S.C. Stat.*, III, 621–629 (1744).   [61] Cecil Johnson, *op. cit.*, p. 179.

[1] *Amer. Hist. Rev.*, I, 90. For conditions in the servant trade in the Shenandoah Valley in 1774, see *Doc. Hist. Amer. Indust. Soc.*, I, 374.

When the redemptioners arrived at colonial ports, servant traders, known as "soul drivers," met the ships and purchased their indentures from the ship captain.[2] Then the party was taken into the back country; sometimes groups of from twenty to fifty immigrants were driven into the interior of a colony "like cattle to a Smithfield market and exposed to sale in public fairs as so many brute beasts," as Peter Williamson eloquently depicted it.[3] In all the continental colonies save for Massachusetts, New Haven colony, New York, and Pennsylvania the master had an almost unrestricted right to sell, assign, or hire out to another his indentured servant for his contracted term of service.[4] Where limitations were imposed, they were chiefly with respect to the assignment of minors bound as apprentices and to the sale outside the jurisdiction of the court of orphans whom the judicial authorities had bound out to service.

In New England the practice of selling or assigning servants and apprentices to other masters was widespread and went back to the early days of settlement. Lechford drew up a considerable number of such assignments for his clients.[5] The assignee would assume the obligations of freedom dues or payment of wages [6] as the case might be.

In the case of apprenticeship, such assignments were out of the ordinary procedure and the apprentice's consent was generally required for their validity.[7] However, sale or assignment was the normal pro-

---

[2] For advertisements of sale on shipboard, see *N.Y. Gazette*, April 17–23, 1739; *N.Y. Mercury*, April 25, 1774; *N.Y. Weekly Post-Boy*, Jan. 7, 1751.

[3] Herrick, *White Servitude in Pa.*, p. 213.

[4] Newspaper advertisements frequently listed for sale at public vendue the time of servants along with dwelling houses, chattels, and the inventory of shops or mills. See, e.g., *N.J. Arch.*, 1st ser., XXV, 512, 2d ser., I, 543; *Pa. Gazette*, Dec. 24, 1768; *Md. Gazette*, Nov. 25, 1746, Feb. 7, 1751; *S.C. Gazette*, March 18–25, May 27–June 3, 1732, Dec. 7, 14, 1734, Feb. 28–March 6, April 17–24, 1736 (14 white servants), Dec. 17, 1753, Sept. 1–8, 8–15, 1766; *N.C. Gazette*, June 6, 1778 (house servants to be hired out by the year or month). For the sale of a white cabinetmaker who had 3 yrs. to serve, along with ready-made tables, chairs, desks, tools, and black walnut plank, see *Md. Gazette*, Nov. 30, 1775.

[5] Lechford, *Note-Book*, pp. 101, 150, 162, 163, 175, 184, 188, 210, 235 (1639), 254 (1640), 389, 390 (1641). See also *Assistants*, II, 119, 122 (1642); *Essex*, I, 48 (1642), 255 (1652), II, 126, 132 (1658), III, 265 (1665), 346 (1666), IV, 8 (1668), VIII, 42 (1680); *Essex Probate*, II, 248 (1671); *Plymouth Col. Rec.*, I, 132 (1639), 158 (1640); *Conn. Particular Court Rec.*, p. 121 (1650). For the later period, see assignment of an Indian servant named Samuel Porridge (1768), Falmouth Hist. Soc.

[6] *Assistants*, II, 129 (1642).

[7] The practice of assigning willing apprentices was not sanctioned by 5 Eliz. c. 4, but by the custom of London. Dalton, c. 58; 1 Salk. 68; 2 Str. 1265; Bacon, *Abridgement*, V, 359. See also Burn, *Justice of the Peace Abridgment* (Boston, 1773), p. 19; William Graydon, *The Justices' and Constables' Assistant* (Harrisburg, Pa., 1803), p. 15. Tapping Reeve, writing in the early part of the 19th century, admitted that the assignment of apprentices was "an usual practice in this country," but contended, "I have not learnt that such practice has ever been sanctioned by the decision of any court." *Op. cit.*, pp. 344, 345. In early Plymouth, willing apprentices were not

cedure for the recovery of passage money from immigrants who had bound themselves to shippers or captains to serve out their transportation costs. Lechford in 1640 drew up the petition of John Askew of Cambridge, who recounted that he had been bound in England for the term of four years and was then assigned by his master to Edward Winslow. Askew claimed that he had served Winslow for three quarters of a year, during which period he had earned enough to pay for the passage money which Winslow had advanced. However, when he sought to buy his freeedom, his New England master asked a higher sum than was demanded of other servants, and, in addition, required him to act as surety for another. He, therefore, prayed relief.[8]

Plymouth colony very early witnessed numerous assignments of servants,[9] in which regular annual wages during the term of the indenture were specified in the contract. In the memorandum recording the assignment by Elizabeth Watson, widow, of her servant, Henry Blage, to Thomas Watson for the residue of Blage's term, the assignee bound himself to pay a total of £11 10s. per annum, of which eight pounds were to go to the widow Watson and £3 10s. to servant Blage for annual wages. In turn, the assignee reassigned Henry over to one John Rogers "upon the same conditions."[10]

Apparently in order to check irresponsible assignment, the Body of Liberties (1641) provided that no servant be assigned for more than one year either by a master or his executors or administrators without the consent of the judicial authorities.[11] This provision was incorporated in the Code of 1648 and the Laws of 1660,[12] but it is doubtful whether the restrictions were faithfully observed by the courts.[13] Where, as in

infrequently assigned. *Plymouth Col. Rec.*, I, 15, 16 (1633), 37 (1636), 110 (1639), 129 (1639). For advertisements of the sale of apprentices' terms in New England, see *Boston News-Letter*, April 15, 1714; April 25, 1715; *Boston Evening Post*, March 9, 1747. For an indenture of apprenticeship specifically prohibiting an assignment, see *Plymouth Col. Rec.*, I, 128, 129 (1639).

[8] *Note-Book*, p. 366 (1640). For the sale or assignment of redemptioners in early West Jersey, see Burlington Court Book, fols. 148 (1697), 163 (1698).

[9] *Plymouth Col. Rec.*, I, 15 (1633), 31 (1634), 33 (1635), 45 (1636), 64, 65 (1637), 110, 119, 122, 129 (1639), 158 (1640); II, 6 (1641), 38 (1642), 66 (1643).

[10] *Ibid.*, I, 102 (1638); see also pp. 132, 133.

[11] W. H. Whitmore, ed., *Mass. Col. Laws, 1660, with the Supplement to 1672* (Boston, 1889), p. 53.

[12] *The Laws and Liberties of Massachusetts* (Cambridge, 1929), p. 39; *Mass. Col. Laws, 1660*, p. 175.

[13] When, in 1649, William Goodwin brought trespass against Samuel Young "for selling of him to Mr. Gott and he to others," the court ordered plaintiff to remain with a third party until his year was up, then to serve one Downing until Oct. 18 "com twelve month," after which date he was to be disposed of as the court should see fit. Three assignees were fined for breach of the court order. The order further provided that, if it appeared that Goodwin was not Downing's servant, he was to have an allowance for clothes, etc. *Essex*, I, 171 (1649). In 1664 the

York County, the servants' indentures were customarily recorded, the practice of masters was to file the assignment as well.[14] In addition to the practice of assigning a servant to another for the remainder of his term, masters frequently hired out servants and received to their own account wages which they had earned.[15]

Where the indenture specifically prohibited assignments,[16] the eighteenth-century Suffolk general sessions ordered masters to take back such servants assigned and fulfill their agreements.[17] Where, as in the case of transported servants, it was unlikely that such a specific prohibition would be embodied in the indenture, the court did not prohibit assignments.[18] In the case of apprenticeship, the eighteenth-century sessions supervised assignments to other masters directly and arranged for compensation by the assignee to the master for the remainder of the apprentice's term.[19] Occasionally the conveyances of Indian servants for life are to be found in Massachusetts along with the sale of fractional shares of Negroes.[20]

Assignments are on record in New Haven of the time of servants [21] much before the order of 1656 which provided that

no master, or other family governor or person, shall sell any servant, male or female of what degree soeuer, out of this jurisdiction, unless it be into some of the other three colonies, wthout leaue and lycense from the authorities of that plantation to wch he belongs, under the penaltie of ten pounds for each default.[22]

Four years later the authorities provided that no agreement made by persons under age, binding themselves for years, should be valid except

Essex court voided all sales of a servant as violating his agreement to serve provided that he was not sold to another man during his term, but the court recognized the first indenture and first assignment in so far as the assignor "had power to dispose of him." Eggon's case, *ibid.*, III, 172 (1664). In Royse's case, New Haven Co. Court, lib. I, f. 264 (1698), an assignment made by a master for more than one year was voided. This case was later settled when complainant agreed to pay costs.

[14] For an assignment duly acknowledged by both parties, properly attested, and subsequently assigned over to a third party with the consent of the servant, see *York Deeds*, Bk. I, Pt. I, fols. 148, 149 (1663). The more usual practice was to make acknowledgment of the "sayle" or assignment in court. *Me. Prov. and Court Rec.*, I, 306 (1667).

[15] See Greeneway v. Lewis, *Me. Prov. and Court Rec.*, I, 5 (1637). See also Lechford, *Note-Book*, p. 58 (1639).

[16] For an early instance, see *Essex*, I, 307 (1653).

[17] See Le Sueur's petition, Suffolk G.S., lib. I, f. 161 (1707); Pitts's case, *ibid.*, I, f. 242 (1711).

[18] Petition of Anne Glyn and Jane Hunt, Suffolk G.S., lib. III, f. 117 (1721).

[19] Armstrong v. Newcomb, *ibid.*, f. 90 (1721).

[20] Conveyances of Juba, an Indian, and Peggy, a Mustee or Indian woman; conveyance of Peggy, Negress (1763), Falmouth Hist. Soc.

[21] *New Haven Col. Rec., 1638–49*, pp. 124 (1643), 370 (1647).

[22] *Ibid., 1653–65*, p. 177 (1656).

with the express consent of their parents or the authorities, and "that no servant shall be assigned from man to man but before the authority of the place and by their allowance." [23]

This second order was doubtless inspired by the case of a lad named Edward House who had been bound to John Strang of Boston with the consent of his father for a term of seven years, beginning in 1652. Another indenture was presented to the governor by Samuel Plum, whereby it appeared that Edward had bound himself to a man named Jeffs for a term of nine years to begin in 1653. This indenture was assigned to Francis Browne, and in turn from Browne to Plum. When House was asked how he came to set his hand to the second indenture, he replied that

he was forced to it in the shipp, being threatened to be throwne ouer board if he would not yeeld to it, and also told him if he would doe it he should go to sea and see his freinds once a yeare, and that Jeffs gave him liquours so that he was not himself, thereby drew him to sett his hand to it, and that this was done when he was about 12 or 13 yeare old.

The court held that, since he had been so young at the time, he "was not capeable of makeing an indenture, wch (by his relation) he was also forced to, and he haveing parents in England, it cannot be thought raitionall that he should be left to himself to dispose of himself, nor can it be judged a valid act." However, Plum asserted that, when he bought the lad's remaining time from Browne, he "then objected not." The court held all the transactions under the second indenture were invalid and left to Plum his remedy at law against Browne. In the ensuing civil action brought by Plum, evidence was introduced that the plaintiff was not teaching House his trade of brickmaker, which was the engagement under the first indenture, and that the boy was being held beyond his term. Plum asked for an allowance in time for healing a festering sore of the lad "wch disabled him for service a moneth or six weeks, besides a fortnights sicknesse in harvest." He further stated that House was not fit for the trade of a brickmaker when he came to him, as he could not bend his knee on account of having contracted scurvy aboard ship. The court ruled that Browne had acted "imprudently" but not fraudulently, and conceded that the lad was infirm in body. It was accordingly decreed that Browne pay Plum £10 current and costs for selling House "beyond what doth appeare to be his right to sell." [24]

[23] *Ibid.*, p. 360.
[24] *Ibid.*, pp. 318, 319, 377-379 (1659, 1660). For a curb on the assignment of debtors to a man "and his assigns," see Swift, *System of the Laws of Conn.*, I, 218, 219.

In New York and New Jersey the sale and assignment of servants was a frequent occurrence. Such transactions were as much run-of-the-mill affairs as the hiring of Negro and Indian slaves at the market house at the Wall Street slip,[25] or the entry in the Ulster Dutch court records of the sale of a Negro without ears.[26] The Dutch records at Kingston record the case in 1663 of a not-too-scrupulous assignor, who, after hiring his manservant to the plaintiff, then went ahead before the plaintiff's arrival and hired him to a third party, making a profit of fifty-two guilders in sewan and six schepels of wheat. The court found that the servant had voluntarily hired himself out to the third party who offered him higher than prevailing wages. The second assignee was permitted to keep the servant for the duration of his term, but required to pay the expenses the plaintiff had incurred in the transaction. However, the court forbade the second assignee from deducting this payment from the servant's wages.[27] Such assignments were also the subject of litigation in the English courts of the province.[28]

The Duke's Laws of 1665 provided that "no Servant, except such as are duly so for life, shall be Assigned over to other Masters or Dames by themselves their Executors or Administrators for above the Space of one year, unless for good reasons offered; the Court of Sessions shall otherwise think fitt to order. In such Case the Assignment shall stand good Otherwise to be void in Law."[29] In view of this provision, and probably to be on the safe side, assignors might attach to the record of the assignment a statement that it was with the "desire and full consent" of the servant."[30] The extra time awarded a master by the court as a penalty for a servant's running away might be assigned to another, apparently without his consent.[31]

The necessity of showing good reason does not seem to have been required by the eighteenth-century courts of the colony to validate a contract of assignment.[32] The legislature provided in 1766 that assign-

[25] *M.C.C.*, II, 458.

[26] Willemsen v. Davenport, Ulster Dutch Transcripts, III, fols. 85, 86 (1682).

[27] Louwrence v. du Mont, "Kingston Dutch Rec.," N.Y. State Hist. Assn., *Proceedings*, XI, 68 (1663). For other instances of the sale of a servant in the Dutch language courts, see *R.N.A.*, V, 204–206, 210; also Swart v. Thusz, *Courts of Albany, Rensselaerswyck, and Schenectady Mins.*, I, 64 (1669).

[28] See, e.g., Wandell v. Hunt, Westchester Co. Court of Sessions, Westchester Co. Hist. Soc., *Coll.*, II, 55–57 (1687).

[29] *N.Y. Col. Laws*, I, 47. This provision was borrowed from Massachuetts law. Cf. Verplanke v. Vanburson, Rec. of Wills, lib. XIXB, f. 353 (1680), detinue of an Indian which the plaintiff "lent unto the Deft wife . . . to boalt a Little Flower."

[30] *Oyster Bay Town Rec.*, I, 17 (1665).   [31] See *Southold Rec.*, I, 377 (1670).

[32] In McKee's opinion the early law was generally ignored and did not afford much protection to servants. *Op. cit.*, p. 103. See also C. M. Haar, "White Indentured Servants in Colonial New York," *Americana* (1940), pp. 387, 388.

ments made in the presence of two witnesses and acknowledged by the servant before any mayor, recorder, alderman, or justice of the peace should be "effectual to transfer" the servant for the remainder of his term, but that no infant should be bound beyond the age of twenty-one except such as were bound to pay their passage money.[33] The assignment and hiring out of indentured servants continued through the Revolutionary period and beyond.[34] However, the courts intervened when the assignment seemed unreasonable or irregular.[35]

The Pennsylvania legislature at the very founding of the colony voted to levy a fine on masters or mistresses who sold their hired servants before the expiration of their time;[36] but this absolute prohibition of assignments was apparently unenforceable, and in 1700 there was substituted for it a statute forbidding the sale of servants outside the province without the consent of two justices of the peace, and an ordinary sale within the province save in the presence of one justice.[37] In Philadelphia such sales or assignments were to be made before the mayor or recorder, and entered in a register.[38]

Some attempt appears to have been made to enforce the early regulations. In 1684 the Chester County court ordered Edward Pritchard, indicted for selling his servant contrary to law, to take the servant home and "allow him all things needfull and requisite."[39] The following year a master who had intended to sell his servant in Virginia was enjoined from assigning him outside the province.[40]

[33] The ostensible purpose of this law was to protect European Protestant immigrants. *N.Y. Col. Laws*, IV, 924 (1766).

[34] See memorial of Loyalist James Murphy, H. E. Egerton, ed., *The Royal Commission on the Losses and Services of American Loyalists, 1783 to 1785* (Oxford, 1915), p. 53.

[35] See Warner v. Banupen and Thomas, Kempe MSS, W–Y (*c.* 1760), for assignment to the commander of a privateer without servant's consent. For the invalidation of a second assignment of a pauper apprentice, see N.Y.G.S., 1772–89, f. 235 (1785); also f. 205 (1784). For widespread instances of assignments in New Jersey, see, e.g., Middlesex Co. Court, lib. I (1692); Monmouth C.P. and Q.S., lib. 1688–1721, f. 458 (1719). See also Burlington Court Book, fols. 148 (1697), 163 (1698). Apprentices were transferred by the court with their consent. *Ibid.*, fols. 138 (1696), 229 (1705).

[36] *Pa. Arch.*, 8th ser., I, 23 (1683). For the appearance of a servant in court to agree to an assignment prior to this act, see *Upland Court Rec.*, pp. 51 (1677), 85, 86, 89 (1678). See also Bucks Co. Court Mins. (1686).

[37] A penalty of £10 to be levied by distress and sale was fixed. *Pa. Stat. at Large*, II, 54–56 (1700); Read, *Abridgment*, p. 346; Graydon, *op. cit.*, p. 283.

[38] *Pa. Stat. at Large*, IV, 170, 171 (1730), 369, 370 (1743). For later acts increasing the penalty, see Bioren, *Laws*, II, 328, 329 (1777), 444 (1788).

[39] The matter was to rest until next court, but no further record of the case is found. *Chester Court Rec., 1681–97*, pp. 38, 43 (1684).

[40] He was bound in the sum of £13 to take his servant to New Castle, where he resided, and to submit the indentures to the magistrates of that town for their determination. *In re* Eleazer Cosset, Pennypacker, *Pa. Col. Cases*, p. 77 (1685). The Bucks Co. court called Stephen Newell to account in 1692 for selling a servant out of the province. Newell pleaded that he had only

In the eighteenth century the Pennsylvania courts held assignees to strict compliance with the letter of the law.[41] In 1757 Mary Bell, a redemptioner who had come in at the port of Philadelphia, petitioned the Lancaster sessions that, in the absence of the person with whom she had contracted, she had been sold by the ship's captain to one Alexander Scott. Scott assigned her over to one John Latey. She was then committed to the Lancaster County prison and sold to Jacob Reigre. None of the assignments were made before any magistrate, and, according to her account, she was compelled to sign a new indenture, the old ones being destroyed without her knowledge. The court held that the last indenture was void and that Mary Bell was still *"the property of Thomas Teaffe, the person with whom she first entered into indenture, as it doth not appear that he hath legally assigned her over to any person or persons whomsoever."* [42] One parent petitioned the Bucks quarter sessions in 1767 asking that a master be required to take back one of his children. According to his story, he had bound two children who were twins and requested that they live together, and yet, notwithstanding his express wish, one of them was sold or assigned by the master. The master pleaded that he made the assignment merely to help out the assignee in time of sickness. As the child returned to the master, the proceedings were terminated.[43]

This judicial surveillance, probably somewhat stricter than in the courts of other provinces, did not deter masters from selling or hiring out their indentured servants.[44] The *American Daily Advertiser* as late as 1793 carried ten advertisements of white servants for sale. The number gradually declines. There were eight such advertisements in 1819, two in 1823, and none the following year.[45]

"lent him to Several for Some time" and would bring him back in 3 mos. Bucks Co. Court Mins., lib. 1688–1730 (1692). See also Phillip's case, *ibid.* (1691).

[41] Parker's case, assigned before a magistrate. Lancaster Road and Sess. Docket, No. 4, 1768–76 (1770). See also Coates' petition, Philadelphia Co. Court MSS, 1732–44 (1732); the court voided an assignment of a redemptioner on the ground that he had already served his original term.

[42] Lancaster Road and Sess. Docket, No. 2, 1742–60 (August, 1757). Similarly in Tucker's petition, Philadelphia Co. Court Papers (*c.* 1760), where the court freed the servant on the ground that he had not been assigned before the mayor of Philadelphia.

[43] Leper's petition, Bucks Q.S., lib. 1754–82, f. 353 (1767).

[44] See Waldron v. Colborne, *Chester Co. Rec., 1681–97*, pp. 129, 130 (1688), 303 (1693); Steer v. Renshaw, Philadelphia Supreme Court Docket, 1772–76 (March term, 1775), case for a servant sold and assigned. Ammerman's petition, Northampton Q.S. (Sept. Sess., 1780). For an advertisement by Andrew Bradford, see *American Weekly Mercury*, July 7, 1720. For the sale of an apprentice shoemaker "to be sold at a Reasonable Price," see *Pa. Gazette*, Jan. 24, 1771.

[45] Hunt MSS, V, 127, 131. Geiser maintains that sales of servants were more frequent in the latter part of the 18th and the beginning of the 19th centuries. *Op. cit.*, p. 73.

The Delaware court records abound in instances of the sale and hiring out of indentured servants. As early as 1678 John Moll sued successfully in the Newcastle court for, among other items, a thousand pounds of tobacco which his servant had earned in the past year working for the defendant.[46] Occasionally the servant's consent to the assignment was made in open court,[47] but generally no mention of such consent is found.[48] In 1698 Philip Benson petitioned the Kent court for his discharge from Dr. Gerardus Wessells to whom he had bound himself for four years upon condition that he should cure his sore leg. Wessells not only failed to effect a cure, but sold the servant to another. The court obtained his discharge.[49] The Sussex quarter sessions discharged one petitioner who revealed that, in consideration of his debts, he had indentured himself to James Culbertson for four years on condition that Culbertson discharge the debt. Culbertson, without so doing, assigned him over to Robert Smith, who again assigned him to Edward Lay. In turn, Lay sold him to Benjamin Easman. The court put an end to this assignment marathon.[50] Where it appeared that a master had been treating a woman servant inhumanly, the court ordered him to "sell" her within one month to any master who would be approved by the justices of the peace.[51] In Delaware, an apprentice could not be assigned without his consent.[52]

In the tobacco provinces the buying and selling of servants and the hiring of them out on wages was as common as the marketing of the sotweed. Lord Baltimore set an example to the planters of Maryland when in 1643 he instructed his commissioners to sell his carpenters, apprentices, and servants "forthwith for my best advantage, which I understand will yeild at least 2000 wt of tobacco apiece although they have but one year to serve." He was given to understand that he could hire ordinary labor at 1,500 wt of tobacco a year, and figured that it was cheaper to engage workmen from year to year to look after his cattle and manage his farm than to have to buy supplies for the maintenance of servants and apprentices.[53] Servants were generally conveyed by a bill of sale, similar to that used in the conveyance of livestock. As a mat-

[46] Noll v. Kittley, *Newcastle Court Rec.*, I, 213 (1678).
[47] Assignment of Claypoole, *Some Records of Sussex County, Del.*, p. 93 (1682).
[48] See Williams v. Dubrois, Kent Court Rec., lib. 1697–98, f. 24 (1697); information against Emmerson et ux., ex'x., ibid., 1703–17, f. 4 (1704); Kent Co. Court, lib. 1718–21, Court of Equity (1721).
[49] Kent Court Rec., lib. 1697–98, f. 36 (1698).
[50] King's petition, Sussex Q.S. and C.P. Docket, 1736–38 (May, 1738).
[51] Mary McMecken's petition, Newcastle Q.S., lib. 1764–65, f. 54 (1764).
[52] Burrows v. Truitt, Boorstin, 1 Del. Cas. 613 (1818); the apprentice was a Negro child.
[53] *Md. Arch.*, III, 141 (1643).

ter of fact, there are recorded exchanges of an orphan boy servant for a cow calf, an indentured man for a boat, and a woman servant for a young mare, a cow and her calf, and 700 lbs. of tobacco.[54] When the transported servants were ready to be turned over to their Maryland or Virginia masters, the indentures properly endorsed would be placed on the record.[55] In fact, the successive endorsements appearing on such indentures might well conceal a dramatic sequence of events. A case in point was that of Mary Simons, who had come to Maryland as a servant in 1677, had been sold, assigned over, and again assigned over, in the last instance to one Richard Jones, "who intended to make her his wife" and bound over his crop as security for her payment. In the meantime he put her with William Guithere until he could the better provide for her, but under promise of marriage and freedom, he "had the use of her body," according to her petition, and then absconded. Jones's assignee insisted that Mary serve out her term, claiming that he had bought her from Jones and had apprehended her by a warrant from the Chancellor. Notwithstanding the grave charges made by the petitioner, the court ordered her to serve out the remainder of her term to the assignee upon his obtaining a reassignment from Jones.[56] The extra time exacted for running away—a substantial item under Maryland law —could be, and frequently was, sold or assigned.[57] Indicative also of the prevailing rule favoring assignments was the occasional stipulation in articles of indenture of the words *"not Assignes."* [58]

[54] Somerset, lib. AW, 1690–91, fols. 133, 154 (1691). A typical contract to deliver servants involved the notorious servant-baiter, Thomas Bradnox, and employs the word "Apprentiship" to mean ordinary bound labor. *Md. Arch.*, LIV, 156 (1658). For sales of servants in exchange for land, see *ibid.*, LX, 147, 169 (1668).

[55] See *ibid.*, LIII, 594, 595 (1665).

[56] Md. Prov. Court Proceedings, lib. 1679–84, f. 51 (1679). Cf. also the case of William Chittwood, who bought a maidservant with intention of marriage. The court ordered him to marry her within 10 days or give her her freedom and 500 lbs. tobacco. *Va. Gen. Court Mins.*, p. 475 (1640).

[57] Ann Arundel, lib. 1720–21, f. 211 (1721). For sales to residents of neighboring colonies, particularly where the servant had fled from the colony, see *Md. Arch.*, X, 214 (1652). Without assignment from the master the apprehender of a runaway servant did not have the right to sell him. *Ibid.*, LIII, 131, 132 (1661).

For a typical agreement of hiring out to work by the day, see *Md. Arch.*, IV, 26, 27 (1638). Normally the servant would be assigned for tobacco or, in rarer cases, specie, but occasionally masters exchanged servants. *Ibid.*, X, 223–225 (1652). The Provincial Court held that a bargain to assign a servant "could not be binding in the Law without a delivery and some pledge or Consideration given in earnest to make good the same." Sturman v. Daynes, *ibid.*, pp. 115–119 (1651); X, 118. In 1699 the legislature decided to buy a servant for James Baker (an employee of the Assembly), such purchase to be paid out of the next public levy. *Ibid.*, XXIV (May 28, 1699).

[58] *Md. Arch.*, LIII, 182, 183 (1661). See also stipulation that unless a servant girl agreed to be assigned the deal was off. *Ibid.*, pp. 168, 169 (1661). The girl in question was considered a good cook, but also a whore and a thief. For litigation and court supervision over the sale and

Except for the restriction against selling or assigning out of the juris-diction of the court orphans whom the commissioner had bound out [59] and statutes denying Jews permission to have Christian servants,[60] there were virtually no restrictions in Virginia upon the sale, assignment, or hiring out of servants.[61] However, after the Revolution, when inden-tured servitude was virtually obsolete in Virginia, a statute was passed prohibiting masters from assigning the contract of a servant to another without the servant's consent.[62] In the case of a servant leased to an-other master, the Accomac court, in an informal suit analogous to det-inue for detaining a cow, decreed that the assignee "deliver into the hands" of the master "the same man againe or as good a man as he was when" the assignee "received him for soe long tyme." [63] An informal action brought by petition would be sufficient to recover an amount due for the sale or hire of a servant. In the absence of an agreement under seal, the court would accept evidence supporting a parol agreement of assignment.[64]

Restraints upon alienation of servants might be imposed by alienors, but the rarity of this practice is indicative of the general freedom of alienation or assignment. For example, one brother, writing to another from abroad in 1659, stated that he was sending over a maidservant for household work on condition that "shee should not be sold unlesse to some planter for a wife." [65] While in general the master had a legal

---

assignment of servants in Maryland, see, e.g., *Md. Arch.*, I, 21 (1638); X, 83 (1650), 55–58, 120 (1651), 119–121, 145, 146 (1650–51); XLI, 9 (1657), 264 (1658); LIV, 302 (1670), 622 (1666); XLIX, 17, 52 (1663). Md. Prov. Court Proceedings, lib. 1679–84, f. 111 (1680). Somer-set, lib. 1670–71, fols. 144, 190 (1671); lib. L, O–7, f. 6 (1683); lib. AW, 1690–91, fols. 33, 34, 159. Somerset, lib. 1692–93, f. 111. Ann Arundel, lib. 1704–8, f. 615 (1707).

Occasionally masters sold servants upon false indentures. After purchase, they turned out to be free men. See, e.g., Somerset, lib. AW, 1690–91, f. 121 (1691). Sales of Negro slaves were like-wise marked by such fraudulent practices. Deceit on a warranty was the legal remedy generally employed. Such frauds were not restricted to Maryland. See Morris, *Sel. Cases, Mayor's Court*, pp. 374–376.

[59] See Lynn's case, Augusta O.B., III, f. 312 (1752). See also Charles, Md., lib. 1689–92, f. 28 (1691); *N.C. Col. Rec.*, II, 392 (1720).

[60] Hening, VI, 359 (1753); VIII, 547 *et seq.* (1748).

[61] For illustrations, see *CSPA, 1574–1660*, No. 26, p. 69 (1624); *Mins. Gen. Court of Va.*, pp. 10, 11 (1623), 30 (1624), 52, 53, 90 (1625), 145 (1626), 407 (1675); Accomac, lib. II, fols. 209 (1642), 296, 297 (1644); Surry, lib. 1645–72, f. 1 (1645); Rappahannock, lib. 1656–64, fol. 50 (1656); York, lib. 1657–62, f. 147 (1659); Henrico County, lib. I, 10 (1677); York, lib. VI, Deeds, Orders, Wills (Henry Tyler to Martin Gardiner, Oct. 4, 1681); Westmoreland, lib. 1675/6–88/9, f. 519 (1686); Augusta O.B., XVI, 253 (1777).

[62] Edmund Randolph, ed., *Abridgment of the Public Permanent Laws of Virginia* (Rich-mond, 1796), p. 350; Ballagh, *loc. cit.*, pp. 65–67.

[63] Jenkins's case, Accomac, lib. I, f. 33 (1635).

[64] Parker v. Downing, Northumberland, lib. 1699–1703, Pt. I, f. 262 (1703).

[65] Hawthorne's indenture, York, lib. 1638–48, f. 366 (1648); lib. 1657–62, f. 145; also *WMCQ.*, 1st ser., V, 269 (1659).

right to dispose of his apprentice to another, provided that the conditions of apprenticeship were met, the court would invalidate assignments when the original indenture was obtained in an irregular manner.[66]

A South Carolina act of 1740 specifically empowered masters to assign indentures of apprenticeship. When the master died, the executor or administrator was permitted to retain the apprentice provided that he carried on the same business. Otherwise he could assign him to someone who did.[67] This was also the practice of the courts of North Carolina.[68] The humane resolution adopted by Georgia in 1749 to the effect that married couples should serve together and that children under certain ages should not be separated from their parents [69] imposed on paper certain practical restrictions on the sale or assignment of servants. In the West Indies the assignment of servants was commonplace.[70]

The Servant as Property of the Estate. In the colonies workmen bound by contracts of indenture were considered chattels. They were often entered in the taxable lists and assessed as personal property. They could be sold, assigned, or hired out. They could be disposed of by will like other personal property or distributed by the administrator as part of the intestate estate of the decedent master. Furthermore, they could be attached to satisfy the debts of their master's estate.

Loyalists, in filing with the British authorities claims of losses suffered at the hands of the patriots, frequently listed their indentured servants. One instance should suffice. Captain Alexander MacLeod settled in North Carolina in 1774, fought with Major MacDonald's Royal Highland Emigrants and escaped to Sir Henry Clinton's forces after suffering military reverses. He claimed that his family and servants were scattered and his property destroyed or seized. He listed his losses, including horses, cows, farm utensils, household furniture, wearing ap-

---

[66] Pelteere's petition, *Mins. Va. Gen. Court.*, p. 109 (1626). But cf. Shult v. Travis, 2 Ky. 142 (1802), where consent of an apprentice is required.

[67] *S.C. Stat.*, III, 544–546 (1750). But see Grimké, *op. cit.*, pp. 8, 13, 14, for the view that the parent's or guardian's consent was required in the later period.

[68] See William Good's petition, Craven, lib. 1757–62 (1758), where the court expressed the opinion that the apprentice's "Mistress has a right to Assign over said Apprentice he chusing his own Master." See also N.C. Gen. Court Mins., lib. 1695–1712, f. 141 (1697); Onslow Precinct, lib. 1734–37, f. 5 (1735); John Jennings, Barbados, to Jonathan Fitts or Edward Mayer, in South Carolina, S.C. Court of Ordinary, lib. 1672–92 (1679).

[69] *Ga. Col. Rec.*, I, 535 (1749).

[70] See Harlow, *Barbados*, p. 293. West Florida forbade the sale of a servant outside the province without his consent and provided that all sales of servants were to be made in the presence of a justice (Johnson, *op. cit.*, p. 179), and Nevis forbade the sale to foreigners of servants, slaves, or utensils for the manufacture of the island's produce without license from the governor. *CSPA, 1681–85*, No. 790, p. 327 (1682).

parel, and six menservants indentured for four years, each indenture valued at £20, and six women servants indentured for four years under contracts valued at £12 each.[71]

Throughout the colonies an indentured servant's or apprentice's unexpired term was considered property which formed a part of the decedent master's estate and could be disposed of by will.[72] An apprentice boy was appraised in one inventory as worth £10, and "a small bed for him" at 20s.[73] In 1664 a value of £5 was set for one year and five months of a servant's time.[74] During inflationary periods valuations in colony money were necessarily far higher. A manservant was appraised in a Connecticut inventory at £100. In accordance with the terms of the will, he made choice in court to live with a particular daughter of the testator.[75] It was not unique for testators to leave their servants a certain freedom of choice as to their future employers. Robert Wilder of Salem left his servant, John Smith, "his choise either to Live with my Brother Woodberry or else my Brother Woodberry to binde him over to a Ship Carpenter." If Smith chose to serve out his term with

71 HMC. *Rep.*, LIX, Pt. II, 7 (1779). See also Egerton, *op. cit.*, pp. 72, 73, 260.

72 The unexpired term of an apprentice was the property of the executor or administrator. See Brit's petition, Philadelphia Q.S., 1779–82 (Jan., 1780); Graydon, *Justice's and Constable's Assistant*, pp. 14, 15. On the other hand, the executor appears merely to have been obligated at common law to *maintain* an apprentice but not to *instruct* him. See Bacon's *Abridgement* (London, 1832), V, 361.

Servants listed in inventories of estates. Essex, Mass., Probate Rec., I, 15 (1642); II, 74 (1666), 103 (1667), 249 (1671), 359 (1673), 407, 409 (1674); III, 180 (1677), 322, 328 (1679). Essex, Mass., Quarterly Court Rec., III, 116 (1663), 174 (1664), 430 (1667); V, 431 (1674). Conn. Probate Records, III, 379 (1742). York Co., Va., Deeds, Orders, Wills, Bk. I, Gill's inventory (Jan. 4, 1655); Bk. V, Dickeson inventory (April 1, 1676); Bk. VI, Hurd inventory (Nov. 16, 1684); Bk. XIV, Charmeson's inventory, June 16, 1712; Bk. XV, Brodnax inventory, Nov. 16, 1719, "Sold to John Hines, blacksmith, his time and tools 5/0/5"; Bk. XIX, Geddy's inventory (Nov. 19, 1744); Bk. XX, inventories of Charlton (Nov. 20, 1749), Bennett (Nov. 22, 1750), Anderson (Dec. 18, 1752), Wells (May 20, 1754). Hening, IV, 21, 22 (1711). Bancks' estate, S.C. Court of Ordinary, 1672–92 (1681).

Servants disposed of by will. Essex, Mass., Probate Rec., I, 147 (1652); III, 79 (1667). Smith's will, Somerset, Md., lib. 1692–93 (1692). *Md. Cal. of Wills*, III, 213 (1711); V, 57 (1721), 136, 149, 160 (1723); VI, 29 (1726), 46 (1727), 178 (1730); VII, 88 (1733). York Co., Va., Deeds, Orders, Wills, Bk. III, Fenne's will (Oct. 9, 1660); Bk. V, Townsend's will (Dec. 20, 1674); Bk. XV, Cunningham's will (Jan. 13, 1719); Allan's will (March 2, 1719). *Abstract of Norfolk Co., Va., Wills, 1637–1710*, pp. 9 (1652), 13 (1654), 17 (1655), 61 (1679). Clark's will, March 3, 1655, Isle of Wight Co. Rec., *WMCQ.*, 1st ser., VII, 221. *VMH*, IX, 197, Robard's will, Goochland County court (1783). *S.C. Hist. and Geneal. Mag.*, XIII, 60 (1709); XXXI, 11 (1799). But cf. Scolly's petition, Suffolk, Mass., G.S., III, f. 127 (1722), for the view that a servant is not bound to serve the heirs or administrators. Where the indentures failed to bind the servant to the master's "heirs and assigns," the servant would be discharged on the master's death. Stansell's case, Queen Ann, Md., lib. 1709–16, f. 147 (1711). An endorsement on indentures that the servant was to be free when his master died was not given effect in Loyd's petition, two of the justices dissenting. Talbot, Md., lib. AB, No. 8 (1697).

73 *Essex Prob. Rec.*, II, 41, 42 (1665).   74 *Essex Quarterly Court Rec.*, III, 174 (1664).

75 *Conn. Prob. Rec.*, III, 379 (1742).

the testator's brother, he was to have £10 at the end of his apprenticeship.[76] Sometimes the remaining term was divided. The will of Richard Ward of Henrico County, Virginia, provided that a servant should spend the first of two remaining years with his son Seth and should divide the last year equally between his son Richard and his daughter Elizabeth.[77] At times very substantial numbers of servants were disposed of in this way.[78] Occasionally a master agreed at the time of entering into indentures with a servant that the latter would not be turned over to the mistress or the estate in the event of the master's death. Such agreements were respected by the courts.[79] On other occasions servants were bequeathed their freedom.[80]

Servants could be and were frequently attached to satisfy the debts of their masters. In an action brought in 1678 in the sessions of Gravesend, Long Island, Captain John Palmer sued the estate of Major Kingsland for debt. Kingsland had owed the plaintiff some £34, for which he attached Elizabeth Burton, one of the major's servants. Her attorney pleaded in her behalf that she was no longer a servant of the defendant and produced a release from Major Kingsland's son and agent. The jury found that the maid was free and that the attachment was illegal, and the court gave judgment in accordance with the verdict.[81] Early Pennsylvania legislation was exceptional in the colonies in that it provided that "no Servant, white or black, within this Province . . . shall be Attached . . . for his Master or Mistress debt or debts, To the end that the means of Livelyhood may not be taken away from the said Master or Mistress." [82]

Enticement or Pirating of Workers and Interference with Contract Relations. The law relating to the harboring and enticement of servants as it evolved in colonial times profoundly reflects the extent of the master's property interest in the services of his employee. Early English law allowed the master an action of trespass for the forcible taking of

[76] *Essex Prob. Rec.*, III, 79 (1677).

[77] *WMCQ*, 1st ser., XXVII, 189 (1682).

[78] See will of John Randolph of Chesterfield County, Va., *VMH*, XXII, 445 (1774), bequeathing 20 working hands, four plough boys, house servants, etc.

[79] Page's case, *Assistants*, II, 104 (1641).

[80] *VMH*, XXV, 141 (1627); XXVIII, 105 (1627); XXIV, 283 (1709).

[81] Gravesend Court Rec., lib. II, f. 90 (1678). For other instances of servants being attached for the debts of their masters or their masters' estates, see attachment of Justassen, *Upland, Pa., Court Rec.*, pp. 145, 179 (1679); Gibson's petition, *Newcastle, Del., Court Rec.*, I, 60, 61 (1677), and Smith v. Moll, *ibid.*, p. 471 (1681); *Pa. Col. Rec.*, II, 148, 151 (1704); *Md. Arch.*, X, 217 (1652); attachment of Dickson, York, Va., O.B., 1664–72, f. 454 (1670); Rose *et al.* v. Smithers, and Donald v. Smithers, Fincastle, Va., O.B., 1773–77 (1774). For the attachment of slaves, see *State Gazette of S.C.*, Aug. 24, 1786.

[82] *Duke of York's Book of Laws*, p. 152 (1682).

his servant.[83] The Ordinance of Labourers provided a statutory remedy for nonviolent enticement.[84] Chapter 2 of the Ordinance set the penalty of imprisonment both for enticers and for servants or workers unlawfully leaving their employment, but ordinarily an indictment would not lie at common law for an enticement, and the injured party was referred to his remedy in "an Action of the case, *per quod servitium amisit."* [85] By the end of the colonial period it was generally accepted in English law that the master's property interest in the services of his servant entitled him to a legal remedy for interference with that service by third parties.[86] Whoever deprived the employer of the benefit of his servant's labor was, according to Zephaniah Swift, the Connecticut commentator writing in 1795, "a wrong doer, and must make good the damages." The word "servant" was broadly interpreted by him to mean "whether hired, or under any other obligation to serve." [87] Such is the law as we find it in our published law reports, but buried beneath this pile of printed decisions lies a century and three-quarters of judicial practice in this country, largely unavailable in published form.

Throughout the British colonies the fugitive servant and his enticer faced markedly similar treatment. The constant labor shortage made the problem of harboring or enticing runaways extremely acute. Everywhere masters were concerned about servants hiring "themselves to one or two or three masters at one time." [88] Servants were not infrequently

[83] Bertha H. Putnam, *The Enforcement of the Statute of Labourers* (New York, 1908), p. 195n. See also Reg. Brev. Orig. 96b (*de nativis abductis*); Y.B. 21 Hen. VI, 31 pl. 8. In the medieval period there were in force restrictions against the unauthorized employment of others than servants. Guild regulations contained stringent orders against the employment of any journeyman who had broken his contract or left his master without good reason. Salzman, *Eng. Industries of the Middle Ages*, p. 343.

[84] 23 Edw. III. For the text, see Putnam, *op. cit.*, Appendix. The form of the writ includes a phrase as to notice. Fitzherbert, *New Natura Brevium*, pp. 167b, 390.

[85] Dalton, *Country Justice*, p. 191; Reeve, *Baron and Femme*, p. 376. By stat. 5 Eliz., c. 4, no person in husbandry or certain specified crafts could depart without a testimonial under penalty of £5 upon conviction in the sessions of the peace (§§ 7, 8), but, according to Dalton (ed. 1727, p. 187), "this is out of Use." See also Bacon, *Abridgement* (London, 1832), V, 379. But see Burn, *Justice of the Peace Abridgment* (Boston, 1773), p. 19, which cites 6 Mod. 182, but no colonial cases. Similarly J. F. Grimké, *The South Carolina Justice of the Peace* (3d ed., New York, 1810), p. 9. For 17th-century indictments in England for enticing a servant, see J. C. Atkinson, ed., *North Riding Quarter Sessions* (London, 1884), I, 41, 59, 60, 164, 237.

[86] For a classic exposition, see 3 Bl. Comm. 142; similarly, Hening, *The New Virginia Justice* (Richmond, 1810), p. 393. See also James Parker, *Conductor Generalis* (Woodbridge, N.J., 1764), p. 23; William Griffith, *A Treatise on the Jurisdiction and Proceedings of Justices of the Peace in Civil Suits* (Newark, N.J., 1797); William Graydon, *The Justice's and Constable's Assistant* (Harrisburg, Pa., 1803), pp. 281, 283. In addition to actions brought against third parties, the master could proceed against his absent servant by an action of covenant for the breach thereof, by a tort action on the case, or he could institute a criminal prosecution. Reeve, *op. cit.*, p. 377. See also *supra*, pp. 399, 400; *infra*, pp. 434–461.

[87] *A System of the Laws of the State of Connecticut* (1795), I, 221; II, 66.

[88] See *CSPA, 1711–12*, No. 149, pp. 128–130 (1711).

induced to run away from their masters by other employers who offered them better terms than were stipulated in their original indentures. Pirating workers was one important aspect of the fugitive servant problem.[89] Workmen, plied with liquor by tavernkeepers, were often dilatory about returning to their jobs. Fugitives were harbored by sympathetic folk. At one time the deputies of Stamford, Connecticut, found it necessary to draw up a complaint against the town of Greenwich for receiving "disorderly Children or servants who fly from their parents or masters."[90] The law placed such harborers and detainers of workmen in the same category as rival employers who resorted to labor piracy. The Director General and Council of New Netherland warned masters who entertained Company servants for longer than twenty-four hours that they would be subject to a substantial fine.[91] The Virginia Company, anxious for the success of enterprises necessitating the use of apprentices in the trades, the sending over of Dutch settlers to build sawmills, water mills, and blockhouses, and the maintenance of a labor supply at the ironworks, instructed Governor Wyatt in 1621 to see that the workers remained at their jobs and were not "enticed away."[92] Captain Mathews truculently warned Captain Yong that his employment of a ship carpenter under contract to Mathews "would breed ill blood in Virginia."[93] Pirating workers was a favorite technique in the iron industry. The superintendent of the Hibernia Iron Works was forced to deny that he had ever "perswaded" workers "out of" the "employ" of a competitor and claimed that he had never "employed a Man" from his rival's works "without being warmly sollicited for that purpose, and enquireing minutely whether they were out of debt and disengaged."[94] Minor differences in the handling of the enticement problem in the colonies were largely rooted in regional economic and social variations.

NEW ENGLAND. One type of legislation, characteristic of New England, where the spirit of exclusiveness was more pronounced than elsewhere, carefully restricted the entertainment of strangers.[95] Supple-

[89] To guard against seasonal workers coming in from other colonies without being released from their employers, Governor Bradford of Plymouth assured the authorities of Massachusetts that henceforth such workers would not be received without certificates of dismissal, but added that "we haue sett no penealtie vpon it as yett, because we hope ther will be noe need." *Winthrop Papers*, III, 64, 65 (1632). See also Geiser, *op. cit.*, p. 82.

[90] *New Haven Col. Rec.*, I, 144 (1655).

[91] The fine was to go to the prosecutor of the complaint. *R.N.A.*, I, 11, 12.

[92] *VMH*, XV, 32, 33; Hening, I, 114–118.

[93] *VMH*, VIII, 156. For other early cases, see *Va. Co. Rec.*, I, 401 (1620); IV, 511 (1625).

[94] Holt to Stirling (1774), Stirling MSS, lib. IV, f. 13, N.Y. Hist. Soc. Cf. G. S. White, *Memoirs of Samuel Slater* (2d ed., Philadelphia, 1836), p. 84.

[95] See *Mass. Bay Rec.*, I, 196, 241 (1637); *Conn. Pub. Rec., 1678–89*, p. 111 (1681). For court and town action, see *Boston Town Rec.*, II, 106 (1651), 135 (1657); VII, 177, 178 (1685).

mentary legislation curbed the entertainment of servants, apprentices, or laborers in taverns or the sale of liquor to them,[96] or enticing them to overstay their time at Indian dances,[97] or even permitting them to game on one's premises.[98] By Massachusetts law, a commander of a war or merchant ship, who hid or received a man's servant or apprentice against the master's consent was liable to a fine of £5 per week.[99] A fine of £50 was set by law for transporting a servant beyond the seas.[100] A Rhode Island act of 1647 provided that any person detaining a servant not lawfully dismissed would forfeit for every such offense £5, which the master could recover by an action of debt. For their authority, the drafters of the act advised, "See 5 Eliz. 4." [101] In affording a penal action of debt in addition to the remedy in case, Rhode Island authorities modeled their labor code pretty closely upon the Tudor pattern.[102]

The problem of the fugitive and the enticer figured in court business from the beginning of settlement. The early cases in the Maine courts often came up by way of petition or "complaint," and, although civil remedies were afforded, it is difficult to decide just what action was employed.[103] At other times the criminal machinery came into operation, and fines and court costs were exacted of convicted entertainers or detainers of servants.[104] In more populous eastern Massachusetts, where legal erudition was a little more common, the orthodox common-law action on the case for enticing a servant was generally employed once the forms of action came to be more clearly differentiated.[105] Even in the earlier period of informal pleading masters stood in fear of possible damage suits for taking away other men's servants. When Henry Lawrence expressed reluctance to take fisherman Batman's daughter as an apprentice on the ground that she might be "a servant of some body," the girl's father assured him "not to feare, for that he the said Batman would discharge him of any trouble or damage that should come upon

[96] *Me. Prov. and Court Rec.*, I, 3 (1636), laborers included; *Mass. Col. Laws, 1660–72*, p. 137.
[97] *R.I. Col. Rec.*, IV, 425, 426 (1729).   [98] *Plymouth Col. Rec.*, XI, 96, 173.
[99] *Mass. Acts and Resolves*, I, 192 (1695); similarly, *Acts and Laws of N.H.*, I, 37 (1714).
[100] *Mass. Acts and Resolves*, II, 419; *Mass. Charter and General Laws* (1814), p. 750.
[101] *R.I. Col. Rec.*, I, 183; Rider, *Laws of R.I., 1636–1705*, p. 10 (code of 1663); *Charter and Laws of R.I.* (1730), pp. 174–175 (1729).
[102] A Connecticut regulation of 1677 made any Indians who hid a runaway servant liable to suffer a fine of 40s. or one month's imprisonment. *Conn. Pub. Rec., 1665–78*, pp. 308, 309.
[103] Cf. Richmond v. Lewis, *Me. Prov. and Court Rec.*, I, 5, 6 (1637); Blakeman v. Broughton, York Co. Court Rec., lib. 1686–1716, VI, f. 2 (1688). For an early "Action of the Case," see Playsteede v. Leighton, *Me. Prov. and Court Rec.*, II, 372 (1661).
[104] See Withers' case, *ibid.*, II, 481 (1673); Arise's case, *ibid.*, I, 212 (1676); Duly's case, York Sess., lib. VII, f. 20 (1720).
[105] For a somewhat unorthodox use of the remedy, see Lechford, *Note-Book*, pp. 403, 404 (1641).

him for carrying" his daughter away, "if it should cost him forty pounds." [106] As a result, the court, "for the present," discharged him of the claims of a third party to the servant.[107] When case actions for enticement or detaining were brought in the Suffolk County court, it was by no means unusual for the court to award the plaintiff specific recovery of the servant.[108] On other occasions damages rather than specific recovery were awarded.[109] Aside from a few instances when the Essex quarterly court awarded specific restitution,[110] damages seem to have been the objective of such civil suits brought elsewhere in Massachusetts.[111]

In the seventeenth century the criminal prosecution of detainers, enticers, and entertainers of servants seems to have been preferred by the Massachusetts Court of Assistants and on occasion by the county courts of the province. Sentences ranged from whipping or sitting in the

---

[106] *Ibid.*, p. 81.   [107] *Mass. Bay Rec.*, I, 265; *Assistants*, II, 82 (1639).

[108] Loatan v. Bonner, *Suffolk*, pp. 152, 153, 165–166 (1672); Danson v. Eliot, *ibid.*, pp. 1086–1092, 1123. *Assistants*, I, 156, 157 (1680), where defendant refused to turn over a runaway servant to the plaintiff's agent on the ground that the bearer did not have a written order or discharge. His rather ingenious analogy to the law of bills and notes was dismissed by plaintiff as mere "Crittical and sophistical assertion." The county court ordered the return of the Indian squaw in controversy, or in lieu thereof £15 and costs. The judgment was twice reversed by the Assistants. See also Rawlins v. Eliot, *Suffolk*, p. 1123 (1680). For other instances of specific restitution orders in suits on the case for detaining a servant, see Shrimpton v. Dowder, Suffolk Co. Court Rec., lib. I, f. 24 (1680); Rawson v. Lilly, *Suffolk*, p. 1142 (1680), in which specific restitution was awarded in a false imprisonment action brought by a master for a servant imprisoned in the course of an execution levied on the servant's person.

[109] See Keene v. Blighe, *Suffolk*, p. 159 (1672); Cooke v. Thornton, *ibid.*, p. 822 (1676). Of these, perhaps the most colorful was the "action of the case" brought against Captain Benjamin Gibbs in 1676 for forcibly taking 25 Indian servants and detaining them from their masters. Verdict for plaintiff masters of £37 10s. and costs. The Assistants also reversed this decision. *Suffolk*, pp. 742, 743 (1676); *Assistants*, I, 77–78. See also *Suffolk*, pp. 139 (1672), 215 (1673); Palmer v. Foy, commander of the *Dolphin*, Suffolk Co. Court Rec., 1680–92, f. 60 (1680); Buckley v. Vernon, *ibid.*, lib. II, f. 380 (1690), for a servant obtained by assignment.

[110] It is not clear from the record which remedy was used in these cases. See Harris's case, *Essex*, I, 197 (1650); Davis v. Swett, *ibid.*, II, 27 (1657); Chandler v. Tayler, *ibid.*, p. 403 (1662), evidence introduced that the apprentice's family had destroyed his indentures in order to obtain his freedom; Buckley v. Quilter, *ibid.*, p. 275 (1665), where specific restitution was ordered despite evidence of the master's failure to teach the apprentice a trade and of injury done to the lad's health by bad living conditions. After the apprentice's widowed mother had nursed him back to health, his master sued to recover him. See Swan v. Morgan, *ibid.*, IV, 53 (1668). In Morgan v. Hutcheson, *ibid.*, IV, 50 (1668), verdict was given defendant in an action brought "for keeping, assigning or selling a boy."

[111] In Hampshire Co. in 1683 case was used "for fellonious takeing away his Goods and for enticing away his Servant." Selding v. Wake, Hampshire Co. Court, lib. 1677–1728, f. 68. In 1698 Samuel Partridge, Jr., brought an action "of the case" in the county court at Springfield against John Montague for entertaining and detaining Mehitable White, plaintiff's apprentice. After a full hearing, the case was sent to a jury, which, though "but Eleven in Number," handed down a verdict for plaintiff of 6s. and costs. *Ibid.*, lib. 1693–1706, fols. 57, 58 (1698). See also Mary Duboys of Ulster County, N.Y., v. Joseph Sheldin of Suffield, case for detaining a Negro man who had run away from her, although it was not clear whether he was a servant or a slave. Plaintiff appealed a verdict for defendant to the Superior Court to be held at Springfield.

stocks for one hour to substantial fines.[112] At times the churches rather than the courts felt impelled to act. The Roxbury church, by way of example, admonished "sister Cleaves" "for unseasonable entertaining and corrupting other folks servants and children." [113]

Criminal penalties, such as fines or corporal punishment, were imposed in the other New England colonies for enticing or detaining other men's servants.[114] In a great many instances, however, a civil suit was substituted for a criminal prosecution, and the master recovered substantial damages.[115]

THE MIDDLE COLONIES. Fairly uniform legislation was enacted in the Middle colonies against enticers, harborers, and entertainers of servants and apprentices. The New York statutes were in many ways typical. An act of 1684 provided that those abetting the transportation of any apprentice, servant, or slave should be fined £5 current money of the province for the use of the county and required to make full satisfaction to the master for the costs, charges, and damages sustained. Whosoever "by promise of freedome Matrimony or by any other ways or means whatsoever" persuaded, enticed, or inveigled a white servant to neglect his employment would, upon conviction, be adjudged to make full satisfaction to the master for the remaining time of service. The convicted person was allowed to serve the master in lieu of the servant's remaining time. By this same act, entertainers of servants, apprentices, or

[112] *Assistants*, II, 51, 52 (1635), 122 (1642); *Essex*, I, 5 (1637), III, 264 (1665), the Essex court "did not accept" a verdict acquitting the prisoner of abetting a runaway; *Suffolk*, pp. 176 (1672), 265 (1673), 1158 (1680); Suffolk Co. Court Rec., lib. 1680–92, I, f. 99 (1681). Frequent entertaining of servants was also the subject of criminal prosecution. *Assistants*, II, 5 (1630). See also Middlesex Co. Court files, folder 115, group 3, cited by E. S. Morgan, "The Puritan Family and the Social Order," *More Books* (Boston, Jan., 1943), p. 17. See also *Essex*, II, 180 (1659); III, 148 (1664), 251 (1665).

[113] Boston Record Commrs., *6th Report* (Boston, 1881), p. 95; cited by Morgan, *loc. cit.,* p. 14.

[114] See, e.g., Kenaston's case, New Hampshire Q.S., lib. 1683–86, f. 13 (1684). Emerson's presentment, *Plymouth Col. Rec.*, I, 118 (1639); Whitney's case, *ibid.*, p. 46 (1636); Billington's and Eaton's case, *ibid.*, II, 58, 59 (1643). Trott's case, *Conn. Particular Court Rec.*, p. 60 (1649); Chapman's case, *ibid.*, pp. 124, 125 (1654). Bradley's case, Conn. Court of Assistants, lib. 1702–11, f. 373 (1702). Searls' case, Hartford Co. Court mins., 1706/7–18, f. 456 (1716), appealed. Gutsell's case, New Haven Co. Court, lib. I, f. 103 (1677); Lancton's case, *ibid.*, f. 155 (1685), in addition to enticing a Negro servant, the prisoner broke gaol and stole a canoe; Lieut. Samuel Pond's case, *ibid.*, lib. II, f. 460 (1710), the fine was divided between the town treasury of Branford and the complainant. On review the judgment was reversed, as defendant's offense appears merely to have been the entertaining of the apprentice on a Sabbath.

[115] *Rhode Island:* see Withrington v. Earle, Newport Q.S., "Aquidneck Quarter Court Records," in Chapin, *op. cit.,* II, 138 (1642), "case," submitted to arbitration; Winsor v. Williams, Newport Court of Trials, lib. I, f. 69 (1684), verdict for defendant. *Connecticut:* Chapman v. Browne, *Conn. Particular Court Rec.*, p. 99 (1651); Grover v. Burret, Conn. Court of Assistants, lib. 1702–11, f. 426 (1704); Robinson v. Charles, New Haven Co. Court Rec., lib. I, f. 84 (1675), brought by servant's husband, acting as attorney for master, for causing his wife's "unlawful departure" from master's service.

slaves, who were aware that they had taken unauthorized leave, would be required to pay the master 10*s*. for every day's enticement and concealment as well as a fine of £5 current for the use of the county.[116]

During the first generation of English rule in New York cases of enticement and harboring of servants were handled very much as in the predecessor Dutch language courts, which normally ordered the servant returned to his master,[117] and which often failed to distinguish clearly between a criminal prosecution and a civil action.[118] In one case before a Dutch language court after the English occupation it appeared that the servant had run away, not through deliberate exhortation, but because of a fight with a third party. The court declined to sustain an action brought against such third party to require him to help search for the servant,[119] from which ruling it might be inferred that in the Dutch language courts malice or intent was necessary to sustain an action for causing a breach of a labor contract.

In the English courts of seventeenth-century New York, harborers and detainers of white servants were liable to be sued in an action on the case;[120] harborers of Negroes were more likely to be criminally prose-

116 *N.Y. Col. Laws*, I, 147. By New Jersey law, enticers of runaways were liable to forfeit £10 and costs to be recovered by the master in any inferior court of common pleas. The same 10*s*. per diem penalty of the New York law was also incorporated in the New Jersey act. Allinson, *N.J. Acts*, pp. 2, 22 (1714). By Pennsylvania law the penalty was 20*s*. per diem. *Pa. Stat. at Large*, II, 55 (1700), 250, 251 (1721); VI, 246–252 (1763); VII, 361–363 (1770). Cf. also *Pa. Col. Rec.*, I, 72, 74, 79 (1683); *Pa. Arch.*, 8th ser., I, 199 (1699); Graydon, *Justice's and Constable's Assistant*. New York carefully restricted the sale of liquor to servants (*N.Y. Col. Laws*, III, 952 [1737]), and forbade tavernkeepers from entertaining seamen after 10 P.M. under penalty of 20*s*. *Ibid.*, I, 866, 867 (1715). New Jersey tavernkeepers convicted of entertaining servants were subject to a fine of 20*s*. current for the first offense, double for the second, and £5 for every offense thereafter. Allinson, *N.J. Acts*, p. 105 (1739). By act of 1751 the refusal of a tavernkeeper to clear himself by oath of selling such liquors was deemed evidence of his guilt. *Ibid.*, p. 191.

117 Cf. Hardenbergh v. Fabricius, *R.N.A.*, VI, 252 (1670); Herregrens v. de Wit, "Dutch Records of Kingston," N.Y. State Hist. Assn., *Proceedings*, VI, 45; Wittekar v. Jansen, Ulster Dutch Transcripts, lib. III, f. 572 (1670), Du Booys v. Wynkoop, *ibid.*, lib. II, f. 603 (1671); Van Alen v. Philipsen, *Albany, Rensselaerswyck, and Schenectady Court Mins.*, I, 75 (1669)—see also *ibid.*, pp. 158 (1676), 466, 467 (1680).

118 Ten Boakans v. Mattysen, Ulster Dutch Transcripts, lib. III, f. 78 (1681).

119 Harmonson v. Louwensen, *ibid.*, f. 109 (1682).

120 Clark v. Musgrove, where defendant was charged with advising the servant that "hee might gitt his freedome if he went to the governor," as he had served one year. While clearing defendant owing to lack of proof, the court implied that such advice, if given, would have been actionable: Gravesend Town Rec., lib. I, fols. 77, 78 (1652). See also Roeloffsen v. Brower, Gravesend Court and Road Rec., lib. II, 1668–1766 (1676). In Sharp v. Brittaine, a suit for breach of contract to deliver a servant, defendant was cleared by arbiters when it appeared that a Frenchman had taken the servant away from him. This complicated suit was tried twice, and, finally, in giving judgment for plaintiff, the court recommended that the governor would "please to appoint some persons to make inquiry how the servant in Question was taken away from both plaintiff and Defendant and by whom," and "how farr they may be lyable to make reparation for the Dammage by that meanes susteyned"—a recommendation which clearly indicated the existence of civil liability for damages on the part of detainers and enticers of servants.

cuted.[121] The English courts by implication held, as did the Dutch language courts under English rule, that, unless the detaining were willful and intentional, no action would lie.[122]

A very revealing eighteenth-century case of enticement—in some respects the most notable dispute of this nature—came up in the New York Supreme Court in 1763 in the January term. In this action John Brinner, represented by John Tabor Kempe, alleged that he had made articles of indenture with John Jarrett in London in 1761 for a term of three years to commence on the latter's arrival in New York, during which time he was to work as a cabinetmaker and chair carver. The plaintiff paid the passage of Jarrett and his wife from England and advanced him some forty pounds. One of the witnesses to this indenture later secured employment with Burns and Melville, defendants. Testimony brought out that Jarrett worked at odd times for Burns and that the latter together with Melville endeavored "to intice him away from my Sarvys." As a result of their efforts Jarrett began to neglect his master's business and to work during his master's time at Burns's shop, and during the last few months he worked irregularly for his master. A warning to Melville through a third party that, if he did not desist, he would be sued, had no effect. Jarrett finally deserted his master completely and Melville retained and employed him with full knowledge of his outstanding contractual obligations. Brinner further charged that

---

Ibid., lib. II, fols. 55, 70, 71; N.Y. State Hist. Assn., *Ann. Report,* III, 245, 246, 249, 327, 408–410. Cf. also Hendrickson v. Peterson, Newtown Court Rec., fols. 243–245 (1670), a strikingly informal complaint in which the court ruled on four distinct issues. Defendant was permitted to keep the servant and no damages were assessed. See also Wessells v. Archer, Rec. of Wills, lib. XIXB, f. 547 (1677).

[121] Kingston Sessions Mins., lib. 1693–98 (1698, 2 cases); Gravesend Court and Road Rec., 1692–1895, lib. I (Flatland Sessions, May 10, 1709); N.Y.G.S., lib. 1694–1731/2, fols. 280 (1714), 517 (1729); Suffolk G.S., lib. 1784–1815 (Oct., 1787).
A somewhat novel variation of the normal enticement situation was the criminal prosecution in general sessions in 1705 of Paroculus Parmyter "for buying the wife of Richard Hunter and Entertaining of her." N.Y.G.S., lib. 1694–1731/2, f. 101 (1705). For other prosecutions for entertaining married women, see J. Goebel and T. R. Naughton, *Law Enforcement in Colonial New York* (New York, 1944), p. 105n.

[122] See, e.g., Meeker's complaint, Newtown Court Rec., f. 141 (1682); Bryant's complaint, N.Y.G.S., lib. 1683–94 (1688). In a sensational action brought in 1681 Edmund Andros, governor of the province, was sued by Robert Story in the mayor's court of New York City for trover and conversion of beaver shipped from London and seized by customs officers, as well as for encouraging plaintiff's servant to desert his master, which latter count also seemed to be part and parcel of the trover action. Damages of £390 sterling were sought. Andros pleaded that this case was not within the jurisdiction of the court, but had been considered in a court of admiralty held three years previously. N.Y.M.C.M., 1677–82, f. 300a (1681).
For later mayor's court suits for detaining or enticing servants, see Robinson v. Lewis, N.Y.M.C.M., 1710–15, fols. 287, 316; Salzer Papers (1711–45) (1713); Francis v. Coleman, N.Y.M.C.M., 1735/6–43, f. 498; Salzer Papers (1711–45) (1741); Readle v. Amstruther, Salzer Papers (1772).

Jarrett had made for Melville "6 or 8 Carved Chairs and a Card Table wch was Carved to the house of one Nathl Marriner a Glasure and painter and Brought from thaire by Mr Melvill and Bourns Servants to his Shop." Burns was likewise informed of Jarrett's legal status as a servant of the plaintiff. Brinner computed the loss of his servant's time at the rate of four or five shillings per day, revealing a comparatively liberal wage scale for skilled craftsmen in this country at that time.[123]

An advertisement in the *New-York Mercury,* under date of May 31, 1762, provides additional background for this case:

John Brinner, Cabinet Maker and Chair-Maker, from London; At the Sign of the Chair, opposite Flatten Barrack-Hill, in the Broad-Way, New York: Where every Article in the Cabinet, Chairmaking, Carving and Gilding Business, is executed on the most reasonable Terms, with the utmost neatness and Punctuality. He carves all sorts of Architectural, Gothic and Chinese Chimney Pieces, Glass and Picture Frames, Slab Frames, Gerondoles, Chandaliers, and all kinds of Mouldings and Frontispieces, &c. &c. Desk and Book-Cases, Library Book-Cases, Writing and Reading Tables, Commode and Bureau Dressing Tables, Study Tables, China Shelves and Cases, Commode and Plain Chest of Drawers, Gothic and Chinese Chairs; all Sorts of plain or ornamental Chairs, Sofa Beds, Sofa Settees, Couch and easy Chair Frames, all kinds of Field Bedsteads, &c. &c.

N.B. He has brought over from London six Artificers, well skill'd in the above Branches.

This small factory operator, with the aid of eleven witnesses, established the fact that Jarrett had worked rather faithfully until June, 1762, after which time he was often absent or idled on the job, complaining that "he could have a great deal more for his Work in another place, That Melvil and Burnes give him 10 sh: a Day. That he would tire Brinner out, unless he would release him from his articles, but would give him £25 for his Time. That he often pretended to be sick in order to be absent from Brinner." One witness who kept the accounts of Brinner's journeymen testified that he saw Melville at Jarrett's lodging and that Melville told Jarrett to complete the work he was doing for him

---

[123] Kempe A–B, N.Y. Hist. Soc. In the original draft of the declaration which Kempe had prepared and which cited Vidian's *Entries,* 8 A, William Smith, Jr., had recommended: "I believe this Draft will do but for greater safety think it would be proper to set forth precisely how long Gerrit bound to serve instead of several years." To this Kempe replied: "I have altered the Draft as you desire—as also in several other places, making it something more special, but nearer to the true State of the Case. If you think there is no Danger in being so special, I think it will be best as it will more agree with our Evidence." The final draft of the declaration stated that Brinner had bound Jarrett to his service until Oct. 29, 1764, but that Burns "unlawfully did sollicit and procure to depart absent and withdraw himself" on July 27 and at other times until Dec. 11, from which date he had completely deserted Brinner's service at Burns's instigation.

and promised him "what Money he wanted." On another occasion Melville treated Jarrett to a bowl of punch and told him "he need not fear Brinner, for he would indemnify him from any Thing that Brinner could do to him." Jarrett was seen in his own lodging at work on some chairs and a card table, subsequently seen in Melville's shop and at his residence. Mistress Marten's testimony disclosed that

> She has often heard Mr Jarret say he should have been very well Contented with Mr Brinner if Melville and Burns had not deluded him away from his Business at Briners to work at home for them by fair promises which they never kept but that they had been his Ruin.

> That Mr Briner Came to our Apartt and askt Mrs Jarrat why her husband was gone who answerd that the Defendants had frightnen'd him away by threatning to Arrest him That was Melville to Come where she was she would give him the devill of a Lesson for that he had been the Ruin of her husband by *inticeing* him from Brinner.

Brinner sued Burns and Melville in separate actions, Melville being defended by Richard Morris and Burns by Whitehead Hicks. Both pleaded not guilty, but subsequently withdrew their pleas, confessed judgment, and agreed to stand as security for such damages as would be awarded by arbitrators.[124] As a result of such awards the total sum recovered on judgments in these suits amounted to some £128—no inconsiderable amount to recover for the services of an artisan appraised at 4s. a day! [125]

New Jersey customarily set her criminal machinery in motion against harborers and enticers.[126] Warnings of prosecution were frequently contained in advertisements for New Jersey runaways: "Whosoever shall Conceal, Harbour, and Entertain the said Servant, or Counsell him to absent himself from the said Service, will be prosecuted according to Law," is a typical example.[127] In Pennsylvania and Delaware from earli-

---

[124] By consent of the parties John Edward Palmer was named by plaintiff as an arbitrator, Jonathan Blake by defendant, and Andrew Gautier by the court. Blake and Gautier were fellow cabinetmakers, and Palmer was probably a member of the craft as well. *N.Y. Mercury*, April 8; *N.Y. Gazette*, April 18, 1765.

[125] The arbitrators awarded plaintiff in each action £42 10s. and costs, which the court fixed at £21 37s. Judgment against both defendants was accordingly obtained. N.Y. Supreme Court Mins., lib. 1762–64, fols. 92, 100, 282, 340 (1763–64). For a similar action brought by a prominent Salem cabinetmaker in 1798, see Sanderson v. Radson, *Essex Inst. Hist. Coll.*, LXX (1934), 335.

[126] Stewart's case, Middlesex Co. Mins., lib. I (1684); Coles' case, Burlington, West Jersey, Court Bk., f. 243 (1707).

[127] *Pa. Gazette*, Dec. 1–8, 1737; *N.J. Arch.*, V, 1 (1780). Cf. *Pa. Gazette*, July 6, 1738. See also *Pa. Gazette*, June 26, 1778, where a master offers a reward of £6 for the arrest and gaoling of a deserter from one of the Jersey battalions who had enticed a servant to indenture himself to him and then took him away.

est times civil actions were instituted against third parties for detaining servants.[128] By the middle of the eighteenth century, cases for selling a servant not one's own, for enticing a servant, or for taking a servant against his master's will were quite usual in the Pennsylvania-Delaware area. Damages rather than specific recovery were by now the end sought by plaintiff masters.[129] In a complaint directed to President Reed during the Revolution for relief against a ship captain who refused to turn over a servant actually under contract to the complainant at the time he bound himself to the captain in France, the President of Pennsylvania gave it as his opinion that the captain, though acting in good faith, had no more right to keep the servant than a man would who had been "so unlucky as to purchase a Stolen Horse." [130]

At times disputes concerning harboring or enticing servants came before the monthly meeting of the Friends. The Philadelphia meeting advised one Christopher White, a servant, to complain to the magistrates in New Castle, but as neither master nor servant belonged to "their religious Societie they wold not Interfere wt the Civill mag'trates office and place." Thereupon the master brought suit against one Philip England for £14 10s., at the rate of 5s. a day, for harboring White contrary to the statute. Evidence was introduced that the servant had been badly treated by the plaintiff, who had withheld necessaries from him, and apparently the jurors' sympathies were with the harborers.[131] In another master-servant dispute the latter acknowledged at the monthly meeting of the Friends at New Harden in 1726 that he had been wrongly encouraged by others to seek his freedom although his time had not expired.[132]

A number of tavernkeepers were prosecuted in the courts of the Middle colonies for entertaining or concealing servants and apprentices,[133]

---

[128] Vanculine's case, *Chester Co., Pa., Court Rec., 1681–97*, p. 84 (1686); Moulder v. Tally, *ibid.*, pp. 110, 111 (1687). Man v. Wharton, *Newcastle, Del., Court Rec.*, I, 211, 212 (1678); Delawood v. Herman, *ibid.*, pp. 399–401 (1680). Clark v. Shattam, *Some Records of Sussex County, Del.*, p. 86 (1682). Where the enticer was also a runaway servant, he was more likely to be punished criminally. Moore's case, *Newcastle, Del., Court Rec.*, I, 386.

[129] Ross Docket, Phila. C.P., 1738–45, Hist. Soc. of Pa.: Stample v. Conrade (1741); Neigley v. Yost, Smith v. Lindsay (1742); McKean v. Miller (1746); David v. Proctor, Phila. Co. Court Papers (June, 1746), Hist. Soc. of Pa.

[130] *Pa. Arch.*, 1st ser., VII, 701.

[131] Guest v. England, Pennypacker, *Pa. Col. Cases*, pp. 96–98 (1686).

[132] Cited by A. C. Myers, *Immigration of the Irish Quakers into Pennsylvania, 1682–1750* (Swarthmore, 1907), p. 231.

[133] See King v. Slyck, N.Y.G.S., lib. 1722–42/3, f. 209; 1732–62, f. 60; N.Y. Supreme Court Mins., lib. 1732–39, fols. 222, 224, 257, 258, 261 (1736). Also *Pa. Col. Rec.*, II, 160 (1704). Because he entertained servants at his public house, George Hooke of York was warned by the court not to sell liquor by less measure than one quart at his peril. York Q.S., lib. I, f. 23 (1758). The Philadelphia grand jury in 1744 called attention to the great increase in public houses, result-

in one instance for allowing a considerable group of apprentices to play billiards,[134] and in another for giving apprentices credit and "encouraging them several times to defraud their masters" in order to make payment.[135] In New Jersey Charles Read, the ironmaster, petitioned the legislature to prohibit licensing of taverns within three miles of any ironworks without the approval of the owners of the works, and to impose a limit of 5*s.* upon the amount of debts contracted by employees of such works, which would be recoverable from the owners. In 1769 the legislature authorized owners of ironworks in Evesham and Northampton townships in Burlington County to furnish their employees with strong liquor "in such Quantity as they shall from Experience find Necessary," but prohibiting any other person or persons residing within four miles of the works from supplying the employees with strong drink.[136] Toward the close of the century the operators of a glassworks in Albany found it necessary to petition the legislature that the number of taverns in the vicinity be limited to one, the keeper of which was to be nominated by the petitioners. They complained that three neighboring dram shops "divert the attention of our labourers from their employment and give them debauched and idle hearts which often disqualify them for executing their business." [137]

THE TOBACCO COLONIES. When tobacco planters advertised warnings that harborers of absconding servants acted at their peril,[138] they did so with the assurance that legislation on the books dealt extensively with such offenses. A Maryland statute of 1649 made it a felony to act as an accessory to the escape of an apprentice from service. Those transporting him out of the province were liable to pay double costs and damages to the party aggrieved.[139] Under Virginia law shipmasters who transported servants out of the province were subject to a penalty of £50,

---

ing in the impoverishment of liquor retailers generally, who were tempted to entertain apprentices, servants, and even Negroes, thus giving the community the opprobrium of "Hell-Town." Ancient Rec. of Philadelphia, 1702–69, Wallace MSS, Hist. Soc. of Pa.

[134] Reg. v. Baulay, N.Y.G.S., lib. 1694–1731/2, f. 137 (1707).

[135] Rex v. Slyck, N.Y. Supreme Court Mins., lib. 1732–39, fols. 222, 224, 257, 258, 261 (1736), found guilty of entertaining servants and apprentices, but not guilty as to crediting them. In 1719 the New York general sessions acted to prevent "Tumults, Disorders and other Mischiefs" on Shrove Tuesday when "Great Numbers of Youth Apprentices and Slaves" were wont to assemble together at cockfights, by ordering the constable henceforth to forbid such sports. *Ibid.*, 1694–1731/2, f. 359 (1719).

[136] Fines collected under this act were to go to road repair. *N.J. Session Laws*, 1769, ch. xix, p. 109; C. R. Woodward, *Ploughs and Politicks* (New Brunswick, N.J., 1941), pp. 92, 93.

[137] Caldwell, Battern, McClallen, and McGregor to Stephen Van Rensselaer (1792), Misc. MSS, N.Y. Pub. Lib.

[138] See, e.g., *Va. Gazette*, July 13, 1775.

[139] *Md. Arch.*, I, 249, 349 (1651). The double penalty was repealed in 1674. *Ibid.*, p. 402.

doubled in the case of slaves.[140] Those who harbored servants without pass or certificate from their masters were liable in both colonies to pay the master damages sustained by such unlawful departure.[141] In Virginia the burden of proof was on the hirer of a servant upon a forged certificate to establish his good faith; otherwise he would be subject to the fines and penalties for entertaining runaways without certificate.[142] Parallel legislation forbidding masters to employ servants without certificate was enacted in the old country.[143] The colonial laws undoubtedly served as a model for a number of Southern states during Reconstruction.[144] The tobacco colonies made innkeepers subject to a fine payable to the master of the servant they harbored, entertained, or provided with liquors without the master's consent.[145]

As a result of these heavy penalties law-abiding tobacco planters hesitated to give food and shelter to a servant even when he had been deserted by his master. Thus, the orphan, John Trundle, apprenticed to a runaway carpenter, appealed for relief to the county court in 1704, reciting "that none dare Entertaine him being a Servant because of the pen-

[140] Hening, III, 270, 271.

[141] Maryland in 1660 fixed a penalty of 500 lbs. tobacco for the first night the servant was entertained, 1,000 lbs. for the second, and 1,500 lbs. for every night thereafter. *Md. Arch.*, II, 146, 147; 500 lbs. was the penalty set by act of 1671 for every night or 24-hour period. *Ibid.*, pp. 298, 299, 524; XXII, 546–553 (1699). Those circumventing the 24-hour limit by entertaining servants or slaves "at dead Times of Night, for several hours together," were later made liable to pay 100 lbs. for each hour of unlawful entertainment. For defaulting, the offender could be whipped not exceeding 39 stripes for each offense and required to give security for his good behavior. *Ibid.*, XLI, 149–151 (1748). In Virginia the penalty was increased per night from 20 lbs. in 1643 to 30 lbs. in 1656 and to 60 lbs. eight years later. Hening, I, 252, 439: II, 239. This was reduced again to 30 lbs. *Ibid.*, VIII, 547–558 (1748); Starke, *Justice of the Peace*, p. 320. For litigation under the act of 1664, see Wallace's petition, *VMH*, XI, 60, 61 (1674?). A penalty of 30 lbs. per diem was imposed upon those hiring or entertaining servants without certificates of freedom. Hening, II, 115 (1662). See York O.B., lib. 1671–91, f. 7 (1671). William Browne, a servant, petitioned the York Co. court that "without his master's leave none will sett him over" the York River which he had to traverse in order to procure his indentures on file at the Gloucester court. Permission was granted. York O.B., 1671–94, f. 219 (1675).

[142] Hening, III, 447. Proclamations by the governors on this subject were customarily read in court and occasionally entered among the court orders. See proclamation of Feb. 21, 1691, Henrico O.B., II, f. 349; precept published, Oct. 10, 1710, *ibid.*, lib. 1710–14, f. 3; Va. Misc. MSS, N.Y. Hist. Soc. For a similar Maryland proclamation, see Somerset, lib. 1695–96, fols. 135, 136.

[143] In 1606 the Scottish Parliament declared that neither coalhewers, bearers, nor salters could be employed by a new master without a testimonial or formal permission from their previous master. *Acts of the Parliament of Scotland*, IV, 286, 287; V, 419; VI, 761.

[144] For example, the Tennessee act of 1875 made the enticer liable to "such damages as [the master] may reasonably sustain by the loss of the labor" of the employee. *Tenn. Code, 1932*, §§ 8559, 8560. See also Landis, *op. cit.*, pp. 101–102.

[145] *Md. Arch.*, XXXIX, 179, 180 (1735); XLIV, 103 (1745). In 1697 the Maryland authorities ordered that, owing to the fact that a certain workman at the State House was constantly drunk and neglected his work, ordinary keepers were cautioned against extending credit to him beyond the limits of the law. *Ibid.*, XXIII, 130 (1697).

alties in the act of assembly against Such Entertainers of Servants." [146]
Again, in 1721, Charles Griffin petitioned that his master had left the
province and that he could not "get a living" as "no person" would
"employ him he being a bound servant." The court ruled "that any
person have liberty of employing" Griffin "until his master returns." [147]

In Maryland a number of different legal devices were employed in
enticement and harboring situations. The master might have recourse
to an informal complaint for detaining, by which his servant was returned to him. This was similar to the informal procedure for specific
restitution found in the Northern colonies.[148] In the second place,
equitable relief might be granted where the wrongful detaining of the
servant was in effect a breach of good faith.[149] Perhaps a more typical
recourse to equity was the use of replevin in suits brought in Chancery
for restitution and damages for the taking and wrongful detaining of
servants.[150] Aside from the informal action for restitution and various
procedures in equity, the principal civil remedy against third parties
harboring or enticing was a damage suit, generally an action on the case,
and occasionally founded on the pertinent statutes.[151] Judgments are on

[146] Ann Arundel, lib. 1702–4, f. 481 (1704).

[147] Peter Rogers filed a similar petition for relief. Charles Co., lib. 1720–22, f. 235 (1721).

[148] Trussell v. Pakes, *Md. Arch.*, X, 15, 16 (1650); Blount v. Copley, *ibid.*, X, 132–135 (1651).
Defendant, a Jesuit priest known also as Father Philip Fisher, later brought an action against
John Hallowes for having influenced a servant to leave him and sought 3,000 lbs. of tobacco
damages. *Ibid.*, IV, 406.

[149] Cornwallis v. Sturman, *ibid.*, X, 235, 254, 371, 372 (1652); Battin v. Smith, *ibid.*, XLI,
368 (1660), defendant was charged with having taken the indentures of certain transported
servants in his own name and disposed of them "contrary to the Fayth reposed in him." A jury
in the Provincial Court returned a verdict for defendant. See also Runnings v. Stokes *et al.*, *ibid.*,
p. 329 (1669).

[150] Thus, according to the writ in Chancery, the widow Verlinda Stone found sufficient security to prosecute her suit for her servant, taken and unjustly detained by Edmund Lindsey, "to
be returned if the return of him be adjudged." The court directed that "the servant . . . Replvyed
to be and delivered you Cause and put by Surety and Safe Pledge the af'd Edmd Lindsey" that
he answer her plea. Stone v. Lindsay, *ibid.*, LI, 81 (1672). See also Wahob v. James, *ibid.*, pp. 103,
104 (1673); Bowdle v. Boteler, *ibid.*, p. 204; Parker v. Tilly, *ibid.*, p. 226; Harrison .v. Pattison,
ibid., pp. 224, 225 (1678).

[151] Cf. Cockschott v. Whitcliff's wife, *ibid.*, IV, 154 (1642); Pope v. Barrett, Clark v. Huett,
ibid., p. 268 (1644); Dorington v. Holman, *ibid.*, X, 523, 524 (1657); Dickison v. Waters, *ibid.*,
LX, 415, 416 (1671). The notorious servant-baiter, Captain Bradnox, brought suit against John
Smith for detaining and concealing Sarah Taylor, who had been forced to flee from the brutal
treatment of her master and mistress. Bradnox claimed that the girl had spent the night in
Smith's house, to which defendant pleaded that, though he had been too tired to take the servant
back that evening, he had intended the very next morning either to return her to her master or
take her before some constable or magistrate. His plea was substantiated by testimony, and the
suit was dismissed. *Ibid.*, LIV, 169, 171, 176 (1659). However, on another occasion the Kent justices ordered John Deare to ask Captain Bradnox's forgiveness for entertaining Sarah and to
promise in open court never to repeat the offense. *Ibid.*, p. 168 (1659). See also *ibid.*, LIII, 592,
602 (1665). For a good illustration of the procedure under the act of 1676 providing that suits
for detaining were to be brought in trespass upon the case, see Rousby v. Spernon, Md. Prov.

record in case for enticing servants in which sums awarded ranged from 6,000 lbs. of tobacco and costs recovered in 1682 to £200 current money of the state in 1779, or as much as £1,500 current in 1781.[152] In addition to case, masters might proceed against enticers or detainers by way of detinue or trover.[153]

As at common law, damages for actual seduction of a servant could be recovered in Maryland courts if the master could show loss of services. In 1671 Captain William Colebourne brought suit in Somerset court "for abusing by carnal copulation" a servant girl and causing her to become pregnant, as a result of which her master suffered a loss of her services. Despite his denial, the jury held the defendant to be the father of the child and returned a verdict for plaintiff for 500 lbs. of tobacco. An additional sentence of twenty-five lashes was meted out to the wrongdoer by the court. Here case for seduction was actually combined with the ordinary bastardy procedure employed in Maryland courts.[154]

Under acts of assembly a large number of *qui tam* suits were successfully brought for enticing and transporting the servants of others, for harboring or entertaining them or for having any dealings with them. As a matter of fact, actions for debt under the acts of 1663, 1671, and 1686 appear more frequently in the records than trespass on the case for enticement or harboring.[155] Notable among these was the judgment for 10,500 lbs. of tobacco recovered from John King for entertaining a runaway servant of Gerard Slye for the space of twenty-one days. By statute half went to the proprietor and half to the complainant master. King petitioned the Governor and Council that the proprietary's share be re-

Court Rec., lib. 1679–84, f. 514 (1682). See also Andrews v. Humphry, *Md. Arch.*, XLI, 351 (1676); Goffe's case, Somerset, lib. 1671–75, fols. 152, 153 (1672), Venables v. Jenkins, *ibid.*, lib. 1689–90, f. 159 (1690), Taylor v. Newbold *et al., ibid.*, lib. AW, 1690–91, f. 171 (1691).

[152] Rousby v. Spernon, Md. Prov. Court Rec., lib. 1679–84, f. 514 (1682); Miller v. King, Somerset, lib. 1689–1701, fols. 494, 495 (1701); Sleycomb v. Garly, Ann Arundel, lib. 1702–4, f. 35 (1703); Moor v. Tully, Somerset, lib. 1775–84, fols. 190, 191 (1779); Tost v. Dorsey, Md. Prov. Court Rec., lib. 1781–82, f. 181 (1781).

[153] Revell v. Poole, Somerset, lib. 1671–75, fols. 133, 134 (1672). See also Bishop v. Mills, Md. Prov. Court Rec., lib. 1688–89, f. 48 (1689); Giuther Admr. of Mary Jones v. Sly, *ibid.*, lib. 1679–84, f. 463 (1681); Miller v. Hill, *ibid.*, f. 516 (1682).

[154] Somerset, lib. 1670–77, fols. 177, 178 (1671).

[155] Under *act of 1671*: Court and Proprietary v. Hartwell, Charles Co., lib. 1674–76, f. 6; *Md. Arch.*, LX, 581–582 (1674); Bookerd and Proprietary v. Thomas, Charles Co., lib. 1678–80, f. 13 (1678); Dent and Proprietary v. Mary Williams, Charles Co., lib. 1688–89, f. 56 (1688). *Act of 1673*: Sly v. King, Md. Prov. Court, lib. 1679–84, f. 807 (1683). *Act of 1676*: Gaunt v. Russell, *ibid.*, lib. 1688–89, fols. 72–74 (1689); Thomas and Proprietary v. Spike, Charles Co., lib. 1690–92, f. 67 (1690); Proprietary v. Guilder, Cecil Co., lib. 1683–92 (1690); Blackstone v. Price, *ibid.* (1692). *Act of 1692*: Smallwood *qui tam* v. Foster, Charles, lib. 1696–98, f. 464 (1698).

mitted on the ground that, unless this were done, it would mean "the total ruin of him and his six small children." His request was granted.[156]

Aside from such penal actions, ordinary criminal prosecutions for enticement were very largely confined to the early years of the province and to instances where the offense bordered on criminal conspiracy.[157] As these prosecutions stressed the fomenting of desertion rather than enticement or detaining, they are considered elsewhere in this study.[158] The chief tribunal of Maryland for the criminal punishment of enticers, harborers, and entertainers of servants was, from the viewpoint of activity, the mayor's court of Annapolis. Between 1753 and 1766 there were forty-two presentments or indictments for harboring and entertaining servants and 322 of innkeepers for entertaining or selling liquor to servants. Of the latter total, a considerable number consisted of multiple prosecutions of innkeepers in which separate indictments were returned for each servant entertained. Thus, in 1765 ten convictions were obtained against Bennett, who was fined 40s. current on each occasion, twelve against Logan, similarly fined, 65 presentments were returned against Peter Strong for selling spirituous liquors and entertaining servants, eighteen against George White, and 72 against Conrad Markell, of which twenty-six were for selling liquor to the servants of John Campbell. He was fined 40s. for each and every case.[159]

In seventeenth-century Virginia enticers and harborers were generally prosecuted criminally. At times the prosecution of the enticer was part of the case against the runaway.[160] Runaway servants who counseled others to abscond with them were dealt with by the criminal process. "Wherefore should wee stay here and be slaves, and may goe to another

---

[156] *Md. Arch.,* XVII, 188, 189 (1684); R. Semmes, *Crime and Punishment in Early Maryland* (Baltimore, 1938), p. 114. For the remission of part of a penalty of 5,000 lbs. because the harborer had acted "innocently and ignorantly," see Smith's case, *Md. Arch.,* VIII, 450 (1692).

[157] See, e.g., White's case, *Md. Arch.,* IV, 165 (1642); also *ibid.,* p. 280 (1644).

[158] See *supra,* pp. 167–169. See also Tony's case, *Md. Arch.,* X, 511, 512 (1657), XLI, 333 (1659); Miller's case, Somerset, lib. 1671–75, f. 157 (1672); Proprietary v. Cattlin, Somerset, lib. AW, 1690–91, fols. 115, 115vso. (1689); Low's case, Prince George, lib. C, 1702–8, f. 96 (1706).

[159] See Annapolis mayor's court: lib. 1753–57, f. 27 (1754, 2 cases), 41, 43, 63, 94 (1755, 5 cases), 96, 99 (1756, 2 cases), 106 (1757, 2 cases); lib. 1757–65, fols. 16, 18 (1758, 2 cases), 79, 144, 151, 155, 157, 159, 162 (1760–61, 7 cases), 194 (1763), 216, 236 (1764, 2 cases), 269, 271–321, 73 cases (of which 72 were against one innkeeper; in all except three he was fined 40s. each, and in three was acquitted), 246 *passim* (198 cases against 17 innkeepers), 322–334 (12 cases), 342–351 (10 cases); lib. 1766–72, fols. 1–45 (37 cases), 105 (2 cases), 257, 258 (1765, 6 cases). From Proprietary v. Stone, lib. 1766–72, fols. 82–84 (1766) it is evident that the town by-law against selling liquor to servants applied even to cases where the liquor was given to satisfy a debt owing to the servant's master. For the recovery of penal damages in Virginia for unlawful entertainment of servants at inns, see Surry O.B., 1645–77, f. 215 (1662); *Va. Gen. Court Mins.,* p. 375 (1674).

[160] Cf. cases of Shelley and Floyd, *ibid.,* p. 194 (1627).

place and live like gent. when our Mr if hee see us durst not own us there," was a statement attributed to one such enticer.[161] In 1640 the General Court ruled that two servants, "principall actors and contrivers in a most dangerous conspiracy by attempting to run out of the country and [by] Inticing divers others to be actors in the said Conspiracy," be whipped, branded, and required to serve the colony seven years apiece, all the while to be required to work in irons.[162] When enticement was aggravated by conspiracy or theft, the penalty was considerably stiffer.[163] If the enticer was a fellow servant he was usually penalized by extra service;[164] if he was a freeman he was either fined and required to satisfy the costs of capture,[165] or enjoined to cease entertaining the servant and to return him forthwith to his master.[166]

In addition to enticement, the mere counseling of servants to seek their freedom by legal means might be considered by the courts as an unwarranted interference with the property interests of others. Masters were expected to tend to their own knitting and neither to have dealings with nor give advice to the servants of others. A mistress who, upon selling her maidservant, told her "that she was a foole if she served soe long as she was sold for, for she had not so long to serve" was promptly haled into court.[167] When John Bradye advised Thomas Jarrett to seek his freedom and even volunteered to appear in court on his behalf, Jarrett's master found it necessary to petition the court that the servant had since become very stubborn and restive and that, "when he finds his hope of Freedome Circumvented, he will run away," to the loss of

---

[161] Abram's case, Accomac, lib. I, f. 115 (1638).

[162] Cases of Wootton and Bradye, *et al., Va. Gen. Court Mins.*, p. 467 (1640). For the arrest of Indians for detaining a servant, see *ibid.*, p. 505. See also Ball's case, Lower Norfolk, lib. I, f. 230 (1643), where enticement was combined with conspiracy, and the culprit was sentenced to receive 30 lashes "as a deserved punishment for his offenses and to deter others from attempting or acting the like hereafter"; for another enticement by Ball, see *ibid.*, f. 234 (1643). From this case Bruce generalizes that enticers of runaways would receive 30 lashes. *Instit. Hist. of Va.*, I, 623. But in 1655 the Northampton court sentenced one such culprit who had run away and enticed another "to have a Confederacy wth him" to 10 lashes and costs. Northampton O.B., 1655–56, f. 9. See also Jenkins' case, Westmoreland O.B., 1675/6–1688/9, f. 619 (1688), where merely six months' extra service was exacted and no corporal punishment.

[163] See complaint of Edward Scarburgh, Accomac O.B., lib. 1666–70, f. 31 (1667). The harborer and concealer of the deserters was accused by the court of "vile and villanous" dealings. *Ibid.*, f. 45 (1667). The Scarburgh enticement and conspiracy case led to a defamation action, in which Martin Moore recovered from John Parker 250 lbs. of tobacco and cask because the latter had "fraudullized" plaintiff, a tanner, by saying that he had counseled one of the servants to run away, with the result that Moore had been expelled "from his livelyhood of imployment with his master Coll Scarburgh." *Ibid.*, f. 64 (1668).

[164] Accomac O.B., 1666–70, f. 40 (1667); Lancaster O.B., 1666–80, f. 353 (1676).

[165] York O.B., 1664–72, f. 496 (1671).

[166] *Ibid.*, 1675–84, f. 661 (1683). Cf. also Spotsylvania O.B., 1724–30, f. 54 (1725); Henrico O.B., V, f. 136 (1690).

[167] Widow Crafton's case, Surry O.B., 1645–72 (1645).

the petitioner's crop and the risk of permanently losing the servant "through the Seducement and Evil councill of the sd Bradye." The court was requested to give due consideration to "such abuses, as men will not be able to Keep servants." [168]

In the seventeenth century, civil suits against enticers and detainers were also brought successfully in the courts of Virginia, although outnumbered by criminal prosecutions. However, the reverse was true in the following century, when civil actions exceeded criminal suits.[169] By the end of the seventeenth century, legislation adequately covered the offenses of enticing and detaining, and the courts then considered this remedy to be founded upon statute rather than common law.[170] As in other colonial jurisdictions and at common law, a similar remedy was available for enticing or seducing a wife or daughter by analogy to case for enticing a servant.[171]

THE RICE AND SUGAR COLONIES. Here legislation imposing penalties for the unauthorized entertainment, harboring, or employment of other men's servants as well as slaves paralleled acts in force in the tobacco colonies.[172] When the harborer actually knew that his guest was a serv-

---

[168] *Ibid.*, fols. 118, 119 (1658).

[169] In the very early years the civil action was seldom designated as "case." Price v. Roe, Lancaster O.B., 1656–66, f. 119 (1660), appealed; also Aduston v. Cholmenby, York O.B., 1657–62, f. 326 (1661). Later, when case was widely used, specific restitution might be awarded in such an action. Cf. Newell v. Croshow, *ibid.*, f. 354 (1661). As time went on damages seem to have been the essence of the action. See Storkdale v. Martin, *ibid.*, lib. 1675–84, f. 30 (1678); Wise v. Hyde, *ibid.*, lib. 1687–91, f. 435 (1690).

[170] Bradford v. Chamberlain, Henrico O.B., lib. III, f. 177 (1698). To "a plea upon his case" for detaining an Indian servant and converting him to his own use, defendant pleaded that the action was brought at common law, "notwithstanding that there is a particular act of assembly for the punishment of such offences." Plaintiff's demurrer was overruled by the court which held the "oppinion that the defendts attorney hath made a good plea," and nonsuited plaintiff with costs. Greater preciseness marked pleadings in Henrico court than elsewhere in the colony in this period. In the previous year Bradford sued Chamberlain in debt for entertaining an Indian indentured to him for seven years. His suit was based on the act of 1666. The amount sued for totaled 10,900 lbs. of tobacco. *Ibid.*, lib. III, f. 165 (1697).

[171] For award of damages for seducing a servant, see Gayne's case, *Va. Gen. Court Mins.*, p. 469. For damages for enticing a wife, see Smart v. Silvester, Westmoreland, lib. 1675/6–88/9, f. 622 (1688), trespass was used although there does not appear to have been a forcible taking.

[172] Generally from £1 to £2 was the penalty for every 24 hours of unlawful detaining. *Jamaica:* C.O. 139:1, fols. 10–11 (1661). This 24-hour period, according to an act of 1675, need not be consecutive. C.O. 139:4, f. 19 *et seq. Antigua:* C.O. 154:7, f. 39 (1669); increased from 50 lbs. of tobacco to £20 in 1716. Servants entertaining other servants were to be whipped or to serve three months at the election of injured party. *Laws of the Island of Antigua, 1690–1798* (London, 1805), I, 186 (1716). *Barbados:* Hall, *Acts Passed in the Island of Barbados* (London, 1764), p. 134 (1696). An overseer, freeman, or laborer entertaining or hiding a servant was to serve the owner one whole year after his time without any salary, except for ordinary plantation clothes, shoes, fish, or flesh. *Montserrat:* C.O. 152:13, fols. 67–72 (1719). See also *CSPA, 1681–85*, No. 2007, p. 750 (1684). *South Carolina:* S.C. Stat., III, 621–629 (1744); Simpson, *Practical Justice of the Peace*, p. 230. *North Carolina:* Davis, *Office and Authority of a Justice of Peace*, p. 313; *Moravian Rec.*, III, 1193, 1194 (1776).

ant a far heavier penalty was imposed by law.[173] Despite legislation enacted in South Carolina against harboring and entertaining runaway
seamen,[174] the Commons House of Assembly declared in 1743 that it
was "notorious that no Prosecutions" had been instituted "against Persons harbouring Seamen Contrary" to this act.[175]

Advertisements of runaway servants in South Carolina newspapers
frequently included specific warnings against the harboring or assisting of such fugitives, and even went so far as to state the statutory penalty for such conduct. It was customary for the master to warn the
enticer or detainer before instituting suit.[176] Unfortunately the loss or
destruction of general sessions minutes prevents our drawing conclusions as to the extent to which criminal prosecutions were actually instituted in South Carolina against enticers and harborers.[177] Generally
speaking, there appears to have been less civil litigation on this subject
in South Carolina than in other colonies.[178]

Summary.—In the period before trade unionism secured a real foothold in this county the courts allowed damages for inducing the breach
of a labor contract. But, as at early common law, the essence of this
action appears to have been the protection of the quasi-proprietary interest which the master had in his servant. Case could be brought for
the wrongful detaining or enticement both of servants and apprentices,
with whom there was a contract relationship, and of slaves, whose status
rested on a property relationship. Furthermore, the occasional use of
detinue and replevin to recover servants stressed the proprietary rather
than the contractual interests. The fact that specific restitution was
awarded in so many of these early actions lends still further weight to
the quasi-proprietary basis of the legal remedy. The nearest emphasis

[173] Baskett, *Acts of Jamaica* (London, 1738), pp. 2–5 (1681); Barbados: C.O. 30:5, fols. 44–45 (1682); revived, 1685–87, 1689, *ibid.*, fols. 133, 166, 192.

[174] S.C. Assembly J., Nov. 24–Dec. 6, 1696, f. 4 (Nov. 25, 1696); Trott, *Laws of S.C.*, I, 53.

[175] S.C. Commons J., 1742–43, fols. 445, 446 (1743); *S.C. Gazette*, May 23, 1743. Cf. also *ibid.*, Feb. 12–19, 1731/2.

[176] See *S.C. Gazette*, Aug. 4–11, 1733; March 30, May 24, July 27, 1734; Feb. 12, 1736/7; Jan. 18–25, Aug. 27–Sept. 3, 1737; Dec. 12, 1743; Jan. 29, 1750. For notices in Georgia papers, see *Ga. Gazette*, May 18, 1774.

[177] For occasional cases, see Mahoon's case, *J.S.C. Grand Council, 1671–1680* (Columbia, 1907), p. 14; Radcliffe's case, S.C. Council J., 1671–1720, f. 23 (1672). For a presentment for entertaining seamen as well as Negroes at unseasonable hours, see *S.C. Gazette*, April 15, 1745.
For North Carolina cases, see Fox's case, *N.C. Col. Rec.*, II, 241 (1716); Rex v. Cotton *et al.*, Misc. Gen. Court Papers (1725). For entertaining vagrants and criminals, see Jones's case, Bertie Rec., 1724–69 (Nov., 1739), where the defense was that a counterfeiter had been entertained "on acco't of his knowledge and skill of Weaving." For fines against ordinary-keepers, see New Bern Town Rec., lib. 1792–1825, f. 54 (1801).

[178] Cf. Drake v. McDowell's Exrs., Charleston C.P., lib. Feb.–Aug., 1767, fols. 299–301, case for harboring four Negro slaves.

upon damage to contract relations was found in the cases of *Brinner v. Melville and Burns* in New York. This approach is in sharp contrast to the stolen-horse analogy advanced in Joseph Reed's opinion. These legal remedies appear to have been generally effective. As Benjamin Franklin's own experience in quitting his apprenticeship in Boston revealed, masters stood together even when brothers could not.

2. The Middle colonies and the South resorted to the criminal machinery to a much greater extent than was the case in contemporary England and chose to place their emphasis upon the punishment of disturbers of the public peace and the maintenance of the master's discipline rather than upon the breach of contract. Where the enticement was brought about by a fellow servant, their chief anxiety was that workers' conspiracies be suppressed. These criminal prosecutions and the statutory penal actions are the early American antecedents of legislation in certain states, notably in the South, that make it a penal offense to employ, knowingly, a servant who has broken his contract with his former master without justifiable excuse.

3. There are no instances in the colonial and Revolutionary periods of these legal remedies having been employed for the breach of other than personal-service contracts. There was no attempt to enlarge the scope of the remedy to include contracts of employment in general, as in the later British decision of *Lumley v. Gye,* where status in the true sense was not involved, but the court expanded the remedies available for disturbing some one's trade or business.[179] From *Lumley v. Gye* the courts moved beyond the field of personal-service contracts, ultimately holding that the action lies regardless of the nature of the contract [180]—a position without support in colonial legal experience. The new weapons fashioned by the courts from the arsenal of common-law remedies seriously checked trade-union activity in this country.[181]

---

[179] 2 El. and Bl. 216 (1853) and Lumley v. Wagner, 1 De G.M. and G., which established the principle in modern law that a person is liable in tort for procuring the breach of a personal-service contract.

[180] F. B. Sayre, "Inducing Breach of Contract," *Harvard Law Rev.,* XXXVI, 663 at p. 671; C. E. Carpenter, "Interference with Contract Relations," *ibid.,* XLI, 728. In a majority of American jurisdictions Lumley v. Gye prevails. Probably its most extreme application in this country was found in the well-known case, Hitchman Coal and Coke Co. v. Mitchell, 245 U.S. 229 (1917). Perhaps the widest application has been in the nonlabor field, as a remedy for inducing breach of competitor's contracts. Most N.R.A. codes contained prohibitions against interference with competitor's contracts. See Handler, *op. cit.,* pp. 1040, 1041.

[181] See Frankfurter and Greene, *The Labor Injunction* (New York, 1930), p. 21; E. E. Witte, "Early American Labor Cases," *Yale Law J.,* XXXV, 825, 832; *The Government in Labor Disputes* (1st ed., New York, 1932), pp. 84–85; J. M. Landis, *Cases on Labor Law* (Chicago, 1934), pp. 25, 26, 77–189. See also R.Y. Hedges and A. Winterbottom, *The Legal History of Trade Unionism* (London, 1930), pp. 134–153; S. and B. Webb, *History of Trade Unionism* (rev. ed., London, 1926), pp. 597–599; Holdsworth, *H.E.L.,* II, 462–463, III, 383–385.

4. Support for both sides of the modern judicial controversy as to whether malice is essential to support an action for procuring a breach of contract might be drawn from the colonial cases. The requirement was generally laid down that, to hold the detainer liable, he must have had knowledge of the existing contract of service. This was the requirement of the medieval writ, and is the root of the position of some modern cases that the act complained of must be "wilfully and knowingly done" or done "for the purpose of injuring another." [182] Even in Barbados, where knowledge was not requisite to liability, the penalty was fivefold in the case of those who had such knowledge. Paralleling common-law developments, the colonial courts held that mere employment of a servant known to be under contract with another was actionable and that actual enticement need not be shown.[183] In fact, in some of the colonies gratuitous advice to a servant to seek his freedom at law would be actionable. But in reality the colonial courts were anxious to check any disturbance of status. Challenging the legality of an existing contract is quite another matter from willfully breaking that contract.[184] Nonetheless, even in the modern law it is very difficult to draw a sharp line separating cases where it is and cases where it is not actionable to exhort a person to break a contract.

Absenteeism and Desertion: the Fugitive Servant Problem. The absentee and the deserter posed a serious problem for the colonial producer. From earliest days bound laborers sought to terminate their contracts of employment unilaterally. John Winter, a pioneer labor overseer in northern New England, reported to his employer abroad that it was extremely difficult to keep the fishermen and husbandmen from leaving their service and that a strict example must be set with deserters. In the case of one workman he complained:

Sander Freythy is going for England, and yf you do not question him for going from your servize, you will not keep a man heare to the plantation no longer than the[y] list [i.e., choose] them selues for. I heare those that ar heare now, though they will not say so much to me for the[y] say Sander Freythy is gon home and we shal se what is donn to him; if their be nothinge

---

[182] Cf. Bowen v. Hall, 6 Q.B.D. 333 (1881); South Wales Miners' Federation v. Glamorgan Coal Co., House of Lords [1905] A.C. 239; Sorrell v. Smith, House of Lords (1925) A.C. 700; also James v. Le Roy, 6 Johns. (N.Y.) 274 (1810); Ferguson v. Tucker, 2 Har. and G. (Md.) 182 (1828); Conant v. Raymond, 2 Aiken (Vt.) 243 (1827); R and W Hat Shop, Inc. v. Scully, 98 Conn. I (1922).

[183] Contrast Adams and Bafeald's Case, 1 Leo. 240 (1591) with Blake v. Lanyon, 6 T.R. 221 (1795).

[184] Cf. also Brimelow v. Vasson, Ch. Div [1924] 1 Ch. 302; State v. Harwood, 104 N.C. 724 (1889).

donn to him we may all go away as well as he and nothing to be donn to vs, for heare about these parts is neyther law nor government. Yff any mans servant take a distast against his maister, away the[y] go to their pleasure.[185]

Fugitives from labor contracts sought refuge in other colonies or escape on board ship. Others merely took French leave to enjoy a few days' dissipation, as is illustrated by the following advertisement in a colonial newspaper:

Whereas, John Powell was advertised last week in this paper as a Runaway; but being only gone into the country a cyder-drinking, and being returned again to this master's service; These are therefore to acquaint all gentlemen and others, who have any watches or clocks to repair, that they may have them done in the best manner, and at reasonable rates. William Roberts.[186]

Frequently such absentees were rounded up at near-by taverns. Franklin, describing in his *Autobiography* his trip from New York to Philadelphia in 1723, narrates that, when he spent the night at a "poor inn," he "made so miserable a figure" that he was actually "suspected to be some runaway indentured servant, and in danger of being taken up on that suspicion."

The loss of time from absenteeism and desertion laid a heavy tax upon the profits of colonial productive enterprise. Throughout the colonies, masters found it necessary to resort constantly to the newspapers to advertise rewards for runaways who were by no means first offenders. One culprit was described as having a string of bells around his neck "which made a hideous jingling and discordant noise," another wore an iron collar, and others bore the scars of recent whippings on their backs.[187]

The early frontier situation described by John Winter was mainly a temporary one. Throughout the colonies, laws were put into operation

[185] "Trelawny Papers," Me. Hist. Soc., *Coll.*, III, 137 (1638).   [186] *Md. Gazette*, Sept. 6, 1745.

[187] Newspaper advertisements inevitably contained other graphic details relating to the appearance and costume of the servants; at times they were even in poetical vein. See, e.g., *Pa. Gazette*, June 22, Sept. 21, 1769; *Pa. J.*, March 12, 1777; *Pa. Packet*, March 12, 1777, April 11, 18, 1788; *Carey's Pa. Evening Herald*, Sept. 3, 1785; *Md. Gazette*, July 5, 1745, March 18, May 27, June 17, 1746, March 17, 1747; *Va. Gazette*, Sept. 22, 1768. For an amusing poem recounting that an Irish servant had run away from Philadelphia and offering a reward of "five dollar bills and half a crown" for his arrest, see *Md. Gazette*, March 16, 1769. For other rewards, see Ancient Records of Philadelphia (Wallace Coll., 1702–69), Hist. Soc. of Pa.; John Gibson, ed., *History of York County, Pa.* (Chicago, 1886), p. 360, wherein a reward of one cent is offered for a runaway servant, a schoolmaster by vocation, addicted to drinking and gambling; offer of six cents, but "not thanks," cited by B. W. Bond, Jr., *The Civilization of the Old Northwest* (New York, 1934), p. 415. Rewards were included in the costs of returning the servant to his master, for which the servant was liable. During the Revolution the Continental Congress allowed rewards for the capture of army deserters to be deducted from the offender's wages. *J. Continental Congress*, III, 325 (1775).

and legal agencies were employed to deal with the absentee and the deserter and to enforce specific performance of the contract of employment. As the fugitive servant and absentee were considered the property of the master, the employer's legal right to his recovery was everywhere recognized. Governor Johnstone of West Florida on one occasion pressed M. Aubry, French governor at New Orleans, to return a mulatto servant who had fled to the French colony in 1766. "As he had sold his Liberty for a certain Term (a thing which is permitted in our Colonies), he surely must be considered during that period, as the property of his Master, as the Contract specifies," Johnstone contended.[188]

The claims of masters in one colony upon fugitive servants in another jurisdiction appear to have been allowed from the beginning of colonial settlement.[189] The articles of the New England Confederation provided that, where a servant ran away from his master to one of the member colonies of the Confederation, upon certification of one magistrate in the jurisdiction whence he fled or upon other due proof, the fugitive should be delivered either to his master or to any others bringing legal proof.[190] By the intercolonial treaty of 1650 this article was extended to claims arising between the United Colonies and the Dutch in New Netherland.[191] Extradition of fugitive servants came to be a matter of general policy,[192] actually carried out in the exceptional case. In many

[188] *Mississippi Provincial Archives: English Dominion* (Nashville, Tenn., 1911), p. 318.

[189] See Hurd, *Law of Freedom and Bondage,* II, 405.

[190] E. Hazard, *Historical Collections* (2 vols., Philadelphia, 1792–94), II, 1–6. Long after the Confederation agreement had expired Rhode Island, not a party to it, was accused of protecting fugitive servants from neighboring provinces. *Ibid.,* III, 76 (1704).

[191] *Ibid.,* II, 172.

[192] For instances of extradition between Mass. and R.I., see Herndon's case, *Providence Town Rec.,* II, 77 (1654), and Betts' case, *ibid.,* pp. 79, 80 (1655); between Massachusetts and New York, see Carter's case, Suffolk Sess., lib. II, f. 242 (1684), where the attorney for Col. Lewis Morris of N.Y. was empowered to transport the servant to New York to stand trial there, provided he posted bond of £10 to answer damages in case Carter were cleared. The Duke's Laws authorized local officers to seize any stranger traveling without a passport and secure him "until hee can Cleare himselfe to bee a free man." He could defray the charges of his detention by work. N.Y. Hist. Soc., *Coll.,* I, 421. For an account of a hue and cry in New York after a Maryland servant, see *R.N.A.,* VII, 128 (1668). Runaway servants from other colonies committed to Pennsylvania gaols might be ordered to serve the sheriff to satisfy the costs of their detention; such periods of service ranged from six months to a year and a half. Lancaster Road and Sess. Docket, No. 1, fols. 228 (1738), 238 (1739); *Chester Co., Pa., Court Rec., 1681–97* (1687). For a proclamation issued by a New Jersey court for the arrest of a seaman deserting in New York, see Middlesex Co. Court Mins., lib. I, f. 192 (1698). In 1697 the Commissioners of Customs agreed with Penn's proposal that runaways of one province ought not be protected in another. Stock, *op. cit.,* II, 203n. Delaware courts were vigilant in apprehending runaways from other colonies. Cases of Edwards and Loyd, Sussex Co. Rec. (1683), Hist. Soc. of Pa.; Naomi Medly's case, Kent, lib. 1699–1703, f. 70a (1702); Johnson's case, Kent Q.S., 1722–25, f. 56 (1724). Masters whose servants had fled Maryland could count upon the cooperation of the provincial authorities to regain them. For the agreement with New Netherland on this subject, see McCormac, *White Servitude in Md.,* pp. 52, 53; *Md. Arch.,* III, 134. For reciprocal legislation

instances servants were successful in finding refuge abroad or in another colony and in evading the long arm of the law.[193] The intercolonial agreements for the recovery of fugitive servants were the pattern for the clause in the Federal Constitution providing that

No Person held to Service or Labour in one State, under the Laws thereof escaping into another, shall, in Consequence of any Law or Regulation therein, be discharged from such Service or Labour, but shall be delivered up on a claim of the Party to whom such Service or Labour may be due.[194]

The colonial authorities dealt far more severely with the absentee and the fugitive than did the courts of the mother country. British eighteenth-century legislation merely required the apprentice to make up his lost time,[195] whereas colonial statutes generally penalized the absentee by requiring him to serve severalfold the period of his unlawful absence, although in New England and New York less drastic penalties were customarily imposed.

NEW ENGLAND. A Connecticut statute of 1644 provided that servants absenting themselves from their masters were to serve threefold the period of their unlawful absence.[196] Massachusetts, whose courts at times

---

with Virginia, see *Md. Arch.,* XIX, *passim* (1694–97); for court orders, *ibid.,* IV, 224 (1643), X, 442 (1655), 515, 516 (1657), LIV, 388 (1665). For extradition in Virginia and her relations with neighboring colonies on this subject, see Hening, I, 539 (1660), II, 187 (1663), V, 556 (1748); *Va. Gen. Court Mins.,* p. 466 (1640), 500, 505. When a Virginia master complained to the Accomac court in 1643 that he had appealed without success to Gov. Calvert of Maryland "for justice and restitution" of some of his servants who had fled thither, Gov. Berkeley directed him to take out an attachment against any Maryland servants or goods "by way of reprisall till [he] have justice" and his servants be returned to him. Plowden's petition, Accomac O.B., II, fols. 233, 234 (1643). For reciprocity with Massachusetts, see Hazard, *Hist. Coll.,* I, 536 (1644); *Winthrop Papers,* IV, 89 (plan to desert to Va., 1639), 463, 464 (request fugitives' return to Va., 1644). At least in one instance a servant who escaped to England was returned to Virginia. Greenfield's case, *Va. Gen. Court Mins.,* p. 274 (1671). Cf. Ballagh's assertion that no case of a runaway servant escaping to England "seems to have occurred." *White Servitude in the Colony of Virginia* (Baltimore, 1895), p. 54n. Appeals to South Carolina from the colonies to the north did not fall upon deaf ears. See S.C. Assembly J., 1703, f. 115. However, Georgia found South Carolina not very cooperative, and was compelled to appeal to the Board of Trade to bring about the return of colony servants who had fled across her frontiers. *Ga. Col. Rec.,* I, 124 (1733); XXV, 440 (1750); XXVI, 20 (1750).

[193] See, e.g., *Pa. Gazette,* Dec. 1, 1743 and *infra,* pp. 445, 448, 458, 460.

[194] Art. IV, § 2, cl. 3. The Northwest Ordinance, art. VI, contained a similar provision. For claims under this provision, see Boaler v. Cummines (1853), *Amer. Law Reg.,* I, 654, applying it to apprentices. This provision, as well as the act of 1793, was held applicable to apprentices as well as to slaves. 9 Ohio 248; *Monthly Law Reporter,* IV, 526, VI, 178, 295; Hurd, *op. cit.,* II, 377 *et seq.*

[195] Stat. 6 Geo. II, c. 25 § 1 (1766). English quarter sessions customarily ordered such offenders to serve out their terms. See "County Palatine of Chester Q.S." Record Society, *Publications,* XCIV (1940), 71 (1611), 88, 89 (1635); "Manchester Sessions, I, 1616–1622/3," *loc. cit.,* XLII (1901), 3, 17 (1616), 22 (1617), *passim.* For an indictment, see J. C. Atkinson, ed., *North Riding Quarter Sessions,* I, 11.

[196] *Conn. Pub. Rec.,* I, 105.

penalized runaways by multiple extra service, authorized constables as early as 1634 to whip any servant who had been previously whipped as a fugitive, if he were found outside his master's farm without a note from his master stating his business.[197] Both Massachusetts and New Hampshire made servants who were absent on shipboard for more than twenty-four hours liable to suffer a penalty not exceeding one year's service.[198] Rhode Island went so far as to place ordinary wage workers or artificers under contract to perform a specific task in the same category as covenant servants bound for a term. Its labor code of 1647 provided that any artificers or laborers lawfully retained for the building or repairing of a house, shop, mill, "or any other piece of worke taken in great, in bulke, or in gross," or who shall agree to finish any specific task

shall continue and not depart from the same, (unless it be for the not paying his wages as here agreed on, or otherwise be lawfully taken off and appointed to serve the Colonie, or by leave and license from the Master, Overseer, or owner of the worke,) untill it be finished according to the agreement upon paine of the forfeiture of five pounds to the party from whom he shall depart, who may recover it by an action of debt, and other ordinary costs and damages besides, in the Courts where such matters are to be tryed.[199]

Classed with "Thieves and other Criminals," the absentee could be pursued by hue and cry [200] on land and over water, and men and boats could be impressed in the hunt.[201] The chief officers of the town were empowered to commit fugitive servants and send them back to the town whence they came, their masters to bear the costs of their return.[202]

---

[197] *Assistants*, II, 43.

[198] *Mass. Acts and Resolves*, II, 419 (1718); *Acts and Laws of New Hampshire*, I, 37.

[199] *R.I. Col. Rec.*, I, 183 (1647); Rider, *Laws of R.I., 1636–1705*, p. 11 (code of 1663); *Charter and Laws of R.I.* (Newport, 1730), pp. 174, 175.

[200] The Essex quarterly court phonetically ordered "Hewghen Crie" for the recovery of Francis Usselton's servants in 1659. *Essex*, II, 192 (1659). For allowance to constables for "hughencry," see *ibid.*, III, 435 (1667). For the English hue and cry procedure, see Burn, *Justice of the Peace Abridgment* (Boston, 1773).

[201] *Mass. Col. Laws, 1660–72*, p. 174. The master was required to pay for the hue and cry. Renold's case, *Essex*, III, 435 (1667). But cf. Pursvall's case, where the charges were deducted from funds found on the servant. *Plymouth Col. Rec.*, V, 68 (1671). One of John Winthrop's runaway servants who sought to escape by sea was placed in irons by the captain of the vessel. *Winthrop Papers*, IV, 499 (1644).

[202] The New Hampshire act of 1701 empowered town selectmen to commit runaways or stubborn children and servants and keep them at work, allowing them 8*d.* out of every shilling they earned. *Acts and Laws of N.H.*, I, 15 (1701); also II, 138, 139 (1714). See also *Mass. Acts and Resolves*, I, 378 (1700); *R.I. Col. Rec.*, I, 183 (1647), 247 (1654); Rider, *Laws of R.I.*, p. 10 (code of 1663). Suffolk sessions ordered the constables and tithingmen to walk the streets of Boston at night and search all houses suspected of entertaining Indian, Negro, or mulatto servants and apprehend them. *Suffolk Sess.*, lib. I, f. 111 (1705).

The remoter regions of northern New England were less troubled by the runaway problem than their more populous neighbors to the immediate south as there were far fewer servants in the colonial outposts. Such unsettled frontier regions offered the runaway a reasonably good chance of starting life anew and with little likelihood of being apprehended.[203]

To determine the policy of the courts of colonial New England toward absentee and deserter, an analysis was made of every recorded fugitive-servant case to come up before the Massachusetts Court of Assistants,[204] the inferior court of populous Suffolk, and the quarterly court of adjacent Essex County for the seventeenth century. These cases reveal that the extra service penalty was never consistently enforced in Massachusetts. In most instances where extra service (double time) was imposed the servant was also charged with theft. Corporal punishment was most consistently meted out to runaways in the seventeenth century, while, in the century following, the absentee was generally returned to the master without a specific decree of extra service. Out of eighty cases studied for the seventeenth century, fines were imposed in merely ten, in quite a number of which the servant was also charged with larceny or contempt of public authority. In fourteen fugitive-servant cases noted in the eighteenth-century Suffolk sessions prior to the Revolution, corporal punishment was imposed in only one instance; as a general rule the fugitive was merely required to serve out his term, with extra service being imposed in only two cases.[205]

These cases cast light on certain other aspects of fugitive servant law. The Essex quarterly court acted on the principle that a manservant could

203 *New Hampshire:* N.H.Q.S., lib. 1692–1704, f. 14 (1693), whipped for theft in addition to runaway attempt; *ibid.*, f. 170 (1702), discharged for being bound without father's consent. *Maine: Me. Prov. and Court Rec.*, I, 81 (1640), whipped and returned; II, 354 (1679), order to seize and return. See also *ibid.*, p. 79 (1659), damages to master; York Q.S., lib. VII, f. 72 (1724), both sides admonished; *ibid.*, X, fols. 62, 63 (1735), to serve 2 yrs. 10 mos, for runaway time and for prosecution costs paid by master.

204 There are no runaway cases recorded in the Court of Assistants between 1643 and 1681. Apparently after 1643 such cases were brought to the county courts.

205 *Assistants,* II, 16 (1631), 27 (1632), 40 (1634, 2 cases), 57 (3 cases), 59 (1635, 6 cases), 71 (1637–39, 2 cases), 97 (1640, 2 cases), 107 (1641), 118 (1642), 122, 123, 126, 132 (2 cases) (1643); I, 200 (1681). *Essex,* I, 3, 4 (1636), 5 (2 cases) (1637), 8, 9 (1638), 20 (1640), 33 (1641), 61 (1643), 91 (1645), 285, 286 (1653), 404, 405 (1655); II, 136 (1659), 240 (1660); III, 148 (1664), 254, 263 (1665), 351, 366 (1666), 435 (1667); IV, 234, 237 (1670), 425, 442 (1671); V, 23 (2 cases) (1672), 140, 230 (1673), 357 (1674); VI, 228 (1676); VII, 74 (1678); VIII, 91 (1681), 301, 365 (1682). *Suffolk,* I, 184 (1672), 484 (1674), 561 (1675); II, 605 (1675), 801, 847 (1677), 884, 894, 958 (1678). Suffolk MS lib. I, 1680–92, fols. 37, 39 (1680), 75, 84, 85, 99 (1681), 140 (1682), 242 (1684), 254 (1685), 290 (1686). Suffolk Sess., lib. 1702–12, fols. 4 (1702), 18 (1703), 177 (1708); II, fols. 5, 10, 252 (1712), 98 (1715), 222 (1718); III, fols. 11 (1719), 69 (1721), 132 (1722), 267 (1724); Unbound, 1737–39 (1738), (1765).

be held liable to extra service for his wife's running away from her master.[206] The Essex probate ruled in one such instance that the estate of an erstwhile servant be kept intact until the court had an opportunity to pass on a claim for the damages incurred by the master.[207] The theft of indentures by a servant was considered by the court as prima facie evidence of an intention to desert.[208]

Extra service was more consistently exacted of runaways in the courts of Plymouth colony, although in some cases the service was in satisfaction of fines. Such service ranged from a half year extra for a year's unauthorized leave, a seventeenth-century sentence, to the harsher double penalty in force in the following century, when Plymouth sessions was part of the Massachusetts inferior court system.[209] Occasionally the seventeenth-century courts substituted whipping for the extra service penalty, especially where the deserter was charged with theft or fornication in addition.[210] By the eighteenth century the court, in the absence of aggravating factors, might either impose an extra service penalty, as at Worcester general sessions,[211] or merely, as in Suffolk, order the servant to return and finish out his term.

Most of the Connecticut runaway cases are complicated by the fact that the servant was also charged with larceny. On a few occasions extra service amounting to treble damages was exacted, aside from the multiple damages awarded for the larceny.[212] At other times runaways were whipped or placed in the stocks and fined. Such fines might be commuted by extra service.[213] Instead of resorting to the criminal process, Connecticut masters often preferred bringing civil actions for

---

[206] Tibb's case, *Essex*, V, 23 (1672); similarly Genning's case, *New Haven Col. Rec., 1638–49*, p. 105.

[207] Estey's case, *Essex Prob. Rec.*, I, 198 (1658).

[208] See Allin's case, Suffolk Sess., lib. III, f. 184 (1722).

[209] In general, Indian runaways were treated more harshly in Plymouth than white servants. *Plymouth Col. Rec.*, I, 128 (1639), 139, 140 (1639), II, 105 (1646), 111 (1647), VI, 152 (1685); Plymouth Sess., lib. 1723–30, fols. 45, 46 (1725); 87, 93 (1728), 129 (1730), lib. 1730–49, fols. 32, 33 (1731). As early as 1639 there was incorporated into a Plymouth indenture a provision whereby the servant bound himself to serve "two years ouer and aboue his terme for every time that hee shall" run away before the expiration of the stipulated seven-year term. *Plymouth Col. Rec.*, I, 129.

[210] *Plymouth Col. Rec.*, I, 15 (1637); II, 30 (1642); III, 204 (1661); VI, 20 (1679).

[211] See Wicker's case, Worcester G.S., pp. 62, 63 (1733).

[212] *Conn. Particular Court Rec., 1639–63*, p. 74 (1649); Hartford Co. court, Conn. "Prob. Rec.," lib. III, f. 111 (1671); New Haven Co. Court Rec., lib. I, f. 121 (1680), fined for theft, to serve three weeks for his week's absence, to pay hue and cry charges as well as court and prison charges, and to be placed under a £10 bond for good behavior.

[213] For New Haven colony, see *New Haven Col. Rec., 1638–49*, p. 162 (1645), 380 (1648). See also New Haven Co. Court Rec., lib. I, f. 91 (1676), 101 (1677), 149 (1683); New London Co. Court Rec., lib. XIV, f. 99 (1725).

breach of indentures. If the court sustained the servant's plea—"not a lawful apprentice"—he would be dismissed from service; [214] otherwise the court would order specific performance of the indentures, and grant the master, as in criminal prosecutions, treble service for the unauthorized period of absence.[215]

THE MIDDLE COLONIES. By a New York statute of 1684 runaways were to be sentenced by any two justices of the peace to double the time of their absence by future service and to make full satisfaction to their masters for the costs and charges sustained by their unlawful departure, items which could also be satisfied by extra service.[216] This was also the penalty in New Jersey,[217] but in Pennsylvania, perhaps in emulation of the experience in the tobacco colonies, the penalty was placed as early as 1683 at five days of extra service for every day's unlawful absence.[218] In penalizing absentees and deserters both legislature and courts of New York displayed much greater moderation than did the authorities of Pennsylvania.

The more conciliatory attitude toward the absentee in New York may be traced at least in part to policies pursued in the Dutch courts of New Netherland, where such culprits were usually ordered to go back to work and pay damages for their absence rather than to serve extra time. It is also quite clear that the Dutch language courts, even under English rule, put the contract laborer in the same category as the indentured servant in so far as unauthorized absence from work was concerned. As early as 1638 all persons in the service of the Dutch were "commended not to quit the Island of Manhattan without the express permission of the Honble Commander." [219] An ordinance of 1640 directed farm and house servants to serve out their time according to contract.[220] At times the Dutch courts awarded the master damages; [221] on other occasions they enjoined the workman from entering upon his trade until he had given satisfaction for the period of his absence.[222] On still others the

---

[214] Wolcott v. Drake, Hartford County Court Rec., lib. 1706/7–18, f. 202 (1712).

[215] Collings v. Heming, New Haven Co. Court Rec., lib. II, f. 92 (1702).

[216] *N.Y. Col. Laws*, I, 147 (1684), IV, 924 (1766); *New Conductor Generalis* (Albany, 1819), p. 30.

[217] Allinson, *N.J. Acts*, pp. 21, 22 (1714).

[218] *Pa. Col. Rec.*, I, 80 (1683); *Pa. Stat. at Large*, II, 54–56 (1700). But cf. *ibid.*, VII, 30, 31 (1771).

[219] Stokes, *Iconography*, IV, 88. A forfeiture of three months' wages was the penalty for disobedience. *Laws and Ord. of New Neth.*, p. 18.

[220] *Ibid.*, p. 24; Stokes, *op. cit.*, p. 92.

[221] *Rensselaerswyck Court Mins.*, 1648–52, pp. 25, 26 (1648).

[222] *R.N.A.*, VII, 224 (1659). See also *ibid.*, V, 205–206, 210 (1665). If the employer could not prove that he had hired the defendant for a term of a year, the court held that the latter's clothes and other property could not be attached. *Ibid.*, II, 37, 38 (1657).

court would order the servant merely to serve out his term.[223] The suit
for damages is illustrated by the case of *Sleghtenhorst v. Keller,* brought
in the Kingston court.[224] The defendant servant pleaded "that he cannot live there any longer, and cannot please her [i.e., the mistress] in
anything," for, in her opinion, he was "not worth the bread he eats."
The presiding overseers handed down individual opinions. Meyer ruled
that Keller be discharged, merely paying costs, because his mistress did
not want him any longer. With this view Ten Broeck and Claesen concurred, the latter, however, holding that he need not pay costs. In
Wittaker's dissenting opinion the principle was enunciated that "if the
complt [complainant] can prove that the servant left her house at an
improper time, he ought to be punished on account of it, as a servant
ought to be punished." Keller was discharged from service without
penalty for damages or costs, a decision which the plaintiff's wife appealed to the next court of sessions.

The effect of desertion upon the employer's liability for the payment
of wages was occasionally litigated in the Dutch language courts. Where
a worker was hired to work up to harvest time and left before the expiration of the stipulated period, his employer maintained in one case
that he was not obliged to pay the balance of wages due. The workman
countered that he left because the employer had paid his wages irregularly and not monthly according to agreement. The court ordered the
employer to pay the balance due and the laborer to complete his term
until harvest, under penalty of losing ten schepels of wheat.[225] In a labor
contract drawn up in 1683 for the building of a stone house, express
stipulation was made that in case the workman should "run away or
die or fall sick," the agreement was to be void, but daily wages were to
be paid for that portion of the work completed.[226] At times English settlers in the early period incorporated into service contracts provisions
for extra time. George Reynolds, to take one example, stipulated in his
indentures that if he attempted to run away, he should serve his master
seven years extra, a provision which was upheld in Gravesend sessions
in 1679.[227]

At least one public official appeared sympathetic to the plight of
servants in the period of English rule, if we are to believe the hostile
charges brought to the attention of the New York authorities in 1675
by a resident of Martha's Vineyard. According to his recital, he took

[223] *Albany, Rensselaerswyck, and Schenectady Court Mins., 1668–73,* I, 183 (1670); *R.N.A.,*
II, 144 (1656), III, 40 (1659); Ulster Dutch Transcripts, lib. II, f. 436 (1667).
[224] Ulster Dutch Transcripts, lib. III, f. 129 (1683).
[225] Doorn v. Paulusen, Ulster Dutch Transcripts, lib. I, f. 352 (1666).
[226] Ulster Dutch Transcripts.   [227] Reynold's case, Gravesend Court Rec., lib. II, f. 108.

a "naked Indian boy" as an apprentice for a four-year term. Within a year his relatives carried him away. Then ensued a period in which the boy shunted back and forth, departing every time his master left the island. If the master's wife had agreed to let the boy go home on Saturdays and return on Mondays he would have been willing to stay, but she made short shrift of this idea. "No, you shall not go to stink of your company but you shall go to meeting with me and do as your master hath apoynted you," she declared. Terrified at the thought of many more interminable Sabbath sermons, the Indian boy again took French leave, only to return once more. This time the master boxed his ears, and then when the lad fled again, he complained to Governor Mayhew, who ruled that the boy was to return to his master, but that there was to be no penalty of extra service, and that, in the event of further corporal punishment being administered by the master, he was to be free. Again "when greene Indian Corne was eatable," the boy departed. When his master tried to sell him, Richard Sarson, an assistant, was alleged to have made a weird ruling that such a transfer was "unlawful because he was bound to serve my heirs or assignees." Sarson further stated it as the official view of Governor Mayhew "that no Master should strik his servant and that if the servant is not willing to abide, the Master should let him goe." From such humanitarian notions the master craved relief, urging that the laws of New York be enforced on the island and that the settlers "be delivered from all rible rable and notions of men." [228]

The course of eighteenth-century sessions proceedings in New York with regard to runaways pretty closely paralleled the New England courts of that period. The principal penalty was the order to return to service; and no case has been found in general sessions in which the penalty of double time was exacted.[229] However, so few runaway cases came up in the courts of New York City that it is doubtful whether the courts ever worked out a carefully articulated policy.[230]

[228] N.Y. State Hist. Assn., *Ann. Rep.*, p. 371 (1675).

[229] In 1684 two justices sentenced Governor Dongan's absentee servant to serve double time and satisfy £23 pursuit costs. Horton's case. Rec. of Wills, lib. XIXB, f. 132 (1684).

[230] Robert Ellis's servants: committed to gaol until they were bound out to serve the terms stated in their indentures. N.Y.Q.S., 1694–1731/2, f. 338 (1717). Welsh's case: committed to the common gaol to remain a prisoner one month unless his master in the meantime conveyed him to Pennsylvania, otherwise to be discharged. N.Y.G.S., lib. 1722–42/3, f. 144; 1694–1731/2, f. 542 (1731). Jenkinks's case, *ibid.*, lib. 1772–89, f. 432 (1789), ordered to return to his master. Wendover's case (master complained also of embezzlement, servant of want of necessaries): the court held that the complaints on both sides were not supported. *Ibid.*, lib. 1772–89, f. 423 (1789). For an early order to serve out a term, see Boyer's case, Newtown Court Rec., f. 245 (1670). For a suit for civil damages for desertion, see Taylor v. Cornish, N.Y.M.C.M., lib. 1674–75 (1675), where plaintiff alleged that through "misinformation" the defendant had obtained "his freedom from the Dutch power." Verdict for defendant.

From a study of the newspaper files of the period it is evident that the apprehended runaways actually brought before the New York courts for sentence were only a small fraction of the total number of such fugitive servants. In any statistical compilation from newspaper advertisements one must guard against considering every advertisement a case *de novo*. In general, it was the practice of masters to repeat an advertisement for several issues. Benjamin Peter Hunt made compilations of such runaway advertisements in the *New York Gazette, or Weekly Post Boy* for the years 1748–57 as follows:

Runaway Advertisements in the New York Gazette

	1748	1749	1750	1751	1752	1753	1754	1755	1756	1757
Whole no. of advts.	22	11	7	18	22	46	96	112	124	100
Different white servants	6	6	5	14	13	17	22	20	18	5
Men	5	6	5	11	10	12	21	19	16	4
Women	1	0	0	3	3	5	1	1	2	1
Apprentices	1	0	0	0	0	0	1	0	1	2
Convicts	0	0	0	0	0	0	0	0	0	0
Servants for sale	1	0	1	0	0	6	0	0	0	0
Servants in gaol	0	0	0	0	0	0	0	1	1	0
Vessels arriving with servants	0	1	0	0	0	0	3	1	1	0

These figures show an appreciable increase in the number of such advertisements with the outbreak of the French and Indian War. Nevertheless, they are not overly reliable. For example, let us compare the advertisements of runaway white servants in the *New York Gazette* and in the *New York Journal, or General Advertiser* for the years 1770 and 1771:

	N.Y. Journal 1770	N.Y. Gazette 1770	N.Y. Journal 1771	N.Y. Gazette 1771
Whole no. of advts.	56	27	43	95
Different white servants	12	9	8	23
Men	12	9	6	23
Women	0	0	2	0
Apprentices	3	0	4	10
Convicts	0	0	0	0
Servants for sale	1	2	0	2
Servants in gaol	0	0	0	1
Vessels arriving with servants	0	0	0	0

Thus, while the available files of the *Journal* indicate a drop in 1771 from the previous year, the *Gazette* shows a sharp rise in the total. For the year 1776 the *Gazette* has sixty-one runaway advertisements representing apparently only nine different individuals, of whom four were apprentices.

During the Revolution, Committees of Correspondence in New York assumed judicial as well as administrative functions and on occasion saw to it that servants on unauthorized leave made proper reparation.[231]

It is astonishing how few fugitive servants came before the courts of New Jersey and Pennsylvania, particularly in view of other sources of information that disclose a multitude of known runaway cases in these two provinces. As early as 1682 the Burlington court ordered that servants absent without leave should serve one week for every day's unauthorized absence, two months for every week, and one year for every month—an extremely high penalty ranging from seven for one to twelve for one.[232] In the eighteenth-century Jersey quarter sessions on occasion ordered runaways to serve extra time, although such instances are far less frequent than in Pennsylvania.[233]

It is quite apparent that few of the New Jersey runaways were ever returned to their masters, forced to serve extra time, or penalized in some other manner by the courts. While it must be conceded that many masters did not put themselves to the expense of advertising when a servant ran away, not wishing to throw good money after bad, there is nonetheless not the slightest correlation between court prosecutions and runaway advertisements in the Jersey press. For the period, 1740–50, some 151 cases have been identified in the newspapers. The rate then doubles between 1751 and 1755, the figures totaling 147 for the shorter period. For the next five years the annual average is about fifteen a year, which jumps to about forty a year between 1762 and 1771. The outbreak of the Revolution and the early campaigns in the Middle states contributed to the problem. Of the 71 advertisements for white-servant runaways between 1775 and 1782, 55 appeared in the years, 1775–77.[234]

An unusual example of cooperation by employers to capture runaway workmen was the program drawn up by the Cordwainers' Fire Com-

231 Adair's case, *Mins. Albany Comm. Corr.*, II, 1143 (1778), on refusal of the servant to appear, she was committed to the Albany gaol until she gave satisfaction to her master or was released by the committee.
232 Burlington, West Jersey, Court Book, f. 7 (1682); also Tregidgon's case, Burlington Q.S., f. 117 (1693).
233 Hunterdon C.P. and Q.S., lib. 1733–36, f. 70 (1734).
234 *N.J. Arch.*, 1st ser., XI, XII, XIX, XX, XXIV–XXVII; 2d ser., I, III–V.

pany of Philadelphia in 1767. Some seventeen years after its organization, the company was harassed by "the frequent losses Sustained by Sarvants and Apprentices runing Away." Under a novel plan a committee of four, regularly appointed to serve for three months, was required to pursue runaways belonging to members of the company and was authorized to expend up to £5 in prosecuting their inquiries at ferries and along highways. In the event that the servant or apprentice should not be recovered, the company agreed to stand the loss up to the amount specified. If the servant were captured the master was obligated to pay the money advanced within three months. Masters were required to notify the society as soon as they found out that a servant or apprentice had absconded. If the master happened to be away from home, the company member first learning the tidings was required to secure an adequate description of the servant and to take other necessary steps. This program amounted in effect to an insurance by members against loss of their workmen. In order to share in the benefits each member was required to pay 5s. to the treasurer. The only persons who begged off were masters who had neither servants nor apprentices.[235]

Was a skilled craftsman who quit his job when his wages were withheld a fugitive who could be forced by law to return to work for his employer? The issue was brought to a head when Henry Stiegel, the fabulous glass manufacturer, offered a reward of five pistoles for the return of an employee. The workman rejoined that he had, along with several others, come to America to make glassware and had been induced by Stiegel to enter into articles of agreement with him. Since, according to his assertion, Stiegel had "forfeited the covenants on his part," the employee maintained that he had "a right to leave his employ and to bring an action against him." He further asserted:

I am not by the laws of nature, to drudge and spend my whole life and strength in performing my part of the articles, and Mr. Stiegel not paying me my wages. I have taken the opinion of an eminent gentleman of the law upon the articles, who declares, no person can be justified in apprehending me, as I am no servant, and that any person so doing will subject himself to an action of false imprisonment.[236]

In some jurisdictions it is clear that the wage earner and hired man was, from the point of view of the runaway laws, in the same category as the

[235] See Cordwainers' Fire Company Mins., 1760–72 (Nov. 9, 1767, March 11, 1771, Nov. 2, 1772), Hist. Soc. of Pa. Parallel organizations appear to have been established in 18th-century Britain. For example, in 1789 an association was formed at Sheffield for the apprehension of absconding apprentices. R. E. Leader, *History of the Company of Cutlers in Hallamshire in the County of York*, I, 51.

[236] *Pa. Packet*, Nov. 11, 1771.

apprentice and the indentured servant, but there is no evidence which would lead us to believe that the fugitive-servant laws were applied in Pennsylvania against wage earners.

On the basis of fugitive-servant cases culled from the dockets of Pennsylvania county courts it is difficult to determine with what degree of consistency the courts enforced the five-for-one extra service penalty of the statute. In many cases the length of the period of absence is not disclosed; in others the extra service penalty also includes service in lieu of the costs of capture. However, it is safe to conclude, on the basis of 94 fugitive-servant cases examined in four of the inferior courts of the province, that Pennsylvania punished her fugitive workmen more severely than any other colony north of the Potomac. Down to 1750 the penalty was generally, but not invariably, five for one, but the exorbitant service periods exacted in satisfaction of capture costs [237] would run up the total extra servitude to the penalties prevailing in the tobacco colonies (ten for one in Maryland), the severest of any in their treatment of the runaway. In fact, capture costs might figure heavily in the sentence. For one day's unauthorized absence the Chester County court sentenced Matthew Boucher to serve five days additional as well as six months in lieu of the expenses of taking him.[238] When John Burck ran away from his master, Edward Barret, victualler, that worthy advertised a reward of £3 and reasonable charges for his return. A pilot who had seen the announcement took the fugitive off a ship. The complainant master filed the following expense account:

Advtsments to the printer	£0: 05: 00
To a man going to the ferry and other plans to put up the advertisement	0: 04: 00
To Samuel Rowling a pilot for taking him up	3: 00: 00
	£3: 09: 00

As he was unable to reimburse his master, Burck was sentenced by the Philadelphia mayor's court to serve another twelve months.[239] Other

[237] As regards the nature of such "costs," it must be borne in mind that court clerks frequently used the word "costs" in cases of absenteeism to include fees for official services as well as certain allowances to a party for expenses incurred in a suit. Under the strict English rule sessions courts could not award costs, merely fees. See also Goebel and Naughton, *Law Enforcement in Col. N.Y.,* p. 731.

[238] Chester Q.S., lib. 1733–42, f. 105.

[239] Barret's petition, Philadelphia Co. Court papers (1754), Hist. Soc. of Pa. Between 1725 and 1734 Mulatto Ben was taken up by the Philadelphia watch some dozen times and thrown into the workhouse, where his master claimed him on each occasion, paying costs. From one of these unauthorized journeys Ben returned with frozen feet, and his master had to place him under the doctor's care for a week. These escapades cost his master some £5. *Ibid.* (c. 1734). For an action on the case against a master for capture costs, see Dyer v. Cloud, *Chester Co., Pa. Rec., 1681–97,* p. 64 (1685).

offenses committed by the runaway, such as bastardy or theft, appreciably increased the total servitude penalty.[240]

Court prosecutions in Pennsylvania, as in the other Middle colonies, represented only a small percentage of actual runaway cases. In the file of the *American Weekly Mercury* for the year 1726 are found 326 different advertisements, 110 of them relating either to runaway servants or to the sale of servants.[241] Out of 11,606 advertisements for runaway servants tabulated by Benjamin Peter Hunt from the files of the *Pennsylvania Gazette* from 1728 to 1784, at least 4,748 were new advertisements. The peak years were 1753, with 555, 1754, with 519, and 1775, when there were 1,055 advertisements of 355 different and distinct runaway cases.[242] Despite discrepancies between newspapers studied, the average for the years of the Revolution declined drastically from the 1775 figure.[243] The decline continued, but somewhat more slowly, between 1785 and 1804, for which period there were 816 advertisements, 283 appearing to be different and distinct ones; but of this total some 193, including 71 different runaway cases, appeared in 1785 and only 27, of which four were new cases, were reported in 1804. Although such advertisements continue to appear down through the 1820s, the number of indentured servants advertised as runaways in Poulson's *American Daily Advertiser* had declined to four by 1824, while the number of apprentices so listed reached a total of 57. Thus, while in-

[240] See Judith Manning's case, York Q.S., lib. XII, f. 89 (1778), 1 yr. 3 mos. extra for 8 days' absence and bastardy. Pennsylvania cases studied include: Bucks Co. Sess., lib. 1648–1730 (1691), (1692, 2 cases), (1726, 3 cases), (1728), (1730, 3 cases); lib. 1715–53, f. 126 (1731); lib. 1754–82, fols. 3 (1754), 20, 29, 30 (1755), 99 (1758), 126 (1759), 196 (1762), 258 (1764), 297 (1765), 409 (1769), 531 (1774). Chester Co. Sess., lib. 1681–97, fols. 95 (1687), (1689), 155, 175, 178 (3 cases) (1689), 206 (1690), 322, 340 (2 cases), 356 (1695); lib. 1714–23 (1718), (1719), (1720); lib. 1723–33, fols. 216, 217 (1731); lib. 1733–42, fols. 99, 105 (1737); lib. 1742–59 (1749), (1752); lib. A (1766), (1767), (1768, 2 cases); lib. B (1770, 4 cases), (1771, 2 cases), (1772, 2 cases), (1773, 3 cases), (1774, 5 cases), (1775), (1776, 4 cases). Cumberland Co. Road and Sess. Docket, No. 1, 1729–42, f. 15 (1736); Docket No. 2, 1742–60 (1747), (1757); Docket, 1750–65, Pt. I, fols. 93 (1760), 111 (1761); Pt. II, fols. 39, 44 (1762); Pt. III (1765, 2 cases), fols. 29, 42, 43 (1766); Pt. IV, fols. 157, 169 (2 cases) (1771); Docket No. 5, 1776–82 (1776, 2 cases), (1778). Philadelphia Sess., lib. 1753–60 (1754), (1755); lib. 1773–80 (1774, 3 cases), (1780).

[241] For the following year, such advertisements number 130 out of a total of 387. See Benjamin Peter Hunt MSS, lib. III, f. 30.

[242] The third Intercolonial War aggravated the problem of absenteeism (*Pa. Gazette,* July 9, 1752), and a sharp rise in the number of runaways was reported for the period of the French and Indian War. For the years, 1752–56, there were 809 advertisements, 444 of which were new. Of this last figure, 494 were men, according to Hunt's tabulations, 57 women, 221 Irish, 119 English, 7 Scotch, 9 Welsh, 100 "Dutch," by which was meant German, 3 French, and 7 Negro. Nine were native born and no nationality was indicated in 70 cases. Benjamin Peter Hunt MSS, lib. I, fols. 222–227.

[243] For 1783 the total number listed in the *Pa. Packet* was 52, of which 9 were different and distinct cases. See Benjamin Peter Hunt MSS, lib. V, fols. 69, 76, 79.

dentured servitude was rapidly on its way out, the institution of apprenticeship continued to show far more vitality at this late period.[244]

As early as 1681 the Newcastle court was advised by a jury to impose an extra service penalty of four days for every day's unauthorized absence,[245] but very shortly thereafter the Delaware courts followed Pennsylvania in the enforcement of the even more severe penalty of five for one, which, when recapture costs were taken into consideration, often approximated a tenfold penalty for each day's leave.[246] In the Newcastle quarter sessions it was not unusual for the master to petition for extra time merely on the basis of capture costs. If costs were sufficiently high—and masters generally claimed expenditures ranging from £5 to £8—the petitioner was certain that the court would greatly prolong the servant's time, even though his daily labor might have been valued at a maximum of 1s.[247]

The requirement that strangers have a passport or certificate to show that they were free men, generally in force in the Middle colonies,[248] effectively implemented the hue and cry procedure in force in that area.[249] Statute or court practice authorized town officials or the sessions to confine runaways to gaol to await claims by their masters.[250] The masters or their attorneys were bound to pay charges arising from the hue and cry.[251]

[244] See *ibid.*, lib. VI, fols. 35–38. Of course, such statistics are subservient to the particular whim of the advertiser in his choice of newspapers. For example, while the *Gazette* lists only 193 advertisements of runaways for 1785, the *Packet* carries 514; and while the former has only 55 such items for 1789, the latter allots space to 185. *Ibid.*, lib. V, f. 101. Of the *Packet* advertisements, 23 out of the 1785 total were apprentices and 22 out of the 1789 total.

[245] *Newcastle, Del., Court Rec.*, I, 455 (1681).

[246] See, e.g., Kent Co. Court, lib. 1697–98, f. 25 (1697), 1699–1703 (1700, 1701), (1702, 2 cases), (1703), 1703–1705, fols. 8a, 22 (1704), 25 (1706, 3 cases), 1718–21, f. 12 (1718); Q.S., lib. 1728 (1); Q.S. and C.P., lib. 1730 (1731), 1731 (1).

[247] Newcastle Q.S., lib. 1764–65, f. 78 (1765); 1774–76 (1775), anywhere from 9 mos. to a year and a half allowed for costs ranging from £5 to £8.

[248] N.Y. *Col. Laws*, I, 94; Stokes, *Iconography*, IV, 333; MS Exec. Council Mins., lib. V, f. 106 (N.Y. State Lib.); P. W. Edsall, *Journal of the Court of Common Right and Chancery of East New Jersey, 1683–1702* (Philadelphia, 1937), p. 175 (1683).

[249] N.Y. *Col. Laws*, I, 157 (1684). See also *Docs. Rel. to Col. Hist. of N.Y.*, V, 410. For a satirically humorous hue and cry appeal, see Misc. Phila. County Papers, 1738–67 (1740), Hist. Soc. of Pa. For a written power of attorney to pursue a runaway, see that of Simon Lobdell of Hartford to Ralph Warner, *Huntington Rec.*, I, 224 (1676). For others, see Newtown Court Rec., f. 4 (1649). For the hue and cry procedure in the case of deserting seamen, see N.Y. Court of Assize, fols. 574, 575, 645 (1670); Gravesend Court Rec., lib. II, f. 108 (Gravesend sessions, 1679); N.Y. State Hist. Assn., *Ann. Report, 1896*, Col. Ser., I, 176 (1672).

[250] In one case where the confinement was by mittimus the court found the writ "defective both in form and substance" and discharged the prisoner. Henderson's case, Lancaster, Pa., Road and Sessions Docket, No. 3, 1760–68 (Aug. session, 1766).

[251] Gravesend Court Rec., lib. II, f. 170 (Gravesend sessions, 1682); *Newcastle, Del., Court Rec.*, I, 455 (1681); Kent, lib. 1699–1703 (orders of Dec. 14, 1699; May 11–13, 1703).

THE TOBACCO PROVINCES. Maryland enacted far more severe legislation dealing with fugitive servants than did any of the colonies to the north. As early as 1641 it was made a felony, punishable by death, to run away from one's master or to assist a runaway.[252] In 1649 the death penalty was dropped and extra service at the rate of two days for every day's absence substituted.[253] The basic fugitive-servant law of 1661 raised the penalty to ten days' service for every day away.[254] Statutes placed severe restrictions on the travel of servants without a pass from master or overseer, and authorized "strangers and other suspicious persons" to be disposed of by a justice of the peace as "he shall think fit." [255] The law made no distinction whatsoever between runaway indentured servants and absentee free workmen under contract, but specifically provided that all servants, "whether by indenture, or according to the custom of the country, or hired for wages," were liable to be taken up as runaways if caught ten miles from home without written permission from their masters.[256] Provision was made for the detention of such runaways,[257] a standing reward offered for taking them up,[258] and ample allowance given to sheriffs for expenditures incurred.[259]

Even though the fugitive law made no distinction between servants and hired workmen, masters sometimes found it expedient to have their employees expressly stipulate that, in case they took unauthorized leave, they could be dealt with as absconding servants. Colonel Henry Darnall freed Arnold Lyvers, a tailor by trade, from an agreement to serve him four years in consideration of £5 sterling, on condition that

---

[252] This sentence might be converted to servitude not exceeding seven years by the governor with extra allowance of double time to the master for the period of absence. *Md. Arch.*, I, 107. Benefit of clergy was allowed. *Ibid.*, p. 71. See also act of 1642, *ibid.*, p. 124.

[253] *Ibid.*, p. 249.   [254] *Ibid.*, II, 146; also p. 298 (1671).

[255] *Ibid.*, I, 451; more stringent in 1669 and again in 1671. *Ibid.*, II, 224, 298, 524. This procedure was made applicable to seamen in 1695. *Ibid.*, XX, 392. See also *ibid.*, XXII, 546–553 (1699); XXVI, 254 (1704).

[256] *Ibid.*, XIII, 451 (1692), XXVI, 254 (1704); Bacon's *Laws*, ch. xliv (1715).

[257] In 1669 the legislature provided for the building of a loghouse prison in Baltimore Co. for committing runaways from neighboring colonies to the north. *Md. Arch.*, II, 224. Later on provision was made for sending runaways to Annapolis. *Ibid.*, XX, 395 (1695). All sheriffs were to be notified and required to post the information at public meeting places. Where the master did not appear after due notice, the sheriff was authorized to dispose of the runaway by sale to the highest bidder. *Ibid.*, XXXIII, 459 (1719). For instances of the return of runaways to their masters in adjacent counties or other provinces, see *ibid.*, X, 15, 24 (1650); Somerset, lib. 1671–75, f. 342 (1674); Charles, lib. 1690–92, f. 2 (1690); Ann Arundel, lib. 1704–8, f. 302 (1706); Md. Prov. Court Rec., lib. 1692–93, fols. 192, 193 (1692).

[258] 200 lbs. of tobacco (*Md. Arch.*, II, 298 [1671]); but Indian captors were to receive a "match-coat," or blanket.

[259] Talbot, lib. AB, No. 8, f. 467 (1697). Runaways seized by private persons were automatically turned over to the sheriff by the court (Somerset, lib. AW, 1690–91, f. 61vso. [1688]), but at times it was necessary to caution sheriffs not to exploit the prisoners for their private advantage. See *CSPA, 1702*, No. 222, p. 150.

Lyvers would relinquish his wages and serve his former master eight weeks a year for six years, during which time he was to be allowed to ply his trade in five specified Maryland counties. However, "in case the said Lyvers shall make an attempt to depart Farther than the Said Counties then it is agreed and it Shall be Lawfull for the said Henry Darnall to apprehend him . . . as one that hath deserted the service of his said Master." [260]

In order to ascertain the extent to which the statutory penalty was carried out by the inferior courts of Maryland, tabulations were made of 267 cases of fugitive servants in the court records of eight counties for the period 1668-1776. In over 90 per cent of these cases the ten-for-one sentence under the act of Assembly was imposed. In a few Talbot County cases in 1705 the absentee was merely required to make up his lost time; and in some scattering cases in Somerset, Baltimore, Charles, and Prince George's counties between 1720 and 1766 penalties ranging from four for one to eight for one were substituted.[261] In addition to

[260] The counties specified were on the Western Shore. Darnell agreed to give Lyvers "the Proffitt of his worke he hath been Imployed in and hath gained since the first day of March last." Prince George, lib. A, 1696-1702, f. 424 (1699). See also indenture made in 1647 between Thomas Greene and Hannah Mathewes, whereby a flat payment by the servant of 1,000 lbs. of tobacco and three barrels of corn was to void the indenture of servitude as well as all extra time the master might be entitled to by his servant's unlawful absence. *Md. Arch.,* IV, 464.

[261] Ann Arundel, lib. 1692-93, f. 330 (1693); lib. 1702-4, fols. 5, 7, 12 (2 cases), 41 (2 cases), 42, 110 (2 cases), 113, 225, 226 (1703); lib. 1703-5, fols. 144 (1703), 303, 419 (1704), 553 (1705); lib. 1704-8 (1706), (1707); lib. 1708-12 (1708, 3 cases), (1709, 4 cases), (1710, 2 cases); lib. 1720-21, f. 180 (1721); lib. 1721-22 (1722, 2 cases); lib. 1745-47 (1745, 2 cases). Baltimore, lib. D, 1682-86 (1683, 2 cases); lib. 1691, 3 cases; lib. LG, 1693-96 (1695), (1696); lib. IS, 1718-21 (1718, 2 cases), (1719), (1720, 2 cases), (1721); lib. HS, No. 7, 1730-32 (1730, 4 cases), (1731, 3 cases); lib. 1772-80 (1772, 9 cases), (1773, 2 cases), (1775, 5 cases). Cecil, lib. 1708-16 (1711), (1714, 3 cases), (1715, 2 cases), (1716, 2 cases); lib. 1723-30 (1723), (1724, 2 cases); lib. 1772-73 (1772), (1773). Charles, lib. 1668-82 (1668, 2 cases); lib. 1680-82, fols. 85 (2 cases), 189 (1681), 224 (1683), 226, 236 (1686); lib. 1686-87, fols. 267 (3 cases), 300 (1686); lib. 1690-92, fols. 39 (4 cases), 40, 103 (2 cases) (1690), 274 (1691, 2 cases), 429 (1692); lib. 1692-94 (1693, 2 cases); lib. 1696-98, fols. 3 (2 cases), 25, 52 (1696), 203 (1697, 2 cases); lib. 1699-1701, fols. 35 (1700, 2 cases); lib. 1704-10, fols. 6, 59, 65 (2 cases) (1704), 347 (1705); lib. 1720-22 (1720, 6 cases), (1721, 3 cases); lib. 1734-38 (1734), (1736, 2 cases), (1738, 2 cases); lib. 1746-47, fols. 31, 141 (1746). Prince George, lib. A, 1696-1702 (1696, 2 cases); lib. 1699-1705, f. 13 (1699), 27 (1700), 153, 216 (4 cases) (1702), 234, 238 (2 cases) (1703), 309 (1704); lib. 1699-1705, fols. 352, 353, 402, 439 (2 cases) (1705); lib. C, 1702-8, f. 89 (1706); lib. 1708-10, fols. 76, 277 (1708), 318 (1710); lib. 1720-22, fols. 10, 82, 83, 245, 247, 378, 417, 651-653 (1720-22); lib. 1730-32, fols. 221, 278, 280, 292, 293 (1731), 529 (1732, 2 cases); lib. 1746-47, f. 385 (1746, 2 cases); lib. 1775-77, f. 506 (1776, 4 cases). Queen Ann, lib. 1709-16, fols. 82, 114, 157 (1710), 190 (1712), 203, 204 (1713), (1714), (1715, 3 cases); lib. 1718-19 (1718), (1719, 8 cases); lib. 1735-39 (1735), (1736, 3 cases), (1737-38, 14 cases), (1739, 2 cases). Somerset, lib. 1671-75, f. 152 (1672); lib. 1675, fols. 537 (2 cases), 538, 573; lib. L, O-7 (1683), (1688); lib. 1692-93, fols. 111 (1692), 226 (1693), (1694); lib. 1701-2, f. 133 (1702, 2 cases); lib. 1722-24, f. 118 (1723); lib. 1730-37, fols. 49 (1731), 279 (1733, 2 cases). Talbot, lib. NIV, No. 6 (1687, 2 cases), (1688); lib. AB. No. 8, fols. 2, 6 (1696), 344 (1697), 521 (1698); lib. 1703-4 (1704, 12 cases); lib. RF, No. 10 (1705, 9 cases). Prior to the enactment of the ten-for-one statute the courts imposed a more modest penalty,

the severe penalty of extra service, the court also meted out whipping, especially where the fugitive had acted in concert with other workmen.[262]

It must be remembered, too, that the court might enjoin workers under contract from leaving their tasks as well as impose extra service upon absentees. John Lewger had agreed to accept dressed skins in lieu of three years service still due on indentures from Thomas Todd. Lewger found it necessary to complain to the court that there was "a vehement suspicion of the intent of the sd Tho. Todd to depart out of the Colony, and defeat the pet'r of the benefitt of the sd bargaine." The court promptly issued execution against Todd for 710 lbs. of tobacco, apparently as security that he would not quit the province.[263]

At times the application of the full penalty would have meant adding many years of servitude. In such cases the court might arrange a compromise. Thomas Vaughan accepted a year's additional service instead of the tenfold penalty for seventy-one day's absence, and Francis Armstrong, even more lenient, agreed to waive any additional service if his servant did not go away again without his permission and would finish out his term.[264] Where a servant's absence was accounted for by his having turned Indians over to the authorities, the court refused the master's petition that he serve ten days for one, but merely imposed a day-for-day penalty.[265] Despite occasional compromises and modifications of the statutory penalty, sentences running as high as 1,530 days, 2,000 days—in the case of William Babbery of Charles County—and even of 12,130 days, which the master generously agreed to commute to five years, were at times imposed by the county courts.

Women runaways with prolonged absences charged against them appear to have fared slightly better than did male culprits. May Harris, who over a period of three years had run away on fifteen different occasions for a total of 195 days, was merely sentenced in Ann Arundel court

---

such as double time according to the previous law. See *Md. Arch.,* IV, 162 (1642); X, 322 (1653), double time but freed on account of cruelty; *ibid.,* p. 416 (1655); XLI, 316, 317 (1659). When, around 1750, the Frederick Co. court was exacting a four-for-one penalty (Frederick, lib. 1748–50, f. 243), the courts on the Eastern Shore were imposing penalties of six-for-one. Charles Co. was perhaps most consistent in observing the statutory penalty. See order of Aug. 10, 1686, Charles, lib. 1685–86, f. 224.

[262] However, in a suit instituted by Elizabeth Hasell's master for damages for satisfaction for runaway time, the jury sustained the contention of defendant's attorney that, as Elizabeth had been corporally punished by her mistress for her absenteeism, plaintiff was not entitled to recover under the act of Assembly. According to the evidence, her mistress had put her in irons, tied her to her bedpost, and whipped her until "there was a puddle of blood in the room and great wounds in her back." Emanson v. Hasell, *Md. Arch.,* LX, 233–235 (1670).

[263] *Md. Arch.,* IV, 243, 283 (1644). See also Tony's case, *ibid.,* X, 511–514.

[264] *Ibid.,* LIV, 398 (1666), 540 (1672).

[265] Casey's petition, Prince George, lib. C, 1702–8, f. 77 (1706).

to serve five days for each day's absence and Jane Parker was required to serve fifty-four days for an unauthorized leave of eighteen days.

Capture costs lengthened the runaway's sentence appreciably. In ascertaining the service due in lieu of payment of such costs, the courts showed little consistency. The very same county court that sentenced a servant to serve nine months extra on account of £3 expenses incurred by the master sentenced another culprit to serve three months extra for a mere 4s. The services of the former, a woman servant, were calculated at the rate of 5s. a week in 1715, and of the latter, a male servant, at the rate of 4d. a week the very next year! In a few instances the rate exceeded 1s. per diem, but, generally speaking, servants' wages were appraised at a far lower rate than in Pennsylvania.

The master had a property interest in his servant's runaway time, which he might sell or assign even before sentence had passed against the servant.[266] The servant was entitled to a record or accounting of such extra time. Silent Ball, who comes up again and again in the Charles County court minutes as a runaway, actually lost track of her extra service liability, and, on petition to the court in 1699, her master was ordered to "allow her time to Come to the Clerke to gett Copyes of the Seuerall Judgments Entred against her for her Runaway time." [267]

Advertisements of runaway servants in Maryland newspapers, contrary to expectations, do not reflect the influence of the French and Indian War, with the notable exception of the year 1759. Although the problem of servant enlistments was acute in Maryland, her experience with runaways in wartime does not appear to have been as exigent as that of the Middle colonies. A closer correlation can be made between advertisements of runaway servants and convictions in Maryland courts than can be drawn for the Middle colonies. There were on an average several convictions a year of fugitive servants in each of the Maryland

[266] See Ridge's case, Cecil, lib. 1708–16 (1713); Margaret Brown's case, Ann Arundel, lib. 1720–21, f. 221 (1721). In 1703 the administrators of James Brookes sued James Watts on an agreement to swap a woman servant for a manservant in consideration of Watts's making oath as to the number of days which the manservant had absented himself, which he was to prove according to law but failed to do. A verdict of 2,500 lbs. of tobacco was awarded plaintiffs, but, "Considering the advantage the Defendant might have by bringing a Writt of Error or by Fileing reasons in Arrest of Judgment which the Defendt had Leave to doe from the Court, they rather Choose to Suffer a Nonsuite." Prince George, lib. B, 1699–1705, f. 243 (1703).

[267] Charles, lib. 1698–99, f. 2. John Edwards, awarded freedom dues in 1706, made claim that his master had not particularized his account for runaway time or specified the exact days on each occasion. The court cautioned "John of the Danger of Swearing to the truth and Justice of Such an account and thereupon the said John desists till he can be better Informed." Ann Arundel, lib. 1704–8, f. 301 (1706). In one instance the court discharged a servant where a master had sold him for runaway time without having brought him into court to have his extra time adjudged according to law. Simmons' case, Prince George, lib. A, 1696–1702, f. 6 (1696).

county courts. Hence, the following table of advertisements compiled from the *Maryland Gazette* for the years 1745–48 and 1756–60 is hardly indicative of any breakdown of the police or judicial machinery set up to deal with the absentee and the deserter:

	1745	1746	1747	1748	1756	1757	1758	1759	1760
Different white runaway servants	31	38	34	38	14	36	26	54	11
Men	27	35	32	37	14	35	24	52 [b]	11
Women	4	3	2	1	0	1	2	2	0
Convict runaway servants [a]	5	16	12	16	7	25	17	40	10
For sale	2	2	3	0	0	2	5	1	0
In gaol (as runaways)	0	0	0	0	0	0	1	2	0
Runaway Negro servants	1	0	0	1	1	0	1	1	0
Imported	0	0	0	. . [c]	0	0	0	0	0

[a] Convicts are also listed in other appropriate categories.
[b] Two of the runaways are described as "apprentices."
[c] "A parcel" (for seven years).

Virginia was as alert and vigorous as Maryland in detecting and punishing absentee workmen. The Dale Code of 1611 fixed the death penalty for any man or woman who ran away to the Indian settlements,[268] and a number of executions were actually carried out under this harsh provision.[269] The act of 1643 provided double time for the first offense, or a greater penalty at the discretion of the commissioners. For the second offense, the culprit was to be branded on the cheek with the letter "R" in addition to double service.[270] By act of 1662 a term in excess of the statutory double time "proportionable to the damage" could be meted out to servants running away during the harvest season or causing their masters extraordinary charges for apprehending them;[271] six years later a statute permitted master or magistrate to inflict corporal punishment in addition to extra service.[272] In addition to the statutory double time, fugitives were required to perform extra service in pay-

---

[268] Force, *Hist. Tracts*, III, No. 2, § 29.   [269] See *supra*, pp. 169–171.
[270] Hening, I, 254, 255 (1643), 440 (1658); "Abridgment of Va. Laws," 1695, *VMH*, X, 154, 155. White servants running away in the company of Negroes were required to serve for the time of the Negroes' unlawful absence as well as for their own. Hening, II, 26 (1661).
[271] *Ibid.*, pp. 116, 117.
[272] *Ibid.*, p. 266; *VMH*, X, 154, 155. Because of some doubt as to the enforcement of the double-service penalty prior to this date, the Assembly pointed out that such "moderate corporal punishment" should "not deprive the master of the satisfaction allowed by law, the one being as necessary to reclayme them from perishing in that idle course as the other is just to repaire the damages sustained by the master." Under the act of 1753 runaways could not be whipped in excess of 39 lashes. Hening, VI, 357–369. For other limitations on the exercise of corporal punishment, see *infra*, pp. 483–497, *passim*.

ment of the charges incurred by their masters in capturing them. Under the act of 1705 they were required to serve one and one-half months for every hundred pounds of tobacco expended by their masters and to make reparation for other recovery costs at the rate of one year's service for 800 lbs. of tobacco.[273]

By the eighteenth century it is clear that these penalties were applied in Virginia, not only to runaway servants, but to virtually all forms of hired labor. An act of 1726 provided that any person imported into the colony as a tradesman or workman fot wages who refused or neglected to perform his duty or absented himself was liable to serve two days for every day's refusal or neglect after his time "and without any wages to be paid for such service."[274] Such legislation effactually outlawed strikes.

To make certain that masters would not condone the conduct of runaways or adopt a lenient attitude toward those who were captured or who voluntarily returned to work, the authorities ordered masters to bring such delinquents to the next quarter court for punishment on pain of losing their servants, who would then be disposed of by the Governor and Council.[275]

Virginia formulated a detailed procedure for the apprehension and return of runaways. The justices of the county courts were empowered to do separately and out of court what could be done in England by a justice of the peace in a like situation. This included the power to issue a warrant of hue and cry for the runaway's capture.[276] In order to apprehend fugitives more easily an act of 1659 provided that the hair of runaway servants be cut close above the ears.[277] As in Maryland, servants were forbidden to leave their homes without license.[278] To induce

[273] Hening, III, 447. [274] *Ibid.*, IV, 175 (1726); V, 556, 557 (1748).

[275] *Va. Gen. Court Mins.*, p. 467 (1640); Lower Norfolk O.B., I, f. 237 (1643).

[276] See Starke, *Justice of the Peace*, p. 320. Where such a warrant was contemptuously tied to the tail of a dog, three persons in Middlesex County were carried to the whipping post, the two male culprits given 39 lashes apiece and the woman 29. Middlesex O.B., Sept. 2, 1677. The fictionalized character, Win-Grace Porringer, eloquently portrayed the terrors of the fugitive in Mary Johnson's *Prisoners of Hope: a Tale of Colonial Virginia* (Boston and New York, 1902), p. 58.

[277] Hening, I, 517, 518.

[278] A servant named William Browne petitioned the York County court for his freedom in 1675, alleging that he had had an indenture recorded at the Gloucester court and asking permission "to gett a passage over York River to see for same," for "wthout his master's leaue none will sett him over the River." The court granted permission without the master's consent, but provided that in case the petitioner was unable to prove he was free he was to make good the time of his absence. York O.B., 1671–94 (1675). No servant was allowed to go aboard ship without a pass, as this was a favorite means of escape. *Exec. Journal of the Council of State of Va.*, I, 258 (1692). In order to prevent their escape on horseback, an act of 1713 forbade overseers or servants from keeping horses without a license; even when licensed by their masters, they were limited to one horse apiece under penalty of forfeiture of the horse to the informer. Hening, IV, 49.

planters to cooperate, an act passed in 1669 offered a reward of 1,000 lbs. of tobacco to be paid by the public for the recovery of servants and to be reimbursed by the extra service of the delinquent.[279] Claims for taking up runaways—white or Indian servants or Negro slaves—were certified to the General Assembly by the county courts.[280] In order to facilitate the return of the runaway to his master the eighteenth-century county courts at times ordered that notice of arrest be entered in the *Virginia Gazette*.[281]

In determining the nature of the penalties imposed by the courts of Virginia for absenteeism and desertion, thirty-five cases were located in the extant records of the General Court for the seventeenth century, and some 160 other cases were examined for the period, 1641–1776, in the records of nineteen county courts of the province. The general pattern here varies considerably from that of Maryland. The penalty of double time prevailed in the courts of Virginia in accordance with the statutes of that province as contrasted with the ten-for-one penalty, pretty generally enforced in Maryland by the latter part of the seventeenth century. On numerous occasions the General Court exceeded the double penalty; but as the length of the unauthorized absence is normally not recorded in the minutes of that tribunal, it is not possible to ascertain the exact ratio of extra service to illegal absence. Between 1625 and 1640 it was not unusual for the court to impose extra service to the colony, at times amounting to as much as seven years. After this date such extreme penalties were abandoned in favor of the statutory penalty of double time.[282]

[279] *Ibid.*, II, 273; also *VMH*, X, 155; Hening, II, 283, 284 (1670), III, 28, 29 (1686).
[280] Lancaster O.B., 1666–80, f. 198 (1671). York O.B., 1697–1704, f. 297 (1700). Spotsylvania O.B., 1724–30, fols. 15 (1744), 2 claims; 78 (1725), 3 claims; 390 (1730), 4 claims; 1730–38, fols. 122 (1732), 9 claims; 435, 436 (1736), 4 claims. Isle of Wight O.B., 1746–52, f. 134 (1748), 397, 398 (1752). On occasion awards were made directly by county courts. Charles City O.B., 1655–65, f. 289 (1661); Northumberland O.B., 1666–78, f. 49 (1670); Henrico O.B., III, fols. 50, 51 (1695), 105 (1696), 225, 227 (1699), 251 (1700). Cf. also Rappahannock O.B., 1686–92, f. 41 (1687).
[281] Henrico O.B., 1767–69, f. 189 (1769). Escapes of runaways from the county gaols were hardly news. See *Va. Gen. Court Mins.*, p. 413 (1675).
[282] *Va. Gen. Court Mins.*, pp. 54 (1625), 105 (1626), 466 (4 cases), 467 (12 cases) (1640), 207 (2 cases), 274 (2 cases) (1670), 330, 348 (1673), 382 (10 cases), 394 (1674). Accomac, lib. II, fols, 97 (1641), 223 (1642), (1643); lib. 1666–70, fols. 31 (8 cases), 35, 38 (2 cases), 65 (1667); lib. 1682–97, f. 93 (1686). Botetourt, lib. 1770–71, Pt. I, f. 40 (1770). Caroline, lib. 1732–40, Pt. II, fols. 445 (1737), 637 (1740). Charles City, lib. 1655–65, fols. 229, 243 (1660), 573 (2 cases), 598 (1665); lib. 1672–74 (1673). Elizabeth City, lib. 1684–99, f. 60 (1695). Fairfax, lib. 1768–70, f. 103 (1769). Fincastle, lib. 1773–77 (1773). Henrico, lib. I, f. 144 (1680); lib. 1677–92, fols. 44 (1682), 59 (1683), 110 (1685), 158 (1686); lib. III (1695), (1696, 2 cases), (1697), (1699); lib. 1737–46, f. 227 (1743, 2 cases). Lancaster, lib. 1656–66, fols. 149 (1661), 179 (1662), 217 (1663, 4 cases), 224 (2 cases), 241 (2 cases), 248, 264, 309 (1664), 339, 346, 355 (2 cases) (1665); lib. 1666–80 (1666), (1670, 2 cases), (1671), (1674,

While in Virginia the extra service penalty was more moderate than in Maryland, corporal punishment was meted out as an additional penalty for desertion far more frequently, especially in the seventeenth century and particularly when a charge of theft was also included. From twenty to thirty-nine lashes was the usual sentence imposed by the old General Court. Magistrates, sheriffs, or constables were authorized by statute to whip the fugitive servant severely before returning him to his master, who would doubtless inflict more corporal punishment.[283] Indeed, it is more than likely that corporal punishment had already been inflicted in many cases where the sentence merely mentioned extra service.[284]

The statutory rate set by the act of 1705 for extra service in satisfaction of the costs of capture seems generally to have been enforced,[285] but exact determination is virtually impossible because in most cases the court clerk failed to note capture costs at all or totaled the extra service penalty and the service imposed in lieu of such costs.

By the eve of the Revolution the fugitive servant problem was far more critical on the frontier, where numerous white servants were still employed, than along the Tidewater, where the institution of indentured servitude was largely displaced by Negro slavery. The court records for the huge, sprawling county of Augusta for the brief period August 17 to November 19, 1773, contain fifteen cases of runaway servants, which was double the rate for the period 1767–69 in the same

2 cases), (1676), (1677, 2 cases), (1678, 6 cases), (1679, 4 cases), (1680). Lower Norfolk, lib. II, f. 7 (1643, 2 cases). Middlesex, lib. 1673–80, fols. 16 (1674, 4 cases), 222 (1680); lib. 1680–94, fols. 3, 5, 33 (2 cases) (1680–81), 121, 134 (1683). Northampton, lib. 1655–56, f. 10 (1655). Northumberland, lib. 1666–78, fols. 10 (1677), 87 (1673); lib. 1699–1713, f. 220 (1702, 2 cases). Rappahannock, lib. 1686–92, fols. 26, 41 (1687), 83, 97 (1688), 130 (1689), 249 (1691, 2 cases). Richmond, lib. 1692–94, fols. 40 (1692), 122 (1693), 136 (1694, 2 cases). Spotsylvania, lib. 1724–30, fols. 48 (2 cases), 62 (2 cases) (1725), 114, 128 (1726), 147 (2 cases), 208 (2 cases) (1727), 258 (1728); lib. 1730–38, fols. 36 (2 cases), 59 (1730–31), 98, 108, 124, 156 (1732), 264 (1733), 334 (1734), 534 (1737). Surry, lib. 1671–84, f. 138 (1675). Westmoreland, lib. 1675/6–88/9, fols. 95 (1677), 544 (1687), 617 (2 cases), 619 (2 cases) (1688). York, lib. 1638–48 (1647); lib. 1657–62, fols. 145, 170 (1647), 233 (1660), 355 (1661), (1663); lib. 1664–72, fols. 138 (1666), 294 (1668), 421, 454 (2 cases) (1670), 496 (1671); lib. 1671–94, fols. 32, 46 (1672), 256, 259 (1675); lib. 1675–84, fols. 410 (3 cases) (1682), 596 (1683), 760 (1684); lib. 1684–87, f. 299 (1687); lib. 1687–91, f. 558 (1690); lib. 1706–10, f. 59 (1706).

[283] *Exec. J. of Council of State of Va.*, I, 149 (1690); *VMH*, X, 154, 155.

[284] In accordance with statute, the penalty of whipping was carried down by the eighteenth-century courts. Charles City O.B., 1655–65, f. 602 (1665); Spotsylvania O.B., 1724–30 (1726). On occasion runaways had iron collars put around their necks and gags in their mouths, and were imprisoned to boot. Augusta O.B., II, fols. 65 (1748), 184 (1751).

[285] See Lancaster O.B., 1666–80, f. 374; Augusta O.B., II, f. 187 (1751). In one instance a master asked that a horse be included in the costs assessed, but the York court denied the claim on the ground that there was "no Law to direct an allowance for the horse but for running away." Elliot's case, York O.B., 1706–10, f. 59 (1706).

county [286] and far in excess of the average for the corresponding period in any eastern county. Washington's overseer and agent, confronted with the problem of constructing a fort neighboring his owner's plantation in western Virginia, reported in 1774 that "Sarvants" were not wanted in such work "as there was a great dale of Companey att the Fort and drink Midling plenty it would be out of his [the builder's] power to govern them and he Said they would Run away from him." [287]

THE CAROLINAS AND GEORGIA. Few runaway servant cases are recorded in the county court proceedings of North Carolina,[288] where the runaway slave problem bulked much larger. Penalties were far milder than in Maryland and more in accord with Virginia practice. By the act of 1715, later incorporated into the general laws of 1741 relating to servants, double service and capture costs were imposed,[289] and seem to have been enforced pretty generally by the courts. As in the tobacco colonies, the extra service in lieu of capture costs often materially increased the penalty. In one case an unauthorized absence of two months was punished by four months of extra service and an added twenty months in satisfaction of costs.[290]

For many years, and until the settlement of Georgia, South Carolina, as the southernmost frontier of British settlement on the North Atlantic seaboard, offered unrivaled opportunities for servants and slaves to escape to the swamplands and forests to the south or to the Spanish settlements.[291] Originally the death penalty was set by statute. In 1672 capital sentence was imposed upon two servants for a mere "discourse" about leaving the province. Their appeal for clemency was granted by the Grand Council on the ground that so severe a penalty "may not

---

[286] See Augusta O.B., XV.

[287] *Letters to Washington*, ed. S. M. Hamilton (Boston, 1898–1902), V, 12–14; *Doc. Hist. Amer. Indust. Soc.*, I, 344, 345.

[288] See, e.g., *N.C. Gazette*, June 25, 1753; June 24, 1768; Feb. 20, 23, May 5 (2 cases), Dec. 2, 1775; June 23, 27, July 17, 25, Aug. 1, 1777 (3 cases). $20 was offered by one master for the head of a runaway Negro slave. *Ibid.*, Nov. 30, 1778. For West Indian precedents for such an offer, see *CSPA, 1693–96*, No. 114, p. 31 (1693). The records provide no support for the view of J. S. Bassett that as many servants ran away in North Carolina as in Virginia. *Slavery and Servitude in the Colony of North Carolina* (Baltimore, 1896), p. 79. For occasional advertisements of white runaways, see, e.g., *Cape-Fear Mercury*, Jan. 13, Sept. 23, 1773; *N.C. Gazette*, May 15, 1778.

[289] Laws of 1741, c. 24, § 2. The courts had latitude in extending the service penalty beyond double time. Davis, *Justice of Peace*, pp. 310, 311.

[290] Smart's case, Bertie, lib. 1724–69 (1724). See also *ibid.* (1735); Cartaret, lib. 1723–47, fols. 23 (1732), 30 (1735), 52 (1742); Chowan, lib. 1730–48, fols. 53 (2) (1744), 89 (1748); Craven, lib. 1730–46, f. 14 (1732), lib. 1757–62 (1758); Cumberland, lib. 1777–78, f. 70 (1778). The mechanics of capture were precisely the same as in the colonies to the north. See Misc. Papers, Edenton Court House (Jan., 1724/5); *N.C. Col. Rec.*, II, 66 (1713).

[291] See *CSPA, 1689–92*, No. 612, p. 187 (1689); *1700*, No. 369, p. 214; *1717–18*, No. 423, p. 206 (1718).

alltogether be a matter soe well approved on abroad as mercy." [292] Later extra service was substituted. [293] In 1701 the legislature went so far as to order that "no servant or slave be sent beyond the Savana Town," [294] but in the eighteenth century the Negro slave came to dominate the labor market of the province and to provide the chief source of concern on the score of the runaway. Between February 12, 1732, and December 20, 1735, the *South Carolina Gazette* carried 110 advertisements of Negroes who had run away from their masters as compared with forty-one white servants and three Indian female servants. This ratio of two or three to one in favor of the Negro fugitive [295] had become exaggerated many fold by the close of the Revolution. Between July, 1783, and July, 1784, thirty-two Negroes were advertised as fugitives, but not a single white servant was listed. These advertisements are also indicative of the gradual supremacy of the Negro artisan in the skilled trades and the virtual elimination of the free white skilled worker from the labor market of South Carolina. [296]

Because of the widespread fear of possible conspiracies by servants or slaves, South Carolina had in effect for a time the most drastic extra service penalty of any of the Thirteen Colonies. In 1686 a term of twenty-eight days was fixed by statute for every day of unlawful absence. [297] This term was sharply increased in 1691, when a statute provided that for every day's unauthorized absence the servant would be required to serve a week, and for every week a whole year—in effect, fifty-two for one! [298] Apparently this penalty proved excessive. In 1744, by which time white servants were no longer abundant in the province, the legislature repealed the act and substituted extra service of one week for every day's absence, provided the penalty did not exceed two years, together with costs and charges not to exceed one year's additional service. Runaways were to be whipped not exceeding twenty-one lashes and conveyed to their masters' home. Such punishment did not deprive the master of lawful satisfaction. [299]

[292] Cases of Nicklin and Rivers. *S.C. Grand Council J.*, pp. 47–49. Execution of the death sentence was also suspended in the case of Richard Batten and William Loe upon "the earnest solicitation of Margaret Lady Yeamans and the rest of the Ladyes and Gentlewomen of this Country." *Ibid.*, pp. 55, 56 (1673).

[293] See Haley's case, *S.C. Grand Council J.*, 1692, pp. 51, 52.

[294] S.C. Assembly J., Aug., 1701, f. 8. See also petition of Thomas Elliot and six others for relief on account of the escape of their slaves to St. Augustine. *Ibid.*, 1727–29, f. 130 (1728).

[295] 29 Negroes were reported as runaways as against 13 whites for the year 1739.

[296] Even as early as the 1730s skilled Negro artisans were being employed in at least as considerable numbers as whites, judging from these advertisements. See also *supra*, pp. 184, 185, 388.

[297] S.C. Stat., II, 22, 23 (1686). The title of an act to prevent runaways (1683) is found in Trott's *Laws of S.C.*, pp. 1–3, but the original is unknown.

[298] S.C. Stat., II, 52.   [299] Ibid., III, 621–629; Simpson, *Practical Justice of the Peace*, p. 229.

The frontier colony of Georgia harbored many fugitive white servants and Negro slaves belonging to masters in colonies to the north.[300] In Georgia, where the freedom dues amounted to a mere twenty acres of land, quitrents and restraints upon the alienation and accumulation of land were already considered by opponents of the trustees' regime as deterrents to settlement. William Stephens reported in 1750 that most of the single men among the German servants had deserted and were believed "to be sculking about the out settlements of South Carolina from whence it is almost impossible to recover them." Despite the practice of most masters of shortening the terms of their servants by a year or two in order to induce them to faithful service, Stephens complained that "there are but few, if any of the single men, that have not run away." [301] Such wholesale desertions, added to the difficulties of attracting white servants to settle, finally brought about the abandonment of the early restrictions on the ownership of slaves. With the authorization of Negro slavery in 1749 the white servant problem ceased to be of serious concern to the legislature and the courts.[302]

THE WEST INDIES. While the chances of making a successful getaway were slimmer on the British Caribbean islands than along the North American mainland, the problem of the runaway white servant was nonetheless, for a time at least, as exigent in the West Indies as in the Thirteen Colonies. In some respects it was even more acute. Penalties were imposed by law upon shipmasters permitting men to embark from the islands without ticket of leave.[303] Extra service penalties were in force throughout the islands—the most severe in Jamaica and Barbados, where an extra month might be exacted for every two hours of unauthorized leave.[304] This penalty was shortly reduced to one month's service for every twenty-four hours' absence, and a year's service for each month.[305] These statutes exceeded by many times the ten-for-one provisions in force in Maryland, but they were reduced by an act of 1672, which provided one week's service for every. day's absence, the total extra penalty not to exceed three years.[306] Rather severe penal-

---

[300] See, e.g., *Ga. Col. Rec.*, I, 363 (1740); IV, 191; XXV, 440, 508 (1750).

[301] *Ibid.*, XXVI, 20 (1750).

[302] See *ibid.*, III, 427 (1739); also L. H. Gipson, *The British Empire before the American Revolution*, II, ch. vi.

[303] Jennings, *Laws of Barbados*, pp. 22–24, cl. 15, 16.

[304] C.O. 139:1, fols. 10–11; Hall, *Laws of Barbados*, No. 30, cl. viii (1661).

[305] C.O. 139:1, f. 34.

[306] C.O. 139:1, fols. 123 *et seq.;* C.O. 139:2; Jennings, *Laws of Barbados*, cl. 60, pp. 81–82. For the enforcement of the maximum three-year sentence, see *CSPA, 1675–76 (Addenda, 1574–1674)*, No. 1216, p. 522 (1672). For constables' runaway fees on a mileage basis, see C.O. 139:1, f. 127 (1672); C.O. 139:7 (1677, 1681). In Jamaica servants forging certificates were to be

ties were also in force in the other British Caribbean possessions.[307]

This severe labor code does not appear to have effectively curbed desertions by white labor.[308] However, as Negro slave labor came to supplant white labor on the islands almost entirely, fugitive servant legislation became a matter of academic interest. Far harsher enactments were then put into effect against Negro slaves escaping.[309] Despite such precautions, many Negroes succeeded in escaping to the French West Indies, whence restoration to their British owners was a slow and involved affair.[310]

DISCIPLINARY PROBLEMS

THE DISOBEDIENT AND UNRULY SERVANT. English law authorized the master to administer moderate correction to his servant for neglect of duty, abusive conduct, or general insubordination.[1] Uprisings of disobedient

---

put in the pillory and lose their ears upon their conviction. *Loc. cit.* In Barbados any white servant who stole aboard a boat with evident intent to leave the island could, under the act of 1701, be adjudged a felon to suffer death without benefit of clergy. The justices of the peace were empowered by that act to press boats for the recapture of such fugitives, and provision was made for reimbursing owners of boats lost in such pursuit or men wounded in the course thereof. *CSPA, 1701* (addenda), No. 1172, p. 742 (1701). For the earlier Nevis law of 1672, see *ibid., 1669–74*, No. 1013, p. 459 (1672).

[307] Antigua, by an act passed in 1669, and Montserrat, by a law enacted the following year, provided an extra week for every day's absence, a month for each week, and a year for a month, or such other penalty at the discretion of the justices of the peace. This penalty could be doubled were the runaway to join forces with fugitive Negroes. Montserrat and Antigua MS Laws, C.O. 154:1, fols. 21, 39. See also *CSPA, 1697–98*, No. 828, p. 444 (1698), woman servant sentenced to thirty lashes and four years' extra service. In Antigua servants planning to run away with slaves might be whipped at the discretion of the justices and sentenced to double time. If the servant were found in the possession of a boat or of goods worth more than 12*d.* and had intended to run away, he was considered guilty of a felony. Any servant free of complicity in a plot which he had revealed was to have as a reward 1,000 lbs. of sugar from the public treasury at the expiration of his term of service. Antigua MS Laws, C.O. 154:2, f. 326 (1677). The Nevis act of 1675 merely imposed double time as in Virginia. See Nevis MS Laws, C.O. 154:2, f. 14. This penalty was later substituted in Antigua also. Baskett, *Acts of Assembly Passed in the Charibbee Leeward Islands, 1690–1730* (London, 1734), p. 160 (1716).

[308] See *J. Commrs. Trade and Plantations, 1718–22*, p. 7 (1718); *A.P.C., Col., Unbound*, No. 374, p. 187 (1727).

[309] For the death penalty by hanging, drawing, and quartering in force at Montserrat, see *CSPA, 1697–98*, No. 995, p. 558 (1698).

[310] See *ibid., 1669–74*, No. 1333, pp. 600, 601 (1674); also *ibid., 1717–18*, No. 763, p. 396 (1718).

[1] See Stat. 33 Hen. VIII, c. 12; M. Dalton, *Country Justice* (London, 1727), c. 58; Bacon, *Abridgement* (London, 1832), V, 378; *New Conductor Generalis* (Albany, 1819), pp. 28, 29. But see 1 Bl. Comm. 428; W. W. Hening, *The New Virginia Justice* (Richmond, 1810), p. 393; W. Graydon, *The Justice's and Constable's Assistant* (Harrisburg, Pa., 1803), p. 281; Reeve, *op. cit.*, p. 374, permitting correction of an apprentice, but not of a servant "of full age." See also Batt, *Master and Servant*, pp. 150, 151. To an action for assault and battery brought by a servant at common law the master might justifiably plead that plaintiff was his servant and gave provocation and that the master moderately corrected him. On the issue of *immoderate castigavit* the master would be acquitted if it appeared in evidence that the punishment was such as was "usual from masters to their servants." Bacon, *op. cit.*, p. 378.

and unruly servants were severely punished.[2] Heavy restraints upon the servant were also imposed in the colonies, where masters generally had a legal right to administer corporal punishment. Governor Wyatt of Virginia issued a proclamation in 1622 providing that masters were to keep a ferule to correct blasphemous servants and made them liable to a fine of £15 for failure to use it. The same proclamation ordered that incorrigible servants were to be burnt in the tongue with a red-hot iron.[3] Even where satisfaction had been obtained from runaways by extra service, masters or magistrates were authorized by an act passed in that colony in 1668 to inflict "moderate corporal punishment" upon such absentees.[4]

We have already considered the attitude of the colonial law toward concerted action by workers to secure better working conditions or to effect their escape from servitude. The courts also had to deal with many individual cases of outright disobedience, sabotage, or deliberate slow-downs, not necessarily instigated by conspiratorial action, and with a variety of acts against masters, ranging from petty pilfering to arson and murder. Aside from the sentences recorded by the court clerks, it must be remembered that the master could penalize his servant without necessarily resorting to the legal authorities.[5]

Discontent was rife between master and servant from the very beginning of New England settlement. Labor trouble flared up in the fishing colony off the Maine coast settled by Robert Trelawny, a Gorges patentee. His agent, John Winter, incessantly complained that the workmen were "unrued peepell," "stubborne," and "lasy," and would

[2] By Stat. 5 Eliz., c. 4, any servant, workman, or laborer committed for having willfully made an assault or affray upon his master or overseer by the testimony of two honest men before any two justices of the peace of the county where the offense was committed was subject to imprisonment for a maximum of one year at their discretion, and, if circumstances warranted, to such further punishment not extending to life or limb. When, in March, 1664, two apprentices were sentenced to the pillory and imprisonment for beating their master, rioting flared for several days until the militia restored order. Execution of apprentices not infrequently provoked serious riots in Britain. Beloff, *op. cit.,* p. 30.

[3] *WMCQ,* 2d ser., VII, 248.

[4] Hening, II, 75, 115, 118, 266; *VMH,* X, 154, 155; J. C. Ballagh, *White Servitude in the Colony of Virginia* (Baltimore, 1895), pp. 59, 60. For a recorded instance of such legal punishment having been inflicted by the master, see the case of Elizabeth Griffin, whipped 21 lashes by her master, William Colston, in the presence of the justices. Rappahannock O.B., 1686–92, f. 267 (1690). For restraints upon this power, see *infra,* pp. 482, 484 *et seq.*

[5] The manager of the Hibernia Iron Works wrote the proprietor in 1774, complaining that a certain "Gillis McPherson is so lazy and impertinent that I cant manage him without useing Violence which would choose to avoid if possible." He asked permission in effect to demote the workman by transferring him to the colliers. Joseph Holt to Lord Stirling, Stirling MSS, lib. IV, f. 26 (1774), N.Y. Hist. Soc. Cf. also *Amer. Weekly Mercury,* Feb. 20, 1729, reporting that a servant deliberately disabled himself from sawing wood by chopping off one of his hands with an axe.

do little or no work "iff therebe not an eye over them." The task of discipline was most disagreeable; cooperation was entirely absent. "I hardly know my friend from my foe," he confessed. He even found it necessary to defend his wife of "yll reports" of beating a maidservant named Priscilla, and gave this convincing picture of the domestic help problem on the early American frontier:

yf a faire way will not do yt, beatinge must, sometimes, vppon such Idlle gir-rells as she is. Yf you thinke yt fitt for my wyfe to do all the worke and the maid sitt still, she must forbeare her hands to strike, for then the worke will ly vndonn. She hath bin now 2 yeares ½ in the house, and I do not thinke she hath risen 20 times before my Wyfe hath bin vp to Call her, and many times light the fire before she Comes out of her bed. She hath twize gon a mechinge [6] in the woodes, which we haue bin faine to send all our Company to seeke. We Cann hardly keep her within doores after we ar gonn to bed, except we Carry the kay of the door to bed with vs. She never Could melke Cow nor goat since she Came hither. Our men do not desire to haue her boyle the kittell for them she is so sluttish. She Cannot be trusted to serue a few piggs, but my wyfe most Commonly must be with her. She hath written home, I heare, that she was faine to ly vppon goates skins. She might take som goates skins to ly in her bedd, but not given to her for her lodging. For a year and quarter or more she lay with my daughter vppon a good feather bed before my daughter beinge lacke 3 or 4 daies to Sacco, the maid goes into bedd with her Cloth and stockins, and would not take the paines to plucke of her Cloths: her bedd after was a doust bed none after that tyme she was found to be so sluttish. Her beating that she hath had hath never hirt her body nor limes. She is so fatt and soggy she Cann hardly do any worke. This I write all the Company will Justify. Yf this maid at her lasy tymes, when she hath bin found in her ill accyons, do not deserue 2 or 3 blowes, I pray Judge You who hath most reason to Complaine, my wyfe or the maid.[7]

Thomas Shepard and Cotton Mather have left us a picture of idle and disobedient servants, who were enjoined to a "Dutiful Behaviour and a Suitable Content in their Station" in accord with the proper attitude of reverence toward authority, religious in inspiration.[8] Industrialists

[6] Hiding out.

[7] "Trelawny Papers," Me. Hist. Soc., *Coll.*, III, 166–168. See also ibid., pp. 86, 91, 113, 136, 137. Cf. also *Winthrop Papers*, III, 221 (1636), IV, 232, 233 (1640). For a complaint against a servant in a later period, see "Diary of Jacob Spicer," N.J. Hist. Soc., *Proceedings*, LXIII, 106 (1755).

[8] Thomas Shepard, *The Parable of the Ten Virgins Opened and Applied* (London, 1660), Pt. II, p. 55; *The Sincere Convert* (London, 1641), p. 164; Cotton Mather, *Brief Memorial of Matters and Methods for Pastoral Visits* (Boston, 1723), p. 13; *The Fisher-man's Calling: a Brief Essay to Serve the Great Interests of Religion among Our Fisher-men* (Boston, 1712), Preface, p. 45; *Bonifacius: an Essay upon the Good, That Is to Be Devised and Designed, by Those Who Desire to Answer the Great End of Life* . . . (Boston, 1710); *A Flying Roll Brought Forth, to Enter into the House and Hand of the Thief* (Boston, 1713), p. 31; *Durable Riches: Two Brief Dis-*

of the Revolutionary period and the early nineteenth-century millowners who supported churches and Sunday schools on the ground that "religion was a very good thing to keep the lower classes in proper subordination"[9] were perfectly consistent with the stand taken by these Puritan divines.

The contemporary files of the New England county courts amply document Shepard's contentions and reveal that Cotton Mather's injunctions to servants too often fell upon deaf ears. One servant struck at his master with a pitchfork;[10] another, an apprentice, was accused of "laying violent hands upon his . . . master, and throwing him downe twice and feching bloud of him, threatening to breake his necke, running at his face with a chayre, and voweing to be the death of some of them," accompanying the assault with profane and contemptuous remarks.[11] The Essex court found one servant to be a "rash, unsettled and indiscreet young man ready to run into divers enormities if Lett free."[12] Master and mistress charged that one insubordinate maidservant was "bad, unruly, sulen, careles, destructive, and disobedient," "fitter for bridewell, or the house of correction, than for any bodyes service."[13]

The early Maine court sitting at Falmouth sentenced disobedient workers or those refusing to work to correction to be administered at the discretion of the constable and selectmen.[14] The Massachusetts Assistants almost invariably punished refractory servants by severe whipping,[15] and the Essex and Suffolk County courts pursued the course taken by the superior court.[16] A fine was substituted for corporal pun-

---

courses (Boston, 1695), Pt. II, p. 13; *A Good Master Well Served* (Boston, 1696), p. 46; B. Wadsworth, *The Well-Ordered Family* (Boston, 1712), p. 115; Samuel Willard, *Compleat Body of Divinity* (Boston, 1726), p. 616. For specific complaints against servants, see *Winthrop Papers*, Pt. VI, pp. 353–354n. (1717); "Diary of Cotton Mather," Mass. Hist. Soc., *Coll.*, 7th ser., II, 537, 538 (1718). Shepard, Mather, and other Puritan divines were to a large extent paraphrasing such English writers on master-servant relations as Fuller and Brathwait. See M. H. Walten, *Thomas Fuller's The Holy State and the Profane State* (New York, 1938), I, 106, 107; II, 19–21.

9 For the views of John Jacob Faesch, ironmaster, see N.J. Hist. Soc., *Proceedings*, 2d ser., I, 37.

10 *Essex*, I, 133 (1647).

11 Rumball's complaint, *ibid.*, IV, 200 (1669); also Deane v. Wade, *ibid.*, II, 62 (1658).

12 Hammon's case, *ibid.*, I, 23 (1640).

13 Elizabeth Woodbury's case, *ibid.*, III, 225 (1664).

14 *Me. Prov. and Court Rec.*, I, 313 (1666); II, 28 (1654), 30 lashes; in the event of further misbehavior the master was authorized to sell the culprit "to Virginia, Barbadoes, or any other English Plantations." See also Parker's case, York Sess., lib. VI, f. 247 (1687).

15 Diffy's case, *Assistants*, II, 8 (1630); Perry's case, *ibid.*, p. 18 (1631); Ropp's case, *ibid.*, p. 62 (1635); Pope's case, *ibid.*, p. 92 (1640), also an "unchast attempt upon a girle, and dalliance wth maydes"; Wilson's case, *ibid.*, p. 104 (1641); Conway's case, *ibid.*, p. 127 (1642); Archer's case, *ibid.*, p. 135 (1643); Hickbourne's case, *ibid.*, p. 107 (1641), also to wear an iron collar.

16 Cooke's case, *Essex*, I, 20 (1640); Harmon's case, *ibid.*, pp. 23, 25 (1641), also fined £5 and sentenced to serve an extra year; Thomas's case, *ibid.*, p. 68 (1644); Farras's case, *ibid.*,

ishment in a number of cases, and in still others the master was awarded money damages.[17] In fact, damages were an alternative to an order for specific performance of a contract of employment. For example, when in 1677 Robert Orchard, a feltmaker, brought an action on the case in Suffolk court against William Gilbert, whom he had transported to New England in return for an agreement to serve for two years, he disclosed that Gilbert, influenced by "evil Counsellors," absented himself, and, when ordered to return to his master's service by the governor, ran away again and tried to get passage to Jamaica. The master had him committed to prison where, according to his petition, "by the Countenance and supply of some Contentious persons hee hath sett up and practices his Trade refuseing to returne again" to the petitioner's employment. Orchard with restrained irony pointed out "what ill Consequences it may bee that the place that is appointed to restraine and punish Refractory Servts should bee Improved for their freedome and Advantage and to the punishment and Injury of their Masters." The jury awarded him £6 4*s.* in money or work and costs amounting to 28*s.* 4*d.*[18] In cases of extreme disobedience the court might choose to order that the servant be sold to the West Indies, providing his master with due compensation.[19]

Eighteenth-century Suffolk sessions were not hesitant about ordering the return of an unruly servant to his master [20] or fining or imprisoning an insubordinate servant.[21] In 1718 John Mackneil and Joseph Rounds complained that on their master's charge of abusing him and neglecting his business they had been committed to prison six weeks earlier and confined to a dungeon where they were kept on bread and water. The court put the case over, meanwhile sending the servants back to prison.[22] The most celebrated instance in provincial Massachusetts of the incarceration of a servant in prison for refractory behavior was the action taken by John Saffin against his Negro, Adam.

---

p. 356 (1654), also extra service. Owen's case, *Suffolk*, p. 412 (1674); Nicholas, Negro, *ibid.*, p. 884 (1678). For corporal punishment for like offenses in the other New England courts, see Godden's case, *Plymouth Col. Rec.*, I, 159 (1640), Thurston's case, *ibid.*, II, 73 (1644); case of Susan Coles, *Conn. Particular Court Rec., 1639–63*, p. 33 (1644), Renolds' case, *ibid.*, p. 42 (1646); Manchester's case, *New Haven Col. Rec., 1638–49*, p. 26 (1639), Davis's case, *ibid.*, p. 46 (1640), whipping "suspended for tryall of his future carryage." See also Smoolt's case, *ibid.*, p. 308 (1647), and Woodcliff's case, p. 35 (1640).

[17] *Fined:* Morris's case, *Essex*, I, 97 (1646); Goodwin's case, *ibid.*, p. 156 (1648), also robbing orchard and lying. *Damages to master:* Larckum's case, *ibid.*, p. 404 (1655); Hilton's case, *Suffolk*, pp. 606, 607 (1675).

[18] *Ibid.*, pp. 800, 801 (1677).   [19] Hancock's case, *Essex*, III, 376 (1666).

[20] Townsend's case, Suffolk Sess., lib. 1702–12, f. 22 (1703).

[21] Cases of Jackson and Baxter, *ibid.*, lib. II, 1712–19, f. 11 (1712).   [22] *Ibid.*, f. 198 (1718).

The issue, however, was complicated by the contention of the master that the defendant was not free, whereas Adam held that he had been manumitted.[23]

Servants who stole from their masters were liable in New England to be whipped, and in addition, to treble damages in money or extra service in lieu thereof.[24] Murders of masters by servants were comparatively rare in New England, where the death penalty was imposed for this crime.[25] On the other hand, disobedient servants appear to have specialized in arson, a crime which was dealt with very sternly by the courts, with sentences varying from corporal punishment [26] to extra service for periods ranging from four years [27] to as many as twenty-one.[28] In one New Haven case in which the latter penalty was imposed it appeared that the servant had set his master's house afire because "he loued not to goe to plow wth his master, because when the oxen went not right he would knock him." The master remonstrated that the sentence of the court that the servant henceforth wear a light lock on his leg would interfere with his work, but the neighbors were not willing even to have such a workman in the vicinity. Accordingly the master was authorized to sell his servant to the proprietor of the ironworks, or, if no satisfactory location could be found for him, to ship him back to England.[29]

The Dutch courts of New Netherland normally relied upon admonition or decrees of specific performance when workmen or servants were

[23] See Superior Court of Judicature, lib. 1700–14, fols. 114 *et seq.* (1703); *Mass. Acts and Resolves,* VIII, 11, 266–270; Samuel Sewall, "Selling Joseph," Mass. Hist. Soc., *Proceedings* (1863–64), pp. 161–165; G. H. Moore, *Notes on Slavery in Massachusetts* (New York, 1866); Samuel Sewall, "Diary," Mass. Hist. Soc., *Coll.,* 5th ser., VI, 64 *et seq.;* L. J. Greene, *The Negro in Colonial New England, 1620–1776* (New York, 1942), pp. 296, 297.

[24] Others than servants were liable to servitude on conviction for larceny in satisfaction of fine or damages. See *supra,* pp. 345 ff. Cf. Budd's case, *Plymouth Col. Rec.,* III, 204 (1661). Bartlett's case, *Assistants,* II, 14 (1631); Shepheard's case, *ibid.,* p. 62 (1636); Bell's case, *ibid.,* p. 121 (1642). Alice Wright's case, *Suffolk,* pp. 751, 752 (1676); case of David, Indian, *ibid.,* p. 778 (1677). Case of Conner *et ux.,* Suffolk G.S., lib. 1680–92 (photostat), II, f. 275 (1685); Lang's case, *ibid.,* f. 289 (1685); Everendon's case, *ibid.,* lib. IV, f. 259 (1730). New Haven exacted double restitution and whipping. Cases of Duhurst and Stewart, *New Haven Col. Rec., 1638–49,* p. 26 (1639); see also Ellice's case, whipping only, and Bromfield's case, stocks only, *ibid.,* p. 28 (1639). Cf. also Conn. Court of Assistants Rec., f. 534 (Oct. 2, 1707), defendant convicted of receiving stolen property from Negro servants.

[25] Cases of Driver and Faevor, *Assistants,* I, 30, 32 (1674). For the death sentence of a servant for buggery, see *Plymouth Col. Rec.,* II, 444 (1642).

[26] Bridge's case, "Conn. Prob. Rec.," lib. III, fols. 70, 71 (1667).

[27] Towlthead's case, *Me. Prov. and Court Rec.,* II, 335 (1677).

[28] Stevens' case, *Assistants,* II, 100 (1640).

[29] Frost's case, *New Haven Col. Rec., 1653–65,* pp. 169–171 (1656). Spite, coupled with the desire to frighten the master into granting release from indentures, was behind a few other arson cases in that colony. Lopen's case, *ibid.,* pp. 384–387, 399, 400; Mary Betts' case, *ibid.,* pp. 504–510 (1663).

insubordinate or neglected or refused to work.[30] Upon complaints to parents or masters, the Duke's Laws authorized constables and overseers, where no justice of the peace dwelt within ten miles of a town or parish, to call before them "rude Stubborne or unruly" children or servants and to inflict such corporal punishment, not exceeding ten stripes, as they should deem deserving, provided that such children and servants had attained the age of sixteen.[31] The eighteenth-century New York sessions court might sentence refractory servants to the house of correction, order them whipped, or merely discharge them from their contracts.[32] Workhouse or prison terms for servants convicted of disobedient and disorderly behavior were set by New Jersey and Pennsylvania law.[33] The Pennsylvania and Delaware courts imposed fine, imprisonment, or extra service.[34]

A servant convicted of stealing from her master was sentenced by the old New York court of assize to make satisfaction and to be whipped and made to stand upon a barrel for half an hour with a paper fixed upon her breast bearing the legend: "For stealing and purloyning of her Masters goods." [35] Abraham, Lewis Ogden's "Negroe Boy," pleaded guilty in 1772 to setting fire to his master's house; he threw himself upon the mercy of the Essex County court, which sentenced him to

[30] Duckingh v. Rentije, *R.N.A.*, VII, 202 (1658); Strycker v. Janzen, *ibid.*, III, 274 (1661); Hardenbroeck and Schol v. Ten Eyck, *ibid.*, p. 280 (1661); Hoochteylingh v. Claesen, Ulster Dutch Transcripts, lib. I, f. 245 (1666). Captain Chambers complained to the Kingston magistrates of his servant, Regard Berry, in 1681, for calling him names and threatening to "turn Foxhall upside down (*dat by Foxhall will het onderste boven Keeren*)." The court approved the assignment of the servant to one Kettel, for which Chambers was to receive 100 schepels of white peas. *Ibid.*, lib. III, f. 79 (1681).

[31] *N.Y. Col. Laws*, I, 26 (1665).

[32] *House of correction and whipping:* Smith's case, N.Y.G.S., lib. 1732–62, f. 155; also in lib. 1743–60 (1743). *Discharged:* Farnell's case, *ibid.*, lib. 1772–89, f. 11 (1772); Everit's case, Queens G.S., lib. 1722–87 (May 20, 1761). Cf. also case of Arthur, Indian apprentice, committed to gaol "Until Such time as he Shall Humble himself" to his master's satisfaction. Suffolk G.S., lib. 1723–51, f. 32 (1732).

[33] Justices in Middlesex and for the town of Elizabeth were empowered to commit to the workhouse to hard labor white servants or slaves brought before them by their masters for rue or disorderly behavior and to have them whipped not exceeding 30 lashes. Allinson, *N.J. Acts*, p. 185 (1748); Parker, *Conductor Generalis* (Woodbridge, N.J., 1764), p. 22. As early as 1682 the Pennsylvania Assembly found it necessary to enact a statute "Against Assaulting and Menacing of Masters." *Pa. Arch.*, 8th ser., I, 11, 34 (1682–83). By act of 1701 a servant was liable to a term of six months' imprisonment for assaulting or threatening his master and was required to give his master such satisfaction for loss of time as the justices of the peace should determine. *Pa. Stat. at Large*, II, 13; *Pa. Arch.*, 8th ser., I, 248. This act was repealed by the Queen in Council in 1706.

[34] *Fined:* Pidcock's case, Bucks C.P. and Q.S., lib. 1684–1730 (1686). *Workhouse:* Jones's case, Chester Q.S., lib. B (Nov. 30, 1773). *Extra service:* Croaning's case, Bucks Q.S., lib. 1715–53 (1751); Sarah Hughes's case, York Q.S., lib. I, f. 25 (1759). *Admonition:* Hurst's case, *Chester Rec., 1681–97*, pp. 59, 60; Kimson's case, Kent Q.S., lib. 1718–21 (1719).

[35] Dale's case, N.Y. Court of Assize, lib. 1665–72 (1668 ?), N.Y. State Lib., MSS Div.

stand in the pillory at Newark with his neck and hands "thro the Holes thereof" for the space of one hour, and then to be tied to a cart's tail and driven around the square, at each corner of which he was to receive twenty lashes on his bare back.[36]

The public authorities in the tobacco colonies held far stricter rules of servant behavior than prevailed in the North. Maryland provided a whipping for servants "refusing to perform the lawful commands" of master, mistress, or overseer or unjustly complaining against their masters, or offending any other wise against their duty or indenture." [37] Virginia enforced similar penalties during the early years of settlement.[38] Harsh statutory penalties were eventually substituted for discretion. A statute of 1660 justified a sentence of two years' extra service for servants laying "violent hands" on master, mistress, or overseer on the ground of the "audacious unruliness of many stubborn and incorrigible servants." [39] This term was reduced to one year in 1662, and as such remained in force throughout the colonial period.[40] Occasionally the court contented itself with a warning,[41] corporal punishment,[42] or imprisonment.[43] One incorrigible and impudent woman servant was ordered by the Accomac court to be ducked, but since her master, in the court's opinion, had "degenerated so much from a Man as neither to beare Rule over his weoman servant nor govern his house, but made one in that scolding society," he was sentenced to be ducked along with the servant and to pay court costs as well.[44]

In eighteenth-century Virginia prosecutions of white servants for refractory conduct became less frequent as white servitude in turn declined, whereas such crimes as larceny and other offenses against prop-

[36] King v. Abraham, Essex, N.J., lib. 1772–81 (April term, 1772).

[37] *Md. Arch.*, I, 53 (1639). Ten to 30 lashes would be the usual penalty. *Ibid.*, X, 439, 440 (1655); XLI, 316, 317 (1659); LIV, 248 (1668); Prince George, lib. B, 1699–1705, f. 237 (1703); lib. 1720–22 (1721).

[38] *VMH*, II, 64, 65 (1619); Lower Norfolk O.B., May 15, 1637; *Va. Gen. Court Mins.*, p. 475 (1640); Accomac O.B., Sept. 7, 1640.

[39] Hening, I, 538.

[40] *Ibid.*, II, 118; *VMH*, 156, 157; Hening, III, 447 (1705), VIII, 547–558 (1748); George Webb, *The Office and Authority of a Justice of the Peace* (Williamsburg, 1736), p. 291; Starke, *Justice of the Peace*, p. 319. For enforcement: York O.B., 1657–62, f. 545 (1662); Tyler, *Mag.*, I, 273; Charles City O.B., 1655–65, f. 367 (1663); York O.B., Feb. 26, 1664; Accomac O.B., 1666–70, fols. 12, 38 (1667); York O.B., 1664–72, f. 420 (1670), 1675–84, f. 135 (1679). Middlesex O.B., 1680–94, f. 36 (1681); Henrico O.B., Dec. 1, 1688. In York O.B., 1664–72, f. 59 (1665), the attack upon the mistress appears to have taken place in England.

[41] Lancaster O.B., 1655–66, f. 149 (1661).

[42] Accomac O.B., 1666–70, f. 48 (1667); *Va. Gen. Court Mins.*, p. 295 (1672).

[43] Henrico O.B., II, 1677–92, f. 41 (1683), where the servant died in prison and the master obtained a court order for his body.

[44] Cases of Elizabeth Leverit and Robert Brace, Accomac O.B., 1663–66, f. 26 (1663).

erty, in which convict servants participated to no inconsiderable degree, mounted rapidly.[45] In the early years the courts of Maryland and Virginia punished by whipping servants who were guilty of stealing their masters' goods,[46] but this was not the invariable rule, and, to the corporal punishment, imprisonment might be added or the death penalty imposed. One servant named Oliver, convicted in the Provincial Court of stealing money, escaped the gallows, although unable to read when the clergy test was given, by the expedient of agreeing to serve for life as "general hangman" of the province and to satisfy his master by extra service for the cost of his imprisonment.[47] The corporal penalty set by Maryland's act of 1663 [48] was not considered by the courts as freeing the servant from the obligation to make restitution, and on occasion fourfold damages were imposed in addition to corporal punishment, amounting in effect to from sixteen to twenty months' extra service.[49] Hog killing and hog stealing were of frequent occurrence, and very severe statutory penalties were attached to these offenses in the tobacco colonies.[50]

In accordance with old feudal law the murder of a master by his servant was in the tobacco colonies denominated petit treason—a capital offense. A number of such trials are found in the court records; [51] perhaps the most notable was the trial at Jamestown in the summer of 1678 of a Dorsetshire redemptioner named Thomas Heller for the brutal murder of his master, mistress, and a maidservant, all of whom he slew with an axe. He charged that he had been set to labor at the hoe instead of being assigned to teaching his master's children and that he had been incessantly abused by his mistress's sharp tongue. He was convicted and hanged, and an account of his *Vain Prodigal Life, and Tragical Penitent Death* was published in London in 1680.[52]

South Carolina in the early years appears to have meted out corporal punishment to refractory servants rather than to have imposed extra

[45] Scott, *op. cit.*, pp. 232, 299.
[46] *Va. Gen. Court Mins.*, pp. 159, 162–164 (1627); *Md. Arch.*, I, 35, 36 (1639), where some members of the Assembly advocated that the servant be laid in irons and even hung. See also *Md. Arch.*, XLI, 328, 432, 433 (1660), 450, 451 (1661); LIV, 213 (1661), 297 (1670), 420 (1668).
[47] *Ibid.*, LI, 214, 215.   [48] *Ibid.*, I, 500, 501; II, 526, 527; XLIX, 495; LIV, 511.
[49] Cases of Jackson and Fernly, Somerset, lib. 1701–2, f. 59 (1702).
[50] *Md. Arch.*, I, 500, 501 (1663), LX, 251–254 (1670), for a surprisingly lenient verdict; Ann Arundel, lib. 1702–4, f. 2 (1703); Hening, I, 244 (1643), 350 (1647), III, 276–279 (1705). Cf. also cases of Page, Boulton, Shelton, Carter, and Higby, Lancaster O.B., 1666–80 (1669–70, 1673).
[51] Mathews's case, *Va. Gen. Court Mins.*, p. 479 (1630); Ayres's case, York O.B., Dec. 20, 1650; *WMCQ*, 1st ser., XI, 37, 38; cases of McGuire, Simmons, and Thoroughgood, *Va. Gazette*, Jan. 24, Dec. 21, 1751; *VMH*, XXIV, 409. For Maryland, see, e.g., *Md. Arch.*, LI, 257 (1676).
[52] See *Doc. Hist. Amer. Indust. Soc.*, I, 357–365.

service. The Grand Council in 1672 sentenced Philip Orrill to be tied
to a tree and given twenty-one lashes for threatening to upset a boat
carrying his mistress, throw his provisions to the dogs, and run away
to the Indians. Two other servants, also involved in this episode, were
admonished "to render a more dutifull obedience to the lawful comands
of their said Mistresse upon payn of condigne punishment."[53] Subsequently statutory penalties of extra service were laid down.[54] The
South Carolina legislation seems clearly modeled upon the severe laws
of the West Indies.[55]

The Oppressive Master. The master's right of discipline at English
law was restricted to correction within the bounds of moderation. Not
only was his disciplinary authority limited, but he was under a duty at
law to give his servant his wages due and to provide him with decent
treatment, adequate food, clothing, and shelter.[56] While a disobedient
apprentice could be punished physically and sent to the house of correction, an oppressive master was penalized merely by the discharge
of his servant. The one-sided character of the English law, freely admitted by contemporary legal authorities,[57] influenced the pattern of
labor relations in the colonies. Swift, in his *System of the Laws of
Connecticut,*[58] suggested that in a progressive society more humane controls on the treatment of young servants and apprentices would some day
be put into effect.

[53] *J.S.C. Grand Council, 1671–80*, pp. 33, 34.

[54] One year, by act of 1686, *S.C. Stat.*, II, 22, 23, 52 (1691). Reduced to six months or
21 stripes in 1744. *Ibid.*, III, 621–629; Simpson, *Practical Justice of the Peace*, p. 229.

[55] In 1661 the Council of Jamaica imposed two years additional service upon persons laying
violent hands on their masters. C.O. 139:1, f. 3; *CSPA, 1661–68*, No. 123, pp. 42, 43. See
also Hall, *Acts of Barbados, 1643–1762* (London, 1764), p. 35. Corporal punishment was set
by the Nevis act of 1701. A servant failing to do his part could, by act of 1705, be sentenced
to be tied by neck and heels, or to ride a wooden horse, not to exceed one hour. For corporal
punishment as the penalty in North Carolina, see Davis, *Justice of Peace*, p. 310.

[56] Fitzherbert, *New Natura Brevium* (London, 1730), p. 392; *New Conductor Generalis*
(Albany, 1819), pp. 28, 29. The redress given to the servant was on grounds of "misuse,
abuse, or evilly treat." The court held that the allegation of using an apprentice "unkindly"
was too loose. 2 Str. 1013; Graydon, *op. cit.*, p. 15. See also "Surrey Quarter Sessions Rec.,
O.B., 1659–61," Surrey Record Society, *Publications*, No. 35, p. 20 (1660); "County Palatine
of Chester Q.S. Rec., 1559–1769," ed. J. H. Bennett and J. C. Dewhurst, Record Society, *Publications*, XCIV (1940), 98 (1640), 109–112 (1641), 129 (1648). These safeguards did not
entirely eliminate cruel and oppressive employers in contemporary England. Mrs. Brownrigg
and the Metyards, mother and daughter, were among the more notorious sadists. See Rosamond
Bayne-Powell, *The English Child in the Eighteenth Century* (New York, 1939), pp. 41–43;
W. M. Cooper (J. G. Bartram), *Flagellation and the Flagellants: a History of the Rod in all
Countries from the Earliest Period to the Present Time* (London, 1868): G. R. Scott, *The History
of Corporal Punishment* (London, 1938), pp. 70, 71.

[57] See Stat. 7 Jac. c. 4; Dalton, *Country Justice*, pp. 178, 190; W. Hardy and C. E. Longmore,
eds., *Session Books of Hertford County*, VII, VIII, *passim*.

[58] I, 221. An early 19th-century traveler noted that masters did not by that time have the
power to confine servants by law, nor would the white or hired man submit to the whip, "had
masters the power to use it." J. Flint, *Letters from America* (Edinburgh, 1822), p. 39.

The British government sought to check brutality to servants on the plantations. Circular instructions to the royal governors, running from 1675 to 1764, requested those officials to "endeavor to get a law passed, if not already done, for the restraining of any inhumane severity which by ill masters or overseers may be used towards their Christian servants and their slaves." [59] Colonial homilists like Cotton Mather and early Federal writers on the law admonished masters to observe moderation in dealings with their servants.[60] American almanac compilers reiterated this advice, cautioning employers to treat their hired hands well and not drive them too hard, and satirizing the master who "drains his Rage" on his help, although considered "Complaisant enough" outside of business.[61]

NEW ENGLAND. As early as 1636 John Cotton in his unacceptable, but nonetheless influential, draft of laws for Massachusetts, known as "Moses his Judicialls," provided that if the servant were maimed or wounded he was "to goe forth free from such a service, and the master further punished by discretion, etc. Ex. 21. 26. 27." [62] This provision was expanded in the Body of Liberties of 1641, the first code of laws in New England. Liberties 85–88 laid down four laws of servitude, humanitarian in character, and based on Deuteronomy 23:15, 16; Leviticus 25:39, 40, 43; Exodus 23:12; 21:2, for which common-law precedent could not readily be found.[63] These liberties provided for the safe harboring of servants fleeing from their masters' cruelty, for the discharge of servants maimed or disfigured by their masters, for adequate freedom dues for servants faithfully serving seven-year terms, and prohibited the assignment of servants beyond the period of a year unless approved by the authorities.[64]

---

[59] In the case of Georgia the instructions substituted: "You are to use your best endeavors to restrain" for the directive to secure passage of legislation. Labaree, *Royal Instructions*, § 733.

[60] For Cotton Mather's views, see "Mather Papers," Mass. Hist. Soc., *Coll.*, 4th ser., VIII, 48; *The Fisher-mans Calling*, p. 45; *A Good Master Well Served*, p. 16. See also Wadsworth, *Well-Ordered Family*, p. 106; Willard, *Compleat Body of Divinity*, pp. 615, 616; E. S. Morgan, "Masters and Servants in Early New England," Boston Pub. Lib., *Bull.*, XII (1942), 315. For similar humanitarian concepts of labor relations in contemporary English literature, see Mrs. Wooley's *The Gentlewoman's Companion or Guide to the Female Sex*, cited by Rose M. Bradley, *The English Housewife in the Seventeenth and Eighteenth Centuries* (London, 1912), pp. 144, 145. See also Walten, ed., *Fuller's the Holy State*, I, 104–106; II, 17, 18.

[61] Briggs, *op. cit.*, p. 276 (1715); Thomas's almanac, 1815, cited by G. L. Kittredge, *The Old Farmer and His Almanack* (Cambridge, 1920), pp. 85, 86.

[62] "An Abstract of the Laws of New England" in "Hutchinson Papers," I, Prince Soc., *Publications* (Albany, N.Y., 1865), p. 203.

[63] See R. B. Morris, "Massachusetts and the Common Law: the Declaration of 1646," *Amer. Hist. Rev.*, XXXI (1926), 450.

[64] *Mass. Col. Laws, 1660–72*, pp. 51–53. These provisions were incorporated in the Code of 1648 and the Laws of 1660. *The Laws and Liberties of Massachusetts* (Cambridge, 1929), p. 39; *Mass. Col. Laws, 1660–72*, p. 175. The liberty providing for the discharge of servants maimed by

From the earliest settlement of the New England colonies the courts were concerned with curbing excessive punishments that were sometimes so severe as to cause the death of a servant. Nicholas Weekes of Kittery and his wife Judith were indicted by a coroner's inquest in 1666 on suspicion of causing the death of a servant whose toes the mistress confessed she had cut off. Nevertheless, the jury cleared them. This flagrant disregard of simple justice caused the Assembly to have the trial proceedings reexamined. The court on review found that the acquittal jury "were noe grand Jury, but a particular Jury of paress," incompetent to find indictments, and that there had been a "mischarage [*sic*] both in bench and Jury, in not taking notice of the charge that had been occasioned by the Coroners Inquest to lay it upon the right persons." The General Court, to whom the case was referred, found that Weekes was "defective in his duty to his servant," and sustained the finding of the coroner's inquest that the punishment administered had been the direct cause of the servant's death. In addition, the court found "the Townes men of Kittery faulty that when Complaynt to them being made they had not caused his Master to provide for him," and proceeded to enunciate an important principle: "Persons defective in their duty from whom comes dammage or charge must of right pay that dammage that cometh through their defect." When the General Assembly ordered that the town of Kittery be discharged of responsibility, the court expressed a desire for "a forbearance of the publication of that order . . . until there bee a further debate thereof at the next General Assembly." [65] In laying down a principle of community responsibility for the proper treatment of servants the General Court went far beyond any accepted standards of that day,[66] and while its virtual suspensive veto of an Assembly order could hardly be construed as judicial review, it clearly is an attempt on the part of the judiciary to influence the course of legislation.[67]

The most celebrated trial of a master for the murder of his servant in the early annals of Massachusetts was that of Marmaduke Pierce. After a trial jury had disagreed in 1639, Pierce was let out on bail. At

---

their masters was incorporated in the New Hampshire acts of 1694 and 1718. *N.H. Prov. Laws,* I, 570; disallowed in 1704; see *ibid.,* pp. 646, 861. *Acts and Laws of N.H.,* I, 99 (1718); despite disallowance, the King in Council had urged the New Hampshire authorities to enact such a law, *ibid.,* II, 27, 183, 235, 292. Cf. also *Laws of R.I.* (1761 ed.), p. 198; (1771 ed.), p. 101.

[65] *Me. Prov. and Court Rec.,* I, 262, 272, 286.

[66] For other early Maine prosecutions for abusing servants, see Colcord's case, *Me. Prov. and Court Rec.,* II, 85 (1659), discharged on payment of court fees; Carpenter's case, *ibid.,* p. 216 (1671), fine to be paid in silver, fish, or other pay; March's case, York G.S., lib. VI, f. 384 (1713), servant to stay with father until next sessions.

[67] For judicial supremacy in the inferior courts of the colonies, see R. B. Morris, "Judicial Supremacy and the Inferior Courts in the American Colonies," *Pol. Sci. Q.,* LV (1940), 429–434.

a second trial new evidence was admitted, including depositions attesting to severe beatings with a rod having been administered the lad "for mooching." Apparently impressed by the character evidence of one deponent, who "did ever and doth still take the said Marmaduke for a moderate and Christianlike man," a jury returned a verdict of "not guilty," to which, Winthrop recounts, two of the jurors dissented.[68]

While fines were occasionally imposed upon masters for immoderately correcting their servants, the courts did not hold them criminally liable for other types of unfair treatment, such as inadequate food, raiment, or shelter. In such cases the courts customarily granted the servant his freedom, provided his petition was substantiated, without penalty to the master himself. Occasional exceptions to the general rule are found in Massachusetts. Eight complaints against masters for abuse of their servants came before the Court of Assistants between 1638 and 1643. In one complaint the master was charged with "swearing Gods foote, and cursing his servant wishing a p[o]xe of god take you!" Three masters were fined sums ranging from £5 to £10, two were admonished, but in only one out of the nine complaints was the servant set free from his master, and in that case he was bound over to someone else for three years.[69] Out of seventeen cases of maltreatment of servants to come up in the Essex Quarterly Court between 1640 and 1682, two alleged inadequate food and clothing, and fifteen undue correction or improper conduct toward a servant, such as calling the servant "base rogue" and "French dog." The two complaints of inadequate food and clothing were disposed of as follows: one master was fined and one enjoined to provide his servant with proper raiment.[70] The following dispositions were made of the fifteen cases of undue correction: four masters were fined; four admonished; in one case where the master was fined the servant was bound out to another employer; in one a verdict was returned for the plaintiff, although the judgment is unrecorded; in three the master was acquitted; in one the servant whipped; and, lastly, in two others no final action is on record.[71]

The depositions in these cases give some insight into the motives of

[68] Lechford, *Note-Book*, p. 229; Winthrop, *Journal*, I, 319; *Assistants*, II, 86, 89, 92. As late as 1784 the Berkshire sessions committed Asa Sparks to gaol on the charge of having been the cause of the death of his Negro man. Berkshire, lib. B., f. 361 (1784).

[69] *Complaints dismissed: Assistants*, II, 82, 83 (1639); Lechford, *Note-Book*, p. 51. *Fined: Assistants*, II, 80 (1638), 81 (1639), 103 (1641). *Admonished: Ibid.*, pp. 88 (1639), 133 (1643). *Discharged: Ibid.*, II, 101 (1640).

[70] *Essex*, I, 57 (643), 69 (1664). For an early complaint against an overseer for withholding provisions which does not appear to have been brought into court, see "Trelawny Papers," Me. Hist. Soc., *Coll.*, III, 168 (1639).

[71] *Essex*, I, 204 (1650); II, 236 (1660); III, 164, 224 (1664), 365 (1666); V, 232 (1673); VII, 149, 241 (1678); VIII, 6 (1680), 91, 184, 222–226 (1681), 296, 302, 315, 371 (1682).

the court. Relief was granted where "the boy was growing thin" because of faulty diet, improper clothing, and a poor bed. While the court held a master to be "justified" in giving deserved correction to his servant, it saw fit to disapprove the specific form of punishment selected by one master, which consisted of hanging the servant "by the heels as butchers do beasts for the slaughter." [72] When John Jackson was fined for "attempting to assault his maid" and for filthy language, the court nevertheless issued a warrant to the constable of Gloucester directing him to return Mary Soames, the complainant, to her master. John Peerce, the constable, refused to serve the warrant and gave the officer who sent it on a piece of his mind. It seems, according to the court testimony, that Jackson's neighbors complained that they had reason to believe that as soon as his wife heard that the maidservant had made the complaint she would either "murder the maid or inflict a deadly wound" upon her. When the warrant was read to the constable, that official retorted: "It shall be the worst dais worke that ever thee didst in thy life." Nonetheless the court fined him for his recalcitrant attitude.[73]

Virtually all the cases of improper treatment of servants in the Suffolk County and sessions courts came up by way of petition for freedom or relief brought by servants and apprentices or their parents. The eighteenth-century record of this court seems far less impressive from the point of view of the enforcement of labor's rights than that of the Essex court for the previous century. In only three complaints of undue correction out of eleven was the servant awarded his freedom, and in three others the master was required to post bond for his future good behavior toward his employee. In two others the master got off with mere admonition. Some of the particulars of alleged maltreatment hardly make pleasant reading. One master used unlawful instruments and grievously bruised and wounded his apprentice. A mother appealed to the court against the "barbarous" usage of her son by his master, who "for very trifles" unmercifully beat him with "an unlawful weapon," until he was "black as a Shoe all over his back and Shoulders." Not only must a servant guard against a beating, but also be shielded from his master's "most hasty temper . . . and passion," which could become "most ungovernable" and "hurry" the servant to destruction.[74] In no case did the sessions discharge an apprentice from his indentures on the ground of insufficient food and clothing; but in three out of

[72] Fowler's case, *ibid.*, VIII, 203, 214 (1682). [73] *Ibid.*, II, 236, 257, 258 (1660).
[74] Suffolk Sess., lib. I, 1702–12, fols. 107 (1705), 214 (1710); lib. II, 1712–19, fols. 3 (1712), 12, 42 (2 cases) (1713), 47, 123 (1714), 250 (1716); lib. IV, 1725–32, fols. 272 (1730), 309 (1736).

seven the servant was assigned to another master for the remainder of his term. In only one complaint does the master appear to have been admonished. Just what the court considered insufficient apparel is illustrated by the allegation that the apprentice was "very ragged and fil'd with vermin." It is not clear that the court would have intervened, however, were the master not also accused of the "incouraging of him in stealing and other evil practises." [75] The Suffolk sessions of 1706 ordered Robert Rust to return to his master to serve out his term, at the same time requiring the master to give security "to behave himself to his said Servant in all Respects, as becomith a master to a Servant of his Degree." [76] This would indicate that servants of a higher social rank were to be given special consideration by their masters—a policy not inconsistent with the hard crust of caste with which Puritan New England was caked in this period.

Other examples of "barbarous and inhumane" conduct are drawn from the early court records of Plymouth colony. One master was indicted for "fellonious crewelty" to his fourteen-year old servant. In addition to administering to the lad immoderate correction, he withheld necessary food and clothing, and subjected him to fatal exposure to the "extremities of season." The grand jury found that the dead servant's body showed the marks of beatings, his hands and feet were frozen, and that he had suffered further injuries by being "forced to carry a logg which was beyond his strength." The master was convicted of "Manslaughter" by "chaunce medley" and was burnt in the hand and suffered confiscation of his goods.[77] On a few occasions masters or members of their household were prosecuted for making improper advances to servant girls,[78] and one master was presented for "Unchast Carriage Towards his Men Servants." [79]

[75] *Ibid.*, lib. I, 1680–92, fols. 39 (1680), 182 (1683); lib. II, 1680–92, fols. 244 (1685), 365 (1690); lib. II, f. 237 (1719); lib. III, 87 (1721); lib. IV, 101 (1727).

[76] Stamford's case, Suffolk Sess., lib. I, f. 128 (1706).

[77] Latham's case, *Plymouth Col. Rec.*, III, 71–73, 82, 143 (1655). The prosecution of the mistress for her part in the servant's death was dropped. For other Plymouth cases (servant either bound to another master or the master was admonished), see *ibid.*, I, 14, 142 (1640); III, 51, 63 (1654), 75 (1655), 91.

[78] Pecke's case, *ibid.*, III, 75 (1655). Pecke was later admitted as a freeman and served as a selectman. *Ibid.*, VI, 167, 206. See also Partridge's case, Hampden Co. Mins., lib. 1693–1706, f. 59 (1698), where the court ordered the girl to return to her master because of "So many Irregularities in the Proceedings." The Hartford Co. court sentenced one such master to be kept in gaol until the next lecture day and then to suffer a whipping to take effect after the birth of the maidservant's child, for which he was responsible. Miller's case, "Conn. Prob. Rec.," lib. III, f. 47 (1666).

[79] Pengiely's case, Hampden Co. Mins., lib. 1693–1706, f. 93 (1700). Upon open confession in court he was fined 20*s.* and required to enter into recognizance in the amount of £10 for his good behavior or until next sessions.

The authorities in New Haven, Connecticut, and Rhode Island were equally concerned about curbing the maltreatment of servants.[80] Sudden deaths of servants were invariably investigated to determine whether they were accidental or attributable to the actions of masters.[81] The New Haven County court found in 1676 that the severe punishment inflicted by a master on his disobedient servant might well, "(together with the boyes naughtiness)," have been "influentiall to hasten his death." The court castigated the master for his "unmercifullness or cruell usage," which it declared to be "a great sin against god, and violation of the wholesome lawes of this colony." The court fined him £10 and witnesses' expenses and made him post bond of £50 for his behavior during "the courts pleasure."[82]

Based on an analysis of the court records, which invariably give a distorted picture of labor and domestic relations,[83] there is nevertheless justification for the conclusion that cruelty and oppression toward servants were less typical of New England than of the Middle colonies and the South. In fact, New England is the only colonial area where the complaints which masters brought against their servants for misconduct equal, if not exceed, the petitions submitted by servants seeking court intervention on the ground of improper treatment by their employers. In notorious instances where the courts failed to grant relief the church might feel impelled to step into the picture and to discipline cruel masters. The First Church of Boston, to cite one example, excommunicated William Franklin "for Rygarous and Cruell Correction

---

[80] One servant's term was shortened by two months because his master had struck him on the head with a hammer. *New Haven Col. Rec., 1638–49*, p. 46 (1640). See also order of the Providence town council for adequate apparel. Dalie's case, *Early Records of the Town of Providence*, XII, 56 (1717). See also presentment of Robert Ballard "for oppression in the way of his Servt." "Aquidneck Quarter Court Rec.," in H. M. Chapin, *Documentary History* (Providence, 1916–19), II, 136 (Portsmouth Q.S., 1641).

The servants at Saybrook collectively petitioned John Winthrop, Jr., against their diet of peas and porridge, their lack of adequate clothing, and the failure to make provision for their religious training. "These things not being performed with the whole consent of the companie," they declared, "we are resolved not to be content without them." *Winthrop Papers*, III, 281, 282 (1636).

[81] See, e.g., Steade's inquest, "Conn. Prob. Rec.," lib. I, f. 152.

[82] Maltbye's case, New Haven Co. Court Rec., lib. I, f. 90 (1676). The witnesses' expenses amounted to £1 6s. 4d. The same court later admonished a master for treating his servant "wth Rashness and Severity, if not cruelty." Royse's case, *ibid.*, f. 264 (1698). A Connecticut Special Court in 1690 fined Samuel Wolcott £3 after hearing that he had stripped his servant boy naked, tied him to a saddle, and beaten him "with the three great stick" until he was badly bruised. The boy was ordered to serve out his time to another employer to be approved by any two of the assistants. "Conn. Prob. Rec.," lib. I, f. 524 (1690).

[83] In one case the mistress alleged that she had cared for the child apprentice as tenderly "as if it wer our own child." *Essex*, VI, 68 (1675).

to his servants, and for sundry lyes in his being dealt withall about it, both pryvately and publiquely." [84] To some extent at least the relatively minor degree of master-servant friction in New England may be attributed to the far less important role played by white servitude in that area than elsewhere along the Atlantic seaboard.

THE MIDDLE COLONIES. The Dutch language courts in New Netherland fined masters convicted of maltreating their servants and generally required them to pay the medical bills for their servants' recovery or held them liable for civil damages. Masters or mistresses were haled into court for putting holes in their servants' heads, for beating them black and blue, and, in one case, for kicking a maidservant from behind when she stooped, causing her to discharge "much blood contrary to nature" and to be confined to bed for a long time during which she suffered "great pain." [85] A master who consistently nagged and bullied a workman, ordered to drill holes in a rail, and "slapped him two or three times about the ears" because "he did not understand boring very well, not being a carpenter," was admonished by the Kingston court to treat his employee "as a helper ought to be treated." While ordering the workman to serve out his time according to contract, the court warned the master that, if there were any further justifiable complaints, the workman would be set at liberty and given his full wages. [86]

English legislation in New York did not furnish the servant with remedies as substantial as had been offered in the Dutch courts. The humane provisions of the Body of Liberties were reflected in the Duke's Laws of 1665, which provided that masters or dames would be admonished by the constable and overseers for oppressive acts against servants. Upon hearing a second complaint, the local officials were authorized to "protect and Sustaine such Servants in their Houses" until the very next session when an order would be given for their relief. After due proof, servants would be freed. [87] An act of 1684 empowered the sessions to require a master convicted of maltreating a servant to

[84] First Church of Boston MS Rec., f. 23, Mass. Hist. Soc., cited by Morgan, *loc. cit.*, p. 14.

[85] Janzen's case, *R.N.A.*, III, 65 (1659), Tonneman v. de Witt, *ibid.*, V, 11 (1664); van Hoesem v. Jeronimus, *Ft. Orange and Beverwyck Court Mins.*, II, 33 (1657), damages awarded. See also Aelberts v. Brat, *Albany, Rensselaerswyck, and Schenectady Court Mins., 1668–73*, I, 99 (1669), where the court submitted to arbitration a suit for one year's wages and release from service on the ground of maltreatment consisting of "beating, cursing, and swearing."

[86] Tenhout v. De Wit, Ulster Dutch Transcripts, lib. I, fols. 291, 292 (1665). See also Jansen v. Wittikar, *ibid.*, lib. II, f. 572 (1670), where a hired hand was beaten by his irate employer because he drove his horses at least three times around the village on a hot day. The complaint of overwork was raised in Beeckman v. Eldes, *ibid.*, f. 456 (1667).

[87] N.Y. *Col. Laws*, I, 47.

give security for his future good conduct. If he refused to do so, the court was then empowered to discharge the servant.[88]

Contemporaries considered the New England codes of master-servant relations more favorable to the servants. Simon Athearn of Martha's Vineyard was moved to petition the New York authorities in 1675 that, while Gardner had enforced the Duke's Laws in his bailiwick, Mayhew refused to follow that code at Nantucket court, and proceeded to restrain masters from striking their servants, apparently on the basis of the humane legislation of Plymouth and Boston. The law of England seems to have been ignored in those early years on the islands, for, according to the petitioner, "the Law of England non of us knew." [89]

In interpreting the act of 1684 the local courts in New York customarily freed servants where the master was found guilty of undue correction, but unlike their Dutch predecessors, they seldom fined such delinquent masters.[90] A great number of complaints came before the court of general sessions of New York County in which servants charged their masters with maltreatment. That tribunal was prompt in granting legal redress. Out of thirty-nine cases of unreasonable correction noted between 1695 and 1789 the complaining servants were discharged from their indentures in twenty-eight and in one the master was fined. In only eight cases did the court find that the complaint was unsupported and order the servant to return to his employer. Even more significant is the fact that in every case prior to 1774 the servant was successful. Between 1774 and 1789, save for the years of British occupation, servants secured relief in merely six cases, masters were successful in eight, and in two there is no record of a final disposition of the complaint. Apparently by the eve of the Revolution the court began to scrutinize much more closely evidence supporting complaints of immoderate correction. All things considered, however, the record of the New York general sessions with respect to according relief to servants abused by their employers remains unsurpassed in the American colonies.[91]

[88] *Ibid.*, p. 157. An act of 1766 provided that Protestant redemptioners were "liable to such Correction as any apprentices are liable to in England, and may be relieved and discharged for Misusage, Refusal of Necessaries Cruelty or Ill treatment in the manner Apprentices are relievable in England for any of the Causes aforesaid." *Ibid.*, IV, 924. For the act of 1703, see Stokes, *Iconography*, IV, 441.

[89] N.Y. State Hist., *3d Ann. Report*, pp. 371, 373. See also *supra*, pp. 442–443.

[90] In one case where a servant was discharged from his master's service before the expiration of his four-year term the court made the servant pay 100 guilders sewan for board received as well as costs. Hardenbrook v. van der Borgh, *R.N.A.*, VI, 288 (1671). See also *ibid.*, V, 243 (1665), 332, 345 (1666).

[91] N.Y.G.S., lib. 1694–1731/2 (1695), (1718), (1720), (1729), (1731); lib. 1722–42/3,

These complaints of immoderate correction, often substantiated by numerous witnesses,[92] reveal oppressive labor conditions to have been imposed by harsh employers. The widow Anne Sewall was charged with "keeping in Chains and Irons for several weeks upon bread and water only and also Cruely beating A Certain Servant Maid of hers." Her defense that "she did not know itt was a breach of any Law" was considered insufficient, although she was released on payment of fees. Henry Brugham was found to have grievously disfigured the face of his apprentice, who stood "in Danger of loosing his Eyes thereby." In addition to having unreasonably corrected his apprentice, an eleven-year old girl, a cordwainer by the name of Benjamin Bates was charged with "not allowing her reasonable time of rest at several times in the Night time." [93]

Where the principal complaint against the employer was that he had not provided his servant with adequate food and clothing, the New York court of general sessions gave affirmative relief by discharging the servant in every case except one in which the complaint was held to be unsubstantiated and the servant was returned to him.[94]

Under New Jersey law the servant was entitled to his discharge if the master had treated him improperly or denied him necessary provisions and clothing.[95] From the few extant cases of maltreatment found in the court records, supplemented by newspaper accounts, it is clear that the servant's lot was not invariably an enviable one. A number of deaths of Jersey servants looked suspiciously like homicide at the hands of master or mistress. Occasionally an inquest put the blame upon the employer, as in the case of the sudden death in 1755 of a servant of Matthias Auble of Roxbury in Morris County, when the coroner's jury found that the death was "occasioned by the cruelty of his Master

fols. 109 (1729), 136 (1731); lib. 1732-62 (1746), (1751), (1756), (1759, 2 cases), (1760, 4 cases); (Kempe J–L); (1762, 3 cases); lib. 1760-72 (1762), (1763), (1765), (1768), (1769), (1770); lib. 1772-89 (1774, 4 cases), (1775, 3 cases), (1785, 3 cases), (1786, 2 cases), (1787), (1788, 2 cases), (1789). In two cases, decisions were not recorded.

[92] See, e.g., Garreau's case, Richmond G.S., lib. 1711–45, fols. 63, 64 (1721), servant discharged; Rex v. Lewis, Queens G.S., lib. 1722-87 (1760), court by divided vote discharged apprentice.

[93] Capt. Christopher Billop was accused in 1693 of kicking and beating William Bryan for refusing to sign his indentures. *Cal. Hist. MSS* (Dec. 5, 1693). For other instances of cruel treatment of servants, see Lauroson's case, Newtown Court Rec., f. 86 (1671); Stokes, *Iconography*, IV, 489.

[94] N.Y.G.S., lib. 1732-62 (1758), (1760), (1762); lib. 1760-72 (1768), (1772); lib. 1772-89 (1774), (1785), (1787), (1789). Similar relief was granted by the law officers in other counties when these grounds were shown. Vaughan's case, Dutchess County Book of Supervisors, f. 63 (1722); Rex v. Ellison, Queens G.S., lib. 1722-89 (1753).

[95] Parker, *Conductor Generalis*, pp. 22, 23; *Laws of the State of N.J.* (New Brunswick, 1800), p. 305.

a few days before in chastising him for some Misdemeanor." [96] A sensitive apprentice lad drowned himself rather than report to the magistrates a beating at the hands of his master, as his mother had advised him to do.[97]

While the county courts normally observed the letter of the law regarding oppression of servants and discharged maltreated servants from their indentures, in a number of instances they merely admonished the master or canceled the indentures after the apprentice's next of kin had satisfied the master in some part for the time remaining to be served.[98]

The laws of Pennsylvania provided in substance the same relief. The servant was to be discharged where the maltreatment had been proven; where he himself was shown to have been at fault, he was liable to be punished "by imprisonment of the body and confinement at hard labor" at the court's discretion.[99] Numerous complaints of unreasonable correction came up before the justices of that province as well as of neighboring Delaware, which, before 1704, was united with Pennsylvania. Suspicious deaths of servants were investigated.[100] Servants were usually discharged when they could substantiate their complaint of being maltreated, but at times the courts assigned them over to another

---

[96] *N.Y. Gazette, or Weekly Post-Boy,* Jan. 13, 1755. See also indictment of James Wills in 1686 for causing the death of a Negro woman servant. One witness stated that the Negress told her that the sores on her back came from "fum, fum," i.e., beating; another that he had administered fully 100 stripes. Wills was acquitted, but the jury found that he should have been more "sparing" as the Negress was "unsound." He was condemned to pay all costs. Burlington Court Book, fols. 47, 48 (1686). In a dying declaration, Ruth Birch charged that her master and mistress were the cause of her death, but the grand jury returned a bill ignoramus. *Ibid.,* f. 79 (1688). In 1702 one master recovered a verdict for damages from a woman who had defamed him by asserting that he was a bad master and had caused the death of his Negro by administering a whipping. Hollinshead v. Gleave *et ux., ibid.,* f. 190 (1702). See also *Pa. Gazette,* Feb. 7, 1738, master held for the murder of a servant.

[97] For a pathetic account, see *American Weekly Mercury,* Sept. 2–9, 1731.

[98] See, *e.g.,* Warne's case, Middlesex Co. Court Mins., Sept. 17, 1684, admonished; Crow's case, *ibid.,* March, 1694, indentures canceled, apprentice's father-in-law to pay master £7 10s. current; Willis's complaint, Essex, lib. B, 1724–39, f. 37 (1726), discharged; master appealed; Bayley's case, Morris C.P. and Q.S., lib. 1740–54, f. 4 (1740), to remain, master to provide necessaries; Mary Williamson's complaint, *ibid.,* lib. 1778–82, f. 53 (1779), discharged; Mount's case, Monmouth Q.S., lib. 1775–83 (July 23, 1776), discharged.

Inadequate apparel: Johnson's complaint, Essex, lib. B, 1724–39, f. 23 (1725), discharged; Hunt's case, Hunterdon C.P. and Q.S., lib. 1733–36, f. 6 (1733). See also Wright v. Duncke, Burlington Court Rec., f. 10 (1682).

[99] *Pa. Stat. at Large,* VI, 247 (1763), VII, 361–363 (1770); C. Read, *An Abridgment of the Laws of Pennsylvania* (Philadelphia, 1801), pp. 10, 11.

[100] Pennypacker, *Pa. Col. Cases,* p. 52 (1685); Pride's case, *Pa. Col. Rec.,* II, 513 (1710). Cf. also Renolds v. Anderson, *Chester Co. Court Rec., 1681–97,* pp. 53, 54 (1685), a suit for defaming the master by stating that he "beate his servt and the next night after shee dyed." As evidence tended to show that the master had beaten the maid for complaining of the victuals, the jury gave defendant a 6d. and costs verdict.

master, or even returned them to their employer with an admonition.[101]

In a petition to the Bucks quarter sessions in 1767 Matthias Kempf, a laborer, set forth that he and his wife had been bound in 1764 by indentures to one Richard Stevens of Philadelphia. When Stevens's lands and estates were taken in execution, the couple were sold to his brother in New Jersey. Kempf charged that, not alone did the brother take him by force to the adjacent province, but that he also failed to provide essential food, clothing, and bedding, and refused to permit him to return to the county from which he had beeen taken. "Your Petitioner humbly conceives," Kempf concluded, "that the Coming of Strangers from another Government with Force and Arms to do themselves Justice when the Laws are Open for them is a Manifest Contempt of the Laws and Insult upon the Government of this Province, and that the assault upon your Petitioner in the manner afores'd is a Breach of the Kings Peace." Accordingly the court turned the petitioner over to an inhabitant of Bucks County in which the suit was brought.[102] When Shephard Kollock complained to the Philadelphia sessions that his master had "used him cruelly," beaten him "without any Reason in the most violent Manner," compelled him to work on Sundays, and denied him sufficient provisions, he was ordered to return to his master's service, but the master in turn was required to post security of £50 for his good behavior for three months and to find two sureties in £25 apiece.[103] Where the servant had been denied food and clothing, the normal procedure was to order his discharge.[104] Occasionally the court directed the master to satisfy the servant's needs, in one case actually issuing a warrant of attachment against him to oblige him to provide his servant with food and raiment and to reimburse the overseer of the poor who had assumed that responsibility temporarily.[105]

In a majority of the complaints for cruel treatment brought against

---

[101] *Chester Co. Court Rec., 1681–97*, p. 45 (1684), assigned to another; *ibid.*, p. 59 (1685), complaint "Rejected for want of Proofe." Bucks, lib. 1684–1730 (1685), master bound to good behavior; Lancaster Road and Sess., Docket No. 2, 1742–60 (1758), and *ibid.*, No. 3, 1760–68 (1766), discharged in both cases; Chester Q.S., lib. 1723–33 (Dec. 15, 1724), discharged; York Q.S., lib. I, f. 24 (1750), returned to master; Bucks Q.S., lib. 1754–82, f. 340 (1767), no final action recorded. York Q.S., lib. XII, 1779–81, fols. 117, 118 (1779), discharged; *ibid.*, f. 210 (1780), servant returned; Philadelphia Q.S., lib. 1780–85 (1784), no final action recorded; Philadelphia City Court, lib. 1785–87, f. 205 (1787), bound to another.

[102] Bucks Q.S., lib. 1754–82, f. 354 (1767).

[103] Goddard's case, Philadelphia Q.S., Docket, 1770, Phila. Co. Court Papers, Hist. Soc. of Pa.

[104] Grainer's case, Philadelphia Q.S., lib., 1779–82 (Oct., 1780); Dehaven's case, *ibid.* (July, 1780). But cf. Brown's case, Cumberland Q.S., lib. 1777–89, f. 165 (1780), servant returned.

[105] Taylor's case, Lancaster Road and Sess. Docket, No. 1, 1729–42, fols. 12, 13 (1729); Enfield's case, York Q.S., lib. XI, f. 59 (1778). Cf. also Stamfield's petition, *Chester Co. Court Rec., 1681–97*, pp. 178, 179 (1689).

masters in the courts of Delaware, servants obtained their discharge.[106] In a few instances the servant was returned to his master on the master's promise to behave in the future,[107] while in still others the servants were denied relief.[108]

THE TOBACCO COLONIES. Maltreatment of servants was most flagrant in the tobacco colonies, where flinthearted employer and churlish redemptioner or convict most frequently came to grips. While it would be unfair to indict the whole planter class, the fact remains that an impressive number of masters led drunken, dissolute lives and were brutal and sadistic in behavior toward their workmen. Even members of the governor's council and county commissioners were not above reproach and set a poor example to their own communities in ruling with a rod of iron. In his secret diary William Byrd recorded that he went with the governor to the latter's home on one occasion, but as the servants were "out of the way," the governor chastised them when they returned. Byrd's first wife, Lucy, led him a tempestuous married life and not infrequently took her fits of temper out on servants and slaves, going so far as to burn them with a hot iron. Juvenal, who among other things was a good psychoanalyist, has given an explanation of the tantrums of such abusive mistresses which seems perfectly valid in Lucy Byrd's case. Byrd himself, though far more restrained than his wife, beat his servants rather regularly, often for very minor infractions—for going to bed before he returned home, not working "on pretense of sickness," or for "a hundred faults" unspecified. Such masters preferred to discipline their servants themselves rather than to bring them into court. Byrd had a manservant whipped for beating his wife and a maid "for being his whore." [109] Court cases are likely, therefore, to represent more serious instances of maltreatment, but the pattern they shape is fairly typical of servant life on the plantations.

Were we to accept as valid the reflections of the redemptioner, George

[106] Howard's complaint, Kent Q.S., lib. 1756–59 (1758); Bropson's case, Newcastle G.S., lib. 1765, f. 15 (1764), referred to arbiter, and Holland's case, *ibid.*, lib. 1778–93, fols. 194, 201 (1782). Homis's complaint, Kent Q.S., lib. 1778–83 (1782); Bennett's complaint, *ibid.* (1783), bound to another.

[107] Kent, lib. 1699–1703, f. 89a (1703).

[108] In 1676 Symon Gibson was cleared by a jury of the charge of raping his maidservant, Sara Jennings. *Newcastle Court Rec.*, I, 16. See also Crayford's complaint, *ibid.*, p. 61 (1677); Sellers' and Cochran's cases, Newcastle G. S., lib. 1778–93, f. 267 (1784).

[109] L. B. Wright and Marion Tinling, eds., *The Secret Diary of William Byrd of Westover, 1709–1712* (Richmond, 1941), pp. 84, 112, 119, 127, 192, 205, 269, 295, 307, 462, 494, 533; *Another Secret Diary of William Byrd of Westover, 1739–41*, ed. M. H. Woodfin (Richmond, 1942), pp. 292–294. However, the later diary reveals that Byrd, as he grew older, treated his servants more humanely and that his second wife, Maria Taylor, was a more self-restrained person than Lucy.

Alsop, or such early literature as the "Sot-Weed Factor" or Hammond's *Leah and Rachel,* we should be forced to conclude that, as compared with England, servants in the tobacco provinces were well treated.[110] For sentimental reasons we should prefer to remember the Maryland master who was out "Playing nine pins with his Servants" and could not be disturbed [111] to malevolent and degraded employers like Captain Bradnox and Henry Smith, whose cruelties filled many pages of the court records.

Virginia, whose early settlement problems were atypical of the English colonies, governed her servants with a Draconian code, the "Laws Divine, Morall and Martiall." The Assembly charged in 1624 that during those early years the few survivors were required to serve the colony for seven or eight years, during which they were put to "as harde and servile labor as the basest Fellow that was brought out of Newgate," were furnished moldy, maggoty rations, and, when they attempted to flee from insufferable conditions of employment, were hanged, shot, or broken on the wheel.[112] Employed primarily in field work under the supervision of exacting overseers, the white servants in the tobacco colonies, especially before the heavy inroads of slavery, did not enjoy that close personal relationship with their masters which marked labor relations in craft and household in the Northern and Middle colonies. Dutch travelers visiting Maryland toward the latter part of the seventeenth century found that servants, after working all day in the tobacco fields, were often compelled to grind and pound grain for the household. Nothing was permitted to interfere with the task of tobacco planting. One master, so they reported, made a dying servant dig his own grave rather than take another from the fields for that task. Their diet was limited to corn and water, and they were required to work hard six days a week, as the members of the Assembly felt that servants should not be permitted to rest on Saturday afternoons.[113] A later critic

110 See John Hammond, *Leah and Rachel, or, The Two Fruitful Sisters, Virginia and Maryland* (1656), reprinted in Force, *Hist. Tracts,* III. George Alsop's letter, *c.* 1659, is found in Md. Hist. Soc., *Fund Publications,* No. 15, p. 94. This rosy picture is uncritically accepted by Scharf, *Hist. of Md.,* II, 14, 15, by Andrews, *Founding of Maryland,* p. 87, and by J. C. Ballagh, *op. cit.,* p. 77, citing Robert Beverley, *History of Virginia* (Richmond, 1855), pp. 219, 220, 222.

111 *Md. Arch.,* XLI, 575, 576 (1661).

112 MS "The Tragicall Relation of the Virginia Assembly, 1624," Lib. of Cong.; also in E. D. Neill, *History of the Virginia Company of London* (Albany, 1869), pp. 407–411, and in *Narratives of Early Virginia, 1606–1625,* ed. L. G. Tyler (New York, 1907), pp. 422–426. See also Neill, *Virginia Carolorum* (Albany, 1886), p. 58.

113 Dankers and Sluyter, "Journal," L.I. Hist. Soc., *Memoirs,* I, 191, 192, 216, 217; *Md. Arch.,* I, 21. Oatmeal, peas, bread, and water comprised the diet of servants "in sickness and in health," according to charges made in 1623. *Va. Co. Rec.,* IV, 231.

corroborated this view and recommended that servants in the tobacco provinces "should have a little more kind usage from their masters, for a man had really better be hanged than become a Servant in the Plantations, most of his food being homene and water . . . I have been told by some of them that they have not tasted flesh meat once in three months." He charged planters with treating their servants so inhumanely in the last months of their terms that they would agree to forego their freedom dues in order to gain their discharge a month or two before their terms ended.[114]

While slavery very largely supplanted white servitude in the tobacco colonies in the course of the eighteenth century, there does not appear to have been any material improvement in the treatment accorded those still in service. Because of the large-scale transportation of convicts, white servants remained under suspicion and subject to the strictest disciplinary measures. The court clerks of the seventeenth century, by their practice of recording testimony or depositions, have left us a more vivid picture of labor grievances for their day and age than are furnished by the meager dockets of the later period. Nevertheless, such complaints, though relatively less frequent, were still insistent, and there is little to indicate that there had been any substantial amelioration of the servant's lot by the late colonial period. "Generally speaking, they groan beneath a worse than Egyptian bondage," observed William Eddis in 1770.[115] The bulk of complaints of abusive treatment brought by the eve of the Revolution came from the western counties, where the less affluent planters still had need for white servants, finding slaves beyond their means.

Before turning to some of the more significant trials, let us examine the law on the books. Virginia, by an act of 1643, empowered the county commissioners to decide cases of maltreatment of servants "as they in their discretion shall thinke fitt."[116] Persons who presumed to whip a Christian white servant naked without an order from a justice of the peace were, by the servant code of 1705, subject to the forfeiture of 40s. sterling to the injured party, to be recovered before a justice upon petition. Masters were expected to provide their servants with "wholesome and competent diet, clothing, and lodging," and, where they failed to comply, the servant could be "sold at an outcry by the sheriff," or else

---

[114] *CSPA, 1701*, No. 1103, p. 693.

[115] *Letters from America* (London, 1792), reprinted in *Doc. Hist. Amer. Indust. Soc.*, I, 343, 344. For corroboration of Eddis's views, see "Intercepted Letters from Maryland and Virginia," High Court of Admiralty Papers, Misc. 1066 (1756).

[116] Hening, I, 254, 255. See also act of 1658, *ibid.*, p. 440; act of 1662, *ibid.*, II, 117.

taken care of by the church wardens until his time had expired.[117] Maryland provided that servants were to have justice done them by way of petition; [118] masters who overworked servants or slaves, deprived them "of necessary rest," or denied them necessaries were subject to a fine of 1,000 lbs. of tobacco; [119] servants who were excessively beaten or abused [120] were to be set at liberty.

To present in all their gruesome details a full account of the trials which took place in the tobacco colonies for oppression of servants would be to heap Ossa upon Pelion. Let us confine ourselves therefore to the major causes of contention and to certain significant trials which may be taken as fairly representative of the trend of judicial decisions in this field. In the first place, it was no easy task to secure the conviction of a master in the tobacco colonies for the murder of his servant, although Maryland's record on this score is far brighter than that of Virginia. According to the act of 1642, such murder trials were to be conducted by the Maryland courts "as near as may be to the law of England." Where the evidence proved the maltreatment and brutality to be flagrant and irrefutable and indubitably the direct cause of the servant's death, juries had no alternative but to return a verdict of guilty. Such a verdict was handed down against a smith named John Dandy, tried in 1657 for beating his servant to death. Dandy was an inveterate servant baiter, but no one actually saw him beat his servant on the last occasion. The lad's naked body, black and blue from blows administered with a switch, was found floating down a small creek near a mill at Newtown where Dandy lived. The most damning testimony was contributed by Dandy's wife, Ann, who described the serious skull wound which her husband had inflicted on the servant on an earlier occasion and which she had dressed, and declared that "in her Conscience She doth Verily believe" that the servant never drowned himself. To such circumstantial evidence was added the accusation, which carried great weight in a superstitious age, that when Dandy touched the corpse, the wounds started bleeding again. Dandy broke gaol, ran away to Virginia, and was brought back to stand trial in Maryland, where he charged he had already suffered "hard usage by those in Authority." He

---

[117] Hening, III, 447 (1705); V, 547–548 (1748); VI, 357–369 (1753); *Executive Journal of the Council of State of Virginia*, III, 110; Starke, *Justice of the Peace*, p. 319.

[118] *Md. Arch.*, XXII, 10, 102, 121, 546–553 (1698).

[119] For a third offense of overworking a servant, the servant was to be discharged. *Ibid.*, XXII, 546–553 (1699).

[120] *Ibid.*, XXVI, 254 (1704). Whipping in excess of ten lashes constituted maltreatment. To exceed this punishment the master had to apply to a justice of the peace, who was authorized to increase it not to exceed thirty-nine lashes. *Ibid.*, XXX, 177.

was found guilty by a jury and sentenced to death, and was hanged on an island in the Patuxent River.[121]

Pope Alvey was convicted in 1663 of being the cause of the death of his servant Alice Sanford, whose body was reported to have been "beaten to a Jelly," and who, in a dying declaration, had cried out: "Take notice that my master has killed me!" He pleaded his clergy and was burnt in the right hand.[122] Despite a finding of a coroner's inquest in 1664 that Jeffery Haggman's death had been due to scurvy, many people believed that his master, Joseph Fincher, had whipped him to death. When the case came to trial, William Gunnell testified that, on the day before Haggman had died, Fincher had given his servant a load of tobacco plants to carry. When Haggman protested, Fincher warned him: "Go or else I will beate you as never was a dogg so beaten!" This threat Fincher literally carried out. Seeing his servant staggering under the load, he kicked and punched him severely and threatened to knock him in the head or starve him rather than put up with such nonsense in the future. The next morning Fincher's wife assisted her husband in administering the finishing touches. Others corroborated Gunnell. Fincher was found guilty by a jury and was sentenced to be hanged.[123] Both Francis Carpenter, a Talbot County planter, indicted in 1666 for the murder of his servant, but convicted of manslaughter, and James Lewis, convicted in 1688 of the murder of a servant some eight years earlier by having "trampled upon his throat with violence so that he died within two hours," pleaded their clergy and were burnt in the hand in open court;[124] but Richard Vanson, a laborer, did not get off so lightly, and suffered death at the hangman's noose for murdering a servant whom he had assaulted with a log.[125]

[121] *Md. Arch.*, X, 522, 534–545. Raphael Semmes (*Crime and Punishment in Early Maryland* [Baltimore, 1938], p. 126), who has made a careful study of these early trials, feels that it was more likely that the servant had drowned himself to escape further chastisement. But the failure to find the boy's clothes or any of his footprints leading to the stream make this supposition rather improbable. Some years earlier Dandy had been convicted of the fatal shooting of an Indian boy. His sentence of death at this earlier trial was commuted on condition that he serve as public executioner in the colony for seven years, in accord with the act of 1642, authorizing such sentence for manslaughter; but later he was freed of this obligation. *Md. Arch.*, III, 146, 187, 188; IV, 254, 255, 260.

[122] *Md. Arch.*, XLIX, 166–168, 233–235. The following year Alvey was convicted of stealing and killing a neighbor's cow, but the governor saw fit to stay execution, and a number of years later he was pardoned by unanimous request of the Lower House, possibly on grounds of irresponsibility. *Ibid.*, II, 370, 377; LI, 121–123, 219.

[123] *Ibid.*, XLIX, 290, 305–307, 311–314.

[124] Md. Prov. Court Rec., lib. FF, fols. 289–297. *Md. Arch.*, LIV, 390, 391, 410; LVII, 59–65, 153 (1666), the master fractured the boy's skull and left him lie on the ground in a thatched cabin, without covering, on a cold February night. Charles, lib. 1680–82 (1681). Md. Prov. Court Rec., lib. 1679–84, fols. 378, 379 (1680); lib. 1682–1702, f. 104 (1688).

[125] *Ibid.*, f. 36 (1684).

Convictions of masters for the murder or manslaughter of their servants were definitely the exception. In a preponderance of such trials
they were acquitted or let off lightly, often in the face of incontrovertible
evidence of guilt. Mistress Thomas Ward whipped her maidservant on
the bare back with a peach tree rod and then put salt in the wounds.
When her servant implored her to use her like a Christian, she retorted: "Do you liken yourself like a Christian?" The girl died shortly
thereafter. The jury found that the punishment was not the direct cause
of her death, but in view of "her weak state," deemed it "unreasonable
and unchristianlike," and Ward and his wife were fined 300 lbs. of tobacco.[126]

The impressive number of servant suicides on record in the seventeenth-century tobacco colonies is a sad commentary on their wretched
condition. Some of these "suicides" took place under highly suspicious
circumstances, but in each and every case the master was able to excul-
pate himself of guilt, even where he had, in defiance of the law,[127]
buried the servant secretly and with undue haste or where the corpse
bore the marks of brutal treatment.[128]

---

[126] *Md. Arch.*, LIV, 9, 10, 125, 126. But see Anne Nevill's case, *ibid.*, XLI, 467, 471, 475,
478–480, acquitted despite servant's dying declaration; Martine's case, *ibid.*, p. 385 (1660),
exonerated by coroner's jury after no blood issued from corpse when he placed his hand on
it. See also John Grammer's case, where the master had his servant beaten 100 stripes with
a cat-o'-nine-tails. Instead of expressing regret for carrying out the order, the overseer declared:
"I could have given him tenn times more." *Ibid.*, XLIX, 307–312 (1663). Again Grammer
was cleared when another servant died under suspicious circumstances, the coroner's inquest
laying it to "want of good dyett and lodging." *Ibid.*, pp. 351, 401 (1665). See also Susannah
Keen's case, Md. Prov. Court Rec., lib. 1682–1702 (1684), f. 5, acquitted. No final disposition
is found of the case of Thomas King, gaoled in 1680 on a similar murder charge. *Ibid.*, lib.
1679–84, f. 379 (1680).

For acquittals of masters in Virginia or instances of failure to prosecute them for the murder
of their servants, see *Va. Gen. Court Mins.*, pp. 22–24; *VMH*, XIX, 388; Scott, *op. cit.*,
p. 201; Howe's case, Accomac O.B., I, fols. 80, 81 (1637); Charles City O.B., 1655–65, f. 357
(1663); Accomac O.B., 1671–73, f. 135 (1672); Givans' case, Augusta, lib. XV, f. 310b
(1774), acquitted on the ground of justifiable homicide.

[127] An act of 1662 in Virginia provided that in suspicious deaths the neighbors were to
be called in to view the corpse and no one was to be buried in other than official burial
grounds except by his own choice. The Assembly justified this act by reciting that, as a
result of private burials of servants, there had arisen a good deal of "scandall against diverse
persons and sometimes not undeservedly of being guilty of their deaths." Hening, II, 53.

[128] See *Md. Arch.*, X, 74, 157–159; LIII, 363; LIV, 360–362; XLIX, 215, 216, 314, 351,
374, 394. For other Maryland suicides, see *ibid.*, p. 216; LIII, 140, 141, 502; LIV, 327,
373; XLIX, 88, 113; LIII, 501, 502. In one year the coroner held three inquests over the
bodies of dead servants. *Ibid.*, LX, xxvi. See also *Md. Gazette*, Aug. 3, 1747, which, after
reporting that Hannah Senhouse was bound over to the next Assize Court on suspicion of
responsibility for a servant suicide, stated its hope and purpose "that all masters may and
will, for the future, use their servants according to their deserts, let the consequences of this
case end whatever manner it will." For deaths of servants by accident or suicide in Virginia,
see Charles City O.B., 1655–65, f. 154 (1658); York O.B., 1657–62, fols. 345 (1661), 477
(1662); *Va. Gen. Court Mins.*, pp. 53, 54 (1625).

In about two thirds of all complaints on the score of undue correction or overwork studied in the Provincial and county courts of Maryland down to the Revolution, the petitioning servant secured some measure of redress from ill-treatment at his master's hands. However, only in a minority of such cases did the court go so far as to grant his discharge. The normal course was to admonish the master, or, in more severe cases of oppression, to assign the servant to another employer. In a number of instances the county courts imposed fines upon masters. When the servant could not substantiate his complaint, he was customarily returned to his master to finish out his term.[129]

Some of these complaints cast a lurid light on master-servant relations. One maidservant accused her mistress of beating her "two hours by the clock." One master was charged with having belabored his servant with a dogwood stick until he broke it in pieces and with having thrown him down and kicked him violently in the stomach and ribs; another, with hanging his servant by his wrists to the gunrack and giving him an unmerciful beating. One servant, who was actually chained to his task, declared that his master and family, after whipping him, placed salt over his raw wounds and held him naked over the fire. In 1721 Governor Calvert sent Alexander Cole, a servant to the bricklayer Thomas Cooke, to Chief Justice Samuel Young to hear his complaint. Justice Young reported his findings as follows:

On viewing the perishing condition he now is in, in respect to his State of health I find his master has not onely Misused him but Neglected to Doe his Duty in getting him Cured of the Aylemt the Servt now has and in order to prevent the sd Servt perishing I therefore hereby recommend to you to administer unto the sd Servt Such Medicine for the recovery of his health as you shall Judge proper, as alsoe to place him wth any Person that will accomodate, for all wch his master will be obliged to pay, or the Justices of Ann Arundel County Court as the sd Justices Shall Judge reasonable.

He then ordered Doctor Alexander Fraser to remove the servant's irons.[130]

[129] Typical examples of relief: *Servant discharged:* Md. Arch., X, 416 (1655), LIII, 410, LIV, 292 (masters to maintain maidservant in the meantime), 167, 178–180, 191, 213, 224, 234 (1659); Prince George, lib. 1746–47, f. 23 (1746). *Servant assigned to another master:* Md. Arch., X, 191 (1652), to be sold or exchanged "with all convenient speed"; XLIX, 318 (1664); Somerset, lib. AW, 1690–91, fols. 48, 49vso. (1688). *Master admonished:* Md. Arch., XLI, 68 (1658), X, 505, 521 (1657); Prince George, lib. B, 1699–1705, f. 434; Queen Ann, lib. 1709–16, fols. 128, 129 (1711), servant also admonished; Baltimore, lib. I.S., No. C, 1718–21 (1719); Ann Arundel, lib. 1720–21, f. 100 (1721); Prince George, lib. 1775–77, f. 164 (1775). *Master fined:* Prince George, lib. B, 1699–1705, f. 50 (1700); Queen Ann, lib. 1718–19 (1719); Baltimore, lib. I.S., No. C, 1718–21 (1720); Somerset, lib. 1730–33, f. 83 (1731), servant discharged also. *Servant to return to master:* Queen Ann, lib. 1709–16 (1712), (1714).
[130] The Ann Arundel County court thereupon ordered the master to pay the physician "as

Among the charges of abusive treatment were accusations of being overworked or forced to work at laborious tasks, or to labor on the Sabbath. William Ireland accused his master, Captain Philip Morgan, of "unhumanly" beating him, of forcing him and the rest of his servants to "beate their Victuals in the Night," and of not giving them enough to eat. The Provincial Court ordered Morgan to stop beating his servant "unlawfully" and not to require him to "beate in the Night time but at a Seasonable time in the yeare or in case of Necessity," and to provide adequate diet for all his servants.[131] Rather than be forced to beat at the mortar and bake bread on Sunday or suffer "hard and cruel usage" John Little's servant ran away, preferring to remain with the savages than "to be starved for want of food and clothing, and have his brains beaten out." [132] When Mary Hobbs petitioned the Queen Ann County court that she was being "putt to more Labour" than she was obliged to by agreement with Robert Colt her employer, the court ordered that Colt find her those necessaries she requested, but that she "Serve her time out according to Contract." [133] William Smith, a mariner out of work, hired himself out to tend the ferry, but his employer insisted that he was hired for all employment. The court directed Smith to "doe only that Buisiness he was hired to doe." [134] When John Smith confessed that he had unreasonably corrected Hugh Brady and Owen Mackdonall and employed them on the Sabbath, denying them leave to go to church, the Prince George County court, under authority of the act of 1678,[135] fined him one hundred pounds of tobacco and required that he give security for his good behavior.[136]

The singular difficulties in the way of a servant seeking justice from a master who sat on the county bench is illustrated by the troubles of one maidservant named Sarah Taylor who petitioned in 1659 to be discharged from Captain Bradnox, a Kent County commissioner. One justice on the county bench thought she deserved to be whipped for running away, but the remainder of the court felt that she had received sufficient corporal punishment already and ordered her to get down on her knees and beg her master and mistress for forgiveness and promise them to behave better in the future. But when she continued to be maltreated, she renewed her complaints. A jury acquitted her of a

---

well for accomodating as for administering physic" to the servant. For the future Cooke was admonished to provide such medicines and other accommodations as the servant's condition demanded. Ann Arundel, lib. 1720–21, f. 100 (1721).

[131] *Md. Arch.*, X, 521 (1657).   [132] *Ibid.*, X, 474, 482, 484, 485.
[133] Petition of Mary Hobbs, Queen Ann, lib. 1709–16, fols. 128, 129 (1711).
[134] Smith's petition, Prince George, lib. 1699–1705, f. 434 (1705).
[135] *Md. Arch.*, VII, 51, 52.
[136] Smith's case, Prince George, lib. B, 1699–1705, f. 50 (1700).

malicious charge brought against her by her master of stealing some clothing. Before three of the Kent County commissioners she dramatically described how, while working in the kitchen one day, her master and mistress suddenly fell upon her, the mistress holding her while the master beat her "with a great ropes end . . . and so unreasonably that theare is twenty on[e] Impressions or blowes, small and great, upon her back and Armes." After administering the beating, her master warned: "Now, spoyle me a batch of bread again!" Further testimony was adduced that on one Sunday morning, when Sarah picked up a book to read, Captain Bradnox hit her over the head with "a three-footed stool," exclaiming, "Youe disembling Jade, what doe youe doe with a booke in your hand?" The county court, upon reviewing the evidence, discharged her from her apprenticeship because of "the imminent danger likely to ensue by the inveterate malice of her master and mistress toward her." Bradnox then appealed to the governor, charging baselessly that the county court had no right to set his servant free. Henry Coursey and Edward Lloyd, whom the governor chose to settle this question, required the Kent County justices to pay Mistress Bradnox two hundred and twenty pounds of tobacco for having discharged Sarah Taylor. On the death of Bradnox his wife pressed a suit against Sarah for conspiracy.[137]

That the county justices, when not restrained by higher authorities, did attempt to curb maltreatment of servants is established by considerable evidence, and is perhaps best illustrated by the trial of Arthur Turner, who was summoned to appear before the Charles County court and "to give a Reason why the orphant John Ward hath bin so ille treated in his hows *in so much that the voyce of the People crieth shame thereat.*" When the orphan lad was brought before the court, he was found to have a "Rotten filthy stincking" ulcer on one of his legs that was loathsome to "all the beholders thereof" and to be clad in rags, his hair appearing "to be rotted of ashes." He was promptly discharged of his indentures.[138]

Servants were almost invariably successful at law when they sought relief on account of improper food, shelter, or clothing. On such grounds the Maryland courts normally ordered the master to see that they were furnished with sufficient necessaries, or else discharged them, on occasion binding them out to other masters. Until such assignment had been effected, someone else at the county seat might be directed to provide

[137] *Md. Arch.*, LIV, 167, 178–180, 191, 213, 224, 234; XLI, 482, 506, 525 (1661).
[138] *Ibid.*, LIII, 410, 411.

the servant with shelter until the master appeared to answer the charges.[139] When John Helme asked his master, the chirurgeon John Meekes, for some clothes, that worthy told him that he might go "whither he would and bee damned." The apprentice took his master at his word and appeared one winter's day before the Charles County commissioners clad in garments very "bare and thin for the time of the year." Meekes was promptly ordered to clothe the youth "from top to toe fit for an apprentice." [140]

The following sentences were meted out by the courts of Virginia in forty-four complaints brought by servants for maltreatment down to 1780: servants discharged, nine; masters warned, six; masters required to give security for their future conduct, six; masters ordered to provide their servants with proper medical attention, five; master forbidden to have a servant, one; servant whipped, one; master cleared, one; no final disposition recorded, fifteen. Thus, servants appear to have enjoyed about the same ratio of success to failure in the courts of Virginia as in Maryland, although there are proportionately fewer instances where servants obtained their discharge and more where masters were required to post bond for good behavior.[141]

At times the higher authorities overruled the county court and brought class justice down to the level of the scandalous Bradnox affair in Maryland. An extraordinary master-servant controversy was initiated in 1668 on Virginia's Eastern Shore, when Mary Hewes complained to the Accomac court against her master, Henry Smith, charging that she was "hard worked ill dieted and bad Cloathed," and was "most

[139] See *Md. Arch.*, LIII, 431 (1663), X, 401 (1654), XLI, 2 (1657), 417 (1660); Somerset, lib. AW, 1690–91, fols. 48, 49vso. (1688); Talbott, lib. NN, No. 6 (1688); Charles, lib. 1680–82, f. 85 (1681), 1696–98, f. 165 (1696), two servants; 1720–22, f. 42 (1720); Prince George, lib. A, 1696–1702 (1698), lib. B, 1699–1705 (1705); Ann Arundel, lib. 1702–4, f. 225 (1703); Queen Ann, lib. 1709–16, f. 83 (1710).

[140] *Md. Arch.*, LIII, 431. For neglecting the cure of his servant's leg and failing to supply him with bedding, John Hawkins, Jr., was fined 200 lbs. of tobacco "for such his Carelessness and Negligence," but the servant was ordered to "go home about his Masters Business." Queen Ann, lib. 1709–16, f. 83 (1710). Stephen Gill was summoned before the Baltimore County court in 1772 for permitting his servant to lie in gaol. Baltimore, lib. 1772–80 (1772).

[141] Accomac, lib. I, f. 2 (1632), II, fols. 76 (1637), 221, 227 (1642, 1643), lib. 1666–70, fols. 17 (1667), 72, 103, 104, 123, 126, 148 (1668–70), lib. 1671–73 (1672); Lower Norfolk, lib. I, f. 141 (1641); York, lib. 1657–62, fols. 4 (1657), 76 (1658), 249 (1660), 317 (1661), lib. 1664–72, f. 385 (1669), lib. 1675–84, f. 638 (1683), lib. 1700 (Tyler, *Mag.*, I, 213), lib. 1774–84, f. 267 (1780); Charles City, lib. 1655–65, fols. 239 (1660), 357 (1663); Lancaster, lib. 1656–66, f. 116 (1660), lib. 1675 (*WMCQ*, 1st ser., VI, 117); Northumberland, lib. 1666–78 (1667); Stafford and Isle of Wight, 1693 (*WMCQ*, 1st ser., VII, 257); Spotsylvania, lib. 1724–30 (1727); Augusta O.B., I (1746–63, 12 cases), XVI, f. 230 (1777); Botetourt, lib. 1766–71, Pt. I, f. 237 (1770); *Va. Gen. Court Mins.*, pp. 465 (1640), 506 (1657), 212, 217 (1668–70), 352 (1673), 520 (1680); *Exec. J., Council of State of Va.*, I, 490 (1682); *Cal. Va. State Papers*, I, 99 (1706).

Cruelly beaten wthout any Cause given him but Only his angry and discontented humors of wch she made severall proofes." In the late fall she found it too cold to work bare-footed, and asked her master for a pair of shoes. For her presumption he gave her several sound thrashings. When she sought to go to the commissioners, he stopped her. She went "to Seeke for Justice" she told him, and he replied that "he would give her Justice." He thereupon dragged her home and administered a further beating. After hearing a good deal of supporting testimony, the court passed a general order to which this complaint was referred. Four other servants of Smith not only supported Mary Hewes but joined with her in further complaints for relief from his cruelty and failure to provide adequate clothing. Joan Powell deposed that Smith made her work barefoot in the snow and allowed the servants nothing but hominy and salt "except wee will eat Stinking fatt." Save for a few pieces of beef or pork, she had had no sweet meat since she came. On the day he beat her for being idle, she claimed to have weeded three hundred corn hills, as against three hundred and fifty, the maximum most menservants could do. The court record shows that

It was debated whether according to the Statute in such Cases provided the Servts Should not be Sett free from so Cruel a Master as was party, Judge, and Executioner, But Considering Servts are mens Estates and the prsident might be of worse Consequence then intended, Doe order that for the future Henry Smith noe more strike any of his Servants but if they doe amisse bring them before some Comissionr to have the Complant examined and proved Then punish the Servts as the Commissionr shall find the fact deserue or reffer the matter to the next Court.

The court also ordered that none of the servants be removed by Smith from Accomac County without permission of the court, as it was feared that he intended to take them to Maryland outside the court's jurisdiction. He was to find them sufficient clothing and not to work them "unreasonably" by night. If he proved recalcitrant, the court agreed to submit to the governor the issue of whether servants "so ill used shall be sold to other masters for their times or set free."

But complaints against Smith continued to mount, and the court condemned him for beating his wife, children, and servants, for begetting two bastards by two different maidservants, for providing his wife, children, and servants with inadequate provisions; for not clothing his maidservant, Joan Powell, and sending her out on an island against her consent; for misappropriating an orphan's estate, for refusing to give security for his good behavior, and for suborning witnesses. Continuing in his refractory conduct, Smith was adjudged by the court "to be one of the most wicked of men." The governor was requested for further directions in this case. In adjudicating a complaint brought by his maidservant, Rachel Moody, whom he had cruelly treated, the court queried how it was that he had not followed the usage of the Bristol Tolsey and gotten an indenture or other contract of service before transporting her. Smith could produce none, and merely contended that "he brought her into the Country and therefore was his Servant." The court ruled that the act of assembly, providing that servants coming in without indentures were to serve according to their respective ages, did not necessarily apply to all those who arrived, some of whom might "in the strictest sense" be considered "but Debitors for Disburst's of passage." It appeared that Rachel had served Smith a number of years, was now over twenty-one, and heiress of an estate in Bristol of £20 per annum. The court therefore ordered Smith to produce by Christmas sufficient legal authority from Bristol to support his claim of service, and in the meantime discharged Rachel, requiring that she give security for her service if he was able to establish it legally. The court frankly distrusted Smith, and in order to prevent his forging Bristol papers, ordered that letters be sent to the mayor, aldermen, and persons of credit in that city to "explicate the present Controversy That when they are informed the Evill Life and demeanor of the sd Smith They may more knowingly treat Rachell Moody's Relations and detect the Errors if the sd Smith falsely pretends a Claim of service."

But Smith refused to mend his ways. Between 1668 and 1670 additional minor as well as more serious accusations were made against him. Richard Chambers and William Nash complained that, by agreement made with Smith in England, they were to have Saturday afternoon free to work for themselves, "which they proved in court to be their due." Despite a court order in their behalf, Smith refused them the agreed time off and denied making any such bargain in England. The court sharply called his attention to a previous confession he had made of such an agreement which was on the record. Therefore, unless he could bring legal proof, these two servants were not to be charged for taking Saturday afternoons off.

More serious, however, were the accusations against Smith of raping two maidservants, Mary Hewes and Mary Jones, and of causing the death of a manservant, "Ould John" by name, by administering a cruel beating. On the rape charges the court heard conflicting testimony, and expressed the opinion that Smith might "be guilty of a Rape though Charged by a Contemptable person who if she were so bad as Smith would Render her is not to Compare wth Smiths proued guilt. Therefore the Court put noe reputation in ballance agt the Charge of Rape, and haue at Large declared the mannor of Discoury wth the Rule for the Reason of their Judgmt that Smith is not Innocent." In determining whether the charges were outlawed by lapse of time, the court took into consideration "the incapacity of the person ravished The feare and dread Shee Liued in The many punishmts she Suffered and also for speaking of the Rape had no releife nor Cognizance taken their might be Reason of feare and prvention in Such a Country as Virginia where remoteness of dwelling did not speedily admitt access to Such as might heare and protect the injured." Accordingly the court committed Smith to prison to await the governor's order as to whether he should be bound over to the next General Court or dismissed with censure. The members of the court, recognizing the importance of this trial and the continued defiance of the prisoner, proposed to appear in person at the trial before the Governor and Council to show that they were not acting with malice toward him. They also ordered that there be drawn up a complete statement of the charges, court procedure, "together wth the Reasons and Rules in Law directing the Court in those their proceedings." The court then particularized the charges and its disposition of them, and, what was far more unusual, cited legal authorities to support its rulings.

As regards the charges against Smith of cruelty to his wife and children, the court attached three thousand pounds of tobacco from Smith's estate for their relief and for the purchase of "a bed to lie upon." As the court could not obtain from the governor a provision for substantial annual maintenance of the wife and children, she was permitted to go to her friends in England. The court sequestered as much of the estate as was necessary for their maintenance, but Smith seized this property and carried it to Maryland, leaving the children dependent upon charity.

The court referred the Governor and Council to Dalton's great treatise on the justice of the peace in order to justify its orders regarding Smith's cruel treatment of his servants and his failure to provide them with necessaries. Their legal defense adopted the following line: Justices of the peace had statutory jurisdiction over such matters. Their records or testimony is "in some cases . . . of as great force as indictment upon Oath of twelve men in Some other cases of greater force than an Indictment."[142] Of special interest, was the citation by the court of a passage from Dalton concerning servants which appears in the record as follows:

Dalton fol. 204 l.45 to l.50. And where the Servant shall bee negligent in his service or shall refuse to doe his worke then the Master may chastise his servant for such negligence or refusall so as hee doth it not outragiously, But if the Servant shall depart out of his Masters service and the Master happen after to lay hold of him yet the Master fol. 205 l.2 to l.4 may not beat or forceably compell his sd Servant against his will to returne or tarry wth him or doe his service but either must complaine to the Justice of Peace for his Servants departure or hee may have an accon against his Servant if being required to doe his service hee shall refuse.[143]

Common law authority was adduced to support the charge against Smith for causing Ould John's death. According to the testimony, John ran away, and when Smith caught him, he stripped him, tied him to a mulberry tree, cruelly whipped him, and put a heavy chain on his leg. He then ordered him, though weak and old, to grind by night and to work in the fields by day. As a result of this treatment, he died three weeks later. The court points out:

And forasmuch as o'r Law books instruct as in Stamfords Pleas of the Crown fol. 16; It is said, "If a man doe any unlawfull thing and kill a man by Mischance it is felony at this day if not Murther Or if a man strike another wth an Intent Only to beat him, yet if he shall dye of the beating it is felony and the Limitacon of Such Consequences of death by beating is declared that the Person so beaten die within a year and a day Stamf: fol 21 etc." In the opinion of the court Smith was no justice of the peace himself and therefore had no authority to punish his servant for running away, but ought to have brought him to a commissioner and "not to haue been Judge party and execuconr himself." Therefore the punishment was illegal and his cutting the hair of John from one side of his head was adjudged "a Malicious and Cruell act" as was his "Unlimitted punishmt of Whipping according to his own rage." Moreover such acts were in contempt of justices, for when Smith took Old John to Capt. Bownson, the latter refused to order him whipped, but told him that "Ould John had more need of a Nurse then to be whipped" and warned Smith to take better care of his servant. Smith thereupon defiantly punished John,

---

[142] The citations are apparently from the original Dalton edition. On these points: fols. 8, lines 46–49; f. 9, lines 22–26 (quoting Lambard 67); f. 10, lines 30–40. The court accepted Dalton's definitions of felony, homicide, and misadventure, citing fols. 179, 295, lines 28–32.

[143] Further citations from Dalton on the subjects of homicide and bailment were made. To justify inventorying Smith's estate on his removal to Maryland, the court cited Dalton, f. 308, l. 2 to l. 5. On forfeiture the court cited Wingate's *Abridgment of the Statutes*, f. 225, § 5, *De cattalis*, and Dalton, f. 363.

and, in the view of the court, it was highly probable that he "died the worst of deaths by being in Long Suffering with hunger hard Labour want of needfull Cloaths and Lodging" in an old tobacco house. The night he died with his very last words he accused his master of having beaten him to death. The court held Smith in custody for presentment to the Governor and Council on suspicion of the murder of his servant.[144]

Of the several charges against Smith which went to the Governor and Council, there is no record of further action having been taken as regards the charge of murdering John. In view of the action taken by the General Court in the rape charges, it is highly probable that Smith went scot free. According to the General Court minutes, although Smith had been indicted for rape committed upon Mary Jones and Mary Hewes, a grand jury returned ignoramus, and he was cleared by proclamation. Thereupon the court, in the face of such damning evidence of Smith's consistent brutality to his servants and family, ordered that both maidservants serve double the time they had been away from him. Smith decided to dispose of these two to other masters. Mary Hewes acknowledged having four years, five months, and fourteen days to serve, and Mary Jones four years.[145]

To relate all the recorded inhumanities of other masters and the calculated cruelties of she-devils among Virginia's mistresses [146] would be to give the screw many a turn and in the long run immunize the reader by harsh repetition. In 1661 Governor Berkeley, hardly famous as a humanitarian, wrote one county commissioner urging that a master be bound over to the county court, whose members were to see that "servants shall be christianly used." When the commissioner talked to the complainant maidservant, Mary Rawlins, she vomited blood several times, "a pint at least each time." A physician reported the marks of blows on her breast and stated that in his opinion her injuries were serious enough "to have rendered hir incapable of hir future happiness." Although the master, one John Russell, had accepted £20 sterling for the girl's release from a carpenter who was in love with her, he refused to let her go and beat her when she insisted upon her freedom. Russell's wife "flew upp" to the commissioner's face "and clapt hir hands at him saying she would be revenged of some of them." The master, equally

---

[144] Dalton, f. 100, l. 28–37; f. 416, l. 11–15, were cited as authority for detaining a prisoner under charge of felony until he came to trial.

[145] Accomac O.B., 1666–70, fols. 78, 82, 85, 95, 103 *et seq.*, 123–127, 132 *et seq.*, 147 *et seq.*, 176–179; *Va. Gen. Court Mins.*, p. 217 (1668–70).

[146] See complaints against Mistress Alice Travelor, Accomac, lib. II, fols. 231, 232 (1643); against Ralph Hunt's wife, York, lib. 1657–62, f. 76 (1658); against John Davis and wife, York, *ibid.*, f. 249 (1660), accused of having forced their servants to steal tobacco plants.

defiant, told the commissioner that "before he would bestow one penny" on Mary in reparation for her condition, "hee would venture a hanging for hir." He was placed under bond to keep the peace, but, on asking the court's forgiveness, was discharged from the bond.[147] Similarly defiant was Mistress Mourning Bray, who had nerve enough to charge the commissioners with bad manners in sending for her, to refuse to appear before them, and to swear very emphatically and profanely that she would not let her help "go to play or be Idle." When her servant told her that he had gone to the magistrate to complain of his lack of clothing and blankets, she ordered him to be stripped and given thirty-one lashes, after which she retorted: "Now you may goe to Justis Marable and Complain agin!"[148] Some masters defied the courts with impunity; others were less successful. There is one cryptic, but nonetheless significant, entry in the General Court minutes under date of September 20, 1680: "Cruel mistress prevented from having servants."[149]

As in other colonies, the courts of Virginia adjudicated complaints of insufficient food and clothing. The wife of Thomas Cork, according to testimony in the Charles City County court, "was a very shrewd woman to her servts" and "fed them wth the huskes that were sifted from the corn that was fitter to be given to horses then to Christians."[150] John Walter petitioned the Henrico court in behalf of his fellow servants that "their victuals being So ill dressed that they Could not Eat it, and their bed So short, and the Cloathing soe mean that they could not keep themselves warm with it."[151] Governor Nicholson shocked some of his Virginia neighbors by living in a low wooden house "worse than many overseers have" and stinting on his servants' food, allowing them just "one small dish a day among them."[152]

THE RICE AND SUGAR COLONIES. Statutes in the Carolinas dealing with oppression of servants reflected the course of legislation in both the tobacco colonies and the British West Indies. Following Barbados and Jamaica, South Carolina provided that ill-treated servants were to be discharged and imposed a fine for whipping a servant naked without

[147] York O.B., lib. 1657–62, f. 317 (1661); also Tyler, *Mag.,* I, 267; *WMCQ.,* 1st ser., III, 151.

[148] *Cal. Va. State Papers,* I, 99 (1706).   [149] *Va. Gen. Court Mins.,* p. 520.

[150] As a result of her hard usage, one of her servants ran away. Charles City Co. O.B., 1655–63, f. 357 (1663).

[151] Henrico O.B., V, f. 285 (1692).

[152] Affidavit of Robert Beverly, *CSPA, 1703–5,* No. 270, p. 103 (1704). For court order to provide suitable clothing, otherwise servant was to be disposed of until master obeyed, see Huddleston's complaint, *Va. Gen. Court Mins.,* p. 465 (1640). See also Spotsylvania O.B., 1730–38, fols. 265 (1733), 383 (1735).

order of a justice of the peace.[153] Later legislation actually limited the unconditional freedom provision. By act of 1717 a servant was not entitled to his freedom until the third complaint,[154] and an act of 1744 provided that, for a second offense, the servant could be sold by the justice for the remainder of his time.[155]

The dearth of extant judicial records for South Carolina and the uninformative, even cryptic, dockets of North Carolina account for the relatively few available illustrations of the way in which these statutory remedies were enforced.[156] On occasion the North Carolina justices discharged a servant who had been abused or placed an oppressive master in custody, but actually a larger proportion of decisions were found in the courts of that colony dismissing the servant's complaint as groundless and ordering him to return to his master than are revealed by the much fuller records of the tobacco colonies.[157]

The authorities in the southernmost seaboard colonies of Georgia and

[153] *S.C. Stat.,* II, 52 (1691); Simpson, *Practical Justice of the Peace,* pp. 17, 18, 231. C.O. 139:5 (Jamaica), fols. 6–9; C.O. 139:2, f. 161; Hall, *Acts Passed in the Island of Barbados* (London, 1764), p. 157 (1703). Antigua laws imposed a fine upon masters who failed to provide their servants with adequate provisions, clothing, or medical care. On the third complaint the servant was to be freed by the justices, which was also to be the remedy for cruel usage. Baskett, *Acts of the Charibbee Leeward Islands,* No. 153, cl. 14 (1716); *Laws of Antigua, 1690–1804,* I, 320, 321 (1755). North Carolina set a fine to the injured party for unauthorized whipping. *N.C. State Rec.,* XXIII, 62, 63 (1715), 192 (1741); James Iredell, *Laws of the State of North Carolina* (Edenton, 1791), c. xxiv; Davis, *Justice of Peace,* p. 310.

[154] The act fixed reproof for the first offense, fine for the second. E. McCrady, "Slavery in the Province of S.C., 1670–1770," Amer. Hist. Assn., *Ann. Report,* 1895, p. 634.

[155] A fine of £4 proclamation money was to be imposed for the first offense. *S.C. Stat.,* III, 621–629.

[156] According to the Chowan, N.C., Rec., lib. 1730–34, 1740–48, Richard Haughton, constable, appeared in court in 1744 "and made oath that he summoned all the Masters and Mistresses of familys in his district." But whether it was to warn them in regard to the treatment of their help can only be surmised.

[157] *Complaint dismissed and servant returned to master:* Frances Beatman's complaint, Onslow Precinct, lib. 1734–37, f. 5 (1735); Lovet's case, Craven, lib. 1730–46, f. 79 (1746); Dr. Fontain's case, *ibid.,* lib. 1747–56 (1751); Gibbs's complaint, Cartaret, lib. 1723–47, f. 54 (1742–43), despite some testimony that, in addition to beating the lad, the master had said he would poison him "if he could get any poison." *Master bound to good behavior:* Wheeler's case, Craven, lib. 1730–46, fols. 63, 65 (1740); Lydle's case, *ibid.,* lib. 1745–56 (1747), where the master was obliged to give security for paying servant her freedom dues and for not carrying her out of the province. *Servant discharged:* Mills' case, *ibid.,* lib. 1730–46, f. 13 (1731), discharged, but the question of "title" was raised here as well as unlawful coercion; Hodgson's case, Pasquotank, lib. 1737–55 (1747); Roberts' complaint, Craven, lib. 1767–75 (1769); Owen's case, Cartaret, lib. 1764–77, f. 74 (1775), where an orphan girl was taken away from her master and mistress and sent to her stepfather on the ground that she "Was in A Likely Way to Gett Corrupted in her morals." See also depositions of Elizabeth and Frances Hodges, Chowan Co. court files, Edenton (1768); Rex v. Alleyn, Robertson's complaint, *ibid.* (1732); Borden's case, Cartaret, lib. 1723–47, f. 72 (1746); Murphy's case, Craven, lib. 1757–62 (1761); Upton's case, Cartaret, lib. 1764–77, f. 39 (1769), servant to be placed in custody of a third party until next court.

the Floridas not infrequently dealt with complaints of bad treatment accorded immigrant servants. Contemporaries differed sharply as to the way in which Georgia's German servants were treated.[158] The fact remains that when they had the chance to redeem their passage money and obtain their freedom, many took advantage of the opportunity. The charges, doubtless highly colored, brought against Dr. Turnbull and his overseers of having harshly disciplined the servants at the New Smyrna settlement in East Florida and of half starving them have previously been considered in connection with the insurrection that broke out in that colony.[159] In many ways this type of settlement was unique to the Southern colonies. Unique also was the exceptionally severe treatment meted out to Turnbull by Governor Tonyn, doubtless inspired in no small part by personal and political antagonism. In fact, the governor himself does not escape from his brush with Turnbull without severe imputations of having dealt harshly with his own workmen.

The British West Indies were no paradise for white servants. As early as 1640 the Council of Barbados ordered one master who had tortured his servant "by hanging him upp by the handes and putting fired matches between his fingers," inflicting severe injury to his right hand, to set the servant free, to pay him 5,000 lbs. of cotton by way of compensation, and to pay for his medical care in addition.[160] Colonel William Brayne of Jamaica wrote the Protector in 1656 urging the importation of African Negroes on the ground that, "as the planters would have to pay for them, they would have an interest in preserving their lives, *which was wanting in the case of bond servants,*" numbers of whom, he charged, were killed by overwork and cruel treatment.[161] Similar concern was expressed by the Barbadian Assembly, which was impelled to enact a law prohibiting the burial of a servant until the body was viewed by the nearest justice of the peace or constable.[162] Complaints continued to mount, and the home authorities were obliged

---

[158] See *Ga. Col. Rec.,* IV, 63, 231; VI, 351; XX, Pt. I, 105, 261; Pt. II, 484; XXIII, 56; XXVI, 47.

[159] See *supra,* pp. 178–181.

[160] The master was to remain in prison during the governor's pleasure. V. T. Harlow, *A History of Barbados, 1625–1685* (Oxford, 1926), pp. 303, 304, citing from Council Mins., May 7, 1640, Davis Coll., Bk. 4, R.C.I. Three other instances—two from 1656 and one from 1657—are also cited from the council minutes. In one the order of release was conditional upon a finding by the justices that the servant had been beaten excessively "and without just and good cause."

[161] Thurloe, *State Papers,* V, 473.

[162] *Laws of Barbados, 1648–1718,* Law No. 21, cl. xiii.

to prosecute investigations from time to time.[163] Despite the testimony of Ligon that Christian servants received worse treatment than Negro slaves because the latter were "subject to their masters forever," whereas the white servants were their masters' property for only five years,[164] the Negro slave was in the long run exposed to more persistent indignities and even harsher treatment. Little moved by "arguments drawn from motives of humanity," West Indian planters, charged one observer on the eve of the American Revolution, were "deadened to every feeling but commercial deductions." [165]

LEGAL AND POLITICAL RIGHTS OF SERVANTS

THE COLONIAL BOUND LABORER dwelt in that shadowland between freedom and slavery. To the author of *Moll Flanders* white servitude and slavery were identical. In fact, the system of indentured servitude differed in certain important essentials from Negro slavery. In the first place, the colonial settlers did not consider the servant inferior as a human being, but recognized him to be a fellow Christian, not differentiated by race. A slave had only those rights which were granted by law. A bound servant enjoyed all rights, whether political or legal, except those specifically denied him by law or contract. His mobility, his freedom of occupational choice, and certain personal liberties were curbed merely for a term of years, whereas a slave was bound for life, and his children inherited his unfree status. Detailed consideration has already been given to certain limitations upon the freedom of the bound servant arising largely out of the prevailing concept that the master had a property interest in his servant's term. Aside from such limitations, it is appropriate to consider as a concluding problem the extent to which the bound servant enjoyed the legal and political rights of free settlers.

The Servant's Day in Court. Not only legal safeguards but also ethical standards imposed by religion served to mitigate class injustice in the colonies and to assure the servant his day in court. The pious settler could not fail to remember the injunction of Job: "If I did despise the cause of my manservant or of my maid servant, when they contended with me,

---

[163] See C.O. 1:30, No. 150. When Sir Richard Dutton urged the Barbadian Assembly to pass an act to "restrain bad masters and overseers from cruelty to their Christian servants," the legislature resolved that masters should be protected against malicious complaints as well as servants against ill-treatment. *CSPA, 1681–85*, Nos. 59, 250 (1681), 1258 (1683); *1685–88*, No. 1858 (1688); *1697–98*, No. 107, p. 62; *1699*, No. 262, p. 122; *1702*, No. 244, p. 167 (1702); *1706–8*, Nos. 173, 175, p. 80 (1706).

[164] Richard Ligon, *True and Exact Account of Barbadoes* (London, 1657), p. 44.

[165] HMC, *Rep.,* XXXVIII, 300–301 (1767).

what then shall I do when God rises up?" Thus the Virginia Company, concerned lest oppression or fraud enter into the making of contracts of employment, sought to prevent masters from holding their servants to "intollerable and vnchristianlike conditions." The magistrate was often regarded as labor's shield against the injustices of the oppressive master. One servant, who had a wife and five children in England, petitioned John Winthrop, "whom the lord hath sett in place to iudge the cause of the poore," asking him "to stand my frend (beeing destitute of any other in this land) that I may part from my m[aste]r without any trouble." [1] Aside from securing from the courts a measure of relief on grounds of undue correction, insufficient food and clothing, and, in the case of apprentices, inadequate instruction or abandonment, servants had considerable success in enforcing the principle that the essence of servitude was service for a limited term specified by contract or prescribed by custom. In suing for freedom on the ground of having completed their service or attained their majority, servants obtained their discharge by the courts in over 60 per cent of such cases.[2]

The servant's suit was generally instituted by petition. In order to protect this proceeding from attack on the ground that it differed from English practices a statute was enacted in Maryland in 1698 which provided that no judgment should be reversed for "want of Judiciall process, or that the same was not tryed by Jury or any matter of form Either in the Entry or giving of Judgment, provided it appears by the Record that the parties defendant were Legally summoned and not condemned unheard." [3] From this procedure evolved the petition for freedom of slaves.

In support of such a petition or in defense of a suit brought by a master the servant appears to have enjoyed full testimonial capacity in

[1] *Va. Co. Rec.*, II, 113 (1622); *Winthrop Papers*, IV, 105 (1639), 238, 239 (1640).

[2] A few typical instances from the many available may be cited: N.Y.G.S., lib. 1732–62 (1759); Middlesex, N.J., Court Mins., lib. I (1689); *Upland Court Rec.*, p. 102 (1678); Lancaster, Pa., Road and Sess. Docket, No. 4, 1768–76 (1774); West Chester, Pa., Q.S., lib. 1733–42, f. 112 (1737), lib. B. (1775); York, Pa., Q.S., lib. I, fols. 1, 2 (1751); Sussex, Del., Rec., f. 182 (1683); Kent, Del., lib. 1699–1703, f. 82a (1703); *Md. Arch.*, XLIX, 82–84 (1662), 331, 332 (1664); LIII, 599–600 (1665), LIV, 485 (1671), LX, 46–47 (1666); Md. Prov. Court, lib. 1679–84, f. 105 (1680); Ann Arundel, lib. 1702–4, fols. 618 (1704), 679 (1705); Cecil, lib. BY, No. 1, 1770–71 (1771); Charles, lib. 1720–22, f. 72; Prince George, lib. A, 1696–99, f. 6 (1696); Somerset, lib. AW, 1690–91, f. 43 (1691); lib. LO–7, f. 224 (1715); Talbot, lib. AB, No. 8, fols. 2 (1696), 196 (1697); Charles City, Va., lib. 1655–65, f. 604 (1665), court failed to sustain defense that the Negro servant had been disobedient, freedom granted; Henrico, Va., lib. II, f. 348 (1692); Lancaster, Va., lib. 1666–80, f. 193 (1671); Cartaret, N.C., lib. 1778–89, f. 43 (1783); *S.C. Grand Council J., 1671–1680*, pp. 62, 63.

[3] *Md. Arch.*, XXXVIII, 117 (1698). See also C. T. Bond and R. B. Morris, *Proceedings of the Maryland Court of Appeals, 1695–1729* (*American Legal Records*, I) (Washington, D.C., 1933), p. xxv.

the colonial courts.[4] The record of proceedings in the master-servant litigation considered in this study fully substantiates the view that the servant was not only considered competent to testify against his master,[5] but was also permitted to be a witness in his behalf. Despite the authority which the master had over his servant, the interests of the two were not considered identical, and hence the servant was not disqualified as an interested party.[6]

Sometimes a servant wished to fulfill his contract and petitioned the court to restrain the master from dismissing him before the expiration of his term. Cases in this category are, however, less frequent than suits for freedom; most disgruntled servants appear to have been anxious to put as much territory as possible between themselves and their masters. The requirement that the master secure the permission of the court before dismissing his servant is evidence that the colonial courts considered articles of indenture bilateral agreements capable of enforcement by either party.[7]

While the colonial courts were open to servant and master alike, they were not always open on an equal basis. The workman or servant who sought the intervention of the courts ran certain heavy risks not shared by the master. Many of the colonies provided that servants who "unjustly" complained or molested their masters would be subject to whipping at the order of the court or to serving extra time, running to from three to six months for each such "causeless complaint."[8] One master was awarded substantial damages by a Maryland court for the unjust molestation by his servant.[9] Symptomatic of the unfriendliness of the bench to litigious servants was the unusual order of the Charles County

[4] In Great Britain, the testimony of servants was admitted by 20 Geo. II, c. 19 (1747). Richard Burn, *The Justice of the Peace* (London, 1800), IV, 244.

[5] But cf. Edmonds v. Pinner, *Md. Arch.*, LIII, 592, 602 (1665). When Jacob Lumbrozo was presented for having brought an abortion upon his maidservant, Elizabeth Wilde, who charged him with responsibility for her pregnancy, he saved himself by marrying her, thus disqualifying her from appearing as a witness against him. *Md. Arch.*, LIII, l–li (1663). For an analogous case, see Smith's case, *Pa. Col. Rec.*, II, 5 (1700). See also R. B. Morris, *Studies in the History of American Law*, pp. 197–199.

[6] Sir Geoffrey Gilbert, *The Law of Evidence* (London, 1769), p. 138.

[7] See, e.g., Philadelphia Q.S., lib. 1779–82 (April, 1780); Kent, Del., Court Rec., lib. 1703–17; Newcastle, Del., G.S., lib. 1778–93, f. 83 (1779). The court ordered one master who asked permission to dismiss an habitual runaway whom he described as acting "like vnto a runagate" to keep him until he could send word to the boy's father "and take further order with him about him." Barnes v. Wade, *Plymouth Col. Rec.*, III, 126 (1657). See also *supra*, pp. 17, 18, 376, 377; *Moravian Rec.*, II 714 (1772).

[8] *Md. Arch.*, I, 53 (1639), whipping at discretion; Hall, *Acts of Barbados*, pp. 35 (1661), double time lost, 157 (1703), whipping; *N.Y. Col. Laws*, I, 47 (1665), 3 mos. extra, 157 (1684), 6 mos. extra. See also Harvye's case, Lower Norfolk, lib. II, f. 62 (1644), 20 lashes; Davis, *Justice of Peace* (New Bern, N.C., 1774), double time lost.

[9] This was Thomas Gerrard, Lord of St. Clement's Manor. *Md. Arch.*, XLIX, 94, 122, 124, 126 (1663).

court of Maryland at the March, 1673 session prohibiting any attorney from appearing for a servant against a master, "but such as the Court shall appoint." [10]

While the servant enjoyed full testimonial capacity, he often had practical difficulties in obtaining corroborative testimony from his fellow servants, who might very well be intimidated by the master. This condition was not peculiar to the colonies. In one contemporary London mayor's court action brought by an apprentice for cruel treatment, the attorney noted in his brief: *"Note that the plts* [plaintiff's] *Witnesses are the Defts* [defendant's] *Journeymen and will be unwilling to discover the beatings."* [11]

Far less favorable treatment appears to have been accorded servants by the West Indian courts than they received in the continental colonies. In 1722 Governor Hart of Antigua criticized "the most unjust usage that was given to artificers and labourers who were not able to go to law with the persons they contracted with for their wages." In his opinion these injustices tended "to the enslaving of the servants and dispeopleing the Island of such labouring men." He strongly supported a statute which put workmen "on the same footing with their fellow subjects in Gt. Britain." [12] From our vantage point the attainment of that goal would hardly have assured a tolerably high standard of justice in labor relations.

Suffrage and Jury Service. Normally the colonial suffrage was confined to freemen with property.[13] Generally speaking, only a small minority of the male inhabitants were legally qualified to vote for the representatives to the legislatures, as the property qualification excluded large numbers of artificers and journeymen. In general, bound servants were excluded from the county and town suffrage.[14] It stands to reason, then, that labor had virtually none of the political power in the colonial period that it has acquired since the Civil War.

There were occasional exceptions to the exclusion of the laboring

[10] The order recited that several attorneys had managed servant causes "to the Mrs and Mrss greate charge and dammage." *Md. Arch.*, LX, 496.

[11] Howard v. Hanson, London Mayor's Court Briefs, 1698–1705 (c. 1704), Guildhall.

[12] *CSPA, 1722–23*, No. 190, p. 91 (1722).

[13] In early Massachusetts and in the old New Haven colony, freemen were also required to be church members, but in the former a property qualification was substituted under the royal charter. The Connecticut regulation of 1659 established a qualification of £30 of "proper personal estate." See C. M. Andrews, *Col. Period of Amer. Hist.*, II, 104, 117; Osgood, *Amer. Col. in 18th Century*, III, 127.

[14] Property qualifications ranged from 50 to 100 acres of land or real estate or personalty worth from £40 to £60 or yielding 40s. income. The Pennsylvania Constitution of 1776 provided for manhood suffrage. For the property qualifications in general, see A. E. McKinley, *The Suffrage Franchise in the Thirteen English Colonies* (Philadelphia, 1905); C. F. Bishop, *History of Elections in the American Colonies* (New York, 1903).

population. The Virginia Company constitution of 1621 granted to all inhabitants of the colony the right to vote for the burgesses.[15] This was in effect until 1655 when a law was passed limiting the franchise to "all housekeepers, whether Freeholders, leaseholders or otherwise tenants."[16] While this law excluded inhabitants who had not served their terms, it provided a more democratic base for the franchise than did the subsequent act of 1670, which confined it to freeholders and housekeepers "answerable to the publique for levies."[17] Just how did this restriction work out in practice? Governor Spotswood complained in 1713 that any one could vote, "though just out of the condition of a servant, and that can but purchase half an acre of ground."[18] As a result of criticism by the conservative interests, the freehold qualification was defined in 1736 as one hundred acres (reduced to fifty in 1769) without a house, or twenty-five acres with a house, or the ownership of a house and lot in any town.[19] In order to make sure that servants working at trades in towns should not qualify, acts of 1742 and 1752, respectively, provided that no servant should be allowed to vote on the ground of his being an inhabitant or resident of Williamsburg or Norfolk. The franchise was restricted to those who had served as apprentices to some trade within the city for a term of five years and were certified by the court of hustings to be inhabitants and householders.[20] Virginia also excluded from the franchise anyone who had been a "convict or any person convicted in Great Britain or Ireland, during the term for which he is transported," even though such a person might be a freeholder.[21]

In South Carolina a substantial property qualification was required of freeholders to vote for assemblymen.[22] Nevertheless, complaints were made that at the election for members of the Assembly in 1701 abuses had been permitted. Not only aliens but "a great number of Servants and Poor and indigent Persons, voted promiscuously with their Masters and Creditors."[23] The opposition also charged that in the elec-

---

[15] Hening, I, 112. This was far in advance of England. Even the Levellers, who favored working class reforms, proposed that servants and those who received alms be barred from the suffrage. D. M. Wolfe, *Leveller Manifestoes of the Puritan Revolution* (New York, 1944), pp. 402, 403.

[16] *Ibid.*, p. 411.

[17] Hening, II, 220. During Bacon's Rebellion this act was repealed (*ibid.*, p. 425), but at the end of the uprising the property requirement was restored.

[18] Va. Hist. Soc., *Coll.*, New ser., II, 1; *WMCQ*, 1st ser., VII, 67.

[19] *WMCQ*, 1st ser., VII, 67; 2d ser., VII, 258 (1776). See also Osgood, *op. cit.*, II, 249, 250.

[20] Hening, V, ch. xxvi (1742); VI, 262 (1752). See also *WMCQ*, 2d ser., VII, 258.

[21] Hening, VII, 519 (1762); *WMCQ*, 2d ser., VII, 257.

[22] Cooper, *S.C. Stat.*, III, 657 (1745).

[23] Daniel Defoe, *Party-Tyranny, or An Occasional Bill in Miniature; as now Practised in*

tion of 1703 "Jews, Strangers, Sailors, Servants, Negroes and almost every French Man in Craven and Berkly County came down to elect, and their Votes were taken." [24] As apprentices and other indentured servants were excluded from voting by the act of 1717,[25] there was a clear implication that they had previously participated in the elections.[26] There is no question, however, as Josiah Quincy later observed, that ultimately neither servants, laborers, nor mechanics were represented in the legislature of South Carolina.[27] Illegal voting by servants appears to have occasionally occurred in other colonies. Servants appear to have participated in the Pennsylvania election of 1705, and there is evidence that even on later occasions members of the servant class attempted by electioneering tactics to influence the course of voting.[28] When the Revolution broke out, the long-standing £50 property qualification in that province was abolished and the franchise put on a democratic basis.[29]

In town elections servants were customarily disfranchised. In Connecticut towns, however, "hired servants" could be admitted as inhabitants along with land- and house-owners provided they were deemed by the majority of the town to be persons of "Honest Conversation." [30] In New York the completion of the term of apprenticeship was one of the ways of obtaining the franchise.[31] As a result of a contested election case in 1773, Albany specifically denied to bound servants the right to vote during the time of their servitude.[32] Nevertheless the town franchise was more widely held than the county franchise. It was obtainable by birth and redemption as well as by apprenticeship. By an act of the common council of New York City in 1762 those unable to pay the price set for the freedom for merchants or artisans were admitted without cost,[33] a practice which had prevailed in the mayor's court for many

---

Carolina (London, 1705), reprinted in A. S. Salley, Jr., ed., *Narratives of Early Carolina* (New York, 1911), p. 239.

[24] W. J. Rivers, *A Sketch of the History of South Carolina to the Close of the Proprietary Government by the Revolution of 1719* (Charleston, 1856), Appendix, p. 459.

[25] *S.C. Stat. at Large*, III, 2–4; McKinley, *op. cit.*, pp. 147, 148.

[26] In county elections in North Carolina Governor Dobbs through an error issued writs empowering the "inhabitants" instead of the "free inhabitants" to take part in elections. *N.C. Col. Rec.*, VI, 303. A freeholder suffrage was also established in North Carolina. See Osgood, *op. cit.*, IV, 151.

[27] Mass. Hist. Soc., *Proceedings*, XLIX, 454.

[28] *Pa. Mag. of Hist. and Biog.*, II, 452; McKinley, *op. cit.*, pp. 284, 285. For the efforts of the colonial workmen of Philadelphia to secure a widening of the franchise, see J. P. Selsam, *The Pennsylvania Constitution of 1776* (Philadelphia, 1936), p. 138.

[29] Selsam, *op. cit.*, p. 138.   [30] *Conn. Code, 1750*, p. 99.

[31] N.Y. Hist. Soc., *Coll., 1885*, p. 52 (1695). See also E. S. Griffith, *History of American City Government: the Colonial Period* (New York, 1938), p. 203.

[32] Munsell, *Hist. Coll. of Albany*, I, 254 (1773).

[33] *M.C.C.*, I, 18, 222; V, 326; N.Y. Hist. Soc., *Coll., 1885*, p. 533.

years before that date.[34] As a result, barriers to the freedom were virtually removed and many journeymen and craftsmen gained admission. In municipal elections in the colonies generally from 20 to 30 per cent of the adult male population participated.[35]

Finally, in the choice of militia officers, which in the Puritan colonies was left in the early years to the soldiers of the company or regiment, servants were specifically disqualified from voting.[36] Plymouth denied the vote to persons under twenty years of age, whether children or servants, but it is by no means clear that bound servants and apprentices who had attained that age were denied the militia franchise.[37] Even as late as the Revolution the New England militia was looked upon as a hotbed of democracy, with a great many officers in proportion to men and the pay of officers and men too nearly equal, although the practice of having the men choose their officers was by no means confined to New England.[38]

The composition of the jury was of the utmost importance to laborers and servants engaged in litigation with their masters. Throughout the colonies servants were excluded from juries and the average workman had little chance to serve on one. Colonial property qualifications for petit juries were patterned after those in force in contemporary England.[39] In Massachusetts and New York, for example, the customary requirement that jurymen be freeholders or possessed of a personal estate to the value of £50 [40] gave a distinct class angle to master-servant litiga-

[34] See R. B. Morris, ed., *Sel. Cases, Mayor's Court*, pp. 34, 178; R. F. Seybolt, *The Colonial Citizen of New York City* (Madison, Wis., 1918), p. 16.

[35] Griffith, *op. cit.*, pp. 210–213. In New York and Annapolis the percentage was closer to the latter figure.

[36] *Mass. Bay Rec.*, I, 188 (1637). For the procedure of nominations or elections in the early period, see Morrison Sharp, "Leadership and Democracy in the Early New England System of Defense," *Amer. Hist. Rev.*, L (1945), 256–260.

[37] *Plymouth Col. Rec., Laws*, p. 39; McKinley, *op. cit.*, p. 366.

[38] J. C. Miller, *Origins of the American Revolution* (Boston, 1943), p. 503. For the procedure by which the company chose its own officers, see C. K. Bolton, *The Private Soldier under Washington* (New York, 1902), pp. 25, 26. For a vote by corps on the subject of changing the rations, see *Pa. Arch.*, 2d ser., XI, 24 (1779). For an agreement to enlist in the Virginia militia subject to the choice of officers by a majority of the subscribers, see *Va. State Papers*, I, 431 (1781).

[39] 4 Wm. and Mary, c. 24, reenacted from Charles II, provided that all jurors at quarter sessions or assize shall have £10 "by the yeare att least."

[40] *Mass. Acts and Resolves*, I, 74 (1692); N.Y. *Col. Laws*, I, 387 (1699), 708 (1710), 1021 (1719), II, 345 (1726). The amount was raised to £60 freehold in 1741. N.Y. *Col. Laws*, II, 185. An alternative of personal estate of like value qualified a man in New York City and Albany. *Ibid.*, III, 599. In Massachusetts the royal province required the juror to have either a personal estate worth £50 or real estate of freehold yielding at least 40*s*. annually. The property qualification for jury service had been fixed in that colony by the act of 1670 (Whitmore, *Mass. Col. Laws*, p. 148; reaffirmed in 1672), although modified on a number of occasions thereafter (*ibid.*, p. 321 [1681]; Emory Washburn, *Sketches of the*

tion.[41] Rhode Island was an exception to the rule. Her statute of 1642 declaring that only freeholders were eligible to serve on the jury [42] was later set aside by an act giving the court "the power to take any man they judge fit for that service." [43] Where, as in New York, certain towns were given the alternative qualification of personal estate, jury panels were in considerable part made up of artisans of the employer ranks.[44] It must be borne in mind that these property qualifications were a carry-over from the mother country. The author of *Lex Londinensis* notes "that an Apprentice cannot sue out his Indenture against his Freeman but in this Court," and remarks quite naively: *"and the Master need not doubt a fair trial; the Juries being all Masters, and the Court constantly shew them all just and lawful favour."* [45]

The bench was recruited exclusively from the property-holding and employer class. In Virginia, where the act of assembly of 1662 provided that the justices of the peace be "of the most able, honest and judicious persons of the county," [46] that office tended to become hereditary. In the list of justices of that province we find such prominent families or personages represented as the Lees, the Robinsons, the Pendletons, the Blands, the Carters, the Stiths, the Chamberlaynes, the Diggeses, the Harrisons, George Washington and other members of his family, George Wythe, Edmund Scarburgh, and Thomas Jefferson.[47]

The Servant's Right to His Own Personalty and Realty. At law the indentured servants had qualified property rights. Protective legislation in their behalf was soon necessary, as many had come to the colonies as immigrants, too easily exploited by masters and assignees. In

---

Judicial History of Massachusetts from 1630 to the Revolution in 1775, p. 97). Typical property qualifications in other colonies: *Del. Statutes*, I, 241 (1741); II, 1072 (1793). Hening, III, 176–177 (1699); *ibid.*, New ser., I, 19 (1792). *N.C. Col. Rec.*, I, 199 (1669); XII, 875–876 (1778).

[41] See also *infra*, pp. 522, 523.   [42] *R.I. Col. Rec.*, I, 124.

[43] *Ibid.*, p. 356. Cf. also attorney general's report in 1693 concerning the petition of Sir Matthew Dudley and others to establish a joint stock company to engage in mining, etc. in New England: "I think that the exemption of their workmen and servants from serving on juries should be conditional." *CSPA, 1693–96*, No. 55, p. 158 (1693).

[44] See J. Goebel and T. R. Naughton, *Law Enforcement in Colonial New York* (New York, 1944), p. 467.

[45] *Lex Londinensis*, pp. 45, 47.   [46] Hening, II, 69.

[47] See "Justices of the Peace of Colonial Virginia, 1757–1775," ed. H. R. McIlwaine, Va. State Library, *Bulletin*, XIV, Nos. 2 and 3 (1921) (Richmond, 1922), pp. 55 *et seq.* Typical of other areas: At a court of quarter sessions held in Tryon County, N.Y., Dec. 13, 1774, the following justices sat: John Butler, trusted agent of Sir William Johnson and father of the notorious Loyalist, Walter Butler; Sir John Johnson, who had just succeeded to the title of baronet and fallen heir to the greater part of his father's estate; and Jelles Fonda, whose family were early settlers in the area. All three were of the substantial propertied class. Tryon Q.S., 1774, N.Y. Hist. Soc.

1662 a law was enacted in Virginia to prevent importers of servants from disposing of servants' goods. The law provided that servants bringing goods into the colony should have the right to dispose of them to their own advantage and to have an absolute property in them.[48] Nevertheless, this qualification was added—permission of their master was necessary to the disposal of the goods.[49] In other words, this unique statute placed indentured servants in the same position as wards and minors. It is by no means clear that this rule prevailed throughout the American colonies.[50]

Headrights were generally given to masters rather than to servants.[51] In 1735 one master memorialized the Board of Trade that the land to be granted his seventeen servants in South Carolina in accordance with the governor's instructions for encouraging newcomers and settling townships be granted in his name.[52] In a great many cases, of course, the servant received a grant of land upon application to the authorities upon the expiration of his term. The Georgia authorities provided the German servants at Vernonburgh with cattle and, when they perished of the "distemper," sent them another herd.[53]

The white servant was the occasional recipient of gifts *inter vivos,* was legally authorized to accept payments for extra work for others with the permission of his master, and very frequently was remembered by benevolent masters when making testamentary disposition of their estates. A good illustration of the gift *inter vivos* is found in the Delaware court records [54] as early as 1679:

> Be itt knowne unto all men by these prsents that I: Thomas Craniton of Duke Creeke in delowar River doe by these prsents freely give unto my servant John Pridgemore the Running of one Sowe during the Terme of his apprentiship and att the End and Expiracon of his said tyme that hee the said Pridgemore shall have free Liberty to take the sowe away wth all hur Increase, as wittnesse my hand in New Castle this 25 of January 1678.
>
> (signed) Thomas X Cramton
> [2 witnesses] his marke

The abovesd Wryting is a true Coppy of the originall by Sam: Land and Robberd hutchinson produced in Cort and by their Request Recorded.

---

[48] See petition of Holmes, Spotsylvania, Va., O.B., 1724–30, f. 258 (1728).

[49] Hening, II, 164 (1662). See also Starke, *Justice of the Peace,* p. 319.

[50] See *contra:* Crumpton's complaint for clothes withheld by master. Prince George, Md., lib. B, 1699–1705, f. 352 (1705). See also Watkins's estate, *Essex,* I, 13 (1641), where the master was allowed to keep the clothes of his deceased servant who died within six or seven weeks after landing, as he had paid for the servant's passage and "had no service of him of value."

[51] See *supra,* pp. 397 f.   [52] *J. Commrs. Trade and Plantations, 1734/5–41,* p. 53 (1735).

[53] *Ga. Col. Rec.,* VI, 134 (1744).   [54] *Newcastle, Del., Court Rec.,* I, 292 (1679).

The quarterly court of Essex, Massachusetts, when it sat at Salem, Hampton, Salisbury, or Ipswich, was generally located at a tavern or lodging house and it was customary for the court to order that sums ranging from five to ten shillings be given to the servants of the establishment "for their attendance."[55] This would certainly indicate that servants had the right to accept gratuities.

Under the circumstances it is not surprising to find that servants occasionally appear in court as creditors to press their legal claims. In one unusual instance a servant advanced to a third party a sum of "eighty pound in Cash," for which a mortgage was given on a windmill and farm.[56] Even more unusual, perhaps, was the gift made in 1634 to his master by Robert Healing, bound to Thomas Young of Accomac, of a manservant he seems to have acquired from a merchant or ship's captain.[57]

When John Davis's will was probated in the Essex court, it revealed total cash gifts amounting to £32, of which £10 went to his "dame Clarke," 20s. to one of his master's daughters, and £5 to another.[58] This was the exception, as inventories of servants' estates generally disclosed clothing rather than cash as the principal item.[59]

While sessions records reveal the seamier side of master-servant relations, the records of probate court and the old colonial will books are indicative of a more intimate and sympathetic relationship. Where a master left a bequest to a servant, it was not merely to comply with the letter of a contract of indenture, but an expression of responsibility and often of friendship and affection. Naturally this practice was not confined to the colonies. In the mother country it had been traditional to leave small bequests to household servants.[60]

First in order of objects bequeathed to servants was clothing, although money, land, tools, cattle, and freedom from indentures were frequently named. When Leonard Calvert, first governor of Maryland, died, he left some of his clothes to two of his servants.[61] In 1665 William Thorne of Somerset County, Maryland, left his servant, John Richards, 300 acres of land, provided that he remained in the service of Mistress Thorne

---

[55] See, e.g., *Essex*, I, 259 (1652); III, 409, 452 (1667).

[56] Petition of Nowell, *et. al., Essex*, III, 9 (1662). See also Goodwin v. Downeing, *ibid.*, I, 161 (1649).

[57] Accomac O.B., 1632–40, f. 46.   [58] *Essex*, V, 160 (1673).

[59] *Essex Probate Rec.*, I, 13 (1641); III, 9 (1675).

[60] See, e.g., HMC, *Rep.*, XIII, 186. See also will of John Colleton, of Whitecomb Rawleigh, County of Devon, Baronet, proved Nov. 30, 1754: "To my servants £5 each instead of mourning . . ." *S.C. Hist. and Geneal. Mag.*, XV, 91; and of Joseph Iles, merchant of Bristol, who left three servants £6 apiece. *Ibid.* (proved April 26, 1750).

[61] *Md. Arch.*, IV, 314.

until he reached the age of twenty-one.[62] When Thomas King of Exeter left his servant, William Willy, fifty acres of land, it was in fulfillment of an earlier promise.[63] Most valued of all grants to a servant would be that of his or her "tyme of servitude." [64] One Virginia planter at the end of the seventeenth century freed his servant and, in addition, left him £5, together with a silver tobacco box, wearing apparel, and other items.[65]

The Servant's Right to Engage in Business. In order to prevent employees from cheating their masters, from working for themselves on their masters' time, or from making outside contacts which might lead to enticement or undue competition, the colonies in general had strict curbs on unauthorized trading with other men's servants.[66] Typical of the New England group was the order of the Massachusetts Court of Assistants as early as 1630 providing a fine and corporal punishment at the court's discretion for any person, man or maid, selling any commodity during his or her time of service without license from his or her master.[67] A similar provision was included in New Haven's comprehensive law of 1656.[68] The Duke's Laws, 1665, provided a fine or corporal punishment for any servant selling a commodity during the time of his service. The person buying from the servant would be compelled to restore the goods to the master and forfeit double the value thereof to the poor of his parish.[69]

[62] *Md. Cal. of Wills, 1635–1738,* I, 51 (1665). [63] *Essex,* III, 409 (1667).
[64] *Abstract of Norfolk Co., Va., Wills, 1637–1710,* p. 22 (1662).
[65] Potter's will, *WMCQ,* 1st ser., XVIII, 193 (1691). For other typical bequests by masters to their servants, see, *e.g., Lincoln, Me., Probate Rec., 1760–1800, p. 241* (1791); *Essex, Mass., Probate Rec.,* I, 9 (1645), 107 (1637), 141 (1650), 161 (1653), 223 (1655), 233 (1665), 333 (1660), 385 (1661), 405 (1662), 439 (1664), II, 56, 61 (1666), 123 (1665), 147 (1669), 242 (1671), 251 (1670), 264 (1672), III, 328 (1679), 382 (1680); *Essex Quarterly Court Rec.,* III, 231 (1665), 363 (1666), IV, 411, 446 (1671); *Conn. Probate Rec.,* I, 18 (1648); *Court of Albany, Rensselaerswyck, and Schenectady Mins., 1675–80,* II, 321 (1678); *Md. Cal. of Wills,* III, 105, 127 (1708), 128 (1709), V, 23 (1719), 30, 94 (1720), VI, 5 (1726), 7 (1725), 227 (1731), VII, 52 (1735), 135 (1735), 258 (1738), 262 (1686); *VMH,* II, 278 (1701), V, 405 (1655), XXXIV, 284 (1671), 347 (1701); *WMCQ,* 1st ser., XVII, 271 (1697), XXIV, 38 (1652); Jackson's will, S.C. Court of Ordinary, 1672–92 (1683); Cottingham's will, *S.C. Hist. and Geneal. Mag.,* VIII, 203 (1683).
[66] See *Some Records of Sussex Co., Del.,* p. 98 (1683). At common law the master had an interest in the labor and acquisitions of his servant, but he could not maintain trover for any property acquired by the servant. However, in the case of an apprentice, his gains went to the master. 1 Salk. 68; Bacon, *Abridgement* (London, 1832), V, 366; Graydon, *Justice's and Constable's Assistant,* p. 15.
[67] *Assistants,* II, 5.
[68] *New Haven Col. Rec.,* I, 601 (1656). For trading with Indian or Negro slaves or servants in Connecticut, see *Conn. Pub. Rec.,* V, 52 (1708).
[69] *N.Y. Col. Laws,* I, 47. A Pennsylvania statute of 1700 provided a penalty of treble the value of the goods traded, the servant to be subject to serve for a term equivalent to double the value of the goods sold. *Pa. Stat. at Large,* II, 54–56 (1700).

A considerable number of *qui tam* suits were successfully brought in Maryland against persons who had unauthorized dealings with servants.[70] By statute such persons were liable to substantial fines and the delinquent servants to corporal punishment.[71] Virginia made those trading with servants liable to a month's imprisonment and security for good behavior, and, for the second offense, to four times the value of the articles traded.[72] In 1672 the General Court of that province sentenced Richard Case for "private and underhand dealing" with the servants of another to make full satisfaction "according to the CVth Act of Assembly," and provided further that the order be entered in the minutes to serve as "a President to deterr others from doing the like and incurring the penalty of the said Act."[73]

Unauthorized trading with servants was forbidden in the rice and sugar colonies. In Barbados the trader would be liable to forfeit to the master treble the value of the goods traded and 500 lbs. of sugar.[74] An Antigua law provided that 500 lbs. of tobacco would be forfeited to the master for such an offense and another 500 lbs. to the public treasury. Servants convicted of unauthorized trading would be "severaly

[70] See Evans v. Foxhall, *Md. Arch.*, LVII, 125 (1668); Norris's Case, *ibid.*, XLI, 511 (1671); Beard *qui tam* v. Sporne, Ann Arundel, lib. 1702-4 (1703); cf. also Majesty v. Hanim, *ibid.* (1705).

[71] Corporal punishment for the servant was provided under Maryland law. *Ibid.*, I, 500 (1663). Philip Fine, carpenter, fined 1,000 lbs. of tobacco for dealing with the servants of Daniel Dulany and William Reynolds. Ann Arundel County, 1745-47, f. 120 (1746). See also Her Majesty v. Collins, Queen Ann, 1710-16, f. 117 (1710), not guilty. Case was occasionally used for this offense. Lane v. Broughton, Somerset AW, 1690-91, fols. 62, 63vso (1688). Such offenders also laid themselves open to the suspicion of receiving stolen goods. Proprietary v. Calahan, Annapolis mayor's court, 1720-84, f. 5 (1720). In 1691 a cooper was prosecuted for dealing with a Virginia runaway and purchasing a 16-foot boat which the servant had stolen from his master "for an invaluable [*sic*] consideration, which might have been Sufficient [*sic*] Suspicion to have Secured both the Runaway and Boat according to Law, but fraudulently and craftily intending to frustrate" the master, he concealed the servant and the boat, which the indictment charged to be "flatt contrary to the laws and institutions of this Province enjoyning and authorizing all persons to take up all such Suspitious persons coming into this Province without a pass, as also agt the Act inhibiting all persons to entertain or deal and truck with any hireling or Servant without the Masters knowledge." Fine confessed to that part of the indictment relating to buying the boat, which he was ordered to deliver into the custody of the sheriff and to give security for good behavior and appearance. Somerset AW, 1690-91, fols. 36, 37 (1691).

[72] *Va. Gen. Court Mins.*, p. 482 (1639); "Abridgment of Virginia Laws," 1694, *VMH*, X, 156, 157. Hening, I, 274 (1643); II, 118, 119 (1662); III, 447 (1705); VI, 357-369 (1753).

[73] *Va. Gen. Court Mins.*, p. 301 (1672). See also Kirton v. Richardson, Northumberland O.B., 1666-78, f. 84 (1672), punishment remitted at plaintiff's request, but defendant ordered to pay 800 lbs. of tobacco and costs; Sarah Hinnes's case, York O.B., 1706-10, f. 149 (1708), remanded to prison on suspicion of dealing with servants and of concealing the goods of another until she gave security for good behavior; sentenced to pay complainant 7s. 6d. with costs. Cowley v. Sulkin, Henrico O.B., 1737-46, f. 10 (1737), judgment for £20 current and costs. See also Wallace's petition, *VMH*, XI, 60, 61 (*c.* 1647) with reference to an appeal to the General Court in an action of trespass brought upon the law against trading with servants.

[74] Hall, *Laws of Barbados*, pp. 35-42; Jennings, *Laws*, p. 17 (1661).

whipped."[75] South Carolina set the extreme penalty of ten times the value of the goods purchased,[76] and North Carolina provided that the sum of £10 would be forfeited to the master.[77]

Servants, unless specifically authorized by their masters, were under a disability to make valid contracts for their employers. They were treated in the law the same as minors and wards.[78] Nevertheless masters could and did specifically authorize their servants to buy and sell for them.[79] However, in the absence of such specific authority the defendant might seek to avoid payment on the ground that he was an indentured servant when he contracted the obligation to the plaintiff.[80]

Occasionally servants were permitted to trade on their own accounts or to work for themselves.[81] John Griggs, a "gentleman" of York County, Virginia, permitted his servant, Andrew James, to work for himself the following year, for which he was to pay his master a specified amount of tobacco and plant and tend to a stated number of corn hills. The master agreed not to hinder his servant in working at his trade of carpentry except during the time when he was expected to plant the corn.[82] A Marylander permitted his servant, bound to him for seven years, "to have the Liberty and priviledge of practising as an Attorney in Baltimore County Court and *the benefitt thereof to Convert to his own use*" and further agreed not to require him to perform any servile labor.[83]

---

[75] Antigua MS Laws, 154:1, f. 39 (1669). See also act of 1693, Montserrat MS Laws, f. 45.

[76] Trott, *Laws of S.C.*, I, 52 (1696); Cooper, *S.C. Stat.*, III, 487 (1738).

[77] This was recoverable by information in any court of record. For prosecutions for dealing with slaves, see *N.C. Col. Rec.*, II, 96, 114 (1713).

[78] See *Conn. Pub. Rec., 1665–78*, p. 50 (1666).

[79] See power of attorney granted by Attorney-General William Calvert to his servant, Robert Simmons. *Md. Arch.*, LVII, 426 (1668).

[80] In Chivers v. Greenby the Maryland Provincial Court held that such a plea was insufficient in law because the defendant's attorney did not join in demurrer in due time. *Md. Arch.*, LVII, 423, 424 (1669).

[81] See *Albany Notarial Papers*, p. 445 (1677), allowing the employee to work "three or four weeks in the harvest for his own profit, provided he serve so much longer afterwards."

[82] York O.B., 1675–84, f. 192 (1679).

[83] Agreement between William Reid and Colonel John Thomas, Ann Arundel, 1702–4, f. 476 (1703). This may have been a case of servitude for debt, as the service was to terminate upon payment of £30 sterling.

PERSISTENT PROBLEMS OF LABOR RELATIONS
IN THE LIGHT OF EARLY AMERICAN
EXPERIENCE

THE EXPANSION of the American economy and its rapidly-changing technology have created vast new problems of labor relations without parallel in our early history. Nevertheless, a great many contemporary labor problems are not really new at all but were significant problems in the colonial and Revolutionary periods. These early problems have been comprehensively treated, not only because a fuller understanding of the relations of government and labor will add appreciably to our knowledge of the first two centuries of American history, but also because the successes and failures of the political and legal measures adopted then may help us in creating and evaluating policies and instrumentalities to deal with certain persistent labor problems of our own generation.

A labor shortage prevailed during the first two centuries of American history. To solve the problems arising from an economy of scarcity the governmental authorities on this side of the Atlantic, from the beginning of colonial settlement, regulated labor as well as productive enterprise and devoted considerable attention to assuring harmonious relations between employer and workman. Prior to the rise of trade unionism, two systems for the control of white labor were recognized by early governments in America—free labor and indentured servitude. The latter system was in fact declining by the end of the Revolutionary era, but it cast its shadow on later trends; the former constitutes the prevailing labor pattern for our modern industrial society.

The manpower scarcity of early days dictated a favorable attitude toward immigration as a source of competent labor. Hamilton in his Report on the Subject of Manufactures declared: "To find pleasure in the calamities of other nations would be criminal; but to benefit ourselves, by opening an asylum to those who suffer in consequence of them, is as justifiable as it is politic." [1] Mass unemployment has con-

---

[1] A. H. Cole, *Industrial and Commercial Correspondence of Alexander Hamilton* (Chicago,

tributed to the scuttling of this cherished American tradition of according a hearty welcome to immigrants—a reversal in attitude reflected in such legislation as the Immigration Law of 1924, which substituted for the earlier policy of selection the new policy of restriction.[2]

By means of the bound labor system the vast majority of European workmen were recruited for this country, in some cases voluntarily, in others by compulsion, down to the end of the eighteenth century. While the practice of formally indenturing immigrants appears to have died out long before the passage of the Thirteenth Amendment,[3] the introduction into this country of contract labor has continued down to fairly recent years. The redemptioner system was in fact revitalized at the close of the Civil War.[4] Owing to the bitter opposition of native labor, particularly organized labor, later legislation was enacted which forbade the importation of workers under contract.[5] Nevertheless, down to the beginning of the first World War the practice of inducing emigrants to come to this country by promises of employment or advertising and promotional literature was a well-established source of Ameri-

---

1928), p. 288. Immigrants were expected to engage in gainful employment. As Franklin pointed out, "America is the land of labour, and by no means what the English call Lubberland and the French *Pays de Cocagne." Information to Those Who Would Remove to America (c.* 1783). Washington, who sought in 1784 to purchase the terms of redemptioners trained as housejoiners or bricklayers, declared: "I would not confine you to Palatines; if they are good workmen, they may be from Asia, Africa or Europe; they may be Mahometans, Jews or Christians of any sect, or they may be Atheists." U.S. George Washington Bicentennial Commission, *Pamphlet Series,* Nos. 1–16 (Washington, 1932), p. 136.

[2] Immigration Act of 1924, Sect. 11, par. (b). U.S. Dept. of Labor, *Immigration Laws, Immigration Rules and Regulations of Jan. 1, 1930* (Washington, 1937), pp. 43–63. See also President Wilson's earlier veto of literacy tests for immigrants (1915). *Cong. Rec.,* 63d Cong., 3d sess., LII, 2481–2482.

[3] The first heavy blow to be struck at the system was administered by the Supreme Court of Pennsylvania in 1793 in Respublica v. Keppele, 2 Dallas 197 (1793). In holding that, under the act of 1700, the only persons who could be bound to service were infants in apprenticeship and imported redemptioners, the court took a position contrary to the previous law and history of the province and state. Another blow was dealt by the Indiana courts in 1821 holding indentures unenforceable under a state constitutional provision based upon the Ordinance of 1787 prohibiting involuntary servitude in the Northwest Territory. Mary Clark's case, 1 Blackf. 122 (1821). Specific performance of contracts or indentures "heretofore existing" was enforced in Illinois under the provisions of the constitution of 1818. Nance v. Howard, 1 Ill. 242, and other cases cited by F. S. Philbrick, ed. "The Laws of the Indiana Territory, 1801–1809," Ill. State Hist. Lib., *Coll.,* XXI (Law Series, II, Springfield, Ill., 1930), p. cxxvin. But cf. Chief Judge Woodward's opinion, *Transactions of the Supreme Court of the Territory of Michigan, 1805–1814,* ed. W. W. Blume (Ann Arbor, 1935), I, 417.

[4] An act of 1864 permitted the immigrant's wages to be pledged for a year for the fulfillment of the contract. This was repealed four years later.

[5] The enforcement of the Alien Contract Labor Law of 1885 was hamstrung by court decisions narrowly defining labor contracts. Congress in 1907 specifically included manual labor and added "offers and promises of employment" to the original "contracts or agreements." Exceptions exist in the case of domestic servants and skilled workers for new industries. During both World Wars these barriers were set aside in the case of Mexican and West Indian laborers.

can immigration.[6] It is interesting to note that just when the formal redemptioner system was disappearing in America it was revived with great vigor in the British sugar colonies after the abolition of slavery, in the tea plantations of the East Indies, and in the world-wide migrations of Chinese coolie labor—not only to the colonies of European powers, but as recently as the first World War to France and Belgium. European migratory labor very largely falls into this category. In fact, contract labor is still widespread in tropical areas.[7] The contract labor system encourages the migration of tractable workers of low standards, which has the effect of lowering wages and breaking strikes. Hence, American labor has a stake in the elimination of such retrograde labor conditions in other parts of the world, not alone on humanitarian grounds but also because these conditions constitute a threat to decent working standards at home.[8]

In colonial times the numbers of bound laborers were augmented by the practice of binding out to service persons convicted of crimes against property and of imposing extra service upon servants for various types of wrongful conduct, including absenteeism and desertion. While this source of labor has long since been abolished, in its stead the convict labor system has evolved to create serious problems of industrial competition.[9] Analogous to the colonial system is the modern institution

[6] The passage of the Immigration Act of 1917, 39 Stat. L. 875, virtually ended this traffic. One of the most flagrant violations of the laws against importing contract laborers took the form of the padrone system, for which see U.S. Industrial Commission, *Reports*, XV (1901), 432.

[7] For the contract labor problem outside the United States, consult, e.g., International Labour Office, "Studies and Reports, Series O (Migrations)," No. 3, *Migration Laws and Treaties* (3 vols., Geneva, 1928–29), No. 5, *The Migration of Workers* (Geneva, 1936); "Series B," No. 26, and *Labour Conditions in Indo-China* (Geneva, 1938); P. C. Campbell, *Chinese Coolie Emigration to Countries within the British Empire* (London, 1923); J. B. Guitera, *Le Contrat-Type pour l'emploi des travailleurs étrangers en France* (Paris, 1924); *American Federationist* (July, 1943); *International Labour Review* (Nov., Dec., 1942; Feb., Aug., Nov., 1943).

[8] Contract labor, peonage, and other forms of debt bondage still exist in some Latin American countries (notably Bolivia), in Africa, and in some areas of India. The Forced Labor Convention of 1930 outlawed forced labor for private purposes completely, but exempted emergency and war situations, and in a number of the British African colonies forced labor has been reintroduced as a war measure. See also American Labor Conference on International Affairs, *Studies in Postwar Reconstruction*, No. 1 (New York, 1944). The employment of German forced labor after the second World War to help reconstruct areas ravaged by the Nazis is thoroughly justifiable on economic, moral, and psychological grounds.

In order to protect contract laborers from exploitation, Carter Goodrich contends that the Australian method of supervising contracts or the placing of immigrants under the protection of government employment exchanges might serve as well as the American attempt to prohibit the system completely. See "Contract Labor," in *Encyclopaedia of the Social Sciences*, IV, 342–344. Cf. Walter Wilson, *Forced Labor in the United States* (New York, 1933), pp. 118–144.

[9] See U.S. Bureau of Labor Statistics, *Bull.*, No. 372 (1925), pp. 2–4, 14–15, 107–108; No. 595 (1933), pp. 1, 13–32; L. N. Robinson, *Should Prisoners Work?* (Philadelphia, 1931), pp. 11, 16; *Monthly Labor Rev.* (July, 1944), pp. 137–138.

of peonage, a system of compulsory service based upon indebtedness, often the result of the payment by the employer of fines and costs in cases of misdemeanors, especially of violations of vagrancy laws.[10] The debtor was a significant source of bound labor in the seventeenth and eighteenth centuries, but this source has in substance been outlawed by abolishing imprisonment for debt and by bankruptcy laws. In recent times state legislatures have attempted to make it a criminal offense for an employee to break a contract of service which he has made and for which he has received money or other personal property, although such statutes have been held to be in conflict with the Thirteenth Amendment.[11] The pauper and the child orphan were customarily bound out to labor by the colonial authorities. Vestigial remains of this practice are still found in the terminology of contracts putting out dependent minors to foster parents,[12] but placing children in orphan asylums, charitable institutions, and foster homes has superseded binding out. The present trend is toward extending public aid to keep dependent children in their own homes in order to maintain wherever possible the original family grouping.

Apprenticeship, a form of bound labor imposing an obligation upon the employer to teach his employee a trade, was, in the absence of vocational schools, the only available method of trade education in the seventeenth and eighteenth centuries. The idea of early training in a craft, strongly endorsed by the political scientist John Locke, was a sound one and not quickly abandoned.[13] Unfortunately the underpaid "green hand" in mills and factories bore little resemblance in fact to the earlier apprentice in the handicraft trades. Despite more formal methods of schooling and changing technological conditions in industry,

[10] The Supreme Court has upheld the right of Congress to outlaw contracts to work out fines. See Clyatt v. U.S., 197 U.S. 207 (1904); U.S. v. Reynolds, 235 U.S. 133 (1914). Cf. U.S. v. Gaskin, 320 U.S. 527 (1944); Pierce v. U.S., 146 Fed. (2d) 84 (1944); Wilson, *op. cit.,* pp. 84–117.

[11] By state laws, juries are allowed to presume that a person receiving money as an advance on an agreement to work and then failing to work received the money fraudulently. On three occasions the Supreme Court reversed convictions obtained under such laws. Bailey v. Alabama, 209 U.S. 219 (1911); Taylor v. Georgia, 315 U.S. 25 (1942); Williams v. Pollock, 14 So. 2d. 700 (1943). See also "Report on Peonage," *Sen. Doc.,* No. 747, 61st Cong., 3d Sess. (1910).

[12] While the binding out of orphans and destitute children under contracts of indenture or apprenticeship had fallen into disuse by the end of the 19th century, New York did not prohibit such binding out until 1923. *N.Y. Laws, 1923,* c. 306. For survivals in Pennsylvania of old apprenticeship indenture forms when children are placed in foster homes, see Grace Abbott, *The Child and the State* (Chicago, 1938), II, 231–234. See also H. W. Thurston, *The Dependent Child* (New York, 1930). From the point of view of the master as well as the child such contracts might well be considered compulsory. The significant point is made in James Parker, *Conductor Generalis* ([Philadelphia, 1722], p. 12) that the power given to church wardens to bind out apprentices "doth necessarily imply, that such who are fit to be Masters *must* take them."

[13] For Noah Webster's ideas, see A. O. Hansen, *Liberalism and American Education in the Eighteenth Century* (New York, 1926), p. 248.

apprenticeship has survived in modified form in the twentieth century as an important source of skilled labor in numerous trades. Modern apprenticeship is no longer based on custom, but on trade agreements. Indentures are not uniformly required. The apprentice no longer lives with the employer nor is he required to perform menial services about the employer's home nor restricted in his private life. He is generally paid a living wage while learning the trade.[14] After the Civil War a number of the Southern states established an apprenticeship system for the emancipated Negroes, rather thinly disguising a permanent semi-servile status for the freedmen.

The employment of women and children was implicit in the colonial labor program.[15] The tendency of the age was to regard the child as a little adult [16] and to train him accordingly. The entire household was employed on the typical colonial farm.[17] Church and state both encouraged family industry as a patriotic obligation. For example, the *Boston Gazette* for August 14, 1753, carried this typical item:

On Wednesday an excellent sermon was preached before the *Society for encouraging Industry and employing the Poor,* by the Rev. Samuel Cooper, after which £453, old Tenor, was collected and in the afternoon near 300 Spinners, some of them children of 7 or 8 Years old and several of them Daughters of the best Families among us, with their Wheels at Work, sitting orderly in three Rows, made a handsome Appearance on the Common.

[14] The apprenticeship period is generally for 4 yrs. or less and runs between the ages of 16 and 21. For apprenticeship agreements, see P. H. Douglas, *American Apprenticeship and Industrial Education* (New York, 1921), pp. 53–84; S. Scrimshaw, *Apprenticeship: Principles, Relationships, Procedures* (New York, 1932), p. 8; A. B. May, *The Problem of Industrial Education* (New York, 1927), pp. 216–222; D. D. Lescohier and Elizabeth Brandeis, *History of Labor in the United States, 1896–1932* (New York, 1935), pp. 270–289. In the founders, metal, machine-tool, building, and printing trades, among others, apprenticeship still has considerable vitality, and in some areas has expanded extraordinarily during World War II. See Abbott, *op. cit.,* I, 239–241; U.S. Bureau of Labor Statistics, *Bull.,* No. 459 (1928). For a proposed uniform state apprenticeship law, see Abbott, *op. cit.,* pp. 247–255. In connection with the postwar reconstruction program, Great Britain has recently established an Apprenticeship and Training Council. The request of organized labor during the second World War that learners receive no less than the common-labor rate of pay was denied by the War Labor Board, although some wage adjustments were made possible by reclassifying learners. *Monthly Labor Rev.* (January, 1945), pp. 41–45. Cf. War Manpower Commission, Apprentice-Training Service pamphlets; *Yale Rev.,* XXVI, 474–490; S. Slichter, *Union Policies and Industrial Management* (Washington, 1941), Chapter II.

[15] See Ola E. Winslow, *American Broadside Verses from Imprints of the 17th and 18th Centuries* (New Haven, 1930), pp. 198, 199.

[16] See Sandford Fleming, *Children and Puritanism* (New Haven, 1933), pp. 60, 61.

[17] Washington used women on his plantations for such tasks as grubbing, carrying rails, putting up fences, leveling ditches, spreading dung, planting corn, weeding peas and pumpkins, picking apples, and threshing rye. Diaries, III, 299, 301, 304, 305, 335, 342, 379, 393 418 (1788). The "Old Farmer" found it necessary to caution his readers as late as 1809 against overworking women in the fields. "Consider the tenderness of her sex, and the delicacy of her frame," he enjoined. Kittredge, *The Old Farmer and His Almanack,* p. 182.

During the Revolution women undertook many of the tasks of men.[18] Many bound servants, other than apprentices, were minors, and an impressive proportion of all emigrants to the colonies were children and young people. The courts sought to safeguard their condition of employment, but, save for restrictions on the term of apprenticeship, there was no legislation comparable with the modern child labor laws, which, in the case of Federal enactments, have had to pursue a thorny constitutional path. As most industrial production in the colonial and Revolutionary periods was still in the home, shop, or putting-out stage, children in the main enjoyed working conditions which were indisputably superior to those prevailing in the early factories, where apprenticeship degenerated into a method of exploiting cheap labor.

After the Revolution the advocates of industrialization regarded the employment of women and children as necessary, because of "the scarcity of hands." Hamilton in his classic survey of industrial prospects remarked that four sevenths of the workers in the cotton mills of Great Britain were women and children, "of whom the greatest proportion are children, and many of them of a tender age." Not only would their employment relieve the prevailing labor shortage in this country, but it would serve to give the farmer a supplementary income, Hamilton maintained.[19] Reporting in 1791 on the progress of his manufacturing venture in Rhode Island, Moses Brown frankly declared that "as the Manufactory of the Mill yarn is done by Children from 8 to 14 years old it is as near a Total Saving of Labour to the Country as perhaps Any Other that can be named."[20] It must be borne in mind that as late as the turn of the present century eight-year-old children were regularly employed in the textile industry of the South.[21]

Many aspects of the master's quasi-proprietary interest in the services of his servant have shown considerable vitality even in our own time. In the seventeenth century servants could as a rule be sold or assigned

[18] For the employment of women in a Virginia munitions plant, see *Cal. Va. State Papers,* I, 41 (1781).

[19] Cole, *op. cit.,* pp. 259, 269.

[20] *Ibid.,* p. 77, and pp. 85, 192, 203, 204, 208, 226, 301. See also Washington, *Diaries,* IV, 37 (1789); Tench Coxe, *An Essay on the Manufacturing Interest of the United States* (Philadelphia, 1804), p. 15; S. Rezneck, "The Rise and Early Development of Industrial Consciousness, 1760–1830," *J. Econ. and Bus. Hist.,* IV, 792, 793.

[21] See U.S. Industrial Commission, *Reports,* VII (1900), 229, 234, 494, 503, 529, 551. In 1899 there were still 24 states which had no minimum age requirements for children employed in manufacturing. See W. F. Ogburn, *The Progress and Uniformity of Child Labor Legislation* (New York, 1912), p. 71. For more recent statistics, see U.S. Bureau of the Census, *Census of Occupations, Abstract Summary* (Washington, 1932), pp. 3–5; *Monthly Labor Rev.* (Nov., 1944), pp. 1034, 1035.

and were deemed the property of the master's estate. The strict laws relating to harboring or enticing them grew out of this property concept of the master-servant relationship. The son of Charles Read, the New Jersey ironmaster, indignantly denied that his father's works harbored an employee from another ironworks. "We have always made it an invariable rule at our Works," he declared, *"never to be assistant in robing a Person of his Property by Secreating* [secreting] *his Servant. The Contrary Conduct is base and unjust as well as ruinus to the Interest of Iron Masters."* [22] Governor Sharpe of Maryland compared the property interest of the planters in their servants with the estate of an English farmer consisting of a "Multitude of Cattle." Franklin's retort in the Continental Congress to Thomas Lynch, who had contended that slaves should not be taxed any more than land, sheep, cattle, or houses, all of which were property, was, in the light of colonial history, even more applicable to the prevailing legal concept of the servant as property than to the slave. There is "some difference between them and sheep," he caustically observed. "Sheep will never make any insurrections."

Vestiges of this property concept survive in modern state legislation prohibiting the enticement of employees although the employment is at will.[23] Colonial experience, rooted in medieval and Tudor labor legislation, provides us with an enlarged historical perspective, essential for an understanding of the origins of the modern civil action for causing a breach of contract. Even today enticement is no academic question. During the second World War the War Manpower Commission endeavored to prevent the pirating of workers in critical areas and set up procedures for employers to curb the "raiding" of workers in certain skilled occupations.[24]

Absenteeism was a perpetually critical problem in master-servant relations. It was most acute in Pennsylvania and the Southern colonies where the heaviest extra service penalties were exacted for it. Comparison of newspaper advertisements with the records of absentee cases in the colonial courts discloses the helplessness of the administrative and judicial machinery to restore fugitive servants to their masters and to keep them at work. In Philadelphia one company of master craftsmen

---

[22] C. R. Woodward, *Ploughs and Politicks: Charles Read of New Jersey* (New Brunswick, N.J., 1942), p. 91. Cf. White, *Slater Memoirs* (2d ed., 1836), p. 84.

[23] Ludwig Teller, *The Law Governing Labor Disputes and Collective Bargaining* (3 vols., New York, 1940), I, 64. Ten Southern states at the present time provide either a criminal penalty for enticement or a civil suit for damages or both.

[24] See *Monthly Labor Rev.* (Sept., 1942), pp. 460, 462.

took the unusual step of insuring themselves against such losses. Although at-will employment contracts have in modern times displaced the older form of long-term service contract, absenteeism remains an acute problem in contemporary industry, even in times of crisis.[25]

In the colonial period, employers could be held accountable to some extent for their servants' criminal misconduct, but in the field of tort liability no sweeping doctrine of the responsibility of masters was ever adopted—despite the implications of isolated and unrepresentative dicta. The colonial courts adhered fairly closely to the contemporary trends of English common law, according to which the master was liable for acts committed by his servant in the execution of the master's authority or for his benefit and without specific command. The colonial courts do not seem to have offered the employer the three loopholes found in modern tort law. These are: 1) the "fellow servant" rule, whereby an employer escaped responsibility for all accidents in which an injury could be attributed to the negligence of another employee;[26] 2) the doctrine of "assumption of risk," whereby an injured employee who had known of the employer's negligence with respect to the hazard causing the injury but who nevertheless voluntarily entered into or continued on his job did so at his own risk;[27] and 3) the doctrine of contributory negligence.[28] It is doubtful whether servants in colonial times could have recovered damages from their masters for injuries occurring in the course of their employment where their fault or negligence could have been proven. On the other hand, masters were expected to provide medical assistance for bound servants who fell ill in the course of their employment. This was the closest approach in the colonial period to any concept now embodied in our workmen's compensation acts.[29]

Finally, a further bar to the recovery for injuries of servants, the common-law rule according to which the right of action for personal

[25] *Ibid.* (Jan., 1943), p. 1.

[26] Priestly v. Fowler, 3 M. and W. 16 (England, 1837); Murray v. S.C. Ry. Co., 1 McMullen (S.C.) 385 (1841); Farwell v. Boston and Worcester Ry. Co., 4 Metcalf (Mass.) 49 (1842). T. A. Street, *The Foundations of Legal Liability* (3 vols., Northport, N.Y., 1906), II, 470. See also American Law Institute, *Restatement of the Law of Agency* (2 vols., St. Paul, Minn., 1933), II, §§ 474–491.

[27] See Harry Weiss, "Employers' Liability and Workmen's Compensation," in Lescohier and Brandeis, *Hist. of Labor in the U.S.*, p. 566; Street, *op. cit.*, I, 157; *Restatement . . . Agency*, II, §§ 521–524.

[28] T. Cooley, *The Law of Torts* (3d ed., 1906), p. 1457. American Law Institute, *Restatement of the Law of Torts* (4 vols., St. Paul, 1934–39), II, §§ 463–466; *Agency*, II, § 525.

[29] These statutes provide for compensation to be paid to servants for harm arising out of and in the course of their employment, irrespective of fault. Restatement, *Agency*, II, § 528.

injury expired on the death of the injured party, was generally operative in the colonies. Departures from this rule usually involved cases of death resulting from criminal conduct or intervention by colonial legislatures, but in no case uncovered was an employer required to pay damages for a fatal accident to a workman. It was left to Lord Campbell's Act [30] and subsequent enabling legislation passed in this country to provide relief where the death was caused by a wrongful act which would, if death had not ensued, have entitled the party injured to maintain an action to recover damages in respect thereof.[31]

More than two centuries before the Granger Cases arose, colonial governments had recognized the principle that certain classes of business of a monopolistic character were subject to control in the interest of the general community. Labor itself, owing to constant shortages, was considered a monopoly and was subjected in the seventeenth century in nearly every colony to maximum-wage controls and in some cases to minimum-hour controls as well. Most persistent of the experimenters with wage fixing were the New England governments. After some two generations the attempt to control wages, either by legislative fiat or by the exercise of administrative discretion, was gradually abandoned, even more rapidly than in England, where the system became largely ineffective by the first part of the eighteenth century.

However, during the American Revolution, as a result of the rapid depreciation of paper money, various state governments attempted to set maximum wages and prices. These regulations were drawn up by state legislatures and regional conventions and relied for sanctions primarily upon the boycott and social ostracism. They failed, not because of the impossibility of regulation per se, but rather because of the failure of the Continental Congress and the states to stem the currency crisis. Without a stabilized currency, control of wages and prices proved impossible of accomplishment. This experience undoubtedly fostered the rise of a laissez-faire program during the Confederation interlude. The abolition of internal restrictions on business, when coupled with provisions for the regulation of commerce between the states and safeguards for the protection of home industries from foreign competition, would, according to American entrepreneurs, lay the foundations for a revival of prosperity.

The Fair Labor Standards Act of 1938 is evidence that the govern-

[30] 9, 10 Vict. c. 93.
[31] F. B. Tiffany, *Death by Wrongful Act,* 2d ed. (Kansas City, Mo., 1913), § 19; *Columbia Law Rev.,* XV, 621.

ment is once more concerned with the regulation of the wages and hours of labor. This act was passed when the country was in the grip of an economy of abundance, which had supplanted the older economy of scarcity, and when labor had attained an influence in political life unparalleled in the first two centuries of American history. The objective of the act was the promotion of high wages and short hours. Hence, except for wartime emergencies, a minimum-wage policy has taken the place of the old maximum-wage policy of the colonial and Revolutionary era. The efforts of the Director of Economic Stabilization in the second World War to control wages through the National War Labor Board and prices through the Office of Price Administration have an objective similar to that of the Revolutionary state legislatures and regional conventions—the curbing of wartime inflation. A realization of the difficulties inherent in executing so vast and complicated a program —despite the more comprehensive and effective controls adopted by this country in the second World War—should give us a more sympathetic attitude toward the pioneer efforts of the Revolutionary fathers.

Overt acts by employees, individually or collectively, to better their working conditions preceded by many generations the formal strike called by the trade union. A note of protest by individual workers runs through our colonial records. Lacking the protective legislation and administrative machinery of modern times to assure them a living wage and satisfactory conditions of employment, disgruntled labor adopted one or the other of two patterns of behavior—incorrigible conduct or legal redress by petition to the courts. The former was a natural way of protesting against conditions of employment by workers customarily tied to long-term contracts. There was truly a method in their madness. In the post-Revolutionary period the story is told of one of Samuel Slater's apprentices who found Slater "too strict." When he told his more experienced fellow worker that he "could not stand it," he was advised to "act like the Devil, and Slater will let you off." [32]

Throughout the length and breadth of the original states, workers were enjoined to obedience to their masters or overseers and strict observance of their contracts. The master had the right to chastise the disobedient servant as well as the slow or incompetent one, provided that the punishment was not excessive or unreasonable. Considering the fact that all servants and most workmen were excluded from juries by property qualifications and that the bench was exclusively recruited from the employer class, an extensive study of the complaints brought against

[32] H. N. Slater's reminiscences of his father, in Weeden, *Econ. . . . Hist. of N.E.*, II, 913.

masters for abusing this power indicates that the courts, especially in the Northern and Middle colonies, made serious efforts to curb employers who were cruel and abusive or callous to their workers' welfare. Nevertheless, as even royal governors and judges were known to resort to the cat-o'-nine-tails when their servants' work was unsatisfactory or their deportment displeasing, these curbs too often appear to have been ineffective, not to say quixotic. As long as John Jay's favorite maxim that "those who own the country ought to govern it" was virtually in effect, justice for the laboring man was precariously dependent upon a fortuitous conjunction of the humanitarian impulses and economic interests of those in power.

Aside from administering corporal punishment, the master could, if he wished, secure specific performance of the labor contract. In some of the Southern colonies, notably in Virginia and South Carolina, he might also, as in the case of absenteeism, be awarded extra service for insubordinate conduct. However, he might prefer to bring a civil suit for damages for breach of contract or else a criminal action, for in some colonies the statutes were sufficiently broad to justify the intervention of the courts to insure discipline and obedience of workers under contract as well as indentured servants.

Because of the fluid character of the colonial labor market, labor combinations were at best temporary affairs, generally confined to the licensed trades, which were regulated as businesses invested with a public interest. Such combinations were generally frowned upon by the authorities and occasionally were prosecuted. In Georgia they were clearly considered illegal. However, the sweeping prosecutions founded upon parliamentary enactments which characterized the industrial history of eighteenth-century England found no parallel in the colonies. While one set of objectives of combinations of mechanics or laborers, masters or journeymen, appears to have been better working conditions, higher wages, fees, or prices for the manufactured product, an equally insistent end was the maintenance of the monopoly of the craft or trade. In this latter objective labor was encouraged by the town authorities, who for a considerable period made the completion of a term of apprenticeship a prerequisite to opening up one's own shop or who limited the trades and crafts to admitted inhabitants. By the mid-eighteenth century, laissez-faire tendencies led to a marked decline in the enforcement of these restrictions, and the outsider began to enter into direct competition. Save for the Hat Act, which was imposed upon the colonial manufacturer by the British Parliament against his wishes, no attempt appears to have been made to limit the number of apprentices a master might employ, in accord with the traditional policy of many English guilds. Employment opportunities were largely unchecked and neither property qualifications nor blood relationships appear to have been prerequisites to admission to the crafts, save where the exaction of entrance fees from apprentices in effect raised a barrier. In this respect the colonial apprenticeship system offers striking contrast to the modern system in some of the trades, where unreasonable conditions of admission to unions are often imposed [33] and where the establishing of a certain ratio of apprentices to journeymen, or the limitation of the number of apprentices permitted each shop or contractor, is perhaps the most significant feature of apprenticeship regulation.[34]

In order to maintain the monopoly of their crafts and to curb the ruinous competition of Negro slaves, white artisans combined in the colonial South, but their efforts were ineffectual. These moves were a forecast of later attempts in the ante-bellum South to keep Negroes from entering the skilled and semiskilled trades,[35] and of more recent opposition to extending vocational and technical training to Negroes, to "upgrading" Negro workers, and to observing the democratic principle of "equal pay for equal work." [36] The lower-class whites have been the principal force behind the economic as well as the political discrimination against Negroes in recent years, thus attesting to the discernment of Gunnar Myrdal's hypothesis that in a society with broad social groupings and a multiplicity of castes in the lower strata, the minorities in the lower groupings "will, to a great extent, take care of keeping each other subdued, thus relieving, to that extent, the higher classes of this otherwise painful task necessary to the monopolization of the power and the advantages." [37]

[33] It is said that in the building trades union in St. Louis "a boy has as good a chance to get into West Point as into the building trades unless his father or his uncle is a building craftsman." "Apprenticeship in Building Construction," Bureau of Labor Statistics, *Bull.* No. 459 (1928), p. 9.

[34] See J. M. Motley, *Apprenticeship in American Trade Unions* (Baltimore, 1907), p. 89; Slichter, *Union Policies,* pp. 20–24.

[35] Exclusion of Negroes from craft unions has by no means been restricted to the South. See S. D. Spero and Abram L. Harris, *The Black Worker* (New York, 1931), pp. 53–86; Herman Feldman, *Racial Factors in American Industry* (New York, 1931), pp. 27–31.

[36] A Federal Committee on Fair Employment Practice was set up by Executive Order No. 9346 of May 27, 1943. The War Labor Board ruled that Negro workers were to be placed "on a basis of economic parity with white workers in the same classification," and the nondiscrimination clause in government contracts was deemed mandatory by the President. See *Monthly Labor Rev.* (July, 1943), pp. 31–33 (December, 1943), p. 1123 (January, 1945), pp. 1–5; H. R. Northrup, "Organized Labor and Negro Workers," *J. Pol. Econ.,* LI (1943), 208 *et seq.;* "The Negro in the North during Wartime," *J. Educ. Soc.* (January, 1944); *Lawyers Guild Rev.,* IV (1944), 32–37; R. C. Weaver, "The Employment of Negroes in the United States in War Industries," *International Labour Rev.,* L (1944), 141–159.

[37] Gunnar Myrdal, with Richard Sterner and Arnold Rose, *An American Dilemma: the Negro Problem and Modern Democracy* (New York, 1944), I, 68, 69, 581, 597.

The chief instances of prosecutions for concerted action by workers occurred in the tobacco provinces and were directed against uprisings by white servants, motivated not infrequently by a desire to better working conditions on the plantations. During the Revolutionary era a perceptible momentum toward labor combinations and concerted action by working-class groups was effectively diverted from economic into political channels. Masters and journeymen joined in protest against British imperial policy and supported the nonimportation agreements, which proved a great boon to local industry and employment. When the war came they left the plow and the work-bench, at least for a time, and joined the armed forces. The really notable uprising against terms and conditions of service in the Revolutionary period was the mutiny in the Pennsylvania Line.[38] As a result, the foundations of permanent trade unionism were not really laid until the post-Revolutionary period.

Except in the licensed trades, the authorities evinced no concern whatsoever with regard to combinations of master workmen to control wages or prices or of merchants to form trade agreements. Beginning with the Philadelphia house carpenters in 1724, master carpenters in most of the colonial towns agreed on a scale of prices for their work, and the practice of entering into and publishing such agreements was widely followed in the post-Revolutionary and Federal periods. The legal and medical associations had by this time well-established professional associations. By the period of the Confederation master silversmiths, coopers, wigmakers, and others were organized by crafts. In addition, master mechanics were already combining in the leading towns to establish intercraft organizations both for economic and philanthropic ends. It was apparent that by the time of the Constitutional Convention there was a clear-cut trend among master mechanics, journeymen laborers, merchants, and industrialists toward the formation of their own associations along economic lines. It was a long, hard, and tortuous road from the society which the Hamiltonian industrialists were fashioning to an industrial democracy in which the policy of collective bargaining is implicit. Actually, employers' trade groups such as the Spermaceti Trust, local chambers of commerce, and the societies of master craftsmen preceded the craft union. The modern peak trade association finds its roots in such colonial economic associations. The period of time from the small local craft union to the giant federations of trades or industrial

[38] See Carl Van Doren, *Mutiny in January* (New York, 1943); also A. Bowman, *The Morale of the American Revolutionary Army* (Washington, 1943), pp. 37-38.

unions covers the entire span of our history from the administration of George Washington to that of the late Franklin Delano Roosevelt.

In the absence of machinery for implementing collective bargaining, the colonial courts repeatedly asserted that the servant or worker should have his day in court, that the master was accountable to the authorities for the conditions of employment, and should even be restrained from dismissing his servant where the contract term had not been completed. This issue of restraint on dismissals is still a paramount one in labor relations today and has been complicated by the spread of union activity.[39] The introduction, to a very limited extent, of power-driven machinery and labor-saving devices in the Revolutionary era does not seem to have created a serious problem of labor displacement. Whether or not there are today automatic compensations for technological unemployment,[40] the continually expanding economy of the colonial and early national periods virtually nullified any displacement of workmen resulting from new technology or from increased operational efficiency. However, where a servant completed his term of service or a journeyman lost his employment, it must be borne in mind that there were no unemployment compensation laws to ease the blow. If the immediate economic situation did not hold the prospect of reemployment or induce the worker to embark upon an economic venture of his own, he would have to wait until he was destitute before obtaining poor relief from his community. The public works projects of the Revolutionary era were very largely inspired by the political and economic contest with the mother country, although they did in a limited way alleviate the unemployment crises in the eighteenth-century towns.

Maritime labor relations in early American history must be carefully distinguished from the ordinary type of master-servant relationship. On the high seas the relations of master and servant were largely determined by a venerable tradition which antedated the common law and found its roots in continental rather than English practice. The essence of these relations was obedience. A strike which might have been treated as an illegal combination at common law would, if participated in by mariners, be deemed a mutiny, for which there were numerous prosecutions in the colonial vice-admiralty courts. This doctrine has survived in modi-

---

[39] See N.L.R.B. v. Jones and Laughlin Steel Corp., 301 U.S. 1 (1937); Phelps Dodge Corp. v. N.L.R.B., 313 U.S. 177 (1941).

[40] For the contemporary problem, see Anderson *et al.*, "Technology in Our Economy," Temporary National Economic Committee, *Monograph*, No. 22 (1941); Lonigan, "Technological Conditions and Employment of Labor," *Amer. Econ. Rev.*, XXIX (1939), 246; Emil Lederer, *Technical Progress and Unemployment* (Geneva, 1938).

fied form to the present day. The Federal courts have held that strikes on ships at sea or even at a port of refuge constitute mutiny or desertion, whereas strikes on vessels moored to a dock or at anchor in a safe harbor are legal.[41] In colonial times desertion or disobedience would subject the seaman to forfeiture of his wages. Federal statutes perpetuate this rule.[42] On the other hand, the colonial and early state tribunals, both common law and vice-admiralty or state admiralty, made a serious effort to restrain masters who were overharsh or who denied seamen proper working conditions aboard ship. Mariners had little reason to complain of the judicial machinery when bringing suit for wages due; at least three fourths of such cases were decided in favor of the mariner. While common-law courts offered them the advantages of jury trials, vice-admiralty gave them the benefit of an *in rem* procedure and priority of wage claims, which more effectively safeguarded their compensation. The Federal courts assumed the maritime and admiralty jurisdiction which the early state courts had inherited from the colonial courts of vice-admiralty. Many of the concepts and procedures of colonial and early state maritime labor law were continued by the Federal courts and, with minor modifications, incorporated in Congressional legislation. The abandonment of some of these earlier concepts in more recent Federal statutes and the introduction of higher standards for the seaman's protection have truly inaugurated a new era for maritime labor in America.[43] While maximum wage scales were laid down by public authorities for many categories of labor in the colonial period, the wage scale of maritime labor was determined by private contract.[44] Hence, the labor provisions of the Merchant Marine Act of 1936 [45] authorizing the Maritime Commission to fix minimum wage scales and minimum working conditions for all officers and crews employed on vessels receiving an "operating-differential subsidy" represents a definite departure from historic practice.

[41] See Rees v. U.S., 95 Fed. (2d.) 784 (CCA 4, 1938); Rothschild, "The Legal Implications of a Strike by Seamen," *Yale Law J.*, XLV (1936), 1181. Southern Steamship Co. v. N.L.R.B., 316 U.S. (1941), went further, declaring that strikes on board a ship away from her home port and lying tied to a dock constituted mutiny.

[42] 46 U.S.C.A., § 701. Accord: Barfield v. Standard Oil Co. of N.J., 172 Misc. 95; 14 N.Y.S. (2d) 684 (1939).

[43] See Rev. Stat., §§ 4511–4519, 4523, 4549–4553, 4556–4569, 4572; 20 Stat. L. 688; 38 Stat. L. 1165; Fed. Stat. Ann. (2d ed.) 151–156; 1920 Supp., 225–226, and other statutes cited *supra*, pp. 240, 259, 264, 268, 269n.

[44] On the other hand, the pay of officers and men in the Continental navy was fixed by the government. G. W. Allen, *Naval History of the Revolution* (Boston and New York, 1913), II, 694.

[45] 49 Stat. 1992 (1936), as amended by Public No. 705 (75th Congress, c. 600, 3d Sess.); 46 USCA, § 1131 (a).

The Intercolonial Wars and the American Revolution raised serious manpower problems. Total wars with their far-reaching effects upon the civilian population, were as yet unknown, but the governmental authorities had to determine policy with regard to the enlistment of servants and workers in the armed forces or the granting of deferments, either as the result of the pressure brought to bear by the masters who were reluctant to sacrifice property rights and profits even in wartime, or in recognition of the need for artificers in war industries. During the Revolution there was always a manpower shortage, both in the Continental Army and in the civilian economy, and short-term enlistments and furloughs to harvest crops or work in war industries were expedients resorted to in order to effect a balance between the competing requirements of the military and civilian economies. Such expedients had to be resorted to in this country in the second World War, when enlisted men were furloughed to return to work in nonferrous mining occupations and in the tire industry. Military conscription was adopted in all of the wars of the colonial and Revolutionary periods, but it never appears to have been employed as a device to control labor. The "Work or Fight" principle, adopted in Massachusetts as early as 1632, was never enunciated with any real clarity, nor was any comprehensive program of labor conscription ever adopted. During the Revolution labor was at times impressed for war work, and, in at least one instance, subjected to a fine and, if the fine were not paid, to imprisonment for noncompliance.

The regulation by the military authorities of the wages of artificers working in the army proved in the long run as ineffective as other wage and price controls and for the same reasons. Even in the Revolutionary period, wage increases were passed on to the general public through the medium of cost-plus-fixed-fee contracts or fixed-percentage-commission contracts. The latter were quite widely employed by the army commissariat.[46] They proved at least as uneconomical as the cost-plus-percentage-of-cost contracts used in the first World War and the cost-plus-fixed-fee system of the second World War.[47] Recent experience has shown that such contracts encourage wasteful manpower practices. Even in peacetime no systematic practice had been inaugurated in the colonial period to provide supplies through competitive bids. The problem of curbing the unconscionable profits of those contracting with the government, whether capital or labor, was as serious an issue during

---

[46] Burnett, *Letters of Members of the Continental Congress*, II, 314.

[47] For recent legislation dealing with labor and war contracts, see T. W. Graske, *The Law of Government Defense Contracts* (New York, 1941).

the American Revolution [48] as it is today,[49] although the amounts then involved may well seem insignificant alongside the stupendous war enterprises of the twentieth century. The taxation of excessive war profits was proposed during the Revolution but not widely put into effect. In short, despite extensive economic controls introduced during the Revolutionary War the government never assumed a measure of control over production or consumers' goods comparable with the controls exercised in the first and second World Wars or to have employed military conscription as a device for promoting essential production.

Finally, recent labor trends are distinguished by certain modifications of the labor contract which afford significant comparison with the colonial and Revolutionary periods. The problem of "incentive wages" is a far more insistent one in the industrial era than in early days. The piece-wage system, while indubitably introduced to stimulate production in the colonial period, does not appear to have been viewed as a form of labor exploitation nor to have been a method of introducing rate cutting, as is often the case today.[50]

In the seventeenth and eighteenth centuries the personal-service contract was specifically enforced as a property right, and it took the Thirteenth Amendment and the Clayton Act of 1914 to terminate this deeply-rooted concept; in its place was set up the principle "that the labor of a human being is not a commodity or article of commerce," and to deny either party specific performance of an employment contract.[51] But as a result of recent court decisions and legislation an employer can

[48] "Speculators are as thick and as industrious as Bees, and as Active and wicked as the Devil himself," wrote Caesar Rodney to John Dickinson in 1779. G. H. Ryden, ed., *Letters to and from Caesar Rodney, 1756–1784* (Philadelphia, 1933), p. 324. "How hard it is," lamented Henry Laurens, "for a rich or covetous Man to enter heartily into the Kingdom of Patriotism!" Declared Charles Carroll of Carrollton, ironmaster and patriot, in 1779: "If members of Congress should engage in trade, their votes in that assembly, it is to be feared, will be often guided by their particular interest." Burnett, *op. cit.*, IV, 163, 223, 238. See also S. W. Patterson, *Horatio Gates: Defender of American Liberties* (New York, 1941), p. 295. For rumors of corruption in the army commissariat, see Burnett, *op. cit.*, IV, 97n. *et seq.*, 214, 235n.; V. L. Johnson, *The Administration of the American Commissariat during the Revolutionary War* (Philadelphia, 1941), pp. 219 *et seq.*; F. Kapp, *The Life of John Kalb, Major-General in the Revolutionary Army* (New York, 1884), p. 143.
The British faced the same problem. Rodney charged that the progress of the war was being retarded "to make the fortunes of a long train of leeches, who seek the blood of the State, and whose interests prompts them to promote the continuance of the war, such as quartermasters and their deputies, *ad infinitum*, barrack masters and their deputies, *ad infinitum*, commissaries and their deputies, *ad infinitum*, all of which make princely fortunes, and laugh in their sleeves at the Generals who permit it." HMC, *Rep.*, XLIX, Pt. II, 191 (1780); also *ibid.*, p. 251 (1782).
[49] See U.S. v. Bethlehem Steel Corp., 315 U.S. 289 (1942).
[50] National Industrial Conference Board, *Systems of Wage Payment* (New York, 1930), p. 38. See also Van Dusen Kennedy, *Union Policy and Incentive Wage Methods* (New York, 1945).
[51] Williston, *Contracts* (rev. ed., 1936), V, § 1423A; American Law Institute, *Restatement of the Law of Contracts* (2 vols., St. Paul, 1932), § 379.

be restrained by injunction from lowering wages contrary to an agreement with a union [52] and can be compelled to enter into an employment relationship with an applicant or to reemploy a former employer or to hire a sufficient number of employers to fulfil his promise under an agreement.[53] Thus in order to provide job security it has been found necessary to create a new labor system establishing a legal duty to employ or reinstate.

The only previous labor experience in American law to which this is comparable is the colonial period, when specific performance of labor contracts was enforceable. However, in the colonial period the chief objective of the courts was the protection of the master's quasi-proprietary interest in his servant, whereas today the law attempts to relieve employees of the necessity of making contracts under economic duress without giving the master a corresponding measure of protection against economic or other forms of pressure brought to bear by the workers, whose bargaining power is being more and more re-enforced by the compulsory support of the state. There is no effective remedy for the employer today when his workers breach their contract and go on strike.[54] The colonial and Revolutionary governments imposed upon the employee a compulsion to accept employment at a legally determined wage. Today we have imposed upon the employer a compulsion to hire or to negotiate. This swing of the pendulum, representing in effect a shift in economic power, does not disturb those who feel that it may be necessary to subordinate freedom of contract in labor relations to freedom of want when or if the two freedoms are incompatible.[55]

Nevertheless, if full employment is to be the major objective of postwar planning, those who will bargain on behalf of labor must share responsibility with the representatives of industry in tempering their demands in order to prevent an inflationary spiral of wages and prices.

[52] Schlesinger v. Quinto, 117 Misc. 735; 192 N.Y.S. 564 (1942).

[53] Phelps-Dodge Corp. v. N.L.R.B., 313 U.S. 177, 188 (1941); Weber v. Nasser, 286 Pac. 1074 (1930).

[54] This point is effectively made by John Dickinson, "New Conceptions of Contract in Labor Relations," *Columbia Law Rev.*, XLIII (1943), 688–704 at p. 696. See also the suggestive article by Arthur Lenhoff, "The Scope of Compulsory Contracts Proper," *ibid.*, pp. 586–602. As a result of emergency conditions in World War II the War Manpower Commission issued a "job freeze" order, which gave employers in essential industries the right to penalize quitting workers by refusing to grant them certificates of availability, without which they were debarred for sixty days from taking other employment.

[55] E. Merrick Dodd, "From Maximum Wages to Minimum Wages," *Columbia Law Rev.*, XLIII (1943), 687. But cf. Sumner Slichter, "The Conditions of Expansion," *Amer. Econ. Rev.*, XXXII (Supp., March, 1942), 4–5.

On the one hand, business must reform trade practices to achieve a more effective utilization of our national resources. On the other, labor must eliminate practices and modify policies which hamper the attainment of optimum output in peacetime.[56] The willingness of both capital and labor to subordinate immediate ends to broader social objectives will in a large measure determine what role the state will play in the postwar period in the settlement of labor problems and the extent to which economic regulation and planning on a centralized scale must be continued.

[56] Sir William H. Beveridge, *Full Employment in a Free Society* (New York, 1945), pp. 200, 201; S. M. Fine, *Public Spending and Postwar Economic Policy* (New York, 1944), p. 153; J. M. Clark, *Demobilization of Wartime Economic Controls* (New York, 1944), pp. 10, 11, 32–34, 147. For a current proposal for dealing with feather-bedding and labor's opposition to mechanization, see Ludwig Teller, *A Labor Policy for America* (New York, 1945), pp. 104–112.

Fisheries, 225; financial return to seamen, 226
Fishermen exempted from military training, 279
Fitch, John, 41, 50
Flaxseed mill operatives exempted from military service, 281
Flogging, aboard ships, 263 ff.; abolished, 264n
Florida, land grants to servants, 396; treatment of servants in, 499; *see also* East Florida; West Florida
Flour mills, 34
Flowers, Benjamin, 298n
Folger, Peter, 50
Food, as compensation, 211, 397n, 398; on colonial ships, 257
Forced Labor Convention, 515n
Forestalling, penalties for, 120
Forni, Carlo, 178
Fornication, problem and punishment, 349-53 *passim*
Forty hour week, *see* Hours of labor
Forward, Jonathan, 329
Fox, William, 317
France, maximum price legislation: anti-hoarding sentiment, 132
Franklin, Benjamin, 36n, 50, 193, 285, 333, 354, 369, 383; on expense of slave labor, 32; quitting of apprenticeship, 433; quoted, 435, 514n, 519
Franks, David, 304
Fraud, contracts vitiated by, 312
Freedom dues, 312, 336, 393, 394; for apprentices, 383; in Maryland, 395, 397n; in Northern and Middle Colonies, 397; in Georgia, 460; in New England, 471
Freedom of contract in labor relations, 530
Freedom of occupation, local regulations curbed, 152
Free labor, 55-309; regulation of wages prior to Revolution, 55-91; regulation of wages during Revolution, 92-135; concerted action among workers, 136-207; terms and conditions of employment, 208-24; maritime labor relations, 225-78; labor and the armed services, 279-309; *see also* Labor
Freemanship, Boston, 148; New York, 149; Albany, 149n
"Free-willers," defined, 315; *see* Bound labor: Immigration
French and Indian War, issue of servant enlistments, 284, 286; effect on absenteeism, 444, 448n, 453
French Caribbean colonies, mercantilist regulations, 91
French colonies, two types of laborers, 316n
Friendly societies, earliest plan in colonies,

157; often a mask for illegal combinations, 198, 204
Friendly Society of Tradesmen House Carpenters, The, 198
Friends, Society of, 283; disputes *re* harboring or enticement, 424
Friendship Carpenters' Company, The, 142
Fugitive servants, *see* Runaway servants
Furnace and forge industries, 39

Gadsden, Christopher, 190n
Gage, Thomas, 189; quoted, 24, 191, 193; workers of Boston and New York refuse to work for, 192; plan to arm Negroes, 293
Gardner, Capt. John, 478
Garnishee, attachment of goods in hands of, 215
Gates, Sir Thomas, 87, 169; quoted, 302
Geiser, K. F., 36n
General Society of Mechanics and Tradesmen, 204
Gentleman's Magazine, 326
Georgia, impressment for public service, 8; restraint on dismissal, 17; wage regulation, 90; forbade employment of slaves and Spaniards in handicraft trades, 186; Negro mechanics barred from building trades, 188; land grants to servants, 396, 508; assignment of servants in, 412; penalties for absenteeism, 460; laws *re* treatment of servants, 471n; treatment of immigrant servants, 498
Germans, immigrants, 29, 178, 316n, 319, 321 f., 392, 460, 499; in Pennsylvania, 36; recruiting of, 320, 322; land grants to, 396, 508
Gifts *inter vivos,* 508 f.
Gillingham, Charles, 34
Girls, apprenticeship: educational requirements, 386-87
Gloucester County, Va., servants' plots, 173
Glovers, labor and commodity costs of, investigated, 68 f.
Goderis, Joost, 157
Godwyn, Morgan, 337
Gold and Silver Smiths' Society, 202
Goldsmith, Oliver, 344
Gooch, Sir William, 331, 332n
Goodrich, Carter, 315, 515n
Goodwin, Major, 172
Gordon, Peter, Prentice and Company, 202
Government, relation between popular associations and, 53; control over production or consumer goods, 529; *see also* States; *and names of Colonies, e.g.,* Massachusetts
Grant, James, 178; quoted, 179
Gratuities to servants, 509

Index